CSWE EPAS 2015 Core Competencies and Behaviors in This Text

Competency	Chapter
Competency 1: Demonstrate Ethical and Professional Behavior	
Behaviors:	
Make ethical decisions by applying the standards of the NASW Code of Ethics, relevant laws and regulations, models for ethical decision-making, ethical conduct of research, and additional codes of ethics as appropriate to context	1
Use reflection and self-regulation to manage personal values and maintain professionalism in practice situations	7
Demonstrate professional demeanor in behavior; appearance; and oral, written, and electronic communication	10
Use technology ethically and appropriately to facilitate practice outcomes	2
Use supervision and consultation to guide professional judgment and behavior	8
Competency 2: Engage Diversity and Difference in Practice	
Behaviors:	
Apply and communicate understanding of the importance of diversity and difference in shaping life experiences in practice at the micro, mezzo, and macro levels	2, 6, 8
Present themselves as learners and engage clients and constituencies as experts of their own experiences	3, 5
Apply self-awareness and self-regulation to manage the influence of personal biases and values in working with diverse clients and constituencies	1, 7
Competency 3: Advance Human Rights and Social, Economic, and Environmental Justice	
Behaviors:	
Apply their understanding of social, economic, and environmental justice to advocate for human rights at the individual and system levels	3, 10
Engage in practices that advance social, economic, and environmental justice	2, 8
Competency 4: Engage In Practice-informed Research and Research-informed Practice	
Behaviors:	
Use practice experience and theory to inform scientific inquiry and research	9
Apply critical thinking to engage in analysis of quantitative and qualitative research methods and research findings	4
Use and translate research evidence to inform and improve practice, policy, and service delivery	1, 3, 6, 7, 11
Competency 5: Engage in Policy Practice	
Behaviors:	
Identify social policy at the local, state, and federal level that impacts well-being, service delivery, and access to social services	10
Assess how social welfare and economic policies impact the delivery of and access to social services	1, 6
Apply critical thinking to analyze, formulate, and advocate for policies that advance human rights and social, economic, and environmental justice	2, 5

Competency	Chapter
Competency 6: Engage with Individuals, Families, Groups, Organizations, and Communities	*Behaviors:*
Apply knowledge of human behavior and the social environment, person-in- environment, and other multidisciplinary theoretical frameworks to engage with clients and constituencies	7, 5, 9
Use empathy, reflection, and interpersonal skills to effectively engage diverse clients and constituencies	3, 4, 6
Competency 7: Assess Individuals, Families, Groups, Organizations, and Communities	
Behaviors:	
Collect and organize data, and apply critical thinking to interpret information from clients and constituencies	4, 8
Apply knowledge of human behavior and the social environment, person-in- environment, and other multidisciplinary theoretical frameworks in the analysis of assessment data from clients and constituencies	9
Develop mutually agreed-on intervention goals and objectives based on the critical assessment of strengths, needs, and challenges within clients and constituencies	9
Select appropriate intervention strategies based on the assessment, research knowledge, and values and preferences of clients and constituencies	11
Competency 8: Intervene with Individuals, Families, Groups, Organizations, and Communities	
Behaviors:	
Critically choose and implement interventions to achieve practice goals and enhance capacities of clients and constituencies	9
Apply knowledge of human behavior and the social environment, person-in-environment, and other multidisciplinary theoretical frameworks in interventions with clients and constituencies	4. 5
Use inter-professional collaboration as appropriate to achieve beneficial practice outcomes	10
Negotiate, mediate, and advocate with and on behalf of diverse clients and constituencies	11
Facilitate effective transitions and endings that advance mutually agreed-on goals	11
Competency 9: Evaluate Practice with Individuals, Families, Groups, Organizations, and Communities	
Behaviors:	
Select and use appropriate methods for evaluation of outcomes	12
Apply knowledge of human behavior and the social environment, person-in-environment, and other multidisciplinary theoretical frameworks in the evaluation of outcomes	12
Critically analyze, monitor, and evaluate intervention and program processes and outcomes	12
Apply evaluation findings to improve practice effectiveness at the micro, mezzo, and macro levels	12

Adapted with permission of Council on Social Work Education

SIXTH EDITION

Social Work Macro Practice

F. Ellen Netting
Virginia Commonwealth University

Peter M. Kettner
Arizona State University

Steven L. McMurtry
University of Wisconsin–Milwaukee

M. Lori Thomas
University of North Carolina at Charlotte

PEARSON

Boston Columbus Indianapolis New York San Francisco Hoboken
Amsterdam Cape Town Dubai London Madrid Milan Munich Paris Montreal Toronto
Delhi Mexico City São Paulo Sydney Hong Kong Seoul Singapore Taipei Tokyo

VP and Editorial Director: Jeffery W. Johnston
Executive Editor: Julie Peters
Program Manager: Megan Moffo
Editorial Assistant: Pamela DiBerardino
Executive Product Marketing Manager:
   Christopher Barry
Executive Field Marketing Manager: Krista Clark
Team Lead Project Management: Bryan Pirrmann
Team Lead Program Management: Laura Weaver
Procurement Specialist: Deidra Skahill
Art Director: Diane Lorenzo

Art Director Cover: Diane Ernsberger
Cover Design: Carie Keller, Cenveo
Cover Art: igor.stevanovic/Shutterstock
Media Producer: Michael Goncalves
Editorial Production and Composition Services:
   Lumina Datamatics, Inc.
Full-Service Project Manager: Prathiba Naveenkumar/
   Murugesh Rajkumar
Printer/Binder: Edwards Brothers Malloy
Cover Printer: Phoenix Color
Text Font: Dante MT Pro Regular, 10.5 pts

Credits and acknowledgments borrowed from other sources and reproduced, with permission, in this textbook appear on appropriate page within text.

Many of the designations by manufacturers and seller to distinguish their products are claimed as trademarks. Where those designations appear in this book, and the publisher was aware of a trademark claim, the designations have been printed in initial caps or all caps.

Cataloging in Publication data is available upon request

10 9 8 7 6 5 4 3 2 1 EBM 19 18 17 16 15

Student Edition
ISBN-10: **0-13-394852-8**
ISBN-13: **978-0-13-394852-3**

eText
ISBN-10: **0-13-394860-9**
ISBN-13: **978-0-13-394860-8**

Package
ISBN-10: **0-13-429012-7**
ISBN-13: **978-0-13-429012-6**

Contents

v

Preface

Twenty-five years ago, three colleagues at Arizona State University School of Social Work decided to write a book to use in two courses in the foundation macro practice sequence in which we were teaching. At that point, we were using "course packs" comprised of readings from professional journals and book chapters, and we needed a textbook that integrated a growing conceptual and empirically based literature on organizational and community change. Through multiple revisions we continued our collaboration, in 2012 adding a fourth author to our team.

Much has changed in 25 years, but our commitment to our original goal remains steadfast. From the beginning, we wanted to recapture a broader definition of *social work practice* that recognizes that all social workers must be able to engage, assess, and intervene with individuals, families, groups, organizations, and communities. In short, we believed (and continue to believe) that active involvement in community and organizational change represents one of the richest and proudest traditions of social work practice over the last century.

New to This Edition

It is our intent in this edition to bring readers abreast of the changes within the field. We have worked to make the sixth edition more practice oriented, integrating more field-based vignettes and examples throughout and elaborating the planned change model originally introduced in earlier editions. We have incorporated more material on international and global content in order to prepare future practitioners for encountering both domestic and international social problems. We have paid special attention to the use of technology such as social media and electronic advocacy, in addition to video links and media asset recommendations. We have reinforced the role of advocacy in all aspects of social work practice. Structurally, we have rearranged chapters, added a new chapter, deleted dated material, added new material, and integrated the most up-to-date conceptual and empirical scholarship into all chapters. Across all chapters, at least one-third of all references are new to this edition. In all changes in this edition, we have tried to be as conscientiously attentive and responsive to reviewers' feedback as possible while ensuring consistency with current professional literature on macro practice.

Specific changes follow:

- **Framing Macro Social Work in an International Context.** In Chapters 1–2, we have framed macro practice within an international context, adding references from international journals and information on international codes of ethics, referring to differences in social work education across multiple countries, adding a case example on international social work, and writing a new section entitled "Global Perspectives on Social Work."

- **Adding Content on Diverse Populations.** Chapters 3 and 4 have been reversed, placing the chapter on populations before the chapter on problems. In Chapter 3, we lead with a new section on "Advancing Human Rights and Social and Economic Justice," including new content on cultural humility, cultural competency, whiteness studies, and critical race theory. Another new section, "Developing Strategies for Authentic Engagement" in Chapter 3, includes new material on working with groups, community organizing, and community engagement.

- **Including Alternative Theories.** New theoretical content has been added as follows: Critical Race Theory, and Identity Theory (Chapters 3 and 9); Framing Theory (Chapter 4); Assets Mapping, Field Interactional Theory, and Power Dependency Theory (Chapter 5); and Organizational Culture, Feminist, and Critical Theories (Chapters 7 and 8). Chapter 7 was entirely restructured to tighten up the content on classical theories in order to focus more on contemporary approaches reorganized within four schools of thought.

- **Updating Practice Frameworks.** All frameworks have been revised, rearranged, and updated in Chapters 3, 4, 6, 8, 9, 10, 11, and 12. New tasks within the frameworks have been renamed to be more congruent with EPAS competencies and graphical representations of each framework are now included. A new task and set of activities on "Identify Focal Community" leads the framework in Chapter 6. A new task on "Assessing the Cultural Competency of an Organization" is now featured in Chapter 8. New material has been added to Chapters 11 and 12 on the logic model in an attempt to strengthen the student's understanding of the relationship between this model and the macro practice procedures we are proposing.

- **Adding Content on Technology.** Chapters 1 and 2 feature updated information on the wise use of technology. In Chapter 9, a new section called "Strengthen Collective Identity" focuses on how use of the Internet, social-networking sites, and mobile technology can be used to facilitate communication among action system members. This is reinforced by a section on the use of technology in advocating for change in Chapter 10.

- **Adding New Chapter on Evaluation.** Our original Chapter 11 has been divided into new Chapters 11 and 12. Each chapter has been expanded in light of reviewers' concerns that more material on the planning, implementing, monitoring, and evaluating aspects of planned change needed more depth. The new Chapter 11 now introduces and focuses on understanding the logic model, illustrated by a series of new figures that demonstrate the model's use. Chapter 12 is almost completely new, focusing in detail on monitoring and evaluating.

- **Chapter Reviews** at the end of each chapter allow students to evaluate mastery of skills and competencies learned.

- **Marginal media assets** are included so that students can search the Internet for relevant content.

Connecting Core Competencies Series

The sixth edition of this text is now a part of Pearson Education's *Connecting Core Competencies* series, which consists of foundation-level texts that make it easier than ever to ensure students' success in learning the nine core competencies as revised in 2015 by the Council on Social Work Education (CSWE). This text contains:

- **Core Competency Icons** throughout the chapters, directly linking the CSWE core competencies to the content of the text. **Critical thinking questions** are also included to further students' mastery of the CSWE standards. For easy reference, a chart in the front pages of the book displays which competencies are used in each chapter.

Interactive Enhanced Pearson eText

The sixth edition Enhanced eText, produced by Pearson, contains new digital elements to enhance student learning and user experiences:

- **Assess Your Understanding Quizzes** appear at the end of each major section within each chapter, with multiple-choice questions to test students' knowledge of the chapter content.
- **Chapter Review Quizzes** appear at the end of each chapter, with essay questions to test student's understanding of major concepts in the chapter.
- **Video links** are provided throughout the chapters to encourage students to access relevant video content.

Instructor Supplements

An Instructor's Manual, Test Bank, and PowerPoint slides are available to accompany this text. They can be downloaded at www.pearsonhighered.com/educator.

The Importance of Macro Practice

We contend that social workers who see clients every day and encounter the same problems over and over are the ones who are most aware of the need for macro-level change, and even if they are not in a position to take the lead in initiating change they need to understand the process and be supportive of others who are involved in macro-level efforts. Macro practice, understood within this context, defines the uniqueness of social work practice. Many disciplines claim expertise in working with individuals, groups, and families, but social work has long stood alone in its focus on the organizational, community, and policy contexts within which its clients function. The concept of person-in-environment is not simply a slogan that makes social workers aware of environmental influences. It means that social workers recognize that sometimes it is the *environment* and not the *person* that needs to change. Mullaly (2007) states that social workers are not simply called to be direct practitioners, but are equally called to be change agents particularly in situations that place service users' best interests first. Our book is designed to prepare social workers to be agents of change for the purpose of improving people's quality of life.

We are aware that the history of social work as a profession has been marked by shifts in and tensions between intervention with individuals and intervention with and within larger systems. Early perspectives on the latter tended to focus primarily on policy-level involvements (especially legislative processes). As the need for content on social work administration and management, and community practice was recognized and incorporated into the curriculum of many schools of social work, these topics were also embraced as an area of concentration for those who wanted to work with and within larger systems. In order to manage oversubscribed curricula, students have often been forced to concentrate in *either* macro or micro areas, creating a false dichotomy, when social work of all professions is uniquely positioned to integrate both.

Therefore, over the years as we taught required foundation-level courses on community and organizational change, and as we worked with students and professionals in the field, we became aware of the changing dynamics of practice and expectations for practitioners. Both students and practitioners were working with populations such as homeless persons, members of teen street gangs, victims of domestic violence, chronically unemployed persons, frail older adults, and other disenfranchised groups. Although social workers will always need casework and clinical skills to help people in need on a one-to-one basis, it was becoming increasingly evident to many in the profession that they were also expected to intervene at the community level. Typical activities included promoting the development of shelters, developing neighborhood alternatives to gang membership and juvenile incarceration, addressing chronic unemployment, and navigating the complexity of long-term care services as a community problem. It was becoming more and more evident that social workers must be contextual thinkers.

These activities are not new; many closely mirror the work of settlement-house workers in the early days of the profession. Yet, many social work students have traditionally seen themselves as preparing strictly for interventions at the individual or domestic level. It is unexpected and disconcerting when they find themselves being asked to initiate actions and design interventions that will affect large numbers of people and take on problems at the community or organizational level if they are not prepared to undertake and support these kinds of professional activities. When social work practice with macro systems is seen as solely the realm of administrators, community organizers, program planners, and others, a vital linkage to millions of people who struggle daily with environmental constraints has been severed. Macro-level change may, but does not necessarily always, involve large-scale, costly reforms at the national and state levels or the election of candidates more sympathetic to the poor, neglected, and underserved members of society. Sometimes useful macro-level change can involve organizing a local neighborhood to deal with deterioration and blight; sometimes it may mean initiating a self-help group and stepping back so that members will assume leadership roles. Thus, the focus of this book is on enabling social work practitioners to undertake whatever types of macro-level interventions are needed in an informed, analytical way and with a sense of confidence that they can do a competent job and achieve positive results.

As this sixth edition goes to press, schools of social work and professional associations are continuing the ongoing debate about the role of macro social work practice in oversubscribed curricula; and making choices about what content to cover, and which courses to offer and methods to use (e.g., classroom, hybrid, and online), in delivering that content. Reports on the state of macro practice social work have been issued, and a Special Commission to Advance Macro-Practice in Social Work is engaged in a multipronged strategic approach to deal with imbalances between micro and macro, the marginality of macro practitioners and educators, and the lack of support for macro practice (Rothman & Mizrahi, 2014). Challenges to professional macro practitioners' identity, recognition of tensions among social work educators, and concerns about state licensing that privilege clinical roles all promise to fuel a continuing dialogue among individuals and groups committed to the field (Hill, Ferguson, & Erickson, 2010).

Amid these debates and challenges about social work as a profession is an increasing recognition that skilled macro practitioners are needed more than ever within a global context (Santiago, Soska, & Gutierrez, 2014). So much has happened in the last 25 years that could not have been predicted. The editors of a special issue of the *Journal of Community Practice* name a few: "global and domestic terrorism, economic adjustments, natural disasters, migration and immigration, new and emerging technologies, globalization … not unique to the United States and … mirrored around the globe" (Gutierrez, Gant, &

Richards-Schuster, 2014, p. 1). Within this international context, we believe it is critical to reiterate our original goal—to recapture a broader definition of *social work practice* that recognizes that all social workers must be able to engage, assess, and intervene with individuals, families, groups, organizations, and communities. Across the world, macro practice skills are needed more than we ever imagined 25 years ago when we started this endeavor. It is our hope that we may contribute to preparing the next generation of social workers to embrace their calling.

References

Gutierrez, L., Gant, L. M., & Richards-Schuster, K. (2014). Community organization in the twenty-first century: Scholarship and practice directions for the future. *Journal of Community Practice, 22*(1–2), 1–9.

Hill, K. M., Ferguson, S. M., & Erickson, C. (2010). Sustaining and strengthening a macro identity: The Association of Macro Practice Social Work. *Journal of Community Practice, 18*(4), 513–527.

Mullaly, B. (2007). *The new structural social work* (3rd ed.). Don Mills, Canada: Oxford University Press.

Rothman, J., & Mizrahi, T. (2014). Balancing micro and macro practice: A challenge for social work. *Social Work, 59*(1), 1–3.

Santiago, A. M., Soska, T., & Gutierrez, L. (2014). Responding to community crises: The emerging role of community practice. *Journal of Community Practice, 22*(3), 275–280.

Acknowledgments

As we finish this sixth edition, much has changed since our original 1993 publication. We are now scattered in four different geographical locations: Virginia, Arizona, Wisconsin, and North Carolina. We are indebted to our colleagues and students at the four universities where we have worked who have given us constructive and helpful feedback throughout the years. We want to thank colleagues who provided feedback as they used our text at other universities. We appreciate as well the efforts of a number of reviewers who provided careful and thoughtful assessments of earlier drafts. For this sixth edition, these individuals are Donna M. Aguiniga, University of Alaska Anchorage; Kathleen Arban, Salisbury University; Iran Barrera, California State University, Fresno; Mark Cameron, Southern Connecticut State University; Adrianne M. Fletcher, University of Wisconsin, Green Bay; and Angela Kaiser, Oakland University.

To our editor, Julie Peters, we express our sincere appreciation for her oversight, patience, interest, and assistance as we began the revision of our text. To Janet Portisch and Megan Moffo at Pearson we thank you for working so hard to facilitate the many transitions we made during this edition. To our project managers at Lumina Datamatics, Doug Bell, Prathiba Naveenkumar, and Murugesh Rajkumar Namasivayam, we extend a round of applause for their diligent oversight about details, constant enthusiasm for the process, and unconditional support. Most of all, we thank those students and practitioners who, often in the face of seemingly insurmountable barriers, continue to practice social work the way it was intended. This book is dedicated to them. They intervene at whatever level is needed. They persist with what may appear to be intractable problems and work with clients who have lost hope until hope can be rediscovered and pursued. Their spirit and dedication continually inspire us in our efforts to provide whatever guidance we can for the next generation of social workers.

1

An Introduction to Macro Practice in Social Work

© E+ / GETTY IMAGES

WHAT IS MACRO PRACTICE?

This book is intended for all social workers, regardless of whether they specialize or concentrate in micro or macro tracks within schools of social work (Rothman & Mizrahi, 2014). Because we believe that all social workers are professional change agents, we use the terms *social worker, professional*, and *change agent* interchangeably throughout this book.

This book is also designed to be an introduction to macro practice as a set of professional activities in which all social workers are involved. Although some practitioners will concentrate their efforts primarily in one arena more than another, all social workers encounter situations in which macro-level interventions are the appropriate response to a need or a problem. Therefore, we define **macro practice** as *professionally guided intervention(s) designed to bring about change in organizational, community, and/or policy arenas.*

Professional identity is a relational concept in that one identifies with a community of colleagues who share a common value base and whose joint efforts work toward "a way of life with public value" (Sullivan, 2005, p. 39). Professions "exist to meet the needs of others" within the larger community (Gustafson, 1982, p. 508). This characteristic has led a number of writers to refer to professions as *callings* because they literally call members to contribute to the civic good. Professions are therefore client oriented and conform to a set of values that encapsulate the community good that is to be served. In many ways, it is this commitment to the understanding and changing of larger systems that defines social work. Sullivan (2005) argues that the very nature of professionalism implies a responsibility to the larger society and to the common good.

In his classic book, *Social Work as Cause and Function*, Porter Lee (1937) described the dual calling of social work—to address systemic social problems and to provide for the needs of individuals and families. Lee acknowledged the inherent tension in trying to do both. In planning for social change while simultaneously responding to immediate need, social work finds its unique "both-and" contribution (Gates, 2014).

This book is based on the assumption that professional social workers will always experience tension as long as they recognize the importance of both providing direct services and addressing organizational and community problems. Social workers must see themselves as problem solvers and do both in order to truly be doing social work. The only other option is to ignore recurring problems. Thus, macro practice is not an option but is an integral part of being a professional social worker. All social workers will engage in some form of macro practice.

The Interrelationship of Micro and Macro Social Work Practice

A broad focus on arenas for change is a feature that makes social work unique among helping professions. When the arena for change is limited solely to casework with individuals and families, an assumption is being made. The assumption is that causal factors associated with the problem or need can be found only in some deficit in the micro system—the client, couple, or family coming for help—or in their abilities to access needed resources. Broadening the problem analysis to include organizations and communities recognizes the possibility or likelihood that, in some situations, the pathology or causal factors may be identified in the policies and/or practices of macro systems—communities and their various institutions. For example, an organization may fail to provide relevant and needed services, or may provide them in a narrow and discriminatory manner. Or some members of a community may find themselves excluded from participation in decisions that affect them.

It is not unusual for direct practitioners to have clients ask for help with problems that at first appear to be individual or interpersonal, but, after further examination, turn out to be macro-level problems. A family that loses its primary source of income, undergoes eviction, and finds that there is no affordable housing and a three-month waiting list to get into a homeless shelter represents a symptom of a community problem. Clearly, the family's immediate shelter problem must be resolved, but just as obviously, the communitywide lack of affordable housing and emergency alternatives must be addressed.

A veteran may report having difficulty getting an appointment to see a specialist at the Veterans Administration and is put on a waiting list. This may seem like an isolated incident until the social worker begins to see a pattern developing among his clients who are service members or veterans. When he watches the news one night to learn that this delay is keeping thousands of veterans from getting health care services and that policies surrounding how waiting lists are handled need to change, what seemed like an individual's problem is quickly seen as a macro problem in the veterans' health care system. Collecting data, advocating at the local level, and joining others around the country to advocate for system reform become necessary if his clients are to receive what they need.

A mother may describe the pressures put on her son to join a gang and become involved in the drug trade. The immediate need of this family can perhaps be met by building a support system for the boy designed to keep him in school, in a part-time job, and in constructive activities. However, this individual/family approach alone would not solve the problem for the many other families who must live daily with the same threats.

In yet another example, a social worker employed by a community-based agency on an American Indian reservation talks about the importance of her work, as she constantly has to ask indigenous people for advice so that she does not make assumptions about the people with whom she works. The concept of community and what it means to this tribe, even the value of the land as a part of their tradition, is so crucial. It is much more complex than she had assumed when she was in school. In her position, this social worker has come to appreciate the false dichotomy between micro and macro social work. Although she works directly with tribal members, she is constantly assessing their environment, asking for advice, and recognizing the cultural context in which all her actions are embedded.

In instances like these, micro-level interventions alone may be inefficient (and often ineffective) ways to address macro-level problems, and they also run the risk of dealing only with symptoms. In some ways, using micro-level interventions to address a macro-level problem is similar to treating individuals who are suffering from a new flu strain one at a time rather than vaccinating the whole population before they contract the disease. In short, it is as important for social workers to understand the nature of individual and group interventions as it is to understand the nature of organizational, community, and policy change.

Macro-Level Change

Intervention in organizations or communities is referred to as *macro-level change*. Managing macro-level change requires a good deal of professional knowledge and skill. Poor management and flawed decision making in the change process can result in serious setbacks that can make things worse for those already in need. On the other hand, many positive changes in organizations and communities have been orchestrated by social workers and others who have carefully planned, designed, and carried out the change process.

Social work students often express the concern that they came into the profession because of an interest in working with individuals and families, not with communities and organizations. This can sometimes present an ethical dilemma, because at times what a client or family most needs in the long run is macro-level change. This does not mean that the immediate need is not addressed. It also does not mean that the social worker is left alone to bring about community or organizational change. Macro practice is a collaborative effort, and change will rarely be immediate. But ignoring the need for change should not be considered a viable option.

Given the complexity of macro interventions, practitioners may begin to feel over-whelmed. Is it not enough to perform good direct practice or clinical work? Is it not enough to listen to a client and offer options? Our answer is that professional practice focusing only on an individual's intrapsychic concerns does not fit the definition of social work. Being a social worker requires seeing the client as part of multiple, overlapping systems that comprise the person's social and physical environment. The profession of social work is committed to seeking social and economic justice in concert with vulnerable and underserved populations, and macro-practice skills are necessary in confronting these inequalities. For example, consider a woman reported for child neglect who lives in a run-down home with structural problems her landlord refuses to fix. A clinical intervention designed to strengthen her emotional coping skills might be useful, but that intervention alone would ignore the context of the problem facing her and other women living in similar conditions. Social workers engaging only in working with their individual cases and ignoring larger scale problems may be doing so to the detriment of their clients. Similarly, social workers who carry out episodes of macro practice must understand what is involved in the provision of direct services to clients at the individual, domestic unit, or group level. Without this understanding, macro practice may occur without an adequate grounding in understanding client problems and needs. One example might be a social worker who conducts a community crime prevention campaign to combat high rates of petty theft in a neighborhood, unaware that most such acts are the work of a relatively small number of residents desperately in need of drug-abuse intervention. The interconnectedness of micro and macro roles is the heart of social work practice.

Macro-Practice Arenas and Roles

This book is not designed to prepare practitioners for full-time agency administration, program planning, community organizing, or policy analysis positions. Social workers who assume full-time macro **roles** will need a more advanced understanding than this text provides. Nor is this a book on how to specialize in macro practice. Instead, it is designed to provide basic knowledge and skills on aspects of macro practice in which competent social work practitioners will need to engage. We also want to raise awareness about how versatile social work is as a profession and about the potential one has to engage at the macro level.

There are different ways to conceptualize the **arenas** in which macro social work practice occurs. Rothman, Erlich, and Tropman (2008) identify three arenas of intervention: communities, organizations, and small groups. We have selected communities and organizations as the arenas on which the majority of this text will focus, folding small-group work in as a critical part of most interventions in both communities and organizations. *Small groups* are seen as collections of people who collaborate on tasks that move toward agreed-upon changes. Small groups are often the nucleus around which change strategies are developed in both communities and organizations, and they are therefore more logically conceptualized as part of the strategy or medium for change rather than the focus of change.

Other writers focus on the policy context in which macro intervention occurs (Gilbert & Terrell, 2013; Jansson, 2014; Karger & Stoesz, 2013). The policy arena is well articulated in other social work textbooks that complement the content here (e.g., Cummins, Byers, & Pedrick, 2011). Organizational and community arenas are deeply embedded in political systems, which are typically the starting points for development of social policies. Although the creation and analysis of these policies are not our main focus, an understanding of how ideologies and values are manifested in local, state, national, and international politics is fundamental to macro change.

The majority of social workers deal with change directly with clients, usually working with individuals one on one, or with families or small groups. Some practitioners focus on communitywide problems. Others work in the areas of planning, management, and administration of organizations. Regardless of the professional social worker's primary practice orientation, it is crucial that all social work practitioners support the position that although some problems can be resolved at an individual or family level, others will require intervention that takes on a broader scope, including the need to effect changes in organizations and communities. Social workers are constantly identifying changes needed to make systems more responsive or sensitive to **target populations**. Other professionals may also see themselves as change agents, and it is important for the contemporary social work practitioner to collaborate and partner with those from other professions so that the knowledge of diverse fields can be used in planning effective change. Macro changes are typically too complex for one to address alone.

It is not uncommon to have social workers describe themselves as *psychiatric social workers*, *geriatric specialists*, *child welfare workers*, and so on. These specialties denote the target populations with whom these practitioners work. Just as common are terms such as *medical social worker* and *behavioral health specialist*, indicating a setting in which these professionals are employed. Within all of these specialities or settings, there are multiple roles one can play as a social worker (Kerson & McCoyd, 2013).

Terms such as *planner*, *community organizer*, *case manager*, and *group worker* describe actual functions performed by social workers. In addition, social workers plan, develop, and coordinate programs; as well as administer, manage, and supervise staff in human service organizations. Social workers develop and organize communities around the world. They advocate for policy change and work as policy analysts in local, regional, national, and even international arenas.

Social work practice is broadly defined and allows for both micro (individual, domestic unit, or group) and macro interventions (organization, community, or policy). See Box 1.1. Social workers who undertake macro interventions will often be engaged in what is called "policy practice" (Jansson, 2014) because policy change is so integral to what happens in organizations and communities. Given this division of labor, some professional roles require that the social worker be involved full-time in macro practice. These professional roles are often referred to by such titles as *planner, policy analyst, program coordinator, community organizer, manager*, and *administrator*.

The micro service worker or clinical social worker also bears responsibility for initiating change in organizations and communities. Workers in micro-level roles are often the first to recognize patterns indicating the need for change. If one or two persons present a particular problem, a logical response is to deal with them as individuals. However, as more individuals present the same situation, it may become evident that something is awry in the systems with which these clients are interacting. The social worker must

Policy Practice

Practice Behavior: Assess how social welfare and economic policies impact the delivery of and access to social services.

Critical Thinking Question: In your field or work experience, what policies have influenced how you practice? How have these policies benefitted or constrained your work?

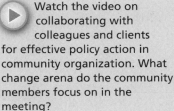
Watch the video on collaborating with colleagues and clients for effective policy action in community organization. What change arena do the community members focus on in the meeting?

Box 1.1	Focus of Intervention	

Level	Primary Focus of Intervention	Examples of Roles
Micro	Individuals	Clinician Care Coordinator
Micro	Domestic Unit	Family Counselor Case Manager
Micro and Macro	Small Groups	Group Worker Supervisor
Macro	Organizations	Human Service Administrator Midlevel Manager Program Coordinator Supervisor
Macro	Communities	Community Developer Community Organizer Community Planner Social Activist
Macro	Policy	Legislative Advocate Policy Analyst

then assume the responsibility for identifying the system(s) in need of change and the type of change needed. The nature of the system(s) in need of change and the type of change needed may lead to communitywide intervention or intervention in a single organization.

Suppose, for example, the staff in a senior center discover that a number of older persons in the community are possibly malnourished because of self-neglect and social isolation. A caseworker could follow up on each person, one at a time, in an attempt to provide outreach and needed services. But this could take a long time and produce hit-or-miss results. An alternative would be to deal with the problem from a macro perspective—to invest time in organizing agency and community resources to identify older people who need the senior center's services and to ensure that services are provided through a combination of staff and volunteer efforts.

Or assume that a social worker begins seeing more and more mixed-status families, composed of members with varying legal status. Parents are fearful of being targeted by deportation laws that could cause them to be forced to leave the country without their citizen-children. Choices are having to be made every day as some parents choose to leave their children in hopes that they will have a better life, whereas others choose to take their children with them even though this will mean taking them into exile. The social worker recognizes how untenable this position is for parents who have to make a choice between orphaning their children or exiling them to an unknown fate (Zayas & Bradlee, 2014). This social worker decides to document these cases, and asks her colleagues to do the same thing, so that they can join forces in advocating for immigration reform.

This may seem like a complex undertaking for someone who came into social work expecting to work with people one at a time. Yet, these social workers know that they have valuable practice experience that can be used to advocate for change . . . and, as a social worker, they are committed to being a voice for those who are unheard.

Although it is true that macro-level interventions can be complicated, we will offer a somewhat systematic approach that attempts to make such efforts more manageable. Remember, too, that these interventions are typically accomplished with the help of others, not alone.

A Systematic Approach to Macro Social Work Practice

Social workers find themselves drawn into episodes of macro practice through a number of different avenues, which we will refer to as (1) population, (2) problem, and (3) arena. The three overlapping circles in Figure 1.1 illustrate the focal points of the social worker's efforts in undertaking a macro-level change episode. As the intervention becomes more clearly conceptualized and defined, political and policy contexts must also be taken into consideration. Figure 1.1 illustrates an approach that can be used by social workers to identify, study, and analyze the need for change and to begin formulating solutions.

Initial awareness that a problem exists may occur in a variety of ways. It might be brought to a social worker's attention by a client. A group of residents within a neighborhood may present issues and concerns that need to be addressed. Issues in the workplace, such as the quality of service to clients, may surface and require organized intervention. Community problems may be so glaring that the need for change comes from many different directions. Social problems may be broadcast around the world, illustrating that multiple societies are struggling with some of the same challenges that one has identified in a local arena. Regardless of how social workers identify change opportunities, they function in a political environment that cannot be ignored.

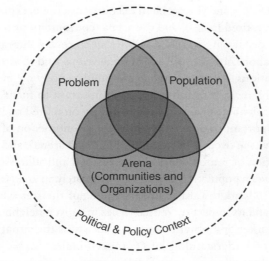

Figure1.1

Macro Practice Conceptual Framework: Understanding Problem, Population, and Arena

More will be said about these interacting factors later in this book, as the analytical and intervention phases of macro-level change are described. The following examples will illustrate these different points of entry into an **episode of change**.

- A social worker working with a senior center discovers that assisted-living resources in the community are limited for low-income seniors. In this instance, the worker's point of entry into the episode of change may be through the *population* of low-income older adults, helping them organize and approach the city council or the state legislature about the need for more options for low-income seniors who can no longer live alone.
- A social worker with a neighborhood service center may discover that among the many families served by the center are five or six single parents who have recently moved from welfare to work but are unable to find affordable child care. Working with this group's *problem* or need (children who need to be cared for while the parent is at work) as his or her point of entry into the episode of change, the social worker and others develop a plan for child care for the children of these single parents.
- A social worker at a community center learns that many apartments in the neighborhood are being used as drop points for undocumented immigrants, where they wait until they are sent to various communities across the country. Concerns are expressed about sanitation, safety, and exploitation. In this instance, the worker's point of entry into the episode of change may be the *community or neighborhood*, perhaps by sponsoring some communitywide meetings to discuss the impact, involving the appropriate community leaders and authorities, and working toward a resolution. This represents entry through the community *arena*.

In the course of engaging with and assessing populations, problems, and arenas, the social worker will inevitably focus on the areas of overlap depicted in Figure 1.1. To engage in macro practice to help a client who is addicted to alcohol, for example, the social worker must understand the problem (alcoholism), the background of the person addicted (e.g., older, retired males), and the arena (community or organization) within which the problem occurs. It would be important to review literature on the **target population**, theory about how alcohol addiction develops, and reports from studies testing various interventions. As the change agent builds a body of knowledge about the population and problem, it becomes especially important to focus on the overlap between the two areas: alcoholism and its unique impact on retired males.

It is likewise important to understand how the phenomenon of alcoholism affects the local community (the overlap between problem and arena), and to what extent the needs of the population of retired males are understood and addressed in the local community (overlap between population and arena). Ultimately, in an episode of macro practice, the objective is to work toward an understanding of the area where all three circles overlap (alcoholism and its impact on retired males in a given neighborhood or town).

As the social worker and other change agents assess the situation, they will gain at least some level of understanding of (1) retired males, (2) basic concepts and issues surrounding alcoholism, (3) the local community and/or relevant organizations, (4) alcoholism as it affects retired males, (5) alcoholism and how it is addressed in the local community, (6) how the needs of retired males are addressed in the local community, (7) available interventions and their applicability to both the population and community of interest, and, finally, (8) the problems and needs of retired males in the local community who are addicted to alcohol.

Social and community problems and needs must also be addressed within a larger context that affects the population, the problem, and the community or organization. Dealing with social and community problems and needs effectively requires an awareness of the political environment within which the change episode will be undertaken. For these reasons, we have placed the three circles (population, problem, and arena) within a large dotted outer circle intended to depict the political environment. The importance of and the need for understanding the political and policy contexts within which macro-practice tasks take place cannot be overemphasized.

 Assess your understanding of macro practice by taking this brief quiz.

THE FOUNDATION OF MACRO PRACTICE

Understanding the professional mission of social work that integrates micro and macro interventions and respects the practitioners who perform those roles is essential to recognizing why macro practice is important. Essentially, social workers have a mission to join the strengths of doing "both-and," being able to intervene with an individual service recipient and then skillfully moving into a larger system intervention that will make a difference in the lives of multiple individuals.

Similarly, the person-is-political perspective underscores the belief that individuals cannot be viewed separately from the larger society. The actions—or lack of actions—of individuals influence those around them and may have broad implications for others within an organization or a community. Thus, micro and macro roles are interconnected.

For those social workers committed to bringing about positive change not only for individual clients but also for whole neighborhoods, organizations, and communities, the question becomes: How is it possible to meet all the expectations of a job and still be involved with larger issues?

In Chapters 3 through 12 of this book, we will attempt to present the building blocks of a planned change model that makes it both possible and manageable to carry out episodes of change. Before we focus on a change model, it is necessary to develop a foundation for macro practice. That foundation is based on an understanding of the relevance of language; theories, models, and approaches; as well as values and ethics.

The Importance of Terminology

It is important to acknowledge terminology used to describe diverse population groups with whom social workers interact. Social workers need to recognize that terms used to define and distinguish special populations can be applied adversely in ways that reinforce stereotypes or isolate the members of these groups.

Abramovitz (1991) called attention to how common speech sends messages beyond those actually spoken. She offered as an example the phrase *feminization of poverty*, which calls attention

Diversity and Difference

Practice Behavior: Apply self-awareness and self-regulation to manage the influence of personal biases and values in working with diverse clients and constituencies.

Critical Thinking Question: Why is language so important in working with diverse clients and constituencies?

to the economic concerns of women but may also imply that poverty is a new issue for women. She argued instead for the term *povertization of women*, which better reflects the long history of women's economic disadvantage. She also argued against the use of the sociological term *underclass*, which has been suggested as a replacement for *multiproblem, disadvantaged*, or *hard-to-reach* poor people, because of its stigmatizing connotations.

Since the 1950s, growing attention has been given to employing more accurate and less historically laden language when referring to special populations. For example, among ethnic and racial groups, blacks adopted the term *black* as a preferred descriptor in the 1960s and 1970s, supplanting the segregation-linked terms of *Negro* and *colored*. Since the Civil Rights Movement, the term *African American* has gained widespread use, and research indicates that African Americans are evenly divided between *black* and *African American* with regard to their preferred term (Sigelman, Tuch, & Martin, 2005). Among Native Americans, the term *Native American* has been promoted as more appropriate than *Indian*. However, the full phrase *American Indian* is considered appropriate to be used interchangeably with *Native American* (Native American Journalists Association, 2006). In Canada, the term *First Nations People* has come into general use, replacing the term *Indian* for the indigenous people of the Americas. The term *Latino* is used as a generic expression to represent persons of Latin American ancestry, including Puerto Ricans, Cuban Americans, Mexican Americans (who also use the term *Chicano*), and others. Advocates of the use of *Latino* or *Latina* contend that *Hispanic* (which was originally created by the U.S. Bureau of the Census) is appropriately applied only to persons with links to Spain (Gutiérrez & Lewis, 1999), but a survey by *Hispanic Magazine* (2006) found that *Hispanic* was preferred by about two-thirds of the more than 1,000 registered voters in the sample. About one-third chose to identify themselves as *Latino* (Granado, 2006). Finally, the term *white*, despite its common usage, is poorly defined, but it remains more broadly applicable than *Anglo* or *Caucasian*. Results from a study to determine the term they prefer to be used when describing their group showed that, among whites, *white* was preferred by a wide margin (62 percent) over *Caucasian* (17 percent) (U.S. Bureau of Labor Statistics, 1995).

The term *persons with disabilities* is considered appropriate as a broad descriptor of individuals who have different physical or mental capacities from the norm. The term *differently abled* has been advocated as a way to avoid categorizing members of this group in terms of their perceived limitations, but this phrase has not yet been commonly adopted. With respect to sexuality, *gay* and *lesbian* have been preferred terms for at least the past three decades, whereas individuals who are *bisexual* or *transgender* have also become better recognized as distinct groups. Members of each group were previously referred to as being distinguished by their *sexual preference*, but the term *sexual orientation* is now considered more appropriate because it reflects research indicating that such orientation is innate rather than a matter of choice. The abbreviation *LGBT* (lesbian, gay, bisexual, and transgender) has become commonplace and is now often expanded to LGBTQ. In some uses, the additional letter stands for "questioning," referring to people who are uncertain about their sexual orientation. In others, it stands for "queer," a once derogatory term that activists have embraced as a sign of defiance against discrimination. With respect to gender, some feminist writers have argued for use of the terms *womyn* or *wimin* on the basis that they are less derivative of the word *men*, but as yet these terms have not gained wide use.

We recognize the importance of language, and it is our intent in this book to reflect that importance in our use of terms. Based on the preceding reviews, we will intersperse the terms *black* and *African American, Native American* and *American Indian,* and *Hispanic* and *Latino.* Our goal is to be sensitive to the convictions and wishes of as many people within diverse population groups as possible, and to reflect what is considered standard terminology by members of those groups. We hope the reader will recognize this as evidence of the dynamic, evolving nature of modern language and as an acknowledgment that social workers need to ask the persons with whom they work about what language they view as respectful terminology.

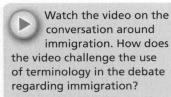

Watch the video on the conversation around immigration. How does the video challenge the use of terminology in the debate regarding immigration?

www.youtube.com /watch?v=tmz9cCF0KNE

Theories, Models, and Approaches

Theories are sets of interrelated concepts and constructs that provide a framework for understanding how and why something does or does not work. *Models* are prescriptions based on theories that provide direction for the practitioner, whereas *approaches* are less prescribed. In other words, theories provide the tools for thinking about a problem or need, whereas models and approaches provide guidelines for action and intervention.

In this book, we develop a practice model of planned change that is fairly prescriptive and derives from systems theory. At the individual level, for example, theories provide explanations about the causes of various types of mental disorders, and practice models arising from these theories suggest ways of helping people affected by the disorders. On a larger scale, sociological theories may describe how communities, organizations, or societies function. A *practice model* for initiating change in communities and organizations (such as the planned change model presented in this book) illustrates how these theories can lead to specific actions.

One theory that seems to have considerable relevance at both the micro and macro levels is systems theory. **Systems theory** contends that there are multiple parts of any entity, whether it is a group, an organization, or a community. Entities can be best understood as systems with interconnecting components, and certain common principles help in understanding systems, whether they are as large as an international corporation or as small as a family. There are resources that the system needs in order to function, and they may come in the form of people, equipment, funding, knowledge, legitimacy, or a host of other forms. These resources interact within the system, producing something that becomes the system's product.

Consider a human service agency that targets gay and lesbian youth. The volunteers and staff, funding from various sources, teachers from local schools, concerned parents, and the youth themselves may all come together within this human service setting. Their relationships and interactions will determine whether the organization functions as a system or merely as a disparate assortment of parts. Functional systems have a dynamic interaction among components that holds them together. The interaction that holds this human service agency together may be the communication that occurs as teachers, parents, and youth come together; their bonding over an important cause; their shared commitment to the mission; and the desire to create a safer, more supportive environment for the youth. Systems expect conflict and have ways to cope when it occurs. For an agency dedicated to gay and lesbian youth, there will be strong community forces that do not agree with what the agency is doing, and organize to challenge the change effort. Depending on the level of conflict, the system may have boundaries that are fairly rigid in order to protect itself from external forces. The product of this system would be youth who are better able to function in the larger environment and who have a sense of who they are.

In an organizational arena, a systems approach reveals the complexity involved in recognizing multiple groups (e.g., professional staff, clerical staff, management, administration, the board, clients, funding sources, neighbors, and others in the community) that have a stake in what that organization does and whom it serves. This theoretical perspective reminds the practitioner that organizations are complex systems embedded in larger community systems, all of which are interacting on a daily basis.

Community researcher Roland Warren (1978) provided a good example of how systems theory can be applied to understanding communities. He built on the work of Talcott Parsons, a sociologist known for defining the characteristics of social systems. He also incorporated the work of others who described how community systems would differ from the groups and formal organizations to which systems theory had previously been applied.

Warren saw the community as not just one system, but a system of systems in which all types of formal and informal groups and individuals interact. Given the diversity among groups and subgroups, communities have a broad range of structural and functional possibilities that do not conform to a centralized goal. The beauty of a community system is that it is a complex arena in which multiple groups and organizations with differing values may simultaneously exist.

Warren's contention that a system endures through time speaks to social work practitioners who work with groups committed to maintaining their communities and grieving over the loss of what their communities used to be. For example, the physical land and the interactions that occurred on that land may render it sacred to indigenous people. Similarly, a widow who has lived on the same street corner for 60 years may hesitate to move even when increasing crime threatens her physical safety.

Systems theory recognizes the importance of formal groups and organizations. For example, in dealing with child maltreatment, child protective service workers, law enforcement officers, hospital emergency staff, teachers, public prosecutors, and others combine their efforts within a community to ensure that vulnerable children receive the highest levels of protection possible. However, it is equally important to recognize and acknowledge "informal linkages." For example, the social support that a female caregiver of an aged parent receives from other caregivers may not be formalized or highly visible in the community. Yet this linkage is vital to whether caregivers will be able to continue the caregiving role. Therefore, systems thinking is value-based thinking; what is selected for consideration will determine what is considered important. Because communities are complex, thinking of them as social systems involves balancing a number of variables that are in dynamic interaction.

Systems theory provides a set of assumptions that undergird the planned-change model in this book. It is important to note that there are multiple approaches to systems theory, some more open to change than others. We assume that social workers will encounter systems of every kind. Some organizations and communities will be more amenable to change than others, some will be more closed, and others will be more open to conflict. Being able to assess these arenas and their openness to change is central to the planned-change process.

In addition, systems theory that informs the planned-changed model implies that there will be goals and outcomes, both of which are important steps in the planned-change process. Our model of planned change assumes that there will be broadly defined goals to guide practitioners' efforts. **Goals** are usually long term and sometimes idealistic. However, goals provide a vision shared by clients and colleagues—a hope of what can be—and they assist the practitioner in maintaining a focus. The identification of these goals should be based on the best knowledge available.

From goals, we assume there will be **outcomes**, defined as quality-of-life changes in clients' lives, based on the interventions planned by practitioners. Much of the history of social work practice has been focused on process—what the social worker does. Interventions of the future will be driven by outcomes—what change is expected to be achieved by and for the target population as a result of this change effort. Balancing the importance of process and the push for accountability through outcome measurement is part of competent, contemporary practice. It is also key to planned-change intervention. Together, goals and outcomes are based on the best available evidence, guided by as complete as possible an understanding of the systems in which change will occur.

The model presented in this book and throughout most of this text is often referred to as a rational planning approach. It is based on a study of the current situation and a carefully developed and prescribed plan for change that leads to predetermined outcomes. In rational planning there is a type of linearity present in that the plan, when produced, goes from one step to the next until the established goal is achieved. This process is called "reverse-order planning" (Brody, 2000, pp. 77–78): establishing a goal and then backtracking to fill in the actions that need to occur to arrive at the selected goal. However, this is not the only approach to community and organizational change available to social workers. The alternative to reverse-order planning is "forward-sequence planning," which begins by asking where can one start rather than what one wants as the final result (Brody, 2000, pp. 77–78). These more interpretive planning processes and emergent approaches are elaborated in other textbooks (e.g., Netting, O'Connor, & Fauri, 2008) if you are interested in exploring alternative ways to plan. Rational approaches to change are typically preferred by funders and regulators; thus, it is important that the social worker be as certain as possible about the course of action to be taken in professionally assisted planned change, because there is often so much at stake. For this reason, we recommend beginning with a rational planning approach and moving to these alternative approaches only when the social worker is confident that an emergent process is necessary.

Underlying any planned-change process is recognition of the potential value conflicts and ethical dilemmas that can occur in macro practice. We now turn to those.

Values and Ethics

Professions require mastery of a large body of theoretical, research-based, and technical knowledge. Having professional expertise means being up-to-date on what theories and practice models are available and integrating the best research evidence into one's practice. Thus, **professional judgment** derives from the ability to skillfully apply and discern the quality of the best knowledge available in a workable manner. Gustafson (1982) argues that professional practitioners prefer guidelines rather than rules because guidelines offer direction instead of rigid formulation. They allow professionals to exercise discretion and to use their judgment. However, professionals also carry enormous responsibility because what they decide and how they act will affect both their clients and the multiple constituencies previously discussed (Cimino, Rorke, & Adams, 2013). In professional practice, every choice is a value judgment.

Being a **professional** implies identification with a set of values that places the interests of the client first; a professional relies on knowledge, judgment, and skill to act on those values. We define *values* as those strongly held beliefs about what is necessary and worthy that many or most members of a social system perceive to be fundamental to quality social work practice. In some ways, values are similar to theories—they provide a framework for understanding and analyzing situations. **Ethics** are similar to models— they provide guidelines for practice in carrying out values. One can feel strongly about something, but acting on that feeling involves ethical behavior, which is the operationalization of that value.

Because codes of ethics serve as guidelines for professional practice, it is imperative that students know the content and limitations of written codes. It is also important for social workers to know that codes of ethics develop over time (they change as new issues arise), that there are multiple codes of ethics for social workers around the world, and that there is an international code of ethics for social workers.

The International Federation of Social Workers (IFSW) has published a Code of Ethics that endorses human rights and social justice as fundamental to the social work profession. Their website links to codes of ethics in over 25 countries throughout the world. Codes in Canada and the United States are very similar, and comparative studies have examined the relationship of national codes to the IFSW Code (Powell, 2009). A commitment to social change is evident across social work codes, even though it is viewed as dangerous for social workers in countries such as China to pursue this agenda (Staniforth, Fouche, & O'Brien, 2011, p. 196). With assistance from the Center for the Study of Ethics in Professions, Buila conducted an online review of 700 professional codes of ethics in health, dental, mental health, and education fields. She selected 55 for in-depth review, using key terms such as *social justice, diversity*, and *discrimination*. She concluded that social work codes are unique in the value they place on social responsibility to pursue social and political action (Buila, 2010).

The U.S.-based National Association of Social Workers (NASW) Code of Ethics is intended to introduce a perspective that drives practitioners' thinking, establishes criteria for selecting goals, and influences how information is interpreted and understood. Regardless of which role the social worker plays—program coordinator, community organizer, political lobbyist, or direct practitioner—these professional actions are not value free.

The NASW Code of Ethics lists six core values on which the ethical principles of social work are based: service, social justice, dignity and worth of the person, importance of human relationships, integrity, and competence. We focus on these core values from the NASW Code to illustrate ethical conflicts that social workers may face when responsibilities to multiple constituencies clash.

Service

Social workers are often simultaneously engaged in both direct and indirect practice, actions intended to help people in need and to address the social problems they face. Closely related to providing service is the concept of **beneficence**, which is based on the desire to do good for others, as well as not doing harm. Persons entering the field of social work will often say that they chose this profession because they want to help others. The core value of service is typically a primary motivator for those professionals who work in health and human service settings.

There is an ongoing debate in the field of social work around the core value of service. Historically, there has been tension over where to direct limited resources, with more radical members of the profession arguing that focusing on delivering social services will create individual dependencies and redirect limited resources away from more aggressive methods of changing oppressive systems and advocating for social justice. Mainstream proponents argue that services must be provided to population groups that are suffering and that collective action is fine as long as the focus on immediate need is not lost (Gates, 2014). This debate and accompanying tension can be framed as a conflict between the desire to provide service (status quo) and the quest for social justice (social change). A social worker may feel there is never enough time to fully provide high-quality services without becoming a part of a system that needs reform and losing sight of the bigger picture. The conflict is that providing services (a responsibility to clients) may be creating dependencies and putting bandaids on social problems that need to be addressed at the broader system level (a responsibility to the profession).

Social Justice

Social justice means being committed to challenging injustice and pursuing social change with and on behalf of oppressed groups. The principle underlying this core value is primarily focused on social workers addressing poverty, discrimination, unemployment, and related issues. Jansson (2014) points out that social justice is based on equality. With the many entrenched interests one encounters in local communities, it is likely that social workers will focus their efforts on oppressed target population groups and will always be discovering new inequalities. Because so many groups face problems related to having enough financial resources, social workers often extend the principle to include economic justice, thus focusing on social and economic justice concerns.

Concerns about social and economic justice are exacerbated when clients cannot pay for services. As long as clients can pay, professional decision making may not conflict with the larger society because resources do not have to be redistributed. Conceivably, as long as clients can pay for professional services, professions can operate within the market economy. Private-practice and fee-for-service agencies conform to this approach. Quality care is exchanged for economic resources, often in the form of third-party payments. The key to this approach is that the client has insurance coverage or access to sufficient personal funds.

This approach breaks down, however, when clients cannot pay. Many social work clients are in problematic circumstances because their income is inadequate to meet their needs and other resources are not available. Social workers face ethical challenges when the practice settings in which they work limit eligibility based on socioeconomic status.

Ethical and Professional Behavior

Practice Behavior: Make ethical decisions by applying the standards of the NASW Code of Ethics, relevant laws and regulations, models for ethical decision-making, ethical conduct of research, and additional codes of ethics as appropriate to the context.

Critical Thinking Question: Can you address issues of social justice and inequality without engaging in macro practice? Why or why not?

Patients with AIDS may find themselves unable to pay for care at the same time that their needs increase because they are fired from jobs when news about their disease becomes known. Older people could avoid institutional care by hiring in-home caregivers, but despite having considerable lifetime savings, medical expenses may leave them with too few funds to meet their needs. Youth who have grown up in poverty may feel there is no way out except to break the law.

Health and human service systems are driven by considerations of whether resources are available to pay for (or subsidize) the services that clients need. If resources are not available, patients with AIDS and older people may be forced to expend all of their own resources before ending up in public institutions, and youth may continue in cycles of insufficient education, housing, health care, and job opportunities.

Dignity and Worth of the Person

Often called *self-determination* or *autonomy*, valuing the dignity and worth of each person means respecting and honoring the right of that person to make his or her own life choices. Concepts such as empowerment are built on the value of dignity and worth, implying that power or control over one's life means seizing the opportunity to make one's own decisions. As an example, the pro-choice proponents in the abortion controversy advocate for autonomy, a woman's right to choose. This stance conflicts with a number of religious codes arguing the immorality of abortion and stating that the right of the unborn child must be considered as well. Although autonomy may be perceived as individualistic and therefore more relevant to direct practice situations, one has only to be involved in the heated debate over abortion to realize the ethical conflict involved in situations where the autonomy of both parties cannot be equally respected.

Similarly, respecting the dignity and worth of people means that social work is committed to addressing the needs of persons who are marginalized. One example is faced by same-sex couples who desperately want their committed relationships to be recognized by the larger society. Access to survivor and spousal benefits, retirement income, and inheritance; hospital visitation rights; adoption; and immigration are just a few of the civil and financial issues faced by same-sex couples. The dignity and worth of persons are disrespected in policies that do not recognize same-sex relationships. Social workers attempting to honor these relationships may be advocating for changes at all levels of policy making and may find themselves in conflict in practice settings that do not recognize the rights of same-sex couples (Pelts, 2014).

Importance of Human Relationships

The NASW Code of Ethics lists the importance of human relationships as a core social work value. This means continually finding new and meaningful ways to facilitate consumer as well as citizen participation in organizational and community arenas. Nurturing relationships is an ongoing and necessary challenge for the dedicated professional.

In macro-change opportunities, the challenge is to include multiple stakeholders who may be both consumers and collaborators in the process. This challenge is grounded in the importance of human relationships, even when people do not agree.

Technological advances help facilitate communication, particularly in mobilizing clients and providers to work toward a cause. Knowing how to engage clients and others in one's change efforts is critically important. As new technological venues emerge, it will be necessary for the practitioner to keep up-to-date so that these tools can be used to communicate with and sustain the central importance of strong relationships with various constituencies.

Reamer (2013) identified a number of ethical and risk management challenges that accompany the new digital landscape. Many intervention methods are available, including but not limited to online, video, and telephone counseling; cybertherapy; web-based self-guided opportunities; social media; email; text messaging; and a host of other possibilities. Macro social workers who administer and manage agencies have an ethical responsibility to clients to be certain that confidentiality is maintained, to monitor potential conflicts of interest and boundary issues that emerge in digital transactions, and to assure that appropriate digital documentation is safely maintained. The ability to connect in multiple ways provides increasing options for maintaining human relationships but changes the nature of those relationships in ways that codes of ethics typically do not address in detail.

Integrity

Integrity is based on trustworthiness and consistency. This core value implies that one's associates (e.g., colleagues, clients, and community groups) should be able to expect consistency in one's thinking and acting. Integrity gets to the character of the person. Professional integrity means that those persons who call themselves professionals will remember that the center of their practice is always the client. Social work is only one of many helping professions, but its unique contribution is to serve as a constant reminder that people are multidimensional and that they must be viewed in the context of their environments.

In professional practice, integrity means that one does not simply do what one would like to do, but fits problems to solutions based on thorough analysis. Defining the problem to be changed requires integrating what clients have to say with what is known from scholarly research and practice results. This analytical process is iterative, dynamic, and interactive, often causing the change agent to reframe the original problem statement because new information constantly requires rethinking. However, once a problem statement is agreed on, social workers must ascertain that their interventions have integrity in relation to the problem at hand. Interventions often require a creative imagination that goes beyond traditional approaches and seeks more fundamental change. Thus, it is hoped that the social worker will be imaginative, will think critically, and will use his or her best judgment as a professional in the process of planned change.

> **Research-informed Practice (or Practice-informed Research)**
>
> **Practice Behavior:** Use and translate research evidence to inform and improve practice, policy, and service delivery.
>
> **Critical Thinking Question:** Why does defining the problem to be changed require integrating what clients have to say with what is known from scholarly research and practice results?

Competence

Professional social workers are expected to be informed and skilled. The competent macro practitioner will approach the need for change with an understanding and expectation that decisions will be based on as complete a set of data and information as time and resources allow. We recognize that there are multiple ways to regard systems, and it is important to carefully assess each arena in which social workers plan to carry out an episode of change. Competence implies that informed decision making is pursued in a systematic and scholarly manner, utilizing the best available theoretical, research-based, and practice-based knowledge. The approach is often called *evidenced-based* or *evidence-guided practice* and applies to whatever level of intervention the practitioner is addressing, whether individual, group, organizational, or communitywide.

In 2001, NASW issued Standards for Cultural Competence in Social Work Practice. These standards were intended to guide practice with individuals, groups, organizations, communities, and societies in respecting languages, classes, races, ethnic backgrounds, religions, and other factors of diversity (NASW, 2001). In addition, the Council on Social Work Education (CSWE) issued Educational Policy and Accreditation Standards (EPAS) called "competencies" that are being used to guide curricular development in schools of social work and are listed at the beginning of this book (CSWE, 2012). These competencies include the ability to engage, assess, intervene, and evaluate practice with individuals, families, groups, organizations, and communities. In other words, the ethical principle of competence means that a social worker should be skillful in working in both micro and macro situations.

> Go to the International Federation of Social Workers homepage and do a search on "Statement of Ethical Principles." After reading the statement of principles, compare and contrast the ethical principles of NASW and the International Federation of Social Workers. What are the implications of their similarities and differences?

Ethical Conflicts

In the NASW Code, social workers have responsibility (1) to clients, (2) to colleagues, (3) in practice settings (typically, organizations and employing agencies), (4) as professionals, (5) to the social work profession, and (6) to the broader society. Inevitably, there will be situations in which these responsibilities interact and create ethical conflicts. For example, a worker who values a child's right to a safe and secure environment must also value the parents' rights to have a say in their child's future. But in a potentially harmful situation, there is the potential for conflict between the worker's responsibility to protect the child's worth and dignity and the importance of a relationship with the parents. The social worker who serves as a public housing administrator may value the freedom of a disruptive resident to play loud music at top volume, but must also respect those in the building who value peace and quiet. Whereas respect for the individual is important, so is creating a fair and just environment for all residents. A social worker who is advocating for diverse client populations may come into conflict with her employing organization that is mandated to set boundaries on who will (and will not) quality for benefits. A choice between equally important values or responsibilities to various constituencies may have to be made when there are no easy or obviously "right" or "wrong" solutions.

During the socialization process of preparing for professional social work practice, each person will have to determine how her or his personal values relate to the professional values being learned. This growing self-awareness includes recognizing one's own privilege and power in being a professional and one's ability to oppress even in attempting to help others (Garran & Rozas, 2013). Integrating one's personal and professional values is a part of professional identification, and it leads to what Sullivan (2005) and others say about professions as communities of identity in which colleagues come together to work toward the civic good. Embracing that identity and approaching one's practice with integrity and competence will contribute to one's ability to join with others in pursuing the values of the profession.

Balancing the values of service, social justice, the dignity and worth of the person, the importance of human relationships, integrity, and competence demands an analytical approach to decision making and intervention. Inevitably, the macro practitioner will face ethical conflicts that go beyond the bounds of codes of ethics. This requires that he or she have a strong professional identity. We now turn to four case examples that illustrate the dilemmas often encountered by social work practitioners.

> **?** Assess your understanding of the foundations of macro practice by taking this brief quiz.

FOUR CASE EXAMPLES

Some of the aspects of social work macro practice that need to be understood by the student and the beginning practitioner can be illustrated by case examples. We selected the following examples because they contain similar themes but focus on different target population groups: children, older adults and disabled persons, immigrant youth, and persons who are homeless. As these cases and the workers' thoughts are presented, we encourage the reader to think about how macro-level change might be approached by beginning with a study of the *population*, the *problem*, and the *arena* within which change might take place. We also hope that these examples will illustrate both the systemic nature of social work macro practice and the types of value dilemmas confronting social workers.

Case Example 1:   Child Protective Services

Child Protective Services (CPS) workers have responsibility for dealing with the abuse and neglect of children. When reports of alleged abuse or neglect come to the unit, the CPS worker must investigate the report and make decisions about the disposition of the case. It is a very demanding and emotionally draining area of specialization within the field of social work. One CPS worker took the time to record the details of a particular case, and also shared a list of dilemmas and contradictions he had encountered over the years, in the interest of helping new workers prepare for what they will face as they enter practice.

Friday, 10:40 A.M. Supervisor text-messaged me about a report of neglect. She felt it should be checked out today because it sounded too serious to be left until after the weekend (as agency rules allow with some neglect allegations). According to the neighbor's report, parents have abandoned three minor children.

11:10 A.M. Got in my car, loading the address in my GPS. I know the neighborhood well. It is the poorest in the city and unsafe at night. A high percentage of families receive some kind of assistance. Homes are run down, streets are littered, and any visible sense of pride in the community has long been abandoned. [*to what extent is this more choice*]

11:40 A.M. The house at the address given is among the most rundown in a seriously deteriorating neighborhood. The house has no front steps—just a cinder block placed in front of the door. Window casings are rotting out for lack of paint. There is no doorbell. I knocked. There was rustling inside, but no answer. I waited and knocked again. I walked around and peered through a window and saw a small child, about 3 years old I guessed, curled up in a chair. An older girl, about age 8 or 9, peeked out from behind a doorway.

I remembered that the oldest child was named Cindy, so I called out to her. After a bit of conversation, I persuaded her to let me in. I quickly recognized that this would not be an ordinary case. A foul smell hit me so hard it made my eyes water. I used a tissue to filter the air. The worst odors were coming from the bathroom and kitchen. The water had evidently been shut off—toilets were not working, and garbage was piled up. The kitchen was littered with fast-food containers, possibly retrieved from the dumpsters of nearby shops.

There were three very frightened children—Cindy (age 9), Scott (age 6), and Melissa (age 3). None would talk.

12:35 P.M. I made arrangements to transport them to the shelter and went back to the office to do the paperwork.

2:15 P.M. A previous neglect report revealed the following:

Father: Stan, age 27, unemployed, in and out of jail for petty theft, public intoxication, and several other minor offenses. Frequently slept in public parks or homeless shelters. Rarely showed up at home anymore. Several police reports of violence against wife and children. Admits paternity for only the oldest child.

Mother: Sarah, age 25, Temporary Aid to Needy Families (TANF) recipient, high school dropout, never employed. Tests performed in connection with one attempt at job training revealed a developmental concern. Child care skills have always been minimal, but there is no previous history of abandonment of children. Whereabouts at this time are unknown.

3:35 P.M. Filed the appropriate forms with agency and the police. Entered field notes into laptop for the record. Children placed at Vista Shelter until a more permanent placement can be arranged. Emailed confirmation of placement to supervisor, copied to shelter staff.

Over the years, as this CPS worker dealt with similar cases, he kept a running list of the kinds of dilemmas, frustrations, and contradictions he and his colleagues regularly faced. These are excerpts from his list:

1. Abused and neglected children desperately need to be loved and nurtured in order to develop into healthy teens and adults. We can see that their needs for shelter, food, clothing, and medical care are met, but we can't insure that they will be loved, nurtured, and given a chance for some type of success. These deficits in their lives present a clear *problem*. Are there people in this community who have the capacity and are willing to invest the time to insure that a child feels loved and valued? Where could we find volunteers willing to take on this type of challenge? Could we approach church groups, PTAs, college or high school organizations, or service clubs?

2. A disproportionately high percentage of lower socioeconomic status teens get pregnant and drop out of high school, go on welfare, parent poorly, and recycle many of their problems to the next generation. In this case, Cindy is a very likely victim. These issues focus on a *population*. How can we interrupt this pattern? Can we develop some type of intervention (maybe a group approach) to help young women make informed decisions during this highly vulnerable time in their lives and find ways to evaluate whether it works?

3. And what about parents like Stan and Sarah? They both appear to be from a culture that doesn't share mainstream values about parenting and taking responsibility for a family. True, they are breaking the law and need to be held accountable, but that approach alone has rarely proven effective in improving parenting skills. Is there some way we can help parents like these overcome their deficits and have some chance of rebuilding a stable family? This might be approached from either a *problem* perspective or a community *arena* perspective.

Case Example 2: Case Management with Older Adults and Disabled Persons

Case managers work in a variety of public and private settings. They are responsible for screening potential clients, assessing client needs, developing care plans, mobilizing resources to meet identified needs, and monitoring and evaluating services provided. The case manager in this example works for a nonprofit agency in an inner-city neighborhood, where many of her clients have lived all their lives. She is assigned to the home and community-based long-term-care unit, and carries a caseload of about 60 older and disabled clients. As part of the program evaluation, she was asked to keep a diary of what happened during a typical day. The following are excerpts from her diary.

Wednesday 7:30 A.M. Arrived early to catch up on email. Entered client data from previous day. Organized three new care plans and five medical reports.

8:00–8:10 A.M. Mrs. Garcia (age 79) called, distraught over a letter received from the Social Security office, thinking it meant her benefits would be cut off. Explained that it was a form letter, a routine change, not affecting the amount of her check. Knowing that she is often forgetful and has a hearing problem, made a note to make home visit tomorrow.

8:10–8:30 A.M. Met with Jim from In-Home Support Services. Mr. Thomas, age 93, fell last night. Is in Mercy Hospital. Home Aide found him when she arrived at 7:00 this morning. He is not expected to live. Aide is very upset. Called his daughter and will meet her at hospital later this morning.

8:30–9:30 A.M. Staff meeting regarding 10 clients discharged from City Hospital with inadequate discharge plans. Discussed how to work better with discharge planners. As I left, another case manager told me that Mrs. Hannibal had refused to let the home health nurse in.

9:30–9:45 A.M. Called Mrs. Hannibal (age 77), no answer. Called lifeline program to meet me at her apartment.

9:45–10:00 A.M. No one answered when I knocked; got manager to let me in. Mrs. Hannibal had been drinking. Threw bottle at me and screamed, "No one is going to get me out of here. I'll never go to a home. I'll die first." Worked with lifeline staff to calm Mrs. Hannibal down. She goes in and out of hospital, and has a severe drinking problem.

10:00–11:00 A.M. Arrived at Mercy Hospital. Met Mr. Thomas's daughter, who was in tears, saying it was all her fault, that if he had been living with her this would have never happened. Talked with her regarding her father's desire to live alone, that this had been his choice. Contacted hospital social worker to work with daughter.

11:15 A.M.**–12:00** P.M. Back to office. Entered notes on visits to Mrs. Hannibal and Mr. Thomas. Called two new referrals, faxed documents to hospital, and set up appointments to do assessments tomorrow.

12:00–12:30 P.M. Ate lunch with Adult Protective Services (APS) worker. Discussed abusive relationship of Mr. and Mrs. Tan, a couple in their 60s living in public housing. Agreed to work closely with APS regarding this situation.

12:45–2:00 P.M. Conducted in-home assessment for new client, Ms. Johnson. She was released from hospital yesterday and is receiving home-delivered meals and in-home nursing. Small house is a mess, roaches everywhere. Needs chore and housekeeping services, but there's a long waiting list. Called and cajoled volunteers at Area Agency on Aging (AAA) to help her temporarily. Ms. Johnson was too weak to complete full assessment, will come back tomorrow.

2:30–3:30 P.M. Attended public hearing preceding the planning process for the AAA. Testified about the need for more flexibility in providing services to disabled clients under age 60. Gave examples of persons in their 40s with severe mobility problems.

3:45–4:15 P.M. Stopped to see Mrs. Martinez, newly admitted to Sunnyside Nursing Home. Has been my client for 5 years. Doesn't know me, seems confused. Checked with social worker regarding her meds and called physician regarding potential drug interactions. Used smart phone to access health department's report card to see if there are complaints about this facility. Texted local long-term-care ombudsman about any issues she might be aware of. Made note to check on Mrs. M's disabled daughter, who is still at home and will need supportive services previously provided by her mother.

4:45–5:15 P.M. Returned to office, found out Mr. Thomas had died. Called his daughter. Tried to call physician about Mrs. Martinez's medications, but his nurse could not reveal any information to me because of the privacy act.

Just as the CPS worker had kept a running list of the kinds of dilemmas he faced through the years, the case manager had kept a list of her dilemmas as well. In preparation for the Area Agency on Aging public hearing, she had updated the list in hopes something could be done. Excerpts from her list follow:

1. Although some of our resources can be used to serve any older person in need, most of our funding is tied to income and age eligibility. Slots for people who aren't destitute are quickly filled, and there are long waiting lists. Disabled clients who are not yet 60 years of age do not qualify for case management, even though physically they may be as challenged as many much older adults. Focusing on the diversity within aged and disabled *population* groups and recognizing the needs of vulnerable subpopulations are critically important. Couldn't we organize population groups to help each other advocate for their needs? How do we familiarize policy makers with the diverse needs of these populations and persuade them to consider changing income and age eligibility criteria?

2. So many of the older people I see have had problems all their lives. You can almost tell what's going to happen in their old age by what happens to them as they go through life. Drug and alcohol problems only seem to get worse. Abusive situations escalate. If someone had intervened early when they began having these problems, it would have been much easier because the behavior patterns are well established by the time I encounter them. I know people can change at any age, but it seems harder when one is under stress or facing hard times. Is there some way we could organize a prevention effort to prepare middle-aged people for their senior years and address *problems* earlier?

3. I'm learning some revealing things about case management. Case managers attempt to coordinate what is really a nonsystem of services. If we had a real system, we wouldn't need to pay people like me and we could put those resources toward client services. We are investing a lot in institutionalizing case management when it often just covers up the real problem—that we don't have an accessible service delivery system in place. Change will require engagement in organizational and community *arenas* to get agencies to collaborate in establishing a coordinated and accessible system of services. Who should be involved in a communitywide coalition to work toward a more integrated system of care for aged and disabled persons?

| Case Example 3:   Advocacy and Organizing with Immigrant Youth |

Numerous nonprofit organizations work to support immigrants in the United States through advocacy and services to facilitate integration into local communities. Two social work students were completing their second-year field placements in an agency that worked to organize and support Latin American immigrants. One of their primary assignments was to help organize Latin American youth around equal access to higher education, opportunities, and a range of civil liberties. The social work students worked with the agency's advocacy director to help support youth leaders and facilitate youth-led efforts. As one of their learning activities, the students kept records of their daily activities and some of the questions and dilemmas they faced or observed.

Monday, 9:00 A.M. At weekly agency staff meeting, the client services director described difficulties her office faces in locating affordable housing for recently arrived immigrant families who have fled violence in their own country. She announced a reception for local landlords to build relationships in order to open up affordable housing opportunities. We described the event we will be leading on Saturday at a local street fair to draw attention to the deportation of unaccompanied youth.

10:00 A.M. The youth advocacy director, also our field supervisor, pulled us aside to discuss a protest he had just learned about. A national anti-immigration group had secured permits to protest outside deportation hearings at the federal courthouse on Thursday. He asked us to research this group's activities and then meet with the advocacy team to discuss our findings.

10:15 A.M. We began research on the anti-immigration group. Juanita focused on the group's website and recent publicity. I focused on descriptions of the anti-immigration group by organizations like the Southern Poverty Law Center that monitor the activities of hate groups. We found the group registered as a 501(c)3 nonprofit organization and with a slightly different name as a 501(c)4 organization. Because the organization is registered as a 501(c)3 nonprofit organization, we were able to get its 990 form, which lists major donors. A local manufacturer that provides numerous jobs in our immigrant community was listed as a major donor.

We discovered that this group was responsible for the blowback that our agency and a number of its collaborators were getting over the "Quit Using the i-Word Campaign." Ever since U.S. Supreme Court Justice Sonia Sotomayor had used the term "undocumented" immigrant to refer to persons who were in the United States without proper authorization, a social media firestorm had been blazing. We had been naïve when we had helped initiate the campaign last year and couldn't believe the angry reaction. This anti-immigration group may have been at least partially behind this harsh reaction.

12:15 P.M. Met with the advocacy team to present our findings. They were surprised to find out about the affiliation of the local manufacturing firm with the anti-immigration agency. The fund development director was particularly concerned about the implications of the discovery. No one was surprised to learn that the group had opposed the i-Word Campaign, and they pulled up a number of irate messages about the campaign that the group had posted on Facebook.

2:00 P.M. We met with field supervisor about mutual interest in international social work. We had located a number of professional resources, including the International Federation of Social Workers, the International Association of Schools of Social Work, NASW and CSWE immigration materials and international publications, and the Global Agenda for Social Work and Social Development. We found job opportunities through the United Nations, the Peace Corps, the World Health Organization, UNICEF, and a number of other nongovernmental organizations (NGOs). We discovered a growing literature on the type of work we are doing. Zayas and Bradlee (2014) explored the detention and deportation of families and the impact on citizen-children born in the United States. Gates (2014) reported lessons learned from an immigrant work center in which the tension between providing services and the crying need for advocacy had to be balanced. The changing face of immigration was studied by the Urban Institute (Gelatt, Adams, & Monson,

2014), and the journal *International Social Work* explored numerous issues challenging social work practitioners and educators in preparing students to practice in a global world (see, e.g., Dominelli, 2014; Hawkins & Knox, 2014; Healey & Wairire, 2014). We need to take advantage of these and other resources as we prepare for contemporary practice.

4:30 P.M. Attended the youth organizing meeting. Youth leaders discussed plans for Saturday, including how participants should handle encounters with individuals who oppose our efforts.

The social work interns discussed a number of questions and dilemmas that had arisen that day. The following excerpts are related to the activities noted above:

1. Juanita is a member of a first-generation immigrant family from Colombia, South America, with roots in Colombia and the United States. I am a White American with roots in U.S. southern culture and tradition. Sometimes our observations are very similar. However, sometimes they are not. How can I become more aware of my own prejudices and of White privilege? What do I need to do to become more culturally competent? One thing is clear. We need to immerse ourselves in learning about the *population* of Latino youth with whom we are working. Meeting with them individually and in groups is essential for finding out how they perceive the problems they face, and including them in every aspect of any change effort is absolutely necessary.

2. Agency staff really struggled with how to address the planned anti-immigration protest, because one of our agency's key donors is a partner in the manufacturing firm that supports the anti-immigration organization that is leading the protest. A number of staff wanted to confront our donor. Others wanted to have a conversation with him about his organization's involvement in anti-immigration efforts. Others wanted to gain more information before deciding on a course of action. How should our team address this *problem* when what is needed by the organization (fundraising) may contradict the advocacy efforts of the organization? What constitutes a conflict of interest here?

3. It is still hard to believe how angry to the point of violence people can become when their beliefs and attitudes are threatened. We're still reeling from some of the comments the anti-immigration group posted for all the world to see. As social workers, we believe that calling someone illegal is dehumanizing and that no human being is illegal. But we also realize that there are people who think we are bleedingheart liberals, and convincing them to use different terminology is like asking them to change their worldview. How do we confront these issues without being intolerant of intolerance within our own community *arena*?

Case Example 4:   Chronic Homelessness

A social worker at a homeless shelter had a caseload of 25 clients and was responsible for orientation, coordinating physical and dental exams, and referral and transportation to community agencies to deal with problems related to income, permanency of housing, employment, counseling, and other problems and needs caused by their homelessness. Excerpts from the social worker's field notes follow.

Tuesday, 8:30 A.M. Jack C., a 3-month resident, had been delivered to the shelter the previous evening by local police after having been cited for drunk and disorderly conduct. I went over the shelter's policies on alcohol and drug abuse, and explained that additional offenses could result in expulsion from the shelter.

His response was very passive and noncommittal, and he indicated that he really didn't care if he stayed at the shelter or not.

9:00 A.M. Went to my office to check my email and return phone calls. Set up two meetings with case managers at a local clinic for homeless individuals. I want to see how the service providers understand the problems faced by homeless adults experiencing serious mental illness. I also want to begin to better identify the strengths of the population—I've noticed that much of our conversations about these homeless adults are about their challenges, not about their resilience and strengths.

10:30 A.M. Met with Trevor L., a 45-year-old man who had been at the shelter for 2 weeks. He had been referred to two different employers and was waiting to hear whether he was still in the running for either job. He had a list of available apartments provided by the shelter, had circled several possibilities in red, and was prepared to follow up if he got one of the jobs. I reinforced his initiative in following his care plan and told him I was available if he needed any help or direction.

1:00 P.M. At the request of my supervisor, met with a community housing committee who were exploring the creation and development of a new shelter. The group reported on two older motels on a major bus route that could potentially be converted into efficiency apartments for chronically homeless individuals.

2:30 P.M. Met with my group of seven residents to discuss progress they were making with their care plans. There is really a wide range of problems and needs even just across these seven, including chronic versus short-term homelessness, drug and alcohol addiction, mental health issues, length of unemployment, and many others. For many, it is challenging just to set goals. For others, they feel they know exactly what they need and are in the process of trying to resolve their problems.

4:00 P.M. Read some materials that my supervisor shared with me on a concept called *housing first*, an innovation in homeless services that differs from the traditional *treatment-first* model. Housing-first models assume that homeless individuals need the stability of permanent housing to succeed in services. Treatment-first models assume that homeless individuals need services to become ready for housing. The article presented compelling evidence that housing first was a promising practice that was reducing chronic homelessness and its associated costs in several cities across the country.

5:00 P.M. Was notified by one of the attendants at the residence that Alan W. was ill and running a fairly high temperature. Since he was in a wheelchair, I took him to see the on-call physician's assistant at the shelter, provided her with necessary information, and left for the weekend.

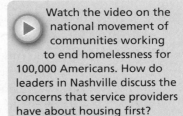

Watch the video on the national movement of communities working to end homelessness for 100,000 Americans. How do leaders in Nashville discuss the concerns that service providers have about housing first?

www.youtube.com /watch?v=LEu2w1FtWME

The dilemmas experienced by this social worker focused on both micro and macro concerns about the homeless population. Reflections from the social worker's notes follow:

1. Homeless people tend to get lumped together in the minds of the general population and even the professional community. Yet, even in my own caseload, there is a wide range of different problems and needs. Some need just a place to live and a job, and they are ready to become self-sufficient again. Others are facing serious mental health problems and addictions, and they are lacking many of the skills needed for employment and independent living. Is there a need to categorize, or can we experiment with placing some of our residents regardless of problems or needs into independent-living situations and allow them to seek the services they need? These issues focus on a *population*.

2. Some of the providers I met with were particularly concerned about the philosophy of the program we were studying, in that they felt that participation in recommended services should be required. How could we help homeless

people if they weren't required to participate in services, quit using substances, and take the medication that would help them recover? How could we justify serving people who weren't willing to follow the rules while so many people were in need and willing to meet eligibility requirements? These are legitimate concerns that need to be thought through, but, at the same time, the treatment-first model has not exactly produced excellent results. And housing first honors self-determination. These issues tend to focus on a *problem*.

3. If we are going to move ahead, we need to focus on developing popular support and the political will to try out the housing-first model. After all, this isn't a particularly popular population to serve—people often assume that people are homeless because of bad choices and a refusal to address their addictions to alcohol and drugs. How can we develop a communitywide effort to promote the positives of this model? These issues tend to lend themselves to being addressed in the *community arena*.

? Assess your understanding of the four case examples by taking this brief quiz.

SURVIVING IN PROFESSIONAL PRACTICE

We have presented these rather lengthy scenarios and the accompanying observations of the workers in an attempt to characterize the kinds of issues and problems social workers face almost every day. The nature of a capitalist system is that some people succeed economically, whereas others do not. For the most part, social workers deal with those who are not able to care for at least a part of their own needs. It should be clear by this time that direct practice interventions alone cannot address large-scale community problems. Social workers must also master the skills involved in organizing people who may want change and have good intentions but need coordination and direction. Faced with these contrasts, a practitioner has a number of options, which can be categorized as follows:

1. **Develop a Strong Support System.** The types of dilemmas that the practitioners in our case examples faced rarely can be handled by one person, no matter how competent that person is. Social workers owe it to themselves to reach out to colleagues and friends, to make connections with persons from other professions, and to create opportunities to use formal and informal teams to solve tough interpersonal and political issues. No one has to work in isolation.

2. **Join with Others to Initiate Change.** Building on a strong support system, social workers can go beyond interpersonal problem solving and join concerned colleagues, clients, and citizens to initiate change. Together with colleagues, workers can form committees and task forces with the intent of changing organizational and community problems.

3. **Prioritize Efforts.** Initiating feasible change means that the social worker must be selective, recognizing that not every problem is solvable and that choices must be made as to which will be addressed. Working toward change calls for sound judgment and discretion. Think about how to channel your energies so that the causes that really matter become the focus of your efforts.

4. **Find Ways to Do Self-Care.** Some practitioners may burn out but remain on the job. Social workers can get caught in believing that they are working at

impossible jobs. They stay in the system and feel powerless, accepting that they, too, are victims of the things they cannot control. They may do the basics of what has to be done with clients and ignore the larger issues, which means that they accept organizational norms and relinquish the advocacy role. This is a tempting option because taking on the larger issues can add many hours of work to an already busy week for what often seems like an impossible task. The profession, then, ceases to be a calling and becomes "just a job." One way to counter these tendencies is to engage in self-care behaviors. This means being intentional about nurturing oneself. Find ways to rest, get away, enjoy the outdoors, or do whatever renews you both personally and professionally.

 Watch the video on how trauma workers maintain and find balance and healing in their own lives. What resources did the workers in the video use to cope with what they observed and experienced in their work?
www.youtube.com/watch?v=CoLupPSmmoU

Much of the work done by social workers who seek to bring about change is what we refer to as *macro practice*, and it is carried out with widely varying degrees of skill. The purpose of this book is to present a theoretical base and a practice model designed to assist the professional social worker in bringing about change in organizations and communities. Not only do we encourage readers to become change agents within the organizations and communities in which they will work, but also we believe that the value base of social work demands it. We believe, too, that surviving the dilemmas requires a strong professional identity.

Do an Internet search for "Self Care Starter Kit" from the University at Buffalo School of Social Work. After reading the article, what key components should you include in your maintenance and emergency self-care plans?

 Assess your understanding of surviving in professional practice by taking this brief quiz.

SUMMARY

In this chapter, we have provided the basic foundations on which students can build an understanding of social work macro practice. We defined *macro practice* as professionally guided intervention designed to bring about planned change in organizations and communities, and we examined the interrelationships of macro and micro practice, emphasizing that all social workers engage in both types of practice in their careers. As long as individuals, groups, and families are viewed in context, there will always be macro aspects to one's job.

We began a discussion of the circumstances leading to the need for planned change. A conceptual framework was provided. Systems theory guides the planned change model that will be elaborated in subsequent chapters. Systems theory contends that there are multiple parts of any entity, whether it is a group, an organization, or a community. These parts have connections, some more closely aligned than others. There are resources the system needs in order to function, and they may come in the form of people, equipment, funding, knowledge, legitimacy, and a host of other components. These resources interact within the system, producing something that becomes the system's product.

The IFSW has published a Code of Ethics that endorses human rights and social justice as fundamental to the social work profession. Their website links to codes of ethics in over 25 countries throughout the world. We focused on the value base of social work, as summarized in the U.S. NASW Code of Ethics, which embodies the profession's orientation to practice. Intervening at any level presents ethical dilemmas that must be faced by the practitioner. In many cases, no right or wrong answer is present, and the appropriate course of action is not at all clear. In such instances, the practitioner's job can be facilitated by analyzing the situation in terms of the six core values in the NASW Code of Ethics. *Service* (sometimes called *beneficence*) refers to the value of helping others. *Social justice* is assuring equal access to resources and equitable treatment. *Dignity and worth of the individual* (often associated with *autonomy*) refers to the value ascribed to an individual's right of self-determination. The *importance of human relationships* recognizes the value of connecting with others to improve quality of life and to facilitate change. *Integrity* and *competence* are values that implore professional social workers to be consistent and skilled in all that they do. Social workers engaged in macro practice may find that their job is one of balancing these values.

From a macro-practice perspective, social and economic justice considerations may demand that one focus not on individual helping but on attempts to alter macro systems that fail to distribute resources in a fair manner. These points were reinforced through four case studies showing how policies, program structures, resource deficits, and other macro-related criteria have much to do with social workers' ability to be effective in their jobs.

One way that social workers sometimes respond to these realities is to give up fighting against them. However, social workers who are skilled in macro practice have other options—to develop strong support systems, join with others to bring about needed changes in these systems, prioritize efforts, and find ways to do self-care. These skills are not and should not be limited to those who are working in traditional macro-practice roles, such as administration or planning. Instead, they are critical for all social workers to know, including those engaged mostly in micro practice.

Working through these dilemmas aids in the development of a professional identity that incorporates both micro- and macro-practice aspects. Just as the profession must be built on social workers who are committed to making a difference in the lives of individual clients, these same workers must also be committed to making a difference in the systems within which clients live and on which they depend. In the chapters that follow, we will provide a macro-practice model to guide social workers in undertaking change processes. But first, Chapter 2 will complete our introduction to the field by reviewing the historical background of social work macro practice.

 Recall what you learned in this chapter by completing the Chapter Review.

Assess Your Competence

Use the scale below to rate your current level of achievement on the following concepts or skills associated with each learning outcome listed at the beginning of this chapter:

1	2	3
I can accurately describe the concept or skill(s) associated with this outcome.	I can consistently identify the concept or skill(s) associated with this outcome when observing and analyzing practice activities.	I can competently implement the concept or skill(s) associated with this outcome in my own practice.

_____ Define macro practice and its relationship to micro practice.

_____ Explain the theoretical and values foundations of macro practice.

_____ Discuss case examples used to illustrate macro practice.

_____ Discuss methods used to survive practice challenges.

2

Historical and Contemporary Influences on Macro Practice

© NORTH WIND PICTURE ARCHIVES / ALAMY

THE CONTEXT WITHIN WHICH PROFESSIONAL SOCIAL WORK EMERGED

As noted in Chapter 1, social workers operate in a complex and rapidly changing society. To understand the problems and opportunities they face, it is important to be familiar with the historical trends that have shaped today's social systems and to recognize forces that will affect the evolution of these systems in the future. Garvin and Cox (2001) call attention to social conditions and ideological influences that influenced professional development. We will examine both in the context of U.S. history, recognizing that there are different stories of social work's emergence in different countries.

Social Conditions

Numerous social conditions set a context for the development of social work as a profession. In the following sections, we focus on population growth and immigration, industrialization and urbanization, changes in institutional structures, and the emergence of the welfare system.

Population Growth and Immigration

The first U.S. census in 1790 revealed a national population of less than 4 million. By 1900, this number had grown to almost 92 million, and the final total from the 2010 Census estimated the nation's population at just under 309 million (U.S. Bureau of the Census, 2010a). The period of fastest growth was in the 1800s, when the nation's population increased by more than one-third every 10 years throughout the first half of the century, and, despite the death and destruction of the Civil War, continued to grow by more than 25 percent per decade during the century's second half. The rate of growth moderated after 1900, with increases diminishing to an average of about 10 percent per decade since 1960. Still, in raw numbers, the nation continues to add almost 30 million people to its population every 10 years.

Immigration has always been a critical element in population growth in the United States. One of the first great waves of immigrants occurred in the 1840s. To the east coast came Irish and German immigrants fleeing famine and political upheaval; to the west coast came Chinese workers seeking employment during the California gold rush. Successive waves followed from southern and eastern Europe as well as Asia, reaching a peak during 1900–1910 when immigrants totaled over 6 million and accounted for almost 40 percent of the nation's population growth.

Industrialization and Urbanization

Accompanying U.S. population growth was a rapid shift toward industrialization of its economy. Stern and Axinn (2012) use the production of cotton in the South to illustrate the effects of this shift. Total cotton production was only 6,000 bales the year before the invention of the cotton gin in 1793, after which it grew to 73,000 bales by 1800, and to almost 4 million bales near the start of the Civil War in 1860. In fewer than 70 years, mechanization thus helped to effect an almost 700-fold increase in production. This type of dramatic change transformed working life throughout the country. The economic opportunity produced by industrialization was a key enabling factor for the rapid growth of the nation's population. The wealth generated by an expanding industrial economy meant that many more people could be supported than in previous agricultural economies. Trattner (1999) called particular attention to the vast growth in national wealth that occurred following the Civil War. In the 40 years between 1860 and 1900, for example, the value of all manufactured products in the country grew sixfold and total investment in industry grew by a factor of 12.

The combination of population growth and industrialization brought about increased urbanization. No U.S. city had a population of 50,000 at the time of the 1790 census. Fifty years later, there were 40 communities in the nation that the Census Bureau considered urban. Most population growth initially occurred in the urban core of large industrial cities.

Changes in Institutional Structures

As the United States became more urbanized and industrialized, its social structure also changed, especially the system of organizations that meet people's needs. In the early 1800s, these organizations were usually few in number, informal, and small in scope (e.g., families, churches, and schools). Engaged primarily in agriculture and living in rural areas, people were forced to be largely self-sufficient and depended on organizations for a limited range of needs. With the advent of industrialization, however, new technologies were linked with advances in methods of organizing, and new patterns emerged.

> Watch the video on the Triangle Shirt Waist Fire. Why had the women who worked in the Triangle shirtwaist factory gone on strike the year before the fire?
>
> www.youtube.com/watch?v=owk_LE1GcKY

Of particular importance was the rise of a complex system of highly specialized organizations. These ranged from accounting firms to satellite communication systems. Their specialization allowed them to do a few tasks efficiently and in great quantity, but they were dependent on other organizations for resources such as power, raw material, and trained personnel, even if they did not always recognize this dependence. Instead of learning the range of tasks necessary for basic self-sufficiency, individuals now concentrated on learning specific skills that allowed them to carry out particular functions— such as social work—that usually occurred within or were provided by an organization. This allowed both individuals and organizations to perform those tasks better and more efficiently, meaning that society as a whole was more productive. But a corollary effect of specialization was that individuals and organizations were no longer able to produce most of what they needed on their own, and the level of interdependence within society became increasingly greater. Moreover, individuals who met their needs through the roles they were able to fill were much more dependent on assistance from societal institutions. This was a principal reason for the development of social work as a profession.

Emergence of a Welfare System

In the United States, organized efforts to respond to human welfare date back to England's Elizabethan Poor Law of 1601. This first written statute established a governmental system of services for the poor and adopted a decentralized approach to service provision. Under this law, assistance to the poor was a local function (as was taxation to pay for the assistance), and responsibility for service provision rested with an individual "overseer of the poor." This model was retained more or less intact in the American colonies, and until the 1800s, relief efforts for the needy were primarily local and small in scale.

The reformist period of the early nineteenth century began a slow transition to larger scale services in the form of state-run asylums for dependent children, the mentally ill, and children and adults with mental retardation. Later, as population, urban concentration, and service needs increased, so did the diversity of both public and private programs. Eventually, it became apparent that a coordinating mechanism was needed for these various efforts. Using Massachusetts in the late 1850s as an example, Trattner (1999) described a hodgepodge of private facilities serving orphaned or delinquent youth, people with physical or developmental disabilities, those with mental illnesses, and others. Each institution tended to be independently governed, and lack of communication

---

Box 2.1   Historical Trends at a Glance

- **Population Growth and Immigration.** From fewer than 4 million in 1790, the U.S. population reached almost 309 million in the 2010 Census. Today, more than 1 in 10 residents in the United States are persons who were born outside its boundaries.

- **Industrialization and Urbanization.** Most Americans 200 years ago were farmers living in rural areas. Now, fewer than 1 in 300 works in agriculture, 80 percent are urban dwellers, and more than half live in the 50 most populous metropolitan areas.

- **Institutional Structures.** Although largely self-sufficient when the nation was an agrarian society, Americans now live in a highly interdependent economy and social system. Most workers are extremely specialized, and relatively young professions such as social work have developed in response to the increased complexity of society.

- **Emergence of a Welfare System.** Dating back to the Elizabethan Poor Law, a local system of providing services to the poor developed in the United States. However, well into the 1900s, the primary focus remained on decentralized private-agency provision of services.

---

between them meant that critical information on matters such as standards of practice or treatment advances was infrequently shared. Trattner argued that this illustrated both the need for and value of having states assume coordination and regulatory roles.

Box 2.1 provides an overview of historical trends.

Ideological Influences

Not surprisingly, changes in broad social conditions coincided with considerable ideological change. Garvin and Cox (2001) identified several viewpoints that arose during the late 1800s in response to these conditions. These included Social Darwinism, Manifest Destiny, the growth of the labor and **social justice movements** (once called "radical" ideologies), and what is today called progressivism.

In the late 1800s, the English writer Herbert Spencer drew comparisons between Charles Darwin's biological theories and social phenomena. Applying the concept of survival of the fittest, **Social Darwinism** suggested that persons with wealth and power in society achieve this status because they are more fit than those without such resources. He also argued that in the biological world, the random appearance of favorable traits leads to the gradual supplanting of less favorable traits, but in societies some individuals or groups remain inherently "inferior." Not surprisingly, this philosophy was embraced by many of the wealthy, who contended that little should be done for the poor and dispossessed on the grounds that such help would simply perpetuate societal problems (Bender, 2008).

The concept of **Manifest Destiny**, first coined by newspaper editor John L. O'Sullivan in 1845, described the belief that God had willed the North American continent to the Anglo-Saxon race to build a utopian world. Such a world would fuse capitalism, Protestantism, and democracy, and in it Anglo-Saxon peoples were not to dilute their superiority by marrying members of other races (Jansson, 2015). Manifest Destiny was used to fuel westward expansion in the late 1800s and to justify seizure of lands from American Indian groups already occupying them.

Partly as a reaction to the racism and classism inherent in these views, but also in response to the growing influence of Karl Marx and other socialist writers, the first flowerings of the labor and social justice movements appeared. The labor movement drew its

---

Box 2.2   Historical Ideologies, Ideas, and Definitions

- **Social Darwinism.** The belief that income differences between rich and poor are natural and arise because the rich are more fit. A corollary is that services should not be offered to the poor since this would perpetuate the survival of those less fit.
- **Manifest Destiny.** The belief that North America was divinely intended for white Europeans, especially Anglo-Saxons, to inhabit and control.
- **Social Justice Movement.** A broad term covering the philosophies of union organizers, anticapitalists, and social

reformers who fought the excesses of the Industrial Revolution and advocated on behalf of laborers, immigrants, and persons living in poverty.
- **Progressivism.** A counterargument (in part) to Social Darwinism that contends that as societies become more complex and individuals less self-sufficient, government must act to ameliorate the problems faced by those less able to cope.

---

strength from the appalling workplace conditions facing most industrial wage earners at the time. A goal of many writers and activists in the movement was to transfer industrial control from capitalists to trade unions (Garvin & Cox, 2001). Meanwhile, the growing number of poor people, their concentration in urban slums, and the desperate conditions in which they lived spurred the growth of what became the social justice movement. Its goal was and still is to mobilize, organize, and empower those who lack equal access to the nation's economic resources.

Progressivism is a complementary ideology that arose partly as a secular expression of Judeo-Christian values of egalitarianism and social responsibility, which were seen as ways to temper the excesses of laissez-faire capitalism. In this view, human rights supersede property rights, and society is seen as responsible for promoting the collective good. One of the early expressions of progressivism was scientific charity, which sought to harness what were seen as "natural" feelings of compassion for the poor to build private systems to provide one-on-one help (Bender, 2008). This view was to contribute to the rise of some of the earliest human service agencies—the Charity Organization Societies—in the late 1800s.

Box 2.2 provides an overview of the early trends discussed in this section.

> **?** Assess your understanding of the context within which professional social work emerged by taking this brief quiz.

THE DEVELOPMENT OF SOCIAL WORK AS A PROFESSION

Women played a major role in building the foundations of social work. Three traditions of women's organizations and programs appeared in the early to mid-1800s: *benevolence*, *reform*, and *rights*. Starting in the late 1700s, women's benevolence primarily took the form of missionary work and the founding of orphan asylums to address immediate human needs. The rise of the reform tradition in the 1830s saw the creation of organizations to advocate for the abolition of slavery, closing of brothels, provision of sex education, and cessation of inappropriate sexual advances. In the 1840s through 1860s, a third tradition of feminist organizing arose around *women's rights* and produced groups such as the National Women's Suffrage Organization (Becker, 1987).

Historically, benevolent work was viewed as compatible with women's nurturing responsibilities, and even social change efforts were seen as an extension of domestic roles into the public arena (Chambers, 1986). Trattner (1999) noted that because elected office was effectively denied to most women, an alternative chosen by many was to pursue their interest in social and political issues through involvement in the settlement houses and other efforts.

Charity Organization Societies and Settlement Houses

The formation of the **Charity Organization Societies** (COS) and **settlement houses** was a partial recognition of the advantages of establishing standard service practices within the framework of a strong organizational base. Local COS agencies, which began forming in the 1870s, were usually umbrella organizations that coordinated the activities of a wide variety of charities created to deal with the problems of immigrants and rural transplants who were flooding into industrialized northern cities in the United States in search of jobs. Ironically, Social Darwinism provided some of the philosophical base of the movement, as the "scientific charity" provided by COS agencies tended to be moralistic and oriented toward persons deemed able to become members of the industrial workforce (Stern & Axinn, 2012). Workers in the COS agencies were often volunteers, especially middle- and upper-class women, who served as "friendly visitors" to poor individuals and families. They tended to share idealistic goals of providing the poor with an opportunity to "better themselves," meaning that they typically viewed poverty as the result of individual failings and targeted their efforts toward reforming individuals rather than systems (Chambers, 1985). Although there was a gradual fading of the attitude that sufferers of problems such as oppression, poor health, or mental illness were somehow at fault for their plight, the focus of the COS movement on serving individuals on a case-by-case basis formed the foundation for social casework and for a modern array of micro-level interventions in social work (McFadden, 2014).

At about the same time that the COS agencies were developing, a different response to human need was employed by settlement houses. Conditions in the crowded slums and tenement houses of industrial cities in the late 1800s were as dire as any in the nation's history, and the goal of the settlement house movement, spearheaded by Jane Addams and others at Hull House in Chicago, was to attack these problems on a systemic level. This meant an approach that emphasized societal as well as individual and group reform. Many of the settlement houses served as religious missions and, like the COS members, did their share of proselytizing and moralizing. However, they were also more willing to meet their mostly immigrant constituents on their own grounds and to believe that chasms of class, religion, nationality, and culture could be spanned. In addition, their societal vision tended to be pluralistic—COS workers feared organized efforts such as the labor movement, whereas settlement leaders tended to support these endeavors. Settlement houses also played prominent roles in the birth of organizations such as the National Association for the Advancement of Colored People, the Women's Trade Union League, and the American Civil Liberties Union (Brieland, 1987). Involvement in these sorts of efforts typifies what is now referred to as *macro-level social work practice*.

Box 2.3 provides a quick overview of how micro and macro practice co-developed.

Go to the "Jane Addams Hull-House Museum" homepage and find "Hull-House History on Call." Listen to "Southern Horrors: Lynching in All Its Phases," presented by Paula Giddings. Why did Ida Wells-Barnett challenge the research of reformers associated with Hull House? How did Ida Wells-Barnett use statistics and other research to challenge Jane Addams regarding some of her assumptions about African Americans?

Watch the video on the settlement house movement. What are the early roots of settlement houses? Why did settlement houses begin to change in the 1920s?

www.youtube.com /watch?v=juz1Jw2UcJ0

Box 2.3   Origins of Micro and Macro Practice

Micro	Macro
• Forerunners were COS agencies.	• Forerunners were settlement houses and state boards of charity.
• Guided by tenets of "scientific charity," focus was on improving the individual.	• Focus was on improving conditions for neighborhoods or other groups.
• Evolved into social casework.	• Evolved into community development and community organization.
• Influenced by books such as *Social Diagnosis*.	• Influenced by books such as *Case Studies of Unemployment*.
• Approach to practice influenced by clinical approaches such as Freudian psychoanalysis.	• Approach to practice influenced by mass-movement approaches of progressivists, trade unionists, and civil rights advocates.
• Influenced by disciplines such as medicine and psychology.	• Influenced by disciplines such as sociology, economics, and political science.
• Motivated by desire to achieve professionalization of practice, including scientific knowledge base.	• Motivated by desire to achieve social reform.

Early Social Work Education

Workers in COS agencies emphasized the need for a systematic approach to service provision, whereas workers in settlement houses demanded training on how to effect social change. Both traditions emphasized efforts to gather information systematically on neighborhood problems (Brieland, 1990), and the resulting need for skilled staff fostered the organization of schools of social work. Service responsibility gradually began to shift from volunteers to paid employees.

The New York School of Philanthropy began in 1898 as a summer training program of the New York Charity Organization Society; the Boston School of Social Work was jointly founded by Simmons and Harvard colleges in 1904, also in response to prompting from local COS agencies (Trattner, 1999). Soon after, persons involved with the settlement house movement helped establish the Chicago School of Civics and Philanthropy in 1907 (Jansson, 2015).

Accompanying these efforts, a debate ensued over whether the fledgling profession should focus on macro or micro social work models. Macro models, concerned with fundamental social policy issues, demanded an academic curriculum based on social theory and an orientation toward analysis and reform. A parallel movement, represented by Jane Addams, emphasized training for political activism and promoted not only economic reforms but also a pacifist agenda (e.g., advocating peace negotiations instead of military involvement in World War I). In contrast, micro models focused on case-by-case assistance and required that caseworkers learn how to conduct fieldwork.

An important turning point in this debate was the 1915 meeting of the National Conference of Charities and Corrections. Abraham Flexner, a prominent national figure in medical education, was asked to address the issue of whether social work was truly a profession. He argued that social work still lacked key characteristics of a profession and could more appropriately be called a **semi-profession**, a view that is sometimes applied to careers in which women predominate (Etizoni, 1969). Flexner's six characteristics of a true profession were that (1) professionals operate intellectually with large individual responsibility, (2) they derive their raw material from science and learning, (3) this material is applied practically, (4) an educationally communicable technique exists, (5) there is a tendency toward self-organization or association, and (6) professions become increasingly altruistic in motivation (Morris, 2008).

Some developments in the field tended to strengthen these characteristics. In 1917, for example, Mary Richmond published *Social Diagnosis*, which brought one-on-one casework practice to the fore and cast it firmly in a traditional, professional mold. By comparing casework assessments with diagnostic work, Reisch and Wenocur (1986) argued that the book opened the door to what is sometimes called the "medical model" in social work. The focus on diagnosis was further strengthened by the influence of Freudian psychotherapy, which became the dominant theoretical basis for casework practice throughout the next half century. On the other hand, Morris (2008) argued that the situation was more complex, and that social work continued to be involved in efforts at both micro and macro levels.

Recognizing the Importance of Macro Roles

Although inconspicuous and not specifically professionally focused, macro-practice models developed alongside the casework method. By 1921, *The Community* by Eduard Lindeman had appeared, and at least five more books on the subject were written within the next 10 years. Organizational theorists such as Mary Follett and social work educators such as Lindeman called attention to the potential role to be played by small primary groups working to strengthen local areas within larger communities (Garvin & Cox, 2001). However, differences had already begun to arise concerning the appropriate focus of macro-level interventions. On one side were advocates of grassroots efforts to effect community change; on the other were those arguing for greater involvement in policy development and agency-based provision of services.

In addition, a social justice agenda emerged in the mid-1920s that reached a peak in the New Deal Era and was embraced as a part of professional identity in the early 1940s. Unionization efforts in the late 1920s and early 1930s resulted in social workers such as Bertha Capen Reynolds collaborating with other professions to reduce management abuses and ameliorate the impact of workforce reductions and pay cuts. Social workers also marched side by side with residents of urban slums, demanding improved housing conditions. These social workers were mostly young, held low-level positions (such as case managers and community action organizers), and did not strongly identify with "professional" social workers (Wagner, 1989).

The Effects of the Great Depression

The Great Depression, which began with the stock market crash of 1929, became a watershed event in the history of macro practice. In the 4-year period from 1929 to 1933, the gross national product of the United States fell by almost half, and the rate of unemployment reached 25 percent. The resulting impoverishment of vast segments of the population raised doubts about traditional notions that poor people were responsible for their own plight and should solve it through personal reform. The realization that one could become unemployed and poor when society malfunctioned resulted in temporary relief programs being developed and eventually the passage of the Social Security Act (Stern & Axinn, 2012).

This was the point that settlement leaders, social reformers, and social justice advocates had long argued, and it was to play an influential role in the development of Franklin Roosevelt's New Deal programs. A number of social workers and agency administrators who had supported New Deal–like reforms during Roosevelt's term as governor of New York later assumed key positions in his presidential administration. Harry Hopkins, head of the Federal Emergency Relief Administration (FERA), and Frances Perkins, Secretary of Labor, were the most visible of these (Jansson, 2015).

Community Organization and Social Reform

In an atmosphere of sweeping change in the late 1930s, social justice advocates and mainstream social work leaders worked together more closely. The journal *Social Work Today* began to pay attention to social work practice, muting its traditional view that casework constituted a bandaid approach to human needs. Social justice elements remained identifiable as social work's left wing, but they were less dramatically differentiated from progressive but professionally oriented leaders. These shifts were enhanced by the achievement of mutual goals such as passage of the Social Security and National Labor Relations acts in 1935. The latter ensured labor's right to organize, strike, and bargain collectively, and it marked the beginning of a period of great success by the labor movement in organizing much of the industrial workforce in the country.

After the mid-1930s, large governmental agencies began to dominate the provision of human services, and the battle of social work roles shifted to this arena. Reisch and Andrews (2002) note that advocates of the casework model were well placed in many of these organizations and developed job specifications that largely excluded community organizers. However, members of the Rank and File Movement of social justice–oriented social workers also became involved in the public services arena, and they brought with them an emphasis on large-scale social reform (Wagner, 1989).

These developments in the 1930s and 1940s set the stage for later social movements. Although the 1950s were not a time of great tumult, key events occurred during the decade that would open the door for considerable social change in the 1960s. A landmark example was the 1954 *Brown v. Board of Education* decision by the U.S. Supreme Court that struck down "separate but equal" policies in public education. Ensuing efforts to ensure the ruling was applied in all schools and to overturn segregation elsewhere became the foundation of the Civil Rights Movement. Beginning with the Montgomery, Alabama, bus boycott in 1955, Martin Luther King Jr. and the Southern Christian Leadership Conference carried out a campaign of nonviolent resistance through sit-ins and demonstrations. Other groups, such as the Congress on Racial Equality (CORE) and the Student Nonviolent Coordinating Committee, sponsored "freedom rides" and trained young whites and blacks from elsewhere in the country to assist with organizing efforts in the South. Both the Voting Rights Act of 1964 and the Civil Rights Act of 1965 were passed largely as a result of these efforts.

In response to the struggles of blacks in the South and elsewhere, social change movements designed to help members of other traditionally oppressed groups began to appear. Cesar Chavez's United Farm Workers began organizing the predominantly Chicano field workers in the Southwest, and the La Raza movement sought to gain political power for Latinos through voter registration drives and other efforts that had worked well in the South.

> ▶ Watch the video on activist Dolores Huerta. What reasons does Dolores give for beginning a career as a community organizer?
>
> www.youtube.com /watch?v=ZR7OV6m6Po0

The American Indian Movement (AIM) called attention to governmental policies that often worsened rather than ameliorated problems in Native American communities. Books such as Betty Friedan's *The Feminine Mystique* (1963) became a catalyst for the Women's Movement, which sought to extend into the social and economic realms the equality that women had gained in voting rights through the Suffrage Movement. Episodes of "gay-bashing" by citizens and police officers in New York City led to a disturbance in 1969 called the Stonewall Riot. This became a catalyst for the Gay Liberation Movement, the first large-scale effort to overcome prejudice and discrimination against <u>homosexuals</u>. Finally, the Counterculture Movement, student unrest (through groups such as Students for a Democratic Society), and protests against the Vietnam War helped make the <u>late 1960s</u> the <u>most turbulent</u> period of the century in terms of mass social movements. Participation in these movements provided on-the-job training for many community activists who later became professional social workers.

Also in the 1960s, expanded governmental social programs, although sometimes ill conceived, provided new opportunities for community-level interventions. One stimulus for these changes was renewed awareness of the plight of poor people, brought on in part by books such as Michael Harrington's *The Other America* (1962). John Kennedy's election in 1960 on a platform of social activism also played a part, resulting in the initiation of programs such as Mobilization for Youth, inner-city delinquency prevention efforts, and (with an international focus) the Peace Corps. These efforts helped create and refine new models of community development (Trattner, 1999).

In 1964, Lyndon Johnson's call for a war on poverty led to the passage of a vast array of social welfare initiatives known collectively as the "Great Society" programs, after a phrase in one of his speeches of the time. These programs left a mixed legacy of results but provided an opportunity for testing macro-practice models. One of the most important examples was the Community Action Program (CAP), part of the Economic Opportunity Act of 1964, a keystone of antipoverty legislation. The goal of CAP was to achieve better coordination of services among community providers and facilitate citizen participation in decision making through "maximum feasible participation" of community members and groups (U.S. Congress, 1964, p. 9). CAP agencies were created in neighborhoods and communities throughout the country, and residents were recruited to serve as board members or paid employees alongside professionally trained staff.

Reflecting this trend, the Council on Social Work Education (CSWE) in 1962 recognized community organization as a method of social work practice comparable to group work and casework. In 1963, the Office of Juvenile Delinquency and Youth Development of the U.S. Department of Health, Education, and Welfare funded CSWE to develop a curriculum for training community organizers. Between 1965 and 1969, the number of schools of social work providing training in community organization rose by 37 percent, eventually including virtually every school in the country (Garvin & Cox, 2001). Community organization thus emerged as a legitimate part of social work practice.

Administration and Planning

Communities are macro systems in which all social workers interact and for which practice models have evolved. However, communities themselves are largely composed of networks of organizations, and it is these organizations that usually assume responsibility for carrying out basic community functions. As such, organizations are a second type of macro system with which social workers must be familiar. We will examine many types of organizations in Chapters 7 and 8, but COS agencies, settlement houses, CAP agencies, and other such organizations that focus on the needs of society's have-nots can be categorized as human service organizations. Their history reveals a pattern of shifting emphasis between centralization and decentralization of agencies and services.

It was not until the Great Depression that public organizations for the provision of human services were established on a large scale. Roosevelt's New Deal programs created an infrastructure at the federal level designed to provide a governmental safety net to protect the poorest and most vulnerable from falling below a minimum standard of living. A key function of these programs was to distribute relief funds to states, and this helped spur the creation of state-level public welfare organizations. Some programs, such as FERA and the Work Projects Administration (WPA), were designed to respond to specific Depression-era problems and thus were relatively short-lived. Others, such as the Social Security Administration, formed the institutional basis of ongoing federal programs, and they continue to play major roles. With the creation in 1956 of the Department of Health, Education, and Welfare (now the Department of Health and Human Services), most of these agencies were combined into a single, cabinet-level organization through which federal insurance and assistance programs were administered.

Since its earliest stages, social work has usually been carried out from within some type of organization. These organizations have varied over time, as have the skills needed for effective practice within them. In the early years of social work education, for example, the focus was on preparing a limited number of macro practitioners to assume roles as administrators of small agencies, usually in the private sector. The skills needed included fundraising, working with voluntary boards, and supervising direct-service workers.

With the growth of large public bureaucracies and nationwide networks of private-sector agencies, the size and complexity of human service organizations changed, as did the role of macro practitioners within them. Trends such as the increased size of human service organizations, the growing complexity and diversity of services, and changes in budgeting policies forced administrators to acquire new skills. Concerns arose that if social work administrators do not acquire these skills, leadership of HSOs may pass to persons from other disciplines who lack training in individual behavior, social systems, and the interaction of person and environment.

Some writers also voiced concerns that administrative decisions in human service agencies might become so dominated by a focus on fiscal or operational efficiency that client needs and service effectiveness would be ignored. In response, Rapp and Poertner (1992) were among a number of voices calling for **client-driven models** of administration in which the achievement of desirable outcomes for clients became the primary criterion for decision making. The intent of this model was to view administrative practice in social work as a unique blend of managerial skills combined with broader knowledge of social problems and the means of addressing these problems. Patti (2000) has argued that the role of administrators in human service organizations is to fulfill instrumental tasks common to all managers (e.g., budgeting, acquiring resources, and hiring and directing personnel) while remaining committed to improving the circumstances of those being served.

Global Perspectives on Social Work

Beyond the early tension between individual versus social change perspectives in the United States and Europe has been a shift from a Westernized viewpoint of what social work is to an international perspective that emphasizes the importance of global economic and political realities. Social work is part of an international arena that was formally recognized as early as 1928 in Paris, when the International Association of Schools of Social Work (IASSW), International Federation of Social Workers (IFSW), and International Council for Social Welfare (ICSW) were founded (Dominelli, 2014, p. 258).

In South America, Chile established social work education programs as early as 1925. India initiated programs in 1936 and has developed special schools of social work for Muslim and Christian minority groups. The University of Cape Town established the first school of social work in 1924 focused on reducing white poverty, with the first nonwhite school founded in 1941 in South Africa. In Cairo, the first school of social work in North Africa opened in 1936. Australia and New Zealand have long social work traditions, and in recent years scholars from these countries have made major contributions to community-based practice with indigenous peoples. The last half century has witnessed an acceleration in schools of social work in the Global South (Weil, Reisch, & Ohmer, 2013).

Globalization has its risks in social work education and practice in that educators and practitioners from the United States and Europe may superimpose their clinical biases onto programs that were designed to respect the traditions and values of indigenous cultures. For example, educational programs in Argentina have largely rejected influences from the United States and Europe, creating their own ideologies and practices with a heavy emphasis on community (macro practice) and social change.

Weil, Reisch, and Ohmer (2013) identified three concerns in light of the increasing interest in and emphasis on international social work: (1) the potential for intellectual colonialism to occur when Western approaches are considered superior; (2) the unsuitability of Western-derived theories that may not respect history, culture, and context; and (3) the need for educators and practitioners from the Global North to recognize the contributions of participatory approaches to community work developed by their Global Southern counterparts. In short, there is much to be learned from other countries in terms of social work practice theories and methods in diverse cultures and contexts.

> ? **Assess your understanding** of the development of social work as a profession by taking this brief quiz.

SOCIAL WORK'S COMMITMENT TO DIVERSE AND OPPRESSED POPULATIONS

Within the context of an increasing focus on international social work, it is important to recognize that within the United States, social workers are constantly working with diverse and oppressed populations. The oppression of ethnic minorities, women, disabled persons, and sexual minorities predated the development of the social work profession. The profession was thus born into an environment in which social change was needed. The effects of discrimination, ideological shifts, and economic and technological changes often intensified prejudicial attitudes and discriminatory behavior toward certain groups and created social pressures that could not be indefinitely ignored. The following sections focus on historical trends affecting populations whose members are important constituents for professional social workers committed to social justice.

Diversity and Difference in Practice

Practice Behavior: Apply and communicate understanding of the importance of diversity and difference in shaping life experiences in practice at the micro, mezzo, and macro levels.

Critical Thinking Question: How can one learn about diverse populations without engaging in stereotyping different groups?

Native Americans

In the 1800s and early 1900s, oppression of American Indians was governmental policy, enacted via war, forcible relocation, deliberate spread of disease, contravention of treaties, and confinement to reservations. The Removal Act of 1830 gave the federal government the right to relocate any native groups living east of the Mississippi River. For many tribes, this meant virtual genocide. Relocation of the Cherokee nation in 1838, for example, led to immense loss of life from disease and exposure, becoming known as the Trail of Tears. Beginning in the 1890s, when many American Indian families had been forced onto reservations, generations of Native American youth were made to attend off-reservation boarding schools where the goal was to blend them into white society so well that their original cultural identity would be unrecognizable. The effect was to damage Native American family life and alienate American Indian youth from their heritage (Coleman, 1999).

> Watch the video on the forced removal of the Cherokee Nation from the Southeastern United States. What state and federal policy decisions led to the removal of Native Americans from their ancestral lands?
>
> www.youtube.com /watch?v=7LSkfmCj8Jg

Native Americans benefited in important ways from the social upheavals of the 1960s, with groups such as the American Indian Movement (AIM) helping to focus attention on the troubled relationship between tribal organizations and the federal government. As a result, tribal governments were able to diminish the paternalistic influence of agencies such as the Bureau of Indian Affairs and gain greater autonomy over their own operations. For example, the Indian Child Welfare Act of 1978 gave jurisdiction of child welfare cases to tribal rather than state courts, thus placing tighter controls on practices such as the adoption of Native American children by non-Native American families. Other federal legislation included the 1978 Religious Freedom Act, which recognized the legitimacy of the Native American Church; the 1988 Gaming Regulatory Act, which confirmed that tribes may create gambling establishments on reservation land if gaming of any other form is allowed in the state; and the 1990 Native American Grave Protection and Repatriation Act, which requires that artifacts removed from tribal lands be returned if requested.

Nonetheless, Native Americans have a more distinct cultural heritage than many other ethnic groups, and the struggle to simultaneously preserve this heritage and integrate with the rest of society has taken its toll. Poverty on some rural reservations is as pervasive and severe as anywhere in the country, and much remains to be done to improve economic conditions in these areas. Another concern is health care. The Indian Health Service (IHS), which was created to meet treaty-based federal guarantees for health care provision to Native Americans, has a record of inconsistent and sometimes dramatically inferior care. In recent years, it has also faced both budgetary cutbacks and controversy over the extent of its responsibility for providing services to urban as well as reservation-based populations (Westmoreland & Watson, 2006). The Indian Health Care Improvement Act, a part of the major health care reform legislation passed in 2010, is designed to help the IHS meet these challenges.

In 2009, Native Americans had the second lowest per-capita annual income, the highest rate of poverty, and the second highest unemployment rate of all racial/ethnic groups. They also suffered the highest incidence of health that was only "fair" or "poor," and they had the highest rates of both alcohol and drug abuse. In their study of at-risk Native American youth, Waller, Okamoto, Miles, and Hurdle (2003) summed up the situation as institutionalized oppression that has continued into contemporary times. Not only are the health care, education, social service, and criminal justice systems based on

Eurocentric models, but also they are consistently underfunded, poorly administered, and culturally insensitive.

Latinos

More than 100,000 indigenous Spanish-speaking people in the Southwest became part of the United States following the Mexican-American War in 1848. The war began primarily as a result of U.S. military incursions into Mexico, and the Treaty of Guadalupe Hidalgo that ended it included specific protections regarding property rights and civil liberties for former Mexican citizens who became part of the United States. Nonetheless, many people were forced from their lands (Griswold del Castillo, 2001). Language was also a common tool of oppression, with Latinos being denied participation in voting and public education because they were not proficient in English. Following the Mexican Revolution in 1910, large waves of Mexican immigrants began to face similar barriers. During the Depression years of the 1930s, unemployment pressures and racism led to large-scale deportations of supposedly undocumented residents, as many as 60 percent of whom were in fact U.S. citizens (Boisson, 2006).

The Hispanic population in the United States is currently growing faster than any other ethnic or racial group in the country, and this trend is expected to continue well into this century. By 2050, for example, Latinos are expected to number more than 130 million in the United States. This would represent about 30 percent of the total population, as compared to 9 percent in 1990 (U.S. Bureau of the Census, 2011a). Latinos tend to be younger than the rest of the population and mostly urban. As of 2006, about two-thirds (64 percent) were of Mexican descent, 13 percent were from Central and South American countries, about 9 percent were Puerto Rican in origin, and 3 percent were from Cuba (U.S. Bureau of the Census, 2011a). Population concentrations are in the West and Southwest for Mexican and Central Americans, the Northeast for Puerto Ricans, and the Southeast for Cuban Americans. Based partly on historic inequality and partly on the effect of many recent immigrants still struggling to gain equal economic footing, income among Latinos is much lower than for the population as a whole. In 2009, Hispanics had the lowest per capita income of any major racial/ethnic group, along with the highest incidence of food insecurity. Because many Latino children have to learn English while in school, dropout rates are high, and the percentage of Latino adults who lack high school diplomas is more than double that of any other group. Finally, lack of health insurance and regular access to health care affects a particularly high proportion of Latino households.

[handwritten margin note: Is that the primary reason? what about economics?]

By far the most prominent and contentious issue involving Latinos is undocumented immigration, mostly by Mexicans and Central Americans crossing the U.S.–Mexico border. Much of the debate centers on how undocumented immigrants should be viewed. Social workers, because of their commitment to human well-being, often take the side of ensuring that undocumented immigrants and their families have access to basic services, whereas others fear that their "limbo" status in society makes them especially vulnerable to exploitation and abuse. Meanwhile, many average citizens feel economically threatened by undocumented immigration and are vociferous in their opposition. Perhaps the best that can be said is that this issue is likely to remain difficult and divisive well into the future.

Do an Internet search on the "History of Chicano Park San Diego." Why did residents of Barrio Logan occupy the park?

African Americans

The Civil War won emancipation from slavery for African Americans, but equal treatment was slow to follow. The Freedmen's Bureau, set up in 1865 to assist the transition of freed slaves, was a rare example of federal involvement in the provision of social welfare services. In its brief 6-year life, it assisted many former slaves in finding employment or gaining access to education and health care. But more typical of the Reconstruction era was the founding, also in 1865, of the Ku Klux Klan. Its reign of terror in the South lasted almost 100 years, effectively denying many freedoms African Americans had supposedly gained. In the courts, rulings such as the U.S. Supreme Court's landmark *Plessy v. Ferguson* decision of 1896 upheld the "separate but equal" doctrine that in essence made discrimination a governmental policy. Trattner (1999) notes that although advocates for better social welfare programs achieved important gains in the first decades of the twentieth century, these often had a much greater impact on poverty among white than among black Americans.

For blacks, victories in the U.S.-based Civil Rights Movement of the 1950s and 1960s meant the rejection of segregationist practices that had prevailed since the Civil War. These gains helped spur electoral successes at both the local and national levels. Since the mid-1980s, five of the nation's six most populous cities—New York, Los Angeles, Chicago, Houston, and Philadelphia—have been led by an African American mayor, and Barack Obama's election as U.S. president in 2008 was an historic event. Nevertheless, grave concerns remain regarding the dramatic gap in economic well-being between African American families and others. In 2009, more than one-third of African Americans households lived in poverty, a rate well above the national average and almost two-thirds higher than that of whites. A contributing factor is unemployment, which hit African Americans especially hard in the recession that began in 2008. At 15.8 percent, the jobless rate among Blacks was almost double that of whites in 2009. Annual income was also low, as indicated by a per-capita rate among African Americans of $17,711, which is more than 40 percent lower than the comparable figure among whites.

Poverty among African American children is even more widespread, affecting more than one in three (ChildStats.gov, 2010). Also, poverty and other historical disadvantages have had negative effects on the structure of Black families, and Black children in 2005 were more likely than those in any other racial/ethnic group to live in a single-parent household or one headed by a grandparent.

Perhaps the most glaring indicators of African Americans' struggle to overcome past oppression and its consequences are in the area of health. Infant mortality rates are much higher among Blacks than in any other racial/ethnic group, and they also have the second highest incidence of health that is only "fair" or "poor." Also striking are statistics from the Centers for Disease Control (2010) regarding annual death rates due to various causes. For example, in 2006 African Americans' annual mortality rate from all causes was more than double that of the healthiest racial/ethnic group (Asian Americans). The gravest threats were heart and cardiovascular diseases and cancer or cancer-related illnesses. Also, because low income and lack of mobility often mean living in dangerous neighborhoods, African Americans in 2006 had a death rate from homicide that was eight times higher than that of whites.

It is important to point out that there are strengths among African Americans that typically receive little attention. Compared to other historically disadvantaged groups, for example, African Americans have a low proportion (about one in five) of persons age 16 to 65 who lack at least a high school education. Perhaps even more noteworthy is the fact that, corrosive stereotypes to the contrary, rates of illegal drug use among Black adults is essentially no different from drug use rates among whites, and African Americans are less than half as likely than whites to engage in problem drinking (defined as the number of days per year in which five or more drinks were consumed).

Efforts continue within the African American community to confront problems and consolidate gains. An ongoing emphasis on strengthening basic institutions such as churches, families, and neighborhoods is one example of this, as are efforts to highlight the unique African American heritage through holiday celebrations such as Kwanzaa. Particular attention is being given to ensuring strong electoral representation, and the latest available Census figures placed the number of black elected officials nationwide in 2002 at 9,430, or more than six times higher than in 1970 (U.S. Bureau of the Census, 2011b).

Asian Americans

On the West Coast, Chinese immigrants were often exploited as cheap labor, but when economic conditions changed they became targets of discrimination and hostility. An example is the 1882 Chinese Exclusion Act, which for more than 60 years outlawed all Chinese immigration to the United States (Orgad & Ruthizer, 2010). Meanwhile, immigration from Japan increased between 1890 and 1907, resulting in changes to California state laws that restricted the ability of Japanese residents to own or even lease property. Finally, in one of the most egregious examples of governmental discrimination by race, hundreds of thousands of Japanese Americans were forcibly relocated to internment camps during World War II (Park, 2008).

Public attention is often directed toward the educational achievements of Asian American youth, who, for example, led all other ethnic groups on indicators such as the percentage of students scoring "Proficient" on national tests in grades 4 and 8, SAT scores in the 12th grade, and rates of college completion (National Center for Education Statistics, 2007). As a group, Asian Americans have achieved other successes in areas such as income, employment, health, and low rates of substance abuse.

Still, evidence of such overall successes has sometimes masked problems facing particular Asian American groups, especially those of Cambodian, Laotian, and Hmong origin who are often among those most recently arrived in the United States and whose numbers have increased rapidly in the past three to four decades. Many were refugees who arrived destitute and without an existing community of prior immigrants available to assist in their transition to U.S. society (Haynes, 2014). Once here, they had to adjust to a different culture and language, and most have had to struggle to overcome lingering problems of poverty, poor housing, and discrimination in hiring. Le (2006) notes that the "model minority" label attached to Asian Americans can sometimes be destructive in that it ignores the fact that it is a heterogeneous population within which some groups still face many social and economic challenges.

model / minority myth

Women

In the 1800s, the status of women had improved little from ancient times, and many women were often treated as little more than chattel. In the United States and other developing countries, outright subjugation had given way to a "fairer sex" stereotype of women as the repositories and purveyors of public virtue. This model was then used as a rationale for denying women access to education, employment, voting rights, and other benefits so that they would not be diverted from their role as moral guardians of society. Some women rose above this and began what has been termed the "first wave" of feminism (Gray & Boddy, 2010). Voting rights were the principal goal of this wave, but it also sought to overcome the homebound nurturer mold into which most women of the time were forced. Other women leveraged these stereotypes to aid in founding societies and associations that became the forerunners of contemporary human service organizations (Carlton-LeNey & Hodges, 2004; McCarthy, 2003).

Women's advancement has been marked by both progress and disappointment. One important gain was the development of women's groups such as the National Organization for Women (NOW), which was organized in the mid-1960s. NOW and other organizations formed the core of the Women's Movement, which had considerable success in calling attention to institutional sexism present in employment, government policy, and language. These efforts constituted what is known as second-wave feminism (Gray & Boddy, 2010), and they led to many tangible gains, such as the narrowing of the difference in earnings between men and women. In 2009, for example, the value of median weekly earnings for women was 80 percent of the value for men. This was up from 62 percent in 1979 but slightly below the peak of 81 percent in 2005 and 2006 (U.S. Bureau of Labor Statistics, 2010a).

Collins (2010) notes that one of the most important pieces of women's rights legislation was the 1964 Civil Rights Act. It included antidiscrimination protections for women that were added as a joke by a pro-segregation congressman, but to his surprise the additions were passed along with the rest of the Act. A disappointment for many was the failed attempt to add an Equal Rights Amendment to the U.S. Constitution. The amendment was designed to offer further protections against gender-based discrimination. It drew vociferous opposition by groups that believed it would undermine women's traditional roles, and in 1982, it failed due to lack of ratification by a sufficient number of states. One successful initiative was the 1994 Violence Against Women Act, which was reauthorized in 2006. It put in place programs to prevent domestic violence, improve law enforcement response to acts of violence against women, and assist the prosecution of offenses such as dating violence and stalking. Another advance was the Lilly Ledbetter Fair Pay Act of 2009, which allows individuals to take action against employers for wage discrimination of the type that has often affected women (National Women's Law Center, 2009).

Watch the video on African American women and the struggle for equal rights. How did the Civil Rights Movement contribute to equality for women?

As with other historically disadvantaged groups, women still struggle to overcome gender stereotypes that cast them in nurturer/caregiver roles rather than as full participants in society. They also have considerable ground to make up in order to achieve parity in economic and career opportunities. They are greatly underrepresented in high-prestige, high-power jobs and overrepresented in those that pay poorly, making them much more likely to have incomes below the poverty line.

Persons with Disabilities

Laws urging charitable and considerate treatment of persons with disabilities date from the Code of Hammurabi and ancient Judeo-Christian writings, yet in practice many societies have dealt harshly with their disabled members. Even in the relatively enlightened Greek and Roman cultures, accepted practices included infanticide, enslavement, concubinage, and euthanasia (Trattner, 1999). More recent societies have renounced these practices, but their treatment of persons with disabilities has still been affected by long-standing tendencies to view a disability as somehow the fault of the disabled person or as punishment for unspecified sins. Terms such as *crippled* or *simple-minded*, which have only recently faded from common usage, are instructive because (1) they describe disabilities through pejorative terms and (2) they define disability as some form of deficit vis-à-vis others in the population, although research has shown that persons with disabilities do not perceive themselves in terms of deficiencies (Wright, 1988).

In the United States after the Civil War, battlefield injuries were one of the few categories of disabilities receiving public attention. In 1866, the state of Mississippi spent one-fifth of its budget on artificial limbs for wounded veterans (Wynne, 2006), yet no public system existed in the state to serve the needs of persons with mental retardation. Even for veterans, available assistance was usually limited and did little to foster independence or integration with the rest of society. Not until the Veterans Rehabilitation Act of 1918 and the Civilian Vocational Rehabilitation Act of 1920 were federal programs established to promote greater participation and self-sufficiency. These were followed by income assistance programs created by the Social Security Act of 1935 (Percy, 1989).

The Rehabilitation Act of 1973 and the subsequent Rehabilitation Act Amendments of 1974 were for persons with disabilities what the Civil Rights Act had been for other groups. The acts prohibited discrimination against anyone who currently has or had in the past "a physical or mental impairment which substantially limits one or more of such person's major life activities" (Rehabilitation Act of 1973). The Rehabilitation Act also was the first to require that public facilities be made accessible to disabled persons, and it laid the groundwork for the expansion of these requirements to all commercial properties through the Americans with Disabilities Act of 1990. Another example of related legislation was the 1975 Education for All Handicapped Children Act, which required children with developmental disabilities to be given access to mainstream public education rather than the traditionally segregated "special education" system. In 1990, the Education for All Handicapped Children Act was renamed the Individuals with Disabilities Education Act (IDEA), and it was reauthorized in 1997 and 2004 (O'Brien & Leneave, 2008).

The IDEA legislation and other initiatives share the general goal of **mainstreaming**, which is defined as providing assistance in such a way as to minimize the need for persons with disabilities to remain apart or operate separately from others in society. Unfortunately, efforts to measure success have progressed slowly. The nature of disabilities varies widely, as do their causes, and thus people affected by a disability cannot be treated as a single group. This means that statistics on the well-being of members of this population are difficult to locate, and it is also difficult to determine whether efforts to maximize their participation in society are bearing fruit.

Lesbian, Gay, Bisexual, and Transgender (LGBT) Persons

Due to long-standing and widespread persecution, members of the gay and lesbian communities, along with persons of other sexual orientations, have historically been the most hidden of oppressed groups. In particular, homosexuality was often viewed through the lens of religious taboos, and some religious authorities placed it in the same category as willful murder (as an example of a "mortal" sin). English law, unlike that of many other European countries, made homosexuality a crime as well, and as recently as 1816, English sailors were executed for the crime of "buggery" (Marotta, 1981). English legal codes on homosexuality were adopted in the United States, and, although not always enforced, were often used selectively as means of harassment. Finally, well into the latter part of the twentieth century, drawing in part on theories advanced by Sigmund Freud, gay men, lesbians, bisexual, and transgender persons were considered mentally ill and could be forcibly subjected to hospitalization or other measures designed to cure their "perversions" (Crompton, 2003). Author Randy Shilts (1987) documented how these views contributed to the AIDS epidemic being viewed as a "gay disease," thus eliciting a painfully slow response compared to what would have been the case if an equal proportion of heterosexuals had been affected.

The task of overcoming prejudice against lesbians, gay men, and others in the LGBTQ population has been slow and difficult. Expressions of homophobic views or displays of what Corsini (2002) terms heterosexism remain surprisingly commonplace in a society that long ago ceased to tolerate such behaviors when directed toward racial or ethnic groups. The advances that have occurred have come about mostly from political activism. Lesbians, for example, were an integral part of the Women's Movement and have both contributed to and benefited from its achievements. Wilkinson and Kitzinger (2005) note that many gay males were inspired by the work of Black civil rights leaders → *like Martha P Johnson?* in the 1950s and 1960s, and this helped to foster the creation of organizations such as the Gay Liberation Front. A unique difficulty facing members of the LGBTQ population, however, is that in order to begin advocating for fair treatment, they must go through the process of recognizing their own sexual or gender identities and overcoming the fear or reluctance that often goes with such acknowledgment.

A major step in legal advocacy was taken with the 2003 U.S. Supreme Court decision that struck down a Texas law prohibiting consensual homosexual acts between adults. In effect, this negated all such laws nationwide, and it represented a significant victory in the struggle for equal rights. Another advance occurred in late 2010, when Congress voted to end the "don't ask, don't tell" policies of the U.S. military. These policies required that service men and women be dismissed simply for acknowledging being LGBTQ.

Human Rights and Justice

Practice Behavior: Engage in practices that advance social, economic, and environmental justice.

Critical Thinking Question: Even with the U.S. Supreme Court's decision about same-sex marriage, there are persons who disagree with the decision. What are the social justice issues concerning this ruling?

By far, the most contentious recent issue affecting the LGBTQ community is the effort to secure legal recognition for gay and lesbian couples. Same-sex marriage is legal throughout Canada, Sweden, Denmark, the Netherlands, Belgium, Spain, Portugal, Iceland, France, England and Wales, New Zealand, South Africa, Mexico City, Argentina, Uruguay, and parts of Brazil. In a 2015 landmark decision the United States Supreme Court legalized same-sex marriage. 2020 - work place D1&c.

In summary, these brief historical overviews of a number of different population groups reveal one of the greatest contemporary challenges for social work—advancing human rights and social and economic justice. In Chapter 3, we will focus in depth on engaging with diverse population groups to address issues of discrimination and oppression.

> **?** Assess your understanding of social work's commitment to diverse and oppressed populations by taking this brief quiz.

CONTEMPORARY CHALLENGES

Since the early days of the profession, changes in the United States have brought about profound improvements in areas such as health, income, and transportation, but not all aspects of the transformation have been ones to which members of society could easily adjust, and in some cases this has led to new social problems. We now highlight a few of these changes, along with their implications for macro-practice social work.

Addressing Poverty and Welfare Reform

In 1995, President Bill Clinton signed the Personal Responsibility and Work Opportunity Reconciliation Act (PRWORA) (P.S. 104-193) into law. Although it was viewed as a set of sweeping changes to public assistance programs, amendments to the Social Security Act of 1935 (P.L. 74-271) had already altered Title IV-A, Aid to Dependent Children (ADC), in a number of previous amendments (Pimpare, 2013). The changes in PRWORA were largely prompted by conservative charges that the existing system promoted welfare dependency and a bloated, bureaucratic service system.

The key changes implemented in welfare reform were (1) the requirement that most recipients had to find work and (2) time limits were placed on their eligibility for assistance. In 2006, 10 years after the act, considerable discussion and debate took place regarding its merits.

Studies also suggested that many families failed to take advantage of benefits available to them not because of improved economic well-being but because of organizational barriers. Parrott (2006) found that more than half the drop in welfare caseloads in the late 1990s occurred less because families earned their way out of poverty than that they simply did not apply for help. A study by Wu and Eamon (2010) illustrated possible reasons for this, showing that families with meager resources who might benefit from help were often thwarted by insufficient information, bureaucratic barriers, and unreasonable eligibility criteria. Similarly, a study by Broughton (2010) found that most of the drop in welfare caseloads cited as evidence of success of welfare reform actually occurred as a result of "bureaucratic churning," efforts to deny applicants who, with help, might have qualified, and other means of restricting service access (p. 155). These problems do not appear to be restricted to large governmental agencies.

Box 2.4   Summary of Pros and Cons of Welfare Reform

Pros	Cons
• Welfare caseloads dropped dramatically in the first five years after passage of the reforms.	• Much of the caseload decline may have occurred because poor families assumed they would not qualify, not because they became less poor.
• More mothers joined the workforce.	• Jobs taken by many recipients who entered the workforce pay too little to allow real self-sufficiency.
• Work earnings as a percentage of household income rose sharply after the reforms, while income from welfare benefits decreased.	• Economic gains by poor families in the late 1990s may have been due to a strong economy rather than reform policies. Low-income families are now facing great hardship following the start of a recessionary period.
• Child poverty rates dropped after reforms were enacted, especially among black children, and some other indicators of child well-being also rose.	• Indicators such as child poverty, percentage of mothers in the workforce, and earnings from work among low-income families have worsened since about 2001.
• Children have benefited from the positive model of a parent who is employed and seeking to be self-sufficient.	• Conditions for the poorest of the poor have steadily worsened, as has the number of children in extreme poverty.

Benish (2010) studied efforts in one state to transfer responsibility for services to the private sector and found that rules and regulations in the new nongovernmental agencies became more rigid and inflexible than had been the case in older governmental agencies.

From a macro-practice perspective, these findings are useful in showing a de facto shift in the role of the federal government from poverty prevention to employment support. Holt (2006) called attention to the growth of the Earned Income Tax Credit (EITC), which distributes federal funds in the form of tax refunds (often more than the amount actually paid) to low-income earners who file a return. From less than $2 billion in 1984, the program grew to about $65 billion in 2012 (U.S. Internal Revenue Service, 2014), and it continues to expand. Ironically, the Internal Revenue Service, which administers the EITC, might thus be said to have become a key agency for meeting the needs of poor people, a role for which many observers might question its suitability.

Box 2.4 provides a summary of the pros and cons of welfare reform. It is important for social workers to recognize how the shifts in federal policies can impact persons who live in poverty.

The pros and cons of welfare reform are highly relevant across industrialized nations. The difficulties inherent in reforming welfare and addressing poverty were heightened by the crash of global financial markets in 2008, which led to an economic recession deeper than the 1930s depression. National governments in the United States and Europe focused on saving the banking system, then quickly turned to curbing public sector expenditures in order to reduce government debt. McKay (2013) argued that spending cuts in Europe disproportionately impacted

Policy Practice

Practice Behavior: Apply critical thinking to analyze, formulate, and advocate for policies that advance human rights and social, economic, and environmental justice.

Critical Thinking Question: What are some ways PRWORA may espouse values similar to those of Social Darwinism? How is it different?

women due to the gendered nature of caregiving work. She discussed the concept of providing a minimum income guaranteed to all citizens, even though no industrialized nation has enacted a Citizens Basic Income (CBI). This type of reform would involve an entirely new way of thinking about social security policy and respond to what feminists have called a **wicked problem**, one that is incredibly complex and cannot be easily tamed.

The United Nations General Assembly reported that 1.5 billion people worldwide were living in poverty in 2011 (U.N. General Assembly, 2011). For an excellent overview of ways to confront global poverty, we recommend Chowa, Masa, Sherraden, and Weil's (2013) chapter on "Confronting Global Poverty" in the *Handbook of Community Practice*.

Recognizing Income Inequality

In the midst of debates about poverty policy, many advocates have become concerned about the increasing income gap between the highest-earning and lowest-earning households in the United States. In the four decades during and after World War II, the economy of the United States expanded rapidly, and households in poor and middle-income families (those at the 90th income percentile or below) enjoyed greater percentage increases in earnings than households in the top 10 percent. Since the late 1970s, however, income increased substantially in the 10 percent of households with the highest earnings, while few gains have been made by households in the bottom 90 percent of income (Shaw & Stone, 2010). In 1977, for example, the highest-earning 10 percent of households received about one-third of all income in the United States, but by 2007 this figure had grown to the point that 10 percent of households earned about half of all income. This represented the greatest income disparity between the bottom 90 percent and top 10 percent of households ever recorded (Piketty & Saez, 2014).

Large disparities also exist between rich and poor with regard to net worth, which is the value of all assets minus the amount of all debts. In 1983, the wealthiest 5 percent of households accounted for 55 percent of all net worth, and this grew to 62 percent by 2007. The least wealthy 40 percent of American households accounted for just nine-tenths of 1 percent of net worth in 1983, and this dropped to two-tenths of 1 percent by 2007. Disparities are even greater if home values are excluded. In 2007 the wealthiest 5 percent of households held 72 percent of nonhome wealth (up from 68 percent in 1983), whereas the least wealthy 40 percent of households accounted for −1 percent (compared to −0.9 percent in 1983). The negative values mean these households' average debt exceeded their nonhome wealth (Wolff, 2010).

Disparities such as these can produce a variety of problems. Studies have shown that increased income inequality is associated with poorer infant health outcomes (Olson, Diekema, Elliott, & Renier, 2010), lower self-rated health status among adults (Hildebrand & Van Kerm, 2009), increased homicide risk (Redelings, Lieb, & Sorvillo, 2010), increased suicide risk (Huisman & Oldehinkel, 2009), political and community disengagement of low earners (Bernstein, Mishell, & Brocht, 2000), and many other concerns. Observers such as David Shipler (2005) argue that as the gap between the affluent and everyone else widens, more Americans will find themselves among the "working poor" who teeter constantly on the brink of disaster. He offers an example in which poor housing aggravates child health problems, which lead to higher medical costs, then late payments, then

> Watch the video on inequality and opportunity in America. What factors contribute to social mobility?
>
> www.youtube.com /watch?v=t2XFh_tD2RA

Box 2.5	U.S. Income and Wealth Distribution in the Twentieth and Twenty-First Centuries

Mid- to Late Twentieth Century		Twenty-First Century
• 1940s to 1970s—poor and middle-income households had greater earnings increases than those in the top 10%.	⇆	• 1980s to present—poor and middle-income households made few gains; earnings increased substantially in top 10%.
• 1977—the highest earning 10% of households received about one-third of all income.	⇆	• 2007—the highest-earning 10% of households received about half of all income.
• 1979 to 1998—households in the top fifth had sizable income increases; those in the middle three-fifths saw little change; those in the bottom fifth had a net *decrease* of 12.5%.	⇆	• 2002 to 2007—households in the top 1% earned two-thirds of the new income from economic expansion.
• 1976—households in the top 1% earned about 9% of all income.	⇆	• 2007—households in the top 1% earned about 21% of all income.
• 1979—households in the bottom fifth earned about 7% of all after-tax income.	⇆	• 2007—households in the bottom fifth earned about 5% of all after-tax income.
• 1985—the wealthiest 5% of households held 55% of all net worth.	⇆	• 2007—the wealthiest 5% of households held 62% of all net worth.
• 1983—the least wealthy 40% of households held 0.9% of net worth.	⇆	• 2007—the least wealthy 40% of households held 0.2% of net worth.

penalties or higher interest rates on an already undependable car. That, in turn, threatens the ability to hold down a job, which increases the likelihood that the family will have to remain in rundown housing. Even minor calamities can intensify a vicious cycle that becomes ever more difficult to escape.

These conditions affect many former welfare recipients who have replaced public assistance with work earnings, suggesting that reductions in welfare dependency have not been accompanied by increases in actual economic security. Box 2.5 provides an historical comparison of trends in income inequality.

Assessing Changing Community Patterns of Affiliation and Identification

A recurring question in community literature concerns whether communities are meeting the needs of their members and whether the traditional benefits of community living are in jeopardy. In 1978, for example, Roland Warren called attention to what he described as the "community problem," which involved a feeling among Americans that the communities in which they lived functioned less well than in the past and were subject to more frequent and serious disorders than before.

Fukuyama (1999) described what he termed a "Great Disruption" in countries within the developed world, where an unexpected growth of social problems occurred during a period beginning in the 1960s and extending into the 1990s. Among these problems were rising disruptions in family systems (high divorce rates and high rates of births to single or very young mothers), increased crime, deterioration of inner cities, erosion of trust in traditional institutions and organizations, and generalized "weakening of social bonds and common values" (p. 56). Putnam (2000) focused on changes in how people associate with each other, calling particular attention to falling participation in local membership groups as diverse as neighborhood bridge clubs, fraternal lodges, and college alumni chapters. Unlike Warren or Fukuyama, however, Putnam argued that these changes were not necessarily ominous. The fact that people affiliate in different ways than before does not necessarily portend a breakdown of social cohesiveness, but some members of society will inevitably adapt less well to rapid change than others.

Among the causes of the above changes are trends we have already discussed, including urbanization and what Warren (1978) called loss of geographic relevance. Large, complex cities offer many benefits, but they can also breed large, complex problems, and the very size and complexity of a city can interfere with solving these problems. Likewise, it is impossible to get to know all of one's fellow residents in a large city, where most people one sees are often blurred faces passing by in vehicles or on busy sidewalks.

Still, many city dwellers love urban life and do not find it alienating. They may define "community" in different ways than in rural areas and apply the term to an apartment building; an ethnic enclave; a neighborhood surrounding a particular factory, church, or school; or even an area of gang turf. As we will discuss, this means that practicing social work at the local level in urban areas requires recognition of a complex arrangement of communities within communities.

Technological advances are also enabling the replacement of locality-based relationships with those that transcend geographic boundaries and make physical distance meaningless. The rapid proliferation of cell phones and Internet access paved the way for advances ranging from text messaging to blogs to videoconferencing to multiplayer gaming. Social networking sites have also grown with incredible speed. As of late 2014, Facebook alone had more than 600 million active users, and it is likely that users of other sites equaled or exceeded that total (Facebook Pressroom Statistics, 2014). These networks exist in cyberspace rather than physical space, so what Warren termed **extracommunity affiliations** now involve not only redefining "place" (e.g., as a web address rather than a street address) but redefining "community" as well.

Extracommunity affiliations are important not just to individuals but to organizations and institutions as well. An automobile assembly plant may be the major employer and economic engine in a small community, but despite its local prominence, its most important ties may be to the home office of its corporate owner in a country far away. A decision to close the plant, or a work stoppage at a supplier of critical parts for its assembly line, might happen far outside the community, but local residents could feel the effects quickly. Communities and their institutions are thus highly dependent on global ties, and the rapid development of new communication technologies sharpens that dependence and adds complexity to social work practice at the community level.

Assessing Changing Organizations and Delivery Systems

In addition to community issues, contemporary developments in the structure of organizations are also important. One parallel between communities and organizations is that both have continued to become larger and more multifaceted. In organizations, this has often been accompanied by the **bureaucratization** of operations.

The problem with bureaucracies is that they sometimes become as machinelike as the tools they employ, and the result can be a dehumanizing environment for employees and unresponsive or ineffective services for those in need. This often grows more pronounced as organizational size increases, and large governmental HSOs have developed reputations (sometimes deserved, sometimes undeserved) for reflecting the negative aspects of bureaucratic structure. Even in small agencies, externally imposed regulations (such as for certain operational practices or financial procedures) may produce a service approach characterized by stringency and rigidity. Lens (2008) demonstrated that work requirements for clients seeking public assistance led line-level staff to adopt a "harsh and punitive" orientation resulting in denial of benefits or unjustified sanctions (p. 217). As we will discuss in later chapters, understanding how organizational structure and rules affect interactions with clients is essential for effective macro practice.

Beyond the issue of structure, a lingering topic of debate concerns which organizations should be responsible for providing services and how this should be financed. From the start of the New Deal through the War on Poverty, public agencies were created to provide human services ranging from mental health care to welfare benefits to child protective services. Beginning in the 1960s, however, proponents of **privatization** became increasingly influential. Privatization calls for reducing or ending direct provision of human services by public agencies and replacing it with **purchase of service (POS)** contracting, whereby governments pay private agencies (both nonprofit and for-profit) to provide those services. This trend might more accurately be called "reprivatization" because it involves returning human services to the sector in which they were mostly based prior to the New Deal.

In the early 1980s, for example, an economic slowdown led to decreased public funding, after which POS funds began drying up. Many nonprofit agencies, which had previously grown larger on public dollars, were suddenly faced with stiff competition for limited resources. Nonprofit agencies had traditionally served low-income clients by offsetting their costs with revenues earned from paying clients. But with government funds more scarce and paying clients being siphoned off through competition from hospitals and for-profit providers, the frequent result was cutbacks in services that fell most heavily on clients most in need (McMurtry, Netting, & Kettner, 1991).

Driven by a desire to reduce the size of government and to encourage competition and cost control, the amount of money flowing into POS has grown enormously. Within the POS model, decision-making and financing functions remain with public agencies, but the actual delivery of services is shifted to the private sector. This can be attractive to service seekers because going to a local nonprofit agency may be viewed as less stigmatizing than asking for "government relief." Advocates of POS also argue that having agencies bid for contracts provides a variety of free-market benefits (e.g., minimizing costs and improving oversight) that would not occur if services were provided directly by the public agency in charge. To further advance the goal of service improvement, contracting agencies are now increasingly using **performance-based contracting**, in which agencies that receive contracts for services are required to meet specific targets for the quantity or quality of services provided (Martin, 2005).

The question of whether privatization has had positive effects on the delivery of human services remains in contention. Critics complain that the narrow focus of POS contracts ignores important client problems and promotes an orientation toward solving problems after the fact rather than preventing them. Others argue that the increased reliance of private agencies on government contracts threatens the independence of the private sector agencies and makes them more vulnerable than in times when their budgets were more diversified, especially when government cutbacks occur. Still other critics question the potential inequitable accessibility of providers. (Marwell & Gullickson, 2013).

Not only has the United States experienced a proliferation of nonprofit organizations, but also economic and political changes in other nations have altered the roles and responsibilities of **nongovernmental organizations** (NGOs). Having widely varying histories and functions across countries, NGOs, self-help groups, and community-based organizations of various types face economic challenges in locating resources to meet community needs. International NGOs such as Bread for the World, Habitat for Humanity, and Save the Children seek to address global issues of poverty, hunger, and housing. The global nature of these concerns means that social workers are constantly engaged in what has been called a **global perspective** in which organizations in communities facing human challenges must communicate across borders and learn from one another in addressing human needs (Moxley, Alvarez, Johnson, & Gutierrez, 2005).

Wisely Using Technology

Anyone who has used a computer or smartphone to make a purchase, schedule a flight, find a restaurant, send a message, locate an old friend, or make a new one knows that rapidly advancing information technology continues to make dramatic changes in our lives. Futurist Alvin Toffler predicted this trend more than 30 years ago, believing that it represented a major new form, or "Third Wave," of human society (1980). In the first wave, it was agricultural products, and in the second, it was manufactured goods. In the third wave, it is information.

Information as a commodity comes in many forms—one example of which is knowledge, such as that acquired and used by professionals. If a farmer was the emblematic figure of the first wave and a factory worker that of the second, in the third it is professionals, who, as opposed to farmers or factory workers, provide services rather than physical goods. The shift to services is becoming increasingly profound, and in the past 50 years the service sector of the economy has grown far more rapidly than any other.

Economies in developed countries seldom grow because new resources are found but because better use is made of existing resources—human or material. When economists refer to "productivity," they typically mean the value of goods and services produced divided by the resources (human and material) available to produce them. In 2002, for example, the U.S. Congressional Budget Office (CBO) examined the question of how much computer technology had to do with increases in productivity nationally. The results were that all net productivity between 1996 and 2001 was attributed to technological changes in the production of computer hardware and the easier access to computer technology this caused (U.S. Congressional Budget Office, 2002, p. viii).

Advances in information technology are transforming the workplace in other ways as well. Increasing numbers of employees are staying home for part or all of the work week, carrying out their tasks over voice and data lines linking them to national and international networks. These changes have the potential to dramatically alter the nature of community life. At a minimum, they are likely to modify traditional commuting patterns by allowing more workers to "go to the office" at home. Eventually they could reverse urbanization trends, contributing to smaller and more decentralized communities.

Technological advances have created a world community across national boundaries. Community activism, mass demonstrations, and social movements are immediately visible to populations around the world, mobilizing resistance and support from far reaches of the globe. Now there is the technological capacity to spontaneously translate needs and issues as they are being identified into public discourse. With this ability to know what is happening as it is happening come multiple challenges for social workers. It is easy to become overwhelmed with so much apparent need and conflict in the world. It is also important to recognize cultural contexts within which needs and conflict are framed and to not jump to conclusions about how to assess and engage "solutions" to complex problems that may seem to work in one cultural setting but might not be feasible or even helpful in another (Reisch, 2013).

Social workers can expect the ongoing changes in information technology to have two types of effects on their own work. One is that the nature of the social problems they encounter will be altered, and the other is that the way they do their work will change. With respect to changes in social problems, we have already noted the income gap between high and low earners in the United States, and a looming shortage of skilled workers to fill information-related and other high-tech jobs is likely to further widen this gap. This will further complicate the task of social workers who are attempting to assist society's poorest members, because few of those individuals will have the skills necessary to qualify for better paying jobs.

The way social workers do their jobs is also changing. They compose reports, write progress notes, exchange messages with others internal and external to the organization, access client records, search for referral options, and perform a variety of other functions that define the technical details of their professional roles. Computers, databases, and other information resources have become essential for these tasks. Smartphones and laptop or tablet computers can be used to take case notes, fill out forms, or administer assessment tools. In most cases, they also provide wireless access to allow workers to email questions to a supervisor, search for referral agencies, or schedule appointments for clients. Access to electronic agency files allows workers to search client records, upload forms and case notes, or input information used to monitor and evaluate services. They can also keep up with professional literature through online access to journals and research reports, post questions to members of a listserv who work in the same area of specialization, or visit websites that provide information on problems with which they are unfamiliar. Perhaps of greatest potential value to macro practitioners is their ability to download data on census tracts or access geographic information systems to plot the distribution of income, crime, age, health status, and many other variables on high-resolution maps of targeted areas. In other words, as in virtually all other fields, rapid change in computer and information technology will continue to change the way that social workers do their jobs. Box 2.6 provides an overview of contemporary challenges.

Ethical and Professional Behavior

Practice Behavior: Use technology ethically and appropriately to facilitate practice outcomes.

Critical Thinking Question: If you were asked to develop several principles for social workers about how to use technology ethically and appropriately, what would they be?

? Assess your understanding of contemporary social work challenges by taking this brief quiz.

Box 2.6   Contemporary Challenges at a Glance

- **Addressing Poverty and Welfare Reform.** Between 1996 (when major federal reforms were passed) and 2001, the number of welfare recipients dropped by more than half, but caseloads then began to stabilize. Poverty is now on the rise—especially child poverty—and children are more likely to be poor now than in the 1970s or 1980s.

- **Recognizing Income Inequality.** Income gaps between wealthy and poor are widening, with the richest one-fifth of families in the United States gaining earning power in the past 20 years and those in the poorest 20 percent having lower earnings. In 2007, the top one-tenth of households accounted for more than 50 percent of all income earned, whereas the bottom one-fifth of households received less than 5 percent of all income earned.

- **Assessing Changing Patterns of Community Affiliation and Identification.** Members of society rely less on local relationships and are less closely tied to their communities than in the past. For example, they are less likely to join local membership groups and more likely to affiliate with national organizations whose other members they may never meet, and they now use social networking and other technology to maintain relationships over long distances. Also, their organizations and communities are much more affected than in the past by decisions made outside the local area and across the globe.

- **Assessing Changing Organizations and Delivery Systems.** Social workers are more likely than in the past to work in organizations, and these are more likely to have formal, bureaucratic structures. They are also more likely to be private rather than public agencies and to depend on POS contracts.

- **Using Technology Wisely.** Computerization of many aspects of society means that the most valuable commodity is information. Moreover, most jobs now involve the production of services rather than food or manufactured goods. Only $1 of every $100 in the economy now comes from agriculture, while $4 of every $5 comes from services. From computer programming to health care to a variety of social work functions, services are increasingly information driven and computer dependent.

THE IMPORTANCE OF CHANGE

The development of social work macro practice has proceeded hand-in-hand with rapid changes in society. In fact, change is one of the few constants in modern life, and its effects are sometimes difficult to evaluate. Is fading participation in local membership groups evidence that people's connections to their communities are dying, or are we simply witnessing the replacement of old modes of affiliation and old definitions of "community" with newer ones? Does the gradual absorption of immigrants into the larger society represent a loss of their cultural identity, or by becoming a part of that society are they adding new flavors to it and guarding its variety and vibrancy? Is privatization a way to use market forces to lower costs and improve the quality of human services, or is it an intermediate step on a path toward abandonment of government responsibility for human services? Viewed up close, questions such as these are often difficult to answer, and sometimes it is only with the passage of years that a consensus begins to form.

In the meantime, social workers involved in macro practice must be aware that change is a constant force in society, and certain consequences of its presence can be anticipated. For lack of a better term, we will refer to these as *axioms of change*. They are:

1. Some individuals, organizations, and communities will be more welcoming to change than others.

Watch the video on health care for Americans with mental illness. How do changes in the mental health care system impact people with a serious mental illness?

www.youtube.com
/watch?v=XCw4PAWf6_U

2. Individuals, organizations, and communities will also vary in how well they cope with change.

3. Resistance to change may occur as individuals, organizations, and communities attempt to hold on to the familiar, but resistance may also be a rational response to changes that have negative effects.

4. The constancy of change, the fact that people and collections of people vary in how well they cope with change, and the fact that the change may be negative create an ongoing need for social workers to assist at both the micro and macro levels.

We believe that a planned change model can be employed to assist social workers in answering these questions and addressing problems in macro systems. Chapter 3 will introduce the basic elements of such a model by discussing how to engage target populations in addressing macro-level problems.

 Assess your understanding of the importance of change by taking this brief quiz.

SUMMARY

The need for social workers to be able to understand and practice in macro systems is based on both the history of the social work profession and the society in which it evolved. Major social changes such as rapid population growth, immigration, industrialization, urbanization, and the rise of modern institutional structures led to concentrations of people in large urban areas. Accompanying these changes were modern problems of urban crime, unemployment, poverty, and blighted neighborhoods. Societal responses to these conditions were affected by new ideologies. Social Darwinism provided a rationale for ignoring many of these problems (through the reasoning that people in need were weak and helping them would in turn weaken society) or to provide paternalistic and judgmental forms of assistance. However, services guided by progressivism and social justice concerns resulted in much more proactive helping efforts, such as the rise of the settlement houses.

Social work as a profession emerged in the United States during the Progressive era. At that time, Charity Organization Societies (with their emphasis on case-level practice) and settlement houses (with their more community-oriented efforts) fostered micro and macro perspectives. Workers in COS agencies emphasized the need for a systematic approach to the work, whereas workers in settlement houses demanded training on how to effect social change, as early social work education emerged.

Recognition of macro roles evolved as social work education developed. These roles included community organization, social reform, administration, and planning. In different parts of the world, these and other roles were emphasized as diverse perspectives about social work as a field of practice emerged.

Social work's commitment to diverse and oppressed populations revealed many issues faced by Native Americans, Latinos, African Americans, Asian Americans, women, persons with disabilities, and lesbian, gay, bisexual, and transgender persons. Complex urban, industrial communities produced vast wealth during the past century, but this was not always shared by ethnic groups segregated (formally or informally) in ghettos or on reservations. Highly bureaucratized organizations became efficient at processing individual clients in standardized ways, but they did not consistently advance in their ability to meet individual needs or avoid practices that actively or passively discriminated against particular groups.

Advancing human rights as well as social and economic justice became one of social work's ongoing challenges. In addition, several contemporary challenges were identified, including: addressing poverty and welfare reform, recognizing income inequality, assessing changing community patterns of affiliation and identification, assessing changing organizations and delivery systems, and wisely using technology.

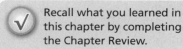

Recall what you learned in this chapter by completing the Chapter Review.

Assess Your Competence

Use the scale below to rate your current level of achievement on the following concepts or skills associated with each learning outcome listed at the beginning of this chapter:

1	2	3
I can accurately describe the concept or skill(s) associated with this outcome.	I can consistently identify the concept or skill(s) associated with this outcome when observing and analyzing practice activities.	I can competently implement the concept or skill(s) associated with this outcome in my own practice.

_____ Identify historical social conditions and ideologies leading to the establishment of social work as a profession.

_____ Discuss how professional social work education and practice developed during the 1900s.

_____ Describe issues faced by diverse and oppressed population groups.

_____ Identify contemporary challenges related to social work macro practice.

_____ Explain why change is so important to social work practice.

3

Engaging with Diverse Populations

CYLONPHOTOFT / FOTOLIA

DIVERSITY AND DIFFERENCE

Figure 3.1, originally presented in Chapter 1, illustrates how the three domains of population, problem, and arena have unique as well as overlapping elements. In order to be effective in bringing about macro-level change, the social worker and collaborators must begin by becoming knowledgeable about (1) the population affected; (2) the problem, need, or opportunity; and (3) the locality or arena where the change will take place. These three domains can also be thought of as three intersecting circles in which the most critical knowledge and information are at the points of overlap.

In this chapter, we will focus on one of the three circles: the population. The following chapters will explore the remaining circles: understanding problems (Chapter 4) and assessing communities (Chapters 5 and 6) and/or organizations (Chapters 7 and 8) with and in which macro practice is carried out. This chapter and the next will be used to guide the practitioner into the study of a particular population that has social, community, or organizational problems or needs. Altogether, these chapters will present a conceptual framework for a model of macro practice and will specify a series of tasks for collecting data and information.

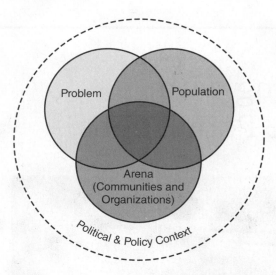

Figure 3.1
Understanding Population, Problem, and Arena

We turn now to diverse and different population groups to provide a context for the framework that follows.

Problems affect people. Solutions, if they are to be effective, must reflect an understanding of and respect for the people affected and the capacity to build on their strengths.

A particular **target population** may be implied or stated as a part of framing a problem. Focusing on a problem such as a high rate of teenage pregnancy and underweight infants immediately narrows the population to young women between the ages of approximately 11 and 19. Addressing a rising incidence of elder abuse narrows the population to people who are usually over age 65 and in a vulnerable and dependent situation. In some cases, a population may be distinguished by shared race, ethnicity, or culture. For example, a focus on health disparities among African American women or resettlement barriers faced by Hmong immigrants suggests factors that may be central to understanding a population and the challenges they face.

Historical and contemporary issues faced by a few oppressed groups were summarized in Chapter 2. The following paragraphs provide a brief overview of why it is important for social workers to engage with diverse and different population groups in order to advance human rights and social and economic justice.

Advancing Human Rights and Social and Economic Justice

Gutierrez and her colleagues (2013) identify issues faced by macro social workers as they work with diverse population groups. For example, the life expectancy of people of color continues to lag behind the general population. and a major public health problem is that the life expectancy for black men continues to decline, with homicide as the leading cause of death for young men of color. Members of the social networks for children of color have become overwhelmed in trying to provide support at a time when it is needed more than ever. With the implementation of welfare reform, women of color have been disproportionately pushed into low-paying jobs with inadequate (if any) child care. Persons who have immigrated to the United States work long hours to send income to members of their extended families in their countries of origin.

Two contrasting views can and often are held when assessing current circumstances affecting historically disadvantaged groups. One view sees progress in the way that racism and, to a lesser degree, sexism are recognized and condemned both informally among society's members and formally through laws, operational rules, and new programs created to address old injustices. The opposing view sees lingering disparities in income, education, and health that continue to affect racial and ethnic minorities; stereotypes and paternalistic attitudes affecting women; neglect and ignorance affecting persons with disabilities; and reactionary legal initiatives designed to label LGBTQ citizens as aberrant and undeserving of equal protection.

The contrast between these views illustrates the way in which ideological differences seem to have become more sharply defined across the political spectrum, with the result that concepts of compassion and caring for vulnerable populations sometimes appear at risk of drowning in a sea of rhetoric. The task facing social workers is further compounded by the fact that their efforts are often portrayed as destroying individual responsibility and fostering dependency among those they serve.

Perhaps the most important point to keep in mind is that social programs tend to reflect the status quo because they address symptoms of oppression rather than causes. Professionals frequently assume they know the causes of oppression—and thus the needs of consumers—without directly asking the people they serve. During recent decades, efforts such as social movements and citizen participation activities have taken steps to address the needs of special populations in a more comprehensive and consumer-involved manner. The task for practitioners remains that of (1) truly engaging population groups in every phase of change efforts that will impact their lives, (2) finding interventions that respond appropriately to the needs of these populations, and (3) keeping in the forefront a genuine commitment to meeting these needs.

 Watch the video on how the social, economic, and physical environments in which we are born, live, and work affect our longevity and health. How does the video explain the causes of health inequality?

www.youtube.com /watch?v=uE7v5cHlHDQ

Human Rights and Justice

Practice Behavior: Apply their understanding of social, economic, and environmental justice to advocate for human rights at the individual and systems level.

Critical Thinking Question: As a practitioner, how do you plan to balance your responsibility to advocate at both the individual and systems levels?

Where Does One Begin?

Social workers engage with populations throughout the world who experience oppressive conditions and are discriminated against on a daily basis. In some cases, the population may not even be clearly defined.

For example, an episode of change may focus on a neighborhood. In this instance, the population may be neighborhood residents within which there are numerous subpopulations such as preschoolers, children, teenagers, young families, adults, and/or elders in multiple racial, ethnic, and cultural groups. When intervening at the neighborhood level, assessing the **arena** (to be discussed in subsequent chapters) will require close collaboration with community members. Without their engagement, false assumptions could easily be made about the needs of this community.

In another instance, the arena could be a long-term care facility in which the lowest paid workers are doing "the bed and body work" of daily patient care. Primarily minority women perform these backbreaking duties every day, often moonlighting in more than one facility in order to make ends meet. Their voices are seldom heard by administrators, even though they likely know more about patients and their daily needs than anyone else. Theirs is an economic justice issue in that they are rarely paid enough to provide for their own families, yet are expected to provide quality care for members of other families. Hearing their stories is crucial if change is to occur.

A word of caution is needed at this point. In this and subsequent chapters, we will provide guidance on how one might begin engaging and assessing situations before attempting to initiate or participate in a change process. Every population group and every problem are complex, no matter how they appear on the front end, and there is no one right way to begin. In fact, even though we will offer you various tasks that may appear to be logical, you may find that some are useful and others are not. You will also find that often there is not enough time to do everything we suggest because timelines and other demands are often superimposed and out of your control. It is important to know that change agents do not have to use every aspect of every assessment tool in lockstep fashion. We provide you with multiple assessment tasks so that you know they are available. When change efforts are made within existing resources, choices can be made about what to use. However, some macro-level changes require special funding, and when additional resources are requested it is very likely that the funding source(s) will specify at least some of the topics to be covered.

Although these tasks are presented in a series, you will find that they are iterative in that you may be working on multiple tasks simultaneously, with each task informing your thinking about another.

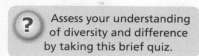

You might be asking at this point: Where do I begin? How is it possible to focus? We recommend that you begin by prioritizing the population's perspectives on the problems and opportunities they face. In the framework that follows, we underscore the importance of engaging in a critical reflection process of self-awareness in preparation for working with any population group.

A FRAMEWORK FOR ENGAGING POPULATION GROUPS

For change to be initiated, there must be an individual or a small group that recognizes the need for change and is prepared to take action. Within this core group, early decisions are made about collaboration and sharing of responsibility. Skills are needed in the areas of interviewing representatives of affected populations, researching the professional knowledge base, collecting quantitative and qualitative data, and making an informed analysis based on findings. Remember that it is likely that the case to be made in favor of change will ultimately be taken to a decision-making body and possibly to a funding source. People who make decisions and allocate funds have a right to expect that those who come before them are knowledgeable and informed, and have "done their homework."

"Doing one's homework" in this instance means taking a disciplined, methodical approach to understanding the population, problem, arena, and political context of the proposed change. Referring to Figure 3.1 as a guide to our study of these domains, we first approach them as separate circles. This means that a social worker might, for example, look first at the population and attempt to understand everything he or she can about this domain within the limited time frame available.

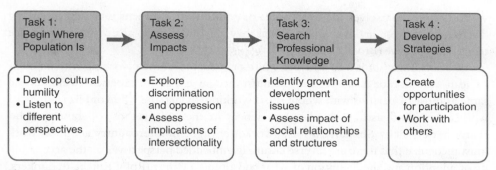

Figure 3.2
Tasks in the Framework for Engaging Population Groups

To begin assessing the population, we propose that the change agent engage in a series of tasks, as depicted in Figure 3.2.

Task 1: Start Where the Population Is

A mantra of social work practice is to "start where the client is." This is as much the case in macro-practice activities as it is in work with individuals and families. Engaging a population and assessing the problems they face require attention to a range of perspectives. Problems can be understood in a number of ways, including (1) experiencing the problem firsthand, (2) working closely with people who have experienced the problem, or (3) exploring the professional knowledge base about the problem. In considering these approaches, it is important to distinguish between the understanding and insight gained by personal experience as contrasted with other methods of learning. For this reason, it is important to communicate directly with persons who know about the problem firsthand, and to remember that early encounters in which one is humble and open will help pave the way for mutual trust and engagement.

Task 1 includes two sets of activities—developing cultural humility and listening to different perspectives from population members.

Develop Cultural Humility

Most, if not all, episodes of macro-level change will involve populations that differ on some dimension from the social work change agent. For this reason, we emphasize listening to members of the target population and gathering a wide variety of theoretical perspectives and empirical evidence in order to develop an effective planned change intervention. But before a social worker engages in these learning activities, she or he must attend to interpersonal attitudes regarding diversity and difference.

Questions to be explored for this activity include:

- What experiences has the social worker had with members of this population group?
- What self-identities and attitudes does the social worker bring to this situation?
- What are the strengths, vulnerabilities, and power imbalances faced by this population group?

Ideally, in each macro-level change effort, there would be a change agent available who reflects the race, culture, ethnic group, gender, age group, and life experiences of the target population. This ideal should be pursued but at times is not possible. Social workers find themselves the focal point or conduit for concerns representing many diverse perspectives, and it is expected that they will find ways to give visibility and voice to each perspective (Brooks, 2001).

If a social worker is a 23-year-old white or Hispanic woman working with an older African American or Asian person, she must recognize that her experiences are not the same as those of persons with whom she is working. In fact, the white or Hispanic social worker should not assume that her experiences are the same as those of someone who shares her ethnicity. Similarly, a social worker engaged in intercountry adoption work must recognize that there are diverse cuturally embedded perspectives on the acceptability of adoption and the definition of what constitutes a family (Roby, Rotabi, & Bunkers, 2013). Effective cross-cultural social work in these situations requires that the social worker be able to hear the voices of persons with different perspectives and to partner with others as they guide one another toward understanding and change.

To become effective in such cross-cultural situations, social workers have been encouraged to develop **cultural competence**. Cultural competence includes interrelated actions, thoughts, and even policies that are joined within a system or organization to facilitate effective cross-cultural work (NASW, 2000, p. 61). NASW (2001) recognizes cultural competence as both a process and a product that includes self-awareness and respect for diversity as well as effective practice behaviors on micro, mezzo, and macro levels.

Cross, Bazron, Dennis, and Isaacs (1989) identified six points on a continuum of competency. The authors suggested a process of growth that includes practitioner and agency awareness, knowledge, and skills. The authors' six points on the continuum are noted in Table 3.1.

Table 3.1   Cultural Competence Continuum

Competency Continuum	Description
Cultural Destructiveness	• Attitudes, policies, and practices that are destructive to cultures are also destructive to individuals within cultures.
Cultural Incapacity	• The person, agency, or system lacks the capacity to help members of a cultural or ethnic group. • The person, agency, or system does not respect the beliefs or traditions of the group being served.
Cultural Blindness	• The belief that culture is not important and that all people are the same. • Use of helping approaches is seen to be universally applicable.
Cultural Precompetence	• The individual, agency, or system recognizes its cultural deficiencies and begins to make attempts to address them through outreach or hiring practices.
Cultural Competence	• Differences are accepted and respected. • Self-assessment of staff and policies are made in relation to culture. • Cultural knowledge and resources are expanded.
Cultural Proficiency	• Culture is held in high esteem. • Cultural practice is enhanced by research. • Cultural knowledge is increased.

Based on Cross, Bazron, Dennis, and Isaacs' (1989) six points of cultural competency.

The assumptions of cultural competence have been questioned in recent inter-disciplinary scholarship, particularly the assumption that competence can ever truly be attained (Hook, Owen, Davis, Worthington, & Utsey, 2013). For example, Johnson and Munch (2009) identified four paradoxes in current understandings of cultural competence. First, despite professional emphasis on *learning from* clients, models of cultural competence often espouse *knowing about* clients and assume specialized knowledge can be acquired about different client groups. Second, although ethical standards emphasize the dignity and worth of individuals, descriptions of difference are by definition stereotypical and may overlook the uniqueness of each individual. Third, the ethical value of self-determination may be undermined by a focus on the group. Finally, the authors questioned if competence can ever be achieved given (1) the lack of clarity about the definition and (2) the numerous unique combinations that comprise individual identities.

Diversity and Difference in Practice

Practice Behavior: Present themselves as learners, and engage clients and constituencies as experts of their own experiences.

Critical Thinking Question: What is the difference between learning from clients and learning about clients? Why does this matter?

In contrast to cultural competence, medical educators Tervalon and Murray-Garcia (1998) proposed *cultural humility* as the goal for cross-cultural practice. Unlike competence, humility does not suggest that one can master everything about a culture. Instead, it suggests an ongoing process that includes a continual commitment to learning and self-reflection, to altering the power imbalances in the interactions between helping professionals and service consumers, and to developing collaborative and equitable relationships with community members. Tervalon and Murray-Garcia and other critics of cultural competence recognize the importance of increasing knowledge and skills, but also recognize the limits and potential dangers of these behaviors if they are not accompanied by ongoing self-evaluative processes and relationship building.

For social workers who practice directly with individuals and families, each encounter with a client provides an opportunity to exercise cultural humility. For social workers who practice with organizations and communities, these opportunities are also readily available. Using Tervalon and Murray-Garcia's (1998) components of cultural humility, Table 3.2 provides critical questions to consider when faced with opportunities to develop and exercise cultural humility.

Although we emphasize cultural humility in this text, we do not discount the value of the work that has been done to develop the concept and practices of cultural competence. Seeking to increase one's understanding of different groups and cultures is a goal worth pursuing and a task required by many professional bodies. Conceptual and empirical works on cultural competence are invaluable resources for professionals. For example, Organista (2009) proposes a practice model with Latinos that synthesizes previous models and methods of culturally competent practice. Using a range of theories and research, Organista contends that practice with Latinos should be attentive to four dimensions in order to practice competently: (1) Increase service availability and access, (2) assess problems in the social and cultural contexts, (3) select culturally and socially acceptable interventions, and (4) increase service accountability (p. 300). These dimensions should assist practitioners as they assess and critique current practices and develop new practices with Latinos. The value of such an integrative model is that it provides a ready tool for practitioners as they work with one of the fastest growing minority groups in the United States.

Table 3.2   Critical Questions about Cultural Humility

Components of Cultural Humility	Critical Questions for Social Workers
Having a lifelong commitment to self-evaluation and critique	• How are my beliefs and values influencing how I view this person, group, or community? • Have I identified and reflected on how my past experiences might influence how I view and treat this person, group, or community?
Attempting to redress power imbalances in the interaction and dynamics between social workers and a consumer of services	• Where is power located in this relationship? • How am I using power in this situation? • Am I using power "over" or power "with" this person, group, or community? • How can I begin and sustain relationships that acknowledge and equalize power differences?
Developing mutually beneficial and nonpaternalistic partnerships with communities	• How are community perspectives incorporated into this partnership? • Have community representatives been a part of this partnership since its early stages? • Were community perspectives sought before solutions were imposed?

Based on Tervalon and Murray-Garacia's (1998) components of cultural humility.

We stress, however, that knowledge acquisition is only one dimension of ethical and effective cross-cultural practice. Drawing from Tervalon and Murray-Garcia (1998), such practice must also address power imbalances, mutuality in relationships, and critical self-awareness.

Listen to Different Perspectives from Population Members

As practitioners continuously cultivate self-awareness and cultural humility within the context of social work values, the imperative to seek population perspectives is clear. Questions to be explored for this activity include the following:

- Identify key informants from the population of interest.
- Include diverse voices and perspectives in articulating the issues faced by this population.

To better understand a particular population, the social work change agent must seek the perspectives of those who are members of the population. This activity is both an application of cultural humility and social work values, as well as a prudent means to gather useful information to inform the planned change effort. Hook and his colleagues (2013) suggest that a humble person has an accurate view of self and is other-oriented as opposed to being self-focused. Humble professionals respect others and do not exert superiority over others. They see members of the population with which they are engaging as experts on the challenges they face. They look for strengths first.

People who live or work in the place that is seen as needing change may not perceive the situation exactly as the change agent does. They may have important social support structures or resources unknown to persons outside that group. They may also have seen previous efforts by well-meaning change agents fail and/or ignore their plans and desires for their own community. Their positions in the community or organization and their perspectives need to be respected. Cues should be taken from indigenous people as to appropriate roles and responsibilities in initiating a change effort.

Many changes involve cultural and ethnic considerations, so the preceding points about cultural humility should be incorporated early in any planned macro-level change. Also important is an awareness of the many ways in which culture can be manifested. For example, in an extended care facility there is a culture-of-care provision. In a high school, faculty, staff, students, and administrators will typically have developed an organizational culture over time. In these and other situations where the change agent is perceived as an outsider, the components in Table 3.2 can help the organizer or change agent build credibility and avoid mistakes with persons who are part of those environments.

Understanding a macro-level problem or need in all its complexity requires skillful eliciting of information from a variety of people who have experienced the problem. Knowledge and sensitivity are required for this type of interview. The work done in macro practice in social work is not like that of a newspaper reporter gathering information for an article. A trusting relationship must be built so that those persons in the community or organization will develop a commitment to the changes needed and participate in the change effort.

Furthermore, if a person who identifies with the population is not already a part of the change effort, seeking input from members of the population may identify a representative or representatives of the population for participation in the planning and implementation of the change. Those who have direct experience with the problem or opportunity might not accept those without similar experience as spokespersons. People who have experienced life on public assistance may not be willing to accept a social worker as a representative of their feelings and needs. Likewise, someone living in an affordable housing development may be more likely to turn to a fellow resident as spokesperson. Describing the experiences that led to posttraumatic stress disorder in the wars in Vietnam, Iraq, and Afghanistan is more credibly done by someone who was there. People of a particular ethnic group may be able to speak for the experiences of their own group but not for another group. A person who is not a transgender may not be able to credibly represent a transgender person. For these reasons, it is important to find spokespersons who are accepted and supported by their peers and who can help to articulate the perspectives of the group(s) involved. Identifying key participants to take lead roles in certain areas doesn't diminish the role of the social worker. It merely changes its focus.

> Go to the Community Toolbox homepage and do a search on "Chapter 7." Read Section 8, "Identifying and Analyzing Stakeholders and Their Interests." What reasons are provided for including stakeholders and their interests?

Task 2: Assess the Impact of Difference, Discrimination, and Oppression

Difference that is stereotyped and stigmatized can result in prejudice, discrimination, and oppression. **Prejudices** are based on preconceived stereotypes, rather than on experience or reason (Hoyt, 2012). **Discrimination** refers to detrimental action or an absence of action because of individual and group differences (Bell, 2007). **Oppression** occurs when an individual, group, or society unjustly uses authority or power over others, and it includes everything from institutional discrimination to personal bigotry (Hoyt, 2012).

Task 2 pushes deeper into examining the impact of discrimination and oppression on the population group. Two sets of activities follow: exploring the discriminatory issues faced by, as well as the intersectionality within, the population.

Explore the Discriminatory and Oppressive Issues Faced by This Population

Questions to be explored for this activity include the following:

- What stereotypes or generalizations confront this population group?
- How has this population group been discriminated against or oppressed?
- Do members of the population group feel marginalized, and if so, why?

Population groups that are recognized as different from the dominant culture are frequently stereotyped. *Stereotypes* are generalizations about a group that suggest that all members of that group are the same and will exhibit the same behavior (Rosenblum & Travis, 2008). Link and Phelan (2001, p. 367) suggest that stigmatization occurs when the following five elements converge:

- Human differences are identified and then labeled.
- Cultural differences and values link labeled people to negative stereotypes.
- A separation of "us" and "them" develops, categorizing people as a group.
- Persons in the labeled group lose status and are discriminated against.
- Because they are stigmatized, the labeled population does not gain access to resources and is disempowered and excluded.

Stereotyping and stigmatizing others provide a rationale for discrimination and oppression. When a difference is construed as abnormal and wrong, individuals, programs, and institutions that identify as normal have a rationale to maintain their perspectives. The change agent must search beyond these normative descriptions of "different" groups to understand a population and its challenges. Constructed categories such as race, class, or gender maintain social hierarchies and power relations, privileging some groups at the expense of others (Sewpaul, 2013). Social workers must recognize how a difference is portrayed and how dominant interpretations of that difference have resulted in discrimination and oppression. Oppression can occur around any dimension of difference, but common "isms" describing specific forms of oppression are defined in Table 3.3.

The "isms" are based on steoretypical thinking that generalizes to a group of people, based on their shared characteristics. Often, these attitudes become barriers to community participation even though they are subtle and difficult to identify. The "isms" exist in the values, norms, and traditions of a society to be translated into local community activities. For example, as children are socialized in their educational, religious, and familial roles, they are given messages regarding what is considered appropriate for women and men. Bricker-Jenkins and Hooyman (1986) proposed that social workers should examine patriarchy within the community. They suggested that the recording of history and the establishment of myths that set direction for succeeding generations are parts of a patriarchal system in which experiences of women tend to be devalued and their contributions subjugated.

▶ Watch the video featuring Camara Jones discussing race and racism. How do Dr. Jones' allegories help you understand the impact of privilege and oppression on you and the populations with whom you may work?

www.youtube.com/watch?v=GNhcY6fTyBM

Table 3.3   Systems of Oppression

System of Oppression	Definition
Ableism	An institutional, cultural, and individual system of disadvantage and discrimination against people who are considered physically or mentally unable to function as well as others.
Ageism	An institutional, cultural, and individual system of disadvantage and discrimination against people because of their age.
Classism	An institutional, cultural, and individual system of disadvantage and discrimination against people who are at a lower socioeconomic level.
Enthocentrism	Ethnic groups share a common language, customs, history, culture, race, religion, or origin. Ethocentrism is an institutional, cultural, and individual system of disadvantage and discrimination that implies that one's ethnic group is superior to others.
Heterosexism and Trans Oppression	An institutional, cultural, and individual system of disadvantage and discrimination against people who are (or are perceived to be) lesbian, gay, bisexual, or transgender.
Racism	An institutional, cultural, and individual system of disadvantage and discrimination against people based on their race or perceived race.
Sexism	An institutional, cultural, and individual system of disadvantage and discrimination because of gender.

The target population may encompass one or more racial or ethnic groups. Information on such factors as rates of employment, educational achievement, and socioeconomic status within these subgroups is important to understanding the effects of institutional racism. Whether persons from different groups within the target population are involved in decision-making roles is an important indicator of sensitivity to ethnic and cultural issues. Services and other resources available to people from diverse ethnicities in the target population proportionate to their numbers in the community comprise another indicator. Statistics on violence against women and resources to deal with this problem are available from such organizations as women's support groups, women's centers, and shelters for battered women (Busch & Wolfer, 2002). Lack of services, such as child care and transportation, may limit women's access to employment.

Cultural attitudes associated with classism frequently blame people who are poor for their own situation. These judgments are based on the assumption that those who are poor lack initiative and are unwilling to work to achieve a better socioeconomic status for themselves and their families. Such perspectives are sometimes reflected in the prejudicial language and popular culture stereotypes used to describe people from lower socioeconomic levels. Terms like *trailer trash, low class, ghetto, white trash*, and *redneck* impugn the character of individuals from lower socioeconomic levels. In popular culture, working-class people may be viewed as ignorant, whereas upper-middle-class lifestyles are seen as normal (Leondar-Wright & Yeskel, 2007).

Homophobia is a term used to describe irrational fears held by people toward individuals who have a same-gender sexual orientation. Homophobia, in the extreme, has taken the form of "gay bashing," a practice of physically beating gay people. In other forms, heterosexism and homophobia result in job discrimination, ridicule, and ostracizing. Like all prejudices (literally, "prejudgments"), homophobia blinds those afflicted with it to the individual qualities of lesbians and gay men and causes them to perceive these populations only in the context of their sexual orientation. Homophobia, along with heterosexism, heterocentrism, and other systems of oppression, have an impact on every aspect of a person's life, including work environment, housing acquisition, access to health services, and religious and community life (Appleby, 2007).

The vast majority of older adults and persons with disabilities are capable of self-sufficiency and productive lives, yet they may be excluded from employment and from playing an important role in the community because of perceptions about their abilities. Persons with disabilities and older individuals may not be hired because employers are concerned about higher than average medical costs. If age or disability is relevant to understanding the target population, statistics on the numbers and age ranges of those persons in the community should be compiled. How many persons are frail older adults (over 85)? How many persons are physically disabled, and what types of disabilities are documented? Is there adequate access to services that engage persons with disabilities in active community roles—transportation and outreach, for example? Are there support services (e.g., nutrition programs, homemaker, and respite) that sustain these persons and their care partners?

"Isms" do not exist in isolation, but rather intersect with other systems of oppression to further impact individuals and populations. For example, many of the "isms" intersect with classism to further marginalize members of affected populations.

Assess Implications of Intersectionality

Questions to be explored for this activity include the following:

- What are the dimensions of intersectionality within this population?
- What issues of power, privilege, discrimination, and oppression are identified by members of this population?
- What frameworks are useful in understanding population dynamics?

Macro practitioners work with individuals and communities that vary along a number of dimensions, including race, ethnicity, gender, socioeconomic status, and religion, among others. In addition to talking to members of various populations, concepts and frameworks have been developed that help practitioners better understand the complexity of these intersecting dimensions and the relationship of a person's identity to majority culture.

An early framework for understanding the complexities of cultural characteristics and the impact of those characteristics on the identity and well-being of individuals was Norton's (1978) **dual perspective**. The dual perspective views an individual at the center of two surrounding systems, which Norton called the nurturing system and the sustaining system. The **nurturing system** includes the values of parents and an extended family or substitute family via community experiences, beliefs, customs, and traditions with which the individual was raised. Surrounding the nurturing system is a **sustaining system**, represented by the dominant society and culture. The sustaining system also reflects beliefs, values, customs, and traditions.

e. generational
mistrust teachers

Sustaining systems are made up of influential and powerful people, including, for example, teachers, employers, and law enforcement and elected officials. Some segments of sustaining systems may reflect ageist, racist, sexist, or other prejudicial attitudes, and can therefore be perceived by diverse population groups as representing alien and hostile environments. An example is the often antagonistic relationships that develop between ethnic communities and the local police. Norton suggested that the more incongruence between a person's nurturing and sustaining systems, the more difficulty she or he would have. She urged social workers to take actions to support the nurturing system and educate and confront the sustaining system when needed.

Years earlier, W. E. B. DuBois (1903) coined the term *double consciousness* or *two-ness* to refer to African Americans' awareness of their identity and the identity ascribed to them by the dominant white society. He and subsequent scholars recognized this dual consciousness as both a "special gift" and a powerful source of maladaptive identity development. As a gift or strength, double consciousness recognizes the bicultural capacity of minority group members that function, by necessity, in both their own culture and the dominant culture. Members of the dominant culture rarely need and are seldom forced to experience and live within minority cultures. Along with that strength, however, is the risk that members of minority groups might internalize the stigmatized and stereotyped messages the dominant culture conveys about them.

In recent years, studies about whiteness and white identities have increased across multiple fields of study. The reification of whiteness has been recognized as the standard against which anyone who is not considered "white" is measured. The unrecognized and unexamined category of whiteness has dominated all aspects of society as the norm against which everyone is judged. The power behind whiteness comes in its lack of acknowledgment, yet its influence saturates every aspect of life. Western film, literature, and other cultural manifestations have perpetuated the institutionalization of whiteness as dominant. Essentially, whiteness functions to project the image that being white is beyond racial categorization, and, when left unscrutinised, it is used to gain white privilege. **White privilege** includes a vast range of unearned social gains that white people have by simply being white, but that are largely invisible (taken for granted) by them (Jeyaskingham, 2012).

Critical race theory (CRT) reveals how policies, laws, and court decisions that abolish the most visible signs of discrimination are often underminded by the deeply institutionalized and less visible values, norms, and cultures of the arenas in which they are implemented (e.g. housing, education, and employment). These arenas have institutionalized norms of whiteness whereby racial groups are marginalized in subtle but nonetheless damaging ways. CRT is used to analyze, deconstruct, and transform those power relationships that marginalize racial groups. Basic premises of CRT are highlighted in Table 3.4.

Perspectives on **intersectionality** emphasize the complexity of multiple dimensions of difference that individuals occupy and the isms related to those dimensions in understanding identity development (Mattsson, 2014). Born out of Black Feminist scholarship (Hill Collins, 2000; Hooks, 1981, 1989), intersectionality suggests that gender alone is an insufficient analytic category to understand the experiences and identity of women of color. In fact, any singular category is inadequate. Instead, when considering life experiences and the development of identity, one must consider the interaction of multiple

---

Table 3.4   Themes of Critical Race Theory

Themes of Critical Race Theory

1. Racism is deeply and perpetually embedded in societal institutions, making it very difficult to identify. Despite the banning of visible signs of discrimination, racial privilege continues. CRT seeks to study and change the relationship between race, racism, and power, questioning the liberal order of things.

2. Racism has become normalized in societal structures and institutions in which whites are privileged and persons of color are not. Thus, race and racism serve psychological, social, and material interests, and in order for change to occur it must benefit majority interests as well as those interests of excluded minorities.

3. Race is socially constructed, having no basis in genetics or biology. Yet, categories of difference have been created by law to normalize race and underscore white privilege.

4. Symbolism and meaning of racial groups have changed over place and time depending on political, social, and economic needs.

5. The intersectionality of multiple identities is recognized, and to solely recognize gender, race, class, sexuality, disability, or any other identity without acknowledging the complexity of their overlap leads to further marginization.

6. The voices of people of color are unique, must be heard, and are often more effective in assessing the intended and unintended consequences of public policies and programs.

Adapted from Freeman (2011); and Kolivoski, Weaver, and Constance-Huggins (2014).

---

categories and isms. Specifically, everyone has a race, gender, and class, and these categorizations intersect to form complex, layered identities (Doykos, Brinkley-Rubinstein, Craven, McCormack, & Geller, 2014). Identity is further developed by other differences, including age, ethnicity, physical ability, and sexual identity.

The dual perspective, double consciousness, and intersectionality provide guidance when working with different population groups, particularly groups that are marginalized. Each of the concepts suggests that the best place to begin to understand a population is with the population itself, especially if the change agent is not a member of that population. In attempting to solve vexing social problems, the social work change agent should assume that oppressed or ignored groups have a better understanding of their culture than the change agent does. Related, the change agent should recognize that members of oppressed groups are more likely to understand and function within the dominant culture than members of the dominant culture are in minority cultures. People who live within a dominant society observe and experience, on a daily basis, the values, beliefs, traditions, and language of the dominant society through personal contact, television, newspapers, and other media. Representatives of the dominant society do not regularly observe and experience the values, beliefs, and traditions of nondominant groups. A social worker must often help representatives of the dominant society understand the strengths and needs of the marginalized populations experiencing a social problem. For example, a young, black, special education student recently testified before the state legislative committee on his experiences with bullying. Special education students are by far the majority of victims. A social worker and a teacher identified this young man and made arrangements for his testimony so that his voice and experience could be heard by persons in decision-making roles.

Most policies, programs, and services, along with their underlying rationales, are designed from a dominant-society perspective. Theories used to explain the problem and the research on which the practitioner builds hypotheses may reflect majority-culture biases. Practitioners with the best intentions of working with a population group bring their own layered identities to the engagement process, and when power differentials are unexamined, they can unwittingly contribute to the institutionalized oppression that already exists. Members of diverse population groups, on the other hand, may have different perspectives of the problem and how to resolve it. These perspectives are crucial in understanding a problem and creating effective solutions for change (Doykos et al., 2014).

Consider, for example, a situation in which some of a community's older adults are experiencing deteriorating quality of life. One culture may value the concept of extended family and wish to maintain older parents in the home, but family members may not be able to afford the expense of taking on another dependent. Another culture may value the independence and privacy of older parents, but its members may not be able to pay retirement-community prices. The community's influential and powerful leaders and decision makers may believe that government should not be involved, and that decisions about aging parents should be left to adult children. It is likely that these types of perceptions will be linked to factors relating to culture and/or gender and to nurturing-system/sustaining-system perspectives.

Theoretical principles should be critically evaluated for their biases and given credibility based on how thoroughly they have been tested, especially in relation to the population being explored. Once selected as a framework for analysis, theoretical assumptions should be stated and shared with those involved in the change effort. Change agents should always stay open to reassessing assumptions as new information is gathered and new perspectives emerge. This is intended to facilitate progress toward shared understandings of the population group and openness toward amending those joint understandings in process.

> Go to the Unnatural Causes homepage and do a search on "Health Equity Quiz." Take the quiz. What does the quiz teach you about the relevance of socioeconomic differences in health outcomes? Did taking the quiz make you reassess some of your assumptions?

Task 3: Search the Professional Knowledge Base on the Target Population

There was a time when compiling information on a topic meant going to a library and scouring journal articles on the topic. The Internet has changed all that, and for this reason we no longer refer to a "review of the literature," but rather use the phrase *exploring the professional knowledge base.* The latest research, essays, case examples, and many other resources can be found online in professional journals and at other sites that specialize in populations and problems. Most journals provide a table of contents, and some provide abstracts as well. Resources can also be accessed by entering key words (e.g., "child neglect," "teenage alcohol abuse," or "dementia") into the search function and getting a list of types of data and information available. Articles in social work journals can also be helpful in directing professionals to useful resources.

It is important, however, for those attempting to compile a credible theoretical and research-based understanding of a population or the problems they face to check the sources of

Research-informed Practice (or Practice-informed Research)

Practice Behavior: Use and translate research evidence to inform and improve practice, policy, and service delivery.

Critical Thinking Question: How can population groups help practitioners use and translate research findings? What if they disagree with the literature?

information provided. Some of what is included on websites and other Internet resources may be opinion or conventional wisdom passed on without regard to authenticity.

The professional knowledge base includes the major contributions to a field of study, beginning with peer-reviewed professional journals in social work and related areas, books and monographs focused on the population, and reliable organizational resources. An Internet search can provide an overview of professional journals at websites such as *Social Work Abstracts, PsychINFO*, and *PubMed. WorldCat* is a valuable source of information on books. In addition to peer-reviewed scholarship and books indexed at the sites listed above, useful data and information may also be provided by groups representing populations such as the American Association of Retired Persons (AARP), the National Alliance to End Homelessness, the Children's Action Alliance, the American Cancer Society, and the National Alliance on Mental Illness (NAMI).

Local studies done within an agency or a community are also valuable sources of data. Although national studies tend to produce findings that are more widely applicable, local studies have the advantage of being specific to the agency or community and are therefore perhaps more precise and relevant to the population being studied. Agency employees and networks of service providers can be helpful in identifying local research projects and reports, as well as needs assessments, that may be available.

An important part of reviewing the knowledge base should be devoted to identifying and applying relevant theoretical perspectives. Theories can be descriptive, helping one to better understand the population group, or prescriptive in helping the change agent know how to intervene (Mulroy, 2004; Savaya & Waysman, 2005). As opposed to the random listing of facts and observations, theories allow for categorizing one's findings, making sense out of them, and turning seemingly unrelated bits of information into explanatory propositions that lead to logical, testable hypotheses.

Understanding populations and framing problems is a professional undertaking that must be approached with care and sensitivity. Without careful attention to the multiple dimensions of populations and problems, descriptions and explanations may be overly simplistic and result in "blaming the victim" (Ryan, 1971). This is always a risk when attempting to understand why a population is experiencing a particular condition or problem. The risk can be addressed, in part, by recognizing that factors ranging from human behavior and development to social relationships and structures contribute to robust explanations of populations and problems.

Task 3 involves seeking additional information about the target population from academic and professional resources. When examining existing literature about a population, sets of activities may include at least exploring issues of growth and development of the population, and assessing social relationships and structures.

Identify Concepts and Issues Related to Growth and Development

Questions to be explored for this activity include the following:

- What sources of the professional knowledge base are available on this population group?
- What theoretical frameworks are available that will help in understanding the target population?
- What factors or characteristics gleaned from the knowledge base on this population will be helpful in understanding the target population?

In studying certain types of problems where human behavior is a factor, at least part of the focus of the study should be on what is known about the various stages of growth and development of the population. For example, problems such as eating disorders, substance abuse, interpersonal violence, and suicide may be understood in a particular population by considering stages of development over the life course.

In other instances, understanding the behavior of individuals within the target population is not as important as assessing the impact of the arena (community or organization) on its members. Organizations and communities can present barriers to full participation. Problems such as overutilization of emergency room services for routine health care or violation of zoning ordinances by housing multiple families in single-family units are examples of situations where the focus should be on understanding how the community or organization functions in relation to the target population. Whether the problem or population suggests attention to human behavior and/or social structures, the knowledge base on diversity and difference discussed previously will contribute to a better understanding of the factors that contribute to the population's experience of a problem.

A useful starting point for understanding a population is a text on human growth and development. These texts are frequently divided into ages and stages of life. For example, Ashford and LeCroy (2013) organized their text on human behavior in the social environment around a multidimensional framework for assessing social functioning, including the biophysical, psychological, and social dimensions. The authors then explore phases of growth and development from pregnancy and birth through late adulthood. Hutchison (2012) explores the changing life course and the person and environment. Santrock (2010) has used the following chapter headings: Beginnings, Infancy, Early Childhood, Middle and Late Childhood, Adolescence, Early Adulthood, Middle Adulthood, Late Adulthood, and Death and Dying. These types of frameworks may be useful in organizing a study of the target population. For example, in attempting to understand a population of teenage methamphetamine users, a study might focus on adolescent growth and development, perhaps using selected biophysical, psychological, social, cultural, and gender characteristics that may, in some combination, contribute to the use and abuse of substances.

Theoretical perspectives may also assist in understanding a population's experience of a problem. One can draw from a range of traditional and alternative theories to do this. For example, focusing on the population of adolescents who drop out of high school, one might draw on the classical works of Skinner (1971), Erickson (1968), or Maslow (1943) to understand the behavior of the target population.

Other traditional theorists provide additional perspectives on how adolescents deal with issues of self-identity as they grow and develop (e.g., Kohlberg, 1984; Marcia, 1993; Piaget, 1972). One can also draw from identity theories offered for various population groups including, for example, the Cross (1971, 1991) Model of Black Identity Development and Cass's (1979, 1984) Model of Homosexual Identity Formation. These two models are described briefly below.

Cross (1971, 1991) suggests a four-stage model of black racial identity development. In the first stage, *Pre-encounter*, the individual views her or himself from a white frame of reference. In the second stage, *Encounter*, the individual confronts experiences that challenge a white frame of reference (i.e., acts of discrimination). In the third stage, *Immersion–Emersion*, the individual adopts a black identity and withdraws from interactions with other cultures, particularly the dominant white culture. In the final stage, *Internalization*, the individual develops self-confidence and security in her or his racial identity and embraces pluralism. Parham (1989) extended Cross' model by suggesting three ways of moving through the stages. First, a person can *stagnate* in any one of the stages. Second, a person can make *Stagewise Linear Progression* (SLP) through the four stages. Third, a person can *recycle* the stages and experience how it feels to struggle with racial identity and the action required to resolve that struggle.

Cass (1979, 1984) developed the Homosexual Identity Formation model based on her research of lesbian and gay individuals in Australia. In stage 1, *Identity Confusion*, the individual is aware of being different and that her or his behavior may be considered homosexual. In stage 2, *Identity Comparison*, the person realizes the she or he might be homosexual and feels alienated because of this possibility. In stage 3, *Identity Tolerance*, the individual accepts and tolerates the possibility of being homosexual and begins to seek community. In stage 4, *Identity Acceptance*, the person accepts her or himself as homosexual and increases efforts to create community. In stage 5, *Identity Pride*, the individual is proud of her or his identity and angry about heterosexism and heterosexist privilege. In stage 6, *Identity Synthesis*, the person is able to recognize heterosexual allies and integrate multiple aspects of her or his identity. Cass emphasized that individuals may progress through the stages at varying paces and that some individuals may stop at a particular stage and not progress further, a process Cass referred to as *Identity Foreclosure*.

The two examples above suggest additional lenses through which to view the problems a population is experiencing. If the adolescents who are dropping out of high school are predominantly African American, perhaps members of that group believe that the school culture, based on dominant-culture assumptions, is hostile to their own experience. Likewise, if those dropping out of high school are lesbian, gay, bisexual, or transgender (LGBT) youth, leaving may be related to the lack of acceptance and fear that she or he feels as someone with a developing awareness of her or his own identity.

A number of other identity and developmental theories provide frameworks that help the social work change agent understand a population and its problems. A growing number of researchers have investigated how stereotypes influence identity development in adolescents. For example, Way and colleagues (2013) interviewed 40 African American, Chinese American, Dominican American, and European American middle school students. Ethnic identities during adolescent were found to reflect the macro culture in which stereotypes about ethnicity, race, gender, and social class were infused into every aspect of students' lives. Thus, identities were constructed by comparing and contrasting sets of stereotypes and attempting to avoid becoming a stereotype. The researchers concluded that stereotypes pervaded identity development and that more attention needed to be directed toward processes of "avoidance" and "negative identity" in constructing identities, a point underscored by Erickson decades ago.

Assess the Impact of Social Relationships and Structures

Questions to be explored for this activity include the following:

- What structural and environmental forces are affecting this population group?
- What theoretical frameworks are available that will help in understanding the interactions between members of the population and the larger social environment?

Understanding processes of growth and development contribute to the social work change agent's understanding of a population, but alone they may be insufficient in understanding a population in relation to the problem(s) they are experiencing. Furthermore, use of these explanatory frameworks alone may inaccurately focus attention and blame for a problem on the people experiencing it instead of on the contributing social factors. In addition to these individually focused explanatory perspectives, theories from sociology and social psychology can also provide insight on how social relationships and structures impact a population and how members of that population act and understand themselves.

Focusing on family homelessness, one might use role theory, agency/structure theories, and conflict theory to better understand families experiencing a housing crisis. Role theory addresses the patterns of attitudes and behaviors typically associated with various positions in society (Turner, 1982, 1990). Roles may be related to gender or age (basic roles), or they may be related to a person's occupation or family positions (structural status roles). When a person fills a certain role, she or he is expected to conform to the behavior patterns associated with that role. For example, a woman is expected to act in accordance with the roles she holds as a daughter, mother, and wife.

Role conflict may be experienced when one or more of the roles that a person holds conflicts with another role. Role strain may occur when one struggles to meet the expectations of a particular role. Single mothers in homeless families may experience role conflict and strain as they attempt to be both an effective parent and provider. Emergency shelter regulations that do not allow dependent male children over a certain age force homeless mothers to contend with the stress of keeping their family together and providing housing for the rest of the family.

Sociological theories that bridge the concepts of agency (the ability of individuals to act and create their own lives) and structural determinism (the inability of individuals to act outside of constraining societal structures) can also be useful in understanding populations. Giddens (1979) proposed structuration theory to integrate agency and structure. He noted that the social practices performed by humans are recursive, that is, as they are repeated, social practices both create social structures and are conditioned by them. Bourdieu (1977) popularized the term *habitus* to refer to the recursive frameworks, often held unconsciously, that help humans function in everyday life. Conflict theory recognizes the inherent power differences among groups in society. Social problems in this perspective are viewed as the result of conflicts among various groups in society vying for control of important resources. Problems are not attributed to the individual, family, or social group, but to the exploitative practices of dominant groups that alienate nondominant groups.

These three theories are only examples of the many theoretical frameworks that may inform your understanding of a population. Along with the community and organizational theories noted in Chapters 5 and 7, respectively, sociological and psychosocial theories may help to explain populations and their problems or opportunities in terms of the interactions between members of the population and the larger social environment.

Task 4: Develop Strategies for Authentic Engagement

Client participation, consultation, community or *civic engagement*, and *stakeholder involvement*, among other terms, have been used to describe population engagement in macro change. **Meaningful participation** is defined as

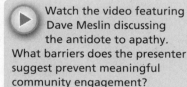

Watch the video featuring Dave Meslin discussing the antidote to apathy. What barriers does the presenter suggest prevent meaningful community engagement?

www.youtube.com
/watch?v=5Knz100ldLM

authentic engagement of participants and the use of their input in decision making throughout the entire process (Woodford & Preston, 2011). The entire process may be a defined episode of planning change or a long-term commitment to change that consists of multiple episodes of change. If a program results from the change process, the entire process includes participation in the design, implementation, and evaluation of that program as well.

In pursuing authentic engagement, practitioners are urged to see beyond binary views of insider and outsider, activist and community, practitioner and population, and a host of other dichotomous ways of conceptualizing participation (Sonn & Quayle, 2013). A culturally humble approach to engagement recognizes that there are a complex range of perspectives within and across groups that will come together in any group, community, or organizational change. The importance of including diverse population perspectives was reinforced by Weil, Gamble, and Williams (1998) when they pointed out that for community members to be empowered, community practice must be conducted "with" rather than "on" communities. Thus, the engagement of diverse population groups and their members will open the door for the emergence of new ways of thinking about the processes and outcomes of change.

Task 4 focuses on engagement with population members. Two sets of activities include creating opportunities for participation, and working with groups of population members, allies, and advocates.

Create Opportunities for Participation

Questions to be explored for this activity include the following:

- Who has been involved in identifying the need for change?
- What principles can be used to guide a meaningful engagement process?
- What methods can be used to engage diverse population groups?

The identification of a condition, problem, or change can come from any direction and at any time. A clinical social worker may see multiple clients who remain in abusive situations because they have no shelter or other resources in the community. A group of African American community members march in protest when an unarmed youth has been shot by police. A social media site features the problems faced by undocumented workers. A health-care social worker discovers that older clients are routinely being labeled as having Alzheimer's disease and written off as untreatable. In each of these situations, an individual or group of concerned persons may search for a place to start addressing needed change.

Getting Started   Gaining access to a population group, an organization, or a community is a critical step in getting started. Sometimes access means following an established protocol such as approval of a board to go about an internal organizational change. If the change requires access to a population group in the community, it may be that there are relationships already established. Oftentimes access is not guaranteed, particularly when social workers work across community, state, and even national borders (Strier, 2013).

For example, Narag and Maxwell (2014) report on lessons learned about doing field research in a slum area of the Philippines. They discussed differences between

Western and non-Western approaches to gaining entry into local communities and the importance of being careful in the use of tried methodological approaches in unfamiliar surroundings in order to avoid confusion, misinterpretation, and doing harm to participants. They concluded that standard approaches of being introduced to the community by a known leader (or key informant) and participating in community life (such as volunteering) to gain access to local people were inappropriate in certain contexts. In cultures where communication is not as direct, population members may convey information beyond stated words. In cultures with collectivistic identities, expressed opinions may reflect a collective stance rather than an individualistic perspective. Differing cultural assumptions about communication must be taken into consideration. Knowing the language that population members use in the community, being cognizant of specific code words, and being familiar with unique symbols are important. Dressing to blend into the community may ease potential barriers. In short, Narag and Maxwell (2014) underscored the importance of being creative and open to difference in approaching a population group, that is, practicing cultural humility.

Getting started in addressing an injustice requires gathering information, assessing what is learned, then reasessing as more information is gathered. For example, a community activist may have taken the lead in the past to ensure that health care for migrant workers is available. If this issue is revisited later in the process, it is important to understand the experiences and perspectives of the first initiator. Was he or she successful? Why or why not? Did he or she alienate any critical decision makers? How did he or she approach the issue, and what would he or she do differently? Has he or she brought certain biases or prejudices to his or her view of the situation? Who else was involved, and what were their roles and perspectives on the proposed change? Change agents are not obligated to utilize the same method or to affiliate with an earlier change effort, but they should at least be aware of the approach taken and the results achieved.

Whether or not the current condition or problem has been addressed before, it is important that the change agent develop an understanding of which local individuals and groups support or oppose the change effort that is being considered. For example, a small group of staff within an organization may want to promote an aggressive affirmative action approach to recruitment and hiring in order to better reflect the changing demographics of a community. It would be a mistake to assume that all staff, managers, and administrators will favor this change effort. Rather than plan only with those who agree, change agents should engage opponents in expressing their opinions. Working with the opposition can present some difficult ethical issues, but the skillful change agent will find ways to identify key local participants who favor and who oppose the change effort, and will make every attempt to keep the process open to all.

Another group of local participants to be identified is those individuals who have the power or authority to approve or reject the change that ultimately will be proposed. Within an organization, this will most likely be the chief executive officer (CEO) or the board of directors, but others throughout the organization may have an important say as well. In a community, the identity of decision makers will depend on the domain identified for change. If the focus is on a school or school district, decision makers will include principals, school board members, parent groups, and others within the system. In a local neighborhood, key people will include city council members or city staff and their constituents. Some exploration will be needed to determine who has this type of authority. It is also helpful to have a complete briefing on local politics by someone who knows the organization or community so that key influential people are not left out, and so that alternative and opposing perspectives are understood. More will be said about this in Chapter 9.

There are many ways in which to engage others in change opportunities. Typical activities designed to gain participant input are surveys, community meetings, focus groups (Letendre & Williams, 2014), and key informant interviews. Increasingly, social media is being used to engage large numbers of people in **cyberactivism** through the use of listservs, websites, message boards, petitions, blogs, text messaging, polling, mapping, and a host of other digital media such as Twitter, Facebook, and YouTube. In organizations, advisory councils, governing boards, task forces, committees, and other vehicles may be in place to serve as a nucleus for addressing the problem. Community coalitions and alliances may be formed if they do not already exist. Intergroup dialogue among diverse population members may provide opportunities for analyzing power and privilege, key elements in raising issues around exploitation and empowerment (Gutierrez, Lewis, Dessel, & Spencer, 2013). Typically, whatever form engagement takes, social workers will need to understand how to facilitate and lead task-oriented groups.

Task-Oriented Groups   Having informally talked with other persons about an injustice that needs to be addressed, the change agent will engage with others in task-oriented group work. An existing group may already be working on the change, and the social worker decides to join with this group. A small informal group of population members may serve as a nucleus for deciding what to do before a larger coalition of stakeholders is formed. A virtual group that shares information online may be already chatting and blogging about the issues. In an organizational change process, engaging a committee or task force may be enough to get a change made, whereas in a communitywide effort a larger alliance with a diverse group of residents may form. No matter what the macro change is, it is essential that the social worker has skills in creating, developing, and leading task-oriented groups (Maidment & Brook, 2014).

Staples (2012) compares a social justice organization without task-oriented groups to a human body without vital organs. Small groups are the vehicles for engaging people in learning new skills, taking action, and experiencing collective power. **Community organizing** engages multiple indigenous community residents using their strength in numbers to participate in empowering themselves to pursue social change. On the largest scale, **social movements** are composed of small and large groups of people coming together for a common cause. **Social action** groups pursue community change and political activism (Dudziak & Profitt, 2012). **Community development** connects people to existing structures to engage in activities such as community building, economic development, neighborhood improvement, and developing affordable housing (Staples, 2012).

In the past, group work was often separated into treatment/therapeutic or task-oriented groups. Dudziak and Profitt (2012) offered a cautionary note about this dichotomous way of thinking. If one sees a task group as solely focused on action, there may be a tendency to neglect the importance of group process in favor of accomplishing change. It is important to recognize that group members will learn from one another and will grow personally and interpersonally just as much as they will take action. Having the opportunity to struggle together, learn from one another, and develop in a collective effort may be particularly healing for marginalized population group members who may be experiencing the potential to become empowered for the first time. Attention to relationship building and interpersonal dynamics is part of a successful group process (Staples, 2012).

Gutierrez, Lewis, Dessel, and Spencer (2013) provide a set of guiding principles for practitioners who are engaging in multicultural group work. They emphasize that practitioners need to be (1) flexible, (2) self-reflective, (3) skilled with theory and practice, (4) skilled in small- and large-group work, (5) inclusive, (6) aware of when the concepts and methods they use were developed, (7) knowledgeable about the use of evidence-based practice from multiple sources, (8) aware of the language used in assessment and intervention tools, (9) consistent in their use and definitions of constructs used to build the knowledge base, and (10) advocates for the use of community-based workers (p. 448).

Woodford and Preston (2011) offer a set of principles designed to engage group members in meaningful participation. Their principles were designed for inclusion of service users in human service agencies but have applicability to task groups in general. They are summarized below:

- **Only Practice Authentic Participation:** Too often population members are told their input is needed, but staff commitment is limited or inclusion is simply based on a funding source requiring consumer participation. Woodford and Preston (2011) advise the practitioner to be certain there are time and emotional commitments before seeking advice from diverse population groups.
- **Include All Stakeholders:** As mentioned earlier, within any population group there are diverse perspectives. Also, there are diverse stakeholders such as staff members, referral sources, advocates, and others who have different views of population needs and issues. Including diverse perspectives will offer alternative approaches to expressed concerns.
- **Include Participation in All Phases of the Change Process:** Critically important is communicating with stakeholders about when and how much they will be included; otherwise, misunderstandings can occur. If it is feasible, inclusion in everything from initial input on a policy or program all the way through the process of implementation is recommended.
- **Communication Needs to Be Ongoing:** Communicating the purpose of participation, the level of involvement expected, how input will be incorporated, when updates will be provided, and a host of other logistics is important so that participants feel that they are truly part of the process.
- **Allot Sufficient Time:** Meaningful participation takes time, and it is suggested that no matter how much time is allotted, there will always be delays. Methods to obtain rapid feedback when unexpected issues arise should be in place so that stakeholders do not feel disregarded.
- **Ensure Capacity:** Change agents work for various groups and organizations, and those bodies must have adequate capacity to engage stakeholders in the process of inclusion. It is incumbent upon the social worker not to set something in motion that cannot be supported by her employer or any other group within whose auspices the process is occurring or whose affirmation is needed for legitimacy.

There are numerous theories about group development with various phases, steps, or stages identified. Tuckman's model of the stages of group development has been used to study small-group and team behavior. His stages are listed below:

- **Forming:** The beginning stage of group development in which members decide to stay or leave, negotiate expectations, and operate on a fairly superficial level.
- **Storming:** Conflicts between group members emerge in this stage, as members begin to feel more comfortable in expressing how they really feel and struggle over what actions need to be taken and how to go about the change process.
- **Norming:** Some agreement (even if it an agreement to disagree) occurs as values, norms, and expectations emerge.
- **Performing (Cohesive Team Building):** Members work on tasks and actions that have come out of the group process, often gaining a sense of collective identity as they achieve (or not) what they are committed to doing.
- **Adjourning:** Task forces, ad hoc committees, and groups formed around specific or time-limited change opportunities have an ending stage. Some groups such as alliances and coalitions may be formed with the intention of moving from one change to another. Whenever the group ends, in the adjourning stage group members may share the meaning of their experiences, engage in final problem solving activities, and look to the future.

These stages are not linear, and they may ebb and flow in an iterative process. The major thing is that facilitators recognize that group dynamics will change over time and that attending to group process is important in achieving a collective identity (Seck & Helton, 2014).

In summary, engagement is a process. Planning, recruitment, and group formation are all part of engaging with population members. Table 3.5 provides a brief overview of potential considerations as you move though that process.

Engagement

Practice Behavior: Use empathy, reflection, and interpersonal skills to effectively engage diverse clients and constituencies.

Critical Thinking Question: How can social workers use empathy, reflection, and interpersonal skills in their macro activities?

Work with Groups of Population Members, Allies, and Advocates

Questions to be explored for this activity include the following:

- Who are the allies and advocates of this population group?
- What can be learned from allies and advocates about the history of experiences with the target population and the pressing problems and opportunities?
- How can relationships be built and maintained?

In addition to involving and listening to members of the population, allies and advocates for the population may also assist the social work change agent in understanding the target population. An **ally** is a person of privilege who actively works to eliminate stigma and discrimination that occur based on that stigma (Rosenblum & Travis, 2008, p. 473). Broido (2000) suggests that allies work to end oppression based on dominant members having greater privilege and power (p. 3). Allies work alongside individuals who are marginalized because of their race, ethnicity, gender, sexual orientation, disability,

Table 3.5   Engagement: Planning, Recruitment, and Group Formation

Phases of Engagement	Potential Approaches
Planning	• Collaboratively involve members of the organization or community in thinking about how to begin. • Minimize the distinction between professionals as expert and service users; the relationship is reciprocal. • View this process as consciousness raising, in which everyone will grow and learn. • Be open to surprises, allowing next steps to emerge in unexpected ways.
Recruitment	• Recognize the power dynamics surrounding group composition. • Obtain organizational or community support, if needed for legitimacy. • Recruit persons who have experienced the problem. • Reach out to existing groups with interests in making a change. • Identify strengths and resources that members bring to the group, and what skills and/or resources need to be sought from outside.
Group Formation	• Meet in a safe, accessible location. • Set a comfortable, inclusive tone for group interaction. • Prepare members for the group: Dialogue about expectations and goals, how decisions will be made, and how leadership is exercised. • Factor in relationship-building opportunities among group members. • Lift up all voices so that they can be heard. • Establish ground rules for how to proceed.

age, or other dimension of difference. **Advocates** are persons who argue for a cause or on another's behalf. A number of ally and advocacy organizations have been formed to confront oppression and support members of oppressed groups by advocating for change. For example, the organization PFLAG (Parents, Families and Friends of Lesbians and Gays) is an organization that engages and develops allies to advocate for equal civil rights and the health and well-being of sexual minorities. The National Council of La Raza is a national civil rights and advocacy organization that seeks to improve opportunities for Hispanic Americans. Local organizations that create opportunities for members of a target population and their allies to work together will be valuable sources of information about a population.

If a social worker is attempting to understand a hidden population, or a population that remains out of public view for fear of physical or psychological harm, an ally may help arrange access to members of the population for research and participation. For example, millions of women refugees throughout the world flee their homelands, searching for freedom and safety from persecution, war, and torture. They are entitled to protection under the 1951 Geneva Convention, yet the United States and Canada frequently deny them protection and deport them to countries where they are in fear of their lives. It is taking the collaborative effort of social workers, lawyers, immigration advocates, and others to lobby for change on behalf of women refugees of color who seek protection from rape, torture, and violence (Haynes, 2014).

If a social worker is attempting to understand a population that is underage or experiencing the acute symptoms of a serious mental illness, an advocate can provide a voice for those who cannot, at that time, speak for themselves. Social workers are familiar with the advocate role and are often involved in advocating for groups that cannot advocate for themselves (National Association of Social Workers, 2000, 2001). The role of ally is discussed less but is a role premised on the assumptions of cultural humility—particularly shared power and nonpaternalistic partnerships (Tervalon & Murray-Garcia, 1998).

Nygreen, Kwon, and Sanchez (2006) discuss the role of adult allies in the youth-led organizing efforts of urban youth. Noting that "urban youth" is a euphemism for marginalized, poor, minority youth, adult allies support youth efforts to engage their peers, change their communities, and, in the process, challenge common stereotypes. Casey and Smith (2010) describe men who become allies in efforts to end violence against women and how they became involved in these efforts. The men indicated that becoming involved as an ally in the fight to end violence against women was a process and that their involvement was influenced by an emotional connection to the issue, by opportunities to make sense of that exposure, and by invitations to join efforts to end violence against women.

Identifying and interviewing allies and advocates can supplement the information gained from the members of the target population. These key stakeholders should aid in understanding the history of experiences with the target population and the pressing problems and opportunities. If there have been relevant past experiences with this population, the change agent can compile a list of key actors and a chronology of interactions between the target population and the community or organizational representatives leading up to the present. These notes will help shape strategy and tactics later in the episode of change.

Engaging individuals and groups in a change effort is an ongoing process. Building relationships takes time, but maintaining those relationships requires ongoing communication. Walker and East (2014) detail the benefits of including engaged residents and professionals in a planning process for low-income neighborhood redevelopment. Successful engagement of residents was based on outreach, inclusiveness, slowing down the process so that genuine dialogue could occur, and increasing resident knowledge as well as opportunities for input. Ongoing dialogue revealed past and present conflicts with the city that had disenfranchised residents. Relationships were forged between residents and city officials through ongoing dialogue, which was even contentious at times. These relationships made it possible for residents to access other resources and allies beyond the group.

However, staff turnover made it difficult to maintain connections as some professional staff and public officials left the group and new persons were assigned. The importance of ongoing communication and reengagement was emphasized in this redevelopment process. Engagement is not simply an initial process; it requires vigilance and attention to maintaining relationships over time.

> **?** Assess your understanding of a framework for engaging with population groups by taking this brief quiz.

SUMMARY

In this chapter, we framed engagement with diverse and different population groups within an overview of advancing human rights and social and economic justice. A framework for engaging with diverse populations was presented. The first task was to start where the population is and involves self-reflective practice. Although cultural competence is extensively cited as a goal, criticism of this concept is that it assumes one can become competent in understanding another culture. Cultural humility makes a somewhat different assumption: It involves a continual commitment to co-learning and self-reflection, and recognizes the power imbalances in interactions between helping professionals and consumers. Throughout this chapter, we emphasized the importance of listening to population group members and recognizing that there will be different perspectives.

Task 2 focused on the impact of difference, discrimination, and oppression. Highlighted were definitions of systems of oppression, including ableism, ageism, classism, ethnocentrism, heterosexism and trans oppression, racism, and sexism. Intersectionality was introduced, along with themes of critical race theory and recognition of the reification of whiteness.

Task 3 focused on using the professional knowledge base to gather information on the population, noting that it is important to fully draw from insider perspectives as well as the theories and studies that inform understandings of the population group with which one is working. What is known about growth and development as well as social relationships and structures was explored as a beginning step in fully accessing the professional knowledge base.

Task 4 elaborated on methods that can be used to engage small and large groups in change episodes. Understanding group development and stages of growth was emphasized, given the fact that macro practice involves an array of task-oriented groups in the change process.

Engaging the population group is a parallel process to problem identification, the subject of Chapter 4. Together, Chapters 3 and 4 provide change agents with sets of interrelated activities that will be helpful in formulating a problem definition. In conjunction with persons who have experienced the problem, and with their full and ongoing participation, the tasks and activities in these two chapters will assist the change agent and others in beginning to move toward an episode of change.

Appendix: Framework for Understanding the Target Population

Task 1: Start Where the Population Is

Develop Cultural Humility

- What experiences has the social worker had with members of this population group?
- What self-identities and attitudes does the social worker bring to this situation?
- What are the power imbalances faced by this population group?

Listen to Different Perspectives from Population Members

- Identify key informants from the population of interest.
- Include diverse voices and perspectives in articulating the issues faced by this population.

Task 2: Assess the Impact of Difference, Discrimination, and Oppression

Explore the Discriminatory and Oppressive Issues Faced by This Population

- What stereotypes or generalizations confront this population group?
- How has this population group been discriminated against or oppressed?
- Do members of the population group feel marginalized, and, if so, why?

Assess Implications of Intersectionality

- What are the dimensions of intersectionality within this population?

- What issues of power, privilege, discrimination, and oppression are identified by members of this population?
- What frameworks are useful in understanding population dynamics?

Task 3: Search the Professional Knowledge Base on the Target Population

Identity Concepts and Issues Related to Growth and Development

- What sources of the professional knowledge base are available on this population group?
- What theoretical frameworks are available that will help in understanding the target population?
- What factors or characteristics gleaned from the knowledge base on this population will be helpful in understanding the target population?

Assess Social Relationships and Structures

- What structural and environmental forces are affecting this population group?
- What theoretical frameworks are available that will help in understanding the interactions between members of the population and the larger social environment?

Task 4: Develop Strategies for Authentic Engagement

Create Opportunities for Participation

- Who has been involved in identifying the need for change?
- What principles can be used to guide a meaningful engagement process?
- What methods can be used to engage diverse population groups?

Work with Groups of Population Members, Allies, and Advocates

- Who are the allies and advocates of this population group?
- What can be learned from allies and advocates about the history of experiences with the target population and the pressing problems and opportunities?
- How can relationships be built and maintained?

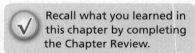

Recall what you learned in this chapter by completing the Chapter Review.

Assess Your Competence

Use the scale below to rate your current level of achievement on the following concepts or skills associated with each learning outcome listed at the beginning of this chapter:

1	2	3
I can accurately describe the concept or skill(s) associated with this outcome.	I can consistently identify the concept or skill(s) associated with this outcome when observing and analyzing practice activities.	I can competently implement the concept or skill(s) associated with this outcome in my own practice.

_____ Discuss issues of discrimination and oppression faced by different population groups.

_____ Use a framework for engaging population groups in a change episode.

4

Assessing Community and Organizational Problems

OLLY / SHUTTERSTOCK

THE SOCIAL WORKER'S ENTRY INTO AN EPISODE OF MACRO-LEVEL CHANGE

Chapter 3 focused on engaging diverse population groups. In that process, a number of problems faced by different groups were introduced. This chapter focuses on assessing problems, one of the three domains through which social workers become involved in community and organizational change. Just as major tasks and sets of activities were identified in Chapter 3, in this chapter, a framework will be provided to guide the change agent in assessing problems faced by diverse population groups. These assessments mark the social worker's entry into an episode of macro-level change.

Over the years, the image of the change agent has developed around some of the early social change pioneers—people such as Jane Addams, a founder of the famous Hull House in Chicago and the second woman to be awarded the Nobel Peace Prize; Ida B. Wells, an African American journalist, newspaper editor, and newspaper owner who was active in the Civil Rights and the Women's Rights movements; Dorothea Dix, a nurse who, in the nineteenth century, became a reformer of prisons and mental health facilities; and Susan B. Anthony, a teacher who, in the late nineteenth and early twentieth centuries, was a champion of suffrage, abolition of slavery, and equal rights for women. Others view change agents as super-organizers—people such as Dr. Martin Luther King Jr., who led the fight for civil rights during the 1960s, or Cesar Chavez, who, along with Dolores Huerta, founded the United Farm Workers to protect the rights of migrant workers. Other, more recent organizers include Cathy Lightner, who, in 1980, founded Mothers Against Drunk Drivers; Ralph Nader, who founded public interest groups on automotive safety, energy, the environment, global trade,

> Go to the National Association of Social Workers homepage and do a search on "NASW Pioneers." Choose the name of a pioneer you don't recognize. What kind of change did the pioneer help bring about? How was the change related to organizations and communities?

health research, congressional oversight, and legal protection of civil rights; Desmond Tutu, the South African social activist who fought apartheid and dedicated his life to peace; and Barack Obama, the first African American president of the United States. These leaders have served as role models and have had great success in bringing about social change throughout nations and the world.

Most social workers have neither the resources, media exposure, experience, followers, nor power that these leaders have had available to them. Yet, in spite of seemingly overwhelming challenges, social workers have been effective in bringing about positive changes in organizations and communities. Effectiveness does not necessarily come from the power of personality or the ability to mobilize thousands to a cause. It can emerge from careful, thoughtful, and creative planning undertaken by a group committed to change, along with the tenacity to see it through to completion. The change effort may be guided, led, or coordinated by a professional social worker, but those involved may represent a broad range of interests. Planned change is often incremental and cumulative. One particular episode of change may appear small and insignificant in view of the scope of the problem, but it should be recognized that others committed to positive change may be working on the same problem or need from different perspectives. In the practice of social work, one finds many avenues or points of entry that lead to the use of macro-practice skills.

Recovery from manmade or natural disasters is a good example. When faced with the enormity of the task, members of any one group could easily feel that their contributions to recovery are insignificant. But taken together, the cleanup crews, the religious groups that house displaced families and help them rebuild their lives, the nonprofits and nongovernmental organizations (NGOs) that mobilize many thousands of volunteers who supply needed services and support, the social workers who provide counseling and resources, and literally thousands of others contribute to the renewal of communities and cities that would have been impossible or much delayed if the tasks had not been shared. Although the one-to-one response with victim families is critically important, so too are the planning and organizing of the macro-practice role that enables large-scale recovery from crises and allows people to get on with their lives.

Conditions, Problems, Issues, Needs, and Opportunities

In assessing problems, there are a number of terms that are often used interchangeably, but they have subtle and important differences for the change agent. A **condition** is a phenomenon that is present in a community or organization and that may be troublesome to a number of people but has not been formally identified, labeled, or publicly acknowledged as a **problem**. It is important that social workers understand whether a phenomenon is a condition that has not been formally recognized, or a problem that has been acknowledged by the organization or community. This status will affect where the social worker places her or his emphasis in early planning efforts. Ultimately, decision makers will have to acknowledge the existence of a problem (either willingly or reluctantly) if formal resources are to be dedicated to alleviating or eliminating the problem.

Every organization and community is full of conditions as well as problems. Social consequences of urban living—such as traffic congestion, exposure to air pollution, dangerous neighborhoods, affordable housing, and other issues—can all be considered social or community conditions if no efforts have been mobilized to address them or if residents have taken them for granted as part of urban living. Similarly, in rural communities, isolation, inaccessible health care, and a declining economic base can all be considered social conditions if they remain unrecognized by any formal or informal efforts toward resolution.

The same concept applies to organizations, where troublesome phenomena are present but have not necessarily been formally identified or labeled as a problem. For example, a social worker in a long-term care facility for older adults may be concerned about what she considers to be overmedication of some of the residents, yet this has never been labeled problematic by residents and families. Similarly, program managers in a family service agency may recognize a trend to extend services to those who can pay while offering only a waiting list to those who cannot. Yet, no one has complained about this discriminatory practice.

To be defined as a problem, a condition must in some way be formally recognized and incorporated into the action agenda of a group, organization, or community. This may mean, for example, that an elected official proposes a study of elder suicide, or that a group of parents concerned about methamphetamine abuse lobbies for a city ordinance to regulate the sale of cold medicines containing pseudoephedrine (an ingredient used to make meth) within the city limits. It may mean that a task force within an organization is officially sanctioned to explore the effects of medication on residents in long-term care. Or it may mean that a neighborhood group experiencing high-speed traffic on their residential streets takes steps to bring about broader recognition of the presence of the condition and its problematic nature. Regardless of the form it takes, formal recognition is important for legitimization.

The distinction between a condition and a problem is significant to a social worker planning a macro-level intervention. If a condition has not been formally recognized in some way, the first task must be to obtain that formal recognition. For example, for many years homelessness was dealt with as a personal employment problem, family violence as a personal matter, and AIDS as a personal health problem.

Watch the video on ACT UP's advocacy for women's inclusion in the CDC's definition of AIDS. Why was it important to change the early definition of AIDS? www.youtube.com /watch?v=VpSXRLE1eDk

Most communities simply viewed these as existing conditions, not as social or community problems. When these conditions began to affect greater segments of society and reached the point at which they could no longer be ignored, national, state, and local community leaders began to identify them as problems and to dedicate resources toward their resolution. Once formally recognized and acknowledged as problems (usually as a result of persistent media attention), these conditions become candidates for organized intervention efforts. The creation of task forces for homeless people in cities across the country, child abuse and neglect reporting laws, and federal funding for AIDS research and services are results of recognizing conditions and defining them as problems.

In addition, we often use the terms *issue, need*, and *opportunity* when we are discussing problems and conditions. One cannot have an **issue** without disagreement. Even when people agree that there is a problem and that some action needs to be taken, at issue may be how to go about taking that action. There may be many issues that emerge in any planned change process as different perspectives and opinions are shared. The important thing is to get those issues on the table, even if there is an agreement to disagree.

Unmet needs are often described as problems. Needs assessments are conducted in local communities in order to identify what needs are not being met. A **need** is something that is necessary for living a quality life. Different types of needs will be discussed in Chapter 5, but important to problem identification is the recognition that many change efforts are attempting to address unmet needs in an organization or community. For example, living wage campaigns are advocating for women who need financial resources to support their families.

Problems and needs emerge in many forms. Some are personal or family problems that can be resolved within an individual or family context; others can be solved only by changing something within a larger system, such as a neighborhood, an organization, or a community. When people with problems or needs request help or are willing to accept it, social work intervention is appropriate.

An **opportunity** occurs when the change agent sees a condition that could turn into a problem and decides to act in a proactive manner. We often hear the expression *window of opportunity*, and this is a good description. A window may open for a time due to funding, advocacy, or other reasons, but the window also may close at some point. For the majority of the time, social workers are reacting to conditions that have already been labeled as problems by diverse population groups, but may not yet be seen as more than a condition by persons in power. This becomes an opportunity for the social worker to be proactive and seize the moment by bringing information to the attention of decision makers. There are many examples of how local citizens have seized an opportunity when a crisis has happened in their lives to inform future action. For example, a child abduction alert system started in 1996 in the United States has since been adopted in a number of other countries. The Amber Alert was initiated by the mother of 9-year-old Amber Rene Hagerman after Amber was murdered. Now this system is used to intercept aductors before children can be harmed.

Narrowing Down to the Most Useful Data and Information

In preparing to engage in a change process, some team members will be gathering information from interviews with people in the organization or community that is the focus of the change effort. Others may be exploring the professional knowledge base, attempting to locate data and information about the problem(s) that population members are facing. The intent is to understand as much as possible about the phenomenon itself—exploring what is known from a scholarly perspective, while at the same time using information from those affected to help rule in or rule out various causal factors and other considerations.

Information on the overlapping areas of population and problem will often be found during the study. While attempting to understand teenagers, for example, you may come across studies on teenage violence. In most cases (but not all), these studies or summaries of existing knowledge about the problem and population will be more informative than studies of the problem alone or population alone. Information and knowledge of the greatest value to local decision makers will ultimately be found where the three circles in Figure 3.1 in Chapter 3 intersect. In other words, knowledge of how the problem, population, and arena overlap will aid in understanding how these domains interact with each other to create the current situation and explain how it is unique to this local community or organization.

The issues facing social workers in their daily practice are not limited to individual client problems. If social workers are to be effective in serving their clients, many problems must be recognized and addressed at the agency, community, and policy levels. Some of these problems require changing the nature of services, programs, or policies. Most require an understanding of funding issues and the complications caused by economic challenges.

> **?** Assess your understanding of the social worker's entry into an episode of macro-level change by taking this brief quiz.

FRAMING AND REFRAMING PROBLEMS

People bring different **frames of mind** to thinking about conditions and problems, some better formed than others. A basic premise behind **framing theory** is that any problem can be viewed from a variety of perspectives and can encompass multiple values. Frames help to organize data and information in meaningful ways so that they can be used to guide action (Borah, 2011; Dewulf & Bouwen, 2012). **Collective frames** are negotiated shared sets of beliefs and meanings that guide and legitimate the course of action. The process of framing occurs when people who have particular conceptualizations of a problem begin to change their thinking about an issue (Chong & Druckman, 2007). Social workers bring their own frames of mind to any potential change opportunity, and as new information emerges, it is important to be open to reframing one's original conceptualizations of the problem as well as potential courses of action that might be taken. Openness to reframing requires a willingness to engage in different ways of thinking as new information informs and updates what one knows about a problem.

> Go to the Frameworks Institute homepage, and do a search on "Sexual Violence." Review the resources based on the research done by the institute. What core set of assumptions do people use to frame sexual violence? How do the frames or dominant cultural models differ from those of researchers?

Core framing tasks are diagnostic (problem identification and analysis), prognostic (determining possible ways to approach the problem), and motivational (figuring out how to gather support for the change). Table 4.1 summarizes these tasks. In the example provided, note that diagnostic framing reveals a target population (caregivers) and a problem (they are in danger of sacrificing their own health). The prognostic frame focuses on solutions, or what might be done as an intervention. Last, motivational framing uses words like *no cure, devastating,* and *urgent* to press for immediate action.

Jumping to prognosis before having diagnosed the problem is extremely common. Community political and civic leaders, activists, and others are often so anxious to make change happen that they begin at the point of proposing solutions. Increased incidence of driving under the influence (DUI)? Hire more police and increase penalties! More homeless families on the streets? Build a shelter! Increased numbers of teen pregnancies? Offer classes on the importance of sexual abstinence until marriage! These simplistic solutions will inevitably emerge in any episode of change. It is the responsibility of the social worker in a professionally guided change effort to make certain that a range of alternative perspectives and possible causes is adequately explored before proposing a solution. This means framing the problem, but being open to reframing as the process proceeds.

There are several reasons for exploring multiple perspectives on the problem. First, leaping to quick solutions without adequate study is the antithesis of professional practice. In one-on-one counseling, for example, telling clients exactly how to solve their problems after only a brief introduction to the facts violates many ethical and professional principles. Second, quick and easy solutions are usually based on the assumption that the problem in question has one primary cause. In fact, as we will discuss in greater detail later in this chapter, virtually no social problem has only one cause. Many different factors come into play in the development of a social condition, and changing

Table 4.1   Core Framing Tasks

Core Task	Description	Example
Diagnostic Framing	A process of problem identification and analysis: How is the problem defined, and what are its causes?	The number of persons with Alzheimer's disease is rapidly increasing, and caregivers are sacrificing their own health to care for loved ones.
Prognostic Framing	Determining proposed solutions to a task and the strategies that will be used to carry out the plan: What approaches can be taken?	Support groups, information, and respite opportunities are being offered to caregivers. In addition, research into the treatment and cure is needed.
Motivational Framing	A "call to arms" or rationale for proceeding in the change effort so that the group will want to move forward in pursuing the change: How can people be motivated to address the problem?	There is as yet no cure for this devastating disease, and it is urgent that every effort be made to inform the public, advocate for Alzheimer's research, and prevent caregivers from ignoring their own health.

Based on Benford and Snow (2000).

that condition almost always necessitates addressing more than one of these factors.

Take, for example, a community in which highway deaths due to alcohol have increased 18 percent in the past 2 years. How might the causes in this case be defined? One group will be convinced that the cause is lack of strict enforcement of existing laws prohibiting driving under the influence of drugs or alcohol, and may want to increase the budget of the police department to crack down on those who are driving while impaired. Another group will describe causes as easy availability of alcohol to teenagers, and may want to see increased penalties to those who sell alcohol to minors. Others will see alcohol abuse as a symptom of increasing stress or family breakdown, and may propose a campaign to promote activities that strengthen families. These represent just a few of the perspectives that might be introduced in an attempt to understand reasons behind driving under the influence of alcohol or drugs.

When a review of the knowledge base and interviews have been completed, a profile should begin to emerge. This profile will assist in better understanding target population members' perceptions and responses to the presenting problem or need. Factors relating to this population's needs or behaviors that must be dealt with in order to bring about needed changes should begin to become evident.

For example, Ashford and LeCroy (2013) identified the following factors as being associated with preadolescents at risk of delinquency: (1) low expectations for education, (2) limited participation in school activities, (3) poor school achievement, (4) low verbal ability, (5) truancy, (6) stealing and lying, (7) high peer influence, (8) nonconformity, (9) hyperactivity and aggressive behavior, (10) limited parental bonding, (11) family history of violence, and (12) living in high-crime, transcient communities. If the population being studied includes this group, some of these factors might be used in compiling a profile that could be used in predicting certain outcomes.

Which, if any, of these factors associated with the particular population under study will be useful in understanding the population can only be determined within the context of an episode of change. Much will depend on the nature of the problem identified and the purpose of the intervention. When a list of relevant factors has been identified, the process is at a point where speculation can begin about the **etiology** of the problem, and the change agent will engage with others in framing and reframing the problem.

We now focus on the parallel process of problem identification and analysis that, combined with what is known about the population group, will lead to an episode of change. For all three assessments (of the population, the problem, and the arena), the core planning team will need to coordinate activities. These will include identifying various roles and responsibilities, assigning individuals according to their abilities, monitoring progress, and dealing with interpersonal, intergroup, and political dynamics.

We are not proposing an exhaustive exploration that goes on for years. There is rarely time or resources for such study, and responding expeditiously is often critical to success. However, plunging into a proposed solution without doing the necessary

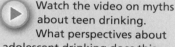

Watch the video on myths about teen drinking. What perspectives about adolescent drinking does this Mothers Against Drunk Driving public service announcement challenge?

www.youtube.com /watch?v=eXUt-QETR_s

Assessment

Practice Behavior: Collect and organize data, and apply critical thinking to interpret information from clients and constituencies.

Critical Thinking Question: Why is it important to gather information about a problem and a population from a variety of sources?

? Assess your understanding of framing and reframing problems by taking this brief quiz.

homework is equally risky. Our intent in the following framework is to lay out a format for systematic assessment of what can be accomplished within a reasonable amount of time (a few weeks to a few months, depending on the people and the skills involved), beginning with a small core team of perhaps four or five people committed to bringing about needed change, and gradually expanding to others willing to carry out specific tasks.

A FRAMEWORK FOR ASSESSING COMMUNITY AND ORGANIZATIONAL PROBLEMS

We have attempted to break down the understanding of what needs to be changed (to the extent that this is possible) into three interrelated tasks depicted in Figure 4.1.

We propose that change agents proceed with a set of tasks designed to gather as much useful information about the problem as is available. These tasks involve direct contact with those who have experienced the problem or need firsthand, as well as a systematic exploration of the professional knowledge base, data summaries, and perhaps a chronology of events leading to the current situation. This approach is designed to produce as thorough an understanding of the problem and population as possible in as short a time as possible, although there are limits to how short this time can be. A hurried and incomplete analysis can be worse than none at all.

These tasks can and should proceed simultaneously, which is where the coordinating work of the change agent becomes important. Those participating in the change effort who have the best credentials for entering the community or organization for the purpose of interviewing and data collection should be assigned to such tasks. Those who have demonstrated skill in searching and synthesizing theoretical and research resources should carry out this task. Those who work well with numerical data should plan to compile the necessary tables and charts. In the end, each of these separate tasks will contribute to a clearer understanding of the problem, need, or opportunity and will provide the basis for a well-designed plan of intervention leading to a positive solution.

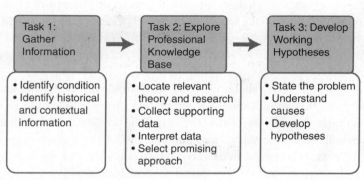

Figure 4.1
Tasks in the Framework for Assessing Community and Organizational Problems

Task 1: Gather Information from Persons within the Community or Organization

A number of authors emphasize the importance of sensitivity in approaching the assessment of communities or organizations (see, e.g., Weil, Reisch, & Ohmer, 2013). The organizer or change agent cannot simply enter a community or organizational culture without careful preparation and attention to the groups represented and to the professional knowledge base necessary to the intervention. For example, knowledge of human behavior and the social environment will assist the change agent in recognizing the importance of personal and collective identities and diversity. Contextual knowledge will provide guidance for the change agent in recognizing the interrelationships between organizational units and the larger organization or between diverse groups within the community.

Task 1 includes two sets of interconnected activities—identifying the condition and identifying relevant historical and contextual information.

Identify the Community or Organizational Condition

Recall the difference between a condition and a problem. A condition is simply "what is" without putting a value label on it. Although the change agent and others may have labeled the condition a problem, it is helpful to step back and see if you can assess the situation without coming to premature explanations of why this may be a problem.

Questions to be explored for this activity include the following:

- What are the conditions in this community or organization that need to be assessed?
- In approaching an episode of change, how could the condition statement be framed?

One of the first tasks in problem identification, then, is to develop a *condition statement*. A condition statement includes (1) a target population, (2) a geographical boundary, and (3) the difficulty facing the population. Statements should be descriptive, as objective as possible, and based on findings to date.

Statements will be adapted depending on whether the condition exists within a community or in an organization. For example, a condition statement might be "Domestic violence in Preston County is increasing." Generally speaking, the more precise the statement is, the greater likelihood of a successful intervention. This statement, for example, could vary from extremely general to very specific, as depicted in Figure 4.2.

A similar process within an organization would begin with a general statement. For example, an organizational condition might be that in a domestic violence shelter, resources are not being used efficiently and many residents are returning to their abusers. Quantitative data such as demographics, incidence, prevalence, or trends, and qualitative data focused, perhaps, on reasons for returning to abusers, would then need to be compiled to help pinpoint the condition as precisely as possible.

We now use Roby, Rotabi, and Bunkers' (2013) work on intercountry adoptions (ICAs) to provide an example of how conditions can be framed and reframed. Intercountry adoptions were originally framed as charitable opportunities to rescue children

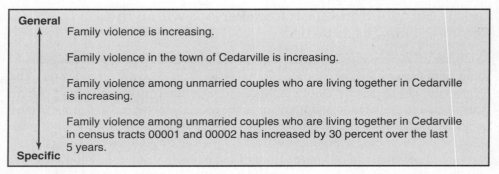

Figure 4.2
Sample Condition Statements

from harmful, even life-threatening environments. The United States received more children adopted internationally than any other country in the world, totaling over 1 million children since World War II. Social workers in several hundred U.S.-based agencies oversee adoption coordinators who negotiate these adoptions. Given this information, the condition could be stated as follows: Over 1 million children have been adopted from outside the United States since World War II. Framed as an opportunity to perform a charitable service of finding children safe and caring homes, one could see this as a very positive condition.

However, Roby, Rotabi, and Bunkers (2013) provide more information, reframing this condition into one fraught with "fraud, coercion, and corruption." Obviously, they have labeled this condition as a problem. They build their case by identifying these facts:

- ICA typically occurs between developed and developing countries.
- ICA usually occurs between resourced and impoverished families.
- Adopted children often have living biological parents.
- Children are removed from familiar cultures.

These facts and other information led the authors to reframe what was originally viewed as benevolent acts of charity into a social justice nightmare. As they continue their analysis of the power and social justice issues they have identified, social workers within the field of adoption are called upon to work with others in addressing the problems posed by these situations. Obviously, local social workers will not attempt to address this problem on an international level, but having this information may help them examine conditions within their own adoption agencies and propose practice changes so that they are more vigilant in their oversight of the selection and placement of children adopted from other countries.

Condition statements are made more precise through a process of research and documentation of the nature, size, and scope of the problem. As one proceeds with subsequent tasks in problem analysis, condition statements will be refined many times as new facts and findings emerge. As in the example above, statements may evolve into an identified problem on which there is consensus or it may be perceived as a need or deficit. It is possible that a change effort can be developed around an opportunity, where there is no identified problem or need, but instead funding or resources become available. The change agent needs to recognize that consensus building is important no matter how the change effort arose.

Identify Relevant Historical and Contextual Information

Questions to be explored for this activity include the following:

- Has the problem been recognized and acknowledged by any community or organizational members?
- If so, when was this condition, problem, or opportunity first recognized in this community or organization?
- What are the important incidents or events that have occurred from the first recognition to the present time?
- What do earlier efforts to address this problem reveal?

The next task is to compile a chronology of significant events or milestones that promotes understanding of the history of the community or organizational condition or problem. This shifts the focus to the area in Figure 3.1 where the problem and the arena overlap.

A condition or problem in any community or organization has its own history. This history can affect the ways in which people currently perceive the condition or problem. It is, therefore, important to understand how key people within the community or organization perceived the condition or problem in the past. If it was seen as a problem, how was it addressed? How effective were the attempts to alleviate the problem? Who were the major participants in any previous change efforts?

If one looks at the condition or problem merely as it is defined at present, much will be missed. Instead, it is crucial to determine the problem's history, particularly in terms of critical incidents that have shaped past and current perceptions of the problem. A task force might, for example, be concerned about a high dropout rate from the local high school. The following chronology of critical incidents could help the group to better understand factors that influenced the origin and development of important issues in the high school over the years.

2003	Riverview High School was a predominantly lower-middle-class high school with an 82 percent graduation rate.
2005	School district boundaries were redrawn, and the student body changed. For 30 percent of its members, English was a second language.
2007	Enrollment dropped 20 percent, and the graduation rate fell to 67 percent.
2008	Riverview High School initiated a strong vocational training program designed to prepare high school graduates for post–high school employment; the college preparatory curriculum was deemphasized.
2010	Enrollment increased; attendance patterns improved.
2012	Local employers hired only 32 percent of the graduates; unemployment rates among Riverview graduates 1 year later were as high as 37 percent.
2014	Enrollment dropped back to 2007 levels; the dropout rate reached 23 percent, its highest mark yet.
2015	Riverview High School was written up in the local newspaper as one of the ten worst schools in the state in terms of quality of education, retention rates of students, and post–high school employment. A blue-ribbon panel was formed to make recommendations to improve the quality of education.

Tracing these historical events lends insight into some of the incidents experienced by the faculty, staff, administration, students, and families associated with Riverview High School. In this case, the task force should expect to encounter a discouraged and cynical response to any sort of a "Stay in School" campaign. The critical incidents list indicates that many of the arguments for staying in school simply did not prove true for those who graduated.

When the employment, career, and financial incentives for remaining in high school are removed, the challenge to keep students in school is greatly increased. This means that the approach to organizational change needs to be tailored in a way that is relevant and meaningful to those who are intended to be the primary beneficiaries. This has clear implications for including in the change effort those who can, for example, positively influence the employment environment for graduates.

Exploring relevant historical incidents also helps establish the credibility of the change agent. Many people are simply not open to supporting change for their communities and organizations if those organizing the change effort are perceived as being "outsiders" who have not taken the time to become familiar with what has gone on in the past.

The types of critical incidents just described are generally gleaned from interviews, discussions, or social media exchanges with long-time residents, activists, community leaders, teachers, and social service agency employees. In tracing the history or antecedent conditions of an episode of change, the change agent hopes to discover (1) what happened in the past to call attention to the problem or need, (2) what the community's (neighborhood, city, county, state, and private sector) response was to the attention focused on the problem or need, and (3) how successful or unsuccessful the response was and why.

Engagement

Practice Behavior: Use empathy, reflection, and interpersonal skills to effectively engage diverse clients and constituencies.

Critical Thinking Question: What would you consider to be effective ways to engage with clients and constitutencies in learning about the historical context of the problem?

Task 2: Explore the Professional Knowledge Base on the Condition, Problem, Need, or Opportunity

In addition to interviewing local people to help frame the condition or problem, those involved in a change effort are also expected to immerse themselves in relevant professional journals and other resources, including theory and research on the problem as well as data and information. There are three types of scholarly resources to be explored here: (1) theoretical and empirical books and journal articles on the problem to be studied; (2) statistical and qualitative data and information that can be used to document the existence of the problem or need, and to help in understanding such factors as size, scope, trends, and other useful information; and (3) practice-based articles and reports on promising interventions used to address the problem. The Internet has become perhaps the most valuable single tool for accessing information of this nature.

Locate Relevant Theoretical and Research Resources

Questions to be explored for this activity include the following:

- What body of knowledge is considered key to understanding the condition, problem, need, or opportunity?

- What frameworks are useful in understanding the condition, problem, need, or opportunity?
- Where and how does one access the knowledge and information needed for this task?

The challenge to the change agent in this activity is to become as much of an expert on the condition, problem, need, or opportunity as possible in the time available. Few experiences are more embarrassing than to be making a public presentation to a decision-making or funding body and to be exposed as less knowledgeable than the audience.

A number of journals reporting empirical testing of theoretical and practice-related questions are available in the social sciences and can be accessed through the Internet. Some journals are now devoted almost exclusively to reporting research in social work and related fields (e.g., *Journal of Evidence-Based Social Work*, *Social Work Research*, *Journal of Social Service Research*, and *Research on Social Work Practice*). Others focus on special populations and/or social problems (e.g., *Child Welfare*, *Journal of Gerontological Social Work*, *Journal of Child Sexual Abuse*, *Journal of Poverty*, and *Bulletin of HIV/AIDS and Social Work*). A computerized search of journal abstracts such as *Social Work Abstracts*, *PsychINFO*, and *Sociological Abstracts* should quickly produce a listing of relevant articles, and a scan of the titles will guide the change agent toward those that appear to be most useful in understanding the condition, problem, or opportunity. WorldCat is a major source of information about books.

Web resources include websites sponsored by advocacy groups that attend to the needs of specific populations such as the American Association of Retired Persons (AARP) for older adults, the Child Welfare League of America (CWLA) for children, the American Cancer Society, and the National Association for the Advancement of Colored People (NAACP). The professional change agent has a special role at this point in separating sound, credible theoretical and research knowledge from opinion and hearsay available on some nonprofessional websites or blogs. Major contributions to the professional knowledge base begin with journals, then books, then web resources.

One feature that can be useful in attempting to understand a phenomenon is the way in which the author has conceptualized the condition, problem, or opportunity. In compiling an article for publication, it is incumbent on the author to present some framework or format for analysis that sheds light on the topic under study. In a study of isolated and neglected older adults, for example, does the author break down the topic by the number of social contacts? By distance from family? By participation in groups? What concepts (and what technical terms) are presented that aid in understanding the phenomenon? Information uncovered in exploring the professional knowledge base should be constantly examined for its relevance to the current situation. Ultimately, a mix of potential causal or contributing factors will be selected as a framework for explaining the phenomenon under study. Achieving this beginning level of understanding of the condition, problem, or opportunity under study prepares the change agent for the next task—collecting supporting data.

> ▶ Watch the video about what grey literature is and how it can expand your research options. Why examine grey literature in addition to peer-reviewed literature?
>
> www.youtube.com/watch?v=m9-0ZYnCmAI

Access and Collect Supporting Data

Questions to be explored for this activity include the following:

- What data are most useful in describing the condition, problem, or opportunity?
- Where can useful quantitative and qualitative data, historical records, agency-based studies, and other types of information be found?

There was a time when a community could become sensitized to a condition and recognize it as a problem based on a few incidents. Churches started orphanages and counties started poor houses with little or no data beyond personal knowledge of a few people in need and the expectation that there would be more. In the complex communities of today, however, with so many social and community problems competing for limited resources, data must be compiled to document the size and scope of a problem or need.

Data Sources.   Basic to all statistical support is the knowledge of the number of people in various demographic categories (e.g., gender, age, racial, or ethnic groups). Valuable information of this type is available in the *County and City Data Book* published by the U.S. Bureau of the Census. As with many census publications, it is available for free online at the Bureau of the Census website. This resource includes such data categories (for both counties and cities) as racial/ethnic breakdown, age, gender, the number of people with less than a high school education, and the number of people in poverty. Additional statistical references based on census data include *USA Counties*, *Statistical Abstract of the United States*, and the *State and Metropolitan Area Data Book*, all of which can be accessed online.

State and/or county departments of social services, health, mental health, and corrections often collect data that can be useful in documenting the existence of social conditions or problems. Other sources include local social service agencies, the United Way, community councils, centralized data-collection resource centers, centralized information and referral agencies, law-enforcement agencies, hospitals, and school district offices. The process of tracking down information is often similar to a scavenger hunt, where one clue leads to another until a point is reached where the quantity and quality of supportive data collected are sufficient to allow the persons initiating change to make their case.

In collecting supporting data, the change agent should think in terms of the entire "circle" of information needed to understand the presenting problem or condition. This means that data collection will not necessarily be limited to the *local* community, neighborhood, or organization that is the focus of the change effort. Although data on the smallest local units of analysis (such as the neighborhood or census tract) are certainly powerful in terms of supporting the argument that something must be done, data on the same conditions or problems at the county, state, or national levels can also be useful in providing a basis of comparison against which local figures can be judged.

Types of Data.   Research scholars have increasingly emphasized the importance of incorporating both quantitative and qualitative data into the understanding of social conditions and problems. Trochim (2006) points out that using multiple types of data (both numbers and words) can provide a rich and diverse perspective.

Tashakkori and Teddlie (2009) make an important case for using mixed methods. By exploring both quantitative and qualitative studies, the social worker can expand and enhance the understanding of problem, population, and arena.

To oversimplify the discussion, quantitative research tends to focus on numbers while qualitative research focuses on words, or the capturing of any data that are nonnumerical in nature. One can readily recognize the value of incorporating both quantitative and qualitative data into the study of a community. For example, a quantitative study would tend to focus on a series of questions with definitive, quantifiable answers in addressing the question "Would you support or oppose the introduction of a program to increase the high school graduation rate?" A qualitative study might attempt to explore a whole range of feelings behind the same question. Qualitative research generally includes such techniques as in-depth interviewing, direct observation, or an analysis of written documents.

Collecting data on a community social condition or problem can be a challenge. Ideally, in promoting a program to educate homeless children, for example, one would hope to find information that clearly demonstrates something similar to the following:

- There are currently 3,279 homeless children in Clifton County.
- Lack of positive early school experience can be expected to result in about 2,000 of these children being unable to read at grade level.
- Inability to read at grade level can be expected to result in 1,500 of this group dropping out of school by the 10th grade.
- Of the 1,500 who drop out of school by the 10th grade, about 1,000 will eventually either be in trouble with the law and become incarcerated or otherwise be placed in a state-supported institution.
- Each person supported by the state costs, on average, $28,000 per year. The cost to the state for 1,000 incarcerated or institutionalized dropouts will be $28 million per year.
- An early intervention program for 2,000 homeless children will cost $6.5 million.
- About 1,800 of these children can be expected to improve their reading skills to grade level, resulting in improved opportunities for employment and self-sufficiency.
- If successful, this program offers a potential annual savings to the state of up to $21.5 million.
- These statistics are undergirded by reports from key informants in the community who report that community residents are aware of and concerned about the problem, and eager for efforts to correct it.

These kinds of quantitative and qualitative data make it clear that it is a case of paying something now for prevention or paying many times more than that amount later for care, maintenance, or perhaps rehabilitation. However, although these kinds of statistics are much desired and preferred, it is rare to find that they have been compiled in a usable format. Instead, individuals initiating change must rely on what is available: census data; community needs assessments; levels of demand for service as reported by agencies; rates of service; data generated by hospitals, schools, and police departments; and any other reliable source available.

A few techniques can be helpful in cases in which quantitative and qualitative data are needed. One resource is national, regional, and state studies in which a percentage or an incidence rate (per thousand or sometimes per hundred thousand) has been established. If, for example, it has been found that 48.5 percent of marriages performed in a state end in divorce, one can apply this percentage to a city or town within that state to calculate the number of divorces that can be expected to follow over time. Obviously, the number will not be exact, but it provides at least a beginning point for projection. When such statistics are used, they would be qualified with a statement such as "If statewide rates for divorce hold for Smithville, then we can expect to see almost half of the marriages in this community end in divorce," or something to that effect.

Make the Data Meaningful for Interpretation

Questions to be explored for this activity include the following:

- What options can be used to display data?
- How should data be displayed in order to clearly and concisely make the case for change?

Comparative data are generally more useful than a single statistic, and several techniques can be used to collect and display comparative data. These include cross-sectional analysis, time-series comparisons, and comparisons with other data units. In addition to these data displays, techniques such as standards comparisons and epidemiological analysis can be useful (Kettner, Moroney, & Martin, 2013). Displays should be prepared and presented in a way that will tell the story effectively.

A number of graphic options are available, including line graphs, bar graphs, and pie charts. Thought should be given to which graphic display will have the greatest impact, given the data to be presented. Most of the graphics needed for these types of displays are a part of Microsoft Office Home Edition. This package includes Word (word processing), Excel (spreadsheets), PowerPoint (presentations), and Access (relational databases). When job descriptions include a requirement for computer skills, in most cases ability to use these types of programs is expected.

Cross-Sectional Analysis.   This approach involves collecting data at a single point in time and describing circumstances at the moment captured in those data. It usually focuses on a single population or sample. For example, a survey might concentrate on gathering information about a need experienced by a particular target population and display the percentage of the population who report a problem in this area, as illustrated in Table 4.2.

The data presented in Table 4.2 can be used to create a more dramatic visual effect by translating the data into graphic formats. Figure 4.3 illustrates age distribution in the form of a bar graph, which presents a picture of an aging population.

Table 4.2   An Illustration of Cross-Sectional Analysis, Examining the Percentage of Each Population Experiencing a Problem

Variable	Population (%)	Housing (%)	Employment (%)	Nutrition (%)	Transportation (%)
Age					
0–18	11	5	N/A	5	N/A
19–30	21	14	7	9	16
31–64	28	17	11	8	19
65+	40	19	33	15	33
Gender					
Female	52	5	7	6	18
Male	48	16	24	11	17

Figure 4.4 uses a pie chart to illustrate ethnic distribution. Side-by-side pie charts using census data 10 years apart could be used as a cross-sectional analysis as well as a time-series analysis.

As community or organizational conditions are identified, subpopulations can usually be assessed by demographic characteristics such as age, gender, and racial/ethnic group. The most serious limitation is that a cross-sectional analysis does not reveal changes over time.

Time-Series Comparisons. When available, data from repeated observations over time are preferred because they display trends. Assuming data were collected on an annual basis, a time-series comparison would look at trends in the variable(s) of interest. For example, the number of nonduplicated individuals requesting overnight stays in homeless shelters in a given city might be displayed in a line graph, as shown in Figure 4.5.

Statistics like these can help project need and cost into the future, based on assumptions about changes over time identified in a series of observations. Comparisons among

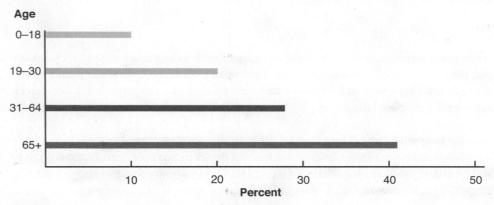

Figure 4.3
A Bar Graph Illustrating Age Distribution and Revealing an Aging Population

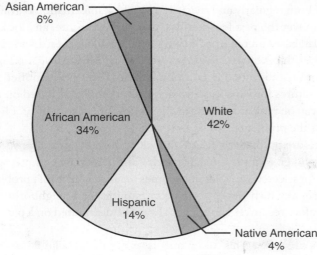

Figure 4.4
A Pie Chart Illustrating Ethnic Distribution

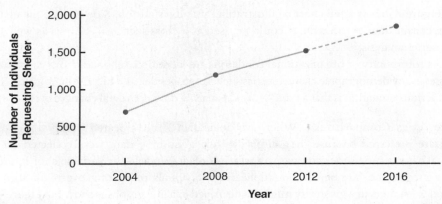

Figure 4.5
A Line Graph Illustrating a Time-Series Analysis of the Number of Individuals Requesting Overnight Shelter by Homeless Persons

these observations can provide the change agent with valuable information. For example, they can be used to document how client need is increasing, what the trends are for the next few years, why additional resources are needed, and the projected dollars necessary to fill anticipated need.

Comparison with Other Data Units.   Even though cross-sectional analysis can provide a snapshot at a point in time, and time series can depict trends over time, questions might still be raised about the legitimacy of a problem, especially when comparisons are being made with other communities or organizations. For example, if a change agent is able to document a current teenage pregnancy rate of 22 percent in a community, and to show an upward trend over 5 years, a critic might reasonably ask if this rate is considered high or low. This is where comparison to other data units is helpful.

A wealth of both regularly and specially assembled information is available for use as supporting data. Over the past few decades, many federal, state, and local agencies have contributed to databases on rates per 1,000, 10,000, or 100,000 on a wide range of social, economic, and health problems. These statistics allow for comparison regardless of the size of the city or neighborhood in question. Studies have also identified state and local per-capita expenditures for various social and health problems. Based on these findings, states and cities can be ranked as to the incidence and prevalence of problems or on their efforts to address the problems.

Comparisons are particularly useful in making a case that a disproportionate share of resources should go to a particularly needy community. By comparing census tracts within a county on selected variables, it becomes readily evident that problems and needs are not always equally distributed across communities and neighborhoods within the county, and therefore resources should not always be distributed on a per-capita basis.

Standards Comparisons.   This technique is particularly helpful when comparative data are not available. A **standard** is defined as an established specification that is widely recognized, used, and accepted by authorities. Standards are developed by accrediting bodies, governmental entities, and professional associations. For example, the Child Welfare

League of America publishes comprehensive sets of standards related to community and agency programs for child abuse and neglect, adoption, and other child welfare services. Similarly, the National Council on Aging has developed case management standards. The National Association of Social Workers (NASW) has developed standards for social work services in a wide variety of settings and with various population groups such as adolescents.

Where governmental units, accrediting bodies, and professional associations have defined standards, conditions considered to be falling below health, educational, personal care, housing, and other types of standards become more readily accessible as targets for change. Community leaders do not like the negative publicity that often results when services offered within their communities are described as being "below standard." These types of standards apply primarily to the quality of services being provided.

Standards of sorts may also be used to define a problem or population. For example, some cities have developed standardized criteria to define a homeless person or a gang member. Where such criteria have been established, they can be useful in interpreting existing records and compiling new quantitative data or other information.

Epidemiological Analysis. This is a technique adapted from the field of public health, where an analysis of factors contributing to a disease helps to establish relationships even when a clear cause-and-effect relationship cannot be demonstrated. This approach can be applied not only to disease but also to social problems.

For example, Sabol, Coulton, and Polousky (2004) examined variables influencing child maltreatment. In this study, the authors looked at age, race, and urban versus suburban location, and found that these factors could be used to predict the probability of a child being reported for an incident of maltreatment before his or her 10th birthday. In another study, Diala, Muntaner, and Walrath (2004) examined rural and urban location; demographic characteristics of age, gender, and race; and social class factors of education, household income, and wealth, and found that some relationships between and among these variables could be useful in predicting the probability of alcohol and drug abuse and dependence.

A useful feature of epidemiological thinking is that, in analyzing problems, it can help avoid simplistic cause-and-effect thinking. Although a single causal factor (e.g., poor education, poverty, or child abuse) may explain current problems faced by a small portion of the population, multiple factors in combination frequently help explain the problem or phenomenon for a much larger portion of the population.

Qualitative Data Displays. Qualitative data can also be presented in the form of tables and figures, allowing word data to tell a thematic story about the problem. Table 4.3 provides an example from a qualitative study on faith-based advocacy organizations (FBAOs). The organization was part of a study examining the activities of FBAOs involved in lobbying on social welfare issues. The table illustrates the policy areas of one FBAO, using examples from the research as exemplars of the policy area.

Search for Promising Practice Approaches to Address the Problem

Questions to be explored for this activity include the following:

- What promising practices related to this problem are identified in scholarly sources and in reports of program/project evaluations?
- What lessons can be learned from these studies/reports that may be helpful in intervening to address the problem?

Table 4.3   An Example of How to Display Qualitative Data

Policy Area	Description	Issue Exemplars
First Amendment	• Preserving the wall of separation between religion and the state • Preventing public policy unduly influenced by singular religious viewpoints	• Prayer in government-funded public institutions • School vouchers • Religious curriculum in public schools • Charitable choice
Bias and Discrimination	• Opposing legislation that promotes bias and intolerance • Supporting efforts that encourage diversity	• Civil equality for same-sex couples • Immigration • Hate crimes • Capital punishment
Health and Social Justice	• Representing those in need in the Jewish and broader community	• Medicaid expansion • Minimum wage • Reproductive choice • Stem cell research

Evidence-based practice (EBP) can be defined as application of research and clinical evidence to decisions made about practice. Social work has had a long history of assessing based on the facts surrounding the case under consideration, but introducing research and clinical findings brings an added dimension. While the field of medicine is credited with the earliest use of the EBP concept, many fields including mental health, child welfare, and education are increasingly incorporating research findings into clinical and macro-level decisions. The NASW indicates that the process of using EBP allows practitioners to use empirically based interventions in every aspect of their practice, including the integration of what is known about culture to inform service delivery (NASW, n.d.).

Gitterman and Knight (2013) recommend replacing EBP with **evidence-guided practice** (EGP) because the concept of being guided is more action oriented than simply being "based on" or "informed." They also argue that if the change agent looks for guidance, flexibility is implied. Being guided does not suggest that there is only one direction; it just provides a starting point. In other words, interventions are suggested rather than prescribed by research findings. This is a good example of how even approaches to gathering information can be reframed. A similar reframe is using the term *promising practices* rather than *best practices*. Promising practices leave room for flexibility as new information emerges in process, whereas best practice terminology implies a one-best-way approach.

Whether one embraces EBP or EGP, it is important to recognize that evaluations of existing social service programs can be informative in gathering information about how to address a problem. Even though these evaluations often lack the methodological rigor of organized research, it is helpful to know what others have done in approaching similar problems. Reports of practice findings tend to be the least formal in terms of their data collection, analysis, and reporting of findings, yet they can be helpful and informative as

Research-informed Practice (or Practice-informed Research)

Practice Behavior: Apply critical thinking to engage in analysis of quantitative and qualitative research methods and research findings.

Critical Thinking Question: What are some strategies you can use to efficiently synthesize what you have learned from multiple sources?

long as the user is cautious in interpreting findings, forming conclusions, and deriving applications.

For example, a rural school system in the northeastern United States identified the following conditions: Engagement of families living in Pleasant Grove in their young children's elementary school experience is very low, and school administrators and teachers do not live in the immediate vicinity. In analyzing the problem, the school social worker reached out to children's parents to see how they perceived the situation. She discovered high levels of poverty within this rural community and a toxic level of stress for parents and children. In the process, she discovered that community residents were surprised that anyone was interested in their opinions and that they referred to themselves as living in "trailers." The social worker referred to their living situation as a "mobile home community," and soon she was intrigued to hear family members refer to their mobile home community, positively reframing the image of their community. The change agent worked with community residents and school staff to develop an intervention to reach out to hard-to-reach families, reduce stress, and engage them in the educational system. Lessons learned from piloting this engagement approach were useful to persons seeking to engage families in their children's education and to build a collective identity within the school system (Blitz, Kida, Gresham, & Bronstein, 2013). From an EGP perspective, this case study is a resource for not only understanding a problem but also determining how to begin changing the situation. It could be useful to other school social workers attemping to engage parents in their children's education, and it could be viewed as a promising practice.

Another example comes from Australia and concerns the marginalization of indigenous people within a cycle of violence, oppression, and dispossession associated with colonialism. Community Arts Network Western Australia (CANWA) was formed to begin a process of community cultural development, using art as a means through which community building could begin. CANWA staff believed that strengthening networks and raising awareness about Indigenous peoples, cultures, and lived experience could eventually work toward more socially just policies. Participants in this change effort described in detail the iterative process in which they worked through CANWA, only to discover how deeply seated racism is within these communities. They outlined lessons learned and ways in which they changed strategies, reframed problem(s) over time, and moved to more aggressive stances (Sonn & Quayle, 2013). Like the previous example, but on a much larger scale, these are the type of practice findings that would be helpful in informing the design of interventions in a social change effort with diverse population groups that face ongoing racial discrimination.

Task 3: Frame the Problem and Develop Working Hypotheses

Is it now time to pull together what was learned in Chapters 3 and 4. The purpose of Chapter 3 was to guide the social worker through an assessment of the population group most directly involved. In this chapter, the problem was assessed.

Etiology refers to the underlying causes of a problem. Speculating about the etiology of a problem is an attempt to arrive at an understanding of cause-and-effect relationships. As one begins to move into this territory, it is important to keep an open mind and let results from searches of the knowledge base, quantitative data, historical information, and the personal experiences of target population representatives inform an understanding of the problem. It is unlikely—in the analysis of social, community, and/or organizational problems—that there will be simple, linear, cause-and-effect relationships. It is more likely that there will be a variety of contributing factors, along with multiple views on what is relevant and applicable to the current situation.

Task 3 includes three sets of activities—stating the problem, selecting factors that help explain the underlying causes of the problem, and developing hypotheses.

State the Problem

Questions to be explored for this activity include the following:

- What are the major concepts, issues, and perspectives identified in the population assessment?
- What are the major issues and perspectives identified in the problem assessment?
- Given what has been learned, how would you now frame the problem?

When examining conditions or problems in the human services, there is often a strong temptation to identify lack of resources as a cause of a problem. For example, in studies focused on an organizational problem, causes often tend to be defined in terms of lack of operating funds, staff, adequate equipment and facilities, and so on. In defining a community problem, causes often are seen in terms of lack of resources for new programs or expanded services, such as more child care slots, more training, and so on. In many cases, genuine resource deficits may exist, but we caution against superficial assessments that look to dollars as the only solution to every problem. There are several reasons for a more thorough approach.

First, resources have to do with the intervention or the so-called solution, and they should be considered only after a specific approach has been proposed and resource issues can be addressed in detailed, not general, terms. Second, "lack of resources" is so universal that it is relatively meaningless as a part of problem analysis. Third, "lack of adequate resources" does not help explain underlying causal or contributing factors. The statement simply assumes that more of whatever is already being done will solve the problem. Additional resources in macro-level change can be critical to success, but the issue should be addressed later in the change process.

The types of causal or contributing factors to be addressed are those fundamental factors that explain why the problem emerged and why it persists over time. They are substantive factors that prevent progress toward solutions. Identifying these multiple causes helps clarify the complex nature of the problem. As a greater understanding of the population, problem, and arena is achieved, these factors will be used to develop a working hypothesis of etiology or cause(s) and effect(s). This working hypothesis will then be used to guide the intervention.

Identification of possible causes is intended to help those who are exploring the need for change to focus their efforts, thereby increasing the chances of success. In most cases, it is unlikely that all contributing factors will be addressed. Selection of a limited number of possible causes should lead either to a narrower, more limited focus or to collaboration with others, with agreement that each change effort will concentrate on different factors. For example, faced with a problem of unsupervised children in a community, a local church might agree to take responsibility for building mutual support systems among single mothers and strengthening the sense of community, whereas a local school may be willing to provide constructive, supervised after-school activities. At this point, however, these decisions would be premature. The purpose of identifying contributing factors is to arrive at an understanding of the problem that is as clear as possible.

Examination of history, theory, and research on the population and the problem comes together at the point at which cause-and-effect relationships are postulated. The change agent looks for patterns of events or factors that seem to be associated so that a case can be made for a working hypothesis on selected causal or contributing factors. For example, in the population assessment, the problem of unsupervised children in a community may have arisen, with the following contributing factors identified:

- There is a high percentage of single, working mothers in the community.
- There are no after-school programs available in the community.
- Children in the community from single-parent families have few male mentors or role models.
- The community lacks a sense of cohesion; for the most part, people know few neighbors.
- No community-based organizations are currently addressing this problem.

In many cases, alternative explanations of cause and effect are all logical and, in a sense, "correct," but they may apply to different groups within a given population. For example, all the following statements are probably logical explanations of why some adolescents exhibit delinquent behavior:

- Some adolescents feel neglected by parents.
- Some adolescents fail to bond with parents.
- Some adolescents are not able to succeed in school.
- Some adolescents choose peers who encourage delinquent activities.
- Some adolescents live in high-crime, high-mobility communities.

Thus, the decision that must then be made is not one of choosing the "correct" perspective on etiology but rather selecting the subgroup(s) to be addressed. As with most populations and problems, one understanding of etiology and one intervention do not fit all. There are multiple rational explanations, and ultimately one or more must be selected to serve as a framework for understanding the problem and the population.

Kettner, Moroney, and Martin (2013) recommend that the framing of a problem contain three statements: (1) a qualitative statement, (2) a quantiative statement, and (3) a justification of action statement. Framed in this way, a problem statement based on the example above might read:

> Adolescents living in the high-crime, high-mobility Catawba community are engaging in delinquent activities and dropping out of school. Furthermore, the dropout and arrest rates in Catawba are three times as high as rates in adjacent communities. Therefore, a multidimensional educational, recreational, and socialization program will target adolescents in order to reengage them and their families in positive community building.

Note that choices have been made in framing the problem. The primary target is adolescents, and the action focuses on developing a program targeted to them and their families. How the problem is framed assumes that the problem and population assessment led to this intervention as a viable option. But assume that the assessment process revealed different information. An alternative problem statement might be:

> Fifty percent of the households in the Catawba community are headed by single mothers who are having difficulty economically supporting their families. Furthermore, the average income for these mothers is 125% of the country's poverty rate. Therefore, a comprehensive women's center is needed in the Catawba community that is specifically designed to build support networks, offer job-counseling and employment services, and locate child care options.

This second problem statement is framed differently from the first. Its target focuses on women rather than adolescents. Given this frame, note that the intervention is different. When reframing the diagnosis, the prognosis changes. Framing, then, guides the change agent into selecting options or priorities.

Intervention

Practice Behavior: Apply knowledge of human behavior and the social environment, person-in-environment, and other multidisciplinary theoretical frameworks in interventions with clients and constituencies.

Critical Thinking Question: When do you have enough information to write a problem statement? What are some potential consequences of not articulating a clear problem statement when planning an intervention?

When those involved in the change effort have defined the problem; reviewed important historical events; completed a review of relevant journal articles, texts, and web resources; and compiled supporting evidence, they should have at least a beginning understanding of what may be causing or at least influencing the problem. The next step is to determine what cause-and-effect relationships must be dealt with in order to bring about needed changes. Preliminary identification of these factors is a necessary step in clarifying the change effort. Before distilling the data and information gathered, however, it is important to understand the types of causes or other considerations to be identified.

Select Factors That Help Explain the Underlying Causes of the Problem

Questions to be explored in this activity include the following:

- What are the causal factors that explain the problem?
- What are the results or effects of the causes identified?

Based on what was learned, a series of statements about probable effects of contributing factors can be generated. For example, in exploring the question of why some adolescents demonstrate antisocial behavior, including committing status offenses (acts that would not be offenses if they were adults, such as truancy or running away from home), a hypothesis of etiology emerges. Other factors could be added that focus on, for example, a specific subgroup of adolescent girls, or a group of Native American boys, in which case gender or cultural factors may be included in the hypothesis.

Another example arises from a growing concern about chronic homelessness among single adults. A study of the homeless services system may lead to the following findings:

- Permanent supportive housing is successful in ending homelessness for chronically homeless individuals with a serious mental illness.
- The majority of the system's programs are focused on emergency shelter.
- Affordable housing is limited.

- Few programs provide permanent supportive housing.
- Eligibility requirements for transitional and permanent supportive housing programs screen out a majority of chronically homeless individuals.
- Ability to remain in housing is linked to service success and program compliance.
- Mental health and substance abuse treatment services are limited.
- Trauma-informed services are rarely provided.
- Chronically homeless individuals who are not stably housed tend to overutilize hospital emergency rooms for health and mental health treatment.

A survey of the population reveals some of the problems and needs faced by individuals who are chronically homeless:

- Some believe that homeless programs do not respect them.
- Some are experiencing severe symptoms of a mental health disorder.
- Some are experiencing acute or chronic physical health conditions.
- Some have difficulty becoming clean and sober.
- Some suffer discrimination and rejection from service providers and community members.
- Some experience trauma because of current and previous experiences on and off the street.

Drawing on these findings from analysis of problem and population, relationships may be proposed between causes and their effects.

It should be clear from these examples that part of the job of creating a clearly focused macro-level intervention involves selecting some contributing factors and setting others aside, at least for the time being, unless enough resources are available to take on every factor within the same project. It is also possible that completely different factors could be identified within these examples if gender or cultural issues emerge during the course of the study. Each episode of change must find its focus within the context of the considerations and dictates of the local situation at the time.

Develop Hypotheses

A hypothesis of etiology should identify what the participants in the change process believe to be the most important and relevant factors contributing to the problem. This may be different from what was identified in the literature or may lead to a particular part of the literature that needs reexamination.

Questions to be explored in this activity include the following:

- Based on the foregoing analysis of problem and population, what seem to be the dominant themes in understanding cause-and-effect relationships?
- How should the hypothesis of etiology be framed?

The hypothesis of etiology frames the change effort in a way that makes it focused and manageable. Example 1 in Box 4.1 leads to a working hypothesis such as the following:

When single, working mothers are unable to meet the needs of their adolescent children for parental guidance, when adolescents lack a positive male role model,

Box 4.1   Selecting Factors from Analysis of Problem and Population: Example 1

Selected Factors Affecting Adolescent First Offenders Who Commit Status Offenses:

1. Some single working mothers have limited ability to meet the many needs of their adolescent children for parental guidance.
2. Some adolescent children of single, working mothers lack male role models.
3. There are no after-school programs for adolescents in the community.

These Factors Appear to Lead to the Following Results:

1. Adolescents whose needs for parental guidance are not met by parents may feel neglected.
2. Lack of positive, male role models for some adolescents leads to bonding with older peers who may encourage delinquent behavior.
3. Absence of organized after-school activities for adolescents results in many hours of idle, nonproductive time every day, which may lead to participation in delinquent activities.

and when no organized after-school activities are available for adolescents, it is likely that adolescents will feel neglected, will bond with older peers who may turn out to be negative role models, and will participate in delinquent acts during idle after-school hours.

Using the hypothesis for Example 1, the change agent will begin to think in terms of framing the intervention around identifying adolescent children of single, working mothers who have been involved in one or more delinquent activities and (1) dealing with their feelings of neglect, (2) finding positive male role models to serve as mentors to the adolescents identified, and (3) providing a program of organized after-school activities for the adolescents identified.

A hypothesis for Example 2 in Box 4.2 might read as follows:

When a homeless services system focuses the majority of its efforts and resources on emergency housing for the homeless; when existing emergency, transitional, and permanent supportive housing programs "screen out" individuals who are chronically homeless and have a serious mental illness; and when chronically homeless individuals use and reuse hospital emergency rooms for health and mental health

Box 4.2   Selecting Factors from Analysis of Problem and Population: Example 2

Selected Factors Affecting Chronically Homeless Adults with a Serious Mental Illness:

1. The homeless service system focuses its resources primarily on emergency housing and services.
2. The eligibility criteria for existing permanent supportive housing screen out most chronically homeless individuals.
3. Chronically homeless individuals tend to use and reuse hospital emergency rooms to meet health and mental health needs.

These Factors Appear to Lead to the Following Results:

1. Little attention and few resources are directed to permanent supportive housing.
2. Chronically homeless individuals who can't qualify for permanent supportive housing programs live on the streets and in shelters.
3. Chronically homeless individual's utilization of health and human services is fragmented and expensive.

services, it is likely that the homeless service system will not develop permanent supportive housing programs, that chronically homeless individuals will not be able to access the permanent supportive housing programs that exist, and that chronically homeless individuals will overutilize expensive health and mental health services.

For Example 2, the intervention will focus on (1) redirecting existing resources toward permanent supportive housing, (2) developing eligibility criteria for programs that are more responsive to the needs of the population, and (3) coordinating immediate and routine health and mental health services to better respond to the health and mental health needs of chronically homeless individuals.

A hypothesis of etiology gives the change agent a beginning point from which to hypothesize further about interventions. An intervention hypothesis will include potential ways to address the problem, moving beyond explaining the problem to providing directions toward change. In Chapter 9, we will return to developing intervention hypotheses after we have fully explored assessing the arenas in which change occurs.

> **?** Assess your understanding of a framework for assessing community and organizational problems by taking this brief quiz.

SUMMARY

Chapters 3 and 4 are companion pieces designed to lead the change agent through an orderly, systematic review of existing knowledge, research, data, information, historical perspectives, and other types of information that may be available on the population(s) affected and the problem(s) they face. A complete study of population and population involves many facets. These studies include personal interviews with local people affected by the problem, and a compilation of quantitative and qualitative data and information to back up the problem statement. The purpose of this compilation of knowledge and information is so that the change agent may develop a clear understanding of the many factors that may have led to the current situation. Based on a study and analysis of these factors, the change agent can narrow a broad, sweeping general definition of the problem to a small number of highly specific factors that lend themselves to intervention and problem resolution. A working hypothesis of etiology can then be framed.

In this chapter, we presented an approach to orderly, systematic, professionally assisted change. Critics may say that this approach takes too long and fails to seize the moment, and we acknowledge that part of the responsibility of a change agent is to make judgments about how and when to act. The study process can be streamlined or extended, depending on the complexity and duration of the problem. But simply ignoring the need for current information and proceeding to action may prove to be irresponsible and detrimental to the very people the change is intended to serve. A change effort worth undertaking is worth approaching systematically and thoroughly. In the next chapters, we will explore communities and organizations, the arenas in which change happens.

Appendix: Framework for Understanding Community and Organizational Problems

Task 1: Gather Information from Persons in the Community or Organization

Identify Community or Organizational Condition

- What are the conditions in this community or organization that need to be assessed?
- In approaching an episode of change, how could the condition statement be framed?

Identify Relevant Historical and Contextual Information

- Has the problem been recognized and acknowledged by any community or organizational members?
- If so, when was this condition, problem, or opportunity first recognized in this community or organization?
- What are the important incidents or events that have occurred from the first recognition to the present time?
- What do earlier efforts to address this problem reveal?

Task 2: Explore the Professional Knowledge Base on the Condition, Problem, Need, or Opportunity

Locate Relevant Theoretical and Research Resources

- What body of knowledge is considered key to understanding the condition, problem, need, or opportunity?
- What frameworks are useful in understanding the condition, problem, need, or opportunity?
- Where and how does one access the knowledge and information needed for this task?

Access and Collect Supporting Data

- What data are most useful in describing the condition, problem, or opportunity?
- Where can useful quantitative and qualitative data, historical records, agency-based studies, and other types of information be found?

Make the Data Meaningful for Interpretation

- What options can be used to display data?
- How should data be displayed in order to clearly and concisely make the case for change?

Search for Promising Practice Approaches to Address the Problem

- What promising practices related to this problem are identified in scholarly sources and in reports of program/project evaluations?
- What lessons can be learned from these studies/reports that may be helpful in intervening to address the problem?

Task 3: Frame the Problem and Develop Working Hypotheses

State the Problem

- What are the major concepts, issues, and perspectives identified in the population assessment?
- What are the major issues and perspectives identified in the problem assessment?
- Given what has been learned, how would you now frame the problem?

Select Factors That Help Explain the Underlying Causes of the Problem

- What are the causal factors that explain the problem?
- What are the results or effects of the causes identified?

Develop Hypotheses

- Based on the foregoing analysis of problem and population, what seem to be the dominant themes in understanding cause-and-effect relationships?
- How should the hypothesis of etiology be framed?

 Recall what you learned in this chapter by completing the Chapter Review.

Assess Your Competence

Use the scale below to rate your current level of achievement on the following concepts or skills associated with each learning outcome listed at the beginning of this chapter:

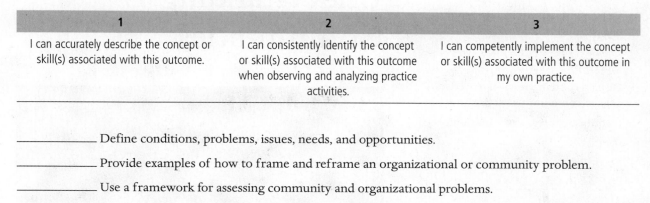

1	2	3
I can accurately describe the concept or skill(s) associated with this outcome.	I can consistently identify the concept or skill(s) associated with this outcome when observing and analyzing practice activities.	I can competently implement the concept or skill(s) associated with this outcome in my own practice.

_____ Define conditions, problems, issues, needs, and opportunities.

_____ Provide examples of how to frame and reframe an organizational or community problem.

_____ Use a framework for assessing community and organizational problems.

Understanding Communities

RSNAPSHOT/SHUTTERSTOCK

CONCEPTUALIZING COMMUNITY

Communities are the arenas in which macro practice takes place, but they are so diverse that no one definition, approach, or theory captures their total essence. Terms such as *global, international,* and *world community* are used in contemporary society to refer to the complex array of relationships among the people of the world (Weil, Reisch, & Ohmer, 2013). Yet, when most people think about communities that are important to them, they usually think on a smaller scale—remembering where they grew up, identifying with where they live today, or focusing on relationships based on affiliations or interests rather than just geographic proximity. These relationships may be bound by characteristics such as shared history, cultural values and traditions, concern for common issues, or frequent communication. Many people identify with multiple communities, thus making "*the* community" a misnomer. For many, affiliation with more than one community is an intrinsic part of who a person is.

Based on life experiences, social workers will have their own perceptions of what a community is, along with expectations about what it should be. These perceptions and expectations will influence how they approach work in communities that are new to them, and it is important to recognize that experiences with and feelings about community as a geographic locality vary. Some communities will be viewed nostalgically as desirable places, evoking warm memories. Other communities will be seen as oppressive, restrictive, or even dangerous to both residents and outsiders. At times, these differing views will be held about the same community, because each person's experience is unique. Community-based groups, ranging from youth gangs to elder rights groups, represent attempts to create specialized communities of interest within geographical communities, sometimes in ways that intentionally run counter to the local culture.

Some observers believe that in the United States, "community" as a geographically relevant concept began to erode with the expansion of suburbs in the 1950s and 1960s (Gerloff, 1992). Others see unlimited human potential lying dormant in inner-city communities that have been rendered dependent on social welfare organizations by an overzealous provision of services (Kretzmann & McKnight, 1993). Still others take an international perspective, revealing the tensions and even violence that can rip apart communities around the world, turning community members into refugees in search of asylum (Haynes, 2014).

One of the big issues we confront in this chapter is whether social workers are best served by looking at communities as places where people's interests are linked by geographic closeness. In an era of mobile phones, email, instant text messaging, Twitter, Facebook, online interactive games, and any number of methods of easy long-distance communication, the whole idea of community needs to be radically redefined.

Also, a problem confronting social workers in helping the poorest members of society is that they are forced to remain in a world where geographic proximity *does* matter because their environment is dangerous and lacks resources such as transportation, jobs, and child care (Abramovitz & Albrecht, 2013). Conversely, proximity becomes ever less relevant to more affluent members of society who can afford the technologies that allow them to transcend geography. Within a single episode of change, multiple definitions of **community** may be needed to help keep commitments and relationships clear. For example, while the target of change may be a specific neighborhood (a geographically bounded community), those needed to support the change may be linked through concern and commitment, and they may come from both the neighborhood and the larger environment (Campbell, 2014).

Marx (2013) calls for a reconceptualization of community for professional social work practice. He identifies 10 types of communities with which social workers may intervene. These types reveal the increasing diversity of geographical and nongeographical ways in which one can envision community. They are:

- Online communities such as MoveOn.org or DoSomething.org or Facebook and Twitter inform the world about movements such as the Arab Spring or Occupy Wall Street;
- Green communities mobilized to spread the message of global warming in which neighborhood organizations, interested citizens, city councils, urban planners, and environmental activists affiliate to promote healthier living;
- Gray communities in which naturally occurring retirement communities and pockets of older adults advocate for needed services and opportunities for meaningful engagement;

- Devastated communities throughout the world in which hurricanes, flooding, tornados, earthquakes, wildfires, and a number of manmade and natural disasters demand mobilization of volunteer and paid personnel to address the needs of victims;
- Hispanic communities, which comprise a growing demographic U.S. trend in which more professional social workers will increasingly engage in Spanish-speaking communities;
- International communities in which nonprofit and nongovenmental organizations (NGOs) seek to address problems that transcend geographic boundaries, joining forces with others to address issues of global poverty, disease, war, and more;
- Innovative communities in which people come together to advance the future through such creative efforts as social innovation, entrepreneurial activities, and diffusion of innovation;
- Electoral communities in which local, state, and national campaigns for public office bring people together with similar ideologies to work for change;
- Cinematic communities, including those for film and the visual arts, and even users of smart phones who make their own videos to use when documenting the need for and advocating for change; and
- Business communities in which the corporate sector can become collaborators with public and nonprofit sectors to solve social problems, such as when United Way Worldwide was formed to encourage links between sectors.

Diversity and Difference in Practice

Behavior: Present themselves as learners, and engage clients and constituencies as experts of their own experiences.

Critical Thinking Question: How do the many conceptualizations of community assist change agents in working with diverse clients and constituencies?

We believe that social workers have a responsibility to recognize that community can be a powerful medium for enfranchisement and empowerment when its potential is understood and skillfully brought to life. We also believe that social workers must recognize that problems and needs can often be addressed more effectively by dealing with them collectively than they can by dealing with them individually.

Defining Community

One of the earliest efforts to conceptualize communities was the work of Ferdinand Tönnies (1887/1957), who discussed the constructs of *Gemeinschaft* and *Gesellschaft*. *Gemeinschaft*, which roughly translates as *community*, focuses on the mutual, intimate, and common bonds that pull people together in local units. These bonds are based on caring about one another and valuing the relationships in the group in and of themselves. The group is valued, regardless of whether its members are creating a product or achieving a goal. Examples are the domestic unit, the neighborhood, and groups of friends. The focus of *Gemeinschaft* is on intimacy and relationship.

In contrast, Tönnies' **Gesellschaft** refers generally to society or association. Examples of this concept are a city or government. *Gesellschaft* is an ideal type representing formalized relationships that are task oriented. In *Gesellschaft*-type relationships, people organize in a more formal way to achieve a purpose, task, or goal. Although they may benefit from the relationships that are established, the purpose of these social interactions is more restricted to accomplishing a particular end, creating some production, or completing some task.

Sociologists in the late 1800s viewed *Gesellschaft* as representing all the negative forces pulling people away from traditional communities built on institutions such as the family and religion. It is important to recognize, however, that the contribution of Tönnies' ideal types is to call attention to the differences between informal and formal systems and to the richness of their interactions. Social workers doing macro practice will find elements of both concepts in the communities with which they work. Tönnies' work is considered a foundation from which community theory emerged in the 1990s.

There are many definitions of community, and we will provide only a sample here. As early as the 1950s, one scholar identified over 90 discrete definitions of community in use within the social science literature (Hillery, 1955). Warren characterized community as (1) *space*, (2) *people*, (3) *shared values and institutions*, (4) *interaction*, (5) *distribution of power*, and (6) *social system*. Conceptualizations of community may be derived from each of these six themes. No matter what definition is selected, concepts such as *space*, *people*, *interaction*, and *shared identity* are repeated over and over again.

One of the most cited definitions of community was provided by Warren (1978), who viewed community as the organization of social activities that affords people access to what is necessary for day-to-day living, such as the school, grocery store, hospital, house of worship, and other such social units and systems. Many people customarily think of social units as beginning with the domestic unit, extending to the neighborhood or to a voluntary association, and expanding to larger spheres of human interaction. Community may or may not have clear boundaries, but it is significant because it performs important functions necessary for human survival.

Irrespective of the changes to be made in community arenas, the social worker will want to be aware of how persons affected by change define and perceive their communities. The social worker must understand alternative perspectives, recognize the assumptions and values that undergird these views, and understand how differing perspectives influence change opportunities (Gamble & Weil, 2010). It is also important to recognize that even persons within the same community will differ in their perspectives of what that community is and what changes are needed.

Communities can be formal or informal, and the variable that usually determines the level of formality is **boundary clarity**. Cities and counties have clear boundaries, whereas neighborhoods are often less clearly defined, and a community based on common interests of its members may not have geographical boundaries at all. The boundaries may be based on a common interest, a cause, and even personal or professional characteristics that transcend space. Not only does the clarity of boundaries vary across different communities, but also, as will be seen in later chapters, the presence of a formal boundary is often a key feature that differentiates organizations and communities.

Dimensions of Communities

Chaskin (2013) contends that community occurs around three dimensions: physical, social or relational, and political. First and most obvious is that people may come together in common physical locations (geography, space, place, or territory). The physical dimension encompasses geographical, spatial, or territorial communities that vary in how they meet people's needs, how social interactions are patterned, and how collective identity is perceived. Local communities are often called *neighborhoods*, *cities*, *towns*, *boroughs*, *parishes*, *barrios*, and a host of other terms. Smaller geographical spaces are nested within other communities, such as neighborhoods within towns or public housing developments within cities.

Warren (1978) identified the structure of internal and external patterns within geographical communities as horizontal and vertical community linkages. The **horizontal community** is geographically bounded and is represented by many linkages between and among organizations and neighborhoods that are located within the area and, in most cases, serve the community. For example, the local nursing home may work with the neighborhood school to develop an intergenerational program for residents and children. This effort may also include a local bookstore that provides children's books, a bus driver who provides transportation, and a staff member from the local multigenerational center. These types of collaborative efforts, which are becoming increasingly common, illustrate the importance of the horizontal community as a concept.

Vertical linkages connect community units (people, groups, and organizations) to units outside the community. These linkages are exemplified by a human service agency with its headquarters in a different community that uses Skype to see its members face-to-face, by local chapters virtually connected through shared information systems with state and national umbrella organizations, and by public agencies that have a central office external to the community from which they receive instruction. The concept of **vertical community** calls attention to the fact that many important decisions may be made by parent organizations outside the boundaries of the local community, and these decisions may or may not be in the best interests of the community.

In earlier times, before people were so mobile and technology transcended space, communities were much more horizontally bound. Today, however, considerations of space must be juxtaposed with other ways of conceptualizing community. Although one often operates within geographical jurisdictions, the influence of vertical forces beyond spatial boundaries is almost limitless.

Chaskin's (2013) second dimension is social or relational. Communities provide opportunities for interaction, making cultural connections, relationship building, and sharing common interests. Social patterns of social interaction can occur in geographical communities, but can also be part of "nonplace" communities (sometimes called *relational* or *associational communities*, *communities of affiliation* or *affinity*, or even *communities of the mind*). These nongeographical communities bring people together based on a variety of identifications and characteristics, including, for example, religion, race, or profession.

Fellin (2001) identified a collective, symbolic relationship that gives meaning to one's identity as a dimension of some place- and nonplace-based communities. In a complex society, people establish constellations of relationships that give meaning to their lives. Often viewed as networks (or webs) of formal and informal resources, it is important for the change agent to recognize, respect, and understand these relationships and what they mean to the person's "sense of community." Community, then, can be seen as those spaces, interactions, and identifications that people share with others in both place-specific and nonplace-specific locations.

Third, Chaskin (2013) indicates that communities can have a political dimension that bonds members together as they engage in action for the good of the community. Chaskin (2013) indicates that political, in this context, has a small (rather than a capital) "p" because it is intended to broadly encompass participation, deliberation, governance, and organizing activities that involve members in ongoing democratic processes and in being a part of civil society. In this last dimension, it is important to note that this coming together may be intentional or might even be facilitated by a change agent who points out what people have in common (Knickmeyer, Hopkins, & Meyer, 2003).

Collins (2010) argues that the concept of community should be reframed as a political construct because it is an arena in which systems of power interact and social inequalities become evident. Collins contends that community is essential to group identity that draws people together and can become the platform from which they join in seeking social change. Since community is such a versatile concept, it is associated with shared culture, race, nationality, ethnicity, religion, and a host of other factors that move people to celebrate their differences (and the power differentials) from other communities. The construct of community, whether imagined or real, has the potential to elicit strong feelings and is central to moving people to action. Thus, even though community may be seen as an apolitical term, even proclaimed nonpolitical communities are engaged in power relations within and among diverse communities.

The political dimension of communities is exemplified in what Gamble and Weil (2010) describe as functional communities, which are formed when people work as a group to jointly address social problems. For the social work practitioner, it is important to recognize and understand communities that are formed around shared concerns, such as AIDS, gun control, terrorism, disaster relief, and political loyalties. It is even more critical to recognize that these communities are formed around deeply held beliefs and values that may conflict with those of other communities.

A functional community may exist when many disparate individuals are working toward a goal or advocating for a cause. Those same individuals may not be aware of the existence of organizations formed to address that goal. In some instances, there may not yet be more formal groups formed to work in a more organized fashion. The change agent's task may therefore involve making members of functional communities aware of one another and furthering the transition from functional community to formal organization. Thus, functional communities may form advocacy organizations that are more structured, with formally stated objectives and the resources, such as volunteers and staff, to get things done (Almog-Bar & Schmid, 2014).

It is important to note that all three dimensions can coexist. For example, persons living in close proximity may develop strong relationships with one another and join together for change. In nongeographical communities, two dimensions may coexist. A professional community of social workers from around the state may develop close relationships and join forces to advocate for underserved population groups, thus bonding as a community through their commitment to change.

Table 5.1 provides a summary of the three dimensions, their definitions, and examples of each. The planned change model presented in later chapters will be applicable to both place and nonplace communities.

Table 5.1   Dimensions of Communities

Dimension of Community	Definition	Example
Space: A place in which one's needs for sustenance are met	A geographical community with defined boundaries where one expects to meet basic needs	A neighborhood in which families fulfill their basic needs and raise their children
Social: Interaction with others	A place or nonplace community of identification and interest	Relationships with others of the same ethnic group, regardless of location
Political: Participation, deliberation, governance, and organizing activities that involve members in a democratic process	Attaching importance to groups and organizations as a means of coming together to effect change	Identification with a religious group, a profession, or a cause for which one is willing to take action

Community Functions

Communities are structured to perform certain functions for their members. Warren (1978) identified five functions carried out by locality-relevant communities: (1) production, distribution, and consumption; (2) socialization; (3) social control; (4) social participation; and (5) mutual support.

Production, distribution, and consumption functions are community activities designed to meet people's material needs, including the most basic requirements, such as food, clothing, and shelter. In modern communities, families seldom produce most or all of what they consume. People are dependent on each other for these and other needs, including medical care, sanitation, employment, transportation, and recreation. The accepted medium of exchange for these goods and services is money, which becomes an important factor in defining the limits of consumption and comes into consideration in almost all community-change efforts.

A second function of community is **socialization** to the prevailing norms, traditions, and values of community members. Socialization guides attitudinal development, and these attitudes and perceptions influence how people view themselves, others, and their interpersonal rights and responsibilities. Attitudes and values also differ from community to community, and they vary across smaller communities that are nested within larger ones. To understand an individual or population, it is therefore critical to understand the norms, traditions, and values of the community or communities in which the person was socialized.

Social control is the process by which community members ensure compliance with norms and values. This is usually done by establishing laws, rules, and regulations, as well as systems for their enforcement. Social control is often performed by diverse institutions such as government, education, religion, and social services. Many social workers serve in practice settings in which they must constantly strive to balance their sometimes conflicting roles as helpers and agents of social control. Examples of such settings include schools, correctional institutions, probation and parole offices, and employment and training programs.

Communities may also exert subtle forms of social control through patterns of service distribution and eligibility criteria that regulate access to resources on the part of vulnerable groups. For example, case managers often find they must deny services due to limited resources. Recognizing how social control can occur both overtly and covertly can be disillusioning, but it is necessary for understanding both the impact of community values and the process of service delivery.

Social participation includes interaction with others in community groups, associations, and organizations. People are assumed to need some form of social outlet, and communities provide opportunities for people to express this need and to build natural helping and support networks. Some find their outlets in local religious groups, some in civic organizations, and some in informal neighborhood groups. Understanding the opportunities and patterns of social participation in a target population is helpful in assessing how well a community is meeting the needs of its members.

Mutual support is the function that families, friends, partners, neighbors, volunteers, and professionals carry out in communities when they care for the sick, the unemployed, and the distressed. As noted in Chapter 2, processes such as industrialization, urbanization, and increased mobility strained the capacity of traditional community units (e.g., families, faith groups, and civic organizations) to meet the mutual-support needs of community members. This led to the growth of different community units, such as helping professionals and government-sponsored programs, that took over some of the roles previously left to informal and smaller scale units.

Building on Warren's (1978) work, Pantoja and Perry (1998) provided a working model of community development and restoration. Citing production, distribution, and consumption as the economic areas on which all other functions are dependent, they identify the remaining community functions as socialization, social control, social placement (participation), mutual support, defense, and communication. Defense and communication are additions to Warren's original list.

Defense is the way in which the community takes care of and protects its members. This function becomes important in communities that are unsafe and dangerous. Some communities have been labeled **defended communities** when they have to focus unusual amounts of effort toward looking after their members. The defense function can also be relevant to nonplace communities. One example is that defense is often critical among gay or lesbian persons because there are groups within the larger society that may seek to do them harm. Similarly, people of color in various communities have had to support one another in defending themselves against the effects of racial hatred.

Communication includes the use of a common language and symbols to express ideas. Although communication may be assumed as part of all functions originally identified by Warren, its identification as a separate function in contemporary society is important. As one example, debate about whether and how forcefully English proficiency should be demanded of immigrants has been a prominent aspect of the broader controversy over immigration in the United States. Similarly, the ability to communicate easily across the country and around the world through email and other rapidly expanding features of the Internet has vastly expanded the definition of community while simultaneously blurring its boundaries.

Table 5.2 provides an overview of community functions.

Functional definitions and understandings of community can also be useful in communities that are not geographically specific. For example, some people may have their communication needs met by keeping in touch with persons in different geographical areas. It is not unusual to have adult children of parents

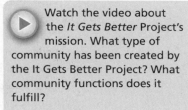

Watch the video about the *It Gets Better* Project's mission. What type of community has been created by the It Gets Better Project? What community functions does it fulfill?

www.youtube.com/watch?v=3lYv1__mSpE

Table 5.2   Functions of Community

Function	Definition	Example
Production, distribution, and consumption	The areas on which all other functions are dependent	Small businesses that provide jobs and goods to a community
Socialization	Learning the prevailing norms, traditions, and values	Understanding how community members perceive their roles vis-à-vis local government
Social control	Ensuring compliance with norms and values	How law enforcement is administered
Social placement	Participation in activities significant to the life of the community	The extent to which parents participate in school-related functions
Mutual Support	Functions carried out in support of each other	The ways in which a community cares for its homeless population
Defense	The way a community takes care of and protects its members	Block watch programs
Communication	Use of a common language to express ideas	The extent to which English proficiency is demanded of immigrant families

Source: Based on the work of Warren (1978) and Pantoja and Perry (1998).

who live miles apart calling daily to check on how their parents are doing. In professional communities, long-distance communication is carried out via telephone, fax, email, or text messaging on a regular basis. However, communication in this form requires access to the technology. In many communities this access is uneven, leading to what has been called **information poverty**. These communities are taking steps such as wiring whole cities for wireless Internet (McNutt, Queiro-Tajalli, Boland, & Campbell, 2001).

When Community Functions Fail

If all functions were performed in a given community in a manner that met the needs of all its members, the community would be considered optimally structured. However, such an "ideal" community probably does not exist. This may be due to inadequate resources for distribution and consumption or to uneven distribution. Socialization may be tied to values imposed by some community members on others but not mutually shared. The social control function may not operate in an evenhanded manner and may even be oppressive. Social participation opportunities may be severely limited, or they may be available to some but not others. Mutual support functions may be undermined by a dominant value system that assumes individuals should be able to fend for themselves. Communication may be limited for members who do not have access to technology. In the case of communities caught between opposing forces in violent confrontations, adequate defense may not be available to protect residents. In short, communities can be considered *healthy* or *unhealthy*, *functional* or *dysfunctional*, and *competent* or *incompetent* based on their ability to meet community needs. This may be particularly true for oppressed populations within their boundaries. We hasten to say that rarely do we find a community that can be labeled so easily one way or another. Most communities are somewhere along a continuum between these pairs of descriptors.

The assumption underlying the identification of functions is that communities serve the needs of members by performing these functions well. Conversely, when communities are dysfunctional, people suffer and change needs to occur. According to Pantoja and Perry (1998), without a stable economic base, the other functions, which are supportive, deteriorate or are impaired. Therefore, it is important for the social worker to carefully assess how communities are functioning and how the needs of people are or are not being addressed.

> **?** Assess your understanding of conceptualizing community by taking this brief quiz.

COMMUNITY THEORIES

Roland Warren's (1978) text on community synthesized the theories that existed up to the early 1970s and provided a valuable resource for identifying studies conducted up to that time. **Theories** are sets of interrelated concepts that explain how and why something works or does not work for the purpose of enhancing one's understanding. Sociological theories of community often describe how communities function. These **descriptive approaches** assist in analyzing what is happening within communities but do not provide the practitioner with methods to change a situation once it has been analyzed. Systems; human or population ecology; human behavior; and power, politics, and change theories will be discussed as sociological theories that assist in understanding how communities function. In contrast, a variety of community **practice perspectives and models** are intended to provide direction or guidance for persons wanting to change or intervene in a community arena. We will focus on strengths, empowerment, and resiliency perspectives, as well as **capacity building** and **asset mapping**, as guides to practice. These **prescriptive approaches** are how-to guides for taking action.

Table 5.3 presents a general guide for distinguishing descriptive and prescriptive approaches, categorized by the use of these theories, perspectives, and models in place-based (geographical) and nonplace-based communities. Note that some approaches are helpful in analyzing both types of communities, whereas others are more geographically based.

Systems Theories

Building on the work of Talcott Parsons (1971) and others, Warren (1978) applied social systems theory to communities. His description shows how the functions identified earlier are typically performed by various groups and organizations within local

Table 5.3 Types of Theories and Perspectives by Place and Nonplace Communities

Types of Theories/Perspectives	Place-Based (Geographical) Communities	Nonplace-Based Communities
Descriptive (to understand communities)	Systems theories Human or population ecology Human behavior Power, politics, and change	Systems theories Human behavior Power, politics, and change
Prescriptive (to guide practice)	Strengths, empowerment, and resiliency perspectives Asset mapping and capacity building	Strengths, empowerment, and resiliency perspectives Capacity building

communities. The planned change model in this book is also based predominately on systems theory, and our discussion of organizations in Chapter 7 will also include information on systems theory.

Boundary maintenance is part of systems theory. Establishing boundaries is critical to system survival. If boundaries become blurred or indistinguishable, the community as a spatial set of relationships may become less viable. For example, as religious congregations in local communities contract with government agencies to provide services to persons in need, the boundaries between what is an agency and a ministry may blur. Moreover, boundaries between long-established, faith-related, nonprofit organizations and congregations within the same faith may begin to overlap in unanticipated ways. Nongovernmental organizations (NGOs) may be so subsidized by government dollars that they become quasi-governmental more than nongovernmental in their orientation. Macro practitioners will witness the struggle for boundary maintenance in their work with communities and organizations. For instance, residents in a neighborhood that has just altered school attendance boundaries may face major changes in how they view their community. The annexation of previously unincorporated areas into the city limits may bring protesters to city hall. The reconfiguration of a planning and service area that alters agency's boundaries may mean that clients formerly considered part of one's community will no longer be eligible for service.

Boundary maintenance has a number of ramifications. First, from a systems perspective, it means that communities are open rather than closed systems, and they are dependent on their external environment for certain resources. Second, not only horizontal but also vertical affiliations and interactions are critical for the community to function properly, and both must be understood in order to have a clear grasp of how the community operates. Third, just as certain groups or organizations play specific roles in carrying out essential community tasks, the community must carve out a role for itself in its larger environment that allows it to provide resources needed by other communities in return for acquiring the resources it needs.

Boundary setting and maintenance are critical to any system's survival. As boundaries become blurred or indistinguishable, the community as a spatial set of relationships weakens and becomes less able to fulfill its core functions. Boundaries are also important to systems within a community, and macro practitioners may often be able to witness diverse examples of the struggle for boundary maintenance in their work (Norlin & Chess, 1997). Youth gangs battling over neighborhood turf offer an obvious locality-based example of boundary conflicts, but others, such as efforts by gay and lesbian residents to secure legal recognition and benefits for their partners, may be less recognizable but are nonetheless boundary issues (Hash & Netting, 2007).

It is important, then, to recognize that there are multiple approaches to analyzing macro situations based on systems theory that can also be used for deeper understandings of how communities function. These include mechanical, organismic, morphogenic, factional, and catastrophic analogies (Burrell & Morgan, 1979; Martin & O'Connor, 1989).

A **mechanical analogy** views a social system as a machine in which all the parts work closely together, are well coordinated, and integrate smoothly. When one part of the system changes, it is expected that other parts will adapt to reestablish equilibrium. In this analogy, order is emphasized over change and conflict. If the practitioner approaches a community using this analogy, his or her task will be seen primarily as one of reducing conflict and restoring a sense of order, connectedness, and mutual purpose. For example, a local community whose members are comfortable with their lifestyles would be disrupted by an influx of immigrants from other cultures who represent difference. Instead of welcoming immigrants, the community members may impose strict boundaries, not be welcoming to outsiders, and work toward maintaining the status quo.

The **organismic analogy** comes from comparing social systems to biological organisms. Communities are viewed much like the human body, with each organ having a different function. This may sound familiar, given our discussion of community functions earlier in this chapter. Assuming that each unit within the community performs its respective role, the organismic analogy predicts that community members will work toward a common good. Parsons' (1971) work on structural-functionalism is primarily grounded in this analogy. It argues that structures arise to serve particular functions, and within the range of normal variability they should allow the community as a whole to function effectively and for community members to agree on what needs to happen. In practice, however, social workers often discover that consensus among diverse community members can be elusive. For example, immigrants coming into this type of community may find that they are cautiously welcomed, but only if they behave in ways that fully acculturate them into established community norms and maintain a sense of stability. As long as they agree to play by the established rules, conflict will be kept to a minimum (at least on the surface).

This leads to the question of what happens when there is conflict that cannot be overlooked, when there is seemingly no articulation of the parts or performance of the functions, or when harmony cannot be restored or perhaps never really existed. In this case, other analogies may need to be explored.

A **morphogenic analogy** is applicable when change is ongoing and the structure of the system is continually emerging. Fundamental change can occur in this type of situation because there may be no chance of returning to a former state of **homeostasis** (balance or equilibrium). This highly open approach to systems thinking means that change may be just as likely to be unpredictable as it is to be orderly. It is this unpredictability that requires the community practitioner to be open to clues about how things are changing and to be open to new possibilities. For example, immigrants arriving in this community can expect some conflict as community members adjust to one another's differences. Expectations will be that the community will change in some ways, and that the acceptable way to incorporate new members into the community will be through open dialogue and recognizing that the community will be changed in the process.

Similar to the morphogenic analogy is the **factional analogy** in which contentiousness in a community system is open and obvious. Conflict may be so basic in some community systems that change is likely to remain disorderly and subject to instability. Approaching this type of system with assumptions that order can be reestablished may be a setup for failure. On the other hand, for the practitioner who can face conflict head-on, this type of community can be a stimulating challenge. Immigrants relocating to a factional community will find local groups in disagreement over how to handle their integration. Conflict will be a normal part of this community's operation, and groups will be trying to convince one another about what approaches should be taken. There will be no attempt to deny that change can be disruptive, and debates over the pros and cons of immigration will be ongoing, sometimes heated.

Last, a **catastrophic analogy** is defined by contentiousness and conflict taken to extremes. Such a community system will be characterized by deep fissures and distress. Without order or predictability, there will be a sense of chaos in which no one can determine future directions. Communication may have broken down in the process, and subsystems are warring. Intervention in this type of community would look different than it would from mechanical or organismic analogies. In catastrophic communities, there will be protests about how to handle immigration and what course the country (and communities) should take with the volatile issues surrounding immigration. The volatility might even lead to violence.

Our point is that, depending on one's assessment of the community system and the degree of conflict, interventions will vary greatly, and in the case of immigration there will be much variation—from wanting to keep immigrants from relocating to a community all the way to full-blown conflict over how immigration should be handled. Gallo (2013) points out how important it is to recognize the complexity in systemic thinking, particularly when one is witnessing conflict. Conflicts exist in local, regional, and international contexts; change over time; and have unintended consequences. We believe that social workers must embrace a mindset that expects complexity and is open to systematically reevaluating conditions and problems.

In addition, it is important to recognize that communities are larger systems and that different views may coexist. Groups, organizations, and associations within the same community may embrace different analogies. See Table 5.4 for a summary of types of systems theory.

Strengths and Weaknesses

Warren's work (1978) synthesized early research on communities, brought a systems perspective to the sociology of the community in the United States, and provided a framework for analyzing ways in which communities can fail in fulfilling one or more of their key functions. There are lessons that systems theory offers to community practice. Hardina (2002) calls attention to four: (1) Changes in one aspect of a system produce alterations in other parts of the community, (2) actions in community subunits influence what happens not only within the unit but also within the larger system, (3) being able to identify how well a community functions means being able to compare its effectiveness with other communities, and (4) the push to return to a steady state in which everyone can participate in community life becomes a driving force in systems theory (pp. 49–50).

As with any approach, systems theory has its critics, and their concerns often focus on the use of mechanical and organismic analogies through which assumptions are made about parts of systems working together to the benefit of the whole. Assumptions about common purposes, it is argued, ignore the role of unexplained change, conflict, and situations in which community members not only disagree but also are deeply divided. These mechanical and organismic analogies are viewed as focused on preservation of the status quo and incremental change, even in the case of unresponsive or oppressive community structures desperately in need of correction. Applying the analogies inappropriately in this way is seen as a refusal to recognize the role of conflict and struggles for power inherent in community life (Martin & O'Connor, 1989). However, as pointed out earlier, there are other analogies of systems theory that do recognize conflict and change.

Table 5.4 Summary of System Analogies and Assumptions

Analogy	Assumptions
Mechanical	Sees the system as a machine
	Assumes all parts work well together in an integrated manner
	Focuses on order over instability
	Avoids conflict if possible
	Maintains the status quo
Organismic	Sees the system as a biological unit (e.g., the human body)
	Assumes each part will perform its prescribed function
	Focuses on making adjustments to maintain equilibrium
	Keeps conflict to a minimum
	Engages in incremental change if needed
Morphogenic	Assumes system must adjust to change (morphing)
	Assumes there is no chance of returning to a former state of homeostasis
	Focuses on adjusting to unpredictability
	Expects conflict
	Is open to new possibilities
Factional	Sees system as composed of competing factions
	Assumes system is rapidly changing
	Expects contentiousness among units within the system
	Sees conflict as inevitable and ongoing
	Assumes that factions will constantly be disrupting
Catastrophic	Sees system as having no recognizable order
	Views change as the only constant
	Is characterized by deep distress
	Sees no sense of order
	Emphasizes chaos over stability

Sources: Adapted from Martin and O'Connor (1989) and Burrell and Morgan (1979).

Even in systems approaches that view disagreements and clashes of viewpoints and interests as parts of human communities, on the whole, systems theory does not focus on power and politics. It provides limited understanding for community practitioners who must face uncertain dynamics among diverse participants. It also fails to explain how to engage community members, how to communicate, or how to use systems concepts to bring about change. Therefore, practice models derived from this theory base must draw from other human behavior theories and perspectives in guiding practitioners about power and politics, group dynamics, and interpersonal communication.

Stanfield (1993) suggests that it is critical to revise sociological concepts that view communities through the lens of structural-functionalism and processes such

Box 5.1 Systems Theory	
Strengths	**Weaknesses**
Changes in one aspect of community produce changes in others.	Assumptions about common purposes ignore many considerations, including disagreements and deep divisions.
Actions in subunits affect the larger community.	Mechanical and organismic analogies are often viewed as preserving the status quo.
Assessing community functions involves comparisons to other communities.	Systems models provide limited understanding of power and politics.
A push to return to a steady state becomes a driving force.	Structural-functionalism and socialization promote a monocultural system perspective that views newly created structures as deviant.

as socialization. He contends that this orientation promotes a **monocultural system perspective** that treats conflict as though it were something deviant. This leads to a view in which communities, associations, and structures created by population groups that do not conform to these accepted standards are seen as underdeveloped, dysfunctional, and pathological rather than as novel, inventive, and understandable responses on the part of segments of a community that have not been well served by its institutions or other members. Thus, systems theory seen from a strictly mechanistic or organismic viewpoint is focused on retaining social structure and function in which change is to be kept to a minimum. Obviously this is the antithesis of what social work practice is all about.

Box 5.1 summarizes the strengths and weaknesses of systems theory.

Human, Population, or Social Ecology Theories

Closely aligned with systems theorists are **human, population, or social ecology** theorists, who also examine structural patterns and relationships within place-based communities. In the mid-1930s, a group of sociologists under the leadership of Robert E. Park at the University of Chicago examined local community spatial relationships. Human ecology theory emerged from this work, and is based on plant and animal ecology, which in turn has roots in Darwin's biological determinism. It was elaborated in the work of Hawley (1950, 1968).

Early human ecologists believed that if they studied one city well enough, they could apply principles of what they learned to most other cities. However, subsequent studies in other metropolitan areas revealed just how difficult it is to generalize. Other cities did not always show the same structural patterns.

Today, ecological theorists focus on the interaction of resident characteristics (e.g., age, gender, and race), the use of physical space (e.g., housing and land use), and the social structures, organizations, and technology within communities. An ecological approach views communities as highly interdependent, teeming with changing relationships among populations of people and organizations (Bessant, 2014). Thus, communities are social systems in which there are subsystems nested within other systems in what has been called a social ecosystem dance (Conn, 2011). For example, social workers have long studied issues of homelessness and inadequate housing in various communities, but research on home ownership possibilities for people with disabilities has been limited. Quinn (2004) reported on programs designed to offer home ownership possibilities for disabled community residents. From an ecological perspective, people with disabilities have often been confined to institutional or group home settings, whereas people without disabilities have had more freedom to choose their housing types. Social workers, however, can educate local communities about such possibilities as Home of Your Own Coalitions and work to change the relationship between resident characteristics, the use of physical space, and how the social structure of communities can integrate people who are disabled.

Human ecologists are particularly concerned about how place-based communities deal with the processes of **competition**, **centralization**, **concentration**, **integration**, and **succession** (Fellin, 2001). For example, a social worker might need to know the history of a new immigrant group coming into a city. Initially, the group may concentrate in a particular area and compete for particular types of jobs in order to establish an economic foothold. At first, they may need to turn inward for mutual support and are isolated due to language barriers. They may also become highly segregated, unlikely to take advantage of existing services, and hard to engage even with diligent outreach efforts. Gradually—often only over generations—they integrate, and a new group moves in and succession occurs as a new cycle begins.

For a summary of human ecology characteristics and issues, see Table 5.5.

Advances in depicting these processes in geographical communities have paralleled the development of management information systems in organizations. **Geographic information systems** (GIS) use data to develop maps and graphics as tools to analyze local communities. Of particular relevance to social service providers, planners, and researchers is the ability to make thematic maps of their communities, geocode addresses, and perform spatial queries and analyses. Social workers can learn to extract and map census variables such as race, poverty, language, education, and health, as well as many other demographic variables, identifying concentrations of need in their communities

Engagement

Behavior: Apply knowledge of human behavior and the social environment, person-in-environment, and other multidisciplinary theoretical frameworks to engage with clients and constituencies.

Critical Thinking Question: What kinds of contextual factors may strongly shape an individual's actions within a community?

Table 5.5   Human Ecology Characteristics and Issues

Human Ecology	Characteristics	Issues
Individual units of a population are in competition, but also must cooperate to ensure that the community can support all its inhabitants (including plant, animal, and human life).	An organized population, rooted in the soil it occupies, and mutually interdependent on other inhabitants.	• Competition vs. cooperation • Centralization vs. decentralization • Concentration vs. dispersion • Segregation vs. integration • Succession vs. status quo

(Case & Hawthorne, 2013; Hillier, 2007; Rine, Morales, Vanyukevych, Durand, & Schroeder, 2012).

Strengths and Weaknesses

Human and population ecologists are cousins of systems theorists. They share the goal of finding ways in which systems can become more harmonious and work better together. However, unlike their systems counterparts, these theorists recognize competition as an ongoing process for which conflict is an inevitable companion. Hardina (2002) identified three community practice implications of ecological theory: (1) recognition that community groups are competing for limited resources, with survival of those in power; (2) realization that groups without power must adapt; and (3) acknowledgment that social structures are heavily influenced by the physical environment, and changes in the physical can make a difference in the social.

Salimath and Jones (2011) reviewed studies conducted on organizational populations within communities, focusing on the convergence of population ecology theory with sustainability practice. They pointed out that as new groups or populations of organizations are born or cease to be part of a community, population ecology theory does not explain the nature of adaptability or fully acknowledge the diversity among population members. Without this understanding, the theory may describe the dynamics among populations but fail to provide direction in how to intervene as changes are occurring. What is missing is an understanding of what to do to encourage sustainability.

The recognition of relationships and their dynamics must be translated into guidelines for practice. Although competition is acknowledged and ecological theorists recognize power dynamics, they do not provide guidance for how to gain power for groups who do not currently have it. More importantly, assumptions that the physical environment influences social structures are somewhat deterministic, leaving the practitioner to wonder if an individual or even a group has the potential to make change within environments that are not conducive to the desired changes. Thus, like some systems theorists, human ecologists could be accused of being inherently conservative and somewhat fatalistic in assuming that populations and sets of organizations must find ways to adjust within resistant environments.

Box 5.2 summarizes the strengths and weaknesses of human or population ecology theory.

Box 5.2 Human or Population Ecology Theory	
Strengths	**Weaknesses**
Recognition that community groups are competing for limited resources	No guidance for how to gain power for groups that do not have it or for how to encourage sustainability
Realization that groups without power must adapt	Implication that physical environment essentially determines the social structure, leaving little potential for change and adaptability
Recognition that the physical environment and social structures are interrelated	Considered by some as conservative and inherently somewhat fatalistic, assuming that there must be accommodation to existing environments

Human Behavior Theories

Parallel to the focus on space, structure, function, and relationships among systems are the issues of how people behave in communities—how they understand and find meaning in relationships, what values guide their actions, and how their needs are determined. There are many ways to examine these factors, and we will address only a few here: interactions and values, collective identity, and needs.

Human behavior theories help social workers better understand why people do what they do, and this understanding is important to skilled practice. Whether communities are place or nonplace based, they are composed of human beings with multiple ways of viewing the meaning of interactions. When social work practitioners interact with community members, they are engaged in direct practice at the macro level.

Interactions and Values

Beginning with rural communities and then expanding to urban environments, early anthropologists and sociologists explored how people related to one another. The Lynds' 1929 study of Middletown and its 1937 follow-up provided a cultural-anthropological view of a small U.S. city (Lynd & Lynd, 1929, 1937). A subsequent study by West (1945) of the fictitiously named Plainville, Illinois, was similar to the Lynds' effort. The anthropological approach to community favored by the Lynds and West attempted to understand the daily lives of people, their behavior patterns, and their belief systems. What emerged from these and other case studies was recognition of the deeply held values that are inherent in community life.

Cohen (1985) viewed the community as rich with values, ideologies, and symbols that people have in common with one another but that also distinguish them from those who hold different beliefs. For example, the colors worn by a youth may symbolize certain values not easily recognized by someone who is not part of a particular culture. But wearing those colors into another community in which the colors are viewed as hostile can incite gang violence.

This relational view of community implies boundaries that are not necessarily tied to place. Boundaries may be physical, but they may also be racial, ethnic, linguistic, or religious. Boundaries may be perceptual and may even vary among those who are part of the same relational community, just as persons who are not part of that community will perceive boundaries differently. Cohen (1985) explains that it is not the clarity of boundaries that are important (for they are always changing), but it is what the boundary symbolizes that is most crucial.

A concept that is gaining particular attention for explaining interaction is **social capital**. Social capital refers to the store of beliefs, values, and practices that are adhered to by members of a community or society and that contribute to the well-being of all. A community with high social capital, for instance, would be expected to have low crime rates because the majority of persons perceive the benefits of not preying on each other. Like economic capital (e.g., investable funds) or human capital (e.g., education or expertise), social capital is a measurable resource that can be considered part of the wealth of a community. A growing body of research suggests that greater social capital is associated with lower levels of poverty (Sun, Rehnberg, & Meng, 2009), lower mortality (Hutchinson,

Putt, Dean, Long, Montagnet, & Armstrong, 2009), increased self-esteem and coping ability (Wahl, Bergland, & Løyland, 2010), more negative attitudes toward violence (Kelly, Rasu, Lesser, Oscos-Sanchez, Mancha, & Orriega, 2010), and many other variables. The role of social workers can be seen as preserving and promoting social capital, but there is a lack of consensus as to what it is or how it can be increased (Lohmann, 2014).

Interactional field theorists hold different assumptions from social capital theorists. Whereas social capital theory is premised on norms of reciprocity and trust, field interaction focuses on building relationships and creating structures to support collective goals. Interactionalists view social capital as a possible by-product of community fields as they emerge, rather than as a preexisting condition. The **field-interactional perspective** is elaborated by Bessant (2014) as a significant way to analyze change dynamics in both place and nonplace communities. A **social field** is an interactional process in which a sense of unity emerges as individual efforts turn toward collective action with common goals. In a social field, individuals' ideas and commitment come together in concerted efforts, and when a number of social fields overlap, a **community action field** emerges. One could say that as social fields interact and explore common ground, a community action field gains momentum. Bessant (2014) identifies several factors that contribute to the building of a community action field: (1) a confluence of awareness about potential connections or links among social fields, (2) making efforts to cooperate despite different interests, (3) developing long-term plans targeting community goals, (4) calls for participation that enhance cohesion, and (5) locating resources to move forward with a comprehensive agenda (Bessant, 2014). As this building process occurs, one can see how norms of reciprocity and trust would develop, eventually tapping into participants' social capital. Lohmann (2014) refers to this process as **voluntary action**, occurring when collective action or group behavior occurs outside the confines of the market or government and away from the privacy of the domestic unit. Voluntary action comes together within the **new commons**, a term used to describe the third or voluntary sector in which collective identity gains momentum.

Collective Identity

Clark (1973) proposes stepping back from the structural approaches to community and looking at the psychological ties that bind people in community. He suggests that community may be thought of as a shared sense of solidarity based on psychological identification with others. Going beyond social interactions, community rests in a sense of *we-ness* that either can be place specific or can transcend place. This approach lends itself to evaluating a community by measuring the strength of its members' perceived solidarity. This can be done whether the community is locality based, as in a neighborhood, town, or city, or whether it is affiliation based, as in a community formed by supporters of a political cause or members of an online chat group.

MacNair, Fowler, and Harris (2000) recognized the psychological ties characteristic of communities in large social movements. Building on the work of Helms (1984), they developed a framework of diversity functions common to three movements by groups seeking greater equality in society: the African American Movement, the Women's Movement, and the Lesbian, Gay, and Bisexual Movement. These six functions are **assimilation**, **normative antidiscrimination**, **militant direct action**, **separatism**, **introspective self-help**, and **pluralistic integration** (p. 73). They represent approaches to organized change that reveal how different people identify with nonplace communities for different purposes.

Needs

Amid these community interactions and values, community members have needs. Abraham Maslow (1962) developed a hierarchical framework for understanding human needs and factors that motivate human behavior. His hierarchy positions the most basic survival or physiological needs (e.g., food and water) at the base of a pyramid-shaped figure. One level above these needs are safety and security needs, followed by social or belonging needs, esteem or ego needs, and then self-actualization needs at the highest level.

In Maslow's model, lower level needs must be addressed before an individual can move to the next level. Anytime a lower level need is not being met, the person regresses down the hierarchy to satisfy that unmet need. Lower level needs usually require a more immediate response and thus have higher urgency. Maslow also reminds us that a satisfied need is not a motivator. Later, Maslow distinguished between self-actualizers and self-transcenders, with the later having a calling beyond themselves. This framework can be useful in assessing the needs of a target population, which can then be used to determine the adequacy of services available to them in the community. The assessment task is one of defining more specifically the problems faced by the target population at each level and identifying the extent of met and unmet need in relation to each problem. In addition, it may be helpful to engage organizers who can self-transcend in responding to the needs of others.

In discussing a community development perspective, Pantoja and Perry (1998) offer a slightly different view of human needs and dimensions. Their list of needs includes:

- **Basic biological needs** to have food, shelter, and clothing for survival and protection
- **Secondary biological needs** to have love, belonging, and identity as a human being
- **Social needs** to engage in relationships, mutual aid, and support
- **Cultural needs** to use language, norms, values, and customs
- **Historical needs** to record the past and to use the past to explore the future
- **Political needs** to gain power, order, and control
- **Creative/spiritual needs** to use words, movements, and art to explain the unknown
- **Intellectual needs** to explore the nature of the environment, to investigate, and to experiment (Pantoja & Perry, 1998, p. 227)

Theoretically, Pantoja and Perry provide a multidisciplinary typology that reveals the complexity of human needs within a social context. Their original intent was to provide a sociological approach to analysis that would lead to deep understandings, primarily of minority communities. But their ultimate intent was to build on this understanding so that these types of needs, once understood, could be addressed. Thus, their theoretical approach, which we have described, is designed to evolve one's understanding of diverse needs into a working model in which each human need is evaluated in light of how well community services and institutions function in meeting it.

Table 5.6 Human Behavior Theories: Foci and Findings

Human Behavior Theories	Focus	Findings
Interactions and values	The daily lives of people; behavior patterns and belief systems.	Deeply held values are inherent in some communities. Collective action fields emerge from social fields and tap into social capital.
	Values bind people together but also distinguish them from those who hold different values.	It is not the clarity of boundaries that is important; it is the symbolic aspect of the boundary created by common values.
Collective identity	The psychological ties that bind people within a community.	People feel a *sense of community* and a *we-ness* when there are psychological ties.
Needs	Understanding needs in a hierarchy from lower order needs to higher order needs.	Higher-order needs cannot be met until lower-order needs are satisfied.

In summary, Table 5.6 provides an overview of human behavior theories, their foci, and findings.

Strengths and Weaknesses

Human behavior theories examine how communities are formed and shaped by factors that motivate human actions. These include the drive to meet basic needs, the drive to affiliate, and the need to be guided by shared values once interactions reach a sufficient level of complexity. Without insight into why people feel and act as they do, community practitioners may see only the big picture, missing critical clues that will make the difference in whether trust and relationship can be established. For example, on one hand, the term *social capital* has become so overused that it may be taken for granted that trust and reciprocity are readily accessible. On the other hand, field interactionists would say that it is critical to understand and study the dynamics of interaction through which trust and reciprocity emerge to release social capital.

Human behavior theories look at the individual or the actions of individuals with others. However, critics of these theories caution that human beings are not robots and that actions are situational. Viewing needs, values, interactions, and relationships without a contextual understanding can lead to misunderstandings about what certain behaviors mean. Theories that focus on individuals must be used with an eye to context so that the person-in-environment is paramount. A related criticism concerns the unit of analysis. Human behavior theories take the position that, if one wants to understand the behavior of communities, one must understand what motivates the behavior of individuals. If one can accurately predict how one member will behave in a given circumstance, it is suggested that one can then predict the likely path to be taken by a collection of actors following the same rules. The argument is that the whole is greater than the sum of the parts, so comparing whole community systems to one another and examining which differences between them predict which actions could be seen as a better approach than focusing on the individual's behavior.

Box 5.3 summarizes the strengths and weaknesses of human behavior theory.

Box 5.3	Human Behavior Theories
Strengths	**Weaknesses**
Examine how communities are formed and shaped by factors that motivate human behavior	Fail to provide a contextual understanding necessary to interpreting behaviors
Help to move past the "big picture" orientation of other theories and pick up on critical factors in the human interrelationships within a community	Often ignore the critical person-in-environment perspective Sometimes overgeneralize from the individual to the collective

Theories about Power, Politics, and Change

Given the diversity within communities, the focus of much of the literature has been on the process by which communities create and build bonds among people. However, it is important to recognize political and social dynamics within communities as powerful forces that can be oppressive as well as supportive.

In her community practice work, Hardina (2002) reviews three theories related to the acquisition of power: power dependency theory, conflict theory, and resource mobilization theory. **Power dependency theory** marks a shift in how sociologists think about power. Originally seen as a personal characteristic, Emerson (1962) conceived power as characteristic of a relationship. The relationship could be between groups or individuals or between a group and an individual, but he shifted the unit of analysis from individuals to relationships. Given this relational focus, there are implications for community practice: (1) Dependence upon others for resources determines the distribution of power in relationships, (2) even if it is not exercised, power is perceived and remains a motivator in relationships, and (3) change occurs within exchange relationships in which people feel obligated to conform when resources have been obtained. In other words, units within local communities become "beholden" to one another and to external sources of resources.

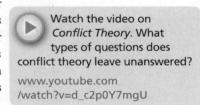

Watch the video on *Conflict Theory*. What types of questions does conflict theory leave unanswered?

www.youtube.com /watch?v=d_c2p0Y7mgU

Conflict theory typically views the community as divided into haves and have-nots, all competing for limited resources. A neo-Marxist view of conflict theory is that social services fulfill a social control function, providing just enough resources to keep the voices of dissent from becoming louder and maintaining the status quo (Hasenfeld, 2010). This casts social workers in the role of social control agents. Alternately, a perspective arising from the work of Alinsky (1971, 1974) might place social workers in the role of organizers who use unexpected sources of power in the hands of the have-nots to upset those in decision-making positions. Hardina (2002, p. 55) identifies basic assumptions of conflict theory: (1) There is competition for resources, (2) the haves hold power over the have-nots, (3) oppression comes largely from the isms (e.g., racism and classism), and (4) government as well as other vehicles of decision making are controlled by the haves. Conflict theory accepts the view that communities may be usefully analyzed in terms of who holds power and how it is applied (Collins, 2010), but it goes further in stating that differences in power and access to resources between the haves and have-nots inevitably lead to conflict and require an understanding of how to manage conflict in order to effect change.

Resource mobilization theory draws from both conflict and power dependency theories to address social movements and the reasons they occur (Benford & Snow, 2000). In order to mobilize, a collective identity must develop (noted earlier in this chapter in the "Human Behavior Theories" section). Nkomo and Taylor (1996) summarized several theories that describe collective identity, including embedded group theory, social identity theory, race/gender research, organization demography, and ethnology (p. 340). Identity group members have common characteristics, have shared histories, and have even experienced some of the same environmental changes. In communities and organizations, identity group membership precedes organizational group membership. Nkomo and Taylor contended that identity must be understood as a complicated concept since individuals have multiple identities that may intersect into an amalgamated identity. Thus, when individuals come together as a community group, their identity (like all others) is constructed rather than something with which they were born. Collective identity then emerges and can change as context changes (Seck & Helton, 2014).

Table 5.7 provides a quick overview of power dependency, conflict, and resource mobilization theory.

Understanding the Politics of Community Diversity

In Chapter 4, we discussed a framework called the *dual perspective*, which viewed the individual in a nurturing system that functions within the context of a larger sustaining system. The *nurturing system* is made up of those traditions and informal relationships in which the individual feels most familiar. The *sustaining system* is made up of traditions,

---

Table 5.7   Themes and Implications of Power, Politics, and Change Theories

Power, Politics, and Change Theories	Themes	Implications for Community Organizing
Power dependency theory	Organizations and communities are dependent on resources, often from outside sources.	• Consumers may limit change for fear of offending resource providers. • Change may be limited to boundaries established within the relationship. • Funding sources and providers of other resources external to the community may limit change.
Conflict theory	The community is divided into haves and have-nots.	• There is competition for resources. • Haves have power over have-nots. • People are usually oppressed because of prejudice and discrimination. • Decision makers, including government, are controlled by haves.
Resource mobilization theory	Social movements need a collective identity.	• Groups not represented in decision making initiate social movements. • Public protests bring public recognition to an issue. • Movements need a structure. • Success depends on a collective identity for those involved in protest. • Strength depends on the quality of the message. • Funding without compromising the group's position is often a problem.

beliefs, values, and practices of the dominant society. This framework is important in understanding how communities contain built-in conflicts. Persons who experience divergence between nurturing and sustaining systems will be aware of community politics, power, and change as part of their daily experience. Even when there is congruence between the nurturing and sustaining systems, it may engender a false perception that communities are benign or supportive of all their members. Because civil society is valued by dominant groups, it reflects the values and norms of those in power; those same groups will resist the development of civil rights associations and other organizations that are dedicated to changing the status quo through political and economic empowerment (Christens, 2012).

Understanding the politics of different communities is critical to social workers as they interact with diverse groups. For example, the meaning of volunteerism in traditional U.S. communities translates to a formalized process through which volunteers are organized and coordinated, but that is a politically dominant view held by the sustaining system. This type of volunteering has seen resurgence in the declining economies of 2009 and 2010, with states and cities attempting to get volunteers to help with functions that were formerly performed by paid staff. Many states and local communities are attempting to keep parks and libraries open, for example, and to supplement many staff functions through the use of volunteers.

Stanfield (1993) contends that volunteerism in African American communities is so much an integral part of the informal nature of caring that it becomes a way of life. Yet, there is no calculation of in-kind contributions or records of volunteer time in this latter definition of volunteerism. It is not captured in anyone's log or volunteer record book. Put simply, it does not appear to exist because it cannot be defined as "volunteerism" in traditional U.S. communities.

Another example of communities that do not conform to dominant criteria was provided by Kayal (1991) in his study of the gay men's health crisis in New York City. Kayal analyzed how volunteerism among those in the gay community became necessary at a time when government support was not forthcoming. He explained how members of the gay community responded to the problem of AIDS, representing the way in which groups become committed to sharing the burden when crises arise. There are many more examples of groups that have formed locally and have responded to problems, but whose work has often not been recognized or valued within traditional understandings of community (e.g., Finn, 2005; Rogge, David, Maddox, & Jackson, 2005). Because social workers advocate with and for these groups, conflict is inevitable when intervening through macro practice.

Politics cannot be ignored as a part of understanding community. Feminist writers have long declared the mantra that the "personal is political," indicating that every action or inaction that one takes is a political statement (Lazzari, Colarossi, & Collins, 2009). There are multiple examples of various interest groups, some more formalized than others, interacting within local communities. In order to fully contextualize their work, social workers recognize the interplay of interest groups competing for resources within the community.

Policy Practice

Behavior: Apply critical thinking to analyze, formulate and advocate for policies that advance human rights and social, economic, and environmental justice.

Critical Thinking Question: Having assessed the interplay of interest groups competing for resources within a community, what strategies might be used to prioritize community needs?

Box 5.4   Theories of Power, Politics, and Change

Strengths	Weaknesses
Introduce important human factors into the understanding of communities and their dynamics.	Typically lack guidance on how to achieve ends without radical initiatives.
Help in understanding the role of power and politics as part of change.	Ignore details in favor of emphasizing the need to push to make changes happen.
Recognize oppression, and make clear that conflict cannot be ignored.	Provide no guidance on how to avoid alienating targets of change.
	Do not present a full range of strategic options.
	Focus too much on mobilizing tangible resources to the detriment of emphasizing social, cultural, and ideological aspects of change.

Strengths and Weaknesses

Understanding power and politics as part of community dynamics is critical to macro intervention. Theorists who focus on power, politics, and change are typically appealing to social work because they recognize oppression and are aware that conflict cannot be ignored. Their language is compatible with social work values and ethical principles, such as autonomy and social justice, and it resonates with social workers who want to make a difference.

Limitations within these theories are that, although they may lead to better understandings about power and politics, they do not offer guidance on how to achieve one's ends without radical initiatives or how to judge when to act and when not to act. The nuances of finessing change are overwhelmed by the push to make change happen. There is no guidance for how to develop and use professional judgment so that targets of change are not alienated, because the assumption is that alienation will inevitably occur. Hardina (2003) indicates that even though these theories provide some guidance for how to deal with power and competition, they do not provide strategies for community or-

 Assess your understanding of community theories by taking this brief quiz.

ganizers to use. Critics of resource mobilization theory argue that tangible resources are overemphasized and that an individualistic, rational, and economic perspective ignores social, cultural, and ideological aspects of advocacy efforts (Greenspan, 2014). Box 5.4 summarizes the strengths and weaknesses of theories of power, politics, and change.

CONTEMPORARY PERSPECTIVES

In the 1950s and 1960s, sociological interest in and research on communities suffered a decline. It was assumed that mass society had replaced the concept of community (Lyon, 1987). This was part of a broader concern expressed by many writers that community had been lost and that there must be a search to regain, revitalize, and reinforce community. Many political candidates also issued calls for decentralizing government, returning control to local communities, and reestablishing family values. Finally, "community lost" became a theme in the popular media, where people used words such as *helplessness* and *disempowerment* to describe their feelings about what was happening to community life.

Putting this in perspective, however, these concerns have waxed and waned since the Industrial Revolution. Hunter (1993) pointed out that social analysts have talked about the demise of local communities for decades and social pundits have feared the social decay of cities. He goes on to say that a number of researchers have reminded practitioners of the resilience of the informal relationships and structures that maintained human relationships long before the advent of modern society. What is hopeful about Hunter's reminder is that he recognized and validated what was once viewed as nonrational, short-lived, unimportant, and invisible. The relationships that women with children formed in local neighborhoods, the plethora of self-help groups that emerged in the last decades, the nurturing systems of racial and ethnic minorities, the voluntary associations to which people flocked, the efforts of natural helpers, and the human bonds that transcend time and space all maintain the functions and roles of community even when the formal structures suffer crises in credibility, integrity, or financial viability. Essentially, Hunter declares that those linkages that are so carefully delineated as "micro" and "macro" are intricately interwoven so that if one works with individuals, one must, by definition, understand community. Perhaps what has changed is that nonplace-based communities have taken on more significance because we have the capacity to transcend geography.

Strengths, Empowerment, and Resiliency Perspectives

In the mid-1980s and into the 1990s, community scholars regained what we believe to be a more balanced set of perspectives, indicating that *both* mass society and community are still relevant concepts. Since the turn of the 21st century, reactions to Putnam's (2000) bestselling book, *Bowling Alone*, brought new attention to the importance of community. Eikenberry (2009) contends that the way in which people engage in their communities and in civic activity may have changed.

We now highlight three interrelated perspectives that are particularly relevant in understanding positive attributes of communities: strengths, empowerment, and resiliency. The **strengths perspective** focuses on identifying the possibilities within individuals and communities, recognizing their assets rather than focusing on their deficits. Building on strengths, there is the potential for empowerment. **Empowerment** comes from within the individual or community as a whole when there is an "aha" realization that there are inherent strengths on which to build and that using those strengths can result in desired change. **Resiliency** is the capacity to maintain a sense of empowerment over time, to continue to work toward community betterment, and to resist the temptation to give up when there are conflicts, struggles, and setbacks—in other words, to bounce back time and again.

The strengths perspective was originally presented by Saleeby (1997). Whereas communities may not appear to be as functional or competent as one would wish, social work practitioners must be careful to recognize and assess the strengths within the communities in which they work. When addressing terrible social problems such as homelessness and violence, it can become too easy to write off entire communities as pathological and beyond assistance. Saleeby reminds us of words such as *empowerment*, *resilience*, and *membership* that can lift and inspire. Empowerment means assisting communities in recognizing the resources they have. Resilience is the potential that comes from the energy and skill of ongoing problem solving. Membership is a reminder that being a member of a community carries with it civic and moral strength.

In the United States, the empowerment perspective can be traced to the concept of citizen participation and the War on Poverty. Having citizens engaged in community planning efforts was seen as a vehicle for social reform. Solomon (1976) refined the empowerment perspective when she acknowledged that empowerment emerged from recognizing the strengths and capabilities of individuals, groups, organizations, and communities in gaining control over actions to change repressive social structures that influenced their lives. Gutierrez and Lewis (1999, p. 11) contend that "empowerment practice must be focused at three levels: the personal, the interpersonal, and the political." In other words, individuals have to feel empowered in order to link with others to engage in change, and together the synergy of their joint efforts can make a difference. Mondros and Wilson (1994) identified four sources in the professional knowledge base that have contributed to the understanding of community power and empowerment: (1) theoretical debates over social protest and discontent, when it arises, and why; (2) a growing body of literature that attempts to classify types of community organizations; (3) a descriptive body of knowledge describing social protest movements; and (4) an extensive literature on community-organizing skills providing practical guidance about how to go about organizing.

Cramer, Brady, and McLeod (2013) provide an example of how an empowerment perspective can be translated into empowerment practice through the I-CAN Accessibility Project, which includes two social work and university centers of excellence and regional Independence Living Centers (ILCs). The ILM began in the 1940s when researchers recognized that the major difficulties imposed on persons with disabilities rested in the negative social construction of disability. Since that time, the ILM established centers throughout the United States, and central to their practice is that consumers must make up 51 percent of their boards of directors, administrative, and service staff. Not only has the disability community recognized the strengths of their members, but also they are empowered to utilize those strengths through Independent Living Centers (ILC) located throughout the United States. Communities, like people, have great *resilience* (Lyon, 1987), the ability to continue to be empowered even in the face of seemingly overwhelming challenges.

Breton (2001) focuses on resiliency in neighborhoods, noting that resilient neighborhoods have a number of characteristics, such as (1) trusting neighborhood networks, (2) residents that spring to action through voluntary associations, (3) stable local organizational networks, and (4) a social infrastructure with needed services available. Of particular relevance is the rapidly increasing literature on the communal nature of people and the resiliency of "the new commons," even in times of great change (see, e.g., Lohmann, 2014). Since the 1990s, the concept of social capital has become a means of exploring power, privilege, and oppression in community settings (Portes, 2000) and is seen as helpful for community practitioners interested in better understanding human behavior within an environmental context (Aguilar & Sen, 2009). Table 5.8 provides an overview of themes in strengths, empowerment, and resiliency perspectives.

Table 5.8 Contemporary Perspectives

Contemporary Perspectives	Themes	Characteristics
Strengths	Communities are assessed in terms of their strengths rather than their deficits.	• Community intervention may emerge around a problem or need. • Assessments identify community strengths (asset mapping). • Solutions come from within the community rather than from "services."
Empowerment	Communities can gain control over decisions that affect them.	• People excluded from decisions gain their voice. • Resources go to the more powerful. • Leadership emerges and promotes an understanding of how decisions can be controlled locally.
Resiliency	Communities have great potential to rebound and to cope.	• Neighbor networks and trust are apparent. • Active voluntary associations participate in community life. • Stable organizational networks are maintained. • Adequate services are provided.

Asset Mapping

Kretzmann and McKnight (1993) have studied resilient communities for years. They use a strengths perspective to develop a model of practice that focuses on community assets rather than limitations. They advocate for strengthening and empowering local community networks and provide detailed guidance for how to do what they call asset mapping. Green and Haines (2002) note that assets have always been available in local communities, but the focus has often been on problems. An assets approach is congruent with a strengths perspective and reframes community development as an empowering process rather than as a problem that needs to be fixed. Focusing on problems, rather than assets, reinforces perceptions that community residents are disempowered and need outside experts, directs funding to services rather than residents, looks to resources outside the community to intervene, emphasizes a client rather than a citizen mentality, forces community leaders to denigrate their own communities, and deepens cycles of dependency (Donaldson & Daughtery, 2011).

Yeneabat and Butterfield (2012) provide an example of building on strengths and assets in their description of "We Can't Eat a Road" in the Gedam Sefer Community Partnership in Ethiopia. This statement was made by a woman who was surprised that a new road was being built when her poverty-stricken community was desperate for food. A top-down approach by decision makers outside the local community had determined priorities, whereas a strengths and assets development effort would have engaged residents in identifying and prioritizing needs. Asset mapping can be used to identify services, programs, resources, staff capabilities, values, and other factors that can be compared with risk factors in determining how to approach a community (Crozier & Melchoior, 2013).

Note that assets can be tangible and intangible. Whereas services and programs are specific intervention assets, values and human interaction are equally important assets

Watch the video where *Angela Blanchard, a* pioneer in the work of asset-based community development, speaks about vulnerable populations. What new questions does the speaker suggest should be asked of communities typically labeled as "broken"?

www.youtube.com /watch?v=XU_vVt298gw

within a community. Donaldson and Daughtery (2011) identify guiding principles and values undergirding an asset-mapping approach:

- All communities have strengths, assets, and resources on which to build.
- It is socially just that community members participate in decisions that affect their lives.
- The central importance of human relationships, which is an ethical principle in the NASW code of ethics, reinforces a collaborative process.
- Before bringing in outside resources, first look toward applying the community's strengths to address the situation.
- Whatever the intervention, it should reflect the input and priorities of community members.
- Cultural humility must guide social workers as they collaborate with community members.
  - All participants in the asset-mapping process communicate in the spirit of collegiality, mutual respect, and support.

In the next chapter the community assessment framework will include the identification of assets and reinforce a collaborative approach. Now, we focus on the multiple types of units within communities that may be capable of building capacity and may be seen as assets.

Go to the Asset Based Community Development Institute homepage, and do a search for "toolkits." What resources are available to guide asset-based community mapping?

Capacity Building

Delgado (2000), Yenebat and Butterfield (2012), and others remind community practitioners that the strength of informal networks within ethnic communities is critical to capacity-building efforts. *Capacity building* is often used interchangeably with terms such as *community building*, *locality development*, and *community empowerment*. All of these terms imply that a process occurs in which persons sharing an identified problem join together to address their own needs as well as the needs of others in a community. Capacity building therefore is an empowerment process at the individual, interpersonal, and community levels as participants gain knowledge and skills to effect action (Cramer, Brady, & McLeod, 2013).

Informal units are those that are not publicly incorporated as legal entities to deliver health and human services. Often, these units have not been recognized for their importance in the service delivery system, whereas they actually perform a vast assortment of mutual support tasks. They include the household unit, natural support systems and social networks, self-help groups, and voluntary or grassroots associations. We briefly examine each now.

Household or Domestic Units

The household unit consists of those persons who share a common dwelling, whether they consider themselves families, significant others, friends, partners, or roommates. In the past, family was often seen as the same as household, but as more and more people live together without being related, the concept of *household unit* is a more helpful term (Smith, 1991). Service provision in this unit generally takes the form of caregiving and tends to fall heavily on women. For example, informal caregivers provide the vast majority of care for persons with disabilities and chronic conditions (Cramer, Brady, & McLeod, 2013). The potential for caregiver burden or strain suggests that mutual support provided by the informal system may require assistance from others within the community. Respite services are often needed in the interest of sustaining the physical and mental well-being of the caregiver.

In assessing the extent of service provided in household units within a given community, one should look for indicators of what is happening within private dwellings of members of the target population. For example, are identified caregivers within the community overburdened? Is there an identified need for respite services for caregivers of physically disabled, developmentally disabled persons and older adults, and/or of young children? Are requests for live-ins and shared housing increasing?

Of particular concern is identifying the importance of the household unit for the target population. For example, if the target population is frail widows living alone, the household unit does not contain others who can assist. Not only are caregivers not available, but also formerly active older women may suddenly find themselves alone after years of providing care to children and spouses. On the other hand, target populations such as inner-city children, who often live in crowded households where privacy is limited and tension is high, may draw support from siblings, peers, and parents. Respite for single mothers may be difficult to locate, and poverty may have reduced opportunities and life choices. Yet the household unit can be a critical source of support for these children, fragile as it may be. Recognizing the household unit as a source of community strength and developing services to support this unit can produce a double benefit in strengthening families and reducing the need for other support services.

Natural Support Systems and Social Networks

Often an unstructured, informal approach to mutual support will evolve as natural or social support systems develop. Most people are part of social networks, but this in itself does not constitute a natural support system. A natural support system, according to McIntyre (1986), exists when resources have actually been exchanged. The existence of natural support systems has been recognized for years. Recent studies and an emphasis on informal support have prompted a more intense examination, particularly in communities with high poverty rates (Saegert, Thompson, & Warren, 2001).

Because networks do not have established boundaries and depend on interaction between informal individuals and groups, they are likely to extend beyond the local community. Mutual support tasks may be provided by geographically dispersed, as well as geographically close, network members. Dispersed networks will depend on linkages such as transportation systems and telephones, and may therefore be vulnerable in times of crisis. Social networks are important because relatives, friends, and colleagues form a support system and respond when there are crises. Social networks are emotionally sustaining and often assist with child care or looking out for neighbors.

Within the local community, there are indicators of the extent of informal neighborhood groups and support systems. Neighborhood associations, child care exchanges, and neighbor-to-neighbor interactions are indicators of the extent of support available within this unit.

Self-Help Groups

Self-help groups are one of the fastest growing elements of community support. They have been formed to deal with a variety of personal and social problems and needs, including substance abuse, bereavement and loss, depression, parenting, and many other issues. A number of self-help groups (of which Alcoholics Anonymous is probably the best known) have formed national and international chapters and are recognized vehicles of service delivery. For example, Weng and Netting (2014) focus on the importance of self-help groups to Asian American populations and their hesitancy in seeking services offered by members of the dominant culture. Because language and cultural barriers can arise in these and other ethnic populations, self-help groups assist in maintaining community identity and involvement.

Self-help groups are often viewed as being compatible with a feminist perspective. Such groups are directed at widows, women who have been exploited or abused, and caregivers. Mutual support provided through self-help groups may assist in protecting the mental and physical health of caregivers.

Depending on the target population identified, self-help groups may be of critical or only modest importance. For example, populations that already have access to the service system and its resources may find such groups less necessary, whereas populations struggling to have their needs recognized may find them extremely helpful.

Voluntary Associations

Smith (2000) identifies what he calls *grassroots associations* that form an interface between informal support groups and more structured service organizations. These associations are typically local in nature, autonomous, and composed of volunteers. Voluntary associations serve as a bridge between informal and formal components of a human service system, and they have been described as very closely tied to the values held by their members and to the causes about which they are concerned (Wollebaek, 2009). A **voluntary association** is defined as "a structured group whose members have united for the purpose of advancing an interest or achieving some social purpose. Theirs is a clear aim toward a chosen form of 'social betterment'" (Van Til, 1988, p. 8). Community groups such as neighborhood associations or local congregations fall within this category. Similar to self-help groups, voluntary associations vary in their degree of formalization. Because they are membership groups, a dues structure will often be in place. Therefore, their boundaries become more clearly defined than informal groups because there is a formal process for joining and providing financial support.

Voluntary associations have several characteristics. Members share a sense of community, which provides a collective identity. Social status may be enhanced by membership, and social control may be exercised over members. A function of the association may be to enhance the well-being of its members in a supportive manner. If the association is strong, it may have a prominent profile from the perspective of nonmembers, even though its influence may be positive or negative. For example, associations such as white supremacist groups can be powerful yet destructive forces within certain communities.

Voluntary associations are a study in both inclusiveness and exclusiveness. Ethnic groups, lesbians and gays, and other oppressed people may use informal and mediating units to a larger degree than other populations. Neighborhood groups, self-help groups,

Table 5.9   Overview of Informal Community Units

Informal Community Units	Composition	Examples of Support Provided
Household or domestic units	Persons who reside within the same dwelling	Informal caregivers of older adults and small children
Natural support systems and social networks	People within a community who exchange resources	People (natural helpers) who provide for a neighbor's need during a crisis
Self-help groups	People who come together to help each other with a problem or need that they share	Parents whose children have been killed by drunk drivers who provide mutual support to one another
Voluntary associations	People who unite for the purpose of advancing an interest	Neighborhood associations and resident councils

and voluntary associations serve as a means of mutual support, as a place for clarifying perspectives, and as a focal point for action. In some cases, these activities lead to recognition and wider support and to improved access to the existing formal units of human service delivery in a community.

Churches, unions, and professional groups are all potential sources of support for the target population. They may not be listed in human service directories, yet they may be the first source to which some people turn when in need (Wineberg, 1992). Trends in the development of what are called **giving circles** illustrate how community members form associations for the purpose of pooling their money and other resources for important causes. These types of fundraising ventures are particularly growing in communities of color and among women (Eikenberry, 2009).

Table 5.9 provides an overview of informal community units. Household units, natural support systems and social networks, self-help groups, and voluntary associations are all community units that interact in informal and sometimes more formalized ways. Capacity building and asset mapping are theoretical concepts that recognize the importance of understanding how these informal units are constructed, the ways in which they are viewed by community members, and the strengths they can bring to community interventions (Chaskin, Brown, Venkatesh, & Vidal, 2001; Hannah, 2006; Nye & Glickman, 2000). Communities rich in informal units have strong capacity, sometimes not previously recognized by community members. Macro practitioners are often engaged in pointing out just how many assets and strengths a community has so that mobilization efforts can occur.

> **?** Assess your understanding of contemporary perspectives by taking this brief quiz.

COMMUNITY PRACTICE MODELS

Whereas theories of community provide an understanding for why communities do what they do, community action and community development writers seek to prescribe how change can occur in communities. Numerous community practice models have been and are being used by social workers to effect community change. These models are heavily grounded in the concepts and language of systems and ecological theories. A summary of the theories that influence many of the community practice models appears in Table 5.10.

Table 5.10   Summary of Contributions of Theories to Community Practice

Theories	Contributions to Community Practice
Social systems	• Reveals that changes in one community unit will impact other units • Indicates that changes in subunits also influence the larger community • Allows comparisons between how different communities function • Recognizes that the push to return to a steady state will depend on the analogy used
Human or population ecology	• Is particularly helpful with geographic communities intent on understanding relationships among units • Recognizes that community groups are competing for limited resources, with survival of those in power • Recognizes that groups without power have to adapt to community norms • Acknowledges the influences of the interconnections and mutual shaping of physical and social structures
Human behavior	• Focuses on the individual within the context of community as the unit of analysis • Provides insight into relationships, interactions, values, and needs of individuals • Provides community practitioners with critical clues about the difference that trust and relationships can make in community interaction
Power, change, and politics	• Reveals the influence of external sources of resources on local communities • Views the community as divided into haves and have-nots • Focuses heavily on the isms • Recognizes the dynamics of social movements and their influence on community change • Acknowledges the role of power in all interpersonal transactions

There are many ways to approach community and social work practice models. As a beginning, Mondros and Wilson (1994) identify components typically found in practice models: (1) a change goal; (2) roles for staff, leaders, and members; (3) a process for selecting issues; (4) the target of the change effort; (5) an assessment of how cooperative or adversarial the target will be; (6) a change strategy; (7) an understanding of resources needed to produce change; and (8) an understanding of the role of an organization in the change process (p. 240). In this book we present a comprehensive practice model, that includes all eight of these elements. This planned change model is elaborated in Chapters 9, 10, 11, and 12 and is somewhat unique in that it can be used in both community and organizational arenas. Best known among community practice models are those by Rothman (2008), who proposed a multimodal approach that builds on the three intervention approaches he originally developed in 1968. These are (1) planning and policy, (2) community capacity development, and (3) social advocacy. Each type has three modes. Policy/planning includes rationalistic planning, participatory planning, and policy advocacy. Capacity development's three modes are capacity-centered development, planned capacity development, and identity activism. Social advocacy's three modes are social action, social reform, and solidarity organizing (p. 14).

The planning and policy approach is task oriented, a data-driven approach in which persuasion with the "facts" prevails. It seeks to address and resolve substantive community problems through careful study of those problems and the applications of rational planning techniques. This approach also seeks to engage community members in the process by hearing their needs and limiting the role of social planners to that of assisting the change process rather than imposing independently determined directives. In its purest form, the model assumes that logic will prevail over political bias. However, planners do not have to be politically naïve, and modifications can be made in the rational planning approach to include political considerations and advocacy.

The goal of capacity development is to develop the community's ability to become more integrated and cohesive through self-help, based on the assumption that broad cross-sections of the community need to engage in problem solving. Empowerment in this mode occurs through collaborative efforts and informed decision making by community residents. The focus is on process, building relationships, and solving problems so that groups can work together. Capacity development fits well with approaches such as asset mapping, capacity building, strengths, resiliency, and empowerment. Its limitations are its time-consuming nature and its assumption that change can occur through consensus rather than confrontation. Thus, theoretical roots fit well with mechanical and organismic analogies of social systems.

The goal of social advocacy is both process and task oriented in that participants seek to shift power relationships and resources in order to effect institutional change. In this approach, pressure is applied and conflict is expected. Beneficiaries of this type of intervention are often perceived to be victims of an oppressive power structure. Empowerment is achieved when beneficiaries feel a sense of mastery in influencing community decision making. Although the language of social action is often espoused by social workers, it is important to realize that this approach to community practice is based in conflict, power dependency, and resource mobilization theories of power and politics. The confrontation required in this model is energy draining and time consuming, and sometimes the focus on task becomes so important that process is forgotten. Because the outcome usually involves a win-or-lose scenario, social advocacy is difficult to complete without creating some enemies. We recommend that it be used when other approaches have failed to be effective.

Intervention

Behavior: Apply knowledge of human behavior and the social environment, person-in-environment, and other multidisciplinary theoretical frameworks in interventions with clients and constituencies.

Critical Thinking Question: How are some community practice models more culturally humble than others? Why or why not?

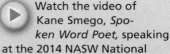

Watch the video of Kane Smego, *Spoken Word Poet,* speaking at the 2014 NASW National Conference. What Rothman model best describes Kane Smego's work in his community?

www.youtube.com /watch?v=J2lrbaPHg4g

Rothman is quick to point out that there are multiple ways in which these three modes can interrelate and overlap. Other writers have expanded on Rothman's work. For example, Mondros and Wilson (1994) identify three practice approaches that come under the rubric of the social action model: grassroots practice, lobbying practice, and a mobilizing approach. Political practice is added by Haynes and Mickelson (2006).

Weil, Gamble, and Ohmer (2013) categorize a larger range of community practice models (eight in all) that incorporate finer distinctions in methods and assumptions. These eight approaches are:

- Neighborhood and community organizing
- Organizing functional communities
- Social, economic, and sustainable development
- Inclusive program development
- Social planning
- Coalitions
- Political and social action
- Movements for progressive change

These models reflect the many different ways in which social workers engage in community work. They range from locality-based grassroots community organizing in which social workers participate with indigenous groups to make change, to social movements that occur across geographical boundaries within countries and even across countries. For example, Broadbent and Brockman (2011) elaborate on social movements in Japan, South Korea, Taiwan, Hong Kong, China, and Singapore, including a range of fields such as environmental issues, women's rights, and political issues. In the United States, social movements such as the Disability Movement (O'Brien & Leneave, 2008), the Gay and Lesbian Movement (Adam, 1995), and the Alzheimer's Disease Movement (Chaufan, Hollister, Nazareno, & Fox, 2012) are usually broad based and include a wide range of people and perspectives (Meyer, 2010). Social movements remind practitioners of Warren's (1978) distinction between vertical and horizontal relationships because they often connect people from multiple communities (vertical) as well as develop local chapters (horizontal).

> Go to the Association for Community Organization and Social Administration (ACOSA) website, and read about the history of this membership organization. How might ACOSA be used as a resource for keeping up-to-date on community practice models in social work?

Our major caution is that readers recognize the absence of any "right" way to categorize community practice models, strategies, and tactics. Planned community change is a mixture of various approaches, based on a careful assessment of the situation to be changed. It is critical also to recognize that because situations and problems are constantly evolving, social workers must be flexible in altering their direction as new information emerges and reassessment occurs. Table 5.11 provides an overview of community practice models (Gamble, Weil & Olmer, 2013; Kettner, Moroney, & Martin, 2013; Rothman, 2008).

Table 5.11   Overview of Community Practice Models

Model	Basic Premise	Reference
Capacity development or neighborhood and community organizing	Focuses on development of community capacity and integration through self-help; very process oriented. Asset mapping and capacity building are used.	Rothman (2008)
Organizing functional communities	Brings together people focused on a particular cause to change people's behaviors and attitudes; not necessarily place based; focus designed to facilitate empowerment.	Weil, Gamble, & Olmer (2013)
Social, economic, and sustainable development	Prepares citizens at the grassroots level to focus on economic and social development that will last; uses intensive asset mapping, particularly in the economic arena, and builds capacity.	Weil, Gamble, & Olmer (2013)
Planning/policy	Engages participants in an interaction designed to address substantive social problems; uses skills of expert planners to guide process.	Rothman (2008)
Program development	Uses organizational base in which programs are designed to address community needs; uses skills of professionals in program design and intervention.	Kettner, Moroney, & Martin (2013)
Political and social action	Attempts to shift power relationships and resources in order to effect institutional change; strengths and empowerment perspectives dominate here.	Rothman (2008)
Coalitions	Joins multiple community units (e.g., organizations, groups) to build a power base from which change can occur.	Weil, Gamble, & Olmer (2013)
Movements for progressive change	Works outside existing structures toward social justice goals that will change existing societal structures; oriented toward broad-scale, structural (even radical) change.	Weil, Gamble, & Olmer (2013)

Keep in mind that we have quickly introduced numerous models that are well developed in the professional knowledge base and can easily be accessed by the reader. You will be reminded of these community practice models and the concepts briefly introduced here when you get to Chapters 9, 10, 11, and 12 and are asked to focus on planned change interventions.

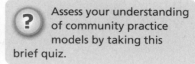

? Assess your understanding of community practice models by taking this brief quiz.

SUMMARY

It should be clear at this point that all professionally assisted change in communities begins with an understanding of definitions, functions, theoretical frameworks, and practice models. These areas of knowledge help to establish the standards by which communities and their problems and needs can be understood. This chapter provided an overview of community theory, perspectives, and practice models used by social workers. There are multiple definitions and types of communities. Three dimensions were briefly examined: (1) geographical, spatial, or territorial communities; (2) social or relational communities that provide opportunities for interaction, making cultural connections, relationship building, and sharing common interests; and (3) political dimensions that bond members together as they engage in action for the good of the community. Geographical communities are obviously place based, but social/relational communities of identification as well as communities bound together by political action may be both place and nonplace based. The planned change model presented in later chapters will be applicable to both place and nonplace communities.

One feature common to many community theories is their attention to structure and function. Five community functions were identified by Warren (1978): (1) production, distribution, and consumption; (2) socialization; (3) social control; (4) social participation; and (5) mutual support. Pantoja and Perry (1998) added two additional functions: (6) defense and (7) communication. Communities are seen as dysfunctional or incompetent when these functions are not adequately performed, especially the economic function. Approaches to community that employ systems theory also have their roots in the analysis of community structure and function.

Human ecology theories, originating with the work of Robert E. Park, view communities as highly interdependent and changing. People, their values, and their interactions were elements of the ecology of communities studied by early anthropologists and sociologists. This work also showed that communities reflect a collective identity rich with symbols, values, and ideologies that people hold in common.

Theories of community that focus on power, politics, and change are important for social work practice. The person-in-environment perspective tends to lead social workers to view communities as political arenas in which the power of dominant groups necessitates a change so that underserved population needs can be addressed. Understanding the politics of different communities is critical to social workers seeking to assist underserved groups.

Last, contemporary community theory and practice reveal a new interest in rethinking the value of community as an arena for future study. Strengths, empowerment, and resiliency perspectives were followed by asset-mapping and capacity-building approaches

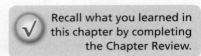

Recall what you learned in this chapter by completing the Chapter Review.

to community practice. A brief overview of community practice models was presented as a way to introduce the reader to the multiple strategies used to foster community change and to prepare the reader for thinking about the planned change model in this book.

Assess Your Competence

Use the scale below to rate your current level of achievement on the following concepts or skills associated with each learning outcome listed at the beginning of this chapter:

1	2	3
I can accurately describe the concept or skill(s) associated with this outcome.	I can consistently identify the concept or skill(s) associated with this outcome when observing and analyzing practice activities.	I can competently implement the concept or skill(s) associated with this outcome in my own practice.

_____ Define community, its dimensions, and its functions.

_____ Explain four theories that describe aspects of community.

_____ Discuss contemporary perspectives used in community practice.

_____ Identify eight types of community practice models.

6

Assessing Communities

IMAGEGAMI/FOTOLIA

ENGAGING COMMUNITIES

There is no single, universally accepted method for understanding all the elements that make up a community. The major focus of this chapter is on engaging communities in an assessment process designed to lead to an informed and skillful community-level intervention. Weil, Reisch, and Ohmer (2013) identify four approaches used by change agents to engage in community practice and to revitalize communities and societies: (1) community development, (2) organizing, (3) planning, and (4) progressive change (p. 11). In Box 6.1, we briefly describe intervention approaches that practitioners use in community work, all of which begin with an assessment process.

There are three reasons why macro practitioners need a systematic approach to conceptualizing and assessing communities and their strengths and social problems. First, the person-in-environment view, which is central to social work practice, requires consideration of how individuals function within larger systems. A person's community has much to do with his or her values, beliefs, problems to be faced, and resources available, so it is difficult to see how social workers can be effective without understanding community influences. The framework for community assessment presented here is designed to assist in conceptualizing the arena within which people experience hope

Box 6.1	Approaches to Community Change
Approach	Description
Community development	Community development connects people to existing structures to engage in activities such as community building, economic development, neighborhood improvement, and developing affordable housing (Staples, 2012). This type of work can include social and economic development as well as strategies of sustainable development (Weil, Reisch, & Ohmer, 2013).
Community organizing	Community organizing (CO) is defined in many different ways and can be used for conservative, liberal, and radical purposes (Brady & O'Connor, 2014). In social work, it involves working with multiple indigenous community residents and using their strength in numbers to participate in empowering the collective to pursue social change (Staples, 2012).
Community planning	Community planning can include program development, coordination and evaluation as well as processes to design projects, programs, and services. The planning focus may be local neighborhoods, states, regions, and even international efforts (Weil, Reisch, & Ohmer, 2013).
Progressive change	Progressive change involves the pursuit of community change through political activism and even radical forms of advocacy (Almog-Bar & Schmid, 2014; Dudziak & Profitt, 2012). Efforts may involve policy practice targeting legislative change, coalition building, and participation in social movements, and it may range from local to global in scope (Weil, Reisch, & Ohmer, 2013).

and draw strength, as well as face oppression and frustration. Note the word *assist*, which means that this framework does not have to be used in lockstep fashion. Instead, it is a versatile tool that can be adapted to the circumstances at hand.

Second, community-level macro change requires an understanding of the significant events in the history and development of a community that influence the ways in which people view contemporary issues. Without this knowledge, the practitioner will have a deficient understanding of important factors such as values, attitudes, and traditions, along with their significance in either maintaining the status quo or allowing for change.

Third, communities constantly change. Individuals and groups move into power. Economic structures and political environments change, as do sources of funding as well as citizens' roles and expectations. A framework for assessing communities can be helpful in recognizing and interpreting these changes.

Two Community Vignettes

Vignette 1   Canyon City

Located in the western United States, Canyon City had a population of 60,000 people in 1975. The most recent data indicated that it had now exceeded 300,000 residents and was continuing to grow rapidly at a time when many older cities were suffering population declines. Because the city was inhabited by many people who had moved to the western Sun Belt to follow job opportunities, most of its residents were not native to the area. Census data indicated that 20 percent of Canyon City's residents were Latino, 60 percent were non-Latino white, 10 percent were Native American, 5 percent were African American, and another 5 percent were Asian American.

Encountering the Community. A recent social work graduate took a position in a multiservice agency in Canyon City. One of her tasks was to develop a program to address the needs of victims of domestic violence in the community. Data from the police department and various other sources revealed a high incidence of domestic violence within the community relative to other communities of similar size. The social worker was new to Canyon City, having lived in another part of the country most of her life. She viewed this chance to assess and understand the community with great anticipation.

She began her work by talking with a number of police officers, social workers, and others who had expertise in domestic violence. Through these contacts, she was able to locate a few women who were willing to talk with her confidentially about their situations. She learned that each woman perceived the situation somewhat differently. Based on numerous conversations, the social worker found that there was a general sense of isolation within the community. Neighbors often did not know one another, and newcomers felt it was hard to form friendships or to feel they were part of a community. Given both the growth and the rapid turnover of Canyon City's population, this was not surprising. It appeared to the social worker that people tended to focus on their own problems and dwell on them within a narrow range of family or friends. The social worker soon found herself looking hard for evidence of any community strengths on which to build.

However, when she got beyond individual interviews and reached out to organizations, she found that Canyon City had many strengths. First, community members seemed willing to acknowledge the problem and were anxious to address it. The social worker encountered few people who denied that something needed to be done. Second, there was diversity within the community that made for a rich mix of customs, traditions, and values. Third, there were several women's groups in Canyon City willing to volunteer their efforts to whatever intervention was developed. Fourth, a local foundation was willing to fund a project if it was well designed.

Narrowing the Focus. In the course of collecting data and defining boundaries, the social worker determined that the problem of domestic violence was being addressed in some parts of the community but not others. Although there were three battered women's shelters within the city, each tended to serve only a limited area. A counseling service for domestic violence victims was available, but only to those who could afford the service. In particular, few Latinas were served by either the shelters or the counseling service. This led the social worker to narrow her focus toward the needs of these women.

The social worker knew she had to take care to recognize the diverse cultural traditions and beliefs of this target population. A number of models were available for developing shelters, safe homes, and services for white middle-class women, but few focused on women of color. The social worker also learned that Latinas in the community often provided shelter for one another, but this often imposed great financial burdens on the host and guest. She began to talk with the women about how to design a program that would be sensitive and relevant to identified needs.

In the process, she discovered additional community strengths. There was a strong sense of community among many Latinas who had lived in the area most of their lives. There were associations of women that were not identified in any listings of services or programs because they were not as formalized as other groups. This informal network was a source of pride in the community, yet these relationships were not known or understood in the larger community. Two Latino churches had identified domestic violence as their focus of concern for the coming year and were willing to work with the social worker and her agency. Also, a support group for women of color had been meeting in one of the churches for several years.

(Continued)

Vignette 1   Canyon City (*Continued*)

Mobilizing Resources. After a few weeks, the social worker realized that there were more resources in the community than she had originally anticipated. However, she also discovered that there were definite locations of power. Community leaders among the women of color were not visible in the larger community and were often left out of any local decision-making processes. Within her own agency, the social worker found that members of the board of directors were not certain they wanted to focus on women of color because the board hoped to serve the needs of all women in the community. The foundation was willing to fund a project that would focus on Latinas' needs, but its board members wanted to be assured that the funds would be used to do something innovative rather than duplicating an existing model. Also, the foundation was willing to fund the project only if it would be self-sufficient within three years. The women's shelters that were already open were cautious about supporting the new program concept for fear that it might call attention to their failure to serve many women of color in the past. The women's support group in the local church was concerned that the group would lose its focus and become part of a bigger project that would take members away from their feeling of closeness and intimacy.

It was the social worker's job to continue to collect information and to determine the project's feasibility. Although this was time consuming, she continued to hear the perspectives of various women who had been battered and to include them in the development of a community project.

Vignette 2   Lakeside

Lakeside was a planned community developed in the 1930s. The downtown area was built around a small lake, surrounded by weeping willow trees. The Baptist, United Methodist, and Presbyterian churches sat side by side along the lake front, forming what was known as "church circle." Each of the Protestant denominations had a children's home, and the Methodist Home for Orphaned Children, built in 1902, was a local landmark.

The population in Lakeside during the 1930s was approximately 20,000 people. The majority of employees worked for a company manufacturing major office products, making Lakeside "a company town." Other businesses in town manufactured paper, building supplies, and various other products.

Assessing Major Changes. By the 1990s, Lakeside had grown to 75,000 persons, and the community was going through a number of changes. Many residents had moved to the outskirts of town and had taken jobs in a larger city nearby, creating problems for the economic base of Lakeside. The various manufacturing companies had experienced layoffs, which made community residents feel uncertain about job security and advancement. One company had closed its doors completely. As manufacturing technologies changed, needed skill sets also shifted. Front-page news in the Lakeside Gazette focused on how local persons were being laid off, whereas new employees with different skills were being recruited to come to the local plants. Both the paper company and the chemical plant had been bought by Canadian companies that were bringing in their own executives. Job competition was becoming much more intense.

Three housing developments for older and disabled persons had been built downtown. Two assisted-living facilities had been completed, and two more were in process. The Methodist Children's Home began providing services to older adults as well as to children, because orphans were few in number but the number of older persons was increasing.

Although Lakeside had been a haven for Protestant families and diversity had been limited, the population was changing. In 1930, the only religious groups other than the Protestant congregations were one Catholic church and one synagogue. By 2005, there was a mosque, two African Methodist Episcopal Zion churches, and a number of new groups that had split off from the original mainline churches. The population was also more racially and ethnically diverse. Whereas in 1930 only 20 percent of the downtown population was African American, by 2005 this figure had grown to 60 percent. The church circle remained a centerpiece in the community around the lake, but many of the members commuted to church from outside the city limits.

Witnessing the Impact of Change. A social worker at the Methodist Home was assigned to work with older persons and persons with disabilities in Lakeside. Her role was to build community and to develop strong support networks for clients. She found that many of her clients lived in the three housing developments in Lakeside, and several more were residents in the assisted-living facilities. The two target populations of older and disabled persons were diverse. With respect to age, for example, residents ranged from 60 to 105 years, and persons with disabilities ranged in age from 25 to 95 years. The housing developments were 55 percent African American, 2 percent Latino, and 43 percent white, whereas the assisted-living facilities were predominantly non-Latino whites.

The majority of the residents had lived in Lakeside all their lives and knew many of the other residents, but this was changing as new employees came to Lakeside and relocated their aging parents to their new community. There was a large senior citizens' center housed in an old department store that had moved to the mall, and the center was trying to reach out to newly relocated older adults who had moved to Lakeside.

The social worker was pleased to learn about these strengths, but she was also aware of the problems that had emerged in Lakeside. There was a definite sense of racial tension in the town. There was also tension between the old and the young persons with disabilities who were living in the same apartment buildings. Older clients complained about loud music and partying at all hours of the night. Younger persons were frustrated by "being forced" to live with old people. Most major stores in the downtown area had relocated, and although mobile community members tended to shop at the mall, persons without transportation were forced to walk to the few remaining downtown stores, where prices were high and bargains were few. Getting Social Security checks cashed at the one downtown grocery store meant paying a $5.00 fee for cashing privileges.

Amid these tensions and concerns, widespread fear of crime had also emerged. Two older women who lived alone had had their purses snatched. In a small community, this was the "talk of the town," and no one felt safe anymore. Older women who lived in the downtown area were being cautioned to keep their doors locked at all times, not to let strangers in, and to call 911 if they had any reason to be suspicious of anyone. A neighborhood crime watch association had been organized, and volunteer escorts were available in the evening hours for anyone having to go out alone. The police department had contacted the social worker so that they could work together, and the senior center was holding self-defense classes. The social worker heard older residents complain over and over again that Lakeside just wasn't the community they had known.

Implications of the Vignettes

Communities change, and it is not unusual for residents to grieve over the loss of what has been. Some changes are planned, such as the deliberate attempts in Vignette 1 to develop a project that would address the needs of Latinas who have been abused. Other changes are unplanned, such as the way in which the "planned" community of Lakeside's downtown area changed. Canyon City addresses a substantive problem (violence against Latinas), and Lakeside faces issues of how to meet the needs of an increasing number of older people and persons with disabilities, as well as how to remain viable as an economic center.

The two vignettes offer a glimpse at what social workers in community practice arenas experience. In Canyon City, the social worker encountered a growing city with much diversity. In Lakeside, the social worker found a city that was changing in different ways. However, both practitioners discovered strengths and problems, tensions and frustrations. Both found that the inclusion of multiple perspectives was important but also complicated the analysis. For example, in Vignette 1, the social worker had to deal with the power dynamics between a possible funding source, local women's shelters that were already established, and Latinas whose voices were not always heard. In Vignette 2, the social worker encountered interracial and intergenerational tensions among residents of a changing downtown neighborhood.

In Chapter 5, we identified three dimensions of communities: (1) geographical, spatial, or territorial; (2) social or relational; and (3) political. Although both vignettes are geographically based, they include elements of all three types of community. They also illustrate how place and nonplace communities can overlap. Canyon City is a "place" or geographical community. Yet bonds of identification within ethnic groups in this community require special consideration. The Latino community has connections that are stronger than geography, and much of the tension in creating a special shelter is tied to nonplace social and relational communities of identification and interest, as well as political collections of relationships that provide meaning and identity. Similarly, Lakeside is a place or geographical community, but within its domain are persons who are moving in from the outside. Their collective relationships that give meaning to their lives may be scattered across other locations from which they have come. These nonplace community ties will not cease when employees and their aging parents move to Lakeside, even though geography separates them from others. In addition, within Lakeside there are communities of symbolic identification that are different, yet at times overlapping, for older and disabled persons. These two groups are tied to differing, and sometimes competing, communities of interest that are much more broadly based than the town of Lakeside. For example, persons with disabilities have formed national networks that advocate for consumer-directed care, whereas older adults are connected by a national political movement calling for civic engagement that is part of the "Age Wave" in a graying society.

Each vignette requires asking many questions in order to know how to intervene. This chapter provides a systematic approach to questions with which one might begin to assess communities like Canyon City and Lakeside from the perspectives of the target populations served. Keep in mind that some questions in this framework may be useful in some communities

Watch the video on how older adults are leading community change. How might the strategies that older adults are using in the video be useful in examining the needs of the Lakeside Community?

www.youtube.com/watch?v=o94wGx__-hk

Diversity and Difference in Practice

Behavior: Apply and communicate understanding of the importance of diversity and difference in shaping life eriences in practice at the micro, mezzo, and macro levels.

Critical Thinking Question: How would you go about engaging two diverse population groups simultaneously (older adults and disabled persons) who live in the same geographical community, but have very different interests and agendas?

and not as useful in others. The identified tasks do not have to be used in the order presented. The point is to find a way to begin to assess a community and to generate additional questions that will provide further direction.

 Assess your understanding of engaging communities by taking this brief quiz.

FRAMEWORK FOR COMMUNITY ASSESSMENT

In any situation in which an assessment is called for, whether for an individual, family, or entire community, it is helpful to use a framework that can help guide the process. With respect to assessing communities, the work of Roland Warren (1978) again provides a useful starting point. He proposes that communities can be better understood if selected community variables are analyzed. Of particular interest are variables that represent characteristics that can be used to differentiate one community from another. For example, some communities are larger than most, some have greater diversity or different kinds of diversity or racial/ethnic mixes, some are wealthier than others, and some are more technologically advanced than others. Each community will have a unique historical context. Thus, a first step in assessing a community can be to create or adapt a framework that will help make comparisons on variables such as these from one community to another.

The following framework builds on Warren's work, and draws on community theories and perspectives introduced in Chapter 5. In Figure 6 we have identified four tasks that incorporate 11 activities to be used in assessing place-based and nonplace-based communities. The process of analyzing a community requires the social worker to go back and forth, returning to refine previous tasks as new data are gathered. Accordingly, the social worker is urged to employ the framework as an interactive guide rather than a rigid formula for community assessment. In subsequent chapters, we will present methods for planning changes based on this assessment.

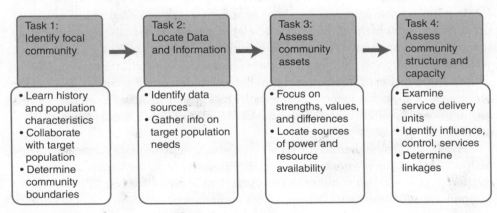

Figure 6.1
Tasks in the Framework for Assessing a Community

Task 1: Identify Focal Community

Many approaches to community assessment contend that the community must be understood in its totality to the greatest extent possible before intervention is planned, and this would be ideal if one had unlimited time. The first activity within this task is to learn as much as possible about the community's history. The task usually begins by gathering basic information on demographics of the community as a whole in order to set a context from which to focus the assessment. However, in order to avoid being overwhelmed with information, the second activity within this task narrows the assessment by identifying a target population. This allows the social worker to collaborate with target population members in gaining their perspectives and concerns in the assessment process.

Learn about Historical Context and Population Characteristics

Questions to be explored for this activity include the following:

- What is known about the history of this community?
- How many persons are members of this community, and what are their demographic characteristics?
- What social indicator data are available about this and similar communities?

Historical Context Gaining an historical perspective is important because it is the foundation on which the community is built. The significance of earlier events and the rootedness of some groups within the community will be seen differently by community members. It is helpful to ask if there are written histories of the community as well as persons who consider themselves to be community historians.

In place-based communities, there may be resources in local libraries, historical societies, or any archival source. Understanding this context of tradition and tension, a change agent can expect to encounter roadblocks to change, but may also gain insight into how to navigate the process in this deeply rooted community. In addition to gathering data-based information about the community, it is necessary to talk with people who understand the history of different population groups as perceived by its own members.

In nonplace communities, there may be someone who recorded a brief history or list of critical dates in the community's development or professionals who have studied that particular community. For example, consider the 2014 outbreak of Ebola in Africa, which affected not only the countries where the disease was concentrated but also the entire world because of international travel, the extreme ease of transmission, and the seriousness of the consequences. Knowing the background of how this global community developed provides context for understanding the complex social and political dimensions of community building.

People may define themselves as part of a geographical or place community based on location (e.g., the town where we live), but ethnicity (e.g., the Latino community), religion (e.g., the Jewish community), commitment to a position (e.g., the pro-choice community), profession (e.g., the social work community), avocation (e.g., the environmental movement community), and many other designations may be nonplace communities with which they strongly identify. Also, as this list suggests, each individual may simultaneously be part of many different communities (both place and nonplace).

Websites can be very useful sources of information about these very different types of communities.

For example, the Latina women in the Canyon City vignette at the beginning of this chapter may view their history differently than the women who are currently being served in domestic violence shelters. Hearing directly from them may raise the possibilities of alternative interventions that are more sensitive to cultural differences (e.g., working through a local Latino Catholic church, where trust has already been established). Similarly, in Lakeside, the older persons who have lived there all their lives and the newly arrived older adults who moved to be near their children will have different historical experiences. The sensitive practitioner will take the time to understand how different characteristics of target population members and their life experiences may contribute to a variety of attitudes and values.

It is also important to note that there are critical differences between urban, suburban, and rural communities. This approach may be particularly difficult in a rural community where community members are geographically dispersed. We also caution the reader not to assume that the target populations can be disengaged or isolated from the larger community, even though one may focus on specific subgroups for the purpose of the change episode. Members of the target population may already feel isolated from the larger community, so the actions of the social worker should avoid reinforcing this perception, while working to strengthen ties and reduce isolation.

Viewed graphically, a community might appear as a series of overlapping circles, representing important elements or reference groups within the community. A given individual could then be represented in a space formed from the overlap of the unique combination of elements relevant to that person, as illustrated in Figure 6.2. It is important to note that within these overlapping circles there are also attitudinal differences, assumptions, and worldviews that may be harder to identify within and between target population groups but need to be taken into consideration.

Target Population Characteristics   Identifying characteristics of the population begins with an examination of available **demographic data**, which refers to variables such as socioeconomic status, age, race, and gender. Information of this sort can be found online from the U.S. Census Bureau, which within cities break down the information by geographic units called *tracts*. Such divisions are relatively small and often incorporate as few as 3,000–8,000 people, making it possible to categorize community units as small as an individual neighborhood. Using this type of source, it is important to identify areas of poverty and high need, as well as to determine whether target populations are heavily concentrated in certain areas or are spread across an entire city or county.

Social indicator data may be helpful in gaining a broad overview of social problems at the international, national, regional, state, and local levels. These data are important sources of information about changes in social and economic trends in communities around the world. Direct measures of phenomena such as infant mortality rates or educational levels may be available for the community. Similarly, indirect measures of complex situations such as the use of divorce rates to indicate family stability or school dropout rates as an indicator of increasing gang membership may provide insight into target population concerns (Estes, 2013). For example, if dropout rates are much higher

> Watch the video where panelists address the barriers that have been put in the way of black males and strategies for how to overcome them. Why do the panelists suggest it is important to address the historical context of black male achievement in order to move toward solutions?
>
> www.youtube.com /watch?v=Eg__-R_Uivw

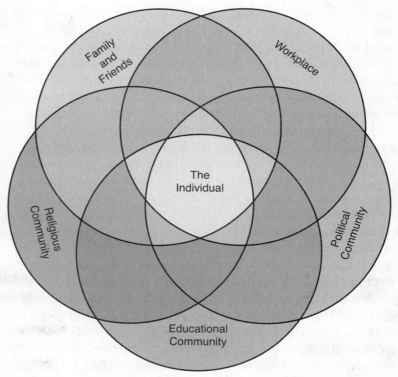

Figure 6.2
The Individual in the Community

for the target population than for other community members, these data may reinforce the need to focus on this group as a high priority.

In this way, the community's social problems can be comparatively assessed using various data displays such as cross-sectional analysis, time-series comparisons, comparison with other data units, and other displays, as discussed in Chapter 4. Other professionals in the community, or at the county or state level, can also be valuable sources of information. They may have firsthand experience with target populations, or their organizations may have conducted surveys or collected statistics of specific social problems. Accessing the websites of these organizations may reveal valuable and useful information. In a global world, there are sources of data about social and economic inequities that transcend national borders and provide regional perspectives for comparison purposes (International Social Work, 2014). In short, in today's world, almost any place or nonplace community has ready access to comparative data that provide a broader contextual perspective than was possible even a decade ago.

Identify and Collaborate with the Target Population

Questions to be explored for this activity include:

- Which community group or subgroup will be the target population of this assessment?
- What are the value and political implications of focusing on a specific group, and how will they be involved in the assessment process?

- Is this target population primarily part of a geographical, social, or political community or a combination?
- What priority is given to the needs of this target population in the community?
- What percentage of the target population is represented by people at risk of being underserved due to their race/ethnicity, gender, sexual orientation, age, disabilities, or other factors?

Identifying a Target Population   Population identification can be a difficult task because populations are varied and often have indistinct boundaries. Individual communities will have their own definitions of target populations, and they may not be congruent with how the target population defines itself. A target population can be narrowly or broadly defined, but the more precise its definition, the more feasible an understanding of its members becomes. Oftentimes, the target population is obvious because it is a group that is already designated as a part of a social worker's workload, or that the worker's agency wants to serve better.

The target population for a particular community assessment could be "people with domestic violence problems who live in Canyon City," or it could be "Latina women who have been the victims of physical abuse by spouses or significant others within the past two years in Canyon City." One is more inclusive, and the other more focused. It is probably advisable, at early stages of the analysis, that a broader definition be adopted, with the expectation that it may be narrowed as a clearer understanding of needed change emerges.

One note of caution is in order here when it comes to nonplace communities. Target population groups may not define their community according to the geographical lines established by planners and designated boundaries. For example, a person who self-identifies as transgender may have a strong symbolic relationship with other transgender persons who are scattered across multiple geographical communities. Yet, the community of transgender persons is as strong and collectively connected as that of persons who live in local neighborhoods, perhaps even more so. Thus, the practitioner who is working with the transgender community will be engaged with a population group that is more vertically connected than horizontally based, as are other groups within geographical communities.

One distinction that may be helpful in this process is offered by Rossi, Lipsey, and Freeman (2004), who distinguish between **populations at risk** and **populations at need**. A population at risk is one in danger of developing a particular problem, whereas a population at need is one in which the problem already exists. In a population at risk, change efforts may be oriented toward prevention; in a population at need, the change may be more focused on intervention or treatment. In the case of a neighborhood plagued by youth gangs, for example, the social worker may identify the target population as those youth who are at risk of being pressured to join a gang, in which case the goal may be to stop this from happening. Alternatively, youth already in gangs may be identified as the target population, in which case efforts might be focused on ways to free them from these gangs or divert the gangs from criminal activity.

A further task facing the social worker in selecting a target population is establishing criteria for deciding which community members are inside or outside this population. In the youth gang example, the social worker may decide to focus on kids at risk of joining a gang. After some study, he or she might propose that the criteria for being considered part of the target population would be to attend one of seven schools serving the neighborhood, to be between 10 and 14 years of age, and to belong to a particular ethnic group that has established gangs in the community. These criteria establish what Rossi and colleagues (2004) call the boundary of the target population.

Individual communities will have their own definitions of target populations. The social worker should determine how the community categorizes client groups for planning purposes. Local and regional planning agencies, United Ways, community councils, and associations of agencies often produce agreed-on classification schemes for data collection and planning purposes, and the social worker will need to decide whether to keep these definitions in establishing boundaries or to establish new definitions. Each approach can be expected to have certain advantages and disadvantages.

Collaborating with the Target Population   The choice of a particular target population is a choice of values. In every community there can be multitudes of groups with varying needs, but in most community change episodes it may only be possible to effectively address one group at a time. In many cases, the target population will be determined by a worker's work assignments or volunteer interests. However, in focusing on a single target, the social worker should think through and understand the implications of examining the community from a limited perspective. The kinds of questions that need to be asked include: How do people in this target population (and others close to them) perceive their concerns, problems, issues, and/or needs? Do they tend to see them in terms of a need for empowerment, freedom from oppression, access to opportunity, the removal of barriers, resources or services, and/or protection? These types of questions focus on the perceptions that target population members have about themselves in the context of their community.

All communities suffer some degree of inequitable distribution of income, opportunity, political representation, personal safety, or other social resources. This means that multiple underserved populations can be expected to exist, and not all can be addressed by a single effort. The initial task facing a social worker when assessing a community is to collaborate with the target population, recognizing that a large variety of populations might be in need of his or her efforts. Once recognized, the social worker is ethically bound to include members of the target population in the assessment process in whatever way is possible so that this becomes a collaborative effort.

Engagement

Behavior: Use empathy, reflection, and interpersonal skills to effectively engage diverse clients and constituencies.

Critical Thinking Question: How would you compare and contrast the engagement process in place and nonplace communities?

Determine Community Boundaries

Questions to be explored for this activity include the following:

- What are the designated boundaries of this community?
- How do members of the target population view community boundaries?
- Where are members of the target population located within the boundaries? Are they highly concentrated or scattered? Or are they a subgroup of a larger community?
- How compatible are jurisdictional boundaries of health and human service programs that serve the target population?

Boundaries are established in many different ways. A community may have legal boundaries, where one town ends and another begins, but if one views communities as systems with multiple overlapping subsystems, there will be social and psychological boundaries in addition to physical demarcations. In nonplace communities, boundaries are defined by who is in and who is out, regardless of physical location. These communities are likely connected in cyberspace and based on relationships or political purposes rather than tethered to a geographical space. Some nonplace communities may have very porous boundaries with limited membership criteria, whereas others may be highly exclusionary.

The practitioner may find that there are a small number of members of the target population concentrated in a particular area, yet if one expands the reach, there are many more persons in the target population across multiple geographical communities. Knowing how geographically contained or dispersed a target population is becomes important when one plans an intervention. For example, it may be hard to convince a funding source that enough people will be served if one defines boundaries too tightly, but if one joins with agencies in other communities across the city, county, or state, or even internationally, then the scope of the problem may be evident.

Earlier in this chapter, we discussed the establishment of criteria for inclusion of individuals in a target population, a process sometimes referred to as **boundary setting**. Another, more common use of the term *boundary* refers to the lines determining the geographical area occupied by a community. For a social worker involved in a macro-level intervention, one important consideration has to do with the extent of the area to be included. If resources are available to focus on the entire city or county, then these may be appropriate boundaries in that instance. If, however, the effort is to be undertaken by a small committee of volunteers who have limited time and resources, it may be better to focus the encounter on the part of a city or even a neighborhood in which there appears to be the greatest need for intervention. In nonplace communities, boundary setting may be around the numbers of members of the target population who can be served rather than their geographical location.

Establishing boundaries for a macro-level intervention is done by determining the characteristics (e.g., age, year in school, and presence of a problem), the geographical area of residence, or the shared interests of a target population. For most interventions in which boundaries involve geographic space, we recommend beginning with clearly recognizable units, such as a city or county, and then narrowing the focus to smaller areas if appropriate. It may be useful at this point to get a map of the geographical area and identify in some ways the areas of high concentrations of the target population. This is not intended to indicate that an intervention at the state, regional, or national level is inappropriate, but for the vast majority of interventions a level of county or smaller will be most relevant and practical. For nonplace interventions, establishing a manageable number of persons who can be served in a pilot approach may be a way to begin.

Figure 6.3 illustrates the boundary-setting process. Knowing that one cannot address all target population needs within large arenas, the encounter focuses on the target population within a manageable part of the broader community.

A target population or community defined by the area its members occupy may be a small section of the inner city or a large rural area containing scattered farms. The notion of community as space is usually applicable to Latino **barrios**, for example, since

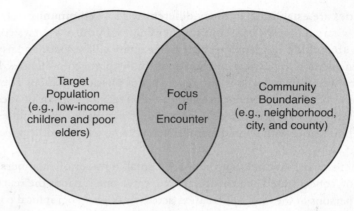

Figure 6.3
Setting Parameters for the Community Encounter

they typically have reasonably well-defined boundaries within a large metropolitan area. Spatial concepts of community are also applicable in less densely populated areas, but they may be more difficult to determine. This was noted by a Navajo social worker who explained how difficult it can be to determine spatial boundaries on a reservation where there may be no street systems, property information, or signs indicating county lines or well-defined human service areas. In a way, this student was experiencing the overlap of place and nonplace communities. The reservation was so dispersed that the major consideration needed to be identification as a tribal member rather than where each person actually lived.

Another characteristic important to understanding community as space are the jurisdictional units established by various government agencies for planning and service provision purposes (e.g., school districts or mental health catchment areas). Because the macro practitioner's focus is frequently limited to a designated geographical area, mapping overlapping jurisdictional units can be important and useful. For example, a change agent may be working with residents of a particular county to establish a prenatal healthcare campaign for pregnant teens, only to discover that he or she is dealing with representatives from multiple city and county governments as well as several school districts. Determining who is responsible within what geographical domain can be extremely important politically. Similarly, a practitioner hired by a mental health clinic may find that the clinic's catchment area overlaps parts of three school districts, requiring letters of agreement with multiple school boards. Being able to anticipate and adjust to these circumstances will aid in both planning and implementation of the change episode. When possible, it may be helpful to set boundaries congruent with established jurisdictional units because data and information will be organized within these boundaries, whereas working across existing boundaries may limit one's ability to compile the necessary information.

In nonplace communities, establishing boundaries will vary depending on how organized the nonplace community is. For example, if one is trying to address the needs of gay, lesbian, bisexual, and transgender persons, many of whom may not want other community members to know who they are, locating the target population may be difficult without assurances of confidentiality. Chances are that the target population will not conform to geographical parameters, and boundaries will have to remain somewhat fluid depending on who feels comfortable making their sexual orientation known. Conversely, in a community of interest based on getting the word out about a devastating disease such as Alzheimer's, the practitioner may have a ready cadre of advocates from the ranks of persons who have had experience with the disease in their families. They may be willing to join forces to work toward change and relieved to tell their stories to the larger public. These boundaries may also be fluid, expanding as more people join the cause from different locations. In both cases, neither community conforms to strict geographical boundaries, but they are held together by the boundaries of shared identities.

In their study of neighborhoods, Coulton and Mikelbank (2011) make an important point. When boundaries are fuzzy or arbitrarily defined, rather than based on a deep understanding of how community members construct meaningful relationships, the change process may unintentionally undermine target population involvement and control. Thus, boundary setting is critical to authentic collaboration with the target population.

Task 2: Locate Data and Information on Community Needs, Issues, and Problems

In communities with severe and/or urgent social problems, the scope of intervention may have to be narrowed in order to address problems in depth. Keeping strengths in mind, as issues and problems are recognized, may help the practitioner maintain a sense of balance (Green & Haines, 2002). In addition, it is important to recognize that there is much criticism of focusing on deficits to the neglect of assessing assets. Therefore, even though Task 2 involves the assessment of needs, issues, and problems, in Task 3 and 4 the focus moves to identifying strengths in the community's assets and capacity.

Identify Community Data Sources

Questions to be explored for this activity include the following:

- What data sources are available about community needs, issues, and problems?
- What methods are used to collect these data, and is this an ongoing process?
- What are the major issues and social problems in this community as perceived by their spokespersons?
- To what extent are these problems interconnected, and must some be solved before others can be addressed?

Ideally, services provided are designed to meet community needs. However, it is important to recognize that people's needs are always changing. This requires a human service system that has flexibility to respond to changing needs. Because the characteristics of community residents vary, there may be subgroups that require special attention. For example, if a community has a high proportion of retirees, one can expect that many of the services will address the needs of older people. If services are not available, the delivery system may not be adequately meeting community needs.

> Go to the Community Toolbox homepage, and locate the toolkit on assessing community needs and resources. What resources does the site suggest you access to understand the history and makeup of a community?

Needs Assessment   Meenaghan, Gibbons, and McNutt (2005) identified various methods of approaching a **needs assessment**. A summary of the advantages and disadvantages of these methods are reviewed in Table 6.1.

...nt Methods: Advantages and Disadvantages

	Description	Advantages	Disadvantages
	Community forums Public hearings Face-to-face interaction Focus groups	Provides opportunities to hear directly from the target population	Often difficult to locate people who fully understand the issues; also time consuming
Collecting servi... statistics	Utilization and rates Waiting lists Caseload data	Provides information from those who serve the target population	Is limited by what is collected and how well data are managed
Locating epidemiological studies (of the origins of problems)	Analyzing existing data	Data are already collected and usually accessible.	Analysis is restricted by what data were collected
Finding studies of the incidence and prevalence of problems	Reporting what previous studies have found	Studies have already been conducted and findings are available	Generalizability of findings may be limited
Accessing social indicators	Reviews of data such as income, age, and occupation	Data are available and provide broad overview of community	Indicators do not provide detailed information
Conducting and locating surveys	Interviews with community members	Provides broad overview of needs	Requires great time and expense

Given limited time, practitioners often have to rely on existing data. Original data collection is expensive and time consuming, and is usually beyond the scope of the macro practitioner unless a particular change effort has widespread community and financial backing. Ideally, the macro practitioner would like to know (1) the number of people who are experiencing each problem and (2) the number of people who are being served by existing resources. The first number minus the second number represents unmet need. Unmet needs, inadequately met needs, or inappropriately met needs are typically the focus of macro-level change.

With special population groups that require multiple services, classification schemes are often based on the concept of a continuum of care. A *continuum of care* consists of a broad menu of services from which items can be selected to address the specific needs of certain individuals or groups. Ideally, each menu will vary based on what is needed for the target population served. Table 6.2 provides one way of classifying continuum-of-care services for those persons requiring long-term care, with in-home services being the least restrictive care environment and institutional services being the most restrictive.

Understanding Collective Needs   As we discussed in Chapter 5, need is an elusive and complex concept that must be understood from a variety of perspectives. What we have discussed thus far are individual needs experienced by many people. When one person is hungry, it is an individual problem; when hundreds of people are hungry and the community is not prepared to assist, it is a social problem. When needs outstrip resources, it is a communitywide problem and may require a human service response. More food banks, more homeless shelters, or more employment training services may be needed.

Social problems are negatively labeled "conditions" recognized by community residents. Identified social problems will vary by community and target population.

Table 6.2   Continuum of Long-Term Care Services by Category

In-Home Services	Community-Based Services	Institutional Services
Outreach	Case management	Alcohol and drug treatment
Information and referral	Transportation	Rehabilitation
Comprehensive geriatric assessment	Senior centers	Psychiatric care
Emergency response system	Senior discount programs	Swing beds or step-down units
Companionship/friendly visiting	Recreational activities	Skilled nursing care
Telephone reassurance	Caregiver support groups	Extended care
Caregiver respite services	Self-help groups	Assisted living
Homemaker and chore services	Counseling	
Household repair services	Foster homes	
Personal care	Adult care homes	
Home-delivered meals	Shared housing	
Home health	Congregate housing	
In-home high-technology therapy	Wellness and health promotion clinics	
Hospice	Geriatric assessment clinics	
	Physician services	
	Adult day care	
	Mental health clinics	
	Outpatient clinics	

Sometimes there are conditions that have not been labeled as problems. It may be the social worker's task to bring these conditions to the attention of people in power so that they are recognized as social problems. This is not always easy because community residents may have a great deal invested in denying that there is a problem. Issues are points over which there are disagreements. Community members may disagree over whether something is a problem, over how resources are to be used to address a problem, or a host of other points. It is helpful to know what the points of disagreement are.

Once major social problems defined by community members have been identified, one can begin to determine their incidence and prevalence. **Incidence** is defined as a phenomenon actually occurring over a period of time (Kettner, Daley, & Nichols, 1985, p. 72). For example, 15 students may have been arrested for drug use in the local high school in the most recent academic year. **Prevalence** is tied to the number of cases of the phenomenon that exist within a community at any one time (Kettner et al., 1985, p. 72). For example, current estimates indicate that drug use among teenagers is as high as 50 percent.

Healthy communities need to ensure adequately functioning systems of service and sufficient support to enable their citizens to achieve basic standards for quality of life. This includes an economic base that produces jobs and income, affordable housing, adequate transportation, sound public health practices, quality education for children, public safety, and freedom to pursue obligations and interests without fear. When these conditions are absent, a service response (more money, or more resources of any kind) may provide temporary relief without dealing with fundamental structural problems.

The long-term need may be for group empowerment, a collective sense of dignity, full participation in decisions that affect the lives of people in the community, self-direction, or self-control. Assessing collective need requires understanding the history and development of the community, an ability to compare economic and social problem data to those of other communities, and sensitivity to the needs and aspirations of those who are part of the community.

Gather Information Specific to Target Population Needs

Questions to be explored for this activity include the following:

- What needs assessment data and other relevant information are available about the target population?
- How do persons in the target population perceive their community's responsiveness to their needs?
- Do some members of the target population experience greater unmet needs due to their race/ethnicity, gender, sexual orientation, age, disabilities, or other factors?
- Are there subgroups of the target population that are experiencing oppressive conditions and discrimination?

People who are identified as being in a target population may be consumers of services or persons in need of services. Macro-level interventions tend to be conceptualized and organized around a selected population and a specific problem they are experiencing. For example, a social worker might discover a lack of child care options for teenaged parents who wish to return to school.

The purpose of establishing a profile of issues and problems in the community is to understand the conditions affecting the target population in context of the broader whole.

Research-Informed Practice (or Practice-Informed Research)

Behavior: Use and translate research evidence to inform and improve practice, policy, and service delivery.

Critical Thinking Question: Why does the professional knowledge base (including practice and research findings) not replace gathering information directly from persons affected by the problem?

This requires both direct contact and searching the professional knowledge base. Direct contact with people who can articulate the problems and needs of the target population gives the practitioner a different interpretation of the issues. The professional knowledge base adds theoretical background as well as practice and research findings based on the experiences of others with the same or similar populations and problems. This is helpful information, but it does not replace gathering information directly from persons affected by the problem.

We cannot emphasize strongly enough the importance of primary sources in understanding a target population. Populations must be understood in terms of their diversity. In family practice, for example, the meaning of family and accompanying role expectations may differ from one culture to the next. Similarly, the ways in which members of the gay and lesbian community define family may differ radically from traditional community values. In border states, many people are expressing strong opinions on illegal immigration. People who live on the border (mayors, law enforcement people, and citizens) are vocal and critical of those who do not take the time to consult with persons who live with the problem every day and have important insights into how immigration should be addressed. A target population will not be adequately understood if these potentially widely divergent views are not respected and taken into consideration.

Identifying needs, issues, and problems helps in two ways: (1) It enables the macro practitioner to appreciate the full range of possibilities as well as difficulties experienced by the target population, thereby helping to prioritize needs; and (2) it should help in proposing more realistic solutions. For example, sometimes there are resources to address a transportation need, and in doing so, a bigger problem of access to services can be addressed.

Some people are uncomfortable with differences, and because they assume that one way must be better than another way, they look on differences as a problem to be solved. An alternative perspective is that differences reflect a variety of ways to view the world, to believe, and to behave. Social workers can employ differences as potential strengths within a target population, but they must remember that differences often include alternative definitions of a successful outcome.

Areas around which oppression often occurs are gender, race, ethnicity, sexual orientation, age, and ability. Depending on the target population, all of the resulting "isms" or selected ones may be relevant. For example, older minority women who live in poverty face triple jeopardy—they are old, female, and poor. Their experience points to generations of blocked opportunities, discrimination, and neglect. Serious damage is done to the fabric of the country, and therefore to the fabric of its communities, when any group of people is discriminated against as a whole category, when an individual is treated only as a member of a group, and when individual differences are disregarded. Thus, recognizing discriminatory behavior from the target population's perspectives is essential in assessing the community.

Task 3: Assess Community Social and Political Assets

In Chapter 5, three dimensions of community have been identified: (1) geographical or place, (2) social/relational, and (3) political (with a little "p"). In this task, we focus primarily on the latter two because both are relevant in both place and nonplace communities. In addition, asset mapping was described in the previous chapter as a process in which change agents engage with community members in identifying both tangible and intangible assets. In this task, activities primarily focus on intangible assets: strengths and values, as well as power and resource availability.

Focus on Community Strengths, Values, and Differences

Questions to be explored for this activity include the following:

- What strengths and resiliencies are evident in this community?
- Are there opportunities (e.g., organizations, rules, procedures, and policies) to engage community members in open communication?
- To what extent are the perspectives of people of color; women; gay men, lesbians, and transgender persons; older persons; and persons with disabilities sought in decisions affecting the target population?

- What cultural values, traditions, and beliefs are important to the target population as individuals or as a whole?
- What are the predominant values (and potential value conflicts) that affect the target population within this community?

Often overlooked are the strengths (assets) of a community. Community strengths are assets from which one can draw (Kretzmann & McKnight, 1993). In addition, understanding dominant values is important in determining community expectations and the "fit" of various population groups with one another. Value characteristics will provide clues to the practitioner about what is important to community members. Clearly, these intangible assets will affect the nature of the macro-level analysis and, ultimately, the intervention.

Values as Assets   For example, the social worker who has discovered a lack of child care options may also discover a strong kinship network and that grandparents are active in their grandchildren's lives. The increasing problem of malnutrition may overshadow the fact that a number of area congregations are ready and willing to provide meals to older people. And African Americans and Latino groups who feel that the city council is willing to be responsive to their issues may have strong motivations to have their voices heard, have a strong sense of community identity, and be eager to mobilize. It is important for the practitioner to identify strengths that may make the difference in determining whether a community can address its issues and problems.

In the previous chapter, we discussed the importance of values in gaining a basic understanding of community. **Community values** are beliefs that are strongly held by persons who make up the community. The idea of shared values requires refinement in today's changing world. At one time, communities without divisions of labor (e.g., farming communities) were more likely to have shared value systems. Early community values had a great deal to do with such issues as self-sufficiency, taking care of one's own family needs, and minimal reliance on government services. Even today, political differences are often defined in terms of one set of beliefs being framed around minimum standards of care for all versus an alternative set of beliefs focused on individuals and families receiving only the standards of care they can afford. These values are often reinforced by the associations and organizations with which community residents affiliate.

One must take care not to assume a single, common, shared value system in contemporary communities or among members of a target population. For example, if the target population comprises persons who have been abused, members of that group will cut across all socioeconomic levels and a host of other differences. They may have completely different perspectives on how abuse is defined and how they define healthy relationships.

Depending on the selected target population, practitioners will find a host of value perspectives. For example, if the target population is people with AIDS, some persons in the community will feel strongly that such people deserve the best possible care and comfort, whereas others will react in fear, not wanting people with AIDS in their local acute and long-term care facilities. Similarly, if the target population is pregnant teenagers, value conflicts may arise between community residents who believe that teenagers should be given contraceptive information and those who believe that this information will only encourage sexual activity.

Jansson (2015) sees value clarification as critically important in asking questions about social welfare responses to various target population groups. He poses questions such as the following:

- Should the target population receive services, and on what terms?
- For what needs and problems is a community responsible, and what target population needs should receive priority?
- What strategies should be used to address specific target population strengths, issues, and problems?
- Should the community give preferential assistance or treatment to the target population?

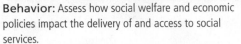

Policy Practice

Behavior: Assess how social welfare and economic policies impact the delivery of and access to social services.

Critical Thinking Question: Why are value clarification questions so important to assessing how policies impact the delivery of and access to social services?

These value clarification questions may be answered differently depending on the population targeted within the community. This series of questions implies that some populations may be valued more than others; that is, some may be perceived as "deserving," and others as "undeserving."

Depending on the target population group, there may be subgroups within the larger whole that are viewed differently. Recognition of the importance of diversity will lead the macro practitioner to check carefully the values of each ethnic or racial group affected; the possible different perspectives of women and men in the target population; and the perspectives of representatives of gay, lesbian, bisexual, and transgender groups if they are affected by the change. It is wiser to take the time to be inclusive of a wide range of values than to find out, too late, that a change effort is not working because differing perspectives were overlooked.

Dynamics of Difference   As one begins to form an understanding of major community value perspectives, one must take care to recognize the fit (or lack of fit) between target population perspectives and dominant community perspectives. Are target population perspectives taken into consideration when decisions are made that affect them? Recognizing value differences and power discrepancies is an important part of the community assessment process.

Regardless of the target population identified, there will be differences between this population and other groups within the community. There will also be differences within the target population. Potential differences include gender, social class, spiritual and religious beliefs, sexual orientation, age, and physical and mental ability.

The "dynamics of difference" (Cross, Bazron, Dennis, & Isaacs, 1989, p. 20) may involve cross-cultural exchanges where groups with diverse histories and values interact. There is always the possibility of misunderstanding and misinterpretation when this occurs. "Both will bring culturally-prescribed patterns of communication, etiquette, and problem-solving. Both may bring stereotypes or underlying feelings about serving or being served by someone who is different" (Cross et al., 1989, p. 20). For example, professionals who serve older adults may rationalize why they do not serve many Latino clients by stereotyping Latino families as taking care of their own and therefore needing few formal services. This oversimplification may ignore the fact that one-fourth of the Latino families in a local community are poor, and caring for an older family member is a tremendous financial burden. It also ignores the fact that not all Latino older adults have other family members residing in the community.

Differences may be subtle or taken for granted, yet they may influence the way in which members of the target population communicate with one another and with other groups. For example, feminist scholars encourage the recognition of gender differences (e.g., O'Connor & Netting, 2009), and Tannen's research indicates that men and women speak in "genderlects" that comprise "cross cultural communication" (1990, p. 18). For example, a male social worker was assessing a community's responsiveness to single mothers with young children. He attended several support groups for the target population and was frustrated that all they did was talk without coming to a consensus on what they wanted from the larger community. He assessed part of the problem as an unwillingness on the part of the target population to face up to their problems and to work on solutions. The women in the support group, however, felt that this was an opportunity to process their thoughts and feelings. They did not view the group as a place to immediately resolve problems. The group was a place to make connections and to achieve intimacy. Note how the support group performed a nurturing function in light of the larger demands of the sustaining community system. Also, observe how important it is to be culturally sensitive to gender, recognizing the strengths of this nurturing system in supporting the women.

Identifying value conflicts is critical to recognizing oppression and discrimination. Values may be based on prejudices, those prejudgments that community residents have about the target group that are not grounded in systematic evidence. The issue of systematic evidence is one that needs to be treated with care and sensitivity. Many people still believe that every individual essentially controls his or her own destiny and that hard work and persistence will overcome any barrier or limitation. This belief is reinforced when severely disabled persons accomplish incredible physical feats or severely deprived persons make it to the top. These accomplishments become "evidence" for local, state, and national leaders that those who need help are simply not trying hard enough. People who hold this belief look at what they consider to be systematic evidence and deny that their beliefs are prejudices. What is overlooked here, however, is generations of differential treatment that have made it difficult for people of color, women, persons with physical and developmental disabilities, and others to have equal access to economic resources and self-sufficiency.

An alternative view is the **capabilities perspective** (Sen & Williams, 1982) in which it is recognized that not all people have the opportunity to start at the same place and that consideration must be given to what it takes to get to the place where they can compete with others (Nussbaum, 2006). So, for example, when a job is available and a homeless person chooses not to take it, one person will see that as evidence that he is lazy, whereas another will recognize it as a response to a lifetime of hopeless, discouraging, dead-end jobs in which skill development was never a possibility. For some, the pain of life on the street is less than the pain of hopelessness in their share of the workplace. In this situation, a practitioner using the capabilities perspective will know to start from where the client is and design a change effort that respects the homeless person within his or her context.

Locate Sources of Power and Resource Availability

Questions to be explored in this activity include the following:

- What funding sources are subsidizing services for the target population, and through what groups, associations, organizations, and agencies?

- How would you describe the power structure (including both formal and informal leaders) and resource availability within this community?
- How accessible are services for the target population?

As local (horizontal) and extracommunity (vertical) ties have expanded in communities, so have bureaucratization and its accompanying impersonalization. Bureaucratic structures are usually adopted by government, businesses, and voluntary organizations as size of population increases. Funding patterns can lead to power brokers external to the community. Being the major source of funding for local service efforts implies the ability to influence and direct provider decisions regarding target population needs. For example, the specialized volunteer-run, community-based agency that once served the neighborhood may have been transformed into a multiservice agency with many paid staff members. This means that there may be a number of leaders within the health and human service system, all representing different sectors (e.g., government, nonprofit, and for-profit). In addition, the larger multiservice organization may have multiple funding sources, including federal, state, and local government funds; the United Way; private contributions; and fees. Each source must be satisfied that its expectations are being met.

Power and Resources   Viewing the community from a power perspective requires identifying the formal and informal leaders within a community. It also means examining their effectiveness. Assessing the political climate requires reading the local newspaper and talking with local community leaders to determine the top-priority issues competing for funding. If a legislative change is needed, it is necessary to identify who may be willing to take the lead on issues affecting the target population.

Community power has been viewed from three perspectives: (1) an **elitist structure**, (2) a **pluralist structure**, and (3) an **amorphous structure**. An *elitist* approach assumes that a small number of people have disproportionate power in various community sectors and that this power remains constant regardless of the issue. A *pluralist* perspective implies that, as issues change, various interest groups and shifting coalitions arise. This perspective increases as more special-interest groups develop within the local community. The *amorphous* structure implies no persistent pattern of power relationships within the community (Meenaghan, Gibbons, & McNutt, 2005). Understanding the community's power dynamics will enable the practitioner to evaluate the community for this task.

Related to community structure is the issue of available resources. Communities can be described as *resource rich* or *resource poor* when it comes to providing for the needs of the target population. Although it is important to consider resources in connection with power, it is also important to compile information on resources so that appropriate sources will be targeted in pursuit of community change.

There are many types of resources to consider. Resources may be tangible, such as a welfare check, or symbolic, such as caring or social support. Resources can include status, information, money, goods, or services. Most early community encounters will focus heavily on the more concrete resources that are exchanged (money, goods, and services) because tangible resources are easier to define and observe. However, as the professional becomes more actively engaged in community practice, there will be more opportunities to learn about symbolic exchanges (status and information) that are equally important to members of the target population.

Resources may be available from a variety of domains. King and Mayers (1984) have developed Guidelines for Community Assessment designed for use in analyzing community resources. They suggest that when assessing community resources available to a particular population, a number of domains should be explored. Within each domain, questions of policy, practice, eligibility, location, and participation must be addressed in order to determine how available each resource is to the target population. Their domains are as follows:

- Health
- Welfare
- Education
- Housing
- Recreation
- Employment
- Business
- Religion

For example, if the target population is low-income children, resources to be explored would include Medicaid (health), child welfare services (welfare), school programs (education), public housing, child care programs provided by parents' places of employment, corporate community service initiatives (business), and faith-based groups involved in serving their communities (religion). One would want to ask: How effective are these systems in meeting the needs of the community's children and satisfying the expectations of the community? How do programs within each of these domains relate to one another?

Service Accessibility   Access is affected by a number of variables, including population density, the distribution of service need, the ability of area residents to pay for services, the existence of competition among service providers, and transportation options available to consumers. Population density is important because service sites tend to arise where enough prospective service recipients are available to ensure steady demand. This is why accessibility is often dramatically more limited in rural areas and thinly populated suburbs than in cities. Similarly, services tend to gravitate toward areas of need; thus, child care centers will be more common where there are concentrations of families with children, whereas senior centers will be more common where more older adults congregate. Gaps arise when no single group predominates, when demographic characteristics are changing rapidly, or when information is scarce regarding population characteristics and needs.

Services also tend to be located where consumers can pay, even if the service is offered by nonprofit organizations. For example, in recent years, many cities have experienced high rates of hospital closures in low-income neighborhoods. These hospitals may be run by charitable organizations and may have existed for many years, but the combination of high costs, lack of health insurance or other resources on the part of local residents, and high demand for costly emergency care may render it financially impossible for the hospital to remain open. Nonprofit organizations must also compete with for-profits for paying customers, and this often leads to steering services and service locations away from those most in need. Finally, low-income residents of a community who require a particular service may still be able to reach it if public transit or other transportation resources are in place. However, transit systems are usually better developed in the most densely populated parts of a community and increasingly scarce in suburbs or newly developed areas. The social worker will need to be aware of these dynamics and the ways they interact in order to understand variations in service accessibility from one part of a community to another.

Having examined the resources available to the target population, those involved in community assessment should examine the structure and capacity of the human service delivery system. This is addressed in Task 4.

Task 4: Assess Community Structure and Capacity

The fourth task in the community assessment is to map its tangible assets and its capacity to effect action. Different structural domains will be important, depending on the defined problem and the needs of the target population. Recall that in Chapter 5 a variety of models were identified, each depicting different organizing structures. For example, one might focus on the city if the problem is homelessness or focus on the school district if the problem is a high dropout rate. The domain may be a mental health catchment area or the planning and service area (PSA) of an Area Agency on Aging. The goal is for the macro practitioner to recognize the units that deliver service; the patterns of influence, control, and service delivery; and the linkages between units that affect the capacity to address target population needs. The practitioner will need to know how community groups advocate for, participate in, and engage in service provision.

Examine Service Delivery Units

Questions to be explored in this activity include the following:

- What informal units (e.g., household, natural, and social networks) are actively engaged in service delivery to the target population?
- What mediating units (e.g., self-help groups and voluntary or grassroots associations) are actively engaged in service delivery to the target population?
- What formal service delivery units (e.g., nonprofit, public, and/or for-profit) are actively engaged in service delivery?
- Are there differences in service delivery that appear to be based on race or ethnicity, gender, sexual orientation, disability, age, or religion?

Part of the community's structure is its human service system and the programs it offers persons in need. Table 6.3 identifies the types of units that should be considered when assessing service provision in a community. These units, taken together, comprise the total health and human service delivery system within the community, and they operate interdependently. A community, depending on the availability of resources, may emphasize the provision of services through one set of units more than another. For example, in a resource-poor community, reliance on informal units may be a necessity until publicly funded formal services can be obtained. However, elements of informal, mediating, and formal service units will be found in each community. The astute practitioner will carefully assess all avenues of service delivery for the target population.

Table 6.3   Units Comprising the Health and Human Service Delivery System

Informal Units	Mediating Units	Formal Units
Household units	Self-help groups	Voluntary nonprofit agencies
Neighborhood groups	Grassroots associations	Public agencies
	Voluntary associations	For-profit agencies

In Chapter 5, we discussed the importance of informal and mediating units in understanding communities. Household units consist of persons who reside within a common dwelling, whether they consider themselves families, significant others, friends, partners, or roommates. Natural support systems evolve around mutual support, going beyond purely social networks, and engaging in resource exchange. Assessing these informal and mediating units is somewhat difficult simply because they are "informal," and therefore less accessible. Yet, any information that can be gathered will be helpful because it is often these less visible activities that make a quality difference for people in need.

Formal vehicles of health and human service delivery are interconnected in numerous ways. For example, one might become a member of the Alliance of Information and Referral Systems (AIRS), which is an umbrella organization for providers of information and referral programs and seeks to enhance the capacity of local service networks (AIRS, 2015). The AIRS program might put you in touch with other communities and how they organize their service-delivery units. We will briefly examine service-delivery units according to three types of auspice: **nonprofit**, **public** (governmental), and **for-profit** (commercial).

Nonprofit Agencies   As voluntary associations become more formal, they may become incorporated as nonprofit agencies, recognized as publicly chartered tax-free organizations. There are many types of nonprofit agencies, but we will focus on nonprofit human service agencies. Nonprofit agencies are formal vehicles of health and human service delivery. They are often viewed within local communities as the agency of choice—a voluntary initiative that targets a specialized clientele.

Nonprofit agencies provide many different services within local communities. Although all nonprofit agencies using government funding serve clients without regard to race or gender, a growing number of agencies are specifically designed to serve the special needs of ethnic communities and families, women who are victims of discrimination and/or violence, and other groups underserved by more traditional agencies. The macro practitioner should identify which nonprofit agencies serve the target population and whether they have particular service emphases.

Public Agencies   The public sector consists of federal, state, regional, county, and city government entities. When the mutual support function is performed by government, it is referred to as *social welfare*. The U.S. social welfare system has been described as a scattered, unpatterned mixture of programs and policies that does not work in a systematic way and is not easy to understand (Karger & Stoesz, 2013).

By the time federal programs are operating within the local community, they have usually gone through several levels of bureaucracy. Depending on the structure, which will vary by program type, there may be several extracommunity levels through which dollars have flowed. There may be regional as well as state mandates, rules, regulations, and procedures that instruct local providers regarding what they can and cannot do. Local decision making and autonomy will vary depending on the policies that drive a particular program. In short, extracommunity sources have a definite influence on the local delivery of public services.

Understanding the political system within the community is a challenge. In the United States, jurisdiction over health and human service programs is distributed across cities, counties, and states. Social workers must contend with federal statutes, regulations, administrative rules, and funding formulas, as well as identify state and local laws and funding procedures (Jansson, 2011).

Professional colleagues, however, can provide perspectives on types of services and whether government is truly addressing the needs of the target population. For example, for macro practitioners working in a public housing development, social workers in other developments will be helpful in interpreting how regulations assist as well as constrain their efforts. Locating colleagues in similar settings is important to developing a professional support system to aid in coping with public policies, procedures, and rules.

For-Profit Agencies   For-profit firms also provide human services, especially in arenas such as hospital and nursing-home care. As of 2015, at least 17 health-related companies (not including pharmaceutical manufacturers) were on the Fortune 500 list of the largest commercial firms in the United States (Fortune.com, 2015), and all of these had annual revenues exceeding the $3.9 billion in charitable donations raised by United Way nationally in its 2012 campaign (Chronicle of Philanthropy, 2013). Other areas in which large human service corporations have developed include child care, home-based nursing care, and corrections. Private counseling firms, though traditionally small in scale, are also a part of this sector. All these organizations share a principal reliance on fee-for-service revenues.

If all these entities making up the structure of a community's social welfare system present a somewhat confusing picture to the student or new practitioner, that confusion is understandable and shared by many. If one looks at structure as a continuum, at one extreme might be the public education system and at the other the entrepreneurial or business system. Education is highly organized with increasingly more challenging curricula at each level from kindergarten through graduate education. In any community, if a parent wishes to have the educational needs of his or her child met, the appropriate educational services can usually be located in relatively short order. The business sector, on the other hand, is made up of large and small organizations where someone perceived a need and proceeded to design some sort of a procurement and delivery system. There is not necessarily any order to it, and finding a particular product or service to meet a need may be a very lengthy process. Human services is somewhere in the middle. Every community includes certain services mandated by some level of government, but there is nothing to prevent an individual from perceiving a need and providing a service as a volunteer, nonprofit, or for-profit organization. The result is often a very complex web or network of services designed to meet the needs of a given population, and a beginning exploration of agencies' websites may be time well spent.

Identify Patterns of Influence, Control, and Service Delivery

Questions to be explored for this activity include the following:

- What groups, associations, and organizations (both extracommunity and in the local community) advocate for and provide assistance to the target population?
- How is resource distribution to the target population influenced by interaction (both electronic and face-to-face) within the community?
- What limits are placed on services to the target population, and who establishes these limits?
- What roles do citizens and consumers play in the control of services to the target population?

When assessing patterns and levels of participation, it is important that the macro practitioner distinguish between citizen and consumer-client participation. There are many citizens who, for reasons of altruism and conviction, are committed to fighting for the rights of the poor and oppressed. They bring a certain perspective to the discussion and make a contribution to constructive change in communities. However, it should not be assumed that interested citizen advocates represent the same perspective as those persons directly affected by the problem. Representatives of the target population should, whenever possible, be sought out to represent themselves in their own words; it should not be left to professionals and other concerned citizens to speak for them.

When dealing with the question of control over service availability to a target population, there can be both intracommunity and extracommunity sources of control—referring to whether the organization's headquarters are within or outside the community. In practice, external and internal patterned interactions tend to develop as community units work together. Examples of extracommunity sources of control are state and federal government funding of community-based health clinics. Resources are typically allocated through contracts that include regulations and performance expectations. Thus, various human service agencies within the local community interact with these extracommunity public entities. Relationships internal to a community have an important part in linking community subsystems together. Organizations with similar interests often form loosely knit federations to accomplish certain functions where there are common interests. For example, several women's groups may form a coalition to establish a battered women's shelter or a political action committee.

There are not only horizontal relationships that tie one to local informal and formal groups and organizations within the community but also numerous vertical ties that transcend geographical boundaries. Local community autonomy may be reduced as extracommunity forces influence what one does and how one thinks. The importance of extracommunity forces on the target population within the local community must be considered in order to understand service distribution patterns. On the other hand, extracommunity forces may actually strengthen communities by providing more options and additional resources as well as requiring performance expectations so important to accountability.

How powerful the controlling entities become in a community often depends on the extent of citizen involvement. Before the Internet, citizen participation was primarily a face-to-face proposition, but today entire webs of relationships can develop sight unseen given multiple forms of electronic access. Citizen participation can take the form of a number of roles, including reviewing and commenting on various materials such as reports and proposals. This review process may be carried out electronically, in committee meetings, through requests for feedback from selected individuals, or through public hearings. Advising and consulting involve giving opinions about what needs to be done, whereas an advisory role usually involves a more formal ongoing mechanism such as a United Way advisory council or planning committee. Although advisory committees do not have the power of policy boards, they can have a strong voice because of their access to decision makers. In addition, their opinions may proactively affect proposals rather than simply reacting to programs designed by others. Governance occurs when citizens and consumers are placed in positions of control over decisions, such as policy statements, or become members on boards of directors. These types of positions allow for the greatest amount of control by citizens and consumers. For example, a consumer who serves on the governing board of a family service agency may convince other board members that quality child care services for single mothers should be a top agency priority.

> Go to the BoardSource homepage and locate the free community resources section. What publications might be useful in understanding and assessing nonprofit boards?

One cannot assume that citizen participation automatically goes hand-in-hand with changes practitioners initiate within the community. The concept of citizen participation is essential to democracy, but it will often involve groups who disagree with one another. Just as citizens may comprise the local board of planned parenthood, there are citizens who believe that some of the services offered by this agency are morally wrong. Whenever interested citizens and consumers participate in community activities, these types of clashes should be expected.

Simply knowing what groups and agencies are available is not enough. It is important for the macro practitioner to know whether they actually work together so that target groups do not fall through gaps in the service delivery system. Thus, the last task in the assessment process examines the linkages evident to the practitioner and requires a judgment as to whether these interacting units truly comprise a system that is responsive to multiple needs.

Determine Linkages between Units

Questions to be explored for this activity include the following:

- How are the various types of service units generally connected?
- What are the established linkages between units that serve the target population within *this* community?
- Where are linkages between service units obviously needed but not currently established?
- Are the interests of people of color, women, gay men, lesbians, transgender persons, and other oppressed groups represented in the network established through linkages between units?

If there are multiple agencies with overlapping relationships and numerous types of services, is there a glue that holds the community's delivery system together? Certainly there may be competition among units, but there will also be connections. Just as the individual is embedded in a social network, group and organizational units are embedded within a service community. These relational patterns may change over time.

Table 6.4   Five Levels of Interaction among Service Providers

Level of Interaction	Type of Relationship	Characteristics	Level of Provider Autonomy
Communication	Friendly, cordial	Sharing of ideas between units, including consultation	High
Cooperation	May be defined as an affiliation	Working together to plan and implement independent programs	High
Coordination	Could be a federation-, association-, or coalition-type relationship	Working together to avoid duplication and to assist one another in sharing information, advertising for one another, and making referrals	Moderate
Collaboration	Could be a consortium, network, or joint venture	Joining together to provide a single program or service, with shared resources	Moderate
Confederation		Merging into one entity	Autonomy relinquished

Sources: Adapted from the works of Tobin, Ellor, and Anderson-Ray (1986); and Bailey and Koney (2000).

A number of writers have created typologies of how organizations relate to one another. Tobin, Ellor, and Anderson-Ray (1986) have identified five levels of interaction between human service agencies within the community: communication, cooperation, coordination, collaboration, and confederation. Bailey and Koney (2000) identify four levels: affiliation; federation, association, or coalition; consortium, network, or joint venture; and merger, acquisition, or consolidation. Table 6.4 provides an adaptation of these various categories, each of which are discussed next.

Communication   Communication can be formal or informal. Information and referral exemplifies formal communication that happens between units on a daily basis. Communication designed to increase interagency information and understanding may be enhanced through the use of websites such as social networking sites like Facebook, brochures, pamphlets, and media. In this sense, it is an affiliation process. Informal communication occurs between units as groups meet to discuss community issues, and as staff engage in email exchanges and text messaging, or even talk about their programs at conferences. Although communication is assumed to occur, breakdowns in the delivery system often happen because this process of sharing information across units is not nurtured, and there are so many ways to communicate that it may be hard to track these relationships. Often, written agreements are developed as a reminder of the importance of constant communication as staff change within organizations and new groups are formed within the community.

Cooperation   Cooperation occurs when units within the community agree to work toward similar goals. A local private child care center may work closely with a public human service agency. Both want to provide support for single parents with young children, yet these units provide different resources. Social workers at the child care center meet with staff at the human service agency once a month to discuss common concerns and to maintain a sense of continuity for parents who are clients of both agencies. The practitioner needs to know that these linkages are established and should also be actively involved in establishing them.

Corporate volunteerism represents a cooperative linkage between the for-profit and nonprofit sectors. The concept of corporate volunteerism is manifested in a number of ways (Brudney, 2005). A business may subsidize its employees by giving them release time to do community service work. Other companies will loan employees to human service agencies for a specified period of time so that the expertise required for a project can be provided at no cost to the agency. As employees near retirement, the for-profit sector often provides preretirement training in which postretirement volunteer opportunities are presented. In this way, the for-profit sector actually performs a recruitment function for the nonprofit service delivery system.

The interchange between the for-profit and nonprofit sectors also occurs in the form of corporate cash and in-kind contributions. Computer manufacturers may donate hardware to a local service agency, assisting in computerizing its information system. Restaurants donate food to homeless shelters. A local for-profit nursing home may open its doors to older community residents who live alone in a large metropolitan area during a time of anxiety over a crime wave.

Coordination   Coordination implies a concerted effort to work together. Often, separate units will draft agreements, outlining ways in which coordination will occur. Federations, associations, and coalitions may be formed.

In a continuum of care system that attempts to address the needs of such populations as older persons, those with disabilities, or people with AIDS within the community, coordination is necessary. As consumers exit the acute-care hospital, discharge planners work to develop a care plan. This requires knowledge of and close coordination with local service providers. Service plans often include a package to support the exiting client's needs—mobile meals, visiting nurses, and homemaker services. Depending on the level of disability and the length of time expected for recovery, this service plan may make the difference between returning home or convalescing in a long-term care facility. Extensive coordination is required.

The growth of case management within local communities reflects the need for interunit oversight as consumers receive services from multiple units. Case management programs attempt to provide a coordination function so that service delivery flows across informal and formal providers of care. Where there are case managers serving the target population, it is useful to learn how they view the relationships between service units that serve the target population and where they see gaps.

Collaboration   Collaboration implies the concept of a joint venture. Joint ventures are agreements in which two or more units within the community agree to set up a new program or service. This usually occurs when no one separate unit within the community is able or willing to establish the new venture alone. Consortia and networks are typically established for collaborative purposes.

Coalition building is another form of collaboration. A **coalition** is a loosely developed association of constituent groups and organizations, each of whose primary identification is outside the coalition. For example, state coalitions have been formed in efforts to prevent child abuse. Community organizations, voluntary associations, public agencies, and interested individuals have joined forces to work toward a common goal—a safe environment for the nation's children. In coming together, a new voluntary association is formed. Even though the diverse members of this coalition represent various interests across community units, their collaboration on child welfare concerns provides a strong and focused network for change.

In some communities, agencies created to serve the needs of a special population collaborate to assess need, to examine the fit between needs and services, and to present a united front and a stronger voice in pursuing funding for programs. Many federal and state contracts require active collaboration or partnerships, even encouraging the sharing of staff and hiring of coordinators in order to ensure full participation. **Requests for proposals** (RFPs) from private foundations typically require grantees to be specific about how they will collaborate with others.

Confederation   Units within the community may actually merge, often when one or both units become unable to function autonomously. A **horizontal merger** occurs, for example, when two mental health centers consolidate into a single organization. A **vertical merger** occurs when a hospital absorbs a home health provider. A **conglomerate merger** occurs when units within the community form a confederation of multiple smaller units under a large umbrella agency. These actions are generally limited to nongovernmental agencies.

Agency interaction inevitably involves competition and conflict. Change agents learn to cope with competition and conflict on a regular basis. These types of interactions will be discussed in Chapters 7 and 8 of this book.

Overall, the preceding tasks may be approached as a series of general questions to be applied to the task of assessing services in a community. Having looked at the community, consider these overriding concerns:

- Is the community generally sensitive to the needs of the target population?
- Are target population needs adequately assessed in this community?
- Is there a "continuum of care" concept or framework that guides service planning and funding for target population needs?
- How adequate is funding to meet target population needs in the community?
- Are services appropriately located for target group accessibility?
- What is the degree of cooperation, collaboration, and competition in providing services to the target population?
  - What gaps in services and problems affecting the target population have been identified in the process of conducting this assessment?
  - How does the race or ethnicity, gender, or sexual orientation of the target population, or some people in the population, affect the need for and provision of services?

? Assess your understanding of framework for community assessment by taking this brief quiz.

SUMMARY

We began this chapter by discussing three reasons why macro practitioners need a framework for assessing communities. First, social work in general and macro practice in particular require an orientation toward the person-in-environment perspective. In this chapter, the community in which the target population functions comprises the environment. Second, communities change and professionals need a framework for understanding these changes. We have discussed four tasks that provide insight into how the target population is served within a changing community. Third, macro-level change requires an understanding of the history and development of a community as well as an assessment of its current status.

The assessment process begins with identifying the focal community within which the target population is located. Learning about the community's history and the characteristics of the population is done in collaboration with members of the target population. Once community boundaries have been identified, a second set of activities focus on the sources of data and information available in understanding the community. Following this, the human service response is explored, and collective needs are considered.

Since assets are both tangible and intangible, Tasks 3 and 4 lead the practitioner into asset mapping, beginning with values, strengths, and differences as well as sources of power and resource availability. A systematic examination of the service delivery units, patterns and influences, as well as linkages among units provides the practitioner with a picture of community capacity. Sources of help can then be addressed, including informal sources such as households and social networks and mediating sources such as self-help groups and voluntary associations. Formal sources of services include nonprofit, public, and for-profit providers, and both the nature and orientation of services may differ in important ways across these auspices. Determining the competence of these systems in combining to meet needs in an effective way is the final consideration.

Based on data and information accumulated in the process of assessing a community's human service system, the macro practitioner must finally exercise professional judgment in evaluating the adequacy of resources devoted to the target population within the community. If the assessment has been thorough and productive, the practitioner will have gained enough understanding of what occurs within the community to identify and begin assessing needed change on behalf of the target population.

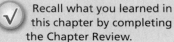

Recall what you learned in this chapter by completing the Chapter Review.

Appendix: Framework for Assessing Community

Task 1: Identify Focal Community

Learn about Historical Context and Population Characteristics

- What is known about the history of this community?
- How many persons are members of this community, and what are their demographic characteristics?
- What social indicator data are available about this and similar communities?

Identify and Collaborate with the Target Population

- Which community group or subgroup will be the target population of this assessment?
- What are the value and political implications of focusing on a specific group, and how will they be involved in the assessment process?
- Is this target population primarily part of a geographical, social, or political community, or a combination?

- What priority is given to the needs of this target population in the community?
- What percentage of the target population is represented by people at risk of being under-served due to their race/ethnicity, gender, sexual orientation, age, disabilities, or other factors?

Determine Community Boundaries

- What are the designated boundaries of this community?
- How do members of the target population view community boundaries?
- Where are members of the target population located within the boundaries? Are they highly concentrated or scattered? Or they a subgroup of a larger community?
- How compatible are jurisdictional boundaries of health and human service programs that serve the target population?

Task 2: Locate Data and Information on Community Needs, Issues, and Problems

Identify Community Data Sources

- What data sources are available about community needs, issues, and problems?
- What methods are used to collect these data, and is this an ongoing process?
- What are the major issues and social problems in this community as perceived by their spokespersons?
- To what extent are these problems interconnected, and must some be solved before others can be addressed?

Gather Information Specific to Target Population Needs

- What needs assessment data and other relevant information are available about the target population?
- How do persons in the target population perceive their community's responsiveness to their needs?
- Do some members of the target population experience greater unmet needs due to their race/ethnicity, gender, sexual orientation, age, disabilities, or other factors?

- Are there subgroups of the target population that are experiencing oppressive conditions and discrimination?

Task 3: Assess Community Social and Political Assets

Focus on Community Strengths, Values, and Differences

- What strengths and resiliencies are evident in this community?
- Are there opportunities (e.g., organizations, rules, procedures, and policies) to engage community members in open communication?
- To what extent are the perspectives of people of color; women; gay men, lesbians, and transgender persons; older persons; and persons with disabilities sought in decisions affecting the target population?
- What cultural values, traditions, and beliefs are important to the target population as individuals or as a whole?
- What are the predominant values (and potential value conflicts) that affect the target population within this community?

Locate Sources of Power and Resource Availability

- What funding sources are subsidizing services for the target population, and through what groups, associations, organizations, and agencies?
- How would you describe the power structure (including both formal and informal leaders) and resource availability within this community?
- How accessible are services for the target population?

Task 4: Assess Community Structure and Capacity

Examine Service Delivery Units

- What informal units (e.g., household, natural, and social networks) are actively engaged in service delivery to the target population?
- What mediating units (e.g., self-help groups and voluntary or grassroots associations) are actively engaged in service delivery to the target population?

- What formal service delivery units (e.g., nonprofit, public, and/or for-profit) are actively engaged in service delivery?
- Are there differences in service delivery that appear to be based on race or ethnicity, gender, sexual orientation, disability, age, or religion?

Identify Patterns of Influence, Control, and Service Delivery

- What groups, associations, and organizations (both extracommunity and intracommunity) advocate for and provide assistance to the target population?
- How is resource distribution to the target population influenced by interaction (both electronic and face-to-face) within the community?
- What limits are placed on services to the target population, and who establishes these limits?

- What roles do citizens and consumers play in the control of services to the target population?

Determine Linkages between Units

- How are the various types of service units generally connected?
- What are the established linkages between units that serve the target population within *this* community?
- Where are linkages between service units obviously needed but not currently established?
- Are the interests of people of color, women, gay men, lesbians, transgender persons, and other oppressed groups represented in the network established through linkages between units?

Assess Your Competence

Use the scale below to rate your current level of achievement on the following concepts or skills associated with each learning outcome listed at the beginning of this chapter:

1	2	3
I can accurately describe the concept or skill(s) associated with this outcome.	I can consistently identify the concept or skill(s) associated with this outcome when observing and analyzing practice activities.	I can competently implement the concept or skill(s) associated with this outcome in my own practice.

_____ Discuss ways in which to engage communities in an assessment process.

_____ Use a framework to assess a community.

Understanding Organizations

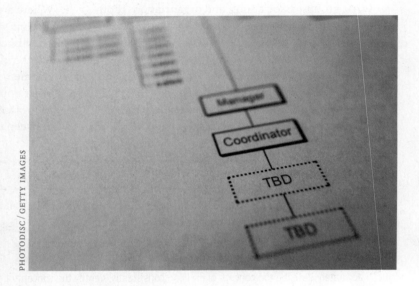

PHOTODISC/GETTY IMAGES

CONCEPTUALIZING ORGANIZATIONS

We live in a society of organizations. Whether they are large or small, or formally or informally structured, organizations carry out the core functions of our social order. In many communities, people's needs are met by specialized organizations, such as voluntary associations, shops, markets, restaurants, religious congregations, municipal utilities, construction companies, schools, hospitals, social welfare institutions, and nongovernmental organizations (NGOs). As we discussed in Chapter 2, today's society was made possible in large measure by the rise of an "organizationalized" structure. From birth (typically in a hospital) to death (under the care of a hospital or hospice, followed by services handled by a funeral home) and at almost all points in between (schools, churches, employers, etc.), people interact with and depend upon organizations throughout our lives.

Organizations also comprise the building blocks of larger macro systems, and individuals engage society through these organizations. Communities are critical societal units, yet individuals tend not to interact directly with their community but with organizations that make up the community. In fact, communities often can be understood not just as masses of individuals but also as networks of organizations. Communities provide the superstructure within which organizations interact, but it is organizations that carry out most basic community functions (see Chapter 5). Macro practice that involves working with communities therefore inevitably requires an understanding of organizations as well.

Of still further importance is the fact that most social workers, as well as most members of society, carry out their jobs from within organizations. In organizations other than the workplace, social workers usually have a consumer–provider relationship, and they are free to turn to alternative organizations if the relationship is unsatisfactory. Workplace environments, however, involve a different type of relationship that is not as easily terminated, and the need for a paycheck may force the social worker to persevere in a less-than-satisfactory relationship with the organization.

The organization may also be one that does not function well. Over time, agencies can stagnate, lose sight of their mission and goals, and begin to provide services that are unhelpful or even harmful to clients. This can occur because of inadequate resources, poor leadership, poor planning, inappropriate procedures or structures, or a combination of these factors. Social workers in these situations may have the option to leave, but doing so can create other dilemmas. We believe that professional social workers have an obligation to attempt to correct problems in their organizations for the benefit of both their clients and themselves. Just as agencies can lose a sense of mission and direction, so too can they regain it. The path to change begins with an understanding of the organization itself—its history, underlying theoretical principles and assumptions, and causes of current problems. The major focus of this chapter will be on understanding organizations in general.

Organizations will be defined here as collectives of individuals gathered together to serve a particular purpose. The key word in this definition is *purpose*. Parsons (1960) contended that organizations are both defined and differentiated from other social constructions by their focus on achieving a particular objective or outcome. As noted in previous chapters, the goals that people organize themselves to accomplish span the full range of human needs, from obtaining food, water, and shelter to achieving personal growth.

Watch this video that conveys the value of human service organizations. Why are human service organizations considered to be so important?

www.youtube.com /watch?v=SUXDkpa7j4o

Using Theories as Frames and Filters

Understanding organizations requires reviewing theories that seek to explain them. Note that the majority of organizational theories were not developed for understanding human service organizations or nonprofit organizations in general. Organizational theories address how organizations arise, why they take certain forms, and how they operate. As with all theories, their value is judged by the accuracy with which they describe things (organizations) and predict events (organizational behavior).

As will become apparent, there are many different organization theories (see, e.g., Shafritz, Ott, & Jang, 2011), and each emphasizes certain variables (e.g., organizational type or managerial style) or explanatory principles (e.g., organizations as open systems or organizations as cultures). By the end of the review, readers may feel overwhelmed by the number of different theories, unsure of how they are applied, or uncertain about which one(s) to choose. Thus, it may be helpful to keep in mind a few basic questions that serve as reminders of what the theories are intended to accomplish:

- What variables emphasized by different theories are of greatest importance in my organization?
- Does my organization resemble or differ from those used as examples in the theories being discussed?
- Does my organization deliberately structure itself or operate in ways promoted by certain theories?
- Which theory best describes the structure of my organization? Which seems best able to predict its actions or decisions?
- Which theories help me understand how my organization differs from others?

Bolman and Deal (2013) discuss the importance of "framing" in making sense of organizations. The picture captured within a frame offers one view of reality, but no frame captures everything, and understanding grows as multiple frames are examined. Each theory we will review frames organizations in a certain way, and the frames themselves fall into larger groups. Bolman and Deal identify four such frames to describe organizations:

- **The Structural Frame:** describes the role of structural architecture in determining roles and relationships and assigning tasks within the organization;
- **The Human Resource Frame:** examines the relationships among people and how people relate to the organization;
- **The Political Frame:** sees organizations as arenas in which power and politics play out among individuals and groups; and
- **The Symbolic Frame:** views the organization as an interplay of artifacts, values, and underlying beliefs.

We have loosely organized the sections of this chapter by frame, keeping in mind that theories in each frame have something to offer in understanding organizations. Our review is by no means complete, as there is such a large body of theory and research that full coverage is beyond the scope of this book. Instead, we will present a brief review of the most important schools of thought about organizations, their main tenets, and their strengths and weaknesses, starting with some of the earliest theories and moving to more contemporary perspectives.

Another distinction we will offer is between **descriptive** and **prescriptive** schools of thought. Descriptive approaches are intended to provide a means of analyzing organizations in terms of certain characteristics or procedures. They often reflect a sociological approach to organizations, which seeks to understand organizations as social phenomena. In contrast, prescriptive approaches are designed as how-to guides, and their goal is to help build better organizations. Not surprisingly, because managers play important roles in deciding how to build and operate an organization, most prescriptive theories are part of the literature on management and leadership.

Table 7.1 illustrates these and other distinctions among various schools of thought about organizations. Primary theorists associated with each school are shown in the left column, after which the date of the first published work in each area appears. Also shown

Table 7.1   Comparative Dimensions of Key Organizational Theories (in order of appearance)

Theory (Theorist)	Dimension				
	Earliest Date	Frame*	Approach	Key Concepts	Conception of Organization in Environment
Bureaucracy (Weber)	1894 (approx.)	Structural	Descriptive	Structure Hierarchy	Closed
Scientific and universalistic management (Taylor; Fayol)	1911	Structural	Prescriptive	Efficiency Measurement	Closed
Organizational goals	1915	Structural	Descriptive	Goal displacement Natural systems	Closed
Management by objectives (Drucker)	1954	Structural	Prescriptive	Setting goals and objectives	Closed
Open systems (Katz & Kahn)	1966	Structural	Descriptive	Systems theory Inputs/throughputs/outputs	Open
Contingency theory (Burns & Stalker; Morse & Lorsch; Thompson)	1961	Structural	Varies	Environmental constraints Task environment	Varies
Human relations (Mayo)	1933	Human Resource	Prescriptive	Social rewards Informal structure	Closed
Theory X and Theory Y (McGregor)	1960	Human Resource	Prescriptive	Higher order rewards	Closed
Quality-oriented management (Deming)	1951	Human Resources	Prescriptive	Consumer/quality Process focus	Open
Decision making (Simon; March)	1957	Political	Descriptive	Bounded rationality Satisficing	Closed
Resource Dependency and Political-Economy Theories (Pfeffer; Wamsley & Zald)	1981	Political	(Varies)	Power Politics	Open
Critical and Feminist Theories (Acker, 1990; Habermas, 1971)	1960	Political	Descriptive	Inequity Social construction Feminism	Open
Organizational culture (Schein, Cross, Weick, & Morgan)	1985	Symbolic	Descriptive and Prescriptive	Values, beliefs, assumptions, diversity, sensemaking, and metaphor	Open
Organizational learning (Argyris & Schön; Senge)	1990	Symbolic	Prescriptive	Learning organization Systemic understanding	Open

*Bolman and Deal (2013).

Go to the Network for Social Work Management website, and read about the development of this network. What journal does this association publish and what topics have recently been covered?

? Assess your understanding of conceptualizing organizations by taking this brief quiz.

are the key concepts associated with each school, along with distinctions relating to whether each theory approaches organizations as **open systems** or **closed systems**. Open-system perspectives are concerned with how organizations are influenced by interactions with their environments, whereas closed-system approaches are more concerned with internal structures and processes.

Theories offer views of organizations from different perspectives, and any given view may sharpen the focus on one part of an organization while blurring others. We suggest that readers return to Table 7.1 regularly to help keep track of the distinctions between different schools of thought, especially with respect to the key concepts that each theory emphasizes.

STRUCTURAL THEORIES AND PERSPECTIVES

Organizational structure refers to the way relationships are constituted among persons within an organization. As we discussed earlier, one of the advantages of organizations is that individuals working in concert can accomplish much more than the same number of individuals working independently. This occurs when the activities of members of a group are coordinated in such a way that the work of one supports or enhances that of the others. Organizational structure is the means by which this coordination is achieved.

Even in informal task groups, members usually do not all attempt to do the same activities. Instead, they divide the responsibilities for tasks among themselves. Recognizing that members also have varying skills and interests, efforts are usually made to match individuals with tasks. Finally, to help ensure that everyone is working toward the common goal and supporting others' efforts, some individuals in the organization may take on management roles. These aspects of organizational functioning—including task specialization, matching of person and position, and leadership—are examples of structural characteristics that are common to virtually all organizations and that provide a means by which they may be analyzed and understood.

Bureaucratic Theory

Among the earliest and most important conceptual work on organizational structure was that of German sociologist Max Weber. Weber coined the term *bureaucracy* and applied it to a particular form of organization. The bureaucracy is an **ideal type**, meaning that it is unlikely that any organization fits perfectly with all the characteristics described by Weber. The bureaucracy typifies descriptive organizational theories in that it provides a model against which organizations can be compared, after which they can be described in terms of the extent to which they fit this model. Also, the organizations Weber described were factories, the military, and the Catholic church, not human service organizations. It should be noted that Weber did not conceptualize the bureaucratic model as a goal toward which organizations should strive, but as a way to understand organizational structure and variation among organizations.

The following characteristics of a bureaucracy are adapted from Weber (1924/1947) and subsequent summaries of his work (Rogers, 1975). They include:

1. Positions in the organization are grouped into a hierarchy.

2. Job candidates are selected for their technical qualifications.

3. Each position has a defined sphere of competence. For example, in a mental health agency, a licensed social worker provides therapy.

4. Positions reflect a high degree of education and specialization.

5. Positions typically demand the full working capacity (in other words, full-time employment) of their holders.

6. Positions are career oriented. There is a system of promotion according to seniority or achievement, and promotion is dependent on the judgment of superiors.

7. Rules of procedure are outlined for rational coordination of activities.

8. A central system of records is maintained to summarize the activities of the organization.

9. Impersonality governs relationships between organizational members.

10. Distinctions are drawn between the private and public lives and positions of members.

In organizations with these characteristics, there may be a single executive selected for his or her technical competence, and the organization is divided into sections by tasks such as client services, budgeting and accounting, and legal services. The organizational structure resembles a wide, flat pyramid in which there are many people at the line level and few at the administrative level, graphically drawn as a hierarchical organizational chart.

Weber was interested in this organizational model because he believed it reflected a change in the values of society as a whole. In fact, his work began with a more general concern about the way power is legitimized in social relations—why people consent to do the will of others. He used **authority** as the term for power wielded with the consent of those being led, and he identified three major forms:

1. **Traditional Authority:** The right to govern bestowed on kings, emperors, popes, and other patrimonial leaders. This type of authority rests in the ruler's claim to historic or ancestral rights of control. It is associated with long-lasting systems and can be passed from generation to generation of rulers.

2. **Charismatic Authority:** Dominance exercised by an individual through extraordinary personal heroism, piety, fanaticism, martial skill, or other traits. Systems based on this type of authority tend to be unstable and transitional because the authority is tied to an individual rather than to a position.

3. **Rational/Legal Authority:** Power assigned on the basis of the ability to achieve instrumental goals. This type of authority derives from the legitimacy given to rational rules and processes and from expertise rather than hereditary claims.

Bureaucracies are the embodiment of rational/legal authority, and the fact that they have become a dominant organizational model reflects societal movement away from systems based on traditional or charismatic authority.

Bureaucratic structure is designed to help an organization complete its tasks by maximizing **efficiency**. As bureaucracies evolved, they provided a blueprint for vast governmental institutions to serve far more people than before. For example, tens of millions receive Social Security payments, Medicare, and other benefits from large bureaucracies.

The machinelike qualities to which Weber called attention can be perfectly suited to manufacturing firms but disastrous in organizations in which the goal is to respond to human needs. One example of the ways that bureaucracies can go wrong was offered by Merton (1952) in his study of employees of bureaucratic organizations. Over time, workers' concern for doing their job well became secondary to meeting procedural and paperwork requirements. Merton called this mindset the **bureaucratic personality** and coined the term **trained incapacity** to describe the ways in which bureaucratic personalities lose focus on the needs of those they serve. He saw the problem as an inevitable consequence of tightly structured chains of command and pressures for rule compliance that eventually forced on all workers the realization that their interests were best served not by doing the job well but by doing it "by the book."

Questions have also been raised about whether racial or ethnic minorities and women are disadvantaged in bureaucratic organizations and whether the bureaucratic model privileges male dominance (Gorman & Kmec, 2009). As employees are promoted through lower and middle levels to upper-level administrative positions, white males have often dominated the highest levels and denied access to others. This phenomenon has been referred to as the **glass ceiling**. Women and minorities can reach a level at which they have a view of functioning at the top but cannot get there because those who select persons for top positions often value sameness and fear diversity.

Box 7.1 provides an overview of bureaucratic theory.

Scientific and Universalistic Management

Some of the earliest writings on managing tasks and functions in the workplace were by Frederick Taylor, a U.S. industrialist and educator whose principal works appeared in the first two decades of the 1900s. Taylor had been both a laborer and a mechanical engineer, and he wanted to identify management techniques that would lead to increased productivity. He also believed many organizational problems were tied to misunderstandings between managers and workers. Managers thought workers were lazy and unmotivated, and they mistakenly believed they understood workers' jobs. Workers thought that managers cared only about exploiting workers, not about productivity.

Box 7.1   Weber's Theory of Bureaucratic Structure

- **Purpose.** Descriptive.
- **Key Features.** Bureaucracies emphasize efficiency of operation. Decision making is done at the top, and authority to do so is based on expertise rather than inheritance. Tasks are specialized, organizational relationships are impersonal, and a "by-the-book" orientation restricts individual discretion.
- **Strengths and Weaknesses.** Organizations with bureaucratic structures are **efficient** at repetitive tasks such as mass production of material goods, but they can be dehumanizing. Also, they are less efficient at variable tasks, in unpredictable environments, and with staff who must exercise professional judgment.
- **Fit with Social Work.** The profession encourages job specialization based on expertise and the promotion of individuals as they accumulate skills and seniority.

To solve these problems, Taylor (1911) developed what came to be known as **scientific management**. One of the first steps to scientifically analyzing a job was to complete a careful study of the work itself, usually by identifying the best worker and studying that person. The goal was to find the **one best way**—to develop the best tools for completing the tasks, fitting workers' abilities and interests to particular assignments, and finding the level of production the average worker could sustain.

The next step was to provide incentives to increase productivity. Taylor's favorite tool for this was the **piece-rate wage**, in which workers were paid for each unit they produced. In this manner, more units were produced, unit cost was reduced, organizational productivity and profitability were enhanced, and workers earned more.

Taylor was seeking an industrial workplace in which the traditional animosity between management and labor could be overcome by recognition of the mutual aims of each. His points in this regard were summarized by George (1968) and paraphrased below:

1. Good management seeks to pay high wages and keep production costs low.

2. To do this, management has to apply scientific methods of research.

3. Workers are scientifically assigned to jobs, and standards are scientifically set.

4. A standard of output means that employees are precisely trained to improve their skill in performing a job.

5. Close, friendly cooperation between management and workers is critical in creating a psychological environment that would make possible the application of the other principles. (p. 89)

As can be seen from these principles, Taylor's interests were as much in the area of organizational psychology as in traditional management theory. Subsequent to his work, other writers focused more narrowly on Taylor's concern with maximizing organizational productivity, and they began to ask whether broader principles could be identified that encapsulated the ideals of rational management. These writers eventually became known as the *universalistic management* theorists. A prominent member of this group was French industrialist Henri Fayol, who focused on specifying the structural attributes of organizations that managers should develop and promote. Scott (1981) and others have suggested ways in which Fayol's ideas can be condensed into a few characteristics that describe organizations that adopt his management principles:

1. **Pyramidal Shape:** Hierarchical management advocated by Fayol produces a structure that has a single decision maker at the top and a gradually widening chain of command.

2. **Single Supervisor:** Each person reports to only one immediate superior.

3. **Restricted Span of Supervision:** No supervisor is responsible for more than a moderate number of subordinates, usually six to eight.

4. **Autonomy in Routine Performance:** Subordinates are responsible for routine matters covered by standard rules; supervisors are responsible for unusual circumstances not covered by those rules.

5. **Specialization by Task:** A division of labor exists within the organization through which similar functions are grouped together (e.g., those that are similar in terms of purpose, process, clientele, or location).

6. **Differentiation of Line and Support Functions:** Line functions are those that are central to the completion of core organizational tasks; staff functions are supportive or advisory.

Although it clearly is not a manufacturing enterprise, social work has adopted a number of "scientific" approaches to practice. For example, many social workers have specialized roles, and within these they follow procedures and protocols for serving certain types of cases. Also, as part of the profession's commitment to research-based practice, individual social workers are expected to study the progress of clients in their caseloads by using methods such as single-subject designs. In a similar way, requirements for outcome evaluation have placed more rigorous demands on the design of interventions and the measurement of success. Although these trends do not embrace the most mechanistic aspects of Taylor's notions, they echo his concern for operations based on careful analysis of the work itself. The evidence-based management (EBM) movement offers a contemporary example of Tayloristic attention to science.

Evidence-Based Management

EBM focuses on the tendency of people to make decisions based on personal experience, overall impressions, and "instinct" or "gut feelings." Managers and administrators often operate this way, and experienced leaders can be in great demand because they are assumed to have gained good "instincts" through years of on-the-job training. Proponents of EBM do not deny that experience has merit, but they caution against assuming that managers can make good decisions based on "practice wisdom" alone (Bolman & Deal, 2013). EBM can trace its roots to scientific management in which the practice of social work is based on the best available scientific research.

In defining EBM, Rousseau (2006) emphasized its goal of improving results by combining three elements: findings from empirical research, the expertise of administrators, and information regarding the preferences of service users. Problems usually arise, she contended, because decision makers typically rely only on their own experiences and fail to systematically collect and use information from the other two sources. Briggs and McBeath (2009) traced the origins of this approach to the accountability movement that appeared first in the health-care arena and then spread to other sectors, and they and other advocates of EBM acknowledged that in many ways this returns to ideas put forth by Frederick Taylor and the scientific management school 100 years ago. However, Pfeffer and Sutton (2006) noted that Taylor called for decisions to be made by managers and then imposed on workers, whereas EBM calls for the entire organization and all staff within it to adopt an orientation toward more informed decision making. The process is also seen as not merely collecting data for its own sake but also gathering it systematically, evaluating it carefully, using it to choose a course of action, and reexamining the decision once its results are known.

Results from studies of EBM principles have provided some empirical support for this approach. Collins-Camargo and Royse (2010) found that the presence of an organizational culture that promotes evidence-based practice, combined with effective supervision, positively influences workers' perception of their self-efficacy. In the health arena, Friedmann, Lan, and Alexander (2010) found that an orientation on the part of managers toward EBM principles was positively associated with their willingness to adopt new techniques for drug-abuse intervention that had received strong support in empirical studies. Findings such as these appear promising with respect to the ongoing diffusion of EBM practices, but whether the approach will prove to be a lasting addition or a short-lived repackaging of old ideas may not be known for some time. It is worth noting, however, that evidence-based practice continues to be an important trend in micro-level social work, and the parallel aims of EBM suggest that the two approaches may prove to be mutually reinforcing.

Box 7.2 provides an overview of scientific management.

> **Research-Informed Practice (or Practice-Informed Research)**
>
> **Behavior:** Use and translate research evidence to inform and improve practice, policy, and service delivery.
>
> **Critical Thinking Question:** What strategies may make it easier for managers in human service organizations to use evidence-based management?

Organizational Goals and the Natural-Systems Perspective

In the early 1900s, Robert Michels (1915/1949) examined political parties as examples of large modern organizations. Noting the rise of oligarchies or small groups of key decision makers within the parties, he suggested that these and other organizations have identifiable life cycles that proceed through the following steps:

1. The organization develops a formal structure.
2. The original leaders move into positions at the upper levels of the hierarchy.
3. These individuals discover the personal advantages of having such positions.
4. They begin to make more conservative decisions that might not advance their original cause as forcefully as before but that are less likely to jeopardize their own security or that of the organization.
5. The organization's original goals are pushed aside, and it becomes mostly a means for achieving the personal goals of upper-level administrators. Examples of this phenomenon abound in political systems at local, state, national, and international levels. Many begin their political careers with lofty aspirations and steadily move toward advancing their own security in office.

Michels called this the "Iron Rule of Oligarchy," concluding that it is an unavoidable fate of large organizations that adopt bureaucratic approaches to structuring themselves.

Writers such as Etzioni (1964) developed a concept which they called **goal displacement**. The formal goals of the organization—*stated goals*—and those of decision makers—*real goals*—may be very different, but through mechanisms such as **cooptation**,

---

Box 7.2   Scientific and Universalistic Management Theories

- **Purpose:** Prescriptive.
- **Key Features:** Although not influenced by Weber, these theories essentially describe how to create a bureaucracy from the management side. Again, the emphasis is on efficiency, top-down control, and specialized work. Managers are also responsible for studying the work itself and teaching staff the "one best way" of doing each job.
- **Strengths and Weaknesses:** Organizations managed by these principles can achieve the original goals of stability, predictability, and efficient production, but, as with bureaucracies, the result can be an oppressive and monotonous workplace.
- **Fit with Social Work:** The emphasis on "best practices" and EBM reflect a "one best way" approach out of the scientific management tradition. The use of flow charting in designing social programs is derived from time and motion studies.

the growth of oligarchies, and the development of the bureaucratic personality, it is usually stated goals that are displaced by real goals representing the interests of decision makers. Selznick (1957) saw this as part of a larger process he called **institutionalization**. An institutionalized organization takes on a life of its own that may have more to do with the interests of its own participants than with the instrumental goals it is supposedly serving.

Recognition of the importance of organizational goals, particularly survival goals, became an important contribution to the development of organizational and management theory. These views have also had considerable influence on the study of human service organizations, such as a well-known analysis of the March of Dimes (Sills, 1957). Organized originally to unify the efforts of volunteers attempting to raise money for polio research, the March of Dimes became one of the vanguard organizations in the fight against polio nationwide. These efforts were eventually successful in that funding from the March of Dimes helped lead to Jonas Salk's development of the first polio vaccine. This and subsequent vaccines proved to be so effective that polio quickly became a rare problem, which meant that the activities of the March of Dimes were no longer needed. Having successfully achieved its goal, the organization could simply have disbanded, but it did not. Instead, it took on a whole new cause—birth defects—and its efforts shifted toward solving this new problem.

Box 7.3 provides an overview of organizational goals and the natural-systems perspective.

Management by Objectives (MBO)

Peter Drucker (1954) proposed that purpose was often assumed by theorists to be clearer than it actually was; thus, a key function of management was to establish what it is that an organization seeks to accomplish. He suggested that organizational goals and objectives should be made the central construct around which organizational life revolves. Instead of focusing on structure, precision, or efficiency and hoping for an increase in productivity and profit, Drucker proposed beginning with the desired outcome and working backward to create an organizational design to achieve that outcome. Termed **management by objectives** (MBO), this approach involves both short-range and

---

Box 7.3   Organizational Goals and Goal Displacement

- **Purpose:** Descriptive.
- **Key Features:** Writers in this school point out that organizational actors tend to be driven more by personal than organizational goals. Organizations can thus be redirected to serve the self-interests of administrators or others. Also, because organizations are made up of many individuals, they act less like rational systems than organic (natural) ones, seeking to protect themselves just as individuals do.
- **Strengths and Weaknesses:** Viewing organizations as organic systems helped draw theoretical attention away from its earlier focus on internal factors, such as structure or management style, and reorient it toward issues of how organizations interact with their environments. Still, some findings showed that goal displacement and the rise of self-serving administrations are not inevitable in bureaucracies.
- **Fit with Social Work:** This theory made organizational behavior a new focus of attention, and it called attention to the potential for goal displacement in human service organizations that function in highly uncertain environments.

long-range planning, and it is through the planning process that organizational structures and procedures necessary to achieve an outcome are established.

Drucker identified several elements of MBO's strategic planning process. **Expectations** are the hoped-for outcomes; an example might be the addition of a new service or client population in an agency, or it might be an improvement in the number of clients served or results of their services (e.g., an increase of 25 percent in client satisfaction over current levels). **Objectives** are means of achieving expectations, such as the steps that must be taken to add or improve programs. **Assumptions** reflect what is presumed about how meeting the objectives will achieve expectations (e.g., that the use of better service techniques will improve outcomes).

Other elements in the process include consideration of *alternative courses of action*, such as the costs and benefits of making no changes. Also, the plan must take into account what Drucker terms the "decision structure," which represents the constraints that exist on how much the plan can do, and the "impact stage," which addresses costs associated with implementing the plan and limitations it may place on other initiatives or operations. Finally, once implemented, a plan will have **results**, and the result of an MBO process is measured by the extent to which actual outcomes match the original expectations.

One theme made explicit in Drucker's MBO model is the assumption that organizations should be directed by rational actions designed to achieve certain goals. This assumption began to be questioned by writers concerned about whether rational, goal-directed, formalized structures are the best way of serving organizational goals, and whether these goals provide a clear direction. In fact, the idea that the goals of an organization and its members could gradually change had been present in organizational literature for some time.

One major advantage of MBO is its emphasis on producing clear statements, made available to all employees, about expectations for the coming year. Techniques are also developed for breaking goals and objectives into tasks, and for monitoring progress throughout the year. An organization that follows MBO principles tends to improve collaboration and cooperative activity.

Many modern approaches to management include various aspects of MBO in their model. For example, organizations often require the development of an annual plan in which goals and objectives in each programmatic area are made explicit. Also significant has been the growth of attention paid to outcomes, in both commercial and human service organizations. Social work as a profession was for many years primarily concerned with process in the development of its practice approaches. Management by objectives, together with the accountability movement, establishes program outcomes as the major criteria for determining funding and program continuation.

Management by objectives adopts a particularistic approach to leadership in which, according to some critics, the attention of managers is concentrated on the trees rather than on the forest. In other words, management requires large-scale strategic thinking in addition to small-scale tactical thinking, yet MBO focuses mostly on the latter. Another criticism is that, although it is sometimes admirable to be clear and direct about organizational expectations, the concept of building organizational life around goals and objectives has its drawbacks. Objectives can serve simply to reinforce existing power structures within an organization (Dirsmith, Heian, & Covaleski, 1997).

Box 7.4 provides an overview of management by objectives.

Box 7.4   Management by Objectives (MBO)

- **Purpose:** Prescriptive.
- **Key Features:** MBO argues that management must ensure the continuing presence of clear goals and objectives for the organization. Once these are in place, the task of management becomes one of decision making regarding how best to achieve each objective. Success is measured by the extent to which objectives were achieved.
- **Strengths and Weaknesses:** MBO focuses attention on results and reorients management toward the question

of how to accomplish desired outcomes. On a day-to-day basis, however, consideration is given mostly to the small steps necessary for reaching intermediate objectives, which may lead to a loss of awareness of eventual end goals.

- **Fit with Social Work:** The accountability structures within human service organizations have become increasingly oriented to outcomes-based approaches, and social workers must be vigilant in engaging service-users in determining appropriate outcomes.

Organizations as Open Systems

In learning about practice with individual clients, most social workers are introduced to systems theory. This approach is based on the work of biologist Ludwig von Bertalanffy (1950), who believed that lessons learned in fields such as ecology, which concerns organisms' interdependence with their surroundings, provide a way to conceptualize other phenomena as systems engaged in environmental interactions. In this light, individual clients are viewed not as isolated entities driven by internal processes but as social beings whose personalities and behaviors emerge from constant interaction with the world around them. As open systems, clients both give to and draw from elements external to themselves. Understanding this ongoing process of exchange with critical elements of their personal environment (e.g., culture, community, and family) is key to understanding clients. In Chapter 5, we discussed how this *organismic analogy* has been extended to communities, and in the 1960s, various writers began to argue that it applies to organizations as well.

One influential example was the work of Katz and Kahn (1966), who noted that earlier theorists approached organizations as though they were closed systems that could be understood simply by studying their internal structure and processes. This approach corresponds to the *mechanical analogy* also mentioned in Chapter 5, and Katz and Kahn considered it naïve. They argued that organizations must be understood as open systems surviving through a constant exchange of resources with organizations and other entities surrounding them. The design and functioning of the system are shaped by the exchanges through which it acts on and responds to its environment.

As illustrated in Figure 7.1, systems are made up of collections of constituent parts (whether cells comprising an organism or people comprising an organization) that receive **inputs**, operate on them through some sort of process called the throughput, and produce outputs. In human service agencies, inputs include resources such as funding, staff, and facilities. Clients who request services are also important inputs, as are the types and severity of the problems for which they seek help. More subtle but also vital are inputs such as values, expectations, and opinions about the agency that are held by community members, funding agencies, regulatory bodies, and other segments of the environment.

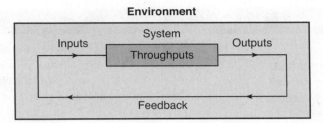

Figure 7.1
The Open-Systems Model

Throughput involves the services provided by the agency—often referred to as its *technology*—and the way it is structured to apply this technology to inputs it receives. **Output** refers to the organization's products. In industrial firms, this is usually some sort of material object; in human service agencies, it is the completion of a service to a client. As we will discuss, the important aspect of service output is often defined as an **outcome**, which is a measure of a quality-of-life change (improvement, stasis, or deterioration) for a client.

Theorists prior to Katz and Kahn implicitly assumed that the key to understanding an organization lies within, and that is where they directed their attention. The open-systems view dramatically redirected attention to external environments and the way organizations must be viewed as dynamic entities constantly involved in exchanges with those environments. Although both organizations and organisms exist within a larger environment, and both engage in exchanges with that environment, organizations are themselves composed of individuals whose goals may differ from those of their organization. The throughput phase of environmental interactions in an organization thus involves the interactions of many organizational members, which adds a new layer of complexity to the model.

Box 7.5 provides an overview of organizations as open systems.

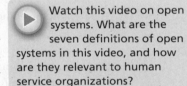

Watch this video on open systems. What are the seven definitions of open systems in this video, and how are they relevant to human service organizations?

www.youtube.com/watch?v=u-x6sNlv01g

Contingency Theory

Partly in response to the new perspectives offered by open-systems thinking and partly because of doubts about one-size-fits-all management theories, a new outlook began to take shape in the 1960s. Its basic premise was that different organizations face different circumstances, so they may need to structure themselves in different ways. Known generally as *contingency theory*, this approach can be boiled down to three basic tenets. Two were proposed by Galbraith (1973), and the first of these, which directly disagreed with Taylor, suggested that there are many ways to organize rather than just a single "best way." The second acknowledged that some ways of organizing are better than others, so effort must be expended to find at least an acceptable approach. Scott (1981) added a third, open-systems principle, which stated that the organization's environment determines which way of organizing works best under present conditions. The unifying theme across all three principles is that the nature of the organization and its management scheme depend on many factors unique to that organization, so expecting to be able to manage a human service agency in the same way as an auto assembly plant, for example, would be naïve.

> ## Box 7.5   Organizations as Open Systems
>
> - **Purpose:** Descriptive.
> - **Key Features:** This theory broadened and extended the natural-systems perspective by showing that all organizations, like all organisms, are open systems. Open systems acquire resources (*inputs*) from their environments, such as funds, staff, and clients, and they return products or services (*outputs*) to the environment. Understanding organizational actions thus requires viewing them as part of a larger environment in which and with which they carry out these exchanges.
> - **Strengths and Weaknesses:** Organizational behavior can be explained as efforts to make beneficial environmental exchanges, and organizations act in ways that seek to reduce uncertainty and make their environments as predictable as possible. This makes organizations themselves more predictable. Still, there are limits to how far the comparisons between organizations and organisms can be extended. A full understanding of how organizations act requires examining both their interactions with their environments and the interactions among their members.
> - **Fit with Social Work:** This view is a natural fit for social workers who understand clients from a person-in-environment perspective. It also echoes the profession's focus on research-based practice, which is necessary to ensure that services remain relevant. For example, in response to a given problem in a community, the social worker might conduct a needs assessment, use the data to design a program to address the problem, implement the program, then gather new data to evaluate and refine it. This meshes well with the input–throughput–output model elaborated in the open-systems view.

Morse and Lorsch (1970) took issue with views such that decentralized, humanistic management models should be the preferred approach across most organizations. Their research showed that high organizational effectiveness and a strong sense of personal competence can be found in organizations with relatively rigid rules and structure. Similarly, some organizations with a loose structure and high individual autonomy were not always effective or satisfying to their workers. The key variable to which results pointed was the nature of organizational tasks. Organizations with predictable tasks, such as manufacturing firms, fared best with a tightly controlled structure. Those with less predictable tasks (such as in a human service agency) appeared much better suited to a loose structure and management style.

A typology of these differences was proposed by Burns and Stalker (1961), who distinguished between two forms of management that they labeled "mechanistic" and "organic." Mechanistic systems, which reflect characteristics of bureaucracies, are commonly found in organizations with relatively stable environments. Organic forms occur in unstable environments in which the inputs are unpredictable and the organization's viability depends on responding in ways that are less bound by formal rules and structures. Table 7.2 compares and contrasts characteristics of organic and mechanistic organizations.

Lawrence and Lorsch (1967) also noted that the stability of the environment is a critical contingency on which an analysis of organizational structure and leadership should rest. Models such as Weber's bureaucratic system are better at explaining circumstances in stable organizational environments, whereas the human relations model (to be discussed in the next section) appears to work better in situations of environmental turbulence. They also called attention to the importance of certainty versus uncertainty in determining organizational actions. Stable environments allow for greater certainty in structuring operations; thus, a human service agency that deals mostly with clients who have a

Table 7.2   Elements of Mechanistic versus Organic Organizations

Variable	Mechanistic Organization	Organic Organization
Focus of work	Completion of discrete tasks	Contribution to overall result
Responsibility for integrating work	Supervisor of each level	Shared within level and across units
Responsibility for problem solving	Limited to precise obligations set out for each position	Owned by affected individual; cannot be shirked as "out of my area"
Structure of control and authority	Hierarchic	Networked
Location of knowledge, information	Concentrated at top	Expertise and need for information assumed to exist at various levels
Character of organizational structure	Rigid; accountability rests with individual	Fluid; accountability is shared by group
Content of communication	Instructions and decisions	Information and advice
Direction of communication	Vertical; between supervisor and subordinate	Lateral and also across ranks
Expected loyalty	To supervisor and unit	To technology and outcome

Source: Adapted from Burns and Stalker (1961).

particular problem (e.g., a food bank) is expected to have fairly routinized operations and formal structure. Conversely, organizations that deal with a wide variety of clients and unpredictable client problems (e.g., a disaster relief organization) can be expected to be structured loosely and have a much less "by-the-book" approach to operational rules.

James Thompson (1967) agreed that a key issue in organization–environment interactions is the degree of uncertainty in the environment, and he noted that organizations seek predictability because this allows the creation of rational (logically planned) structures. However, because environments are never perfectly predictable, an organization that structures itself too rigidly will not survive long. Understanding how an organization has structured itself to respond to environmental uncertainty is therefore critical to understanding it as a whole.

Similar to Morse and Lorsch, Thompson focused on organizations' technology. As illustrated in Figure 7.2, he described three levels of functioning: (1) the technical core, (2) the managerial system, and (3) the institutional system. The **technical core** includes the structures and processes within an organization's boundaries that allow it to carry out the principal functions for which it was created (e.g., the manufacture of an object or the delivery of a service). Theoretically, the technical core works best when environmental inputs never vary and the same work can be done in the same way repeatedly. But because environments are constantly changing, the rational organization seeks to accommodate such variations without endangering its most vital elements (the technical core). The **managerial system** includes those structures and processes that manage the work of the technical core. The **institutional system** deals with interactions between the organization and the environment.

Adaptive responses to environmental change are crucial in Thompson's analytical model, and he hypothesized that these fall into a three-part sequence: (1) actions

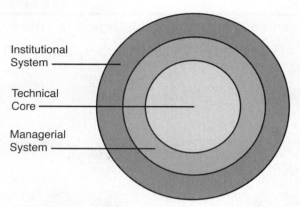

Institutional
System

Technical
Core

Managerial
System

Figure 7.2
Thompson's Organizational Model

to protect the technical core, (2) actions to acquire power over the task environment, and (3) actions to absorb key elements of the environment by altering organizational boundaries. Actions to protect the technical core involve responses that allow the organization to contain necessary changes within itself, such as by increasing or decreasing output, hiring or laying off staff, or shifting resources among different internal units.

The **task environment** is the term Thompson used to describe external organizations on which an organization depends, either as providers of needed input (money, raw materials, and client referrals) or as consumers of its output. If internal responses are unsuccessful in adjusting to change, the organization will attempt to alter its relationships with members of the task environment to gain more control over the change. Examples of this might include negotiating long-term funding agreements or arranging for regular referral of clients (e.g., a residential treatment center may become the exclusive provider of treatment for a particular school district).

Finally, if the organization cannot adapt to change by any of these methods, Thompson predicted that it would seek to incorporate into itself parts of the environment that relate to the change. For example, a human service organization that serves substance-abusing clients whose costs are paid by contracts with a public agency would be endangered if funding priorities shifted toward prevention rather than treatment. If a smaller agency in the area appears to be in line for much of this funding, the older, larger agency may seek to acquire the smaller one in an effort to maintain its funding base. But because such a move involves changing at least part of the older agency's technical core, this response would likely occur only after other tactics were tried and proved inadequate.

Contingency theorists accepted the premise of the open-systems model that the environment is critical in understanding how organizations behave. They argued that organizations develop their structures not so much through the application of management principles as by being forced to react to ever-changing environmental conditions. These ideas

Engagement

Behavior: Apply knowledge of human behavior and the social environment, person-in-environment, and other multidisciplinary theoretical frameworks to engage with clients and constituencies.

Critical Thinking Question: How would contingency theory be helpful in analyzing organizational behavior?

Box 7.6 Contingency Theory

- **Purpose.** Descriptive.
- **Key Features.** A one-size-fits-all approach to organizational analysis or management is doomed to fail because organizations have different purposes and exist in different environments. The question is not how closely an organization adheres to a particular form (e.g., the bureaucratic model) but how well it structures itself to accommodate to its unique environment. Also, contingency theory calls attention to an organization's *technology*, referring to the ways it carries out its tasks. Predictable environmental input and routine tasks are amenable to more traditional, hierarchical structure, whereas unpredictable environments and nonroutine technology require less rigid structure.
- **Strengths and Weaknesses.** Contingency theory has influenced many subsequent works, and its contention

that organizations must be understood in terms of how they structure themselves in response to their environments remains widely accepted. Most concerns about this approach address the role of decision makers. Although proponents argue that their response to the environment tends to be planned, predictable, and based on the rational application of management principles, critics contend that the evidence for this is scarce and that responses to environmental change are often unstructured and reactive.

- **Fit with Social Work.** Since human service organizations are typically more organic than mechanistic, contingency theory offers alternative ways of thinking about how to structure agencies to be more responsive to diverse groups within the larger environment.

---

continue to have considerable influence on organizational analysis, and research continues to demonstrate the applicability of contingency theory principles.

Box 7.6 provides an overview of contingency theory.

? Assess your understanding of structural theories and perspectives by taking this brief quiz.

HUMAN RESOURCE THEORIES AND PERSPECTIVES

As the field of organizational management and analysis grew, the works of Taylor, Weber, and others were criticized for their focus on rational, structural approaches to understanding organizations. The earliest of these criticisms addressed Taylor's assumptions about factors that motivate organizational actors. Critics took issue with the notion that workers are oriented to the instrumental goals of the organization and respond most readily to material rewards (e.g., piece-rate wages) designed to further those goals. One such group sought to test Taylor's principles concerning productivity enhancement. Its members eventually concluded that organizations must be viewed as social institutions, and it is social factors—friendship, belongingness, and group solidarity—that are most important in understanding how organizational actors behave.

Human Relations Theory

Often referred to as the *human relations school*, this view had its origins in the so-called Hawthorne studies conducted in the 1920s. Experimenters placed a group of workers in a special room and varied the intensity of the lighting and other environmental factors to observe the effect on productivity. Initially they found that the greater the intensity of lighting, the more productivity rose. However, when they reduced the lighting, expecting to find reduced productivity, they found that productivity continued to grow even in dim lighting. The researchers concluded that increased productivity was caused by *social factors.* Workers appeared not to respond to the lighting but instead to the fact that they were members of a group for which they wanted to do their part, and it was this sense of social responsibility that prompted better performance.

Subsequent experiments on the effect of social factors on organizations, including many from the field of industrial psychology, examined broader questions about the behavior of groups. The basic tenets of the human relations approach that developed from these findings are listed below (adapted from Etzioni, 1964):

1. It is not the physical limits of workers that determine output levels but expectations among workers themselves regarding what levels are reasonable and sustainable.

2. The approval or disapproval of coworkers is more important than monetary rewards or penalties in determining how workers act, and coworker approval or disapproval can negate or enhance monetary rewards.

3. Individual employees' behaviors or motivations tend to be less important than those of employees as a group. Attempts by management to influence workers' behavior are more successful if aimed at the whole group rather than at individuals because the latter may be unwilling to change unless accompanied by everyone.

4. The role of leadership is important in understanding social forces in organizations, and this leadership may be either formal or informal.

Important implications of these tenets were that individuals were equally or more likely to draw satisfaction from social relationships in the organization than from its instrumental activities. Also important was the notion that workers' willingness to follow management came from their willingness to follow members of the work group. The key to making effective changes in organizational operations was not in rules and formal structure but in the quality of personal affiliations and the coherence of informal structures. Managers who succeeded in increasing productivity were most likely to have been responsive to workers' social needs.

Another writer associated with this school, Mary Parker Follett (1926/2005), noted that social relations also came into play with regard to how managers treated their subordinates. Arguing that "probably more industrial trouble has been caused by the manner in which orders are given than in any other way" (p. 153), she urged managers to recognize that workers remained people rather than parts of a machine, and retaining basic standards of interpersonal communication ultimately facilitated productive functioning.

Human relations theory has had an important effect on organizational thinking. With respect to management practice, its tenets have provided a counterbalance to the formalized and often rigid approaches of other management theories. It has also influenced descriptive approaches by serving as a reminder of how the needs and interests of individual employees can be critical determinants of organizational behavior. Later theories would develop around genuine empowerment for employees, but human relations management eventually died out as an approach to running an organization when it was recognized that a happy workforce was not necessarily a productive one, and other variables began to enter the equation. Nevertheless, human relations called attention to factors such as teamwork, cooperation, leadership, and positive attention from management that remain relevant today. Its emphasis on these aspects of interpersonal relations made it the first of several schools of thought to employ what Bolman and Deal (2013) term the "family" metaphor of organizations.

A number of writers have raised concerns about the methodological soundness of the studies on which these views are based. For example, the original Hawthorne experiments have earned an infamous place in the history of research methodology. The term **Hawthorne effect** refers to the fact that experimental subjects may perform in certain ways simply because they know they are being studied. In this case, workers in the Hawthorne plant may have raised production not because of lighting or a sense of group solidarity but because of self-consciousness about being observed. Other critics have argued that the design of these studies was such that expectations about economic incentives might still have influenced the subjects, further undermining the supposed effect of social factors (Sykes, 1965).

A second line of criticism argues that it is possible to overestimate the importance of social factors in organizations. For example, various studies have indicated that informal organizational structures may not be as prevalent or powerful as human relations writers suggest, that democratic leadership is not always associated with greater productivity or worker satisfaction, and that economic benefits *are* important to many employees. Also, Landsberger (1958) argued that emphasizing worker contentedness at the expense of economic rewards could foster an administrative model that is even more manipulative and paternalistic than might be the case with scientific management. This is because human relations theory, like other management approaches of the time, concentrated power and decision making at the top and was never intended to empower employees or assist them in gaining genuine participation in the running of the organization. If people were treated more humanely under human relations management, it was because proponents believed this would lead to greater productivity, not because of a desire to create a more democratic workplace. Finally, an emphasis on strengthening personal and social relationships within the workplace may also have disadvantaged some groups of employees over the years. Social relationships within organizations play a role in identifying and securing jobs and promotions for people, but women and ethnic minorities have often been excluded from personal networks that control these rewards.

Theory X and Theory Y

Later writers drew on the work of human relations theorists but incorporated them into more general frameworks addressing human motivation. One example is the work of Douglas McGregor (1960), who adopted Abraham Maslow's hierarchy of needs as a framework for understanding workers' actions. To McGregor, organizational actors were not just social creatures but also *self-actualizing* beings whose ultimate goal in organizations is to meet higher order needs. To illustrate this point, he identified two contrasting approaches to management that he labeled "Theory X" and "Theory Y." **Theory X** includes traditional views of management and organizational structure such as those of Taylor, Weber, and others, which, McGregor argued, make the following assumptions about human nature:

1. Human beings try to avoid work at all costs (p. 33).
2. Since they dislike working, human beings must be pressured into working toward organizational goals.
3. Because they have little initiative, human beings need close supervision (p. 34).

These assumptions led to what McGregor saw as the domineering, oppressive aspects of Theory X management.

In contrast, **Theory Y** assumes that the task of management is to recognize workers' higher order needs and design organizations that allow them to achieve these needs. Its assumptions are as follows:

1. People naturally like to work.
2. Human beings like to take initiative and enjoy working toward goals to which they are committed.
3. Human beings typically seek responsibility and can be trusted to get a job done.
4. Most human beings have the capacity to be creative in solving organizational problems.
5. People do not normally require close supervision. (McGregor, 1960, pp. 47–48)

The critical feature of this approach is its break from the management-dominated orientation of previous theories in favor of placing decision-making power with lower level actors. Such loosely structured organizations are seen as best for promoting productivity by allowing employees to meet higher order needs through their work.

McGregor's analysis was supported by the research of Frederick Herzberg (1966). Herzberg studied motivation among employees, dividing motivational elements into two categories: **extrinsic factors** and **intrinsic factors**. Factors extrinsic to the job include wages, hours, working conditions, and benefits. Intrinsic factors have to do with motivators that lie within the work itself, such as satisfaction with successful task completion. Herzberg discovered that, in the long run, extrinsic factors tended to keep down the levels of dissatisfaction with the job, but they do not motivate workers to work harder. Only intrinsic factors, such as the ability to use one's own creativity and problem-solving skills, motivate employees to become more productive. Herzberg's work helped foster ongoing interest in **job redesign**, which, broadly defined, seeks to increase the intrinsic rewardingness of work. Research has shown that appropriate job design positively influences effectiveness in service-related realms (Hakanen, Schaufeli, & Ahola, 2008; Leana, Appelbaum, & Shevchuk, 2009). In addition, better job design has been linked with decreased absenteeism (Pfeiffer, 2010), decreased turnover (Simons & Jankowski, 2008), and increased job satisfaction (Chang, Chiu, & Chen, 2010).

Box 7.7 provides an overview of human relations and Theory Y.

> ▶ Watch this video that explores the puzzle of motivation. What organizational theory do you think Dan Pink's discussion on motivation reflects? How do you think his discussion applies to human service organizations?
>
> www.youtube.com /watch?v=rrkrvAUbU9Y

Quality-Oriented Management

Shortly after World War II, U.S. college professor W. Edwards Deming traveled to Japan to assist with a proposed national census there. He stayed to help Japanese managers, who were working to rebuild the country's industries and learn new ideas for control of the manufacturing process as a means of improving the quality of goods produced. Two important outcomes arose from this work. First, within only 30 years, Japanese management techniques had gained such a reputation for effectiveness that they were being reimported to the United States and touted as a model for improving U.S. management. Second, Deming and others realized that principles being used to improve manufactured goods could be applied to service organizations as well. These were the earliest stirrings

---

Box 7.7   Human Relations and Theory Y

- **Purpose.** Prescriptive.
- **Key Features.** These theories assume that workers are motivated by factors other than wages. Social relations among staff can enhance production, and they seek to enhance performance by promoting group cohesion and adding social rewards to the range of reinforcements available in the workplace. Others added needs such as self-actualization to the list of additional motivating factors.
- **Strengths and Weaknesses.** Managers are more likely to recognize workers' higher order needs (beyond merely a paycheck) and expand their awareness of potential

motivating factors. Flawed early research overestimated the effect of social influences on production, and the model continued to place discretion and authority solely in the hands of administrators. Later writers argued that increased worker participation would enhance both productivity and workers' ability to meet their needs.

- **Fit with Social Work.** The importance of human relations theory is that social factors are recognized. Workers' tasks are often loosely defined and seemingly well suited to Theory Y management, yet many human service organizations are still operated with a Theory X mentality.

---

of a set of related movements that featured a focus by management on quality and ongoing quality improvement. Two of the most influential schools of thought associated with this approach are *Theory Z* and *Total Quality Management*.

Theory Z

Due in part to the quality-control procedures they had perfected, Japanese firms in the late 1970s and early 1980s began capturing markets long dominated by U.S. businesses. This aroused curiosity about how Japanese companies had overcome their prior reputation for poor products and were now setting worldwide standards of quality.

William Ouchi attempted to capture Japanese-style management in his 1981 book, *Theory Z*. The message of the title was that the philosophical and theoretical principles underlying Japanese management went beyond McGregor's conceptualization of Theory Y. An organization in Japan, said Ouchi, was more than a structural or goal-oriented entity—it was a way of life. It provided career-long employment; intermeshed with the social, political, and economic systems of the country; and influenced organizations such as universities and public schools, even to the lowest grades.

The basic premise of Japanese-style management was that involved workers are the key to increased productivity. Although this may sound similar to the human relations school, that was only partly so. The Japanese were concerned about more than whether workers felt that their social needs were met in the workplace. They wanted workers to become a demonstrable part of the process through which the organization was run. Ideas and suggestions about how to improve the organization were regularly solicited and, where feasible, implemented. One example was the **quality circle**, where employees set aside time to brainstorm ways to improve quality and productivity.

In contrast to U.S. organizations, Japanese organizations at the time tended to have neither organizational charts nor written objectives. Most work was done in teams, and consensus was achieved without a designated leader. Cooperation rather than competition was sought between units. Loyalty to the organization was extremely important, and it was rewarded with loyalty to the employee.

These approaches had considerable influence, and among the organizations that were early adopters of these principles were several research and development offices in the U.S. military (Chenhall, 2003). Even more interesting is the fact that, although Ouchi and others were promoting Japanese adaptations of quality-oriented management, a parallel movement in the United States that also had roots in Deming's work was beginning to gain attention: total quality management.

Total Quality Management

A U.S. writer, Armand Feigenbaum, coined the term "total quality" to describe management practices designed to direct all aspects of an organization's operations toward achieving and maintaining maximum quality in goods or services. Feigenbaum (1951) developed many of the principles of this approach independent of Deming's work and at about the same time, beginning with a book published in 1951. But it was not until the 1980s that the work of these and other writers gained prominence and began to be known under the general title of **total quality management** or **TQM**.

In its definition of TQM, the American Society for Quality (2006) emphasizes that the fundamental orientation of TQM is toward maximizing customer satisfaction. This definition is useful in two ways. First, it highlights the breadth of applicability of the concept of quality, which is intended to apply not only to, for example, a machine that holds up under years of use but also to services that are accurately targeted toward meeting the needs of the purchaser. The second way the definition is useful is in its reference to customer satisfaction. Defining quality as satisfaction imposes a requirement that organizations stay in touch with their customers, use the information gleaned from them to assess performance, and fine-tune their operations based on this input.

Although some principles are unique to TQM, others reflect earlier schools of thought. For example, TQM adopts McGregor's view that workers are more productive if they are allowed discretion in determining how the job is to be done. The model also favors using quality circles and other team-building approaches described by Ouchi. In other cases, though, TQM explicitly rejects prior theoretical views. Among these are bureaucratic (rule-oriented) structures, which TQM adherents view as a threat to the flexibility needed to respond to consumer input and engage in ongoing quality improvement. Saylor (1996) also notes that TQM is incompatible with Drucker's management by objective (MBO) guidelines, because TQM considers customer satisfaction a moving target. This again demands a continual process orientation designed to anticipate and adapt to new customer needs, whereas MBO, Saylor argues, focuses on achieving static outcomes that may ignore the changing needs of customers.

Because TQM has its origins in commercial manufacturing firms, its applicability to human service organizations in the public or private sectors may be questioned. However, results of studies in which TQM principles were applied in human service agencies suggest that this concern is unfounded (Kelly & Lauderdale, 2001; Williams, 2004). In addition, Moore and Kelly (1996) have suggested that TQM principles can be useful if tailored to the unique needs of the organization when implemented.

Box 7.8 provides an overview of Theory Z and TQM.

Advocates of quality-oriented management argue that it represents truly new ideas due to its emphasis on process rather than exclusively on outcomes. Through this process orientation, they contend, fundamental changes can occur in the way organizations work. Such changes may include increased involvement by line staff in the design of procedures and services. They might also include a definition of quality operations that effectively incorporates workforce diversity as an organizational resource.

? Assess your understanding of human resource theories and perspectives by taking this brief quiz.

Box 7.8 Theory Z and Total Quality Management (TQM)

- **Purpose.** Prescriptive.
- **Key Features.** These theories underscore quality as the primary organizational goal and customers as determining what quality is. Change is ongoing and requires teamwork, and communication is top-down, down-up, and sideways (Martin, 1993).
- **Strengths and Weaknesses.** Focusing on quality and consumer input is empowering, and the principles of Theory Z and TQM are aligned with social work values. However, these approaches are paradoxical to other approaches such as MBO in which objectives are set from the top down and organizational charts are hierarchical. Thus, quality management requires a paradigm shift that challenges deeply held underlying assumptions.

- **Fit with Social Work.** Quality management principles that can benefit human service organizations are (1) using quality circles to improve staff involvement and make services more relevant, (2) carefully monitoring whether consumer needs are being met, (3) hiring and training staff in ways that ensure front-line staff have both the skills and interests necessary for their jobs, and (4) having management staff who can define a quality orientation and move the organization toward that goal.

POLITICAL THEORIES AND PERSPECTIVES

Recall that in Chapter 5, we examined community politics with a little *p* (denoting informal relationships as opposed to a capital *P*, denoting electoral political systems) because we were referring to those multitudes of interactions in which people engage that are not always related to government or legislative activities. Thus, organizational theories and perspectives within the political frame are inclusive of internal as well as external politics with a little *p*. Even though decision-making theory originally described a very closed system, focusing on internal decision making, theorists were clear from the beginning that decisions are inherently political because they involve human dynamics and power differentials (the politics that occur within organizations). Thus, in this section, we begin with decision-making theory and move on to more open-systems perspectives.

Decision-making Theory

During the time that natural-system perspectives were gaining prominence, other writers continued to explain organizations as rational systems by exploring the process of *decision making*. One of these, Herbert Simon (1957), began by changing the unit of analysis from the organization to individual actors and focusing on their decision making. A strong influence on his thinking was the work of psychologists who studied the importance of stimulus–response connections as explanations for human behavior. He believed organizations can be conceptualized as aggregations of individual decisions within them, and organizational behavior as decisions made about how to respond to certain stimuli. Because every decision carries some risk, decision making in organizations was thought of as a risk management process within the context of organizational politics.

March and Simon (1958) argued that the key to understanding organizational decisions is to recognize that there are constraints that limit decision making. They termed this phenomenon **bounded rationality** and identified three major categories of constraints:

1. Habits, abilities, and other personal characteristics that individuals bring with them into the decision-making process and that influence their actions in certain ways, irrespective of the circumstances surrounding a specific decision;

2. Loyalties toward a certain group (inside or outside the organization) that has values that conflict with the values of the organization as a whole; and

3. The inability of the decision maker to know all the variables that might influence the decision or all possible consequences of the decision.

The goal of the decision maker is not necessarily to achieve a perfect outcome, because this may never be possible. Instead, the decision maker seeks to reduce uncertainty as much as possible in order to make a decision that has a reasonable likelihood of producing an acceptable outcome. In this way, key decisions are computed to handle uncertainty and inherently political in how to obtain cooperation. March and Simon called this process **satisficing**, and they argued that understanding how satisfactory outcomes are pursued via decisions made in the context of bounded rationality is key to understanding organizations.

Subsequent works expanded on these ideas. Cyert and March (1963) suggested that decision making in aggregate is a process of bargaining between individuals and units that have different views and goals (a political process). The eventual actions of the organization can be understood as the outcome of these ongoing negotiations among organizational members. March and Olsen (1976) proposed a **garbage can analogy** to describe the rather chaotic process in which decisions emerge from a mixture of people, problems, ideas, and "choice opportunities" that are unique to every organization and situation.

As a means of understanding organizations, the decision-making approach has a number of limitations. For example, in a critique of March and Simon's work, Blau and Scott (1962) argued that the model focuses too narrowly on formal decision making, ignoring the interpersonal aspects of organizations and the influence that informal structures can have on decisions that are made. Champion (1975) noted that little attention is paid to situations in which a particular individual may not seek overall rationality but personal or local-unit gain. Most important, the decision-making model has been criticized for its focus on internal factors that lead to particular decisions. This emphasis ignores the fact that, often, influences external to the organization are the most important to eliciting and determining a decision.

Box 7.9 provides an overview of decision-making theory.

Resource Dependency and Political-Economy Theories

Jeffrey Pfeffer (1981) argued that organizational actions are best understood in terms of power relationships and political forces. He defined **power** as the ability to influence actions, and politics as the process through which this influence is used. Asked where power originates, Pfeffer would contend that it arises from an individual's position within the organization, meaning that power and organizational structure are closely tied.

To illustrate the relationship of power and structure, Pfeffer compared three models of organizational analysis: (1) the bureaucratic model, (2) the rational-choice model, and (3) the political model. The *bureaucratic model* is based on the classic Weberian approach that assumes an organization both acts and is structured in a manner that maximizes its production efficiency. Pfeffer's criticisms of this model were essentially the same as those detailed earlier in this chapter. The *rational-choice model* derives from the work of decision-making theorists such as Simon. Pfeffer agreed with their points concerning constraints on rational

> **Box 7.9   Decision Making**
>
> - **Purpose.** Descriptive.
> - **Key Features.** Much of what organizations are and do is the product of decisions made by individuals throughout the hierarchy, but especially at the administrative level. These decisions are only as good as the information on which they are based, however, and complete information needed to make informed decisions is seldom, if ever, present. Because of this lack of information, organizations can never be fully rational. Decision makers thus learn to *satisfice*, meaning they do not expect optimal outcomes but merely acceptable ones.
> - **Strengths and Weaknesses.** These writers showed that the quality of other aspects of management is irrelevant if the quality of decision making is poor. They also accurately anticipated the computer age, which demonstrated the importance of information as an organizational commodity. The better the quality (though not necessarily quantity) of information available, the better the decisions and, eventually, the outcomes. The drawback to this approach was that it remained focused on the politics of internal decision making and failed to give sufficient attention to the larger environment in which an organization operates.
> - **Fit with Social Work.** Discretion and professional judgment are trademarks of human service work, and decision-making theory provides insight into the nature of satisficing, the myth of rationality, and the political nature of internal dynamics.

decision making, but he noted that these models still assumed that decision making is oriented toward a clear organizational goal, whereas in most organizations a range of goals and motivations may exist. Pfeffer urged the use of a *political model* of structural analysis, which calls attention to the manner in which organizational actions may be either instrumental (serving the presumed goals of the organization as a whole) or parochial (serving the perceived self-interest of a particular individual or organizational unit). These goals may differ, as does the power of the decision maker to effect his or her choice of action. Pfeffer thus believed that organizational actions must be understood in terms of the complex interplay of individuals working together—sometimes toward mutual goals and sometimes toward personal goals—in a manner analogous to what happens in the political arena.

All organizations rely on elements in their environment from which they can obtain resources needed for survival. In the terminology of systems theory, this is called **resource dependence**. Because of it, organizations try to form relationships with other organizations that can provide needed resources reliably and predictably. Cash and non-cash funds represent one type of resource, but human service organizations need other types such as services (e.g., accounting), skilled staff, and clients.

Wamsley and Zald (1976) argued that structure and process in organizations are best understood in terms of the interplay of political and economic interests, both internal *and* external to the organization. *Political* means the processes by which the organization obtains power and legitimacy. *Economic* means the processes by which the organization gets resources such as clients, staff, and funding.

The goal of this **political-economy perspective** was to incorporate much of the work of previous schools into a more general conceptual model. Within this model, elements such as individual interests and goals, the power wielded by the holders of these interests, and environmental resources and the relative influence of those who control them are all seen to interact in a way that creates the unique character of an organization. This character is not static but changes as the political economy of the organization changes. With respect to the metaphors proposed by Bolman and Deal

Box 7.10   Political-Economy and Resource Dependency Theories

- **Purpose.** Descriptive.
- **Key Features.** These theories underscore how important it is to recognize that organizations are influenced by external and internal political and economic dynamics. Since the environment is constantly changing, organizations must develop adaptive strategies.
- **Strengths and Weaknesses.** Power and politics perspectives affirm the highly complex nature of organizational survival, and illustrate how important

it is to recognize the multiple forces within the environment. However, they tend not to focus on values and ideologies that may transcend power and money in shaping behavior (Hasenfeld, 2010).

- **Fit with Social Work.** Because human service organizations are highly dependent on external resources, it is incumbent upon social workers to be aware of the political and economic forces that impact internal behavior and service delivery.

(2013), this fits the "jungle" model, in that the organization is seen as an environment of competing interests where those holding the power determine whose interests are given priority.

The topic of power has also been discussed with respect to its effect on ethnic minorities and women in organizations. For example, evidence suggests that the gap in pay between white males and others does not arise solely from the fact that white males typically occupy better paid positions. Instead, it also appears to result from white males holding power that allows them to protect their earnings advantage. Castilla (2008) demonstrated that merit pay systems designed to award salary adjustments on the basis of job performance could be manipulated to benefit those in power. Cohen (2007) found that having a higher proportion of women in an organization had little effect on correcting the male–female wage gap. What did begin to narrow the gap was having at least a few women in positions with high prestige and influence. This supports Pfeffer's contention that power and influence—rather than procedures or numbers—determine how organizations behave.

In Chapter 5, we discussed theories about power, politics, and change that pertain to communities (see Table 5.7). Note that because political-economy and resource dependency theories view organizations as open systems, they focus on understanding organizations within their communities. Box 7.10 provides an overview of political-economy and resource dependency theories.

Critical and Feminist Theories

Political-economists recognize the politics surrounding organizational-environmental relationships and attempt to identify strategies used to negotiate and reconcile differences among diverse organizational interests. Critical theorists, on the other hand, not only recognize these politics but also see organizations as instruments of exploitation in capitalist economies in which powerful, elite political systems carry out social injustices. Since organizations are seen as institutionalizing political exploitation, critical theorists call into question their social construction as vehicles in which discrimination and inequity marginalize certain interests (primarily women and minorities) (Hasenfeld, 2010).

Inspired by Karl Marx, as opposed to Max Weber, critical theorists question the assumptions held by traditional organizational theorists. Critical philosopher Habermas (1971), sociologist Giddens (1984), and planners Forrester (1980) and Bolen (1980) have all influenced the development of this perspective. The goal of critical theory is to create workplaces (and whole societies) free from oppression and in which all members have equal opportunities. Recognizing that client–worker relationships are based on power differentials, workers are seen as instruments of discrimination even with the best of motives. Since a leader, manager, practitioner, or worker represents a system that has structure, processes, and services designed with dominant assumptions, critical theory points out that each party may be carrying out assumptions that can do harm. An example is **bureaucractic disentitlement**, a term coined by Michael Lipsky (1984) to describe situations in which workers within social welfare agencies neglect to take action or to inform clients about what they are qualified to receive, thus disempowering the very persons they are there to serve.

 Watch this video where Michael Lipsky discusses street-level bureaucracy. Who are the "street-level bureaucrats," and why are they significant to social welfare organizations?

www.youtube.com
/watch?v=ZX1livgPspA

During the late 1960s and early 1970s, feminist scholars joined with critical theorists in criticizing traditional organizational theory and research that ignored the relevance of gender in the working world. Terms such as *gendered* and *gendering* entered the literature, and a focus on gender inequalities emerged (Acker, 2012). Acker (1990) argued that both traditional and critical approaches to organizations emanate from male conceptualizations and therefore view reality from a male standpoint. These conceptualizations are often assumed to be gender neutral, when in fact women and men are differently affected by organizations. She further argued that traditional organizational theory assumes an ideal worker and divides the world of work into productive and reproductive activities, privileging work within organizations over domestic work that occurs outside formal organizations. Thus, organizations are gendered structures built on dominant logics, and they inherently oppress any group that does not conform to male privilege. Building on Acker's argument, other feminist writers have examined the ways in which organizations inherently oppress women as well as any other non-dominant population group (Britton & Logan, 2008). Fenby (1991) contended that feminist ways of knowing could be combined with critical theory and "used as an alternative theoretical base for management" (p. 21).

Theorizing about gender has become more complicated with the recognition of intersectionality (introduced in Chapter 3), acknowledging that gender does not stand alone but intersects with other forms of inequality and exclusion. Acker (2012) called for a critical review of organizational change related to gender, race, and class. She asked what counts as part of an organization. For example, are outsourced functions part of the organization, such as having young female workers in China produce a product for an American company? In other words, if one organization contracts with another one that exploits women or minorities in some way, is the original organization responsible? She asked about what positions are part of the workforce of a particular organization. In other words, are part-time workers or even volunteers who do not receive benefits considered employees? It is these groups that may be exploited and treated differently, yet they may be invisible in employment statistics. Acker (2012) considered the schism between the paid work sector and the domestic (unpaid) work sectors as the "most enduring gender, race, and class substructures" (p. 222) because it reinforces the differential between the masculine and the feminine. The masculine is carried out in formal organizations as legitimate settings for paid work, whereas the domestic sector in which many women work is often informal, unpaid, and thus subjugated.

Box 7.11   Critical and Feminist Theories

- **Purpose.** Descriptive.
- **Key Features.** These theories question dominant theories of organizations, asking who controls organizations and who benefits. Organizations are seen as instruments of domination in a society that exploits women, minorities, and lower level employees.
- **Strengths and Weaknesses.** These theories raise important issues about power, control, domination, marginalization, and subjugation. Their intent is to expose inequalities and to press for progressive change. They serve to raise consciousness, but are less helpful in prescribing ways

to move from theory to practice. Whereas liberal feminism does not challenge mainstream ways of thinking about organizations and attempts to work within existing structures, radical feminists push for alternative organizations.

- **Fit with Social Work.** These theories fit well with the social justice orientation of social work. They pose questions that raise consciousness and require self-awareness, facilitating human service practitioners to recognize when they may have unintentionally become part of systems that control and exploit rather than emancipate and empower.

In the social work literature, Fenby (1991) used critical and feminist theories to question management's "romance with the technical." She used an action theory approach to encourage managers to be more self-reflective, paying attention to the use of self and forming networks in which alternative ways of looking at managerial actions can take place.

In order to expose dominant systems, Hasenfeld (2010) proposes undertaking an ideological critique of four ways in which ideologies are integrated into human services work:

1. The ways in which human service clients are morally constructed (how clients are viewed within the organization);

2. How desired ends (outcomes) are defined (and who defines them);

3. What technologies are used to deliver services (how sensitive or insensitive they are); and

4. How and by whom organizational staff are socialized and controlled. (p. 47)

If, for example, a human service organization adopts more and more business-like practices based on efficiency and accountability, values of social justice and the culture of care may become subjugated. In short, these theories question everything about the status quo in organizations and call for critical thinking about the unintended consequences and potential ethical conflicts that may be overlooked in every aspect of organizational work.

? Assess your understanding of political theories and perspectives by taking this brief quiz.

Box 7.11 provides an overview of critical and feminist theories.

SYMBOLIC THEORIES AND PERSPECTIVES

The symbolic frame primarily focuses on theories that address artifacts, values, underlying assumptions, and organizational culture and identity. Although we have placed critical and feminist theories within a political frame, they straddle a line between political and symbolic. Similarly, symbolic theories recognize the political nature of organizations (both internally and externally). For example, organizational culture works as a political blanket in organizations and can be constraining (and even comforting) in that it shapes virtually every move an employee makes.

Organizational Culture Theory

The concept of **organizational culture** has shaped the development of many other contemporary theories and perspectives. To describe this concept, different writers have used familiar expressions such as "the way we do things around here" and the "unwritten rules" that constitute intelligent behavior in an organization. A prominent writer on the subject, Edgar Schein (2010), explains that an organizational culture develops through shared experiences. Newly formed organizations are heavily influenced by leaders who bring their perspectives to the organization and around whom assumptions and beliefs emerge. Thus, leadership and culture are intimately related, and understanding what assumptions leaders bring to organizations is central to analyzing how change occurs.

Schein (2010) defines organizational culture as "a pattern of shared basic assumptions learned by a group as it solved its problems of external adaptation and internal integration, that has worked well enough to be considered valid and, therefore, to be taught to new members as the correct way to perceive, think, and feel in relation to those problems" (p. 18). In his definition, Schein starts with "shared basic assumptions." Yet, most practitioners first enter organizations in which those basic assumptions are so ingrained that persons who have been there for a while no longer consciously recognize them. Entering a new organization, you may have had a sense that you had said or done something wrong. You were surprised at the reaction you received, but you didn't have a clue about what it meant. Chances are that you tripped over a basic underlying assumption that everyone else held as the correct way of behaving in that culture. Have you ever tried to change an organization and wondered why you met resistance, when the change seemed so logical to you? Perhaps what you considered valid was not what others considered valid. Perhaps the espoused values were not the same as the norms guiding behavior in that organization.

When entering an organization, one quickly perceives that established patterns occur within that system even if they are not explicitly stated. The social worker who assumes a new place in an organization must be aware that these patterns may be central to organizational functioning. When violated, members may respond emotionally because they are so invested in the "way things have always been done."

Schein (2010) identified three levels of culture. **Artifacts** reflect the climate of the organization and are the most visible structures, processes, and behaviors. The term "artifacts" is particularly appropriate here. Merriam-Webster's (2015) first definition is "something created by humans usually for a particular purpose," and the second is "something characteristic of or resulting from a particular human institution, period, trend, or individual." Both definitions are applicable here.

Espoused beliefs and values are what members of the organization say are important and are typically reflected in mission or vision statements. They are embedded in the culture when a leader convinces others that certain beliefs and values are important

> Watch this video featuring a slideshow presentation by Bill Strickland. What cultural artifacts do you observe in the video? What do you think they say about the organization?
>
> www.youtube.com /watch?v=xoHBiHFV9SA

Box 7.12   Levels of Organization Culture

Level 1: Artifacts (the climate of the organization)

- The organization's constructed physical and social environment (e.g., signage, building or office space, stairs, and elevators)
- Use of physical space (e.g., location and condition of waiting rooms, and private spaces or lack thereof)
- Organizational outputs (e.g., reports, statistics, treatment plans, etc.)
- Written & spoken language (e.g., jargon used, key phrases, code words, and metaphors used)
- Items on the wall (e.g., artwork, photos, signs, and posters)
- Members' behavior (how people interact [or not] among themselves and with clients)

Level 2: Values and Beliefs

- Cognitively transformed into a belief when holding that value works
- Ultimately, some values will be transformed into assumptions.
- "Espoused values" are what people say they believe, but they don't always act in accordance with them. This would be a separation of culture from behavior.

Level 3: Basic Underlying Assumptions

- So taken for granted that one finds little variation in a unit
- Theories-in-use
- Often hard to assess whether one is dealing with organizational culture or professional culture, disciplinary culture, regional variations, ethnic or gender differences, or group subcultures within the organization

---

to embrace. Last, over time, these values become validated (if they seem to be working) and become **basic underlying assumptions**, which are often taken for granted as how the organization should go about its work. Examples of each level are found in Box 7.12.

Solving problems of external adaptation and internal integration refer to the ways in which organizational members go about working on their relationship with the larger external environment and dealing with issues internal to the organization. Schein (1992) contended that adapting externally includes gaining consensus on the following elements: (1) mission and strategy, (2) goals, (3) means to attaining goals, (4) measurement criteria to document how the work is going, and (5) corrections in the form of strategies to keep focusing on goals. According to Schein, these five areas are minimally necessary for an organization to structure itself to survive in its environment without misunderstandings when persons from different backgrounds enter the organization.

Schein also elucidated the factors required for internal integration of an organization's culture. These include (1) developing a common language and means of communication, (2) establishing group/unit boundaries, (3) recognizing power and status dimensions, (4) establishing norms of appropriate interaction among members, (5) determining how to award success and discipline inappropriate behavior, and (6) finding ways to explain uncontrollable events (Schein, 2010, p. 94). Schein explains that cultural assumptions provide a filter for how workers view the world and that, if stripped of that filter, anxiety and overload will be experienced. Cultural solutions offer routine answers to what would normally be complex problems. The major reason why organizational members resist cultural change is because it challenges deeply held assumptions that stabilize one's world—it questions the status quo. This is why members of a dysfunctional culture might choose to retain current assumptions rather than risk having their cultural roots challenged.

Glisson, Williams, Green, Hemmelgarn and Hoagwood (2014) developed the Organizational Social Context (OSC) scale focusing on three dimensions of culture: proficiency, rigidity, and resistance. In organizations with proficient cultures, a concern for client well-being predominates, and employees are evaluated on two elements relating to their ability to improve client well-being. The first is competency, which has to do with the quality of their professional skills and their commitment to keeping those skills at a high level. The second is responsiveness, which refers to employees' attention to clients' individual needs and ability to adapt service to address them. Their research has also shown important differences in the quality of client services provided by human service organizations in the proficient category as compared to those in other types.

Organizations with rigid cultures tend to be averse to change and oriented toward maintenance of the familiar and predictable. Because of this, they tend to be more bureaucratically structured and have an array of rules and policies governing how employees are supposed to do their jobs. Similarly, decisions tend to be made by one or a small number of administrators, and opportunities for employee input into decisions is limited. Finally, resistant organizational cultures are those in which employees are expected to be apathetic toward change or actively antagonistic to it. Training and other service-improvement efforts are seen as futile because staff members oppose trying new things or are pessimistic that different approaches will achieve useful results.

Diversity as an Element of Culture

In many organizations, the culture was dominated by a particular gender group (usually men), a particular racial/ethnic group (usually whites), and a particular socioeconomic class (usually wealthy elites). As with much of the rest of society, organizations were far from level playing fields, and, to an even greater degree than in the rest of society, those in power were able to shape rules, structures, and operations in ways that preserved their privileges. As Brazell (2003) notes, change came about only as social action and large-scale social movements began to change society as a whole. The Civil Rights Movement, the Women's Movement, and the Disability Rights Movement are examples of efforts that heightened awareness of discrimination and made it less likely to go unchallenged. The movements also helped establish antidiscrimination laws that extended new legal protections into the workplace. In addition to these forces, changing economic conditions and better access to education sent women into the workforce in unprecedented numbers, whereas changing demographics, such as the rapid growth of the Latino population, made the workforce more heterogeneous.

In an early work on diversity in organizations, Roosevelt Thomas Jr. (1991) identified three forces acting on organizations in the United States:

1. The need for corporations to do business in an increasingly competitive global market

2. Rapid changes in the United States that are increasing the diversity of its workforce

3. The demise of the "melting pot" concept in favor of a recognition that diversity is a strength rather than a weakness

Behavior: Apply self-awareness and self-regulation to manage the influence of personal biases and values in working with diverse clients and constituencies.

Critical Thinking Question: How might diversity management help strengthen social workers' abilities to work with diverse client populations?

Thomas believed that effective management of diversity is crucial to improving productivity. This is because, in a global economy, organizations with a diverse workforce are more likely to be those with novel ideas and adroit responses to changing circumstances.

Cross (2000) noted the usefulness of the organizational culture approach for developing methods of harnessing and managing diversity. To the extent that culture in organizations involves shared understandings about "how things are done," those understandings must incorporate the differing frames of reference that diversity entails. Carr-Ruffino (2002) sums up many of the key points of diversity management by arguing that administrators must take the lead in changing an organization's culture toward one that embraces diversity. To accomplish this, she proposed seven strategies or responsibilities that administrators must assume:

1. Promote tolerance.

2. Be a role model of respect and appreciation.

3. Value empathy (e.g., by training oneself to see things through others' eyes).

4. Promote trust and goodwill.

5. Encourage collaboration (to break through cliques and promote interaction among organizational members).

6. Work toward synthesis (seek to benefit from new insights offered by bringing diverse perspectives to bear on an issue).

7. Create synergy (use diversity to achieve as a team more than the sum of what could be achieved by individuals working alone). (pp. 118–119)

The framework in Chapter 8 includes analyzing the culture of an organization with respect to its friendliness toward diversity and addresses many of the elements in Carr-Ruffino's list, among others. These include culture-reinforcing elements such as mission statements that embrace diversity and participatory approaches to decision making.

Pursuing Excellence

Another important management theme linked to organizational culture was the "excellence" theme, pioneered by Thomas Peters and Robert Waterman (1982). Both authors, after working at a management consulting firm, became leaders of a project on organizational effectiveness. They created a definition for what they considered excellent companies, then selected 62 for study. They also immersed themselves in the philosophies and practices of excellent companies, and they discovered that the dominant themes were elements of organizational culture such as a family feeling among employees, a preference for smallness, a preference for simplicity rather than complexity, and attention to individuals. In effect, they found that management practices in these organizations focused on personal elements such as those noted by human relations theorists and McGregor's Theory Y.

Their findings were organized into eight basic principles that have become the focal point of the "excellence approach" to management:

1. **A Bias for Action.** A preference for doing something—anything—rather than sending a question through cycles and cycles of analyses and committee reports

2. **Staying Close to the Customer.** Learning preferences and catering to them

3. **Autonomy and Entrepreneurship.** Breaking the corporation into small companies, and encouraging them to think independently and competitively

4. **Productivity through People.** Creating in all employees a belief that their best efforts are essential and that they will share the rewards of the company's success

5. **Hands-On, Value Driven.** Insisting that executives keep in touch with the firm's essential mission

6. **Stick to the Knitting.** Remaining with the business the company knows best

7. **Simple Form, Lean Staff.** Few administrative layers, few people at the upper levels

8. **Simultaneous Loose/Tight Properties.** Fostering a climate where there is dedication to the central values of the company, combined with tolerance for all employees who accept those values

Sensemaking Theory

In addition to the "excellence" theme, another body of work that meshes well with organizational culture theory is the analytical approach termed "sensemaking." Proposed by Karl Weick (1995), this approach is based in part on communications theory, which is concerned with how people process information and make sense of what they see around them. Its relevance to organizations and its connection to organizational culture come from the assumption that individuals draw clues from their environments, engage in internal conversations designed to make sense of these clues, then form conclusions about what they have seen and heard.

Weick, Sutcliffe, and Obstfeld (2005) described various aspects of this process. First, sensemaking arises as a natural effort by individuals to process what is going on around them, which at first may seem random and disordered. Events are "bracketed" (differentiated from others and categorized), after which the category into which they are placed is labeled, again using some form of internal shorthand. Sensemaking is retrospective (meaning that it requires interpreting events *after* they occur), and the necessity to act typically precedes sensemaking done to gauge the results of the action. Although sensemaking may appear to be individualistic, it is actually a social process for it is contingent on interactions and relationships with others (Mikkelsen, 2012).

To understand the value of the sensemaking approach, it is helpful to keep in mind that organizations may be seen as collections of individuals who are constantly engaged in sensemaking to allow them to meet the expectation that they work together toward mutual goals. We noted earlier the definition of organizational culture as "the way things are done around here," and people's understanding of how things are done arise from their sensemaking processes within the organization. Weick and colleagues (2005) describe sensemaking as small-scale mechanisms that in time can lead to large-scale changes, meaning that the shared understandings and modes of operation comprising organizational culture develop from ongoing thought processes on the part of each individual. At a larger level, leaders of an organization engage in sensemaking processes to evaluate the position of the organization as a whole within its environment.

A theme related to sensemaking is offered by Gareth Morgan (1986), who emphasizes the value of metaphor in understanding organizations. Morgan notes that metaphor was often used (explicitly or implicitly) by earlier organizational theories, and he considers it a valid heuristic tool (that is, a device or method used to help understand something). Weber deliberately compared bureaucracies to machines, Morgan notes, and this metaphor was also used by Weber's critics to decry the mechanistic and impersonal aspects of bureaucracies. For open-systems theorists, the metaphor of choice was *organization-as-organism*, and it was from this metaphor that descriptions and studies of the "survival instinct" of organizations arose.

Morgan's ideas fit comfortably with the use of "culture" as a metaphor to describe how organizations work. The concept of culture is used by anthropologists seeking to differentiate societies of people on the basis of their shared beliefs, values, and histories, and Morgan considers this a similarly valid tool for differentiating organizations. This view has been supported by studies showing that the metaphor of organizational culture can be used by managers to reinforce shared perceptions among members of organizations (Gibson & Zellmer-Bruhn, 2001) and to promote team building (Kang, Yang, & Rowley, 2006).

Organizational Learning Theory

An open-systems approach views organizations as cybernetic systems, meaning they gather information from their environments and use it to decide on their next actions. Acting on input in this way involves *single-loop learning*, whereas taking action and then monitoring its effect to alter later actions are termed *double-loop learning*. For organisms, the action–feedback–learning process tends to be immediate and comparatively straightforward: a small hand extending to a countertop and encountering a cookie yields one lesson; the same small hand encountering a hot stove yields another. Argyris and Schön, in two books on organizational learning (1978; 1996), called attention to the constant way in which organizations receive feedback from their environment and attempt to correctly interpret it. They also noted that this feedback is often less immediate and more ambiguous than in the case of organisms. As Senge (1990) explains, organisms receive feedback directly, whereas in an organization it may be one division that takes an action (e.g., a decision by the case management department to engage in more outreach) but a different division that encounters the feedback (such as the administrative team).

In addition to horizontal (department-to-department) distance between decision and effect, there is also vertical distance. Most of us have been in situations where we or others around us have bemoaned being the lowly "grunts" suffering the consequences of decisions made by higher-ups. This dynamic leads to two serious problems. First, decisions gone wrong cause deterioration of morale, which in turn initiates a "blame game" cycle in which everyone in the organization thinks everyone else is responsible for things that go bad. Second, because the effects of a decision—good or bad—tend to be out of sight of the decision maker, more and more decisions are made in the absence of information about their effects. Bolman and Deal (2013) refer to this as "system blindness." Its key characteristics are a delayed feedback loop in which information about decisions filters back to management only slowly, and short-term thinking, in which managers begin to favor decisions that make them look good at the moment even if they have long-term negative consequences.

Peter Senge is most closely associated with the concept of the "learning organization," because in his 1990 book he proposed that the solution to the above dynamic is to build organizations that mirror the learning process of a single organism. Organisms have nerve pathways that rush information quickly from one part of the body to another, and body systems work in tandem to, for example, quickly withdraw the small hand from the hot stove. Senge's learning organization has similar capacities. It is oriented toward gathering, processing, and sharing information both vertically and horizontally. It also places responsibility for creating the learning organization on leaders. They must provide guidelines, incentives, and examples to staff members to help develop the pathways and procedures needed for rapid movement and absorption of information. They must also become fully familiar with the organization that results from this process—replacing system blindness with "systemic understanding."

The concept of the "learning organization" seems to mesh well with the outlook of many administrators and staff members in human service organizations, and Senge's work continues to be cited frequently in this literature. In addition, findings tend to confirm that Senge's ideas are well received when implemented. Latting et al. (2004) found that the problems of mistrust across vertical levels of a human service organization can be overcome if administrators begin with efforts to create a learning- and innovation-oriented climate within the organization and then move to employee-empowerment efforts supported by supervisors. In their study, these efforts were rewarded with increased organizational commitment on the part of employees. This is consistent with results from a study by Beddoe (2009), who found that even in a time of relatively high environmental turmoil, social workers in a human service agency were receptive to efforts to adopt the learning-organization model. Receptiveness was diminished, however, to the extent that the change was perceived as a top-down mandate rather than a grassroots-led innovation. Finally, Bowen, Ware, Rose, and Powers (2007) examined educational settings and developed a measure of a school's capacity to function as a learning organization. Results validated the ability of the instrument to measure theoretically predicted organizational performance. This offers empirical support not only for the validity of the measure but also for Senge's conceptualization of how learning organizations operate.

Box 7.13 provides an overview of the symbolic theories.

The perspectives discussed here come together in interesting ways. Clearly, one trend coming out of the 1980s was the move toward a better, more thorough understanding of organizational culture. Often this begins with an identification of the locus of power and an understanding of the effectiveness of various individuals or groups in exercising political and leadership skills. These factors, together with the development of an organization-wide sense of shared purpose and ways of operating, make up what has come to be understood as organizational culture. As Morgan (1986) points out, "culture" can in turn be used as a powerful metaphor for understanding how people come together in an organization to define and pursue mutual goals.

Ethical and Professional Behavior

Behavior: Use reflection and self-regulation to manage personal values and maintain professionalism in practice situations.

Critical Thinking Question: How might the concept of the learning organization assist you in using reflection and self-regulation in managing your personal values and maintaining professionalism in the workplace?

Box 7.13   Symbolic Theories

- **Purpose.** Most approaches are prescriptive and offering guidance for deeper understanding of organizations.
- **Key Features.** These theories often build on ideas from earlier works that have been generally accepted. All assume, for example, that environmental circumstances are critical to understanding organizational behavior, that no one structure works equally well for all organizations, and that the personal interests of individuals within organizations powerfully influence how they operate. Contemporary theories tend to differ in their choice of variables that have been ignored or underestimated in prior work. Examples of these include *culture* (Schein), *sensemaking* (Weick), *diversity* and the increasing heterogeneity of the workforce (Cross), *quality* (Peters

and Waterman), and the fostering of an organizational orientation toward learning from and responding to the environment (Senge).

- **Fit with Social Work.** Organizational theory continues to evolve, as new theories either supplant older ones or build on their strong points and extend them in new directions. As in the past, many contemporary ideas arose first in studies of commercial firms, and some are easier to adapt to social work organizations than others. Also of note is the fact that work from fields as diverse as political science, biology, and engineering have influenced contemporary organizational theories. Given the increasingly interdisciplinary nature of scientific work, this trend is likely to continue.

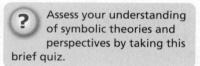 **?** Assess your understanding of symbolic theories and perspectives by taking this brief quiz.

An increasingly important factor in the development and evolution of organizational culture is the diversity of the workforce. Organizations of the future will continue to grow more diverse, and this means they will need to continuously address the question of whether their culture embraces this diversity and uses it in ways that benefit the organization, individual members, and clientele.

SUMMARY

As with Chapter 5 on community theory, it should be clear at this point that all professionally assisted change in organizations begins with an understanding of organizations including theoretical frameworks, structure, worker motivation, management–worker relationships, diversity, organizational culture, and other variables. The goal of this chapter has been to introduce theories about organizations that may help social workers make sense of the organizations in which and with which they work. These theories can be understood partly in terms of how they differ among themselves (Table 7.1). Some (such as scientific management and human relations) are prescriptive, meaning that they provide guidelines on how to organize. Others, such as bureaucracy and decision-making, offer conceptual strategies for analyzing organizations and their operations.

Theories can also be differentiated in terms of their approach to explaining organizational behavior. Some adopt a rational approach in which behavior is seen as the result of logical decision making about how to achieve instrumental goals. Others employ a natural-systems approach, in which the organization is seen as analogous to a biological organism and its behavior as responding to survival and self-maintenance needs. Yet both theories are focused on understanding structure.

Theories also differ as to whether they adopt a closed- or open-systems perspective regarding the role of the organization's environment. Closed-systems approaches implicitly focus on internal structure and processes within organizations and tend to pay little or no attention to the role of the environment. Open-systems models emphasize organizations' dependence on their environment and adopt analytical strategies that view internal structure and process as the product of interactions with the environment.

Each theory can also be understood in terms of one or a small group of organizational variables toward which it directs attention. We have used four frames developed by Bolman and Deal (2013) to loosely categorize theories (structural, human resource, political, and symbolic). Together, all these factors are important because understanding structure, people, politics, and values make for a more complete picture of organizational life.

The history of organizational and management theory has been, in many ways, the history of a search for insights into the best ways to organize and manage—a search for the theory that will unlock the secrets of productivity. It could be said that each theorist examined organizations through an eyepiece with a different filter than others.

Recent decades have witnessed the introduction of a number of alternative perspectives. Although none has dominated the field, each contributes to one's ability to analyze and understand organizations.

 Recall what you learned in this chapter by completing the Chapter Review.

Assess Your Competence

Use the scale below to rate your current level of achievement on the following concepts or skills associated with each learning outcome listed at the beginning of this chapter:

1	2	3
I can accurately describe the concept or skill(s) associated with this outcome.	I can consistently identify the concept or skill(s) associated with this outcome when observing and analyzing practice activities.	I can competently implement the concept or skill(s) associated with this outcome in my own practice.

_____ Define organizations, their characteristics, and their functions.

_____ Discuss at least three theories that focus on organizational structure.

_____ Discuss at least two theories that frame organizations from a human resource perspective.

_____ Explain the importance of examining organizations from a critical perspective.

_____ Discuss the importance of using symbolic theories in understanding the values and underlying assumptions in the cultures of human service organizations

Assessing Human Service Organizations

STOCKBYTE / GETTY IMAGES

ENGAGING HUMAN SERVICE ORGANIZATIONS

Having reviewed in Chapter 7 a variety of approaches to understanding organizations, we now focus on engaging and assessing **human service organizations** (**HSOs**), where most social workers are employed. Regardless of which approach one takes in an organizational change effort, it is important to understand that HSOs can be conceptualized in many ways and to have a workable knowledge of organizational theories and perspectives. The major focus of this chapter is on engaging organizations in an assessment process designed to lead to an informed and skillful intervention.

HSOs have goals to improve the quality of life of persons outside the organization (e.g., helping someone resolve a drinking problem, or providing in-home services to help older adults prolong independent living). In each case, the organization exists because, as a collective, it makes possible the accomplishment of tasks that could not be completed as well or at all by a single individual.

Hasenfeld (2010) identified attributes of HSOs:

- In HSOs, people are the raw material to be worked with in a transformational process, as opposed to organizations that process inanimate materials.
- In HSOs, moral values guide the process of service intervention in which great discretion must be exercised.
- Because HSOs engage in moral work with people, they must be legitimized by their environment. In other words, they may be highly regulated, and workers may be credentialed in order to assure humane treatment of clientele.
- Practice technologies (e.g., counseling, therapy, and macro interventions) must be institutionalized and vetted so that no harm is done to clientele.
- HSOs must manage indeterminacy as their technologies are subject to change, and workers must use considerable discretion and judgment in working with diverse human beings.
- At the core of human service work are client–worker relationships. Thus, practitioners in HSOs are engaged in emotional work.

HSO clients often seek help because they have been unable to obtain education, employment, assistance, or other resources from organizations in their community. In turn, the services that social workers provide often involve interacting with these same organizations on clients' behalf or helping clients improve their own ability to interact with these organizations. Doing this well requires considerable effort spanning a range of agencies and service systems. Social workers with little or no idea of how organizations operate, how they relate to each other, or how they can be influenced and changed from both outside and inside are likely to be severely limited in their effectiveness and disempowered to make changes in their workplaces.

Although HSOs have characteristics that distinguish them from other organizations, these are not always clear-cut. Hasenfeld (2010) indicates that HSOs operate in some way on the people they serve. They may distribute or even produce certain goods (as do food banks or workshops for people with disabilities), but they focus on improving the quality of life of their constituents, consumers, or clients. The problem in defining HSOs, however, is that organizations from barber shops to bistros work with or on people and seek to enhance at least their perceived well-being. But, in Hasenfeld's definition, the defining feature of HSOs is that they are designed to promote human welfare. In particular, they must conform to societal expectations that the services they provide both assist clients and enhance the overall welfare of the public.

Many different types of organizations still fall within this definition, and to make sense of such variety, one important issue is the sector in which the organization operates. As discussed in Chapter 6, the three major sectors of the economy are public, nonprofit, or for-profit. These categories are important because the mission, service orientation, and nature of practice in HSOs often vary substantially across sectors. However, distinctions between sectors are not always clear-cut, either. For example, some public agencies now pay private agencies to perform services that were once exclusively governmental, such as child protection and corrections (Xu & Morgan,

2012). Similarly, some private agencies have created for-profit subsidiaries or launched joint ventures with for-profit organizations in different sectors (Levitt & Chiodini, 2014; Reeves, 2013). While the concept of "sector" remains a variable worth considering when assessing HSOs, it also demonstrates the difficulty of neatly fitting organizations into any single category.

Two Vignettes of Human Service Organizations

The following vignettes illustrate the issues and problems encountered by social workers in governmental and nonprofit settings in the Canyon City and Lakeside communities we introduced in Chapter 6. Vignette 1 focuses on a large public child welfare agency and its development within Canyon City. The concerns the agency encounters involve factors such as the growth of bureaucracy and a hierarchical organizational structure, the role of elected officials, frustrations concerning slow change processes, constrained creativity, and barriers to client services.

The second vignette describes a medium-sized, nonprofit, faith-related agency established in the 1930s at the time the Lakeside community was first developed. As times change, the organization grows through the receipt of government grants and contracts. Issues related to working with boards of directors and sponsoring groups, attempts to address the needs of multiple constituencies in an increasingly regulated environment, and the use of volunteers are illustrated.

We hope these vignettes will show how social workers can begin to analyze circumstances in their own agencies or others with which they interact. Immediately following the vignettes, we will discuss some of the issues raised and then present a framework for assessing HSOs.

Vignette 1:   Canyon County Department of Child Welfare

Canyon City is the seat of Canyon County. The Canyon County Department of Child Welfare (CCDCW) had long considered itself a unique and innovative organization. Created in the early 1960s, its initial years of development came during a time when national attention was focused on the creation of high-quality human service programs designed to address both client needs and community problems. The department's director was hired after an extensive national search. She built a strong reputation as a person who ran successful programs and was well liked by the community, her staff, and clients.

Creating a Dynamic Organization. The director took the job at CCDCW because she was excited by the challenge of building a department from scratch with resources made available from federal, state, and county governments. She hired staff members who, like herself, were committed to teamwork, collaboration, and problem solving. Middle managers and supervisors were professionals with many years of experience, most of whom had master's of social work (MSW) degrees, and many line workers were recent graduates of MSW programs. In selecting among job applicants, the director stressed high energy, enthusiasm, collective effort, mutual support, esprit de corps, and competence.

From the 1960s through most of the 1990s, CCDCW built a reputation for high-quality services, a high rate of success, and a positive work environment. It was an organization other counties looked to for leadership in dealing with prominent problems of the time—not only child abuse and neglect but also domestic violence, drug and alcohol abuse, and other family-related problems.

Dismantling a Dynamic Organization. Toward the end of the 1990s, two things happened that changed the direction of the department. First, as a county in a state with one of the fastest growing populations in the country, Canyon County doubled its population between 1985 and 2000. Increasing fiscal and political conservatism influenced decisions of the county board of supervisors, and the child welfare budget became the focus of a major budget reduction effort. Second, the original director reached retirement age.

The board of supervisors used this opportunity to appoint a person who had spent his career in the insurance industry. They saw this as an opportunity to introduce "hard-nosed business practices" into the running of human service programs. At the same time, state and federal regulations governing child welfare services became increasingly more extensive and strict. Because of CCDCW's strong reputation, employment there served as a solid reference and helped make staff members more marketable in other counties and states. Many managers and supervisors took advantage of this to accept other employment offers, and some of their positions were filled by individuals who had political connections to the board or to the director. The team approach that had dominated for two decades was replaced by a more rigid bureaucratic structure, and collegial practices were replaced by strictly enforced administrative policies.

Within about five years, CCDCW bore little resemblance to its original form. The most noticeable change was in its structure. Its organizational chart reflected clearly defined work units, with reporting lines from entry level all the way to the director. Standardized workloads were assigned regardless of the difficulty or complexity of cases, and standardized performance criteria were used to judge success. Individual discretion in decision making was curtailed, and employee-oriented efforts such as job rotation, job sharing, and flex-time were eliminated.

Involvement of the County Board. Members of the county board of supervisors began to receive complaints about CCDCW. Although most child maltreatment reports were investigated, many children for whom an initial report was judged invalid were later re-reported as victims of recurring abuse or neglect. Also, annual reports revealed a steady decline in the successful resolution of problems for families served by the department. Eventually, a consultant was hired to do an organizational assessment and to make recommendations to the board of supervisors.

The consultant found that staff expressed low levels of commitment to the organization and its objectives. Line-level workers felt their opinions did not matter, so most either kept comments to themselves or complained to colleagues. When problems were identified, few visible efforts were made to analyze them or to propose solutions. Most staff members believed that success was defined in terms of adherence to policies and procedures rather than achievement of appropriate case outcomes. Ambitious staff members who sought upward mobility in the department became experts on internal policies, not on family problems or service provision.

Among those in management positions, the consultant found that most emphasized control. Virtually all decisions about cases had to pass through and be signed by a supervisor and administrator. Managers felt that staff ignored their efforts to adhere to policies and procedures, especially when it came to keeping paperwork up to date. Compliance with rules and completion of required reports and forms were the main criteria by which staff members' performance was judged. Also, although managers expressed a desire to achieve successful client outcomes, such criteria were not part of the internal system by which managers and caseworkers were evaluated.

Ethical and Professional Behavior

Behavior: Use supervision and consultation to guide professional judgment and behavior.

Critical Thinking Question: What effects to you think rigid bureaucracy and limited autonomy have on supervision, consultation, and professional judgment and behavior?

Vignette 2:   Lakeside Family Services

Historical Development. The Lakeside Family Services agency was originally incorporated as the Methodist Home for Orphaned Children in Lakeside in 1935. Begun by the United Methodist Church, the home served children with no living relatives. Because it was situated on a large parcel of donated land on the outskirts of a metropolitan area, the home became the site of many church gatherings as well as fundraising events over the years. Volunteers from the church and community were part of almost every activity at the home.

During the 1930s and 1940s, the home was the recipient of generous contributions from wealthy church and civic leaders, and it was also helped by the Red Feather fundraising campaign, a forerunner of what is now the United Way. As donations increased, so did the scope of the home. By the mid-1950s, it had expanded to include family counseling and services for unwed mothers, and it had hired several professionally trained social workers. Originally, the 15-member voluntary board of directors was elected by the Annual Conference of the Methodist Church. The bylaws specified that the executive director and at least 75 percent of board members had to be members of the church. Although it was not required, most staff were also church members, and there was an active volunteer auxiliary of over 100 persons.

Major Changes Occur. During the 1970s, the board held a number of controversial meetings to determine the future of the home. In addition to changing service needs, fewer and fewer orphans were present and in need of placement. The United Way was putting pressure on the home to merge with two other family service agencies in the same city, and the percentage of the home's budget that came from the United Methodist Church dwindled each year, even though actual dollar amounts increased. Several board members encouraged the home to rethink its mission and seek state and federal funding. By 1980, after a decade of controversy, the home changed its name to Lakeside Family Services (LFS), disaffiliated with the United Methodist Church, and became a nonprofit provider of government contract services to children, families, and the aged. The agency relocated, and the property on which the home stood reverted to the church, which owned the land. LFS remained a United Way agency, and its funding from them increased yearly, but by the mid-1990s almost 70 percent of the agency's budget came from government contracts and grants.

Board members who had supported these changes in the agency's mission, funding, and structure were joined by others carefully selected for their expertise in fundraising and politics. They chose an executive director with an MSW and hired a director of development to search for new funds.

The agency was composed of three main program components: (1) children's services, (2) family services, and (3) aging services. Each component received funds from government contracts, along with United Way funds and private contributions, and within each component there was service diversification. For example, aging services included homemaker/chore services, home health, and adult day care.

Program directors began complaining that contract dollars never covered the full cost of services and that state and federal regulations were restricting their ability to provide adequate care to their respective clientele. The executive director searched for strategies to deal with these complaints and spent considerable time conferring with directors of other nonprofit organizations.

The Search for Strategies. When the recession of the late 2000s hit, LFS experienced major cutbacks in two of its program areas. In talking with other providers, the executive director detected a new sense of competitiveness she had not noticed before. When staff suggested using volunteers to help keep services in place, the executive director realized that the active volunteer pool of earlier days had not been nurtured and maintained. In fact, only the aging services program was using volunteers, who did home visits to frail adults. Even this was limited, because the volunteers' activities were carefully structured and greatly restricted by state regulations. At the executive director's request, the board approved a fee-for-service schedule and instructed the director of development to create a plan for recruiting fee-paying clients. Staff were angered by the agency's new focus on private fee payers, fearing this meant that the poorest clients, who were often those in greatest need, would go unserved. By 2014, the agency was in serious financial difficulty, and in desperation the executive director approached United Methodist Church officials about taking the agency back under the church's wing.

Implications of the Vignettes

It is not unusual for organizations, over time, to display inconsistent or counterproductive behavior such as that described in the vignettes. When this happens, it is tempting to opt for seemingly simple solutions such as changing directors (Vignette 1) or competing for high-paying clients (Vignette 2). However, changes in organizational culture do not occur rapidly, and prevailing attitudes and behaviors tend to permeate all levels of staff. Efforts to solve problems through sudden and dramatic change are thus seldom successful, especially if the changes conflict with the mission (perceived or actual) of the agency.

The two vignettes differ in that one organization is public and exists because of a government mandate, whereas the other evolved in the private, nonprofit sector. There are also many parallels. Both organizations developed in growth climates, only to face severe financial and political constraints in later years. Whereas CCDCW became more bureaucratic, LFS became more professionalized. Just as rigid rules developed within CCDCW, LFS experienced the constraints of state and federal regulations when it began receiving more and more governmental funds. Both organizations searched for answers to complex problems that could not be easily solved.

Both vignettes illustrate the importance of learning about the history of human service organizations and the development of their cultures so that changes they have made can be viewed in context. As described in Chapter 7, organizational culture is a concept that seeks to capture the fact that each organization has a character and ways of operating that embody its unique qualities and differentiate it from others. Another way of thinking about organizational culture is that it is a way of conceptualizing the often unwritten rules within a workplace that new staff members learn gradually over time. In both vignettes, staff, board, and administrators experienced what happens when the norms within their workplaces change.

In this chapter, we propose a method of conducting organizational assessments that will enable practitioners to understand more fully what is happening in agencies such as CCDCW and LFS. The framework we propose for assessing organizations is presented in the form of tasks to be completed and questions to be asked within each task. No listing of

Watch this video that discusses how organizational assessment can be an important starting point for nonprofit planning. What did Operational Fuel learn about its board of directors by engaging an outside consultant to conduct an organizational assessment?

www.youtube.com /watch?v=KVsb4qctB2A

Assess your engaging human service organizations practice by taking this brief quiz.

tasks and activities can be comprehensive for every type of organization, so we will address the major elements and considerations as they relate to HSOs.

FRAMEWORK FOR ORGANIZATIONAL ASSESSMENT

As discussed in Chapter 7, contingency theorists propose that organizations are best understood by examining both external and internal forces that influence their functioning. Similarly, Schein (2010) explains that organizational culture develops in response to two archetypical problems faced by any collective—how to adapt to and survive in the external environment, and how to create internal processes that will ensure capacity to adapt and survive. Beginning in Task 1 by gathering contextual information, we then move to Task 2 (external) and Task 3 (internal) aspects of the focal organization. Having learned about the external and internal work of the organization, one is better able to assess the organization's cultural competency in Task 4. See Figure 8.1 for an overview of the tasks in the framework for assessing an organization.

Task 1: Identify Focal Organization

It may be that you work in a particular organization and are knowledgeable about its background. Or you may be approaching an organization from the outside in an attempt to effect change. Regardless, it is important to identify the history, cultural artifacts, and domain of the organization.

Search for Cultural Artifacts

Questions to be explored for this activity include the following:

- What is the history of this organization?
- How would you describe the organization's identity, and is it congruent with its image?

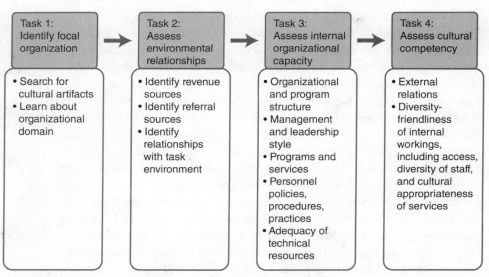

Figure 8.1
Tasks in the Framework for Assessing an Organization

- What are the basis for and extent of the organization's corporate authority?
- What is its mission?
- What physical, social, and behavioral artifacts are observed?

History   Every organization has a history, some much longer than others. A chronology of events in the life of the agency may be listed on the agency's website. Older agencies may have donated their historical records to archives in a local library or historical society. Others may have had a staff member, former leader, volunteer, or scholar write an historical monograph. Whatever form that history takes, it is an important cultural artifact that provides clues to cultural values and assumptions and how they have changed over time.

Equally important are the historical narratives that organizational members tell. Chen (2013) asserts that these stories promote organizational memory and change. Stories provide information on past events and the persons involved as well as interpretations of what happened. They reveal the symbolic meaning in challenges faced and in relational conflicts. Chen goes on to say that sharing historical perspectives is part of relationship building in that organizational members engage newcomers (e.g. new staff, consumers, or other groups and organizations in the community) in communicating about the organization's narrative. Some organizations will have grand narratives vetted as their dominant stories, and others will focus on pivotal events that symbolize the organization's legacy.

Founders frame and shape the beginnings of organizational cultures. They, too, become cultural artifacts and icons either through continued participation or through legend. Their actions may become the touchstone with a set of values to which newcomers are oriented even after the culture has changed (Netting, O'Connor, & Singletary, 2007).

Identity and Image   **Organizational identity** refers to a co-constructed vision for the agency shared by people who play founding, development, staff, and leadership roles (Gioia & Thomas, 1996). Identity is what is unique, core, and enduring to the organization and to which organizational members cling when faced with major challenges (Schmid, 2013). In HSOs, identity may be tied to serving the needs of various population groups, to advocating for system-wide change, or both, depending on how programs are designed and implemented (Almog-Bar & Schmid, 2014). Identity pertains to what insiders want to believe about their organizations or their programs, which becomes particularly important in holding people together in times of change or great uncertainty.

Whereas identity is how organizational members see themselves, **image** is constructed by persons beyond an organization's boundaries. Images shift as public perceptions change. For example, a health care organization may be proud of its identity as a leader in the field, but when incoming patients feel they are not well treated, image will not align with identity. Also, as many child welfare organizations have discovered, years of building up a positive reputation for protecting vulnerable children can be damaged literally overnight when one case of a child's death hits the media. Thus, as organizational identity emerges and changes, so do the images held by multiple constituencies who hear about or come in contact with an organization and the programs it sponsors.

Projecting an organizational identity is often done through branding, selling the organization. Some organizations are iconic, such as the American Red Cross or UNICEF, in that images immediately come to mind. Artifacts that project identity and impact image include documents such as strategic plans, public relations materials, websites, Facebook postings, tweets, and other social media postings. In preparation for a revisioning or strategic planning process, organizations may have conducted an analysis of strengths, weaknesses, opportunities, and threats (**SWOT analysis**). SWOT analyses reveal a great deal about organizational identity.

Corporate Authority and Mission   An agency's corporate authority forms the legal basis for its operations, and this represents one of the ways it defines its **domain**. If the organization is public (governmental), its legal basis rests in a statute or executive order. If it is private, its legal basis is in its articles of incorporation. It may be important to examine these documents firsthand, since organizations that are incorporated for one purpose, such as operating the orphanage from which LFS arose, may gradually add new populations and services, such as help for pregnant teens. The changes may be reasonable and well intentioned, but may still result in the agency operating outside its legal authorization. Important sources of information for analyzing corporate authority and mission include the following:

1. Articles of incorporation, statutes, or executive orders
2. Mission statement
3. Bylaws of the organization
4. Minutes of selected board meetings
5. Interviews with selected administrators, managers, and staff

A good statement of mission specifies the problems, needs, and/or populations the agency serves, along with client outcomes to be expected. It also states the reason for the agency's existence, which should not change in fundamental ways unless the reason for existence also changes. Lack of clarity in a mission statement or disparities between the mission and current activities can be signs of a problem. For example, LFS is a prime candidate for reexamining its original mission, which was established when orphanages were both necessary and commonplace. If LFS has not revised this mission, it is unlikely that its current work has any connection to its stated reason for existence. Revisiting and, if necessary, reconceptualizing the mission can begin the process of redirecting operations or sharpening their focus. Box 8.1 illustrates what the wording for the mission statement for LFS might be.

Evidence suggests that clear mission statements can have beneficial effects on employees. For example, results from a study by Clark (2007) showed that familiarity with an organization's mission statement was positively associated with job satisfaction and with behaviors that tend to strengthen relationships among employees. Table 8.1 depicts a tool for use in assessing agencies' corporate authority and mission.

Multiple physical artifacts become part of organizational functioning, and they will become evident as one moves through the assessment process. These include

---

Box 8.1   Example Mission Statement for Lakeside Family Services

The mission of Lakeside Family Services is to help members of our community solve problems facing them. This includes a special concern for families, children, and older adults. Our goal for families is to strengthen relationships and help each family support and care for its members. For children, we work to promote good parenting, quality education, safety, and growth. In collaboration with older adults, we seek to support continued growth and to ensure basic standards for health, health care, housing, and income.

Table 8.1   Assessing Corporate Authority and Mission

Checklist	Yes	No
1. Are articles of incorporation on file?	___	___
2. Is there a written set of bylaws?	___	___
3. Are board members and agency director familiar with bylaws?	___	___
4. Is there a mission statement?	___	___
5. Is the mission one paragraph or less?	___	___
6. Does the mission make a statement about expected client outcomes?	___	___
7. Are staff aware of, and do they practice in accordance with, the mission statement?	___	___

---

organizational products such as annual reports, organizational charts, job descriptions, case records, and a host of others. The physical environment, pictures on the wall, the language used, the clothing staff wear, rituals and events, and the social interactions between staff and with clients are all cultural artifacts. The question to ask about these artifacts is do they reflect the espoused values within the organization's mission statement or are there potential discontinuities in what is espoused and actual behavior. Many times, change is needed because there are disconnects. For example, an organization with a mission to serve the neediest clients may have begun focusing primarily on marketing to clients who can pay. Similarly, an organization with a well-written diversity plan may not be serving diverse clients.

Assessment

Behavior: Collect and organize date, and apply critical thinking to interpret information from clients and constituencies.

Critical Thinking Question: What ethical responsibility does a social worker have when she or he discovers discontinuities between espoused values and organizational behavior?

Learn about Organizational Domain

Questions to be explored for this activity include the following:

- What is the organization's domain (e.g., the populations served, the technology employed, and services provided)?
- What target populations are recruited or mandated to participate?

- How are the costs of client services covered, and how does the organization deal with those clients who cannot pay?
- Are there defined legal, geographical, or service areas that establish organizational boundaries?

Without consumers of its services, an organization has no reason to exist. However, some clients are a good fit with an organization's services while others are not, so most agencies establish definitions of the types of clients they serve. These often take the form of **eligibility criteria** that clients must meet in order to be considered a fit. Clients who meet the criteria are said to be within the organization's **domain** (Levine & White, 1961). An organization's domain may be understood as a boundary it draws around itself to define what it does and whom it serves.

Domain setting refers to the process by which organizations create a niche for themselves and establish their roles among others within their environment. One part of the process is **domain legitimation**, in which the organization gains acknowledgment of claims it makes as to its sphere of activities and expertise. Legitimation is not always immediately forthcoming, and there may be gaps between what an organization says are its boundaries, the *claimed domain*, and what these boundaries actually are, the *de facto domain* (Greenley & Kirk, 1973).

Consistent with the resource dependency theory, organizations seek to attract clients who fall within their domain, while referring or rejecting those who don't. This improves operational efficiency but can result in some client groups being systematically disadvantaged by certain criteria or the manner in which they are applied. When assessing organizations, therefore, it is important to address questions such as whether enough clients apply to fill the capacity available, whether many applicants are declared ineligible and turned away, and whether, even after services commence, the number of unserved clients in the community remains large.

Also important in understanding which clients an organization views as resources and which it does not is the financial relationship it has with its clients. In commercial firms, consumers usually pay directly for goods or services they receive, and the organizations carefully design their outputs to meet consumer needs. In human service organizations, however, those who consume the services may be different than those who pay for them. For our purposes, we will define the clients of HSOs as those who receive services, not necessarily those who pay. Clients who cover the cost of their services, either personally or through third-party reimbursement, will be termed **full-pay clients**. These clients are important resources that agencies seek to attract and are most likely to serve, because the revenues they provide can be used to offset the cost of serving other clients.

Human Rights and Justice

Behavior: Engage in practices that advance social, economic, and environmental justice.

Critical Thinking Question: When contracting with private agencies, what are some strategies that may help to ensure that vulnerable populations still are served?

Clients who pay less than the cost of their services or who pay nothing at all are termed **non-full-pay clients** (Netting, McMurtry, Kettner, & Jones-McClintic, 1990). Because revenues for serving these clients must be generated from other sources (e.g., charitable donations or profits earned from full-pay clients), agencies often do little to attract these clients and may erect eligibility barriers to restrict their numbers. A prominent example of this is the tendency of health-care providers to restrict or refuse services to

Medicare or Medicaid recipients because of reimbursement rates viewed as insufficient to cover service costs (Bisgaier, Polsky, & Rhodes, 2012). Restrictions or refusals can also occur with clients who seek relatively costly services or services the agency does not provide.

A complete agency assessment should include a determination of whether the organization makes appropriate efforts to direct clients it rejects to organizations that may be able to serve them. It should also identify formal and informal arrangements among agencies for exchange of clients, whereby those that do not fall within one agency's domain are referred to others, and vice versa. This increases the likelihood that clients will receive services and that agencies will receive clients they need. Interorganizational relationships of this sort are often viewed as being of equal importance as those with funding sources. Table 8.2 depicts a tool that may be helpful in identifying client populations.

Organizational boundaries may not be as clear-cut as one might think, and boundaries may change over time. Like communities, organizations may have geographical or nonplace parameters. For example, an international advocacy organization has the goal to assist victims of human trafficking (Hodge, 2014). Since this is a global problem and victims are likely to be identified anywhere there is illegal activity, the target population transcends geographical boundaries. Thus, the agency's domain is geographically broad in scope, even though it is more narrow in terms of whom it targets. In contrast,

Table 8.2 Identifying Client Populations

Client Groups Served

1. Couples or individuals relinquishing children
2. Couples wanting to adopt
3. Foster parent applications
4. Foster parents
5. Individuals in need of personal counseling
6. Families in need of counseling
7. Drug abusers

Demographic Makeup of Client Population

Age (years)	Percentage	Ethnicity	Percentage	Gender	Percentage	Fees	Percentage
Under 20	5	American Indian	3	Female	64	Full pay	26
20–29	15	African American	14	Male	36	Some pay	38
30–39	22	Asian American	4			No pay	15
40–49	29	Hispanic	19			Contract	21
50–59	19	White	60				
60–69	8						
70+	2						

agencies may have defined geographical boundaries (e.g. jurisdictional boundaries, school districts, planning and service areas, and catchment areas) within which they are mandated to provide services.

Agencies seek to take advantage of available resources, and most are constantly adjusting their domains in order to do so. Trends in the availability of funds from charitable or governmental sources are usually closely watched, and in order to ensure resource flow some agencies may attempt to compete for funds in areas where they have little experience or expertise.

Task 2: Assess the Organization's Environmental Relationships

As mentioned, organizations have to be able to navigate the external environment beyond their domains and build internal capacity to adapt and survive within that environment. Thus, Tasks 2 and 3 may be thought of as collecting information about organizations' environments, how they behave in those environments, and how they internally structure themselves (see Figure 8.2).

To understand considerations external to the organization, we use the concept of an organization's **task environment**. As noted in our review of the work of James Thompson (1967) in Chapter 7, the task environment consists of elements outside an organization that enable it to operate and that set the basic context for these operations. Thompson notes that, as originally defined by Dill (1958), the task environment includes four key components: consumers, suppliers, competitors, and regulators (pp. 27–28). These are illustrated in Figure 8.3.

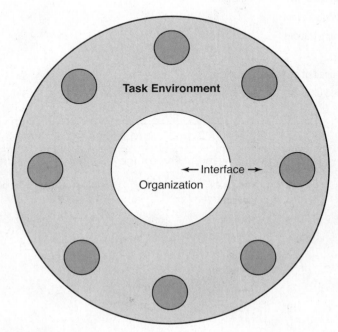

Figure 8.2
Organization, Task Environment, and Interface

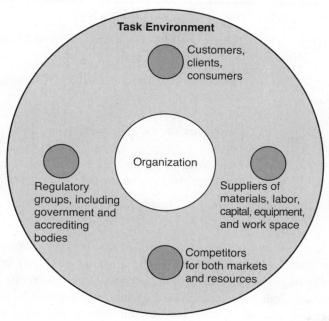

Figure 8.3
Typical Task Environment for an Organization

Identify and Assess Relationships with Revenue Sources

Questions to be explored for this activity include the following:

- What are the agency's funding sources?
- How much and what percentage of the agency's total funds are received from each source?
- What are the nature and quality of the relationship between funding sources and the agency?
- Does the organization use volunteers? If yes, how many, and for what purposes?
- What in-kind resources (e.g., food, clothing, physical facilities) does the organization receive?
- What tax benefits does the organization receive?

In a study of nonprofit agencies' involvement in political lobbying, Twombly (2002) compared more than 2,000 secular and faith-based organizations and found that the latter tended to have a lower diversity of services and slower rates of service expansion. This appeared to be a result of these organizations' greater dependency on private contributions, which offers less predictable funding than the more diversified funding base typical of secular organizations. Ruggiano and Taliaferro (2012) found that lobbying occurred in ways that allowed agencies to maintain access to resources while not endangering relationships with other key elements in the environment by appearing to be too aggressive in seeking them. Table 8.3 summarizes these and other points, and it can be helpful in assessing agencies' relationships with revenue sources.

Table 8.3   Assessing the Relationship to Funding Sources

Relevant Funding Sources	Nature of Communication, Length of Relationship, and Changes in Funding
Contract with State Department of Social Services	Quarterly site visits; have contracted for 12 years; funding has always stayed steady or increased.
Client Fees	Most clients are seen on a weekly basis; they either pay directly or through their insurance plan; client fees have declined 2% in the past three years.
Charitable Donations	Largest donations come from church groups; agency staff visit church representatives once a year; donations have increased 3.5 percent in the past year.

Chaidez-Gutierrez and Fischer (2013) studied the dynamics between grassroots organizations in communities of color and philanthropic funders. They found that these relationships may be particularly challenging because of accountability requirements that are developed by dominant cultures that may not mesh well with local communities. Power dynamics and status differentials may result in misunderstandings. It is important to assess these relationships from a critical theory perspective in order to address needed changes in communication and relationship building.

Cash Revenues   Understanding how an agency is financed is often essential to understanding the agency itself, but this process can be difficult because HSOs typically obtain funds from a multitude of sources. Also, many do not make detailed funding information readily available except where public funds are used and budget documents are a matter of public record.

The first step in assessing organizational funding is to determine the sources from which funds are acquired. The following list details potential sources for HSOs:

Major Cash Revenue Sources for Human Service Organizations

1. Government funds

    Direct government appropriations

    Government purchase-of-service contracts

    Government grants

    Matching funds

    Tax benefits

2. Donated funds

    Direct charitable contributions (from individuals, groups, and associations such as religious groups)

    Indirect contributions (e.g., via United Way)

    Private grants (e.g., foundation monies)

    Endowments

3. Fees for service

   Direct payments from clients

   Payments from third parties (e.g., private or public insurers)

4. Other agency income

   Investments (e.g., interest, dividends, and royalties)

   Profit-making subsidiaries

   Fundraising events and appeals

The sources of an organization's funds affect its flexibility in responding to proposed change. Governmental agencies that depend on direct appropriations are likely to have most of their activities rigidly specified by public policy. Nonprofit agencies, which usually receive funds from a wide variety of sources, may have greater flexibility. But with this comes greater uncertainty about the reliability of each source, and even donated funds may come with strings attached. For-profit agencies that depend on paying clients also have greater flexibility than public agencies, but their decision making is driven by demands to return profits to their investors.

Among government organizations, direct appropriations are usually the only source of revenue, including federal, state, county, and local agencies. State, county, and local organizations also may use a mixture of funds from higher levels of government. In general, the lower the level of government, the larger the variety of funding sources used. Among the most important mechanisms for dissemination are block grants (lump-sum federal appropriations in which specific allocations are left to state or local governments), matching funds (which typically provide a certain amount of federal funds for each dollar expended by the receiving agency), and grant programs in which funds are targeted for a specific use and are restricted accordingly. In the vignette regarding Canyon County Child Welfare Department earlier in this chapter, the agency was funded solely by government funds, although from a combination of direct appropriations, block grants, and matching funds.

Many people assume that nonprofit agencies such as LFS in Vignette 2 obtain most of their revenues from donations, but those contributions often make up only a small portion of annual budgets. The most recent figures available show that in 2010, nonprofit organizations received an average of 13 percent of their funds from charitable contributions, 50 percent from fees paid by individuals or other privates sources, 24 percent from fees paid by government sources, 8 percent from government grants, and 5 percent from other sources (Blackwood, Roeger, & Pettijohn, 2012). The 13 percent of nonprofit budgets accounted for by charitable donations is half as much as in 1977, partially due to dropoffs in donations resulting from the economic downturn that began in 2008 (Association of Fundraising Professionals, 2010). This suggests that "charitable organizations" may be more accurately viewed as quasi-public or quasi-fee-for-service organizations, and the most important elements in their task environments will be public agencies with which they contract, along with paying clients or members.

Clients themselves sometimes pay for services from HSOs, but because many are unable to pay it is more common for their costs to be covered by other organizations. This can mean that consumers are a less important part of the task environment of private agencies than insurance companies and other third-party payers who establish criteria and rates for reimbursement. For example, a for-profit counseling agency may draw most of its clients from the employee assistance program of a nearby manufacturing plant; thus relationships with the manufacturer are likely to be the key environmental consideration for the counseling agency. More generally, almost all revenues of HSOs come with strings attached, and decisions on how to spend them often rest more with the funding agency than with the recipient.

Using governmental organizations as an example, a county agency that appears to be subject to local decision-making processes may in fact operate more like a local extension of the state agency that provides the bulk of its funds. A change episode that attempted to influence the use of these funds would be unlikely to succeed unless those seeking change recognize that decision-making power rests with organizations in the agency's task environment rather than inside its own boundaries.

The number of sources from which an agency's funds are drawn is also a key consideration. Some agencies with many funding sources may have greater autonomy and flexibility than one with few, because the loss of any single source is less likely to jeopardize the organization as a whole. But the greater the number of funding sources, the more complex the agency's operations become, as each new source adds another layer of regulatory constraints, program diversity, and accountability expectations. Agencies with a single funding source risk becoming rigid and overspecialized; those with many sources may have difficulty defining or focusing on their mission. Either way, there are advantages and disadvantages.

Noncash Revenues   When considering resources, it is important to remember that actual dollars coming into an HSO are not its only form of resources. Many other assets on which agencies rely are less obvious than cash revenues but sometimes equally important. Three such assets are volunteers, in-kind contributions, and tax benefits.

Volunteers have traditionally been a mainstay of HSOs. As noted in Chapter 2, the entire nonprofit human service sector originated with individual volunteers working together to make their efforts more productive. In the Lakeside Family Services vignette, volunteers were critical to the organization's early development. Today, the contribution of these individuals to HSOs is enormous. The U.S. Bureau of Labor Statistics (BLS) reports that "about 62.6 million people volunteered through or for an organization at least once between September 2012 and September 2013" in the United States (2014). This number included about 22 percent of adult men and 28 percent of adult women. The median number of hours per years devoted by each volunteer was about 50. Multiplied by the total number of volunteers, this corresponds to 7.7 billion hours of volunteer work which, at an estimated value of $23.07 per volunteer hour during 2013 (Independent Sector, 2014) produces a total monetary value of $173 billion for all volunteering in the United States. According to the BLS report, religious organizations benefitted from the largest number of volunteer hours (33 percent of all hours), followed by educational or youth-oriented services (26 percent) and social or community services (15 percent).

Another type of resource is **in-kind contributions** of material goods. Examples include food, clothing, physical facilities, real estate, vehicles, and office materials. Sometimes, these are provided for use directly by the agency; at other times, they are intended for resale to generate cash revenues, or for distribution directly to clients. The dollar value of these resources is difficult to calculate, but estimates suggest it is substantial.

For example, in 2011 about 23 million individual federal income tax filers claimed non-cash charitable contributions, the monetary value of which totaled almost $44 billion (U.S. Internal Revenue Service, 2014).

Tax benefits such as these are particularly important for private, nonprofit HSOs, which are defined in part by their official designation as charitable organizations under section 501(c)(3) of federal Internal Revenue Service regulations. Meeting the requirements of this section allows nonprofit agencies to avoid income taxes that for-profit firms must pay, and this can be a critical benefit in service arenas such as health care, where nonprofit and for-profit hospitals often engage in intense competition for patients and physicians. Tax laws also have important effects on other revenue sources, such as charitable contributions. Changes to state and federal tax codes may encourage or restrict contributions to nonprofit agencies by individuals who itemize deductions on their tax returns. For example, tax deductions claimed for cash contributions (beyond the noncash contributions mentioned in this chapter) totaled more than $31 billion in 2011 (U.S. Internal Revenue Service, 2014), and it is likely that this source of funds for HSOs would drop precipitously if changes in tax laws were to make charitable contributions no longer deductible.

Any assessment of an organization needs to consider noncash resources because its behavior may be understood as efforts to acquire and maximize these assets. For example, organizations that rely heavily on volunteers may seek to protect this resource even over objections by professional staff that volunteers are ill trained for some types of work. Similarly, agencies may alter their structure to take advantage of one of these resources, as with the sizable number of nonprofit agencies that have begun raising funds by collecting donated material goods and reselling them through thrift stores. Attention to noncash resources may also be important in initiating change efforts, as when administrators are presented with opportunities to use noncash resources to add or augment services for which cash resources are not available.

Identify and Assess Relationships with Referral Sources and Other Providers

Relationships with Referral Sources Questions to be explored for this activity include the following:

- What are the major sources of client referrals?
- Does demand for services outstrip supply, or is there unused capacity?
- What types of clients does the organization refuse (e.g., are there disproportionate numbers of poor persons, senior adults, persons of color, women, persons with disabilities, gays/lesbians, or other groups that are typically underserved)?

As noted earlier, clients are important resources, but individual clients may be viewed as liabilities if they do not fit within an agency's domain or are unable to pay for services. This may lead to certain groups of clients, including the most needy, being deliberately excluded from access to services, as well as to **creaming** (taking on less needy clients who can pay or are more likely to succeed). Evidence of creaming has been observed in situations ranging from the allocation of services to cases in child protection (Jud, Perrig-Chiello, & Voll, 2011), to the awarding of training vouchers to the unemployed (Hipp & Warner, 2008), to the rejection of overweight and obese applicants by nursing homes (Zhang, Li, & Temkin-Greener, 2013).

Selection of clients is also driven by the types of clients an agency's contracts with governmental providers allow it to serve. These dynamics relate to the issue of *boundary control*, which refers to the ability of the agency to reject clients it does not wish to serve. Boundary control is generally highest in for-profit organizations, where the primary goal is making money, and lowest in governmental organizations, which are intended to provide a safety net for clients who cannot obtain services elsewhere. However, since the early 1980s, governmental policies have favored **privatization**—the shifting of more services to the private sector. A guiding assumption has been that private sector organizations can provide services more efficiently and effectively than large governmental bureaucracies, and that, in the case of nonprofit organizations, they can also draw on their traditional commitments to addressing poverty to ensure that these clients are served.

Human service agencies adjust their boundaries due to a many factors, and a misunderstanding of these may lead to critical service gaps. One key criterion in boundary setting is the nature of the clients themselves, and being poor or having complex, long-standing problems are characteristics that simultaneously increase the level of need yet decrease the likelihood of being served.

Relationships with Other Providers   Questions to be explored for this activity include the following:

- What other agencies provide the same services to the same clientele as this organization?
- With whom does the organization compete?
- With whom does the organization cooperate?
- Is the organization part of a coalition or an alliance?

Relationships among agencies that occupy each others' task environments can be competitive, cooperative, or a mixture of the two, depending on the circumstances. Table 6.4 in Chapter 6 gave examples of five levels of interaction that represent some of those mixtures.

Competitive relationships characterize circumstances in which two or more agencies seek the same resources (clients, funds, volunteers, etc.) from the same sources. Nonprofit agencies compete among themselves for charitable donations as well as government and private foundation grants, and in some cases government agencies have sought to improve the cost-effectiveness of services by encouraging nonprofits to compete for grant funding. This has not always been successful, however. For example, Howard (2013), found that as dependence on fee-paying clients in nonprofit HSOs increases, their likelihood of serving nonwhite clients decreases, as does the range of service they offer to non-English speakers. Additional consequences included greater competition not only with other nonprofits but with for-profits as well, along with an increase in the frequency of some vulnerable clients being forced to seek services elsewhere.

Direct competition for funds is not inevitable. Cooperative arrangements are also common, as in the case of referral agreements between agencies, which are used as a means of exchanging clients who do not fit the referring agency but are considered resources by the agency to which they are referred. Other agencies have implemented large-scale coalition-building efforts to improve their ability to meet client needs (Eilbert & Lafronza, 2005).

Identify and Assess Relationships with Other Units in the Task Environment

Questions to be explored for this activity include the following:

- What state and federal regulatory bodies oversee programs provided by this organization?
- With what government agencies does this organization contract for service provision?
- What professional associations, licensing and certification boards, and accrediting bodies influence agency operations?

Within an organization's task environment are groups that may not provide resources but that set the context in which the agency operates. One example is regulatory bodies responsible for establishing acceptable service practices. Some of these may be governmental licensing agencies that inspect and certify the services and physical environment of organizations such as nursing homes, child-caring institutions, and residential treatment facilities. Others may be contracting agencies that enforce adherence to procedural guidelines in order for the organization to be reimbursed for services it provides. Still others may be government revenue departments that levy taxes and monitor financial accounting procedures. Extensive accounting and funding-usage requirements are also imposed by nongovernmental funding sources such as the United Way.

Other organizations that impose some sort of regulatory boundaries include professional associations, labor unions, and accrediting bodies. In general, accrediting bodies certify the operation of organizations as a whole, whereas professional associations and licensing bodies certify the work of individuals. For example, the Joint Commission on Accreditation of Health Care Organizations (JCAHO) establishes requirements for how member agencies must operate, and loss of accreditation can threaten an agency's viability by restricting its funding and client referrals. On the other hand, professional organizations such as the Academy of Certified Social Workers (ACSW) or state licensing agencies impose standards on how individuals carry out their work within agencies, whether or not the agencies themselves are accredited.

The "general public" is a constituent of almost all organizations, and by their nature HSOs are dependent on societal approval for their activities. The views of members of the general public are not always apparent, however, and public opinion is seldom unanimous, so organizations must decide which of a wide variety of expressed views represents the prevailing attitude. Still another complication is that agencies may be forced to stand against public opinion, as in the case of advocacy organizations that must confront ignorance or discrimination against particular clients or groups.

Within the task environment, public opinion is often conveyed through elected representatives, interest groups, civic organizations, and many others. Another indirect but important indicator of public views is funding sources, where patterns in the availability of dollars can reveal much about topics of interest to wealthy donors, private foundations, and ordinary citizens. Finally, mass media are critical purveyors of public attitudes, although they may highlight the extreme rather than typical opinions. In some cases, this can undermine the effectiveness of umbrella organizations such as the United Way in assessing community needs and distributing funds in more measured and planful ways (Cordes & Henig, 2001).

Table 8.4   Identifying Regulatory, Professional, and Media Organizations

Example Organization	Programs Affected
Regulatory Bodies	
State Department of Child Welfare	Day care
County Health Department	Meals on Wheels program
Organizations Issuing Grants and Contracts	
Federal Demonstration Grants (www.grants.gov)	Respite care
State Department of Developmental Disabilities	Vocational training
Professional Associations	
National Association of Social Workers (www.nasw.org)	Individual and group counseling
American Association for Marriage and Family Therapy (AAMFT) (www.aamft.org)	Couple and family counseling
Accreditation Organizations	
Joint Commission on Accreditation of Healthcare Organizations (JCAHO) (www.jointcommission.org)	Home care
National Association for the Education of Young Children (NAEYC)	Day care
Licensing and Certification Boards	
State Social Work Licensing Board	Individual and group counseling
Public Media and Advocacy Organizations	
Local Network Television Affiliate	Child maltreatment investigations
ARC (www.thearc.org)	Vocational training

Child protective services offer an example of the relationship between agencies, public opinion, and mass media (as both a carrier and shaper of public opinion). Deciding whether to remove an at-risk child from his or her home involves a delicate balancing act between concern for the child's well-being and concern for parental rights. Egregious cases in which the abuse of a child resulted in death have led to public outcry, followed by legislative changes directing protective service workers to favor the safety of the child when investigating new reports. In other locations, protective service workers have been characterized as "child-snatchers," prompting elected officials to impose stricter guidelines governing the removal of children.

The key point is that public opinion is dynamic rather than static, and agencies at different times or in different places may encounter widely divergent attitudes and expectations. Identifying important elements in the task environment is thus an ongoing process as public attitudes change and funding methods evolve, and Table 8.4 depicts a tool for use in this process.

Task 3: Assess Internal Organizational Capacity

Consider the examples of Canyon County Department of Child Welfare (CCDCW) and Lakeside Family Services (LFS) presented at the beginning of this chapter. When public organizations such as CCDCW experience problems in productivity, quality of client service, morale, or worker–management relationships, one response might be for an oversight body, such as the county board of supervisors, to hire a management consultant to evaluate the department and its problems. Similarly, in a nonprofit organization such as LFS that has become more professionalized, increased its dependence on government funds, and altered its mission, and now is experiencing funding cutbacks, a consultant may be engaged by the board of directors to conduct a study and recommend strategies for the organization to regain economic self-sufficiency.

Ideally, after interviewing representative staff, consumers, board members, and others, the consultants would be able to document problems such as those identified in the vignettes, formulate working hypotheses about their causes, and recommend solutions or remedies. Following from this approach, consultants often recommend short-term solutions such as staff development and training, employee incentive programs, morale-building activities like social events, relationship-enhancing activities between management and staff, attempts to humanize the chief executive officer, and so forth. The problem is that these steps rarely solve the kinds of fundamental concerns that brought about the need for a management consultant in the first place.

An alternative approach to organizational assessment is to conduct a systematic examination of key organizational elements. Within each element, one could examine ideal models or optimal levels of functioning, as illustrated in current theoretical or research literature. Using this ideal as a basis of comparison, the review proceeds to an examination of data that depict the actual situation as well as gaps between the ideal and real. The goal is to understand causes before proposing solutions and to solve long-term problems rather than treating present symptoms.

Under Task 3, we identify key elements to be examined within an organization. Readers may find it useful to consider how each elements might apply to an HSO with which they are familiar as an intern, employee, or even service recipient. The elements we address include the following:

1. Organizational and program structure
2. Management, and leadership style
3. Planning, delivery, and evaluation of programs and services
4. Personnel policies, procedures, and practices
5. Adequacy of technology and resources

Understand Organizational and Program Structure

Questions to be explored for this activity include the following:

- What are the major departmental or program units in this organization?
- Is there a convincing rationale for the existing organizational structure?
- Is the existing structure consistent with and supportive of the mission?
- Is supervision logical and capable of performing expected functions? Are staff members capable of performing expected functions?
- What can you learn about the informal structure (people who carry authority because they are respected by staff, and thus exert influence) that is different from those in formally designated positions of authority?

When we think of organizational structure, we often envision a pyramid-shaped chart with boxes and lines indicating a hierarchy that extends from the top administrator's level down to many line-level positions. This helps visualize the organization in terms of who reports to whom, who is responsible for which divisions of the organization, and how the chain of command proceeds from bottom to top. As noted in Chapter 7, this system is patterned after the bureaucratic model described by Weber (1946). It is widely used because it is easy to understand and apply, ensures that everyone has only one supervisor, and provides for lines of communication, exercise of authority, performance evaluation, and many other functions necessary to ensure smooth operation.

As we also noted in Chapter 7, however, many critics of bureaucratic structure believe it is not the best design for human service agencies. Their central point is that bureaucratic structure was designed for organizations in which both inputs and operations are predictable and repetitive, whereas the individual clients and client problems served by HSOs are unique. Rules such as those that govern the production process in manufacturing enterprises may be helpful in ensuring consistent quality of the goods produced, but in an HSO these rules may simply constrain workers' abilities to exercise professional judgment.

A number of terms have been used to describe the pitfalls that can accompany bureaucratic structure. Merton (1952) warned of **learned incompetence** that develops among employees in bureaucracies who rely so heavily on a policy manual to make their decisions that they cease to think logically or creatively about their jobs (such as addressing client problems in an HSO). Lipsky's (1984) bureaucratic disentitlement describes situations in HSOs where clients fail to receive benefits or services to which they are entitled due to decisions based on rigid and sometimes illogical internal rules rather than client needs. Jaskyte and Dressler (2005) found that innovativeness in nonprofit HSOs was negatively associated with an organizational focus on stability, which is typical of bureaucratic structures.

Contingency theorists contend that structure depends on what the organization is expected to produce. Morse and Lorsch (1970) demonstrated that higher productivity in one type of organization (a container-manufacturing plant) was achieved through a traditional structure with clearly defined roles, responsibilities, and lines of supervision. A different type of organization (a research lab) achieved higher productivity through a very loose structure, which allowed researchers maximum flexibility to carry out their own work unfettered by rules, regulations, and supervision. Examples of alternative structures are depicted in Box 8.2.

No single organizational structure is likely to fit all HSOs well. For large public agencies, some type of bureaucratic structure may be useful because of size, predictability of operations, and accountability considerations. For a small, community-based agency, a collegial model might be best. As discussed in Box 8.2, much depends on variables such as the nature of the work and the background and roles of staff. Employees of HSOs often come from a wide range of specializations, including health, mental health, substance use, developmental disabilities, child welfare, services to older adults, residential treatment, adult and juvenile corrections, and many others. Disciplines in which they are trained include social work, counseling, psychology, child care, medicine, nursing, rehabilitation, and education, and their work may be supported by people from fields such as accounting, management, public relations, and finance. To bridge these differences the organization must have clear standards governing hiring and job expectations, such as specific requirements for education, experience, and licensure or certification for each position, along with documentation of adherence to these requirements.

Box 8.2   Options for Organizational Structures

Organizations can structure themselves in many different ways:

Hierarchical structure: This traditional, bureaucratic structure is quickly recognized in large organizations where multiple layers of units are depicted on an organizational chart.

Linking-pin structure: Originally named by Likert (1961, p. 11), this approach emphasizes the role of collaboration between work units, which is accomplished by selecting one or a few persons who are fully functioning participants in both and who ensure the flow of communication between them (Wager, 1992).

Matrix structure: In this model, staff members have different supervisors for different functions they perform. For example, direct supervision of a social worker for his or her activities on the ward of an inpatient mental health facility might come from a physician or nurse who is the ward leader, whereas a different supervisor might oversee the social worker's efforts with outpatients. Matrix structures have been criticized because staff report to different people for different functions.

Project team structure: This model is used when work is organized by teams that work relatively independently on specific projects. For example, in starting up a community project one team might conduct a needs assessment, while another looks for funding, and a third locates a facility. Each team has a leader, and overall coordination is done by a committee of team leaders (Miles, 1975).

Collegial or network structure: This is most common in organizations composed of professionals who operate relatively independently and come together only in circumstances in which their work overlaps. Colleagues' status is related to their professional competencies, and thus status differentials are removed. One example would be a private counseling clinic in which a small partnership of psychologists and social workers purchase a building and equipment and hire support staff. No single partner has more authority than others, and each generates her or his own income (Kaldis, Koukoravas, & Tjortjis, 2007).

Still, even a well-designed and clearly defined job will be the source of problems if it rests within a rigid bureaucratic structure or dysfunctional organizational culture. Cramm, Strating, and Nieboer (2013), in a study of nurses, found that organizational solidarity was greater in organizations with less hierarchical structure, more individual autonomy, and more formal and informal information exchange. At the level of service effectiveness, however, desirable results sometimes require the presence of at least some elements of bureaucratic organization, such as job routinization and precision of repeated steps. Regardless of how the formal organizational structure is designed, there will be a second structural level, often referred to as *informal networks* or *emergent structures* (Rank, 2008). Informal networks arise to compensate for what cannot be formally structured, and recognizing this important element of organizational culture is important in any assessment.

> Watch this video that discusses the features of the Organizational Culture Assessment Instrument (OCAI). How might you use the OCAI in a human service organization?
>
> www.youtube.com /watch?v=VyVfqJi6Tus

Documentation and data to be examined in order to understand organizational structure might include the following:

1. Organizational charts
2. Job descriptions
3. Relevant policy and procedure manuals
4. Interviews with selected administrators, managers, staff, and representatives of each discipline

A tool such as the one depicted in Table 8.5 can be used to assess the appropriateness of organization and program structure.

Table 8.5   Assessing Organizational and Program Structure

	Total Organization	Program A	Program B	Program C
1. Would you describe the structure as rigid or flexible?	——	——	——	——
2. Is the structure appropriate to the needs of the organization or program?	——	——	——	——
3. Is communication primarily top-down, or in all directions?	——	——	——	——
4. Are staff competent to do the jobs expected of them?	——	——	——	——
5. Is supervision appropriate to the need?	——	——	——	——

Understand Management and Leadership Style

Questions to be explored for this activity include the following:

- How is the workplace organized, and how is the work allocated?
- Are appropriate authority and information passed on along with responsibility?
- How close is supervision, and what exactly is supervised? Is it tasks, is it functions, or is it the employee?
- How are decisions made? Is information solicited from those affected?
- Do employees feel valued at every level? Do they believe they are making a contribution to the success of the organization?
- How is conflict handled?

A wealth of theoretical literature exists concerning approaches to administration, management, and leadership. One useful way to organize and understand them comes from Miles (1975), who classified managerial theories or models into one of three categories: (1) the traditional model, (2) the human relations model, and (3) the human resources model.

The *traditional model* is characterized by very closely supervising work, controlling subordinates, breaking work down into simple tasks that are easily learned, and establishing detailed work routines. Similar to McGregor's characterization of Theory X, the assumptions of this model are that people inherently dislike work, they are not self-motivated or self-directed, and they do it only because they need the money. The traditional model would include such theorists as Weber (1946), Taylor (1947), and others committed to the basic tenets of bureaucracy or scientific management (as discussed in Chapter 7).

The *human relations model* is characterized by efforts on the part of management to make each worker feel useful and important. Management is open to feedback, and subordinates are allowed to exercise some self-direction on routine matters. Assumptions are that people want to feel useful and important, that they have a need to belong, and that these needs are more important than money in motivating people to work. Theories that support the human relations model would include Mayo's human relations theory as well as many of the theorists who expanded on Mayo's work and focused on employee motivation.

The *human resources model* is characterized by a focus on the use of untapped resources and potential existing within employees. Managers are expected to create an environment in which all members may contribute to the limits of their abilities, full participation is encouraged on all matters, and self-direction and self-control are supported and promoted. It is assumed that for most people, work means more than merely earning a paycheck and that they are willing to contribute to the success of the total work effort. Furthermore, people are assumed to be creative, resourceful, and capable of contributing more when given the opportunity. The theories that support the human resources model are drawn essentially from the work on contingency theory (Burns & Stalker, 1961) and supported by a number of contemporary authors (Forcadell, 2005).

Management practices are important to analyze because they influence so many facets of organizational life. They can affect, for example, whether adult protective service workers are instructed merely to collect facts from a battered older person and then turn to a supervisor who will direct the next steps, or whether they are allowed to use professional judgment to intervene as they believe is needed. Recent research supports the value of approaches that fall within the category of the human resource model in HSOs.

Some more important sources of information to be examined in understanding organizational administration, management, and leadership style include the following:

1. Job description of the chief executive officer (CEO) and other leadership staff
2. Interviews with board members (if the agency is private) or the person to whom the CEO is accountable (if the agency is public) to determine the expectations of the CEO
3. Criteria used for performance evaluation of the CEO and other leaders
4. An interview with the CEO to determine expectations for leadership staff
5. An organizational chart
6. Interviews with staff in various roles to determine perceptions about the job, the workplace, supervision, and administration

A tool such as the one depicted in Table 8.6 can be useful in assessing the agency's management and leadership style.

Assess the Organization's Programs and Services

Questions to be explored for this activity include the following:

- What programs and services are offered, and are the services consistent with program goals and objectives?
- Are staffing patterns appropriate to the services to be provided? Are workload expectations reasonable given expectations for achievement with each client and within each service and program?
- Is there a common understanding among management and line staff within each program about problems to be addressed, populations to be served, services to be provided, and client outcomes to be achieved?
- Are expected outcomes identified with sufficient clarity that program success or failure can be determined?

Table 8.6   Assessing Leadership and Management Style

	Carried Out by Management Only	Input Allowed but Ignored	Input Solicited and Used	Group Consensus and Full Participation
1. How are organizational goals established?	——	——	——	——
2. What is the climate for supporting the achievement of goals?	——	——	——	——
3. Where are program-level decisions made?	——	——	——	——
4. How does information flow throughout the organization?	——	——	——	——
5. Who has involvement in providing feedback about performance?	——	——	——	——
6. Who is responsible for generating ideas about how to make improvements?	——	——	——	——

> Go to the Foundation Center website, and search the free online database of funding sources. How might a human service organization use this resource in locating new sources of revenue?

Small HSOs may have one program with multiple services, whereas larger HSOs may have numbers of programs targeted to multiple population groups. Each program may have its own funding sources with different rules and regulations, each may have specialized staff, and some may share staff across programs. Informational brochures, funding applications, and strategic plans, may contain detailed program plans complete with goals and objectives. Accessing materials that describe programs, their rationale, and their designs will be important to understanding what services are available.

Each program should have a clear statement of the problem(s) it is intended to address and the population(s) it is intended to serve. In reviewing this statement, it is not unusual to find that in some long-standing programs, there has been a shift in emphasis over the years. For example, a program that was designed to deal with heroin use may have begun with an emphasis on detoxification and long-term intensive therapy, later shifting to provision of methadone, and finally to intensive self-help groups. HBOs must typically report data on efficiency, quality, and effectiveness that reflect a commitment to providing the best services possible at the lowest cost. In particular, government contracting agencies often have detailed service standards and requirements for performance monitoring as a condition of receiving funds (Abramovitz, 2005; Polivka-West & Okano, 2008).

Standards typically emphasize three types of accountability: efficiency accountability, quality accountability, and effectiveness accountability (Martin & Kettner, 2010). **Efficiency accountability** focuses on the ratio of outputs to inputs or, more specifically, the ratio of volume of service provided to dollars expended. If Agency A provides 1,000 hours of counseling at a cost of $75,000 and Agency B provides 1,000 hours of counseling at a cost of $100,000, then Agency A is more efficient. **Quality accountability** focuses on the provision of services and differentiates between organizations that meet a quality standard and those that do not. For example, one quality standard might be to require that no more than 20 percent of clients given counseling services drop out before the counseling program is considered to be complete. Recent works emphasize that quality indicators must often be specific to particular services, and an increasing array of standardized quality-assessment tools are becoming available.

Effectiveness accountability focuses on the results, effects, and accomplishments of human service programs. While an assessment of quality accountability might ask whether standards for program completion were met, an assessment of effectiveness accountability would ask whether, across clients, measurable and clinically significant improvement occurred in the problem toward which the counseling was directed. In addition, effectiveness assessments also ask whether the programs and services offered resolved the client problems they were funded to address.

As suggested by the evidence-based practice approach discussed in Chapter 7, programs should also be designed, monitored, and evaluated using the best available information about "what works." In fields such as child welfare, researchers and federal funders are increasingly focusing on child and family well-being as a measure of "what works" (Samples, Carnochan, & Austin, 2013). Also, family courts are also using well-being as a focus for decision making about dependent children (Casanueva et al., 2013). This is being made possible by improved tools for measuring well-being and other indicators of quality of life. Accordingly, it is important in assessing effectiveness to review the professional literature and become aware of the most recent trends and tools. Examples of relevant databases available in most university libraries include *Social Work Abstracts*, *Medline*, *PsycINFO*, and others.

Some of the more important documents and data sources to be examined to understand the planning, delivery, and evaluation of programs and services might include the following:

1. Program plans
2. Organizational charts
3. Roster of staff and job descriptions
4. Annual reports of programs and services
5. Needs assessment surveys
6. Evaluation findings, including client satisfaction surveys
7. Case records
8. Current research on outcome measures

A tool such as the one depicted in Table 8.7 can be useful in assessing an agency's programs and services.

Assess Personnel Policies, Procedures, and Practices

Questions to be explored for this activity include the following:

- Is there a written human resources plan?
- Is there a job analysis for each position?
- Is there a plan for recruitment and selection?

Table 8.7   Assessing Efficiency, Quality, and Effectiveness

	Program A	Program B	Program C
1. Does each program specify and monitor measures for efficiency (e.g., productivity per worker)?	____	____	____
2. Does each program specify and monitor quality measures (e.g., reliability and consistency of services)?	____	____	____
3. Does each program specify and monitor client outcomes (e.g., standardized scales that measure the severity of problems before and after treatment)?	____	____	____

- Is there a plan for enhancing agency diversity?
- Is there a plan for staff development and training?
- Is a performance evaluation system in place?
- Are there written procedures for employee termination?

Most organizations go to great lengths to ensure that their equipment will be in good working order, such as by purchasing maintenance contracts for their photocopy machines, computers, printers, vehicles, and other essential items. Ironically, not all agencies invest the same level of concern or resources in their employees, even though employees also have a variety of needs to be met if they are to function optimally. One way to assess how effectively an organization is addressing its personnel needs is to understand how an "ideal" personnel system might function.

Schmidt, Riggar, Crimando, and Bordieri (1992) propose a human resources system that begins with **strategic planning** to establish broad goals, processes, and actions for the future. These, in turn, guide human resource planning—the forecasting of personnel needs to implement the mission. A human resources plan becomes critical to the success of an organization by ensuring that new employees are added in a way that both meets projected personnel needs and maximizes the likelihood that the employees themselves will be successful and productive.

> Search for strategic planning examples and templates on the Internet. Can you locate helpful tools that a human service agency might use in the planning process?

At the core of a good human resources plan is a set of job analyses. Each analysis should include (1) an itemization of tasks that characterize the job; (2) the knowledge and skills needed to understand the tasks, methods or techniques for carrying out the tasks; and (3) a statement of the results expected. From this, a briefer, more concise job description is developed.

The next step is to design a recruitment and selection plan. Elements of this include specification of the recruitment territory (local, statewide, or national), consideration of labor market conditions, determination of recruitment audience, and description of the search and recruiting efforts. These elements are crucial to successful staffing, since employee selection can be made only from the pool of applicants generated by the recruitment plan. The plan must also be evaluated in terms of its likely success in producing applicant pools that are appropriately diverse across categories such as race/ethnicity, gender, sexual identity, age, and disability status.

Proceeding from recruitment to selection involves a three-stage process. In the first stage, applicants' résumés and letters of reference are reviewed to eliminate those who do not meet the stated qualifications. The second stage involves assessing the merits of the remaining applicants to identify three to five finalists who best fit the job description and are most likely to be able to do it well. In the third stage, finalists are interviewed, and a job offer is made to the top candidate. Screening criteria and interview questions are developed ahead of time so they match the qualifications and expectations described in the job analysis.

After hiring, new employees should receive a complete orientation to the job, workplace, and community, following from a plan for supervision, training, and development that is already in place. Interestingly, research suggests that there is no single "personality" that fits particular types of work within the field, and job applicants of many different backgrounds and personal characteristics may adapt well to the work. While an increasing number of employers are using screening tests that sometimes attempt to assess specific personality traits, the value of this has come into question, as has the possibility of its use in discriminatory ways (Weber & Dwoskin, 2014). Retaining quality employees appears to be most closely tied to the ability of the organization to moderate the stresses of the work through supervisor and peer support and to build commitment to the organization through participatory decision making and opportunities for advancement (Glisson et al., 2008; Hopkins, Cohen-Callow, Kim, & Hwang, 2010).

In order to ensure that employee performance is appropriately monitored and evaluated, a well-designed personnel or human resources system will have a performance appraisal system based on tasks identified in the job analysis. This will ensure that the work for which the employee is evaluated is the same as was described during recruitment, hiring, and training. Criteria and procedures for performance evaluation should always be specified in writing and given to employees at the time of hiring. In a well-designed performance appraisal system, it should be a rare occurrence for employees to be surprised by the written evaluation.

Policies, procedures, and grounds for termination should also be clearly defined and distributed in writing at the time of hiring. These may relate to unsatisfactory job performance or to unacceptable behavior, such as sexual harassment, and should be specified in objective, measurable terms. Procedures and time frames for notifying employees of poor performance long before reaching the stage of termination should also be delineated. Doing so is both a matter of fairness to the employee and a means for avoiding grievances or litigation (Bach, 2009).

In assessing an agency's effectiveness in the area of personnel policies and procedures, these are the types of elements one would want to examine. Helpful and informative documents for conducting the assessment include the following:

1. Manual of personnel policies and procedures
2. Copy of a human resources plan, including affirmative action/equal employment opportunity plans
3. Job analysis and job descriptions
4. Recruitment and selection procedures
5. Staff development and training plan
6. Performance evaluation forms
7. Statistics on absenteeism, turnover, and usage of sick leave
8. Grievances and complaints filed with the human resources department
9. Interviews with representative staff who perform different roles

A. Does the organization have a job analysis for each position within the agency that includes the following?

Responsibilities and Tasks	Methods	Knowledge and Skill	Results
Counseling			
1. Counsel individuals	One on one	Human behavior; group and family dynamics; understand professional role	Client develops independent living and social skills
2. Counsel families	Family treatment		
3. Lead groups	Group treatment		
4. Consult with self-help groups	Occasional group meetings		

B. Is this job analysis consistent with the following?

1. The job description
2. The recruitment and selection plan (or procedures)
3. The plan or practices relative to hiring a diverse workforce
4. Staff development and training plans or activities
5. Performance evaluation criteria
6. Plans for involuntary termination

Figure 8.4
Assessing an Organization's Human Resources System

Figure 8.4 may be useful in assessing the quality of an organization's personnel or human resources system.

Assess Adequacy of Technical Resources and Systems

This task encompasses the assessment of (1) budgetary management, (2) facilities and equipment, and (3) computer technology and information management. Additional questions arise that are specific to these three categories.

Budget Management   Questions to be asked include the following:

- Are program staff involved in a meaningful way in providing budgetary input? Do they get useful feedback about expenditures and unit costs during the year?
- Do resources appear to be adequate to achieve stated program goals and objectives?
- What type of budgeting system is used by the agency?
- How are unit costs calculated? Do staff members understand the meaning of unit costs? How are they used?

Budgeting and budget management is an activity often left to upper administration and treated as though line staff, first-line supervisors, and other persons involved in service delivery need not be included. However, good financial management practices involve all levels of staff. Fiscal soundness and budgeting practices affect programs and services in a profound way.

For many years, human service agencies were limited to an elementary type of budgeting called **line-item budgeting**. This involved identifying expenditure categories and estimating the dollars needed to cover expenses in each category for one year. Categories typically included personnel; operating expenses such as rent, utilities, supplies, and travel; and other items.

Since the 1970s, increasingly sophisticated budgeting techniques have been developed for application to human service agencies (Kettner et al., 2013). These techniques, referred to as *functional budgeting* and *program budgeting*, are based on program planning and budgeting systems (PPBS) (Lee & Johnson, 1973). Both approaches produce cost and expenditure data in relation to programs rather than to the entire agency. Based on this, they produce data such as total program costs, cost per unit of service, cost per output (client completion of program or service), and cost per outcome (the cost of producing measurable change in a client's quality of life). Martin (2000) terms this last approach "outcome budgeting" and describes its use in state-level human service agencies. It can help with conducting cost–benefit and cost-effectiveness assessments as well as helping agencies maintain a focus on measurement of outcomes.

Some of the more important documentation and data sources to be examined in order to understand the agency's approach to financial management and accountability include the following:

1. Annual reports

2. Audit reports

3. A cost allocation plan

4. Program goals and objectives

5. Communitywide comparative studies of unit costs

6. Interviews with all levels of program staff

Facilities and Equipment   Questions to be asked are as follows:

- Is the physical work environment attractive and conducive to high productivity? Do employees feel they have enough space and space of an appropriate type?
- Have problems been identified with current facilities and equipment? If so, is there a plan to address the problems and to fund solutions?
- Are there conditions related to facilities or equipment that appear to act as barriers to productivity or work flow?
- Are the facilities accessible to clients?

Considerations with regard to facilities include quantity of space, physical condition and maintenance of facilities, and geographical location. In assessing physical space, client needs should be a central consideration. "Welfare offices" and other HSOs are often caricatured as dreary, fortress-like, and dehumanizing places. Offices occupied by most HSOs will never resemble corporate boardrooms, but an organization's facilities should reflect earnest efforts to make them as pleasant as possible. They should also be located in places that maximize client access, and ongoing measures should be in place to make them safe environments. Finally, they should feature private space or interview rooms sufficient to ensure protection of client confidentially, plus areas for children if services require them to be at the agency for more than brief periods.

Information Technology and Information Management   Questions to be asked are as follows:

- Does the agency have integrated systems for mailings, payment, case-tracking, and management data?
- Does the agency maintain a website, a Facebook page, a Twitter feed, or any other form of social network presence?
- Does the agency use external information resources for fundraising, grant applications, volunteer coordination, or other activities?
- Do all line staff have desktop, laptop, or tablet computers, personal data assistants (PDAs), and/or smartphones? Do they have access to the Internet, word processing, email, text messaging, data security and firewall software, and other applications? Is this technology up to date?

Advances in computer technology have made possible many of the substantial gains in productivity enjoyed by both commercial firms and HSOs during the past few decades. At the organizational level, even small agencies will need both software and hardware (such as a network server) to establish and maintain systems that allow entry and retrieval of client, management, and fiscal data; Internet access; and email and text-messaging capabilities. Many will also need websites that are not merely informational but also allow online completion of forms, provide links to resources, enable clients to communicate with staff, and offer other features. Others may also add Facebook pages or other social networking efforts. Miller and Tucker (2013) describe both opportunities and potential drawbacks of seeking to increase an agency's social media profile. Guo and Saxton (2014) reveal how tweeting has been used by advocacy organizations to influence international change.

Human service organizations have followed the lead of commercial firms by creating positions for information technology (IT) staff. Their responsibilities include system maintenance and security, staff training, and planning for regular upgrades of software and hardware. In addition, IT specialists are increasingly needed to serve as modern versions of reference librarians, acquainting themselves and then informing staff about the constant flow of new resources. These may range from specialized software for fundraising, website development, or production of newsletters to Internet resources such as nonprofit-agency listservs, donor databases, subscription services that track funding opportunities and assist with preparation of grant applications, and many others. IT specialists are also needed for maintaining data security in an era of increasing use of "cloud" data storage and hacking threats that accompany its use (Wiegand, 2014). Table 8.8 shows examples of websites that provide information on these and other resources for HSOs.

All professional-level employees and most support staff at HSOs should have access to a desktop, laptop, or tablet computer in their workplace. Mobile devices are typically preferred by those who make frequent client visits or travel to multiple office sites. Mobile devices can also be used to access and update agency files, forms, and case notes, but as the convenience of this technology advances, so do the challenges for keeping case records secure. Tools such as the one depicted in Table 8.9 can be useful in assessing the adequacy of technical resources and systems.

Table 8.8   Selected Internet Resources for Human Service Organizations

Description
CompassPoint Nonprofit Services—a nonprofit consulting organization that serves nonprofits
GuideStar—a Web-based information clearinghouse for nonprofits
HandsNet—a news and information website for human service organizations
Grants.gov—Central clearinghouse for information about grant opportunities from the U.S. government
Website for nonprofit agencies and volunteers to advertise and locate volunteer opportunities
The Independent Sector—a coalition to support nonprofit organizations
National Organization for Human Services—provides support to human service professionals
National Council of Nonprofit Associations—a membership organization for nonprofits
American Public Human Service Association—an organization of public human service providers
TechSoup—technology assistance for nonprofits

Table 8.9   Assessing Adequacy of Technical Systems and Resources

	Staff Involved in Design and/or Given Access to Resource?	Up-to-Date Technology?
1. Budgeting process	____	____
2. Location and accessibility of office	____	____
3. Design and décor of office space	____	____
4. Management information system	____	____
5. Client data system	____	____
6. Use of Internet databases for fundraising, donor development, and grant writing	____	____
7. Computer hardware for line staff	____	____
8. Computer software for line staff	____	____
9. Access to Internet and email for line staff	____	____

Task 4: Assess the Cultural Competency of this Organization

Now that internal workings and external relationships have been assessed, one can begin to develop a better understanding of how culturally competent (or not) the organization is. For example, in examining environmental relationships the extent of outreach efforts to diverse constituencies will emerge. Internally, programs that target different population groups and staff characteristics may provide indicators of how sensitive the organization is to diversity. Thus, Task 4 builds on what has been learned thus far.

Assess Cultural Competence in External Relationships

Questions to be explored for this activity include the following:

- What efforts does the organization make to familiarize itself with the diversity that exists in its environment?
- Does the organization recognize and seek to overcome barriers to service access?
- Does the organization take steps to ensure that its staff reflects the diversity of its clients?
- Do the organization's services fit well with the needs of minority as well as nonminority clients?

In earlier chapters, we called attention to some of the disparities in health, income, education, and other factors that affect traditionally underserved or vulnerable populations, including ethnic/racial minorities. At the most fundamental level, culturally competent HSOs are ones that are aware of these problems and oriented toward addressing them. They also collect information systematically to understand the diversity of needs in their environments. This applies to clients and other groups such as donors, client advocates, and citizens' organizations. Gathering this information is usually done through needs assessments carried out via individual and group interviews; focus groups; mail, telephone, or Internet surveys; or analysis of census data or school or court records. In conducting needs assessments, the organization should demonstrate awareness that diversity arises not only from differences in race/ethnicity, gender, sexual orientation, and age, but also with respect to physical and cognitive abilities, socioeconomic background, education, receptiveness to services, and other dimensions. We use the term *cultural competence* with reference to all these factors, and recent studies offer a variety of ways to evaluate this capacity in HSOs (Fung, Lo, Srivastava, & Andermann, 2012; Smith, McCaslin, Chang, Martinez, & McGrew, 2010; Sussman, Skara, & Pumpuang, 2008).

Access   As we discussed earlier, organizations may establish eligibility criteria that ensure a steady flow of needed resources but that exclude some clients who are most in need, including those from traditionally underserved groups. Marchevsky and Theoharis (2008) provide an example of how this occurred with regard to the determination of benefit eligibility among mostly Hispanic immigrant families in southern California. Other research has shown how organizational behaviors discussed earlier can exclude and disentitle certain groups. For example, Herbst (2008) found that low-income African Americans were significantly more likely than others to fail to receive child-care subsidies for which they were eligible. This was due in part to "creaming" processes in which efforts were made to make more remunerative clients aware of their eligibility, while little was done to recruit less remunerative—but no less eligible—clients. Shaefer (2010) found that low-income and minority workers accessed unemployment benefits for which they were eligible less often than others because past experiences of being denied services made them assume they couldn't qualify.

Problems of access affect other groups as well. Despite gains associated with the Americans with Disabilities Act of 1990, people with physical, developmental, and other disabilities still lack physical access to many facilities and services (McColl, Jarzynowska, & Shortt, 2010). Also, due to distance and transportation difficulties, clients in rural areas have substantially greater difficulty reaching needed services than those in urban locales (Fletcher, Garasky, Jensen, & Nielsen, 2010). Even in populous areas, transit problems magnify the effect of distance.

Provider Characteristics   One measure of an HSO's fit with its environment is whether its personnel are reasonably well aligned with the clients they serve on variables such as age, race/ethnicity, gender, and other characteristics. Social workers are trained to bridge gaps between themselves and their clients, and agency personnel do not have to be identical to clients on all or even most dimensions in order to be effective. Still, research suggests that these differences may influence service outcomes. For example, Smith (2013) found that African American patients who had African American physicians adhered to prescription drug protocols better than if they had non-race-concordant physicians. However, in a study of a large national sample of patients, Chen, Fryer, Phillips, Wilson, and Pathman (2005) found that 75 percent of African American patients saw non–African American physicians, whereas for white patients this ratio was reversed. Perhaps not surprisingly, white patients were significantly more likely to report satisfaction with their services.

Another aspect of cultural competence in an organization involves whether appropriate efforts are made to diversify its workforce. Aversive racism, which we discussed earlier, exists in the form of stereotypic attitudes that can lead to inadvertent but real discrimination. These attitudes affect behaviors such as hiring decisions, where perceptions of group characteristics may overshadow individual qualifications (Rodenborg & Boisen, 2013). Beyond race/ethnicity, research shows that hiring biases can also be based on age (Dennis & Thomas, 2007), disabilities (Shier, Graham, & Jones, 2009), and seropositivity (Rao, Angell, Lam, & Corrigan, 2008).

Chow and Austin (2008) describe operations and activities carried out by organizations that help to ensure they are responding appropriately to the diversity in their environment and that serve as makers of cultural competence. Adapting material from Cross and Friesen (2005), their list of activities includes the following:

* Specifying the population to be served, and knowing their characteristics
* Ensuring that staff and board members are representative of the community served
* Locating staff who reflect community characteristics, and establishing staff supports (e.g., orientation, job descriptions, and evaluation protocols)
* Using guidelines for culturally competent practice
* Recognizing diversity and difference in service delivery
* Offering supervision that supports and trains staff to be culturally competent
* Using consultants who understand the cultures of service recipients

One important asset of this list is that it calls attention to provider characteristics such as board composition, job design, and staff development to underscore the fact that cultural competence involves more than simply hiring a diverse workforce.

Diversity and Difference in Practice

Behavior: Apply and communicate understanding of the importance of diversity and difference in shaping life experiences in practice at the micro, mezzo, and macro levels.

Critical Thinking Question: How can social workers assist their workplaces in becoming more culturally competent?

Service Characteristics　　The development of **culturally sensitive interventions (CSIs)** has helped human service organizations provide better services to traditionally underserved groups. CSIs are defined as interventions into which important elements that define a culture, such as values, practices, and standards of conduct, are incorporated. Examples of CSIs can be found in many service arenas, including counseling, substance use, and child maltreatment, and reviews suggest they are effective (Hodge, Jackson, & Vaughn, 2012; Jackson, 2009).

A particularly important quality of a culturally competent agency is an ability to recognize and respond to high-incidence problems in client groups that are numerically small. Bubar (2010) notes that the risk of sexual assault among American Indian women is the highest of any ethnic/racial group, but few agencies, even in areas with large concentrations of American Indian women, employ counselors with special skills in treating this population. This dynamic extends to many other service needs and populations, from counseling of LGBTQ youth, to language training and housing assistance for refugees, to help with insurance premiums for people with treatable but rare and costly illnesses.

Assess Whether the Internal Workings of the Organization Are Diversity Friendly

Questions to be explored for this activity include the following:

- Are the organization's structure and operation conducive to cultural competence?
- Does the organization promote an environment that retains diverse employees?

As we discussed in Chapter 7, highly bureaucratic organizations tend to provide low levels of autonomy or decision-making authority to their staff and are oriented toward making tasks as routinized and predictable as possible. This is seldom a good recipe for cultural competence, since highly routinized services may be a poor fit with the needs and expectations of a diverse client population.

Chow and Austin (2008) provide a framework for enhancing the cultural competence of agency policies and procedures. It begins with a mission statement that makes explicit the organization's commitment to being responsive to diversity. Another element addresses the need for the agency's information systems to gather data in sufficient variety and detail to facilitate understanding of the diversity within the environment and organization. In particular, the data should allow administrators to address questions, such as which services are most in demand by which groups and which services are underutilized. Policies and procedures should also outline intake mechanisms and service standards that are culturally relevant. For example, assessment scales for measuring client problems and progress often perform differently across race/ethnicity, socioeconomic status, English proficiency, and other dimensions.

Box 8.3 provides an overview of ways to promote a diversity-friendly workplace.

Personnel management practices also play a key role in creating a productive environment within organizations. A survey of social workers by Acquavita, Pittman, Gibbons, and Castellanos-Brown (2009) found that being a member of a minority group did not predict respondents' satisfaction with their job. Instead, the important factors for predicting higher job satisfaction were whether respondents viewed their organization as being diverse and inclusive. Mallow (2010) also points to perceptions of inclusion and

---

Box 8.3   Promoting a Diversity-Friendly Workplace

Studies suggest that only 17 percent of employees of commercial firms rate their organization as "very diverse," while nearly 60 percent say their workplace "needs improvement" in this area (Lebel, 2008). Below are some examples of steps that can be taken to increase the likelihood that an organization will be viewed as diversity friendly.

- Include commitment to diversity in the organization's mission statement.
- Ensure recruitment efforts take meaningful steps to attract diverse applicants.
- Offer benefits such as maternity/paternity leave, childcare subsidies, flexible work schedules, observance of cultural and religious holidays, and quality retirement options.
- Ensure all personnel actions (hiring, promotion, salary adjustments, and job termination) are based on merit.

- Emphasize transparency, and ensure easy access to criteria for personnel actions.
- Review personnel actions regularly to ensure proper criteria are applied.
- Ensure enforcement of ADA regulations in all facilities.
- Create an organizational climate committee to advise on diversity issues.
- Ensure supervisors, managers, and administrators receive training in diversity and inclusion.
- Train mentors and ensure they are available to new staff.
- Offer same-sex domestic-partner/spousal benefits.
- Encourage formation of employee resource groups to provide assistance and support to employees from traditionally disadvantaged populations.

---

having a voice in decision making as critical predictors of organizations' ability to retain staff members in general and, in particular, staff members from traditionally disadvantaged or underrepresented groups.

The history of efforts to create organizations that are both diverse and diversity-friendly has often been fraught with tokenism. Success is not achieved by simply including the word "diversity" in an organizational mission statement, attracting a few minority job applicants, or promoting a lesbian woman or person with a disability to a midlevel managerial post. It is achieved by examining the modern workforce in all its variety and making sure that the organization has a good grasp of who its members are and whom it serves. It also means creating an organizational culture that treats diversity as an asset and employees as full participants in decision making.

 Assess your understanding of framework for organizational assessment by taking this brief quiz.

SUMMARY

To fully understand an organization, with all its strengths and weaknesses, one would have to spend years reviewing documents, analyzing data, and talking to people familiar with it. However, an overview of selected elements of the organization and its relationship to its environment can provide a sufficiently detailed understanding to detect the presence of problems that may need to be addressed, why they exist, and steps that might be taken to resolve them.

In this chapter, we proposed that understanding an organization involves four tasks: (1) identifying the focal organization, its cultural artifacts, and its domain; (2) identifying the organization's environment, and understanding relationships between the organization and significant elements of this environment; (3) understanding the inner workings of the organization itself; and (4) assessing the organization's cultural competency.

Significant elements of the task environment include sources of resources such as cash funding, noncash resources, clients and client referrals, and other needed organizational inputs. Also important in the task environment are regulatory and accrediting bodies that set standards for the organization, and professional associations or licensing boards that set standards for the organization's staff. Strong and positive relationships with these entities make an important contribution to the overall strength and stability of the agency.

Assessing the internal functioning of the organization also includes understanding elements such as organizational and program structure; management and leadership style; organizational and program structure; personnel policies, procedures and practices; and adequacy of technical resources and systems. Using the tools discussed in this chapter as means of assessing the organization offers an opportunity to understand the organizational context within which problems are identified and changes are proposed.

 Recall what you learned in this chapter by completing the Chapter Review.

Appendix   Framework for Assessing a Human Service Organization

Task 1: Identify Focal Organization

Search for Cultural Artifacts

- What is the history of this organization?
- How would you describe the organization's identity and is it congruent with its image?
- What is the basis for and extent of the organization's corporate authority?
- What is its mission?
- What physical, social, and behavioral artifacts are observed?

Learn about Organizational Domain

- What is the organization's domain (e.g., the populations served, the technology employed, and services provided)?
- What target populations are recruited or mandated to participate?
- How are the costs of client services covered, and how does the organization deal with those who cannot pay?
- Are there defined legal, geographical, or service areas that establish organizational boundaries?

Task 2: Assess the Organization's Environmental Relationships

Identify and Assess Relationships with Revenue Sources

- What are the agency's funding sources?

- How much and what percentage of the agency's total funds are received from each source?
- What are the nature and quality of the relationship between funding sources and the agency?
- Does the organization use volunteers? If yes, how many, and for what purposes?
- What in-kind resources (e.g., food, clothing, physical facilities, etc.) does the organization receive?
- What tax benefits does the organization receive?

Identify and Assess Relationships with Referral Sources and Other Providers

Relationships with Referral Sources

- What are the major sources of client referrals?
- Does demand for services outstrip supply, or is there unused capacity?
- What types of clients does the organization refuse (e.g., are there disproportionate numbers of poor persons, senior adults, persons of color, women, persons with disabilities, gays/lesbians, or other groups that are typically underserved)?

Relationships with Other Providers

- What other agencies provide the same services to the same clientele as this organization?
- With whom does the organization compete?
- With whom does the organization cooperate?
- Is the organization part of a coalition or an alliance?

Identify and Assess Relationships with Other Units in the Task Environment

- What state and federal regulatory bodies oversee programs provided by this organization?
- With what government agencies does this organization contract for service provision?
- What professional associations, licensing and certification boards, and accrediting bodies influence agency operations?

Task 3: Assess Internal Organizational Capacity

Understand Organizational and Program Structure

- What are the major departmental or program units in this organization?
- Is there a convincing rationale for the existing organizational structure?
- Is the existing structure consistent with and supportive of the mission?
- Is supervision logical and capable of performing expected functions? Are staff members capable of performing expected functions?
- What can you learn about the informal structure (people who carry authority because they are respected by staff, and thus exert influence) that is different from those in formally designated positions of authority?

Understand Management and Leadership Style

- How is the workplace organized, and how is work allocated?
- Are appropriate authority and information passed on along with responsibility?
- How close is supervision, and what exactly is supervised? Is it tasks, is it functions, or is it the employee?
- How are decisions made? Is information solicited from those affected?
- Do employees feel valued at every level? Do they believe they are making a contribution to the success of the organization?
- How is conflict handled?

Assess the Organization's Programs and Services

- What programs and services are offered, and are the services consistent with program goals and objectives?

- Are staffing patterns appropriate to the services to be provided? Are workload expectations reasonable given expectations for achievement with each client and within each service and program?
- Is there a common understanding among management and line staff within each program about problems to be addressed, populations to be served, services to be provided, and client outcomes to be achieved?
- Are expected outcomes identified with sufficient clarity that program success or failure can be determined?

Assess Personnel Policies, Procedures, and Practices

- Is there a written human resources plan?
- Is there a job analysis for each position?
- Is there a plan for recruitment and selection?
- Is there a plan for enhancing agency diversity?
- Is there a plan for staff development and training?
- Is a performance evaluation system in place?
- Are there written procedures for employee termination?

Assess Adequacy of Technical Resources and Systems

Budget Management

- Are program staff involved in a meaningful way in providing budgetary input? Do they get useful feedback about expenditures and unit costs during the year?
- Do resources appear to be adequate to achieve stated program goals and objectives?
- What type of budgeting system is used by the agency?
- How are unit costs calculated? Do staff members understand the meaning of unit costs? How are they used?

Facilities and Equipment

- Is the physical work environment attractive and conducive to high productivity? Do employees feel they have enough space and space of an appropriate type?
- Have problems been identified with current facilities and equipment? If so, is there a plan to address the problems and to fund solutions?

- Are there conditions related to facilities or equipment that appear to act as barriers to productivity or work flow?
- Are the facilities accessible to clients?

Information Technology and Information Management

- Does the agency have integrated systems for mailings, payment, case-tracking, and management data?
- Does the agency maintain a website, a Facebook page, a Twitter feed, or any other form of social network presence?
- Does the agency use external information resources for fundraising, grant applications, volunteer coordination, or other activities?
- Do all line staff have desktop, laptop, or tablet computers, personal data assistants (PDAs), and/or smartphones? Do they have access to the Internet, word processing, email, text messaging, data security and firewall software, and other applications? Is this technology up to date?

Task 4: Assess the Cultural Competency of This Organization

Assess Cultural Competence in External Relationships

- What efforts does the organization make to familiarize itself with the diversity that exists in its environment?
- Does the organization recognize and seek to overcome barriers to service access?
- Does the organization take steps to ensure that its staff reflects the diversity of its clients?
- Do the organization's services fit well with the needs of minority as well as nonminority clients?

Assess Whether the Internal Workings of the Organization Are Diversity-Friendly

- Are the organization's structure and operation conducive to cultural competence?
- Does the organization promote an environment that retains diverse employees? Clients?

Assess Your Competence

Use the scale below to rate your current level of achievement on the following concepts or skills associated with each learning outcome listed at the beginning of this chapter:

1	2	3
I can accurately describe the concept or skill(s) associated with this outcome.	I can consistently identify the concept or skill(s) associated with this outcome when observing and analyzing practice activities.	I can competently implement the concept or skill(s) associated with this outcome in my own practice.

_____ Define human service organizations, their functions, and their attributes.

_____ Use a framework to assess a human service organization.

9

Building Support for the Proposed Change

STOCKBYTE/GETTY IMAGES

DESIGNING THE INTERVENTION

The professionally assisted change efforts discussed in chapters 9–12 are intended to fall into two general categories: (1) those promoting improved quality of life for the clients or communities served, or (2) those promoting improved quality of work life for employees as a means of helping them provide the best possible services to clients and/or communities. In order to accomplish these type changes, macro practice in social work can be viewed as having five major parts: (1) understanding the important components to be affected by the change—population, problem, and arena; (2) preparing an overall plan designed to get the change accepted; (3) preparing a detailed plan for intervention; (4) implementing the intervention; and (5) monitoring and evaluating its effectiveness. Chapters 3 through 8 focused on understanding the components. Chapters 9 and 10 concentrate on distilling the information gathered into a clearly thought-out plan to get the change accepted, and on making decisions about strategy and tactics. Chapter 11 focuses on developing and implementing an intervention, and Chapter 12 follows up to ensure its success.

Before developing a change strategy, however, it is first necessary to be clear on the nature of the proposed intervention. Strategy and tactical planning would be premature in the absence of an understanding of what the change entails. This understanding can be achieved by developing a working **intervention hypothesis**. Note that the original hypothesis may evolve as new perspectives influence the change effort; thus, change agents need to be open to adjusting the hypothesis as it emerges throughout the planning process.

Beginning with the task of further developing and refining an intervention hypothesis, this chapter presents a series of four tasks. Together, these four tasks provide the foundation for moving toward the strategies and tactics one may choose in order to effect change. First, in order to ensure that there are some common themes in the way that participants frame the problem and proposed interventions, it is important to refine the hypothesis of etiology (developed in Chapter 4) and to develop a working intervention hypothesis. When the change agent and other participants are able to reach an agreement on these hypotheses, the second task is to identify some of the major participants who are likely to be critical to the success of the proposed change. After identifying key participants, the third task is to examine organizational and/or community readiness for change. Figure 9.1 summarizes the major tasks and activities involved in reaching consensus on building support for an intervention.

Task 1: Develop the Intervention Hypothesis

During the early phases of problem identification, many people involved in change efforts (paid staff, service users, volunteers, and others) are eager to propose a specific intervention. They may have experienced the frustration of working in what they perceive to be flawed programs, under perceived oppressive community or organizational policies, or as participants or members of communities that seem powerless to bring about meaningful change. Understandably, they are eager to propose immediate change and may be impatient with the idea of carefully thinking through the alternatives. This can be a great temptation and a potential pitfall if change agents do not insist on dealing with the findings developed to this point and avoid straying too far off course.

A well-informed, professional approach to macro-level change requires that the foregoing tasks associated with problem identification and analysis in Chapters 3 through 8 be

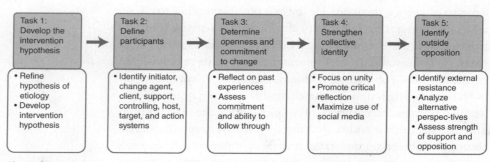

Figure 9.1

Tasks in the Framework for Building Support for an Intervention Strategy addressed first. However, it is the unusual change agent who is not constantly mindful of a preferred intervention and who is not continually molding and shaping it as the analysis unfolds. Yet, if one engages in a process with others who have their own ideas about what needs to happen, original thoughts about preferred interventions may change as new ideas emerge. It is important to trust the process. Final decisions about the design and specifics of the intervention should wait until the analytical work has been completed. When an acceptable degree of consensus is achieved about the nature of the problem and its etiology, an intervention hypothesis can be proposed.

Refine the Working Hypothesis of Etiology

The key questions to be explored are:

- What factors gleaned from the population analysis, problem analysis, and arena analysis help in understanding cause-and-effect relationships?
- What themes seem to fit best with the current situation?
- How should the working hypothesis of etiology be framed?

Study and analysis of the problem, population, and arena invariably produce a wide variety of quantitative and qualitative data. To avoid being overwhelmed with too much information, change agents must be able to identify those factors that are critical to understanding the situation at hand. But how does one know what to look for, what to keep, and what to omit in this process? It may be helpful to briefly review Chapters 3 and 4, considering the tasks associated with understanding populations and problems. These considerations may provide guidance on how to refine one's thinking. Once this sorting process is complete, one is ready to frame a working hypothesis.

Take, for example, a situation where the problem identified is an increase in gang violence in a community, leading to rapid increases in the number of young men and women in the area who have become physically disabled due to gunshot wounds. A study of the problem may provide facts and figures, such as the incidence of disabling gunshot wounds over the last five years, the demographic makeup of the community, poverty rates, high school dropout rates, comparisons with similar communities, a history of the development of gang activity in the community, and various researchers' findings about the nature and causes of violence (Berg, Stewart, Schreck, & Simons, 2012; Decker, Melde, & Pyrooz, 2013; Huebner, Martin, Moule, Pyrooz, & Decker, 2014; Papachristos, Hureau, & Braga, 2013; Slocum, Rengifo, Choi, & Herrmann, 2013).

A study of the population may reveal that violent youth in this community tend to cluster within lower socioeconomic strata, that many are from families having difficulty meeting basic needs, that parental neglect is common, that few have had positive experiences with education, that most are in a stage at which they are struggling to develop an identity, that peer relationships are critical to their social development, and that almost all find few incentives to conform to societal expectations.

Interviews with parents and community leaders may reveal that there is a sense of hopelessness or resignation among adults in the community, that many are unemployed and have low skill levels, that education is not highly valued, that parents rarely support the efforts of teachers, and that associations among both teens and adults are almost exclusively along ethnic lines. Patterns of participation in extracurricular activities reveal higher participation rates among white students, whereas Latino/a and African

American students, who feel the programs are not relevant, are left to develop their own activities. When talking with social service leaders in the community, it may become obvious that providers' perceptions of what to do are different from those of community residents (Kissane & Gingerich, 2004).

Not everything discovered can be used. To be useful, the quantitative and qualitative data gathered in the analysis phase must be distilled into a working hypothesis about etiology (cause-and-effect relationships). In short, the change agent must ask: Having studied the problem, population, and arena as well as their areas of overlap, what do I now believe to be the *most significant* contributing factors leading to the need for change? A working hypothesis of etiology, drawn from analysis of the problem, population, and/or arena, can be expressed in a statement or series of statements similar to the following example.

Example of a Working Hypothesis of Etiology

Because of the following factors (drawn from analysis of the population, problem, and/or arena):

1. A trauma that led to a disabling physical condition
2. Limited basic education and marketable skills
3. Limited job opportunities
4. The need, during the teen years, to develop a positive, socially acceptable identity while, at the same time, being denied opportunities.

The following problems have developed:

1. Limited physical activity and declining health
2. Little to offer prospective employers
3. Discouragement and hopelessness regarding prospects for developing economic and psychological independence
4. Onset of a negative, antisocial identity and behavior pattern.

This example is oversimplified for the sake of illustration. Completion of this task should result in a draft statement that reflects some level of agreement among participants regarding cause-and-effect relationships underlying the need for change.

Develop a Working Intervention Hypothesis

The key questions to be explored are:

- What interventions are implied by the hypothesis of etiology?
- Does it appear that these interventions are most likely to reduce or eliminate the problem?
- What results can be expected from these interventions?

Based on a distillation of the information gathered in the problem analysis phase and expressed in the working hypothesis of etiology, a working **intervention hypothesis** is developed. This hypothesis is a statement or series of statements proposing a relationship between a specific intervention and a result or outcome. It should have an "if A, then B" format, which indicates that if certain changes are made, certain results would be likely to follow. Within this framework, the statement should identify the following: (1) a target population (or specific subgroup) and problem, (2) the proposed change or intervention, and (3) the results expected from the intervention. These elements combine to form a complete package that makes clear the expected relationship between problem, intervention, and result. A working intervention hypothesis to deal with rehabilitation of physically disabled teens might read something like this example.

Example of a Working Intervention Hypothesis

If the following interventions are implemented for physically disabled teens:

1. Increase physical activity and exercise
2. Provide opportunities for education and development of marketable skills
3. Pair with a mentor who has overcome a physical disability
4. Work with local employers to identify job slots.

   Then the following results can be expected:

1. Improved physical health and self-esteem
2. Increased incidence of acquiring a GED or equivalent
3. Development of a positive identity as demonstrated by articulation of life and career goals
4. At least a 50 percent increase in successful employment.

This would be considered a testable hypothesis. The strength of this approach is that it encourages change agents to focus on a specified set of contributing factors and expected results that form a set of cause-and-effect relationships (Mullen, 2006). There should be clearly understood relationships between causal factors and results in the hypothesis of etiology, and between the proposed intervention and expected results in the intervention hypothesis. Furthermore, the relationships between causal or contributing factors in the working hypothesis of etiology and proposed interventions should be clear, as should the relationships between results specified in etiology and results expected of the intervention. These relationships are diagrammed in Figure 9.2.

It is not necessary that each factor match precisely. The point in developing these hypotheses is that the intervention be designed to address the problems or needs specified

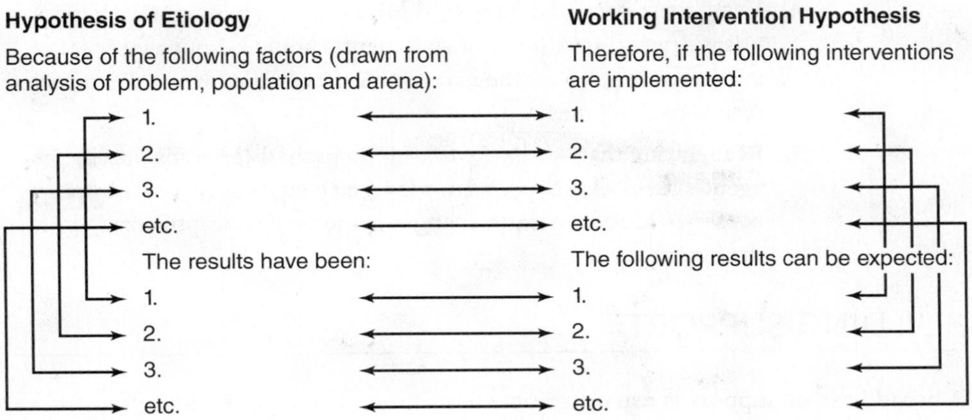

Figure 9.2
Relationship of Factors and Results in Working Hypotheses

and that the results be clearly defined so that they can be tracked. Using this format, one can establish the relationship between intervention and results. If this step is ignored or skipped, one runs the risk that the change intervention cannot be evaluated or demonstrate effectiveness.

An important issue in relation to developing working hypotheses of etiology and intervention is that their development arises from findings gathered in the population, problem, and arena analyses. It is not unusual for people involved in change to attempt to impose their own perceptions and agendas on change efforts. Every effort must be expended to resist having these pat solutions imposed. Solutions should come from well-researched analysis.

It is not necessary at this point to flesh out the intervention in detail, as that will be addressed in Chapter 11. However, for the change effort to proceed, it is necessary to make at least a preliminary decision about the nature and form of the intervention so that building support for a strategy to introduce the change may proceed.

Summary of Steps in Developing an Intervention Hypothesis

Because the information presented may be new to the reader, we recognize that these steps may seem daunting at first, but with practice, skills in writing intervention hypotheses can be developed. The following is a summary checklist reviewing the important points made so far about developing an intervention hypothesis:

1. A representative group should reexamine all relevant findings from analyses of population, problem, and arena.

2. Relevant quantitative data and other types of information should be distilled into a clear working hypothesis of etiology, establishing an understanding about cause-and-effect relationships.

3. Based on the working hypothesis of etiology, creative ideas should be generated about interventions that appear to be relevant to the need as it is currently understood.

4. Using these proposed interventions, a working intervention hypothesis is developed. A series of statements should lay out a clear set of understandings about the nature of the intervention and the expected results or outcomes.

5. Recognizing that this is a "working" hypothesis reminds the change agent(s) that, as support is built for the change effort, new perspectives may introduce slight changes in the final conceptualization of the hypothesis.

BUILDING SUPPORT

A broad base of support is usually critical to successful change. Building support requires planning and effort, and it begins with understanding the major participants or stakeholders (Staples, 2012; Walker & East, 2014; Woodford & Preston, 2011). A

Sidebar content:

Do an Internet search for the "Child Welfare Information Gateway." Locate the "Evidence-Based Practice" page. What resources are available to help agencies research, choose, and implement evidence-based practices to address identified problems?

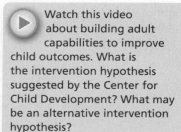

Research-informed Practice (or Practice-informed Research).

Behavior: Use practice experience and theory to inform scientific inquiry and research.

Critical Thinking Question: When analyzing a problem, how would you use practice experience and theory to generate a meaningful working hypothesis?

Watch this video about building adult capabilities to improve child outcomes. What is the intervention hypothesis suggested by the Center for Child Development? What may be an alternative intervention hypothesis?

www.youtube.com/watch?v=urU-a_FsS5Y

? Assess your understanding of designing the intervention hypothesis by taking this brief quiz.

systematic effort to identify the major participants begins with understanding each of the systems to be considered. These are discussed in the following sections.

Task 2: Define Participants

Up to this point in the change process, it is not unusual for the people involved to be a small core of committed individuals, possibly even close friends or colleagues, who recognize a condition or problem and are concerned enough to take action. It is appropriate for members of this group to tackle some of the early activities of problem identification and analysis, as long as they avoid becoming prematurely committed to a particular perspective.

In order for effective macro change to occur, it is necessary to have allies. A good deal of strategy development involves building **coalitions**. People willing to commit themselves to change rarely accept someone else's perspectives on problems and solutions without some negotiation and accommodation. It is often true that the greater the level of participation in the problem identification and analysis phases, the greater the likelihood of consensus on the problem and proposed solution (e.g., Campbell, 2009; Majee & Hoyt, 2009; Peerapun, 2011).

It is important that participants critical to the success of the change effort be identified in a systematic manner. One risk is that group members may assume that they represent a full range of perspectives and fail to identify everyone who needs to be included. If participation is to be representative of a wide variety of groups and interests, change agents need to understand all of the systems involved. Careful attention should be paid to insuring that a wide variety of perspectives is included throughout the process. This would include all relevant ethnic groups, women, and any other populations that are considered relevant to the change effort.

We will use the term *system* to describe these critical participants. This term is used in the context of systems theory, implying that participants should be viewed as more than simply a collection of individuals with common interests and characteristics. As a system or subsystem critical to the success of the change effort, they represent a complex set of interrelationships having system-like attributes that must be recognized and attended to by the core planning group. One of these attributes, for example, is **entropy**, which refers to the natural tendency of systems to expire without input and regeneration from outside the system. The concept is directly applicable to the types of systems involved in planned change.

Given the community and organizational arenas in which change occurs, it is important to emphasize how diverse the identification of participants can be. For example, in a human service agency that has identified an unskilled and potentially insensitive staff who are unprepared to work effectively with immigrant families, it will be necessary to include persons with knowledge about immigration issues and skills in the planned change design. Although this could be initially viewed as an internal agency problem, staff members will want to include participants beyond agency walls,

> Watch this video on building support for policy change at the community level. Why does the Director of Prevention for the Cherokee Nation suggest that the coalitions involved in the policy change effort were successful?
>
> www.youtube.com/watch?v=OGEHI38GCh0

> Do an Internet search for the "Open Society Foundation." The founder, George Soros, believes that individuals throughout the world can make a difference and that critical perspectives are important in order to make change. How do the mission and values of this foundation fit with social work values?

such as immigrants and others with expertise in this area. Another example is a grass-roots community change effort in which multiple domestic violence shelters have been identified as unprepared to deal with lesbian, gay, bisexual, and transgender clients. In this community, participants would include representatives from multiple organizations that house shelter programs as well as constituencies who have an interest in solving this problem.

The systems to be considered include the (1) initiator system, (2) change agent system, (3) client system, (4) support system, (5) controlling system, (6) host and implementing systems, (7) target system, and (8) action system. It should be noted that these terms are used here solely for conceptual purposes to assist in understanding who should be involved and why. They are not commonly used among people involved in change efforts. It is more likely that terms such as *agency, officeholder, position, committee,* and *task force* will be used to designate individuals and groups, but the professional who coordinates the effort should be aware, conceptually, of which systems need to be represented and why.

Identify the Initiator System

The key questions to be explored are:

- Who first recognized the problem and brought attention to it?
- How should or can the initiators be involved in the change effort?

The **initiator system** is made up of those individuals who first recognize the existence of a problem and call attention to it. For example, staff in a state agency had complained among themselves for years about the rigidity within the bureaucracy in which they worked. A social worker was hired to start a new program. When she became an employee of the state agency, she encountered a culture of playing "ain't it awful" that seemed to be the expected norm. Seizing the opportunity, she began to talk informally with staff members who had been there a long time. Whenever they started complaining, she would say, "What examples of rigidity are you talking about?" Staff members would stop for a moment and try to come up with a specific example. Sometimes, in resignation they replied, "It's just the nature of the bureaucracy!" Others, however, would come up with specifics such as the rules about copymachine use or the time it took to fill out a work voucher, submit it to multiple sources, and finally get help with an IT problem that had held up their work for days. Still others talked about how they were "always in the dark" and there was little communication across programs. As the social worker discovered a number of potential issues and concerns, she decided to tackle the "communication problem." By bringing this to the attention of her supervisor, she was the initiator even though she was functioning as the voice of an initiator system composed of multiple staff members who had been complaining for years and had become part of a culture that didn't expect change to occur.

The initiator system may not be part of the organization they want to change. In comparison to change being initiated from within, these types of changes may be precipitated by outside groups or individuals who serve as the initiator system. Many changes are initiated because a potential client group cannot gain access to a program or service, or, even if they have access, program staff may be insensitive to their needs. Changes in access, how services are delivered, or what services are provided may come from external constituencies that advocate for underserved population groups.

> **Box 9.1   Potential Members of an Initiator System in a Community Effort to Promote Safe Sex Practices**
>
> - Concerned citizens committed to change
> - Community leaders
> - Victims of HIV/AIDS
> - Parents
> - High school counselors
>
> - Planned parenthood staff
> - County health staff
> - Other interested and committed community representatives, insuring that all relevant ethnic groups and other special populations are represented

Note that many people inside or outside a system may see a problem that needs to be addressed, yet nothing is ever done. An individual or members of a group do not become an initiator system until they begin taking steps to bring about a change. For example, a group of citizens recognized high rates of HIV/AIDS and teenage pregnancy in their south Florida community and decided to take action (Weiss, Dwonch-Schoen, Howard-Barr, & Panella, 2010). They initiated a participatory action project that was highly successful in achieving its goals. Using this project as an example, a list of potential initiators in such a community action project might include those identified in Box 9.1.

Individuals who first raise an issue may or may not also become a part of the initial planning process. If possible, key roles in the change effort should be assigned to initiators because, having already demonstrated an interest in the issue, they may be in a position to bring other supporters along. This becomes especially important if the initiators are indigenous to the community (Cohen & Hyde, 2014) or a respected part of an organization that needs to change. People who have lived with the problem or need are likely to be knowledgeable about the problem but may see themselves as powerless to affect the system. Empowerment strategies such as teaching, training, group counseling, or consciousness-raising efforts can pay rich dividends in the long run and can place appropriate spokespersons in leadership positions (e.g., Everett, Homstead, & Drisko, 2007). In any case, it is important for change agents to be aware of the person or persons who first raised the issue and to keep in close contact as the problem or need is framed for public consumption.

Identify the Change Agent System

The key questions to be explored for this activity are:

- Who will be responsible for leadership and coordination in the early stages of the change effort?
- Is it necessary to gain approval(s) in order to move forward, and if so, from whom?

For a professionally assisted change effort to be successful, there must be one or more individuals designated as coordinator or coordinators of the change effort. We will refer to this person or persons as the *change agent*. The change agent, together with an initial core planning committee or task force, comprise the **change agent system**.

Hardina (2014) suggests using a variety of skills to engage potential participants. These include expressing empathy, interviewing, building relationships, engaging in group dialogue, using basic group work skills to recruit members of the change agent system, organizing coalitions and other partnerships, developing mutually agreed-upon approaches, and preparing for action. The change agent system serves as a sort of steering committee to guide the change effort in its early stages. The makeup of this system is critical to the change effort because much of what is accomplished will be framed in the perspectives of these individuals. Ideally, this system will include representation from the initiator system—people who have experienced the identified problem, people who have had experience in trying to solve the problem, and people who can be influential in getting the change accepted. Again, representation is important.

If the change activity will require drawing on the resources of an organization, it is essential that the organization sanction the change and also be identified as part of the change agent system. This may involve getting formal approval from an executive director or a board and may require release time from other duties, secretarial support, use of copying machine, mailing privileges, computer access, and other such resources. Depending on the scope of the change, support may require written approval to insure that all contingencies are covered or simply an agreement among supervisor and colleagues that certain staff will be devoting some of their time to the project.

In community change efforts, approvals may be less formal than in organizational settings. For example, a grassroots organizing effort may be comprised of citizen-volunteers who are neighborhood residents but are not tied to formal organizational settings. The grassroots group may be loosely structured, not having executive committees and perhaps not having many resources. General agreement among the members of the group may be the full extent of sanctioning in this arena (Staples, 2012).

The function of the change agent system is to act as an initial coordinating or steering committee until a wider range of participants can be incorporated into the change effort. Many participants in the change effort will be taking on different activities at the same time. It is the job of the change agent system to ensure that the change effort is properly organized and carried out from its early conceptualization to the point it is turned over to others for implementation. As the major systems and perspectives are identified and the action system (discussed later in this chapter) is formed, the coordinating functions are shifted to the action system.

The work of the change agent system begins with coordinating and carrying out the population, problem, population, and arena analyses, as described in Chapters 3 through 8. This may involve setting up project teams, doing research, interviewing, and coordinating all of the study effort through a steering committee. Then there is the work of agreeing on a general strategy. As new participants are added, responsibilities are assigned until the analytical work is complete and a strategy is developed for getting the change accepted and implemented. Examples of people who might serve as part of the change agent system are included in Box 9.2.

Identify the Client System

The key questions to be explored for this activity are:

- Who will be the primary beneficiaries of change?
- Who will be the secondary beneficiaries of change?

The **client system** is made up of individuals who will become either direct or indirect beneficiaries of the change if it is implemented (Linhorst, Eckert, & Hamilton, 2005). They may desire the change but not yet be actively involved in making it happen. Depending

Box 9.2	Potential Members of the Change Agent System in a Community Effort to Promote Safe Sex Practices
• Chair	A county staff person with good organizational skills
• Teens (2)	Knowledgeable about HIV/AIDS with time available to devote to the project
• Concerned citizens	Well known in the community; who can get others to support the effort
• County board member	Someone who can run interference and get the county to support the effort
• Other interested and committed community representatives	

on the change, members of the client system may become the service users. For example, if the change results in a new prevention program for persons with diabetes, the primary beneficiaries will be those persons who use the new program. User involvement in the change process can take many different forms. Calls for participation by users in any decisions that affect their treatment, service development, and evaluation have been the subject of a growing literature on accountability to the consumer (e.g. Leung & Lam, 2014).

In Chapter 3, we pointed out that macro change efforts begin with identification of a target population and a problem. The client system is always in some way linked to the target population for whom the specific change effort is being undertaken. In some cases, it is possible that the target population and the client system could even be synonymous. For example, if the target population is all homeless people in the town of Liberty, and they ask a local housing agency for help in organizing for the purpose of requesting housing and services for all homeless people in Liberty, then the target population and client system are the same. However, if drugs are being sold out of a house in a neighborhood, and if the neighborhood residents ask for help in organizing to get rid of the drug dealers, then the neighbors represent the client system, and the drug dealers become the target population. Different terms are used for conceptual purposes. A target population brings focus to the population analysis and usually represents a broader spectrum of people. A client system refers to the people who are intended to benefit from the change effort. Sometimes they are the same, sometimes they are not.

In defining the client system, the change agent should resist the temptation to jump to the easy and obvious definition of the primary beneficiaries and should patiently and carefully analyze details. For example, if the identified problem is rising vandalism in an elementary school, the client system could include several potential beneficiaries. A partial list of those likely to benefit by eliminating vandalism from the school would include students, teachers, administrators, parents, local police, campus security, neighbors, the school board, and the community as a whole. The question, then, becomes one of establishing priorities for direct benefits and distinguishing between primary and secondary beneficiaries. The decision will have an important impact on the change effort. If "students who want a good education in a vandalism-free environment" are identified as primary beneficiaries, then the intervention may be directed toward tighter security and stricter discipline. If, on the other hand, primary beneficiaries are described as "students who commit acts of vandalism and are unable to maximize their educational opportunities due to antisocial attitudes," then the intervention may be directed toward treatment. In either case, secondary beneficiaries would be "others" on the list (teachers, parents, neighbors, etc.), who would not be the direct targets of an intervention but would benefit from the reduction in vandalism the change effort brings about.

The boundaries for macro-level changes tend to be defined in a way that the primary focus is on a segment of a community or organization. Entire communities (such as towns, cities, or counties that have formal political boundaries) or entire organizations (from small human service agencies to large, for-profit corporations) are rarely the focus of a professionally directed change effort led by a social worker, but it is not out of the question that they could be.

No matter how the primary beneficiaries are defined, the remaining groups should be identified and listed as secondary beneficiaries. It may be important to call on secondary beneficiaries when the change effort needs public support. We will refer to secondary beneficiaries as also being part of the support system (to be discussed in the next section). Remember that systems frequently overlap, and it is possible for individuals or groups to be part of more than one system. Potential primary and secondary beneficiaries in a project to promote safe sex practices and reduce the incidence of HIV/AIDS are included in Box 9.3.

Identify the Support System

The key questions to be explored for this activity are:

- What other individuals and groups (in addition to the primary and secondary beneficiaries) will support the change effort?
- Are there associations, coalitions, alliances, or organizations (local, statewide, or national) that are particularly interested in resolving problems associated with this population group or identified problem? Can their help be solicited if needed?

The **support system** is a catch-all system that refers to everyone in the larger community or organization who has an interest in the success of the proposed change. Some may receive secondary benefits, and others may be socially concerned about the quality of life of primary beneficiaries. The support system can be expected to be positively inclined toward change, and may be willing to be involved in supporting and advocating for the change if they are needed. They may be part of already established collaborative efforts. For example, the Health for Oakland's People and Environment (HOPE) Collaborative engages residents in finding ways to assess healthier, locally grown food

---

Box 9.3   Potential Makeup of the Client System in a Community Effort to Promote Safe Sex Practices

Examples of Possible Primary Beneficiaries

- All teens within the identified boundaries not knowledgeable about safe sex practices
- Selected high-risk teens within the identified boundaries
- All sexually active adults within the identified boundaries not knowledgeable about safe sex practices

Examples of Possible Secondary Beneficiaries

- Families of all who learn about and adopt safe sex practices
- High school teachers, administrators, and health providers
- The entire county-wide health provision system
- Community leaders concerned about HIV/AIDS

options and safer places to live and play. HOPE would provide support for any community change that would align with its goals (e.g., Luluquisen & Pettis, 2014).

Membership in the support system is often a matter of proximity to the problem and/or to the target population or client system. People may be interested in the change because a loved one is affected by the problem, a job brings them into close contact with those affected, or a religious or service organization with which they are affiliated has selected this population for assistance. They are sometimes described in terms of their nearness to the concern or issue by a phrase such as the *mental health community* or the *foster care community*. People who might logically be considered a part of the support system may or may not actually be identified by name and involved in activities. Sometimes a representative is the main contact to others who may be called on at a later time to lend support. They are the people the change agent will count on to become involved if decision makers need to be persuaded that the change is necessary.

Communities of practice (CoP) are increasingly being used to engage groups and individuals in addressing common concerns such as violence in the community or health disparities, particularly when problem solving is needed across locations, organizations, disciplines, or professions. CoP develop when practitioners join members across organizations, coalitions, and communities to share what they have learned in addressing the same or similar problems. Whatever form a CoP takes, there are a number of factors that appear to contribute to its success – developing and having strong leadership, identifying objectives with defined measures for the change effort, and having appropriate technological supports. For example, a CoP supporting the implementation of the Strategic Prevention Framework in Kansas used web-based tools and technology to provide virtual support. Social media such as Facebook and Twitter were used to connect coalition members, along with a Prevention Wiki to assist in creating a common language and definitions for promoting the cause. Their workstation included web-based tools to support virtual co-learning and information sharing included a platform for posting announcements, documents, digital success stories, and a blog (Anderson-Carpenter, Watson-Thompson, Jones, & Chaney, 2014). Important to the development of a support system is having accessible means of communication.

Because certain types of problems may have been identified in other locations, there may be state or national groups dedicated to their resolution. For example, if there is a state or national child advocacy group interested in the problem of child abuse and neglect and it is an area you have identified, their members may be an extended support system on which one can draw (Rycraft & Dettlaff, 2009). Similarly, in a naturally occurring retirement community in which older adults have aged in place for many years, there may be a number of coalitions and service groups already established to advocate for resident needs (Ivery, 2014). Potential support groups and individuals in a community effort to promote safe sex practices are included in Box 9.4.

Box 9.4 Potential Support System Members and Groups in a Community Effort to Promote Safe Sex Practices

- Concerned citizens
- Teachers, counselors, and school administrators
- Health providers
- Planned parenthood
- High school students

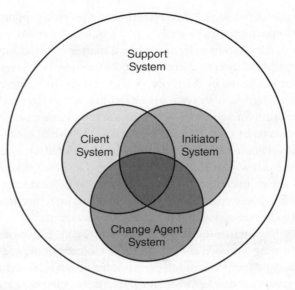

Figure 9.3
Relationship of Systems

Initiator, change agent, and client systems can be seen as incorporated within the boundaries of the support system in that they all have an interest in addressing the need for change. Initiator, client, and change agent systems may overlap or may represent separate and distinct constituencies. Figure 9.3 illustrates the relationship between initiator, change agent, client, and support systems.

Identify the Controlling System

The key questions to be explored for this activity are:

- Who has the formally delegated authority and power to approve and order implementation of the proposed change?
- Who ultimately has the authority to say "yes" to the change?

The **controlling system** is the person or group of individuals with the formally delegated authority to approve and order the implementation of the proposed change. Macro-level change almost invariably involves approval by some formally designated authority. If the change involves a public agency or publicly funded or regulated services, control may rest with a body of elected officials. If the change involves a private agency, control may rest with a board of directors. The question that must be answered in defining the controlling system is: What is the highest level to which one must appeal in order to receive sanction and approval for the proposed change? Also, because these individuals or bodies are critical for allowing the change to move forward, another important question is: What is their position on the proposed change?

The controlling system in a given episode of change is not necessarily the individual or group at the highest level of authority. It is common for a certain degree of authority to be delegated to individuals at lower levels, which means that not every proposed

---

Box 9.5   Potential Controlling System Members or Organizations in a Community Effort to Promote Safe Sex Practices

• Education of high school students	High school principal and possibly the school board
• Community education	Station managers of TV and radio stations and newspaper editor(s)
• Distribution of literature	County health director

---

change must be approved at the top. For example, if staff in a domestic violence shelter find it necessary to add legal consultation to the shelter's counseling program, it is possible that the controlling system might be the organization's board of directors, but it might also be the director of the shelter or the program manager of the counseling program. Much depends on the pattern of delegation within the organization and on the extent to which additional resources will be required. If residents in a long-term care facility are seeking changes in the provision of care, it may be difficult to know exactly who constitutes the controlling system (Kruzich, 2005). Some probing will be necessary to determine who has the authority to approve and order implementation of the proposed change because each situation is unique. Potential controlling systems in a community effort to promote safe sex practices are listed in Box 9.5.

Identify the Host and Implementing Systems

The key questions to be explored for this activity are:

- What organization or organizational unit will be responsible for sponsoring and carrying out the activities of the change effort?
- What individuals will be involved in direct delivery of services or other activities necessary to implement the change effort?

The **host system** is the organization or unit with formally designated responsibility for the area to be addressed by the proposed change. If there is an organizational chart, it should provide some guidance in identifying the host system. Typically, the host is located below the controlling system on the organizational chart. Within the host system is one or more employees and/or volunteers who will have day-to-day responsibility for carrying out the change. These employees or volunteers are referred to as the **implementing system**. In most instances of macro-level change, the host system will be a subunit of an organization that will be expected to implement a policy change, a new program, or a project. The listing of systems in Table 9.1 identifies controlling, host, and implementing systems. Again, as with the controlling system, there may be multiple host and implementing systems, depending on the complexity of the project.

The change agent should be careful not to assume that the positions and perspectives about the proposed change on the part of the controlling system, host system, and implementing system are identical. It is not unusual for those involved in the execution

Table 9.1   Examples of Controlling, Host, and Implementing Systems

	Controlling	Host	Implementing
School System	School Board	A particular school and its principal	Teachers in the school involved in the change
Law-Enforcement System	City Council	Police Chief and department	Police officers involved in the change
Social Services	State Department of Social Services	County department of social services	Social welfare workers involved in the change
Health-Care System	Corporate board of directors	Local hospital	Hospital staff involved in the change

of policy to disagree with the policy makers and vice versa. In some cases, changes may be imposed upon reluctant implementers. Figure 9.4 depicts relationships of the controlling, host, and implementing systems when structures are somewhat formalized.

In grassroots community change episodes involving coalitions and alliances or groups of volunteers, the host system may be loosely formed without a formal organizational structure. Change agents may have to assist volunteers in determining who the controlling and implementing systems are and how to access them from a position of being "outside" the system. In these cases, the "host system" may or may not be neatly nested within the concentric circles depicted in Figure 9.4. Therefore, each system should be assessed separately. Potential host and implementing system representatives in a community effort to promote safe sex practices are illustrated in Box 9.6.

Identify the Target System

The key questions to be explored for this activity are:

- What needs to be changed (e.g., individual, group, structure, policy, and practice) in order for the effort to be successful?
- Where (within the organization or community) is the target system located?
- Are there multiple targets that need to be pursued in multiple episodes of planned change? If so, what are they?

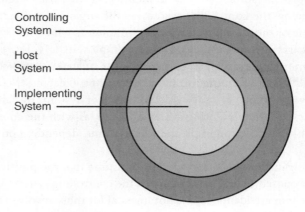

Controlling System

Host System

Implementing System

Figure 9.4
Relationships between Controlling, Host, and Implementing Systems

Box 9.6	Potential Host and Implementing System Members in a Community Effort to Promote Safe Sex Practices
• Education of high school students	Department chair and teachers responsible for the sex education curriculum
• Community education	Persons in charge of public service announcements; news reporters and columnists willing to write articles about the project
• Distribution of literature	County health supervisors and front-line personnel willing to identify patients in the target group and provide brochures and other literature

The **target system** is the individual, group, structure, policy, or practice that needs to be changed for the primary beneficiaries to achieve the desired benefits. The target system (not to be confused with *target population*) is a complex concept that cannot always be defined in clear and simple terms. What needs to be changed may often be philosophy, values, attitudes, practices, and policies as well as the provision of services. Another complicating factor is that many change efforts must address multiple targets. For example, in addressing the issue of "deadbeat dads," it may be necessary to educate the state legislature about the costs to the state of failure to pay child support before lawmakers are willing to support proposed legislation. The expected beneficiary is single mothers who are not receiving court-ordered child support, and the remedy is to pass legislation that allows officials to pursue delinquent parents across state lines and to seize assets until delinquent payments are made. In the process, reluctant legislators may resist government involvement in what they perceive as private matters and may need to be persuaded that the proposed legislation is appropriate. In this case, reluctant legislators become the first target system and, if efforts with them are successful and they propose and support the passage of appropriate legislation, efforts can then be focused on the second target system, delinquent parents, so that the client system of single mothers can finally receive the child support payments due to them.

Three questions need to be answered in defining the target system: (1) What change (or series of changes) needs to take place in order for the primary beneficiaries to achieve the desired benefits; (2) what individuals or groups need to agree to the change (or series of changes); and (3) given the working intervention hypothesis, what needs to be changed in order for the intervention to be successful? We have defined these individuals or groups as controlling, host, and implementing systems. The target system may lie within the boundaries of any or all of these systems, or it may lie entirely outside of any of them. The target system in a school experience may include selected school board members, a principal and assistant principals, a subgroup of teachers, or a selected group of students. The decision will be made based on what change is proposed and who needs to be convinced to support it.

For example, in the community effort to promote safe sex practices, the client system or primary beneficiaries were identified in a number of ways: (1) All teens within the identified boundaries not knowledgeable about safe sex practices, (2) selected high risk teens within the identified boundaries, and (3) all sexually active adults within the identified boundaries not knowledgeable about safe sex practices. This is an illustration where the client system and the target system would very likely be the same. The objective of this effort would be to change these groups from people who are unknowledgeable about safe sex practices into people who are knowledgeable and who adopt safe sex practices.

Identify the Action System

The key question to be explored for this activity is:

- Who should be represented on a central "steering committee" or decision-making group that will see the change effort through to completion?

At some point in the change effort, the central planning and steering committee moves from being the change agent system (a small group to get it started) to an action system (a larger, more inclusive group to take it through implementation, monitoring, and evaluation). Thus, as all other systems are being defined and participants selected, an **action system** is being formed. The action system is made up of individuals from other systems who have an active role in planning the change and moving it toward implementation. There may be considerable overlap between the action system and the change agent system, which was defined earlier as the professional change agent, a sanctioning organization, and sometimes a core planning group. Although the change agent system often forms the core of the action system, other actors also have important roles in providing input into decision making and should be added as the change effort proceeds. The action system should include representatives from as many other systems as possible, especially those systems in need of change, if the relationship is not excessively adversarial.

For example, if the social problem under consideration is the unmet needs of homeless persons, this need might first be voiced by a person who passes by a few old men sleeping in doorways every day on her way from the bus to her place of work (*initiator*). She finds that several other employees at her workplace have the same concern, and she takes the issue to the city council (*controlling system*), where it is assigned to the City Department of Human Services (*change agent system* and *host system*). The social worker from the department forms a task force that includes those who brought the issue to the council. As research and analysis proceed, more people are added to the task force. Professionals who work with homeless persons (*support system*) would be asked to join, as would some current or former victims of homelessness (*client system*) and someone from the city's political or administrative structure who understands the potentialities and limitations of the city's participation (*controlling system*). When all significant participants have been identified, the members of this group would become the central decision-making body in the change effort and would be defined as the action system. At this point, they would most likely be designated as a formally appointed task force or committee and given a name such as Shelter Alternatives for Everyone (SAFE). These same principles would be applied to our ongoing example of the community effort to promote safe sex practices. As key people emerge during the change process, many will be added to form the action system.

Engagement

Behavior: Apply knowledge of human behavior and the social environment, person-in-environment, and other multidisciplinary theoretical frameworks to engage with clients and constituencies.

Critical Thinking Question: Ideally, an action system will include leaders, staff, community members, and families. How can you ensure all voices are valued?

Systems in Interaction

In examining these systems in interaction, it is important to remember that we distinguish among them and define them separately for conceptual purposes only. In actual practice, all systems could be within one organization or community arena, and it is probable that many systems will overlap.

Individuals and groups critical to the success of the change effort can be depicted by diagramming those identified as being included in Figure 9.3 (those assumed to be in favor of the change) and those identified as being included in Figure 9.4 (those assumed to be in control of the decisions and resources needed to make the change happen).

The target system may lie within any of these systems or even outside all of them. The action system may overlap any or all of these systems.

An example illustrating all systems within one organization would be a situation in which an organizational change is proposed. A human service agency may have a special program for "crack babies" (babies born addicted to cocaine) and their mothers (the *client system*) that includes detoxification, rehabilitation, counseling, and parent training. After six months, a community child welfare advocate (*initiator system*) notices that the case managers (*implementing system*) have been practicing "creaming"—in other words, providing the bulk of services to the most highly motivated clients and ignoring the needs of the least motivated. In this example, this practice of "creaming" is the target—that which is to be changed (*target system*). The child welfare advocate calls the problem to the attention of the executive director (representing the *controlling system*), and the executive director directs the program supervisor (*change agent*) to form a small task group to study the problem and propose alternative solutions. The task force (*action system*) is made up of the supervisor, a case manager, a board member, an administrator, a representative of the child welfare advocacy group, and a former client now volunteering for the agency. Together they explore the problems and possibilities of directing more service to unmotivated clients.

All these have taken place within the boundaries of a single organization with some input from extra-organizational sources. Because of shifting boundaries among systems, the eventual target could become some entity completely outside the agency (e.g., focusing on working with the police to interrupt the flow of drugs to this population or supporting a community-wide drug prevention program). The reason for retaining conceptual clarity in defining the systems is that the change agent can ensure that each important perspective is represented even if the focus of the change effort changes over time.

Even though the terms *controlling*, *host*, and *implementing* may never be used, it is important that the change agent understand the domain, authority, and power of each, and that he or she keeps roles, responsibilities, and expectations for each clear and distinct. A roster such as the one illustrated in Table 9.2 may be useful in keeping track of systems and their representatives.

In Table 9.2, note how systems overlap. For example, the initiator system is women who experienced the problem, and they also become part of both the change agent and action systems. In addition, both community and organizational arenas overlap in this change effort, including organizations such as the City Department of Human Services NSD, the Mayor's Office, and the City Council, as well as community members of the neighborhoods in which the change will be implemented.

 Assess your understanding of building support by taking this brief quiz.

Table 9.2   A Roster of Systems and System Representatives

Proposed Change: To develop an orientation program and a self-help network for newly arrived immigrants who move into the local neighborhood.

System	Definition	System Representative
Initiator	Those who first brought the problem to attention	Two women who struggled through the experience of coming to this community from another country with no help available to make the adjustment
Change Agent	The professional social worker, agency, and others coordinating the change effort	The social worker employed by city, initiators, and several community members
Client	Primary and secondary beneficiaries	Immigrant families (both adults and children); local schools; employers; neighborhood residents
Support	Others who may be expected to support the change effort	Churches in the neighborhood; community organizations that deal with immigrants; city officials; selected politicians; people from other, similar neighborhoods
Controlling	The person or persons who have the power and the authority to approve the change and direct that it be implemented	The mayor, city manager, and city council, who are being asked to extend some city services, provide bilingual staff, and donate some funding
Host	The part of the organization or community that will provide auspices for administration of the intervention	The City Department of Human Services, Neighborhood Services Division (NSD)
Implementing	The staff and/or volunteers who will carry out the intervention	One staff member from the NSD (a community organizer) and 10 volunteers who were once newly arrived immigrants
Target	That which must be changed for the intervention to be successful	The majority of the City Council opposes this effort because of the precedent they feel will be established and the number of neighborhoods that will subsequently ask for funding for special needs
Action	The expanded planning and coordinating committee responsible for seeing the change effort through to completion	The Coordinating Committee will be made up of the initiator system representatives, the change agent, two representatives of the client system, one City Council member, one teacher, one employer, the community organizer from NSD, and two volunteers

EXAMINING SYSTEM CAPACITY FOR CHANGE

As the change process unfolds, participants in the systems (defined earlier) should be assessed for their readiness to support the proposed change. An assessment of readiness should include determining openness and commitment in pursuing the proposed change; strengthening the collective identity of the action system; and identifying the degree of outside resistance likely to be encountered. These considerations should be assessed based on what is known about participants who comprise each system and their previous relationships.

Task 3: Determine Openness and Commitment to Change

The key questions to be explored for this activity are:

- What has been the past experience with each of the system's participants with regard to organizational or community change?
- What levels of commitment to the proposed change and abilities to follow through are anticipated from each of the system's participants?

Reflect on Past Experiences

In organizational arenas, this assessment may be a little easier if the participants are known to one another. In community arenas, participants may be more scattered and loosely affiliated, representing constituencies that do not work together on a regular basis. Assessing the capacity of the groups that form each system to follow through with what needs to be done may make the difference in whether the proposal can successfully move forward.

Building trust among participants is central to developing openness and commitment to change. Blitz and her colleagues (2013) write about their project, which was designed to engage parents with rural schools in which their children were enrolled. Several components were identified in the engagement process that contributed to building trust among participants. First, they were intent on modeling a democratic process in which the voices and authority of families and school staff were equally respected, paying particular attention to their roles and responsibilities. They were careful to recognize and respect diverse perspectives, and to articulate shared assumptions about why the project was being developed. In the beginning they established a common language with shared meanings about the project, and reinforced this by developing accessible ways in which to communicate throughout the change process.

Openness to change involves an informal assessment, based on experience, of how people in decision-making positions have dealt with earlier proposals. Even for those systems that are promoting the change, there are considerations. Much has been written about the difficulties of getting organizations (especially bureaucracies) to change and to collaborate (see, for example, Campbell, 2009; Parrish, Harris, & Pritzker, 2013). Analyzing past experiences and general openness to change may be helpful in finding the subsystems or individuals that are most likely to be responsive to the proposed change.

Discovering openness to change is not a simple matter of asking people in decision-making positions if they are open to change. Background information such as the position taken by an individual in response to earlier proposed changes is also needed. Other pertinent questions are: Have there been community-wide issues or initiatives that included (or could have included) this set of participants? Did the host organization participate? What was its position? Have leaders who are part of the change been willing to take stands on public issues? Or do participants prefer to keep to themselves and continue business as usual? Answers to these questions will help determine general openness to change.

Assess Level of Commitment

Commitment to the proposed change could be examined in terms of each system's enthusiasm in endorsing the change as proposed (as specified in the working intervention hypothesis). It is characteristic of community and organizational change that there will be differences in perspective on what form changes should take, even when there is strong agreement that change is needed. Low levels of commitment to the change as proposed can have a negative effect on its acceptance and eventual implementation. Assessment of commitment should involve examining the degree of enthusiasm as well as the degree of internal consensus about the design of the proposed change. Open meetings—or more refined techniques, such as focus groups with parties affected by the proposed change—are useful for gaining a sense of support and degree of consensus.

Luluquisen and Pettis (2014) describe community engagement for policy and systems change. Their work in Oakland, California, focuses on community residents' capacity to collaborate over time in a series of policy changes intended to improve access to healthy food and make their neighborhoods safer places to live and play. Lessons learned in this capacity-building process are extremely relevant for social workers engaged in community change efforts. Reaching out to residents includes hosting neighborhood engagement events, interviewing community members, and asking residents to serve as team leaders in early change opportunities. Involvement of residents in every aspect of decision making is based on a belief that community leadership and ownership are necessary for successful change. Focus groups are conducted to dig deeper in understanding barriers to community participation, and partnerships are developed with local organizations. Champions are selected to promote policy and systems change. These community residents are chosen because of their communication and relationship-building skills. Involvement of youth is considered critically important because a youth lens contributes new perspectives on how problems are experienced. Small changes are selected first so that the coalition can experience early success and deeper commitment to the work. All these participatory efforts are seen as contributing to sustainable engagement.

Task 4: Strengthen Collective Identity

The key questions to be explored are:

- Does it appear that the participants in the various support systems will be able to speak with one voice and successfully work together?
- What methods can be used to strengthen and support unity?
- How can critical reflection be used to form a collective identity and purpose among action system members?
- How will the Internet, social-networking sites, and mobile technology be used to facilitate communication among action system members?

Focus on Unity while Respecting Diversity

The action system was defined as those individuals from other systems who have an active role in planning the change and moving it forward. Thus, the action system will be diverse, representing a number of different interests and not always in agreement about how to go about the change process. The action system has to be able to disagree and reflect, then function in a cohesive way, focusing on the change. In other words, there will be unity among diversity.

The social worker must be savvy about group development and group dynamics, recognizing who are the leaders within the action system and what they bring to the change effort (Seck & Helton, 2014). Does the group of people who comprise the action system have a track record of getting things done? Do they have a group identity that already bonds them over having successfully accomplished previous change episodes? If the group has not worked together before, or does not know one another well, the social worker will need to focus on team building and group development. It may be helpful to return to Chapter 3, where stages of group development and group dynamics are discussed. However, participants in an action system who have previously worked together will have experience performing as a team and may be comfortable arguing among themselves because they have developed trust and established a collective identity (Hardina, 2014; Majee & Hoyt, 2009). It may be that some participants have worked together but others have not. Helping new participants become integrated into the group may be important so that the group functions well as a whole. This may especially be the case for recently formed community coalitions with members who come from different organizational cultures, without having yet established a jointly embraced coalition culture. Ideally there should be agreement that participants in the action system will argue about their differences in meetings but will attempt to speak with one voice in any communication with public media. It takes strong interpersonal skills and political savvy to work with an action system, whether it is an internally focused organizational change, a community-wide change, or even a state policy change. The politics will vary, as will the group dynamics. Before the action system confronts the target system, it will be critical that they gel as a group. This is not to imply that they will always agree; in fact, there may be contentiousness among members when they confront difficult issues. Recall the storming process that occurs in teams discussed in Chapter 3. Regardless of what happens in the team-building process, action system members will need to trust one another enough to form a collective force to pursue an episode or multiple episodes of change.

Promote Critical Reflection

Dialogue has been used to guide group decision making in community and organization practice. Based on a postmodernist approach that calls for thinking differently about the way in which knowledge is created and understood, dialogue can be used to generate new ways of thinking about the problem at hand and to recognize how political power changes individuals' ways of perceiving problems. Experiential knowledge of members of oppressed population groups may differ from the literature on the problem that professionals may use to view the situation. Experiential knowledge comes from being embedded in social networks and having relationships with others who have experienced the problem in different ways, thus providing a range of interpretations and shared meanings (Hardina, 2014). Both experiential and professional knowledge are important in the action system's dialogue.

Hardina (2014) refers to Freire's work in the classic *Pedagogy of the Oppressed* (1970) as a basis for a dialogical approach in which action and reflection intermingle as organizational or community members engage with a professional planner as equals and co-learners. Group dialogue may occur through meetings, focus groups, and community forums with the purpose of encouraging interpersonal relationship building and the construction of shared meanings. Hardina (2014) contends that the critical reflection in which the action system engages in forming a collective identity and purpose is often neglected in the planned change process, even though it is incredibly important if the action system is to move forward in a concerted effort, and it does not stop during the implementation process. Opportunities for reflection and critical dialogue continue as long as the members of the action system are working together. The action system may face disagreement and even need to alter their best thought-out plans based on what is learned in the process, as group members have opportunities to state their views, exchange ideas, and debate issues.

There are multiple purposes of dialogue for the action system. First, in talking through strategies and tactics to be used, individuals learn from one another about options they might not have individually considered. This builds capacity. Second, in group decision making (as opposed to one expert making a decision), the authority of the group is legitimized. Third, ownership of the change process occurs when everyone's voice is heard. Together, capacity building, legitimacy, and ownership create a strong collective identity that will serve the action system well in assessing and engaging political and interpersonal dynamics (Hardina, 2014).

In engaging the action system, it is helpful to recognize the importance of psychological contracts that participants have with the organizations they represent and with other members of the action system. **Psychological contracts** are the individual's beliefs and expectations about the obligations a group or organization has to them and that they have to the group or organization. Because psychological contracts are based on perceptions, there is always room for misinterpretation. When change occurs, psychological contracts may appear to be violated because expectations may be perceived to shift (van der Smissen, Schalk, & Freese, 2013). For example, members of the action system may find that their obligations to the groups they represent are in conflict with the expectations that other action-system members have of them. They may have to assess their first responsibility to an organization, a community, or an action system when each holds a different view of the problem or how to go about addressing the problem.

For example, low-income communities often face financial exploitation and marginalization. This is not new, but what is new is the proliferation of payday lending and check-cashing services, often referred to as *predatory financial services*. Caplan (2014) suggests three community-based strategies to address these exploitive practices including (1) working with mainstream banking establishments to be more inclusive, (2) establishing alternative financial services, and (3) community advocacy for policy change. An action system formed to address issues related to predatory lending will likely include members who represent established banking systems in the community. These members represent established systems and may prefer the first strategy of working with mainstream banks to become more accessible. However, members of the low-income community may want to establish alternative financial services so that

Assessment

Behavior: Develop mutually agreed-on intervention goals and objectives based on the critical assessment of strengths, needs, and challenges within clients and constituencies.

Critical Thinking Question: In the dialogical process, what principles might guide your effectiveness in assessing and engaging diverse groups?

Watch this video on building allies. How does the speaker suggest that those interested in food justice can build relationships with community members most impacted by the problem?

www.youtube.com
/watch?v=3o_qCjAS_2Y

they do not have to engage fringe-banking services or established financial institutions. It is important to recognize these different perspectives and dialogue about them before engaging the target system.

Maximize Use of Social Media

Preferred methods of communication among action system members must be established if they are not already in place. If this is an organizational change, chances are that members are already linked through email and social media channels. A survey of several groups that have been particularly savvy in using Internet, social media, and mobile tools to strengthen their volunteer recruitment and engagement was conducted by AARP, Inc. (formerly the American Association of Retired Persons). These groups included The American Red Cross, The Alzheimer's Association, The National Council of LaRaza (NCLR), the United Way of Central Iowa, and Feeding America (Conroy & Williams, 2014).

The American Red Cross uses virtual volunteers (sometimes called online or digital volunteers) to do what is called e-volunteering or cyber services. **Virtual volunteers** describe those persons who complete their tasks, in whole or in part, off-site from action team members, using the Internet and a computer, tablet, smart phone, or other Internet-connected device. This organization developed a Team Red Cross app, so that participants could become familiar with what it's like to work on a disaster team. When an action team needs to be formed, they are already engaged and ready to join a change effort. The Alzheimer's Association has formed an online community called ALZConnected, uses Twitter to engage policy makers in their advocacy efforts, and engages Peer Volunteers to provide support on message boards to online community members. The National Council of LaRaza, an Hispanic civil rights and advocacy association, updates its members through a Mobile Action Network through which calls for action in the form of text messages keeps their support system abreast of causes. The United Way of Central Iowa has a volunteer mobile app that informs community members of local change efforts in which volunteers are needed. Feeding America stimulates conversation and action regarding hunger through its social media pages. During Hunger Action Month in 2013, they posted a Facebook application displaying a map of the United States. As users took more action to increase hunger awareness, the more orange their state would become (Conroy & Williams, 2014).

AARP (Conroy & Williams, 2014) recommends the use of social media for engaging volunteers and staff in change efforts. This requires that the action system assess members' comfort levels and establish among themselves how they will communicate with one another. Social media not only becomes a connection for action system members, but also can be used for the action system to communicate more broadly with the support system about how the change is going. Mobile technology such as smart phones and tablets are increasingly being used by diverse population groups to access the Internet. Text messaging is another way to keep everyone in the loop. Thus, action systems will likely be incorporating mobile devices into their communication network as well as developing mobile applications as an interactive way to engage members in keeping focus on the planned change effort.

Task 5: Identify Outside Opposition to Change

The key questions to be explored in this activity are:

- What individuals or groups outside the systems identified can be expected to oppose the change effort?
- What alternative perspectives are being promoted to support opposing positions?
- What individuals and groups are supporting and opposing the change, and how much strength is there on each side of the issue?

Identify External Resistance

Another factor to be explored with each system is the degree of external resistance or opposition experienced. There may be instances in which a controlling system—elected local officials, for example—supports a proposed change, but the constituency it represents—certain local neighborhood groups, for example—is opposed. Almost any proposed change that requires public funds will find external resistance from groups that are competing for the funds. If pressure tactics are to be used, the change agent should ascertain whether the pressures that can be brought about through this change effort will be able to offset pressures brought by those resisting the change. Details about these tactics will be covered in Chapter 10.

To illustrate how diverse opposition can be, Schneider and Lester (2001) identify the following categories of people from which opposition may arise: (1) individuals or groups who need more knowledge about an issue but who with adequate information might support it, (2) individuals and groups who are indifferent or neutral and would have to be convinced, and (3) those persons who are certain about their disagreement and may even be hostile (p. 125). These categories underscore the necessity of recognizing intensity of feeling, rather than just recognizing who opposes the change.

For systems promoting change, it is important to identify possible vulnerable points in overall strategic considerations. Weaknesses in supporting data or other information, illogical arguments, or people who can be pressured to back down may represent liabilities, and those promoting change should be aware of them. A summary of considerations is illustrated in Table 9.3.

Has anyone important to the success of the change effort been left out? This question is particularly important from a political perspective. Failure to involve people who can help is as potentially damaging as involving people who may harm the effort. During the data-collection phase within the organization or community, efforts should be made to solicit names of those whose support is needed to succeed.

Analyze Alternative Perspectives on the Issue

Perspective is an important consideration; it refers to the slant or "spin" individuals or groups choose to put on an issue. People involved in change in the field of human services are often amazed to learn that there is almost no concern raised that does not have an opposing view. For every advocate of a woman's right to make decisions about her pregnancy in consultation with her own physician, there is one who will support a fetus's right to survive. For every person concerned about child abuse or neglect, there is one who is equally concerned about perceived abuses of parental

Table 9.3 Assessing System Readiness For Change

	Systems Promoting Change Initiator, Client Change Agent, Support, Action	Systems to Be Changed Controlling, Host, Implementing, Target
General Openness to Change	Probably not an issue, since these groups are promoting change.	If these systems have shown tendencies in the past to resist changes of this type, this should serve as an early warning.
Anticipated or Actual Response to Proposed Change	How committed are those promoting change to the type of change being proposed? What are the differences, if any? Are some committed only to a highly specific solution?	Is there consensus or disagreement about the type of change being proposed? How strong are feelings for or against it?
Opposition to Change	What forces outside these systems are opposing change? How strong is the opposition?	What is the source of outside opposition? How strong are the pressures to reject the proposed change? What significant actors are most vulnerable to pressures?

prerogatives by child welfare workers. It is tempting to dismiss opponents' views as uninformed and unenlightened, but in undertaking macro-level change it is unwise to do so. Alternative perspectives should be carefully analyzed for their merit and their potential or actual political appeal. Plotting a spectrum of opinions, together with some educated estimates of levels of public support of each, can be an informative exercise for action system participants.

Each perspective should also be weighed for the intensity of its support. The likelihood is that the closer to the extremes, the fewer the adherents but more intense the feelings. Figure 9.5 illustrates a continuum of possible perspectives on unauthorized immigration (Cleaveland, 2010). It should be noted that as one moves along the continuum, strong feelings may be accompanied by greater conflict and contentiousness.

Intervention

Behavior: critically choose and implement interventions to achieve practice goals and enhance capabilities of clients and constituencies.

Critical Thinking Question: How might differences in perspectives about the problem change the proposed intervention in the working hypothesis? What knowledge might you use to be as inclusive as possible in rethinking the intervention?

Unauthorized migrants are trying to improve their economic status and should be encouraged to work in the United States.	Unauthorized migrants are necessary to the economy and should be granted a guest worker status.	Unauthorized migrants are costly to states. Since federal laws mandate services, federal funds should underwrite the costs.	Employers should be fined and lose their licenses if they employ unauthorized migrants.	All unauthorized migrants have broken U.S. laws by crossing borders and should be deported as quickly as possible.

Figure 9.5
A Continuum of Perspectives on Issues Related to Unauthorized Immigration

Assess Relative Strength of Support and Opposition

Once those with vested interests have been identified, a force-field analysis model can be applied (Medley & Akan, 2008). This can be done in an orderly fashion by adapting Kurt Lewin's (1947) classic techniques of force-field analysis that was originally used in understanding planned change in organizations and then applied to the emergent field of organizational development (Medley & Akan, 2008). The issue for consideration here is whether to invest additional time, energy, and resources in seeking change. The experienced change agent recognizes that there is little value in moral victories. If a change effort is to be undertaken, it should have a reasonable chance of success. Lewin's force-field analysis model identifies three steps: unfreezing, moving/changing, and refreezing. Using this model can help determine the potential to "unfreeze" the situation and transition to moving and changing (Lewin, 1947) We propose a modification of Lewin's framework that examines two areas: (1) support from individuals, groups, and organizations and (2) support from facts and perspectives. Support for or opposition to the change from individuals, groups, and organizations can be laid out in three columns. Column 1 represents the driving or supporting forces; column 2 represents neutral forces; and column 3 represents the restraining or opposing forces. Identifying each of the systems involved, together with key individuals or groups within them, provides a graphic depiction of supporting and opposing forces and will help in determining the possibility of success if the change effort goes forward. Figure 9.6 illustrates a force-field analysis.

Following the identification of individuals, groups, and organizations supporting and opposing the change effort, facts and perspectives should be identified in the same way. It is unlikely that any new research or analysis is necessary at this point, although it may be worth the effort to go online to search for updates on current debates about the proposed change and how other organizations or communities are dealing with it. Identifying supporting and opposing facts and perspectives involves drawing on everything now known and available in terms of statistics, history, theory, research, etiology, interpersonal and political factors, and resource considerations. This information is then examined for its potential driving or restraining effects on the change effort through use of the same force-field model. Figure 9.7 illustrates examples of support from facts and perspectives.

Using this force-field approach, action-system participants should initiate dialogue focused on making the "go/no-go" decision. One outcome might be a decision to gather more facts or to postpone deliberations until a more opportune time. This step is considered advisable only if the additional fact gathering is highly focused and time limited. Such proposals sometimes arise simply as delaying tactics or as ways of avoiding difficult decisions, and if so, they should be recognized for what they are and rejected. It should also be noted that this may be the point at which some participants will believe the proposed change to be unattainable and will decide to drop out, whereas others may choose to continue. Here again, it should be emphasized that the professional person acting as change agent must make as sound a decision as possible in the interest of achieving the change objectives. Necessary changes that have a good chance of success should be supported. Causes that are likely to be defeated as currently conceptualized should be tabled until they are more fully developed or until the timing is better.

? Assess your understanding of examining system capacity for change by taking this brief quiz.

SUPPORT FROM INDIVIDUALS, GROUPS, AND ORGANIZATIONS			
System	Driving/Supporting Forces ⟶	Neutral Entities ⟵	Restraining/Opposing Forces

Initiator System	• Homeless Advocates
	   T. Johnson
	   L. Stearns		

Change Agent System	• St. Catharine's
	  Parish youth worker
	  J. Foster		

Client System	• Homeless teens in Douglas County		
Support System	• Homeless Advocates • Parents of Runaway, Inc. • Existing homeless programs		

Controlling System	• City Council
	  Members supporting
	  change
		• City Council
		  Members not yet
		  taking position
			• City Council
			  Members opposed
			  to teen shelter

Host System		• City Department of Human Services	
Implementing System	• Potential contract agencies		

Target System		• City Council member
		  votes in favor of
		  funding proposed
		  teen shelter	

Action System	• Advocates
	  (T. Johnson and L. Stearns),
	  youth worker (J. Foster),
	  two homeless teens,
	  two social workers
	  from existing shelters		

Others		• A large percentage
		  of the general public
			• Taxpayers Against
			  Increased Public
			  Social Services
			  (TAPS)
			• City Newspaper
			• Task Force on
			  CMI Homeless
			  (who are competing
			  for funding)

Figure 9.6
Force-Field Analysis of Individuals, Groups, and Organizations Supporting and Opposing a Proposed Project to Serve Homeless Teens

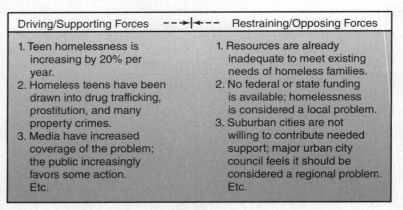

Driving/Supporting Forces -- → |← --	Restraining/Opposing Forces
1. Teen homelessness is increasing by 20% per year.	1. Resources are already inadequate to meet existing needs of homeless families.
2. Homeless teens have been drawn into drug trafficking, prostitution, and many property crimes.	2. No federal or state funding is available; homelessness is considered a local problem.
3. Media have increased coverage of the problem; the public increasingly favors some action. Etc.	3. Suburban cities are not willing to contribute needed support; major urban city council feels it should be considered a regional problem. Etc.

Figure 9.7
Support from Facts and Perspectives on the Problems of Homeless Teens

SUMMARY

As we have discussed in earlier chapters, planned change requires careful study and analysis before action is taken. We proposed in this chapter that the information compiled during the study and analysis phases be summarized into a working hypothesis of etiology and a working intervention hypothesis. This process ensures that the intervention will logically flow from an understanding of the known factors that contribute to the problem, need, issue, or opportunity.

Once a clearly conceptualized intervention has been proposed, it is necessary to begin a systematic process of enlisting support of critical participants. We have used the term *systems* and have identified eight of these that play roles of varying importance to the success of the intervention. Change agents need to know which individuals and groups make up each of these systems, who speaks for these groups, and what the groups' positions are on the proposed change. Without this knowledge, a change agent will be severely limited in getting the change accepted. A series of assessments will help the change agent understand the positions of each of the systems on the proposed change.

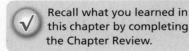

Recall what you learned in this chapter by completing the Chapter Review.

Appendix: Framework for Developing an Intervention

Task 1: Develop the Intervention Hypothesis

Refine the Working Hypothesis of Etiology

- What factors gleaned from the population analysis, the problem analysis, and the arena analysis help in understanding cause-and-effect relationships?
- What themes seem to fit best with the current situation?
- How should the working hypothesis of etiology be framed?

Develop a Working Intervention Hypothesis

- What interventions are implied by the hypothesis of etiology?
- Does it appear that these interventions are most likely to reduce or eliminate the problem?
- What results can be expected from these interventions?

Task 2: Define Participants

Identify the Initiator System

- Who first recognized the problem and brought attention to it?
- How should or can the initiators be involved in the change effort?

Identify the Change Agent System

- Who will be responsible for leadership and coordination in the early stages of the change effort?
- Is it necessary to gain approval(s) in order to move forward, and of so, from whom?

Identify the Client System

- Who will be the primary beneficiaries of change?
- Who will be the secondary beneficiaries of change?

Identify the Support System

- What other individuals and groups (in addition to the primary and secondary beneficiaries) will support the change effort?
- Are there associations, coalitions, alliances, or organizations (local, statewide, or national) that are particularly interested in resolving problems associated with this population group or identified problem? Can their help be solicited if needed?

Identify the Controlling System

- Who has the formally delegated authority and the power to approve and order implementation of the proposed change?
- Who ultimately has the authority to say "yes" to the change?

Identify the Host and Implementing Systems

- What organization will be responsible for sponsoring and carrying out the activities of the change effort?
- What individuals will be involved in direct delivery of services or other activities necessary to implement the change effort?

Identify the Target System

- What needs to be changed (e.g., individual, group, structure, policy, and practice) in order for the effort to be successful?

- Where (within the organization or community) is the target system located?
- Are there multiple targets that need to be pursued in multiple episodes of planned change? If so, what are they?

Identify the Action System

- Who should be represented on a central "steering committee" or decision-making group that will see the change effort through to completion?

Task 3: Determine Openness and Commitment to Change

- What has been the past experience with each of the system's participants with regard to organizational or community change?
- What levels of commitment to the proposed change and abilities to follow through are anticipated from each of the system's participants?

Task 4: Strengthen Collective Identity

- Does it appear that the participants in the various support systems will be able to speak with one voice and successfully work together?
- What methods can be used to strengthen and support unity?
- How can critical reflection be used to form a collective identity and purpose among action system members?
- How will the Internet, social-networking sites, and mobile technology be used to facilitate communication among action system members?

Task 5: Identify Outside Opposition to Change

- What individuals or groups outside the systems identified can be expected to oppose the change effort?
- What alternative perspectives are being promoted to support opposing positions?
- What individuals and groups are supporting and opposing the change, and how much strength is there on each side of the issue?

Assess Your Competence

Use the scale below to rate your current level of achievement on the following concepts or skills associated with each learning outcome listed at the beginning of this chapter:

1	2	3
I can accurately describe the concept or skill(s) associated with this outcome.	I can consistently identify the concept or skill(s) associated with this outcome when observing and analyzing practice activities.	I can competently implement the concept or skill(s) associated with this outcome in my own practice.

_____ Write intervention hypotheses.

_____ Identify and list participants within systems.

_____ Discuss methods used to build system capacity for change.

10

Selecting Appropriate Strategies and Tactics

WB/SHUTTERSTOCK

ASSESSING THE POLITICAL AND ECONOMIC CONTEXT

In Chapter 9, we emphasized that initiating planned change can be a time-consuming process. Although many people may agree that a problem exists, getting agreement on just how the situation should be changed is seldom easy. Therefore, social workers should be open to the possibility that practices in many of the arenas in which they operate will be well entrenched and there will be a tendency to resist change.

At the community level, decision-making bodies such as city or town councils, boards of education, parks and recreation boards, or community development boards can become entrenched in their thinking and planning. Decisions made earlier may be seen as positions to be defended rather than topics for open discussion. At the organizational level, policies and practices become a part of the culture, and change may be seen as a threat. Fellow social workers may even be a part of the commitment to business as usual.

It is likely that those affected will respond to the prospect of change based on three main criteria: perceived self-interest, perceived responsibility within a formal or informal position they may hold, or concern for how constituents may perceive the position they take on the proposed change. Sometimes the personal and public positions of the same person may differ or even be in conflict. For example, a city council member may have a relative who is homeless and knows the city needs better shelter, yet votes against a proposed new structure because business interests in the neighborhood are opposed. These kinds of actions may be taken for partisan reasons, or as a way of trading favors among decision makers. This includes consideration of partisan politics but is not limited to that arena.

Political and economic considerations add complexity to the change effort. Dealing with the political dimensions of a change effort often comes down to negotiating among competing interests. Pooling knowledge and information among those supporting the change will help in understanding how best to approach each of the decision makers who are critical to its success.

As stated in Chapter 9, the target system is the individual, group, structure, policy, or practice that needs to be changed for the primary beneficiaries to achieve the desired benefits. Analyzing the target system means assessing the systems involved. Given the discussion in Chapter 9 of various systems (initiator, change agent, client, support, controlling, host, implementing, target, and action) and their readiness for change, the change agent should have an increased awareness of the politics of the organization or community within which the change intervention is to occur. Even if a change agent believes she or he is in a situation in which there is little contentiousness or conflict, that view may not be held by others.

For example, a school district may be overwhelmed with non-English-speaking students, and the community may have factions with divergent opinions on immigration and the use of language in the classroom. In this situation, attention should be focused on creating linkages among groups before any planned change can occur. However, if the organization or community system is fairly closed, with long-standing, entrenched leadership, then attention will need to be focused on changing some of the organization's or the community's policies or practices. This will require a different approach to change because change will probably not be welcomed. Some groups, organizations, and communities will be more amenable to change than others, some will be more closed, and others will be more prone to conflict. Assessing arenas and their openness to change is central to the planned change process (Shier & Handy, 2015).

No matter how one defines the problem or how one views conflict, a certain level of conflict is inevitable. Whenever change is proposed, no matter how simple it may seem, there will be resistance. Even with willing target systems that agree to collaborate, there will be points of disagreement, even combativeness, over details or specifics of the proposed change.

Selecting appropriate tactics requires recognizing the reasons that community and organizational leaders take the positions they do. At the same time, the change agent must also think analytically about how to get the proposed change accepted and implemented. Brilliant ideas don't mean much if they end up in notebooks gathering dust in some agency's archives. For this reason, it is incumbent on the change agent to study

Watch this video about advocating for tribal HIV/AIDS education and legislation. What political considerations did the advocate make when approaching his tribal council?

www.youtube.com/watch?v=ddq4c8aC3S4

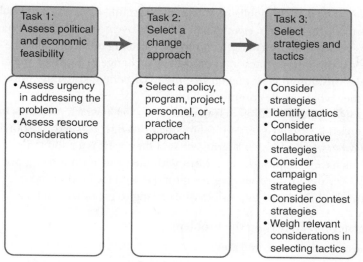

Figure 10.1
Tasks in the Framework for Selecting Appropriate Strategies and Tactics

the makeup of the target system and to decide how individuals and groups can best be approached to ensure the ultimate success of the change episode.

In this chapter, we present three tasks leading to the selection of strategies and tactics one may choose in order to effect change. Task 1, in order to assess political and economic feasibility, examines the urgency (duration, intensity, and frequency) of the problem along with resource availability (the costs of making the change, as well as the costs of doing nothing). Task 2 focuses on which approach is most feasible to pursue in the first episode of change, with the potential for there being multiple episodes that take different approaches. Task 3 involves the selection of strategies and tactics to be used and adjusted later as one episode of change leads to another. Figure 10.1 summarizes the major tasks and activities involved in selecting appropriate strategies and tactics.

Task 1: Assess Political and Economic Feasibility

Earlier, we discussed the importance of politics in bringing about change. We address these considerations more directly in this section. **Politics** as used here refers to the reasons or motivation behind the different ways individuals respond when asked to support a change effort. Preparing a list of participants in each system and assessing the political and economic strengths and liabilities of each participant can assist the change agent and action system in making the best use of each participant's skills. This raises a number of questions. Who is involved in promoting the proposed change, and how are they perceived by decision makers? Who can serve as effective spokespersons for the proposed change? Who should keep a low profile when the proposed change is presented to decision makers? Some people with valuable technical expertise may be seen as highly controversial and a liability when viewed from an interpersonal or political perspective. Previous negative experiences with decision makers should serve as a warning but should not necessarily rule someone out from assuming a high-profile role. Regardless of who is designated as the public spokesperson, careful consideration should be given to whether this person is perceived positively, negatively, or as a neutral party, and by whom. This principle applies to both community and organizational change efforts, but it may be even more important in organizational change because of the closeness of working relationships and the greater likelihood of people knowing more about each other than they would in the community arena.

Change agents have to be very clear about the ways in which proposals might be experienced by decision makers as diminishing their prestige, power, or resources available to them, or otherwise negatively altering what in their view is a good thing. Additionally, change agents have to approach their work with interests but not being overly wedded to positions; they need to find ways to compromise with facilitating and critical actors to achieve as much of their goal as possible while trying to get others on board.

Assess Urgency in Addressing the Problem

The key questions to be explored are:

- How long has the problem existed?
- Is the problem considered an emergency?
- If the problem is episodic or recurring, how often does it occur?

Community and organizational conditions can be referred to as varying in duration, intensity, and frequency. **Duration** is the length of time the condition or problem has existed. **Intensity** is the extent to which it is considered threatening to individual, organizational, or community survival. **Frequency** refers to the number of times the condition is likely to occur within a given time frame.

Long-standing problems are hard to change. People become desensitized, and community and organizational leaders are not easily persuaded that there is really a problem that needs attention. For example, it took a class action suit on behalf of the chronically mentally ill citizens in one state to force the legislature to address their needs. Yet, threats to immediate survival such as terrorism, contagious diseases, and natural disasters are recognized as emergencies and will receive priority attention. But even acute episodes can turn into chronic conditions, and in those situations it takes skilled advocates to keep the public's attention focused on the long-term recovery, cleanup, and rehabilitation efforts that are needed over the long haul.

Frequency of occurrence presents an interesting dilemma. One example is disaster preparedness in a community. Many experts in New Orleans raised concerns over the years about whether the infrastructure there was capable of handling the effects of a Category 4 or 5 hurricane, but such threats were so infrequent that efforts to strengthen barriers were delayed, eventually leading to disaster in 2005. Similarly, experts were always aware that offshore drilling held great risks and emergency plans had to be in place, but the push to drill for oil in the Gulf of Mexico appeared to have been more important than a realistic plan in the event of an oil spill since the frequency of such occurrences are low. A problem of relatively low intensity but high frequency will often be seen by community members as a higher priority than more intense, less frequent problems.

For newly emerging or newly defined problems, the change agent should examine the issues of duration, intensity, and frequency. The closer the problem is to threatening survival needs such as food, clothing, shelter, safety, or medical care, the more likely those in a position to make changes will attend to it. Occasionally, long-standing problems can be presented in a new way, as has been done with alcohol abuse in the campaign against drunk driving over the past decades, framing it as a problem of life and death rather than simply a minor indiscretion. Similarly, police shootings of unarmed Black youth have been a long-term condition in the United States, but the tipping point came in 2014 when a young Black man was shot in the middle of the street in daylight in Ferguson, Missouri. Protests began around the country, with thousands of people redefining the condition as a problem in need of immediate attention.

> ## Human Rights and Justice
>
> **Behavior:** Apply their understanding of social, economic, and environmental justice to advocate for human rights at the individual and system levels.
>
> **Critical Thinking Question:** In concerns about the shootings of unarmed Black men in the United States, how would you apply your understanding of social and economic justice to advocate for human rights at the individual and system levels?

Within organizations, problems that directly or indirectly affect the budget, and therefore the capacity of the organization to survive, tend to receive a relatively higher priority than nonbudget-related problems. The proposed change should be weighed in terms of its duration and urgency, with these factors used appropriately in selecting tactics for promoting the proposed change.

Assess Resource Considerations

Cost is often decision makers' primary concern when considering a proposed change. Social workers may not agree with this value perspective, but they must face the fact that people operate within a money-oriented system and one in which decisions are made constantly regarding how to allocate scarce resources. Decision makers often consider cost even before considering the urgency or necessity of a change. This means the change agent must understand how such decisions are made and must be prepared to address cost issues in advocating for the change. It is therefore important to determine the cost of change and the cost of doing nothing.

The key questions to be explored are:

- What anticipated costs related to the proposed change can be itemized? What must be estimated?
- What sources of financial support or in-kind donations should be approached?
- What will this problem cost the organization or community if nothing is done?
- How can this cost be framed so that it will be persuasive to decision makers as a good investment to support the proposed change?

For reasons already stated, the change agent must attempt to calculate costs associated with the proposed change. This can be difficult because in many cases the details of the intervention design are not even worked out until there are some assurances that the change will be accepted. Take, for example, a situation in which the parents in a community want the school board to sponsor more organized and supervised after-school activities. Some may want arts and crafts, some athletic activities, and some drama and music programs. When the school board is approached, these details have probably not been addressed. The change agent must be prepared for a response that "the proposed change will cost too much and resources are not available." To counter this concern, some preliminary calculations must be done, at least to the point of estimating the number of staff persons, approximate salaries required, computer equipment necessary to do the job, square feet of space needed, cost per square foot, and other rough computations. Technical expertise may have to be consulted to ensure cost estimates are realistic.

Box 10.1	Example of a Simple Line-Item Budget for an After-School Program

Personnel	Cost per Semester (in Dollars)
Arts and Crafts Instructor[1]	1,800
Music Teacher[2]	1,200
Sports and Game Supervision[3]	3,000
Operating Expenses	
Rent and Utilities	1,000
Printing and Publicity	250
Equipment & Supplies	500
Insurance	500
Total	$8,250 per semester

[1] 3 days per week @ 3 hours per day for 20 weeks.
[2] 2 days per week @ 3 hours per day for 20 weeks.
[3] 5 days per week @ 3 hours per day for 20 weeks.

A valuable statistic for comparative purposes, if it can be calculated, is the cost of nonresolution of this problem or nonimplementation of the proposed change. Such calculations may start with a simple line-item budget that demonstrates what is needed to mount a program. Box 10.1 provides an illustration of how one social worker constructed a budget for a much needed after-school program in an inner-city neighborhood.

It is important to impress on decision makers that there are long-term costs associated with doing nothing. For example, costs for in-patient or residential services can run as high as $6,000 to $7,000 a month. At first blush, an intensive vocational training program for high-risk adolescents costing $12,000 per participant per year may appear outrageously expensive. However, if presented side by side with data demonstrating that 90 percent of the service users who complete this program become self-sufficient and do not need residential treatment, decision makers may be persuaded that it really represents a long-term cost savings.

Also, a traditional "ounce of prevention" or "pay me now or pay me later"-argument may be a valid way to build support for changes designed to prevent unlikely but potentially disastrous events. The difficulty is that, too often, these calculations make sense to decision makers (and taxpayers) only in hindsight.

? Assess your understanding of assessing the political and economic context by taking this brief quiz.

SELECTING APPROACHES TO CHANGE

As the change agent completes the process of thinking through what it might cost, the nature of the problem and significant supporting information should be coming into focus. This makes clear *what* needs to be changed. This process of brainstorming together, developing a problem statement, sorting through different perspectives on how to reframe the statement, and using whatever data and information are available has been labeled **concept mapping** (Miller et al., 2012).

An important question yet to be answered is *how* the change should come about. For example, an agency's funding may be in jeopardy because its drug treatment program has been unable to demonstrate effectiveness for the past three years. Changing the ways in which these services are provided may require a policy change (e.g., redefining eligibility). Or circumstances may call for a program change (e.g., altering the type of treatment provided) or a project change (e.g., testing a new treatment approach with a limited number of clients). Changes in personnel and practices are also options, but we recommend that their use be limited to situations in which policy, program, or project approaches are determined not to be effective or feasible. These five change approaches will be discussed next.

Task 2: Select a Change Approach

The key question to be explored for this activity is:

- What approach (or combination of approaches) is most likely to achieve the desired change?

The professionally assisted change efforts discussed in these chapters are intended to fall into two general categories in which effective services are provided by healthy organizations: (1) promoting improved quality of life for the clients or communities served or (2) promoting improved quality of work life for employees as a means of helping them provide the best possible services to clients and/or communities. In order to address these two categories, we propose five approaches to change. The approach selected determines the focus of the target system.

A Policy Approach

Policy is represented by a formally adopted statement about what is to be done and how it will happen—in other words, a course of action. Policy concerning what is to be done may include broad goals and/or specific objectives, but it should be clear in establishing a direction for operational efforts. In organizations, policy about how something will happen often takes the form of an operational manual or set of guidelines for operations. Most organizations, for example, establish policies that govern accounting, personnel matters, purchasing, and other tasks.

Policies may be established by elected representatives, boards, administrators, or a vote of the people affected. In some instances, a new policy may be needed in order to change a situation. For example, establishing a policy that outlines a grievance process for staff may be empowering to employees who feel they have no recourse when they disagree with agency practices. In other situations, existing policy may need to be amended in order to make operations more effective. For instance, a family member may be the best and most appropriate caregiver for an older adult or disabled person, but agency policy may allow for paid services for professionally licensed caregivers only.

Policy Practice

Behavior: Identify social policy at the local, state, and federal level that impacts well-being, service delivery, and access to social services.

Critical Thinking Question: If you were told that "agency policy does not allow a family caregiver to be paid," where would you go to find the actual policy statement?

Program Approach

Programs are structured activities designed to achieve a set of goals and objectives. In macro practice, programs are usually intended to provide services directly to communities or groups of clients. They may also be of a supportive nature, such as fundraising, advocacy, or public relations programs. In general, programs tend to be ongoing and long term, assuming they continue to achieve their objectives.

Program change efforts differ in the type of change being sought. Some result in the establishment of new programs to serve a special population group. For example, a coalition of child-care workers recognized a growing number of homeless, runaway youth in their urban community. No existing program served this population group. Programs for homeless persons served families with children and adults but were not equipped to deal with the care of minors. Police officers could arrest the youth for loitering and curfew violations, but this was not a solution. The coalition created a new program targeted specifically to this growing population group. Other change efforts might focus on altering existing programs to make them more responsive to client or community needs. Had existing shelters been willing to accept minors, or had it been feasible to do so, the change effort might have focused on redesigning current programs to be sensitive to the special developmental and legal issues faced by the youth.

Watch this video about adapting evidence-based programs. What factors must you consider if the change you are implementing adapts an evidence-based program?

www.youtube.com /watch?v=8DDrg00dd78

A Project Approach

Projects are much like programs but may be smaller in scale, have a time-limited existence, and be more flexible. They can also be adapted to the needs of a changing environment. Projects, if deemed successful and worthwhile, are often permanently installed as programs. The term **pilot project** came into use to illustrate this type of preliminary or experimental effort.

Often change agents will find that initiating a short-term project to demonstrate a new or untested intervention is more palatable to decision makers than making a long-term program commitment. For this reason, it is common to select a demonstration or pilot project as a first approach, and then to attempt a more expansive program change if the project is successful.

Many community-wide, ambitious change efforts are dependent on project approaches. Because they may have multiple steps that will occur over several years, each step in the change process may need to be viewed as a pilot. For example, after two years of intensive pressure from a state organizing coalition, the state legislature enacted a statute requiring all law enforcement officers to document the race of anyone stopped for a traffic violation. The intent was to prevent racial profiling, but the implementation of this mandate met with resistance. The coalition to prevent racial profiling conceptualized the next steps as follows: First, assist officers in local communities to set up data collection and tracking systems; second, use reports summarizing the data generated at community law enforcement forums to talk about the findings; and, third, follow up the forums with retraining on proper procedures, and sensitivity training as needed. Although the coalition had three steps in mind, they presented each sequentially as a project so that the overall plan did not overwhelm the community and also because each step was somewhat dependent on the outcome of the previous step.

A Personnel Approach

Communities and organizations are made up of people (**personnel**) who are constantly interacting with each other. When these interactions go well, the quality of functioning and the productivity of the organization or community are enhanced. When there are problems with these interactions, however, the best policies, programs, or projects may be undermined. This means the professional change agent must be prepared to identify problems and undertake change at the personnel level, which is where people in organizations and communities come together.

Problems at this level may take many different forms. Community residents or members of a unit within an organization may experience seemingly irreconcilable differences and engage in ongoing conflict. A unit supervisor or neighborhood organizer may lack the knowledge or skill to form an effective working group. Authoritarian administrators or unresponsive elected officials may engender attempts to depose them. What these situations have in common is that they require caution on the part of the professional change agent who confronts them, recognizing that personal agendas may be involved. When a personnel approach is adopted, it is always important to recognize that there is a risk that the situation that prompted the change effort could end up worse and more firmly entrenched than it was at the outset. When taking this approach, certain questions should be asked. First, is the proposed personnel-related change effort being considered because of the reasons stated earlier—improvement of the quality of life of clients or communities, or improvement of work life so that clients or communities can be better served? Second, will the proposed change be dealt with through regularly established channels? When the target of a change effort is an individual, there is often a temptation to proceed "underground."

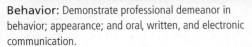

Ethical and Professional Behavior

Behavior: Demonstrate professional demeanor in behavior; appearance; and oral, written, and electronic communication.

Critical Thinking Question: Can you demonstrate professional demeanor and go underground? What ethical considerations are involved in deciding to go underground?

Practice Approach

The fifth focus of change, **practice**, applies mostly to organizations. It refers to how an organization or individuals within it carry out basic functions in ways that are less formal than written policies. At the organizational level, for example, a domestic violence shelter may have developed a common practice of having an experienced resident serve as "big sister," and orient newly admitted residents to the daily routines at the shelter. This is not a policy; it's simply the way they choose to help new residents learn the ropes. Planned change might be needed if it is discovered that some of the more cynical experienced residents have been encouraging negative attitudes toward shelter staff and shelter programs. A study might reveal that screening is necessary for the role of "big sister," and standards might be established for selection. This all remains within the relatively informal domain of practice and does not become policy until that point is reached where there is confidence in the effectiveness of the practice, and it needs to be implemented in the same way agency-wide.

Table 10.1 provides a summary of the definitions of these five approaches to change.

Table 10.1	Approaches to Change
Approach	**Definition**
Policy	A formally adopted statement that reflects goals and strategies or agreements on a settled course of action.
Program	Prearranged sets of activities designed to achieve a set of goals and objectives.
Project	Much like programs, but have a time-limited existence and are more flexible so that they can be adapted to the needs of a changing environment.
Personnel	Persons who are in interaction within the change arena.
Practice	The way in which organizations or individuals go about doing business. Practices are less formalized than policies and may be specific to individuals or groups.

Approaches in Interaction

Decisions about the change approach are obviously closely tied to decisions about the nature of the problem, the target system, and the arena. The important issues to be resolved in defining the change approach are as follows: (1) Who or what needs to be changed in order for the problem or need to be resolved? (2) What is the appropriate point of entry to address the problem or need? and (3) what approaches, or combinations of approaches, are most likely to yield the desired results?

Some changes may require multiple approaches in order to be successful. For example, a community center in a poor, Latino/a community is committed to improving the quality of life for residents. The center provides many services to the community, including a health clinic, back-to-school clothing, a food bank, after-school programs, and other community services. The social worker and several interns have completed a needs assessment to determine what the community sees as priority needs. The workers have also completed an asset assessment to determine what talents and interests community members can contribute toward strengthening the community. At an informational meeting, center staff informs community members about grants that have been applied for and about negotiations with the city to become a neighborhood targeted for specialized services. The residents express dissatisfaction that they have not been involved in these decisions and accuse the staff of having elitist attitudes about participation in decision making. Community leaders threaten to appeal to funding sources if they are not more actively involved by the center in decision making.

This issue can be approached in a number of ways. A *policy* approach would focus on creating a policy, to be passed by the board of directors, designed to ensure that community residents are involved in program and budget decisions. A policy, if monitored and enforced, would be the strongest assurance that the participation issue would be addressed, but it could become cumbersome and lead to micro-management of even small decisions within the center.

Another alternative would be to create a formal volunteer *program*, directed to continue ongoing asset assessments and to actively pursue community members to encourage and facilitate involvement in the various programs and decisions of the center. Although this approach may increase the number of residents involved in the center, it may not ensure that community members' voices are truly heard when decisions are made. Having community members present is certainly important, but the concerns are whether they are empowered to speak up and if their suggestions will be taken seriously by paid staff.

A *project* might also be undertaken that is designed to survey participants periodically to determine whether they support pursuit of various special grants or contract-funded efforts. Results of surveys could be compiled and disseminated through the community newsletter. This may satisfy some of the concern about participation, but it might also eliminate some projects that require short time frames for response.

Another option may focus on *personnel.* The social worker and other staff could be sent for training to ensure that they understand how to work with community members and how to involve them at critical points in the decision-making process. Involvement of community members could be made a part of their job descriptions and could be incorporated into their annual performance evaluations.

Finally, the focus could be on the specific *practices* identified in the community meeting, such as grant writing and collaboration with the city. Community representatives could be identified to work with agency staff on an ongoing basis to ensure that appropriate local input was a part of each decision about new programs, projects, policy changes, funding, or other activities of the organization.

An innovative change agent could probably come up with many more options and may even find ways to use a bit of each approach, if that is what it would take to bring about greater empowerment and participation. Deciding on who or what needs to be changed and what systems need to be involved is an important component of successful change. When these decisions have been agreed on, the change process is ready to move to selection of tactics, which will be discussed next.

 Assess your understanding of selecting approaches to change by taking this brief quiz.

SELECTING STRATEGIES AND TACTICS

Writers who deal with macro practice in social work sometimes use the terms *strategy* and *tactics* in different ways. Brager, Specht, and Torczyner (1987) linked strategy to long-range goals and tactics to the short-range and specific behaviors of groups.

When we use the term **strategy** in this text, we are referring to the *overall efforts* designed to ensure that the proposed change is accepted. The term **tactics** refers to the *specific techniques* and behaviors that are employed in relation to the target system and designed to maximize the probability that the strategy will be successful and the proposed change adopted. As will be seen, selecting strategies and their accompanying tactics is a process that requires careful, professional judgment.

Task 3: Select Strategies and Tactics

In Chapter 9, we provided guidelines on how to develop an intervention strategy based on what is known about the identified opportunity or problem. Strategies involve a long-range linking of activities to achieve the desired goal.

Consider Strategies

The key questions to be explored are:

- With which strategy will the change effort begin?
- Will it be necessary to consider sequential strategies, if a single strategy isn't working?
- If there are multiple, sequential targets, which strategies will be used with each target?

Change almost always involves influencing the allocation of scarce resources—authority, status, power, goods, services, or money. Decisions about strategies, therefore, must take into consideration whether the resources would be allocated willingly or whether someone must be persuaded to make the allocation. If there is agreement on the part of the action and target systems that the proposed change is acceptable and that resources will be allocated, a collaborative strategy can be adopted. If there is agreement that the proposed change is acceptable but a reluctance or refusal to allocate resources, or if there is disagreement about the need for the proposed change, then a more conflict-oriented strategy may be necessary if the change effort is to proceed.

For example, a change effort may focus on the inability of persons with physical disabilities to get around the city and travel to needed service providers. A thorough study documents the problem, and a dial-a-ride transportation service is proposed. The planning commission and city council accept the report, agree on the need, and thank the Transportation Task Force for Disabled Persons. Three city council members favor funding, three are opposed, and one is undecided. If the undecided council member can be persuaded to favor funding, then collaboration is possible. If, however, she decides to oppose funding or if a compromise would undermine the change effort, then a different strategy may be used to aggressively push for her support. For a collaborative strategy to be adopted, there must be agreement on both the proposed change and the allocation of needed resources.

In the social work literature, strategies have been categorized under three broad headings: collaboration, campaign, and contest (Brager et al., 1987; Cohen & Hyde, 2014; Schneider & Lester, 2001). In this chapter, we use these strategies to describe the relationship between the action and target systems. **Collaboration** implies a working relationship where the two systems agree that change must occur. **Campaign** is used when the target must be convinced of the importance of the change, but when communication is still possible between the two systems. The effectiveness of the "campaign" may determine whether collaboration or contest follows. **Contest** is used when, because of the strength of the opposition, neither of the other two strategies is possible. Although we organize these strategies into categories, they may also be thought of as a continuum in which the lines separating one from another may sometimes blur:

$$\text{Collaboration} \longleftrightarrow \text{Campaign} \longleftrightarrow \text{Contest}$$

In selecting an initial strategy, it almost always makes sense to begin with attempts at a collaborative strategy, and to move from left to right if it appears that collaboration will not work. Collaboration aims for win–win solutions. Once a contest strategy has been adopted, it may be difficult or impossible to recreate collaborative relationships.

What begins as a collaborative relationship may move toward conflict when new issues arise during the change process. Relationships tend to ebb and flow, depending on the nature of the change proposed, the strength of the persuasive efforts, the resources required for implementation, and other compelling issues.

Because of this ebb and flow in support for the change, the social worker should not take the relationship between the action and target systems for granted. To assume that the target is immovable before communication has been attempted would be poor professional judgment. To assume that the target will embrace the cause once the facts are known is naïve. Making assumptions about how members of the target system think without actually communicating with them may lead to misconceptions that will threaten the change effort with failure from the beginning.

There may be tension among members of the action system as persons representing established institutions may bring certain assumptions about which strategy is most appropriate to use and which ones are perceived to violate beliefs held by the groups and organizations to which they are tethered. Hoon and Jacobs (2014) coined the term **strategic taboo** to describe "those strategic options initially disqualified and deemed inconsistent with the organizational identity beliefs of strategic actors" (p. 244). For example, nonprofits struggling to sustain their niche in a local community may be averse to embracing a conflict strategy even if this seems like their only hope of effecting a needed change. In their cultures, conflict strategies may be associated with civil disobedience and radical change, whereas their cultural norms have been formed around collaboration. Conversely, radical advocacy groups may expect to encounter conflict and are comfortable with using contest strategies. Because they are so used to contentiousness, they may view collaborative change as too incremental. Their strategic taboo is against strategies that appear compromising and slow.

> Do an Internet search for "The Community Toolbox." Locate the "Toolkits" page. What resources would fit within each of the strategies discussed in this section?

Identify Tactics

The key questions to be explored are:

- Given the strategy most likely to succeed, what tactic (or combination of tactics) is needed first?
- As the change progresses, is it anticipated that changing strategies may lead to the use of different tactics?

Within each of the categories are tactics typically used to further those strategies. The choice of tactics is a critical decision point in planned change. Tactics are active steps taken on a daily basis that become the building blocks of a strategy and move participants toward the change effort's goal (Tropman, Erlich, & Rothman, 2001). As the change agent engages in tactical behavior, it is important not to lose sight of the intervention toward which these behaviors are directed or the overriding strategies that guide the change process (Rothman, Erlich, & Tropman, 2008).

The framework in Table 10.2 guides our discussion. Some of the following conceptualization is drawn from previous literature (Brager & Holloway 1978; Brager et al., 1987; Schneider & Lester, 2001), whereas in other areas we offer different perspectives or add new tactics. Throughout the following discussion, our goal is to provide an analytical framework to guide an action system in selecting the most appropriate mix of tactics.

Consider the Pros and Cons of Collaborative Strategies

Questions to be explored include:

- Is it certain that there is little or no opposition?
- Can the desired change be achieved by identifying appropriate roles for participants and implementing the change?

Collaborative strategies include instances in which the target and action systems agree that change is needed. Using a collaborative strategy implies developing a

Table 10.2 Strategies and Tactical Behaviors	
Relationship of Action and Target Systems	Tactics
Collaboration	

Target system agrees (or is easily convinced to agree) with action system that change is needed and supports allocation of resources.	1. Implementation
	2. Capacity building
	   a. Participation
	   b. Empowerment

Campaign	

Target system is willing to communicate with action system, but there is little consensus that change is needed; or target system supports change but not allocation of resources.	3. Education
	4. Persuasion
	   a. Cooptation
	   b. Lobbying
	5. Mass media appeal

Contest	

Target system opposes change and/or allocation of resources and is not open to further communication about opposition.	6. Bargaining and negotiation
	7. Large-group or community action
	   a. Legal (e.g., demonstrations)
	   b. Illegal (e.g., civil disobedience)
	8. Class action lawsuit

partnership of some sort that goes beyond what one person, group, or unit could achieve alone. This process involves communication, planning, and sharing of tasks, but it goes farther. Collaboration requires commitment among members of an action system to move toward a joint effort that will create change and achieve desired results in a community or organization. The collaboration could take a policy, program, project, personnel, or practice approach, but it requires the formation of a working relationship among all members of the action system.

The definition of the term *collaboration* varies in the professional literature. It can be used to refer to informal communication, cooperation, or coordination. For the purposes of planned change, however, collaboration must be more than just a loose affiliation. This planned change strategy requires a committed partnership among action-system members to see the change process through passage, implementation, monitoring of progress, and evaluation of success.

Formal collaboration of a number of groups leads to coalition building. A coalition is a loosely woven, ad hoc association of constituent groups, each of whose primary identification is outside the coalition (Haynes & Mickelson, 2010). Coalitions can be especially effective in response to disasters. Responses to natural disasters such as tornados and floods often illustrate the consequences of a failure to establish working coalitions. Instead of establishing areas of responsibility and lines of communication, local, state, and federal authorities often end up pointing fingers of blame for the painfully slow pace of rescue, relocation, and rehabilitation.

There is a substantial body of literature on the varying degrees of effectiveness of collaboration in enhancing service delivery and capacity building within organizations and communities (Chen & Graddy, 2010). One study examined collaboration among 10 geographically close neighborhood associations. Results showed that all 10 were struggling to address the same issues with a small core of active participants. Although they expressed a commitment to collaboration, the neighborhood associations failed to translate that commitment into actual joint efforts (Knickmeyer, Hopkins, & Meyer, 2004). A second study demonstrated that coalitions can be successful when there is a neutral, external agency willing to take the lead in supporting collaboration among coalition partners (Waysman & Savaya, 2004). A third study describes successful collaboration designed to help people with disabilities live in the community. In this study, a coordinating agency brought together home buyers, financial institutions, realtors, and other agencies to successfully move people with disabilities into independent living situations (Quinn, 2004).

Studies have also indicated a number of challenges inherent in the use of collaborative strategies, such as dealing with turf issues, recognizing when organizational cultures clash, addressing poor communication, and managing logistics. Facing these challenges can be time consuming (Takahashi & Smutny, 2002, pp. 166–167). This suggests that communication between the action and target system is only a beginning and that sustaining collaborative efforts over the time needed to complete the change may be one of the greatest challenges of their use. Nonetheless, when possible, collaborative strategies are highly desirable because they allow participants to focus their energies and resources on the change itself rather than on resolving their disagreements about what should happen.

Two primary tactics used with collaboration strategies are implementation and capacity building.

Implementation   Implementation tactics are used when the action and target systems are willing to work together. When these systems agree that change is needed and allocation of resources is supported by critical decision makers, the change can move toward implementation. Implementation will most likely involve some problem solving, but it is not expected that highly adversarial relationships will be a concern in these types of collaborative efforts.

Schneider and Lester (2001) identify activities such as conducting research and studying the issue, developing fact sheets and alternative proposals, creating task forces or subcommittees, conducting workshops, and communicating regularly with the opposition (p. 129). Depending on how far along the change effort progresses, implementation tactics may also involve such activities as creating job descriptions for employees or volunteers and ensuring that training and other work-related arrangements are made.

Although implementation may move forward by means of communication, cooperation, and coordination occurring among systems, it is important to recognize that this does not guarantee the change will be sustained. Ongoing monitoring following initial achievement of the change should thus be considered an integral part of the overall process.

Capacity Building   Capacity building includes the tactics of participation and empowerment. *Participation* refers to activities that involve members of the client system in the change effort. *Empowerment* refers to the steps needed to free members of the client system from real or perceived barriers to participation. Using an empowerment perspective means recognizing the power differentials within a community and working to promote positive change among all community members (Gutiérrez, Lewis, Dessel, & Spencer, 2013). Empowerment can be viewed as both a process and an outcome in which people actually gain a psychological view that it is possible to make change happen.

For example, a problem may be defined as the exclusion of members of a neighborhood from decisions affecting them (such as rezoning, street repairs, installation of lighting, or selection of city-sponsored recreational programs for the neighborhood). The focus of the intervention is on building capacity for greater self-direction and self-control—that is, actually teaching people how to get involved in decision-making processes in their communities and taking greater control over those that affect their lives. This approach often emerges in situations where disenfranchised communities become targets for development, freeways, airport expansion, and other encroachments, or when a neighborhood is neglected and allowed to deteriorate by apathetic local authorities.

Professionally assisted change efforts in this example would focus on bringing together selected systems. In the example, a neighborhood social service agency may serve as the change-agent system, a neighborhood resident may represent the client system, and the city council may be the controlling (and perhaps target) system. The objective is to get all to agree that citizens should have a greater voice in developments that affect their community. The focus of the empowerment tactic, however, is not on changing the target system (city council/planning commission) but on educating, training, and preparing citizens for a fuller participation in decisions that affect their communities.

Empowerment involves enabling people to become aware of their rights, and teaching them how to exercise those rights so that they become better able to take control of factors affecting their lives. Mobilizing the efforts of self-help groups and voluntary associations identified in Chapter 5 as well as the client system's informal support structure may also help guide the target system toward consensus with the change effort.

Consider the Pros and Cons of Campaign Strategies

The key questions to be explored are:

- Who needs to be convinced that the proposed change is needed?
- What persuasive techniques are most likely to be effective?

Campaign strategies are used when members of the target system do not necessarily agree that the change is needed but may be willing to listen to arguments on its behalf. This is likely to require a good deal of skill on the part of the change agent and action system, in part because it will first be necessary to determine why members of the target system don't agree with the change. Is it because they lack information about its need and potential benefits? Is it because they mildly disagree but are not yet immovably opposed? Or is it because they prefer to remain uncommitted until clearer evidence is available about the wishes of their community or organizational constituents?

Campaign strategies require an understanding of the target and a calculation of what tactics are most likely to succeed. Elected officials are likely to be motivated by issues important to constituents. Agency executives must be responsive to a governing board, consumers, staff, and funding sources. Understanding the context in which the target system functions can be helpful in shaping the campaign. Specific tactics most commonly used with campaign techniques address these different possibilities.

They include education, persuasion, cooptation, lobbying, and mass media appeals designed to influence public opinion.

Education   Educational tactics involve various forms of communication from members of the action system directed toward those in the target system. These communications may include face-to-face meetings, formal presentations, or written materials. The goal is to present perceptions, attitudes, opinions, quantitative data, or other information about the proposed change, and to inform members of the target system in ways that may lead them to think or act differently about the proposed change. This often involves specialized skills such as compiling statistics and developing PowerPoint presentations. The assumption is that more and better information will lead to a change in behavior.

Education can be a difficult tactic to use because opponents of the change can also be expected to attempt to provide decision makers with different information, and there is no absolute "truth" in dealing with complex organizational or community problems. In many cases where education fails to produce the desired result or falls short of having the desired impact, the change agent turns to persuasion.

Persuasion   Persuasion refers to the art of convincing others to accept and support one's point of view on an issue. Social workers must frequently use persuasive tactics in addition to collaborative tactics because their belief that a change is worth pursuing is not always shared by decision makers. This means that the change agent must understand the motives and reasoning of the target system in order to identify what incentives or information might be considered persuasive by members of the target system.

Skillful communication requires that the action system carefully select as leaders those individuals who have the ability to persuade. Persons who are seen as nonthreatening by members of the target system and who can articulate the reasoning behind the planned change are particularly useful. For example, in a change effort, certain actors may be seen as unreasonable, as troublemakers, or as chronic complainers by members of the controlling system. Although this may be an unfair characterization, it is still best not to use those individuals as primary spokespersons for the change. Credibility with representatives is an important consideration in selecting a spokesperson. Service users can sometimes be powerful spokespersons, providing both information and a viewpoint that convinces people of the need for change.

Framing the problem statement to make it more palatable to target-system members is also a useful persuasive technique. This requires thinking as the target thinks. For example, a social worker hired as a long-term care ombudsperson was working closely with a coalition of advocates for nursing home reform to end abuse in long-term care facilities. Nursing home administrators were upset over the nursing home reform coalition and perceived the members as not understanding the difficulties with which the administrators coped on a daily basis. Although sincerely wanting to provide quality care, they were frustrated by having to hire staff who were not properly trained to work with geriatric populations. By framing the problem as a training problem designed to better prepare employees and reduce turnover, the ombudsperson was able to persuade administrators to cooperate with the action system. When the ombudsperson met with the local nursing home association, she made it clear that she believed administrators shared her goal of wanting high-quality facilities. She also noted that recent studies showed that high staff turnover rates led to lower quality care and sometimes to abuse. She explained that she and her colleagues would be willing to develop training for nurses' aides because they were the staff who interacted most closely with patients yet were most vulnerable to turnover. The result was that a key factor leading to abuse was being addressed, but it was framed as reducing an administrative problem—high staff turnover.

Cooptation   Cooptation is closely related to persuasion and is defined as minimizing anticipated opposition by absorbing or including members of the target system in the action system. Once target-system members are part of the planned change effort, it is likely that they will assume some ownership of the change process and may be able to recruit others from the target system into the action system. Where there is a hierarchy of power, authority, and influence within the target system, cooptation efforts can be effective if they can find a role for influential people in the change effort. For example, allowing their names to be used in publicity materials may sway others who respect their opinions and may also give the supporter a high profile associated with a worthy cause. Cooptation is most effective as a tactic when opponents or neutral parties can be shown how supporting the change may serve their own interests as well as the interests of those who will benefit from the change.

Cooptation can be formal or informal. **Informal cooptation** refers to gaining support from an individual. **Formal cooptation** involves a group agreement, through vote or some other formal means, to support an issue. Depending on the prestige or prominence of the individual or group, a public statement of support can be helpful to the cause.

Lobbying   Lobbying is a form of persuasion that targets decision makers who are neutral or opposed to a proposed change. Full-time lobbyists are paid to represent a special interest; typically, they target elected officials to get their support and their votes. Nonprofit organizations sometimes pool resources to hire a lobbyist to support or oppose legislation affecting the human services industry.

The Democracy Center (2004) identifies five types of decision makers with whom lobbyists typically deal. Champions are dedicated advocates for your cause. Allies are on your side but not outspoken advocates. Fence sitters are uncommitted and are key targets for lobbying. Mellow opponents are clear votes against your cause but not inclined to be active on the issue. Hardcore opponents lead the opposition.

Haynes and Mickelson (2010) delineate three essential concepts for social work lobbyists to consider. First, one should always be factual and honest. Trying to second-guess or stretching the facts to support one's position can be devastating to one's professional reputation as well as to the change effort's credibility. Second, any presentation should be straightforward and supported by the available data. The problem identification and analysis process discussed in Chapter 3 will assist the change agent in organizing the rationale for change. Third, any discussion should include the two critical concerns of decision makers: the cost and social impact of what is proposed. If the cost is high, the change agent may still be able to gain leverage by providing evidence that allowing the problem to remain unresolved will also be costly.

Mass Media Appeal   Mass media appeal refers to the development and release of newsworthy stories to the print and electronic media for the purpose of influencing public opinion.

Direct mail, phone calls, texting, email, websites, and social media sites are all viable ways to get the word out. Instead of selecting one outlet for one's appeal, multiple ways of reaching out can be simultaneously used. Word of mouth is still considered to be the most effective method of inciting people to action, but it is important to note that using social media is a form of word of mouth. Thus, social networks offer an efficient way to get the word out to many people simultaneously (McPherson, 2015).

This tactic can be used to pressure decision makers into a favorable resolution to the identified problem. It is expected that if the proposed change can be presented to the public in a positive way and decision makers' refusal to support the change can be presented as obstructionist or somehow negative, decision makers will feel pressured to change their position. Because decision makers often occupy high-profile positions, such as elected representatives who depend on a positive public perception, this can be an effective tactic. However, it is also important to note that sometimes elected representatives want the public to know that they are opposed to a particular action, and mass media appeals may cause them to become even more firmly committed to their opposition. Initiating a mass media campaign through print and television media will depend on convincing a reporter or editor that the proposed change is a newsworthy story. On the other hand, more and more information is being disseminated through social media outlets and there are no editors monitoring what is released. A consideration for advocates is the importance of launching their stories from sites that have credibility (Deschamps & McNutt, 2014).

Using the power of the Internet means more than simply creating a Facebook page or uploading a story onto YouTube. Extensive evidence suggests that electronic advocacy is being used more and more to rapidly reach large numbers of people. Deschamps and McNutt (2014) cite several fundamental differences between traditional civil society and virtual civil society. First, **flash activists** have emerged to mobilize large numbers of people to promote causes. They are using Twitter, blogs, and Facebook. Often they are mobilizing people across large geographical areas. Second, because they are not always connected to specific organizations or coalitions, **free-agent activists** are more evident. They are connected to causes rather than groups or organizations, and their credibility depends on how they present their message. An emotional message or horrific picture may incite a following. Third, social media allow people to evaluate how much they like the content. For example, hits on a YouTube can actually influence others to view the content simply by the numbers of persons who have viewed the content already. Fourth, as nonprofit and public organizations bring their brands to social media channels, they face a dilemma. They can certainly influence more people, but they decrease the control they have over their message. For example, Menon (2000) reports how one online discussion group developed a campaign to educate others about the issues faced by persons with severe mental illnesses. In the process of being transformed from a discussion group to a virtual community, participants learned how important it is to deal with issues while they are "hot." They also recognized the importance of having a campaign plan when numerous messages are posted in a short time frame. Social networks thrive on user-generated content, and sending electronic messages allows others to pull content into their streams and feeds for their personal network to consume. Soon, the word is out, but like gossip it may become comingled with data and information that can be misinterpreted or has not been verified by a reliable source.

Intervention

Behavior: Use interprofessional collaboration as appropriate to achieve beneficial practice outcomes.

Critical Thinking Question: In interprofessional collaborations, how can social media be used to achieve beneficial practice outcomes?

Internet forums using websites and blogs have become increasingly important tools of communication on various issues, making members of the action system less reliant than in the past on traditional print or broadcast media. Whatever mass media option is used, professional ethics require that the change agent ensure that information on the change effort is presented accurately and that any use of media includes consideration of clients' rights to privacy.

Consider the Pros and Cons of Contest Strategies.

The key questions to be explored are:

- Is opposition to the proposed change so strong that it can only be successful by imposing the change on an unwilling target system?
- Can the proposed change be effective if it is forced?
- What are the potential consequences of conflict?

A contest strategy is used in situations where (1) target system representatives cannot be persuaded by the action system, (2) target system representatives refuse to communicate with the action system, or (3) members of the target system pose as being in favor of the change but do nothing to further it or secretly work against it. Use of a contest strategy means that the change effort becomes an open, public dispute as attempts are made to draw broad support and/or to coerce the target system into supporting or at least accepting the change. Once this occurs, the action system must be prepared to face open confrontation and potentially be the subject of varying types of backlash from those in the target system.

Conflict is inevitable in social work practice. There will be times in the experience of every practitioner when formidable resistance is encountered in addressing the needs of oppressed population groups. To some extent, conflict is inherent in a profession that developed in response to a basic societal conflict—the persistent antagonism between individualism and the common good.

Schneider and Lester (2001) offer a list of specific tactics used with contest strategies that includes the following: seeking a negotiator or mediator; organizing large demonstrations; coordinating boycotts, picketing, strikes, and petition drives; initiating legal action; organizing civil disobedience and passive resistance; and arranging a media exposé. For easier discussion, we will group contest tactics into three main categories: bargaining and negotiating, large-group or community action, and class action lawsuits. The second tactic, large-group or community action, can be further divided into legal and illegal actions.

Before our discussion of these tactics, it should be noted that their use will require widespread commitment and possible participation from members of the support system. To illustrate this point, Rubin and Rubin (2008) refer to contest tactics as confrontational approaches, and confrontation implies the possibility of strong negative reactions that are less likely with other strategies. Because of these risks, it is critical to the success of contest strategies that the support system and its subsystems—initiator, client,

Watch this video about the battle for a living wage. What strategy and tactics do fast food workers take in the video? Why do you think that strategy was chosen?

www.youtube.com /watch?v=Jqzq5Kxcr7U

and change agent—are comfortable with confrontation and aware of its ramifications and potential consequences. It is likely that the time and energy necessary for effective change will increase and that relationships can become disrupted.

When collaborative and campaign strategies have been employed and either stalemated or failed, tactics can move toward contest. However, once a contest strategy is underway, it is not likely that one can return to collaborative or campaign tactics. For these reasons, contest strategies should usually not be considered as a first option.

Bargaining and Negotiation   Bargaining and negotiation refer to situations in which the action and target systems confront one another with the reasons for their support and/or opposition to a proposal or an issue. There is typically a recognized power differential between parties, and compromises need to be made. These tactics are more formalized than persuasion and sometimes involve a third-party mediator. Members of the target system will usually agree to negotiate when the following factors are in place: (1) there is some understanding of the intentions and preferred outcomes of the action system, (2) there is a degree of urgency, (3) the relative importance and scope of the proposed change are known, (4) there are resources that facilitate the exercise of power, and (5) the action system is seen as having some legitimacy. In order to negotiate, both the action and target systems must believe that each has something the other wants; otherwise, there is no reason to come together.

Schneider and Lester (2001) suggest that the involvement of a third-party mediator becomes advisable when alienation between the action and target system occurs. For example, a domestic violence shelter receives a donation of a building in a transitional area between commercial and residential areas. Both residents and business owners angrily oppose rezoning this area for this use because they fear possible violent confrontations that might erupt from angry spouses or partners. A mediator in this situation would attempt to lay out the concerns of all parties and find a middle ground that protected the interests of both sides. Perhaps the shelter could provide assurances that disgruntled spouses' or partners' concerns could be kept off the streets and managed within a "safe room" within the shelter. If a solution could not be worked out, the business owners may agree to buy a building in another area and exchange it for the one in their neighborhood.

If handled well, bargaining and negotiation can lead to win–win solutions, where both target and action systems are pleased with and fully support the outcome. However, the result can also be a win–lose, where one system is clearly the victor, or a lose–lose, where both systems give something up, are disappointed in the results, and are possibly worse off than before the change.

Large-Group or Community Action   Large-group or community action refers to the preparing, training, and organizing of substantial numbers of people who are willing to form a pressure group and advocate for change through various forms of collective action such as picketing, disruption of meetings, sit-ins, boycotting, and other such confrontational tactics. Peaceful demonstrations are legal activities, often used by groups on either side of an issue to express their views. The pro-life and pro-choice movements are examples of groups that regularly use this tactic.

Civil disobedience activities intentionally break the law. For example, Rosa Parks deliberately defied a local ordinance when she refused to move to the back of a bus in Montgomery, Alabama, in 1955. Environmental advocates have blocked access to construction sites when forests or endangered species were jeopardized. Animal rights groups have sprayed paint on fur coats, destroying property in protest. Antiabortion activists have harassed physicians and patients at abortion clinics. A critical line, first articulated by Mohandas Gandhi while leading the struggle against British rule in India in the first half of the twentieth century, is usually drawn between illegal but nonviolent protest and actions that involve violence against others. Social work principles strictly forbid the latter but recognize the former as a legitimate tactic in cases such as the oppression of disadvantaged groups. Still, when action-system members deliberately engage in illegal activities, they must be ready to accept the consequences of their actions. The change agent is responsible for making potential participants fully aware of these risks before the decision is made to proceed.

Class Action Lawsuits   Class action lawsuits refer to those instances where an entity is sued for a perceived violation of the law and it is expected that the finding of the court will apply to an entire class of people. These tactics are often used with highly vulnerable populations such as persons with severe mental illness, homeless persons, and children, who are unlikely to have the capacity or the resources to protect their own rights. Public interest law organizations may be resources for the action system in developing class action tactics.

Class action suits have been used by a variety of groups on behalf of many different client populations. They are a particularly common tool of advocacy and watchdog organizations seeking to ensure that certain service standards are met. In the child welfare arena, an organization called Children's Rights, Inc., has filed class action suits against child welfare agencies in more than a dozen states in the last 25 years, alleging failure to provide adequate services. The defendants have often been city, county, or state governments. When successful, these suits have forced the defendants to upgrade staff and facilities, improve or implement new programs, and invest other types of resources to correct service deficiencies. A follow-up study of a small community in New Hampshire where a class action lawsuit challenged inequitable funding for education revealed a side benefit of a sense of community empowerment through involvement and participation in the action (Banach, Hamilton, & Perri, 2004).

Weigh Relevant Considerations in Selecting Tactics

The key questions to be explored are:

- What is the purpose of the change effort, and has that purpose been altered during the change process?
- What is the perception (by those promoting change) of the controlling and host systems?
- What is the perception (by those promoting change) of the role of the client system?
- What resources are needed and available for each tactic?
- What are the ethical dilemmas inherent in the range of tactical choices?

Selecting the proper strategy and tactics is an important but difficult task, and several considerations need to be weighed in determining which approach is best. We briefly address each of these considerations next.

Purpose   Change goals often evolve as the change process moves along; therefore, a reexamination prior to selection of tactics is in order. For example, with the problem of domestic violence, the condition may have been brought to public awareness by the perceived need for additional emergency shelter space for battered women. However, as the problem is analyzed and better understood, the purpose may shift toward consciousness raising for all women in the community who are at risk of violence. Thus, strategy and tactics would move from advocating for service provision to educating for empowerment.

Because tactics can change as purpose and goals change, it is worthwhile to make a final check to ensure that members of all the relevant systems are clear and in agreement with the working hypothesis as it has evolved. If any system members, especially those in the action system, have concerns about the goal or nature of the change, further dialogue should take place before proceeding. Certain types of goals tend to be approached through certain types of tactics, and this can help ease the selection process. A variety of goals and their typical accompanying tactics are displayed in Table 10.3.

Controlling and Host Systems   The controlling and host systems can be perceived in a variety of ways. If they are active supporters or sponsors of the change, it may be possible to move quickly to implementation tactics (as part of a collaboration strategy) to bring about the change. If members of these two systems are supporters but not participants in the change, capacity building (through participation and empowerment) may be the tactic of choice. If they appear to be neutral or indifferent, one or more tactics in the category of campaign strategy may be in order. Finally, if the members of these systems are oppressive or unresponsive to their primary clientele, then one or more tactics related to a contest strategy are likely to be needed. Table 10.4 illustrates the various perceptions of roles that might be assigned to the controlling and host systems, and the logical tactic for each.

Primary Client   The role of the primary client can vary, and the way in which this role is perceived can affect selection of change tactics. Sometimes it may be difficult to

Table 10.3   Relationship of Goals to Tactics

Type of Goal	Relationship of Target and Action System	Possible Tactics
1. Solving a substantive problem; providing a needed service	Collaborative	Implementation through joint action
2. Self-direction; self-control	Collaborative	Capacity building through participation and empowerment
3. Influencing decision makers	In disagreement but with open communication	Education, persuasion, mass media appeal; large-group or community action
4. Shifting power	Adversarial	Large-group community action
5. Mandating action	Adversarial	Class action lawsuit

Table 10.4   Relationship of Controlling and Host System Roles to Tactics

Perception of Role of Controlling and Host Systems	Relationship of Controlling, Host, and Action Systems	Possible Tactics
1. Sponsors; supporters; co-participants; colleagues	Collaborative	Implementation through joint action
2. Neutrality or indifference	Collaborative	Capacity building through participation and empowerment
3. Uninformed barriers, or not sure about change	In disagreement but with open communication	Education and persuasion
4. Informed barriers, or opponents to successful change	Adversarial	Bargaining; large-group or community action
5. Oppressors	Adversarial	Large-group community action
6. Violators of rights	Adversarial	Class action lawsuit

determine who the primary client really is. For example, in addressing the needs of older persons, the change agent may learn that many caregivers are suffering from stress and fatigue and are unable to provide quality care to the older persons for whom they are responsible. In this situation, one must ask if the primary beneficiaries of a change effort will be the older persons themselves or their caregivers.

If the primary client is seen as a consumer or recipient of services, an implementation tactic (as part of a collaborative strategy) will usually be the most suitable approach. When clients are primarily residents of a community or potential participants in an effort to achieve self-direction and control, then a capacity-building tactic (as part of a collaborative strategy) might be preferable. If the primary client is a group in need of a particular service, but this need is not acknowledged by the controlling system, one or more tactics within the realm of a campaign or even a contest strategy may be needed.

For these reasons, it is important to know how members of the action system perceive the primary client, how those in the client system perceive their roles, and if the perceptions are in agreement with those of members of the action system. Having clients as action-system members (overlapping the client and action systems) can go a long way toward providing a medium for information exchange between clients and change agents. Table 10.5 displays client roles, approaches, strategies, and tactics.

Resources   Key considerations in choosing tactics are the nature and quantity of resources available to the action system because some tactics require more or different types of resources than others. If collaboration is the strategy of choice, for example, one necessary resource will be technical expertise capable of understanding whether the change is being properly implemented, monitored, and evaluated. In order for a capacity-building tactic to be used, grassroots organizing ability, together with some teaching and training expertise, must be available to the action system. If there is disagreement calling for a campaign or a contest strategy, either skilled persuaders, media support, large numbers

Table 10.5 Relationship of Client System Role to Tactics

Perception of Role of Client System	Relationship of Client and Target Systems	Possible Tactics
1. Consumer; recipient of service	Collaborative	Implementation through joint action
2. Resident of the community in need of greater self-direction and self-control	Collaborative	Capacity building through participation and empowerment
3. Citizen-taxpayer not permitted full participation	In disagreement but with open communication	Education and persuasion
4. Victim; underserved needy person	Adversarial	Mass media appeal
5. Victim; exploited person	Adversarial	Large-group community action
6. Person denied civil rights	Adversarial	Class action lawsuit

of people willing to do what is necessary to bring about change, or legal expertise will be needed.

Earlier in this chapter, we discussed the importance of determining the cost of change by putting together a budget of expenditures that would be needed for the change to be successful. A similar exercise can be helpful in relation to determining the resources needed for the preferred tactics to be successful. Costs for such items as expertise, supplies and equipment, postage and mailing, training, meeting rooms, and other such needs should be itemized at this point, and calculations made of anticipated costs. Volunteers and in-kind contributions should be sought to fill as many needs as possible. Resource considerations are illustrated in Table 10.6.

Table 10.6 Resources Needed by Action System for Each Tactic

Tactic	Resources Needed
1. Collaboration—joint action or problem solving	Technical expertise; monitoring and evaluation capability
2. Capacity building	Grassroots organizing ability; teaching and training expertise; opportunities for participation; some indigenous leadership; willing participants
3. Persuasion	Informed people; data and information; skilled persuaders or lobbyists
4. Mass media appeal	Data/information; newsworthy issue or slant; access to news reporters; technical expertise to write news releases
5. Large-group or community action	Large numbers of committed people (support system); training and organizational expertise; informed leadership, bargaining and negotiating skills
6. Class action lawsuits	Legal expertise; victims willing to bring action and provide information; at least enough money for court costs

Professional Ethics   In Chapter 1, we discussed the importance of values in social work practice. Ethics are the behaviors that bring values into action. An **ethical dilemma** is defined as a situation in which a choice has to be made between equally important but seemingly conflicting values. Tactical choices may often present actual or perceived ethical dilemmas in that they usually involve a clash of values between members of different systems. This is especially true in the case of conflicting action- and target-system values that can lead to the selection of contest tactics.

Ethical principles were highlighted in Chapter 1, and these principles are of great significance to macro-level change. A clash between the principle of dignity and worth of the person (autonomy) and the principle of service (beneficence) can occur when members of the client system are determined to resist risking what little they have (autonomy), whereas action-system members want to push for a quality-of-life change on the clients' behalf (beneficence). When such a conflict emerges, the rights of clients take precedence over the wishes of the action system.

This clash was illustrated in a social work intern's first field experience. Working for a small community center in the Southwest, she discovered that many of her Latino clients lived in a crowded apartment complex with faulty wiring and inadequate plumbing. With the backing of her agency, she began talking with clients to see if they would be willing to engage in a change process directed toward correcting these problems. As she analyzed the situation, she realized that any change process would involve housing and public health personnel in the action system. Her clients begged her not to involve these authorities because many members of the client system were undocumented and they feared this fact would become known and could lead to their deportation, which they considered worse than the poor housing conditions. The client system's autonomy was in conflict with the change agent system's beneficence.

The clash between social justice and autonomy is exemplified when the members of the action system demand redistribution of resources and members of the target system believe that, in giving up their control over valued resources, they will have less freedom. Macro change frequently appeals to the principle of social and economic justice, for it is usually through the redistribution of valued resources (for example, power, money, and status) that change occurs. Because social justice is a basic ethical principle that raises emotions when it is violated, change agents can become so obsessed with injustice that any tactic is viewed as appropriate if it leads to a successful end.

It is our contention that this type of thinking can lead to professional anarchy, whereby tactics are perceived as weapons to punish the target system rather than as actions to enrich the client system. In these situations, it may be too easy for the change to take on a life of its own and for the professional to blindly wrap him- or herself in a cloak of beneficence while ignoring other actors. Righteous indignation may overtake sound judgment. The foregoing points should not be interpreted to mean that factors such as horrible living conditions or basic needs should be ignored because clients fear change. The issue is client system rights. If clients can be persuaded that conditions can be improved without risk or that the risk is worth it, then it is acceptable to proceed. If they cannot be persuaded, then campaign or contest strategies may need to be discontinued, unless some means of protecting clients can be identified.

Use of Covert Tactics The concept of "transparency" has become increasingly important in transactions that take place within both government and private organizations. **Transparency** refers to keeping actions and decision-making processes in the open and available to scrutiny by the public and the media. It is intended to protect the public against self-serving actions or ethical lapses. The question is whether the concept of transparency also applies to individuals or groups attempting to initiate change in organizations or communities. When change is being considered that requires those in power to give up some to those not in power, there may be some risk that openness or transparency will result in failure of the change effort. In situations like these, the need for secrecy must be carefully weighed against the risk of mistrust and possible charges of ethical violations. When actions are begun in secret, those involved in initiating the change episode must recognize that at some point they will be made public, and all actions should be handled in a way that they will pass the ethics test when they are brought out into the open.

An example of use of covert tactics arises when an employee feels there is a need for a "whistleblower" within the organization due to perceived unethical or illegal activities. If, for example, a child welfare worker believes that all complaints of child abuse and neglect are not being investigated in accordance with established protocols, he might begin by keeping a log and recording perceived violations. At some point, the worker would compile his data and perhaps take it to the director of child welfare services. The worker may agree to a plan and a timetable for correcting the practices, while letting the director know that if deadlines were not met he would turn his data over to Children's Rights, Inc., and the issue may end up in court.

Selecting the Proper Tactics There are few situations in which there is clearly a "right" or "wrong" tactic. Berlin (1990) explains that thinking in terms of bipolarizations can make people vulnerable in that they look for specific answers to what are highly complex questions. In fact, there are many gray areas in which simple answers will not suffice and in which differences must be respected. Box 10.2 raises a number of questions to guide consideration of professional ethics in selecting the proper tactics.

It is common to think dichotomously (e.g., win–lose, right–wrong, good–bad, or consensus–conflict). In conflict situations, it may be useful to force confrontations and bring opposing views into the open. However, dichotomous thinking about the

---

Box 10.2 Questions to Guide Consideration of Professional Ethics

1. What are the value conflicts between the target and action systems?
2. What ethical principle(s) appear to be guiding the activities of the action system?
3. Is there the potential for a clash of ethical principles between the client and action systems?
4. If covert tactics are being considered, what conditions have led to this decision?
   a. The mission of the target agency or the community mandate is being ignored.
   b. The mission of the target agency or the community mandate is being denied for personal gain.
   c. Change efforts have been tried through legitimate channels, but the target system will not listen.
   d. Client system members are fully aware of the risks involved but are willing to take the risks.
   e. Other.

situation may reinforce the beliefs of a radicalized change agent that the target system represents "evil" and the action system represents "good." Although this achieves the objective of fueling confrontation, it may undercut any potential progress by making it more difficult to find common ground and accept realistic accommodations. For this reason, we believe that the professional social worker has a responsibility to avoid dichotomous thinking and to carefully analyze circumstances surrounding a change episode before making assumptions that lead directly to the use of contest tactics. This means the majority of change efforts will utilize collaboration and campaign tactics as the action and target systems attempt to achieve mutually acceptable solutions. Although collaboration—contest is a dichotomy, we believe the majority of interactions happen in the various gradations in between. When all the foregoing tasks have been completed, the proposed change should be written up in the form of a short, concise plan. Chapter 11 is devoted to a discussion of this process.

> **?** Assess your understanding of selecting strategies and tactics by taking this brief quiz.

SUMMARY

In this chapter, we began with the political and economic contexts within which change occurs. In order to fully assess context, it is necessary to examine how various parties view the urgency of the proposed change. This involves assessing the duration, intensity, and frequency of the problem. Equally important is considering the feasibility of change in light of resource considerations, which include determining the cost of change and the cost of doing nothing. Within this context, we proposed a systematic approach for identifying strategies and accompanying tactics to bring about successful change.

The professionally assisted change efforts discussed in this chapter are intended to fall into two general categories: (1) those promoting improved quality of life for the clients or communities served or (2) those promoting improved quality of work life for employees as a means of helping them provide the best possible services to clients and/or communities. In order to address these two categories, we propose five approaches to change: policy, program, project, personnel, and practice. Decisions for what approach or approaches used are driven by what one has carefully learned about the population, problem, and arena (context). As with all professional practice, the approach may need to be adapted to the situation by the practitioner. If conditions dictate immediate action, some procedures may need to be abbreviated or streamlined. But if time allows, and especially if the proposed change is highly significant, best results are achieved by carrying out each task with careful attention to detail.

Collaboration, campaign, and contest strategies were introduced, along with a number of tactics designed to carry them out. The relationship between the action and target systems is often used to gauge which strategy and its accompanying tactics should be used. Some changes will always be needed in the field of human services, both in organizations and in communities. These changes, we believe, require the professional assistance and consultation of social workers knowledgeable about macro-level change. They require informed, and sometimes scholarly, participation and guidance in order to ensure that what is achieved is what is most needed to meet the needs of the target population.

We believe that social workers are well positioned to lead or coordinate the planning stages of such change efforts and to bring them to the point of action and implementation. Chapter 11 is intended to assist in that process.

 Recall what you learned in this chapter by completing the Chapter Review.

Appendix   Framework for Selecting Appropriate Strategies and Tactics

Task 1: Assess Political and Economic Feasibility

Assess Urgency in Addressing the Problem

- How long has the problem existed?
- Is the problem considered an emergency?
- If the problem is episodic or recurring, how often does it occur?

Assess Resource Considerations

- What anticipated costs related to the proposed change can be itemized? What must be estimated?
- What sources of financial support or in-kind donations should be approached?
- What will this problem cost the organization or community if nothing is done?
- How can this cost be framed so that it will be persuasive to decision makers as a good investment to support the proposed change?

Task 2: Select a Change Approach

- What approach (or combination of approaches) is most likely to achieve the desired change?

Task 3: Select Strategies and Tactics

Consider Strategies

- With which strategy will the change effort begin?
- Will it be necessary to consider sequential strategies, if a single strategy isn't working?
- If there are multiple, sequential targets, which strategies will be used with each target?

Identify Tactics

- Given the strategy most likely to succeed, what tactic (or combination of tactics) is needed first?
- As the change progresses, is it anticipated that changing strategies may lead to the use of different tactics?

Consider the Pros and Cons of Collaborative Strategies

- Is it certain that there is little or no opposition?
- Can the desired change be achieved by identifying appropriate roles for participants and implementing the change?

Consider the Pros and Cons of Campaign Strategies

- Who needs to be convinced that the proposed change is needed?
- What persuasive techniques are most likely to be effective?

Consider the Pros and Cons of Contest Strategies

- Is opposition to the proposed change so strong that it can only be successful by imposing the change on an unwilling target system?
- Can the proposed change be effective if it is forced?
- What are the potential consequences of conflict?

Weigh Relevant Considerations in Selecting Tactics

- What is the purpose of the change effort, and has that purpose been altered during the change process?
- What is the perception (by those promoting change) of the controlling and host systems?
- What is the perception (by those promoting change) of the role of the client system?
- What resources are needed and available for each tactic?
- What are the ethical dilemmas inherent in the range of tactical choices?

Assess Your Competence

Use the scale below to rate your current level of achievement on the following concepts or skills associated with each learning outcome listed at the beginning of this chapter:

1	2	3
I can accurately describe the concept or skill(s) associated with this outcome.	I can consistently identify the concept or skill(s) associated with this outcome when observing and analyzing practice activities.	I can competently implement the concept or skills(s) associated with this outcome in my own practice.

_____ Assess the political and economic contexts of an episode of planned change.

_____ Identify and define five approaches to change.

_____ Select appropriate strategies and tactics to use in an episode of planned change.

11

Planning and Implementing the Intervention

ROSALRENEBETANCOURT 2/ALAMY

UNDERSTANDING THE LOGIC MODEL

At this point, it should be evident that a professionally assisted macro-level intervention involves careful research, data collection, and data compilation. The process begins with the study of community and organizational problems and populations. Next steps focus on understanding the community or organization where change is being sought. Stakeholders are then carefully identified and engaged to build support for the change, and alternative strategies and tactics are explored.

Clearly, not every step in a macro-level intervention can be completed as described here, and much depends on the time frame and resources allocated to the effort. For example, a multimillion-dollar grant application will capture much greater detail than a proposed change in policy by a local school board. Yet both proposals will follow the same general pattern of data collection, compilation, and presentation. Both may use what has been called the **logic model** to systematically capture what needs to happen.

First introduced in the 1960s and 1970s, the purpose of the logic model was to streamline the cumbersome process of evaluating federally funded social programs that, prior to this time, could take many months (Anderson, Petticrew, Rehfuess, Armstrong, Ueffing, Baker, Francis, & Tugwel, 2011; Savaya & Waysman, 2005; Wholey, 2010). The use of its basic concepts became widespread with the United Way of America's publication of *Measuring Program Outcomes* in 1996. Instead of monitoring finances, the logic model shifts the emphasis to evaluating program outcomes. In the context of social work macro practice, application of the logic model requires taking the data collected and compiled to this point, and organizing them in a way that makes three things clear. These are:

1. what resources and raw materials (such as funding, personnel, material resources, facilities, equipment, and target population) will be used;

2. in what manner (process) will they be used; and

3. the specific outputs (completions of service) and outcomes (results) that will be achieved.

Figure 11.1 illustrates this model.

In 1993, the **Government Performance and Results Act (GPRA)** altered how the federal government monitored and evaluated its grants and contracts. It did so by focusing less on how funds are spent and more on whether stated outcomes are achieved, such as reduction of unemployment or increases in graduation rates. Then, in a 2013 update of GPRA requirements, the federal Office of Management and Budget (OMB) further refined this process. Now, programs receiving federal funds are required to identify performance and outcome measures in their initial proposal for federal funding. Also, they are paid only for achievement of results—not simply activities—and they must certify their performance and results in writing.

Research-informed Practice (or Practice-informed Research)

Behavior: Use and translate research evidence to inform and improve practice, policy, and service delivery.

Critical Thinking Question: How does the logic model engage the change agent in practice-informed research and research-informed practice?

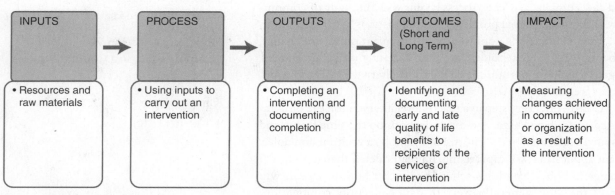

INPUTS	PROCESS	OUTPUTS	OUTCOMES (Short and Long Term)	IMPACT
• Resources and raw materials	• Using inputs to carry out an intervention	• Completing an intervention and documenting completion	• Identifying and documenting early and late quality of life benefits to recipients of the services or intervention	• Measuring changes achieved in community or organization as a result of the intervention

Figure 11.1
The Logic Model as Applied to Social Work Macro Practice

It is critical, therefore, that the change agent understand the logic model and be able to apply the concepts of input → process → output → outcome → impact to every macro-level intervention. From the smallest neighborhood project to large-scale changes at the city, county, or state level, the success of the planning, implementation, monitoring, and evaluation phases rests on understanding this sequence, its components, and their relationships.

> ▶ Watch this video on how Performance-based Standards (PbS) help juvenile facilities. How do proponents of PbS suggest the standards have improved juvenile correction facilities?
>
> www.youtube.com /watch?v=yhKgZgMPn7w

Applying the Logic Model to a Case Example

As we discussed in Chapter 9, macro-level change can take place in the form of policy, program, project, practice, or personnel approaches, and some changes may require a sequence of multiple approaches. For example, what starts as a project approach may move to a longer term program approach. Or what starts as a policy approach may lead to a program approach that carries out the mandates of the policy change.

In this and the following sections, we will attempt to illustrate how a problem that has emerged and been presented to the City Council might be approached. Box 11.1 provides a case example of a project to find housing for selected homeless persons in Centerville. This case will be used throughout the chapter to illustrate how an intervention plan is developed.

Box 11.1 Case Example of a Project to Find Housing for Selected Homeless Persons in Centerville

At a meeting of the City Council in Centerville, a city of about 150,000, a group of business leaders placed on the agenda the issue of the increasing number of homeless men who sat on the sidewalks outside their business establishments in a downtown neighborhood and were having a major impact on potential customers, who were avoiding this rapidly deteriorating area.

The police chief immediately stepped up and stated that he would increase patrols in the area to ensure that homeless persons were not camping out on the sidewalks. The department head of social services pointed out that this type of enforcement often just moves the problem from one location to another. She proposed that her staff take a closer look at the problem in an attempt to find more permanent shelter for this population. The Council agreed and asked for a report at the next meeting.

City employees were assigned to research the problem and discovered that there were about 250 homeless people living on the streets at any given time. About 30% were temporarily homeless and usually found shelter within a month. The remainder tended to be homeless for longer periods, and they suffered from a variety of problems. More than 60% had a serious addiction to drugs and/or alcohol, for example, and almost 20% were found to have some type of mental illness. Another 23% were older men with multiple chronic health problems. Federal funding was available for help with housing costs for these groups, but was not being used at this time.

Recognizing that there could be no "one-size-fits-all" solution to the problem, staff members recommended that bids be put out to local, not-for-profit agencies that could specialize in working with each of these populations, while city staff themselves took responsibility for securing the necessary federal, state, and city funding. These actions would most likely require that some policy changes be passed by the Centerville City Council. Among these were to grant authority to the social services department to assume responsibility for providing services to homeless persons, including securing funding and issuing Requests for Proposals (RFPs) to community agencies to provide direct services to the populations identified.

Community Senior Services, Inc. (CSS), decided to bid on the contract for services to the population of older men with chronic health problems. In responding to the RFP, its staff members developed the following working hypothesis:

If single, homeless men over 65 with chronic health problems in Centerville:

1. Can be identified, screened, and recruited to participate;
2. Appropriate individual and/or group living facilities can be secured;
3. Necessary funding can be obtained; and
4. Needed health and social services can be provided.

Then the following results can be expected:

1. At least 40 persons in the target group will be brought into the program;
2. Will be moved into approved facilities with rents paid by the CSS grant; and
3. Will demonstrate improved health and social adjustment.

After taking extensive social and health histories by engaging a sample of the population and interviewing key stakeholders, CSS staff decided to propose a three-pronged project that included securing apartments, screening potential residents, and moving in candidates, and, for those in need, providing and/or referring for needed health and social services such as monitoring, referral, and follow-up. On paper, the proposed project would be diagrammed as indicated in Figure 11.2.

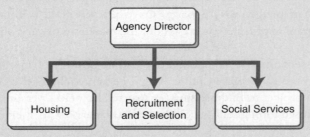

Figure 11.2
Structure of the Proposed Housing Intervention with Homeless Senior Adults

When planning and designing the services described in Box 11.1, it would be necessary for CSS staff to begin at the input and process side of the logic model. See Figure 11.3 to illustrate.

We will refer to the CSS intervention as a project in order to be consistent with our earlier definitions. The term *program* is typically reserved for services that are permanent parts of the organization and have a regular funding source. This effort would tend to be more experimental, hence the term *project*.

Much of what will be designed will depend on resources and raw materials. Resources (largely determined by the funding allocated) will include staff, material resources, facilities, and equipment. In manufacturing, raw materials such as wood or steel are what a factory uses to create output in the form of a physical product. In the service sector, raw materials are program participants who need the proposed intervention. In the example in Box 11.1, homeless people represent "persons with a problem or need." When services are complete, their status will change to "persons whose problem has been resolved or need has been met." Because macro-level interventions may involve policy, program, project, personnel, or practice approaches, the change agent may need to exercise flexibility in defining raw materials on the input side.

Following the defining of resources and raw materials, the change agent will proceed to designing the intervention. The Centerville example will involve specifying the resources to be allocated to each part of the project, along with developing policies and procedures for implementation. As we move into the next sections, we will refer back to the Centerville case and how it fits with subsequent steps in using the logic model.

 Assess your understanding of the logic model by taking this brief quiz.

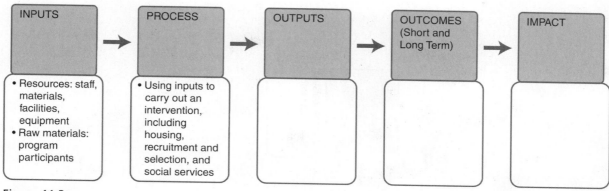

Figure 11.3
The Logic Model as Applied to the First Steps in the CSS Intervention Plan

A FRAMEWORK FOR PLANNING THE DETAILS OF THE INTERVENTION

An important point to remember is that implementation is not an event; it is a process that must be carefully planned, monitored, and evaluated. In the following sections of this chapter, we will discuss what goes into the detailed planning and implementation of a change effort. In Chapter 12, we will focus on its monitoring and evaluation.

It is tempting to assume that, with all the planning and consensus building that have gone into the change effort thus far, little can go wrong. But even carefully planned change can fail because of lack of attention to detail during the implementation phase. Accordingly, a critical factor in the implementation phase is ensuring that each step has been thought through, and that those responsible for its completion understand their responsibilities. All of the data collection, compilation, research, and analysis accomplished to date will culminate in a plan with an agreed-upon set of goals and objectives. The six tasks in planning the details of the intervention and the steps required for each are summarized in Figure 11.4.

Whether one is taking a policy, program, project, personnel, or practice approach, a written plan will be required for a number of reasons. Weinbach and Taylor (2015) recommend careful planning so that managers do not leave too much to chance, warning that activities tend to get sidetracked within organizations unless people or processes are put in place to keep them moving forward.

Plans can also get diverted outside the organization in its interactions with various community constituencies and with other formal organizations. As noted by Hardina (2002), "Planners need political and administrative skills to ensure that plans are actually implemented. They must use all the steps in the problem-solving model—problem identification, assessment, goal setting, implementation, and evaluation—to create appropriate plans" (p. 272). The most skilled administrators may still be unsuccessful if their plans ignore or misunderstand political considerations outside the organization.

Planning the details of the intervention includes establishing goals, writing objectives, listing all the activities that will need to be carried out, and setting time frames, due dates, and responsibilities. When completed, the plan should be distributed to all

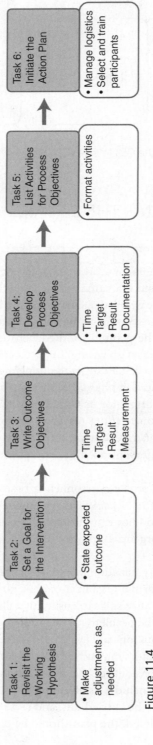

Figure 11.4
A Framework for Planning the Details of the Intervention

stakeholders who have various roles and responsibilities and whose participation and support are important to the success of the intervention. The plan will be used as the basis for orienting and training the implementers and later as a basis for monitoring and evaluating the effectiveness of the intervention.

Task 1: Revisit the Working Hypothesis of Intervention

The key question to be explored is:

- Does the working hypothesis of intervention need adjustment?

In Chapter 9, the reader was encouraged to develop a working intervention hypothesis to use as a guide in explaining how to approach the identified problem and in recruiting potential participants in the change process. This is called a working hypothesis because it is subject to change as new data and information arise in the process of building support for the change and in assessing the political and economic context. In addition, as approaches to change were considered in Chapter 10, the selection of strategies and tactics may reveal new information about the feasibility and sequencing of the original intervention hypothesis. Therefore, as the process unfolds, it may become clear that some rethinking of the working hypothesis is needed.

For example, in the Centerville example (Box 11.1) a working hypothesis had been developed. In the process of building support for the change and identifying new information, a number of possible changes may have occurred. The target population was originally single, homeless men over 65. However in the process of learning more about the target population, the age might need to be lowered to 55 if it is discovered that younger people living on the street were suffering from as many chronic conditions as the average 65 year old. Or perhaps it is found that a number of older women are among the homeless population and the change needs to be more gender inclusive. Potentially, in investigating the problem further, it is discovered that a pilot project cannot realistically accommodate 40 people as specified in the working hypothesis and that 30 is a more feasible number to include. In short, the change agent system may decide to adjust the working hypothesis prior to writing goals and objectives since these will flow from the hypothesis.

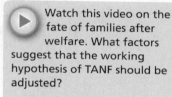

Watch this video on the fate of families after welfare. What factors suggest that the working hypothesis of TANF should be adjusted?

www.youtube.com /watch?v=8wINwIE1WdU

In the Centerville example, the working intervention hypothesis may become: If single, homeless men and women over age 55 with chronic health problems in Centerville:

1. Can be identified, screened, and recruited to participate; and
2. Individual and/or group living facilities can be secured; and
3. Necessary funding can be secured; and
4. Needed health and social services can be provided.

Then the following results can be expected:

1. At least 30 persons in the target group will be accepted into the program;
2. The 30 participants will be moved into approved facilities with rents paid by the CSS grant; and
3. At least 75% of participants will demonstrate improved health and social adjustment.

Assessment

Behavior: Select appropriate intervention strategies based on the assessment, research knowledge, and values and preferences of clients and constituencies.

Critical Thinking Question: How does revisiting the working intervention hypothesis reflect satisficing? If reassessment is ongoing, how does the change agent determine when to move ahead with an intervention strategy?

This working intervention corresponds to the three-pronged project proposed by CSS that includes securing apartments, screening potential residents, moving in the best candidates, and referring for or providing needed health and social services, as diagrammed in Figure 11.2. It has been slightly modified by the change agent system and is now ready to be translated into goals and objectives.

Task 2: Set a Goal for the Intervention

The key question to be explored is:

- What is the overall purpose that is expected if the intervention is successful?

A quote attributed to baseball player Yogi Berra says, "If you don't know where you're going, you'll end up someplace else." **Goals** state where it is you're going. They provide a beacon or focal point for the change effort that serves as a reminder of its purpose. They also provide a starting point for stakeholders with diverse views to begin building consensus. A well-stated goal focuses on the outcome to be achieved and also identifies a target population and a boundary for the change effort (Brody, 2005; Montana & Charnov, 2008). However, because of this focus on what is to be achieved, the processes or methods to be used in reaching the goal should be identified separately and not included in the goal statement itself. For example, the Community Senior Services project in Box 11.1 hopes to achieve the following goal:

- To reduce the number of homeless men and women over age 55 with chronic health problems living on the streets of Centerville.

Other illustrations of goal statements for other change efforts might be:

- The goal of this project is to increase the number of Latino/a students who remain in high school and earn their diplomas in the Jefferson School District.
- The goal of this program is to reduce the number of isolated older adults in the town of Elwood.
- The goal of this change effort is to pass and implement a policy that will ensure a positive and productive lifestyle for first-time offenders in Washington County.

Note that these goal statements do not indicate how they are to be accomplished, and they are not measurable as stated. Building in measurement criteria is a part of the development of objectives. Returning to the sequence illustrated by the logic model, we are in a sense temporarily moving toward the end of the model, as illustrated in Figure 11.5.

At this point, however, we are writing goals and outcome objectives only for the purpose of identifying what we hope to achieve, and to provide a framework for monitoring and evaluation. The actual carrying out of monitoring and evaluation processes will be addressed in the next chapter.

Task 3: Write Outcome and Process Objectives

Setting goals and objectives requires translating concepts and ideas from the abstract phases of the logic model into concrete terms. More specifically, this method of planning

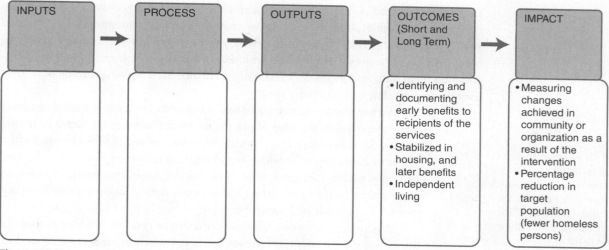

Figure 11.5
The Logic Model as Applied to the Last Steps in the CSS Intervention Plan

simplifies a potentially complex undertaking by breaking it up into manageable parts. Alternately, **objectives** serve as an elaboration of goals. They spell out the details of the planned intervention in measurable terms, including expected outcomes and the processes needed to achieve them. **Activities** are lists of tasks that must be undertaken and completed in order to achieve each objective.

Objectives can be developed around each of the proposed interventions. The purpose of an objective is to lay out a clear path that moves the change effort toward the goal, and the most important attribute of a good objective is that it is specific and measurable. Objectives stated in such a way that their accomplishment cannot be determined are useless as guides for action.

Two main types of objectives are (1) outcome objectives and (2) process objectives. An **outcome objective** specifies the *result or outcome* to be achieved on behalf of the target population. While outcome objectives describe what is to be achieved, **process objectives** describe the procedures to be followed to accomplish that result.

Each outcome objective should have one or more process objectives that accompany it, and once these are written out it should be evident that (1) completion of the process objectives will lead to achievement of the outcome objective and (2) completion of the outcome objective will move the effort toward the goal. For a more complete discussion of goals and objectives, see Kettner, Moroney, and Martin (2013, chap. 7); and Hardina (2002, chap. 11).

Outcome Objectives

Goals are written with intermediate and long-term outcomes in mind, whereas objectives tend to focus more on what can be accomplished within a program or fiscal year. When it comes to monitoring and evaluation, short-term outcomes serve as milestones for marking progress toward achievement of long-term outcomes.

In keeping with the logic model discussed earlier, the desired result specified in an outcome objective may be short-term or intermediate to long-term. These two different time frames remind us that, in designing an intervention, planners must be careful not to overpromise by establishing the expectation that all hoped-for outcomes can be achieved within a short time. But when working with people in need, it is also unacceptable to focus only on objectives that won't be achieved for many years. Identifying both short- and long-term outcomes helps planners strike a balance between what can be done relatively soon and what will take more time.

Writing outcome objectives well takes practice. Writing a good outcome objective requires thinking about the impact of services on clients or participants. An outcome, in this model, involves a quality-of-life change for the client or consumer of services. For example, it is not the objective of a counseling or training program that clients participate in counseling or training, but rather that they strengthen and improve their relationships or that they master a new body of knowledge.

A complete objective, whether outcome or process, has four parts: (1) a time frame, (2) a target, (3) a result, and (4) a criterion for measuring or documenting the result (Kettner et al., 2013). The following sections will explain how each of these parts is applied to outcome objectives as well as process objectives.

> Do an Internet search for "The Urban Institute Center on Nonprofits and Philanthropy." Locate the Perform Well project on the site. Under "Identify Outcomes," what measures may be useful in the agency where you work or would like to work? What measures are missing?

Establish a Time Frame for the Outcome Objective

The key questions to be explored are:

- Is it possible to establish a day, month, and year when results should be evident?
- At what point in the future is it reasonable to expect to see measurable results from this intervention?

Ideally, a **time frame** should be stated in terms of the month, day, and year by which the result will be achieved, because this information will later be needed for monitoring purposes. The end of a fiscal or calendar year is often used ("By June 30, 20XX, . . ." or "By December 31, 20XX, . . ."). When a start date is unknown, the time frame may be specified in terms of time elapsed from the beginning of the change effort (for example, "within three months of the beginning of the project," or "by the end of the first year"). Once a start date is known, it is wise to go back and fill in actual dates, because objectives are often also used as monitoring tools.

The time frame for an outcome objective should not exceed one year, as funding and sponsoring sources usually expect at least annual reporting on progress and results. In situations where it is expected to take more than a year to achieve results, thought should be given to what kind of annual milestones can be established that will indicate that the project is on track. In some instances where shorter time frames are important, reporting milestones can be established at 3-, 6-, 9-, and 12-month periods.

In the CSS project in Box 11.1 that we are using as a case example, there are three parts: housing services, recruitment and selection, and social services. Each part would have a separate set of objectives and activities. Using the social services unit as an example, the time frame for this part of the project might be stated as follows:

- No later than six months after all participants have been selected; or, if known,
- By June 30, 20XX.

Define the Target Population

The key question to be explored in defining the target population is:

- Who or what group will experience a quality-of-life change as a result of this intervention?

The second part of an objective, the target population, specifies the individuals, groups, and even communities for whom the change effort is being made. Outcome objectives should indicate how this population will benefit or what sort of quality-of-life change will occur. By the time the change agent reaches this point, there should be no doubt about the makeup of the target population, but it should be specified in writing so that everyone involved can express their agreement and support or propose amendments.

Statements should be as precise as current knowledge will allow. An outpatient drug treatment program, for example, might specify "24 cocaine addicts at least 18 years of age and currently employed" as its target. In the Centerville example, it is clear from the goal statement that the target is intended to be:

- Single, homeless men and women over age 55 with chronic health problems living on the streets of Centerville.

Specify a Result or Outcome

The key question to be explored for this activity is:

- What benefits or quality-of-life changes are expected for the target population from this intervention?

The third part of an objective is a statement of the expected result or *outcome* to be achieved when all activities are completed. *Outcome objectives* refer to desired accomplishments such as improved knowledge and skill, improved relationship with spouse, reduction of alcohol abuse, or more input into community decision making. For now, the activities necessary to achieve the outcome do not need to be identified. That will happen later.

Desired outcomes for a jobs program might be stated as follows: "Improvement in computer knowledge and skills, increased employability, or qualifying for higher earnings." Results from a parent training program might specify such outcomes as improved family stability, increased self-esteem expressed by children, and/or improved performance in school and extracurricular activities. Note that we have not yet specified how these outcomes will be measured. That is the next step.

The exact phrasing of an outcome is determined by the goal of the program or project. Long-term results or outcomes for the overall Community Senior Services project will focus on ensuring that participants are stabilized in their apartments and connected to all community health and social services available to support independent living. However, each part of the project will have different short-term objectives. Housing services will focus on securing apartments or appropriate shelters. Recruitment and selection will focus on attracting participants to the program. Social services will identify health and social adjustment needs and connect clients to existing community service agencies. The following wording might be used to establish an expected outcome for social services:

- By [date], at least 80% of [target population] will have no more than one incident of disruptive behavior reported. . . .

Define a Criterion for Measuring Success

The key questions to be explored are:

- How will the result as stated in the objective be measured?
- Are there observable criteria readily available for measurement, or will criteria need to be designed?

The final part of an objective is a criterion to be used in determining whether the objective has been achieved. Objectives must be precise and measurable, yet sometimes the result to be achieved seems vague and elusive. Some programs, for example, are designed to improve self-esteem. The question is: How does one know if self-esteem has been improved? Clearly, opinion alone is not sufficiently valid or reliable.

Specifying a criterion in the objective ensures that only one standard will be used by all who monitor and evaluate the program. If improving self-esteem is the desired result, then some measure must be used to determine if that happened. One example of such a measure would be a standardized scale for which there is good evidence of validity and reliability. For self-esteem, one example is the Rosenberg Self-Esteem Scale (SES; Rosenberg, 1965). Although this scale is more than 50 years old, it continues to be used widely with both adolescents and adults, and evidence continues to show that it measures self-esteem accurately (Mullen & Resnick, 2013). Using this as a criterion, an outcome objective might begin, "To increase self-esteem by an average of 10 percent as measured by scores on the Rosenberg Self-Esteem Scale . . ." Outcome criteria can also involve other types of measures such as observation of behavior, collection of information from secondary sources such as school attendance or arrest records, and so forth.

In the Centerville example, successful housing services to move homeless people into independent shelter will require that enough housing units be secured to accommodate all the participants, and that participants be recruited, screened, and informed of all the standards and expectations they will be expected to meet in order to remain in the project. The most important criterion for success will likely be the number of participants who are able to remain in their independent living situations and become self-sufficient, with the help and support of community services. Additional indicators could include stabilized health status (as documented in medical records), social adjustment (as documented by the number of complaints by other residents in the apartment building), participation in a job-training program (as documented by attendance records), and ability to manage finances (as demonstrated by keeping current on all financial obligations). The outcome objectives in Box 11.2 are illustrative of what might be used to monitor and evaluate the health and social services provided.

Both of the objectives in Box 11.2 serve as milestones toward the goal of reducing the number of single homeless men and women over age 55 with chronic health problems living on the streets of Centerville.

Process Objectives

Each outcome objective is followed by a number of process objectives designed to spell out how the outcome objective will be achieved. Process objectives should identify the major components of a planned intervention, not the specific details. The logic behind a process objective is that everything needing to be changed or accomplished in order to achieve the outcome objective should be identified in sequence. To accomplish this, members of the change agent system break down an objective and delegate responsibility

---

Box 11.2   Examples of a Goal and Two Complete Outcome Objectives

- To reduce the number of single homeless men and women over age 55 with chronic health problems living on the streets of Centerville.

The first outcome example focuses on participant health:

Time Frame:	Within six months of the time the participant is placed in independent living,
Target:	At least 75% of the participants
Result:	Will demonstrate improved health
Criterion:	As measured by test results from the clinic (with permission from the participant).

Since having a chronic health problem is a criterion for selecting the participants, it would be appropriate for the case managers to focus on getting health conditions stabilized to the greatest extent possible and as quickly as possible.

A second objective might address social adjustment. The assumption would be that norms of behavior when living on the street are different than when interacting with clerical staff, professional staff, and neighbors in new housing. Assistance in the form of social-skills training might be needed to avoid complaints leading to participants being disqualified from the program.

The second outcome objective on social adjustment might read as follows:

Time Frame:	By June 30, 20XX,
Target:	At least 80% of participants
Result:	Will have no more than one incident of disruptive social behavior reported
Criterion:	As measured by the results of observational data from providers

---

for each step or task to different individuals or units (Montana & Charnov, 2008). When all those tasks are completed, then the objective should be successfully accomplished. Returning to the logic model, this part of planning and developing the intervention will focus on outputs, as illustrated in Figure 11.6.

Each major component of the intervention is translated into a process objective. For example, if the outcome specified is "self-sufficiency," then the process might include such activities as (1) enrollment of participants in night classes leading to completion of a GED, (2) enrollment of participants in a skills training course, (3) job counseling, (4) job placement, and (5) follow-up. Details, such as setting up GED preparation or the skills training courses, become part of the activities, to be discussed in a following section

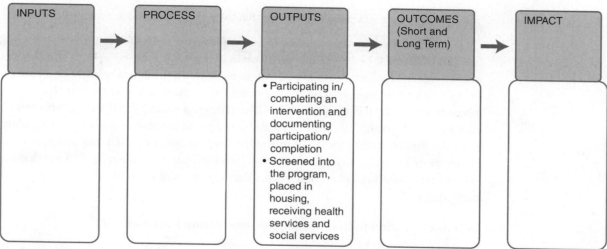

Figure 11.6
The Logic Model as Applied to Outputs in the CSS Intervention Plan

of this chapter. A complete process objective includes the same four parts as outcome objectives: time, target, result, and criterion.

Establish a Time Frame for the Process Objective

The key question to be explored is:

- When will the actions specified in this objective begin and end?

Time frames are specified in the same way for both outcome and process objectives. Ideally, target dates or milestones are established in terms of specific dates—day, month, and year. When this information is not known, the time frame can be defined in terms of the number of weeks or months from when the intervention begins. The actual date selected for a process objective should be the date when the process is expected to be completed, such as: "By March 31, 20XX, . . ." Time frames for process objectives must, of course, be synchronized with those for the related outcome objective.

Define the Target

The key question to be explored for this activity is:

- What individuals, groups, or products will be the focus of this objective?

Process objectives break down the change effort into a series of tasks. The focus is on what steps need to be taken in order to achieve the outcome objective. For some process objectives, the steps may focus on an individual or a group of people. For other process objectives, it may be that the steps address things rather than people, such as a training curriculum to be produced or a policy to be enacted. Examples might include "a computerized record on all participants. . ." or "at least 80% of the participants will attend . . ." In the first example, the target is a document; in the second, it's a group of people.

Specify a Result for the Process Objective

The key question to be explored for this activity is:

- What result will provide evidence that the objective has been achieved?

Results in process objectives involve completion of a service or intervention process, and this must be stated in a way that is concrete and observable. If the process involves services to people, the result might be something like completion of a course, completion of at least six counseling sessions, or attendance at no less than three job-training sessions. If the process involves changing some part of an organization or community, the result might be described as a completed report, a new strategic plan, or a new data collection form. An example using the computerized data system might be "entry of basic identifying information into each participant's record." One that involves participant activities could read, "Participants will have completed their initial clinic visit . . ."

Define a Criterion to Be Used for Documentation Purposes

The key question to be explored for this activity is:

- What observable or measurable factor(s) can be used to determine whether the process objective has been achieved?

Box 11.3 Process Objective Example

Continuing with the example of the Centerville homeless project, a process objective might read as follows:

No later than six months after all participants have been selected, at least 90% of all participants will have completed their initial screening appointment with appropriate health and social services programs as documented by follow-up telephone calls to providers.

Time Frame: No later than six months after all participants have been selected,

Target: at least 90% of all participants

Result: will have completed their initial screening appointment with appropriate health clinics . . .

Criterion: as documented by treatment plans obtained from providers at the clinic.

Process objectives typically focus on the completion of something. This might involve participants completing a portion of the service process (such as training or counseling sessions), or it might be the creation of products (such as a policy or training manual). Many different criteria can be used to document the result of a process objective. The focus in writing process objectives is on determining if a particular step toward an outcome has been achieved, and documenting that fact.

In most cases, process objectives will use the phrase "as documented by" or "as demonstrated by." Completion of a classroom course, for example, can be documented by receipt of a certificate of completion, by attendance records, or by a formal transcript. Development of a new form or formulation of a new policy can be documented by submission of these items in writing to a specified person by a due date. The key is that some indicator exists that will allow for complete agreement as to when the process objective has been achieved. Examples could include "as documented by a review of the computerized records . . ." or "as documented by reports from participating health clinics . . ." Box 11.3 illustrates that when all four parts—time frame, target, result, and criterion—have been written, the objective is complete.

Typically, a set of goals and objectives will include one goal, a number of outcome objectives, and several process objectives for each outcome objective. These components, as stated earlier, are reproduced in Box 11.4 to illustrate the relationship between a goal and its outcome and process objectives.

Because each outcome objective usually requires a series of process objectives, it is important that each step in the implementation process be put into writing so it becomes a clear and visible part of the plan. This commitment to written documentation allows implementers to know precisely what was intended so that they can follow the plan without skipping important elements or assuming that everything is on track. It should also be obvious how completion of each process objective will lead to achievement of the outcome objective.

Intervention

Behavior: Negotiate, mediate, and advocate with and on behalf of diverse clients and constituencies.

Critical Thinking Question: How does the development of objectives engage the change agent system in a process of negotiation, mediation, and advocacy?

Task 4: List Activities for Process Objectives

The final step in developing the intervention plan is to itemize activities. Activities represent the highest level of detail incorporated into the plan. Each activity represents something that someone does that, when accomplished, will advance the change effort toward achievement of a process objective. Activities should specify the work to be done, the person responsible, and a time frame.

Box 11.4   Illustration of the Relationship between a Hypothesis, Goal, Outcome Objective, and Process Objective

Working Intervention Hypothesis:

If single, homeless men and women over age 55 with chronic health problems in Centerville:

1. Can be identified, screened, and recruited to participate; and
2. Appropriate individual and/or group living facilities can be secured; and
3. Necessary funding can be secured; and
4. Needed health and social services can be provided,

Then the following results can be expected:

1. At least 30 persons in the target group will be accepted into the program;
2. The 30 participants will be moved into approved facilities with rents paid by the CSS grant; and
3. At least 75% will demonstrate improved health and social adjustment.

Goal:

To reduce the number of single, homeless men and women over age 55 with chronic health problems living on the streets of Centerville.

Outcome Objective #1:

Time Frame:	Within six months of the time the participant is placed in independent living,
Target:	At least 75% of the participants
Result:	Will demonstrate improved health
Criterion:	As measured by test results from the clinic (with permission from the participant).

Process Objective #1.1

Time Frame:	No later than six months after all participants have been selected,
Target:	At least 90% of all participants
Result:	Will have completed their initial screening appointment with appropriate health clinics
Criterion:	As documented by treatment plans obtained from the providers at the clinic.

Outcome Objective #2:

Time Frame: By June 30, 20XX,

Target: At least 80% of participants

Result: Will have no more than one incident of disruptive social behavior reported

Criterion: As documented by a tracking system included in the monthly social services report, and

Criterion: As measured by the results of observational data from providers.

Format Activities for Easy Monitoring

The key questions to be explored for this activity are:

- What activities or tasks must be successfully completed in order to achieve the process objective?
- When should each activity begin and end?
- Who should be assigned responsibility for completion of the activity?

Activities should be organized in ways that promote orderly, systematic implementation. Such an approach might lead to organizing by individuals, by types of tasks, or by the sequence of tasks. One useful format for this type of organization is a Gantt chart, developed by management pioneer Henry L. Gantt (1919). A Gantt chart is a table in which each row represents an activity, and each column indicates a span of time over which the activity is to be completed. Additional columns before or after a particular activity may be added to identify the activity number and the person responsible. Gantt charts can be essential for keeping track of what steps need to be done when, and they also establish a hierarchy in which each task is clearly located within a larger activity (Brody, 2005). Also, because beginning and ending points are projected

Process Objective: No later than six months after all participants have been selected, at least 90% of all participants will have completed their initial screening appointment with appropriate health and social services programs as documented by follow-up phone calls to providers

Activity Number	Activity	Person Responsible	Months 1	2	3	4	5	6
1.	Take a social and medical history on each participant	Case managers	---					
2.	Identify health and medical needs and have necessary consent forms signed	Consulting nurses	---					
3.	Identify social adjustment needs and have necessary consent forms signed	Case managers	-----					
4.	Identify participating medical clinics	Consulting nurses	--------					
5.	Match participants to appropriate clinic and schedule appointment	Consulting nurses		---------				
6.	Identify participating social service agencies	Case managers		------------				
7.	Match participants to appropriate agencies and schedule appointment	Case managers			-----------			
8.	Arrange transportation	Case managers			----------------			
9.	Follow up with medical clinics to determine if appointments were kept	Consulting nurses						-------
10.	Follow up with social service providers to determine if appointments were kept	Case managers						-------

Figure 11.7
Gantt Chart Used to Monitor Activities

for each task, project managers can see at a glance what actions need to be taken next. Continuing with the example of the Centerville homeless program, a Gantt chart is illustrated in Figure 11.7.

It is helpful in constructing Gantt charts to identify needed activities, determine which ones must precede or follow others, and then, once a sequence is established, assign time frames. Since the final activity must be completed by the date shown in the process objective, it is best to set time frames by beginning at the bottom of the list and working backwards. This ensures that earlier activities will be completed in time to ensure the final deadline is met.

In preparing an action plan for a macro-level change, each subsection of the intervention should include an outcome objective, process objective(s), and activities. When these are developed at an acceptable level of precision, with responsibilities and time frames clearly specified, the action plan is complete. The relationships between a goal, outcome objectives, process objectives, and activities are illustrated in Figure 11.8. Appendix 2 provides an example of an action plan developed for a change effort in one county's foster care system.

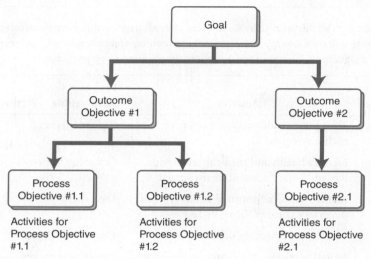

Figure 11.8
Hierarchy of Goals, Outcome Objectives, Process Objectives, and Activities

The last steps in preparing for macro-level change involve the details of implementation. Monitoring of the plan and the evaluation of its effectiveness will be covered in the next chapter.

Task 5: Initiate the Action Plan

A common oversight in planning for organizational and community change is leaving out of the planning process those who will ultimately be responsible for implementation of the program. Fogel and Moore (2011) discuss the importance of collaboration among community agencies. In any change effort, it is common to feel that the standard approaches that have been used have not been effective in getting the job done, so something new needs to be tried. At the same time, it is likely that at least part of the implementing system will be made up of people who have been using the standard approaches for a long time. This creates the possibility of conflict between "traditionalists" and "innovators." Traditionalists may feel that their previous work is being discredited or that those seeking change don't understand the realities of the situation. Innovators may feel that long-time employees are set in their ways and unable to consider a fresh approach. The key to addressing these potential problems is to arrange for overlap between the action system (planners) and the implementing system. Ideally, implementers should be involved in the planning process. If this is not possible, members of the action system must make extra efforts to work with members of the implementing system to understand the facets and complexities involved. The goal is to craft a change process in which all parties believe their voices have been heard and that they have a stake in the change effort's success.

Implementation of policy changes has been the subject of research for a number of experts in the field. A prominent theme in the findings is the potential for failure between the planning stage and implementation. One project tracked spending to educate children and support families in local communities and discovered that some available resources were not getting to their intended target populations (McCroskey, Picus, Yoo, Marsenich, & Robillard, 2004). Another project explored how elite perceptions of poverty often influence policy in ways that interfere with effective problem resolution (Reis & Moore, 2005). Yet another showed that poor monitoring of how well local agencies implemented a new substance abuse prevention program led to widespread rejection of the entire effort (Dickson-Gómez, 2012). On the other hand, a different project showed that collaborative policy advocacy led by social work researchers, practitioners, advocates, and students was successful in placing an issue on the state agenda and instrumental in its passage (Sherraden, Slosar, & Sherraden, 2002). The message is that the implementation process must be managed every bit as carefully as the earlier stages of the change episode.

Putting the plan into action usually requires completion of a number of tasks prior to involving clients, consumers, or participants. For the success of change efforts such as the ones described here, it is critical that they be well organized at the point of implementation and that they have a clearly defined leader or coordinator. The primary tasks for this person are to ensure that everyone's job gets done, to maintain morale, and to motivate participants (Dessler, 2011).

Up to this point, the major phases of the change effort (researching the change in Chapters 3 to 8, creating the design and soliciting support in Chapter 9, developing strategy and tactics in Chapter 10, and planning the details of implementation in Chapter 11) have been carried out by many groups of interacting and overlapping individuals and systems. When preparing for implementation, it is necessary that the intervention becomes more formalized. For example, in addition to designating the lead or point person, it is now time to address logistical considerations, such as facilities and equipment. Some early participants may now form a policy-making or advisory board to provide consultation and guidance. Also, in the case of project or program approaches, planning must begin regarding personnel issues such as hiring and training. Finally, coordination and communication among new and old participants may prove critical to successful implementation. See Winter and Ohmer (2014) for an example of how one family service agency used an outcome measurement framework to implement a new program.

> **Intervention**
>
> **Behavior:** Facilitate effective transitions and endings that advance mutually agreed-on goals.
>
> **Critical Thinking Question:** In designating a lead person to guide the action system, how might she or he negotiate effective transitions and endings?

Manage Logistics

The key questions to be explored are:

- What facilities, equipment, record-keeping system, and other resources, including staff and volunteers, will need to be made available prior to implementation?
- What steps or phases need to be implemented, and in what order, in order to maximize efficiency?

The planned change will likely involve some combination of existing staff and volunteers, new services, new staff, and perhaps new clients, consumers, or participants. If new personnel are to be involved, appropriate space and equipment will have to be arranged. If existing staff and volunteers are to be used, decisions need to be made about sharing of space and equipment between the old and new programs. Returning to the Centerville example, let's assume that the homeless seniors project is funded and staff are selected to head the various phases of the program. Box 11.5 describes the scenario.

| Box 11.5 | Implementing the Community Senior Services Homeless Project |

The Senior Homeless Project as designed has three components, as previously illustrated in Figure 11.2. The target is to recruit and place 30 homeless seniors over age 55 who have chronic health problems. Work will be carried out by three units. First, the Recruitment and Selection unit will be made up of one professional staff member who will have primary responsibility for developing standards and expectations for participants, along with one formerly homeless person who is familiar with parts of the city where homeless people congregate. Next, the Housing unit will be made up of one former property manager who is familiar with apartment managers and owners, assisted by one clerical person who will help develop and record agreements. Finally, a Social Services unit will be made up of two social workers and two consulting nurses who will operate as a team. The social workers will serve as case managers and will each carry a caseload of 15 homeless seniors. The two nurses will be responsible for identifying health problems among the participants, identifying ways to address those, and assisting the social workers with completing referrals. After participants have been recruited and selected and housing agreements have been signed, other staff members will be made available as consultants on an as-needed basis, but they will not be kept on full-time.

Managing logistics will include checking the budget to determine how much is allocated for all personnel and operating expenses; locating a center or headquarters for the project; securing necessary furniture, computers, telephones, and other equipment; and establishing a data collection and aggregation system to track progress of participants. Most likely, the homeless project staff will coordinate with existing agency business management staff to make contacts and get everything properly housed and installed. Housing program and Recruitment and Selection personnel will need to be brought on board first, and as soon as they are trained they can begin their responsibilities. Early coordination between these two units will be critical.

Selecting and training staff, volunteers, and participants will require writing job descriptions for each paid staff or volunteer to clarify roles, responsibilities, supervision, performance evaluation criteria, benefits, and other considerations. The person in charge of these tasks will need to work closely with human resources personnel to be certain that everything is handled properly. Once these "behind-the-scenes" procedures are carried out and all the structures are in place to initiate the program, staff can begin locating apartments and recruiting participants. Next comes the process of matching participants to appropriate housing arrangements until all 30 participants are in their apartments or other housing arrangements. As each participant is settled into housing, the process of matching them to health clinics and social service agencies begins. From this point on, regular case management and nurse consultation will take over through the monitoring and evaluation phases. These logistics and staffing functions are depicted in a flowchart in Figure 11.9.

Select and Train Participants

The key questions to be explored are:

- Who will have overall leadership and management responsibilities for the intervention?
- Will existing or new staff and/or volunteers be used in the intervention?
- What preparations need to be made to bring new participants on board?
- What type of orientation and training will be needed?

One of the first steps in getting the intervention underway is the selection of an overall program leader as well as lead persons for each subunit of the change effort. Because these individuals will be critical to the success of the intervention, careful screening will be required, using standards established in the job descriptions for these positions.

If the intervention is designed as a new initiative, with its own funding and other resources, and if people filling key positions will be employees, then formal job descriptions and job announcements will need to be written. In large-scale changes, where time permits, it is desirable first to go through the recruitment, selection, and hiring process for the overall manager or coordinator, and then to have that person take a lead role

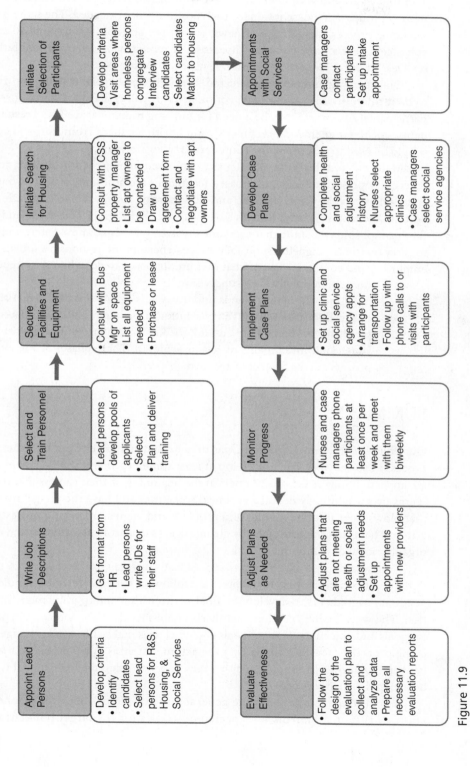

Figure 11.9

Flowchart for Use in Implementing the Centerville Community Senior Center Senior Homeless Project

in selecting other staff. Consultation with human resources professionals will be necessary because of their familiarity with often-complex laws and regulations. Whether additional staff and volunteers will be new or drawn from current employees or community groups, a job description for each position will be needed. The same is true for a screening process, including interviews, even if the positions are to be filled by nonpaid volunteers. (For a more complete discussion of recruitment, selection, and hiring issues, see Dessler, 2011; Kettner, 2013; and Weinbach & Taylor, 2015.)

Once personnel have been selected, they will need initial training to orient them to their roles. In order to maintain continuity, this will be necessary even for very early participants. Also, there may be a need for ongoing training as well, and results for evaluations of the implementation process, along with feedback from staff and volunteers, should be used to determine the content of ongoing training.

Many different tracking techniques can be used to help the implementation process succeed. Sophisticated, computer-based techniques are becoming available, but standard approaches such as Gantt charting and flowcharting also continue to be effective. The bottom line is this: When planners have finalized all the goals, objectives, and activities, they cannot simply assume that everyone involved will begin immediately and with ease to carry out their assigned responsibilities. Lead persons are responsible for ensuring that employees and volunteers know what they are supposed to do, when it is supposed to be done, and under whose supervision.

Once the action plan is underway, it is important that responsibilities be assigned for monitoring and evaluation. Ongoing monitoring ensures that the plan will be implemented as designed, and evaluation ensures that there will be periodic assessments of results achieved. These phases of the intervention process are the subject of the next chapter.

> **?** Assess your understanding of a framework for planning the details of the intervention by taking this brief quiz.

SUMMARY

Our objective in writing this book was to help students understand the macro-practice process in social work and to develop at least some beginning skills as these principles are applied. It may strike practitioners at the beginning of their careers that this process seems overwhelmingly detailed at times. Some may still have the image of the activist that plows right into the middle of a problem and begins organizing protests or other action. That is not the role taken by change agents in a professionally assisted episode of organizational or community change.

Good planning is much more likely to lead to successful change. If all the procedures described in the first 10 chapters are followed, the change agent should have the necessary ingredients to develop the final, written plan and to implement an intervention. The working intervention hypothesis establishes the direction and the parameters for goals and objectives. Writing goals and objectives makes the whole change effort become proactive, which is to say that the action system is in a position to make things happen rather than to simply hope that they happen. Using the logic model is helpful in depicting the change process.

A goal statement provides the general sense of direction for the planned change effort. It is stated in terms of expected outcomes for the target population. As the intervention is implemented, there should be some general sense of positive movement toward the goal, but goal achievement as used in this context is not actually measured.

An outcome objective is a statement of expected outcomes that is intended to operationalize the goal, and it is written in a way so that the outcome can be measured, monitored, and evaluated. An objective includes four parts: time, target, result, and criterion. Process objectives are used to describe the major components of the intervention that will be necessary in order to achieve the outcome objective. Once the outcome expectations are clear, phases or components necessary to successful achievement of the outcomes should be itemized, followed by a complete process objective written for each phase or component. When examining the process objectives as a whole, the planner should be convinced that, if they are all completed as planned, their completion will add up to successful achievement of the outcome objective.

Activities are then written for each process objective. Activities or tasks should be planned sequentially so that, when all activities are completed, the process objective will have been achieved. For each activity, a time frame and the person responsible for completion of the activity should be specified. Thus, the overall plan becomes an intricate set of goals, objectives, and activities designed to work together. If the plan is devised in this manner, the chances for success are greatly increased. If all the activities are completed within the specified time frame, then process objectives should be achieved. If process objectives are achieved, then outcome objectives should be achieved. Finally, if outcome objectives are achieved, the change effort will have moved toward its goal.

> ✓ Recall what you learned in this chapter by completing the Chapter Review.

Appendix 1: A Framework for Planning the Details of the Intervention

Task 1: Revisit the Working Hypothesis
- Does the working hypothesis of intervention need adjustment?

Task 2: Set a Goal for the Intervention
- What is the overall outcome that is expected if the intervention is successful?

Task 3: Write Outcome Objectives

Establish a Time Frame for the Objective
- Is it possible to establish a day, month, and year when the first results should be evident?
- At what point in the future is it reasonable to expect to see measurable results from this intervention?

Define the Target Population
- Who or what group will experience a quality-of-life change as a result of this intervention?

Specify a Result or Outcome
- What quality-of-life changes are expected for the target population from this intervention?

Define a Criterion for Measuring Success
- How will the result as stated in the objective be measured?
- Are there observable criteria readily available for measurement, or will criteria need to be designed?

Task 4: Develop Process Objectives

Establish a Time Frame for the Process Objective
- When will the actions specified in this objective begin and end?

Define the Target
- What individuals, groups, or products will be the focus of this objective?

Specify a Result for the Process Objective

- What result will provide evidence that the objective has been achieved?

Define a Criterion to Be Used for Documentation Purposes

- What observable or measurable factor(s) can be used to determine whether the process objective has been achieved?

Task 5: List Activities for Process Objectives

Format Activities for Easy Monitoring

- What activities or tasks must be successfully completed in order to achieve the process objective?
- When should each activity begin and end?
- Who should be assigned responsibility for completion of the activity?

Task 6: Initiate the Action Plan

Manage Logistics

- What facilities, equipment, and other resources will need to be made available prior to implementation?
- Where will new personnel, including volunteers, be housed?
- How can the steps or phases be depicted in flow-chart form?

Select and Train Participants

- Who will have overall leadership and management responsibilities for the intervention?
- Will existing or new staff and/or volunteers be used in the intervention?
- What preparations need to be made to bring new participants on board?
- What type of orientation and training will be needed?

Appendix 2: Action Plan Example: Jackson County Foster Care

The following example illustrates the major components of a written action plan for a macro change effort.

Background

Jackson County incorporates a major city, several medium-sized suburbs, and a small amount of rural area. The Child Welfare Services Division of its Department of Social Services recently undertook an analysis of foster children for which it had responsibility during the past five years. The findings revealed that there were a disproportionately low number of white children in this population and a disproportionately high number of children from other racial or ethnic groups.

In response to a newspaper article that reported these results, over 30 representatives of various ethnic communities attended an open hearing held by the County Board of Supervisors. They expressed serious concerns about the findings. The County Director of Child Welfare Services was instructed to appoint a task force to study the situation and to make recommendations. The fourteen-member task force included:

- Three parents of ethnic minority foster children;
- Four leaders from minority communities;
- Two foster parents;
- Two foster care social workers;
- A foster home recruitment coordinator;
- A child welfare researcher from the local university; and
- The top administrator from the foster care program.

Analysis of the Problem

The task force began with an initial statement of the problem that focused on the fact that ethnic minority children comprised a higher proportion of children in foster care than would be expected based on the overall proportion of these children in the county. The literature review the group conducted uncovered the following facts:

1. Children of color were overrepresented in foster care not only in Jackson County but elsewhere in the country as well.
2. Racial or ethnic minority children can become overrepresented in foster care in two ways: (a) they can be placed in foster care at a higher rate than white children and/or (b) they can leave foster care at a

slower rate than white children and thus account for a greater number in care at any given point in time.

3. Research reports suggested that ethnic minority children, once placed in foster care, were adopted or placed in other permanent arrangements at the same rate as white children. However, ethnic minority children who were returned to their parents' homes did so much more slowly than did white children.

4. Placing children in foster care may be necessary if it is the only way to ensure their safety, but all possible efforts should be made by workers to avoid the need for foster care by facilitating solutions to family problems while the child is still in the home.

5. If it still becomes necessary, foster care is supposed to be temporary. Workers should attempt to facilitate solutions to problems in the family in order to allow the child to return home as quickly as possible. If this cannot be done, the next best option is to find some other permanent placement such as an adoptive home.

Analysis of the Population

The task force members then directed their efforts toward gaining a better understanding of ethnic minority children in foster care. To accomplish this, they reviewed five-year statistics from the department's child welfare division, studied in detail the findings of the division's recent report, and examined other research on minority children and families. The most important results they found were:

1. Foster care that is intended to be temporary but that continues indefinitely is harmful to children. This is because it jeopardizes their ability to form developmentally critical attachments with a parent or permanent parent surrogate.

2. For healthy development, children need to go through a series of stages and successfully complete developmental tasks. Completion of these tasks can be interrupted by going into foster care. This can result in delayed development for the child.

3. Placement of a child from an ethnic group with a foster family from another ethnic group can be detrimental to the child if the foster family is unaware of or insensitive to important cultural factors.

Based on these findings, the task force refined its problem statement to focus on the specific concerns of children of color being too likely to be placed in foster care and too unlikely to be reunited with their biological families in a timely fashion.

Analysis of the Arena

Initial findings of the research efforts of the task force also implied that the arena in which a change effort would need to take place was not the community as a whole but the Jackson County Social Services organization. Under this assumption, the task force collected the following information from departmental records and from interviews with current and former clients and professionals in community agencies:

1. The proportion of persons of color who held professional positions in Jackson County's foster care services division was much lower than the proportion of children of color who were placed in foster care in the county.

2. Foster parents licensed by the division were also much less racially and ethnically diverse than the population of foster children in the county.

3. Many child welfare workers and foster parents were seen as lacking an in-depth understanding of the meaning of culture and tradition to ethnic minority families. This meant that children's behavior tended to be interpreted from a white perspective, which might be inconsistent with norms established and understood in minority communities.

4. Once child welfare services in Jackson County had commenced, white children were less likely to be placed in foster care than were nonwhite children.

5. Support services offered to help families deal with problems when a child was removed were seen as lacking the cultural sensitivity necessary to help strengthen ethnic minority families.

As shown in Figure 1.1 in Chapter 1, the change effort that task force members began planning therefore assumed that the situation was one involving an overlap of problem (too great a likelihood of children entering foster care and staying too long), population (children of color), and arena (Jackson County Social Services, its employees, its foster parents, and its clients). It was thought that biological families served by the department's foster care division needed more resources and supportive services. Also, the division's professional staff and its foster parents needed a better understanding of family norms and the variables critical to healthy family environments for minority children.

Hypothesis of Etiology
Based on the preceding findings, the task force developed the following hypothesis of etiology:

Because of the following factors:

1. The low number of staff from ethnic minority populations;
2. The low number of foster parents from ethnic minority populations;
3. The limited knowledge of culture on the part of staff and foster parents; and
4. The high number of ethnic minority children being removed from their homes.

The result has been:

1. An organizational insensitivity to and unawareness of the importance of culture in foster care;
2. A preference on the part of foster parents for white children;
3. Low levels of cultural competence throughout the agency; and
4. A disproportionate number of ethnic minority children in foster care.

Intervention Hypothesis
Based on the preceding analysis, the task force proposed the following as their intervention hypothesis:

If we can do the following:

1. Recruit a more diverse child welfare staff;
2. Recruit more ethnic minority foster parents;
3. Train staff and foster parents; and
4. Support ethnic minority families in the home.

Then we would expect the following results:

1. Improved communication and understanding between ethnic minority families and staff;
2. Families better able to meet the cultural and ethnic needs of ethnic minority foster children;
3. Increased cultural competence on the part of white staff and foster parents; and

4. Increased number of successful returns of ethnic minority children to biological families.

After proceeding through each of the tasks outlined in the earlier chapters of this book, the task force produced the following written plan.

Part I: The Problem and the Proposed Change
In the Jackson County Division of Child Welfare Services, it was recently discovered that the rate of return of minority children from foster care to their natural families was significantly lower than the rates for white children. A task force was appointed, and a study was undertaken. A number of causal factors have emerged from the study.

There is some evidence that minority families whose children go into foster care have more serious economic, social, and emotional problems and are in need of a network of supportive services that will enable them to strengthen the family and better parent the child. On the whole, such services, with a special emphasis on serving ethnic minority families, have generally not been available to these families.

Also, there is evidence that child welfare workers and foster parents lack knowledge about culture that could be important in the decision-making process about the needs of ethnic minority children and what should be considered realistic behavioral and performance expectations for return to natural families.

The task force proposes a series of interventions aimed at improving the cultural sensitivity of child-care workers and foster parents and strengthening families who place children in foster care.

The first set of interventions will be directed toward child welfare workers and foster care parents. Recruitment activities will include:

- Contact with graduate schools of social work
- Advertising in urban agencies where there are large numbers of ethnic minority child welfare workers

Cultural sensitivity training for child welfare workers and foster parents will include:

- Assessing one's values and perceptions as they relate to work with minority children and their families
- Understanding African American families and children
- Understanding Latino families and children

- Understanding Native American families and children
- Understanding Asian American families and children

Foster parents who complete cultural sensitivity training courses will:

- Receive a higher level of payment
- Be certified to receive ethnic minority foster children

The second set of interventions will include support services, under contract with agencies that have demonstrated an understanding of and sensitivity to ethnic minority cultures. These services will be directed toward minority families. They are:

- Individual and family assessment and counseling
- Case management

- Economic incentives
- Parent training
- Self-help groups

Part II: Key Actors and Systems

Table 11.1 provides an overview of the systems, their definitions, and the representatives of each system. Note that there is intentional overlap between systems.

Part III: Goals, Objectives, and Activities

This change effort is proposed as a three-year pilot project, during which time the Division of Child Welfare will experiment with and correct any problems discovered in implementing the original design. Following the three-year trial period, it is to be implemented as a permanent part of Jackson County Child Welfare Services.

Table 11.1 Systems

System Representative	Definition	System
Initiator	Those who first brought the problem to attention	Black Families United, a community organization that organized the effort to meet with the County Board of Supervisors
Change Agent	The professional social worker, agency, and others coordinating the change effort	The task force, staffed by an experienced child welfare supervisor
Client	Primary and secondary beneficiaries	Ethnic minority children who are placed in foster care, and their parents
Support	Others who may be expected to support the change effort	At least eight ethnic community organizations, two child welfare advocacy groups, several ethnic minority clergy and their congregations, many child welfare professionals, and the foster parents' association
Controlling	The person or persons who have the power and the authority to approve the change and direct that it be implemented	The County Board of Supervisors
Host	The part of the organization or community that will provide auspices for administration of the intervention	The Jackson County Division of Child Welfare
Implementing	The staff and/or volunteers who will carry out the intervention	Three units within the Jackson County Division of Child Welfare: (1) the foster care unit, (2) the staff development and training unit, and (3) the purchase of services contracting unit

(continued)

Table 11.1   Systems (*continued*)

System Representative	Definition	System
Target	That which must be changed for the intervention to be successful	Since this will be a multiphase process, there will be phase-specific targets. The initial target will be the funding sources needed to underwrite the proposed interventions. This includes the Board of Supervisors and several local foundations. Subsequent targets include (1) child welfare workers and foster parents who need to become more ethnically sensitive and (2) ethnic minority families with children in foster care.
Action	The expanded planning and coordinating committee responsible for seeing the change effort through to completion	The task force, together with key representatives from the Division of Child Welfare and potential service providers

Goal

To reduce the disproportionate number of ethnic minority children in foster care in the Jackson County Child Welfare system.

Outcome Objective 1

By December 31, 20XX, to increase the knowledge of four ethnic minority cultures of at least 50 trainees (including child welfare workers and foster parents), as measured by a 50 percent increase between pretest and posttest scores on tests developed for the training course.

Process Objectives

1.1 By July 31, 20XX, to present a proposal to the County Board of Supervisors for funds to develop culturally sensitive curriculum for child welfare workers and foster parents in Jackson County.

1.2 By September 30, 20XX, to develop four training courses on understanding African American, Latino, Native American, and Asian American families designed for child welfare workers and foster parents who serve ethnic minority children.

1.3 By October 31, 20XX, to produce 50 copies of all handouts associated with the training courses and distribute them to the Child Welfare Staff Development and Training Unit.

1.4 By November 30, 20XX, to recruit at least 50 child welfare workers and foster parents to take the training courses.

1.5 By January 31, 20XX, to administer pretests and to train at least 50 child welfare workers and foster parents in cultural sensitivity.

1.6 By March 31, 20XX, to administer posttests to trainees and to analyze the pretest/posttest results.

Outcome Objective 2

By September 30, 20XX, at least 100 ethnic minority families with children in foster care will demonstrate improved family strength and parenting skills as measured by at least 30 percent higher scores on the Multidimensional Parenting and Family Assessment Inventory.

Process Objectives

2.1 By November 30, 20XX, economic, social, emotional, and family support resources needed to serve African American, Latino, Native American, and Asian American families in Jackson County will be inventoried.

2.2 By April 30, 20XX, at least 100 ethnic minority families with children in foster care will have been initially assessed to determine what resources are currently used and what resources are needed but not available or accessible.

2.3 By June 30, 20XX, gaps between available and needed resources for minority families will be documented in writing.

2.4 By September 30, 20XX, formal proposals for funding services designed for minority families will be presented to the Jackson County Board of Supervisors and at least two local foundations.

Part IV: Tactics

It is anticipated that this change effort will proceed through a series of phases, as shown here.

Phase 1

The purpose of phase 1 is to get the change accepted by potential funding sources. The focus of this phase is on the County Board of Supervisors, several private foundations interested in minority concerns, and people capable of influencing their decisions. Campaign tactics will include education, persuasion, and lobbying. In the event that campaign tactics are not successful and that funding sources are not open to change, contest tactics may be used. These tactics would include mass media appeals to mobilize the support system as well as bargaining and negotiation and large-group social action.

Phase 2

The purpose of phase 2, if the project is funded, is to increase cultural awareness, knowledge, and competence. The focus of this phase is on child welfare staff and foster parents who serve minority children and their families. Collaborative tactics will include joint action, capacity building, and education.

Phase 3

The purpose of phase 3 is to ensure that improved services are provided to minority families who have placed children in foster care. Services should be adapted to the unique needs, concerns, interests, and traditions of each ethnic group and will involve application of knowledge and skill gained in phase 2. The focus of this effort will be on child welfare workers, foster parents, and contracted service providers. Collaborative tactics will include capacity building and joint action.

Monitoring and Evaluation

The child welfare supervisor who served on the task force will be assigned the responsibility of monitoring the implementation of the project and producing evaluation reports. She will use the project's goal, outcome objectives, process objectives, and activities as a basis for ensuring that all tasks and activities are carried out on time and at an acceptable level of quality.

The evaluation report will focus on outcomes related to (1) increased cultural awareness, knowledge, and competence of workers and foster parents; (2) improved levels of comfort and understanding between ethnic minority families and child welfare workers; (3) strengthened families and parenting skills on the part of participating ethnic minority families; and (4) increasing rates of successful return of ethnic minority children in foster care to their biological families.

Assess Your Competence

Use the scale below to rate your current level of achievement on the following concepts or skills associated with each learning outcome listed at the beginning of this chapter:

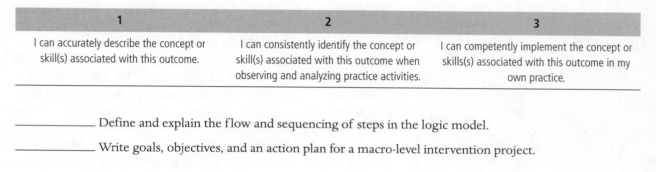

1	2	3
I can accurately describe the concept or skill(s) associated with this outcome.	I can consistently identify the concept or skill(s) associated with this outcome when observing and analyzing practice activities.	I can competently implement the concept or skills(s) associated with this outcome in my own practice.

_____ Define and explain the flow and sequencing of steps in the logic model.

_____ Write goals, objectives, and an action plan for a macro-level intervention project.

Monitoring and Evaluating the Intervention

RAWPIXEL / FOTOLIA

THE IMPORTANCE OF MONITORING AND EVALUATION

In Chapter 11, we discussed the process of planning and implementing the change effort, along with applying the logic model to help understand the necessary tasks (see Figure 11.1). The purpose of this chapter is to describe how to complete a change effort by monitoring and evaluating its success. We will use the term **monitor** to describe the collection of information on activities leading to the achievement of objectives. *Monitor* comes from a Latin word meaning "to warn," which accurately reflects the purpose of data collection. **Lead persons** in charge of the change effort cannot simply assume that activities will be accomplished; they must systematically gather information to confirm that this is the case.

Monitoring and evaluation are fundamental parts of both the scientific method and evidence-based social work practice, and ongoing improvement is seldom achieved in the absence of ongoing monitoring. Governmental grants typically require that 5–15 percent of direct costs be allocated to evaluation efforts (GrantsNorthwest, 2015; U.S. Department of Education, 2015), and organizations themselves may allocate up to 20 percent of operating expenses to evaluation (Better Evaluation, 2015).

Evaluation is also at the heart of social work ethics, since one of the most important responsibilities of practitioners, whether at the micro or macro level, is to be certain that the services they provide clients are effective. Also, clients are neither the only beneficiaries nor the only purchasers of services, and practitioners have both ethical and practical reasons for ensuring that funding sources are also provided with accurate and timely evaluation results. Finally, the mandate for evaluating services holds for change efforts as well, since the ultimate goal of change efforts in social work is to improve clients' lives.

> Watch this video introduction to monitoring and evaluation. What differences between monitoring and evaluation are highlighted in this video?
>
> www.youtube.com /watch?v=Y_z9H0alSqQ

Types of Evaluation

Evaluation efforts are often conceptualized as having three types: formative, process, and outcome evaluations. **Formative evaluation**, also referred to as developmental evaluation, will not be discussed here, since it occurs at earlier stages of a change effort to ensure that the necessary information is available to plan well. In effect, much of the discussion in preceding chapters addresses tasks typically undertaken in formative evaluation. Our concern in this chapter will be with **process evaluation** and **outcome evaluation**, both of which fit well with the logic model.

Process evaluation, also referred to as program monitoring, tackles the question of whether the intended changes were those that were actually implemented. In the Centerville example from the previous chapter (Box 11.1), the types of changes planned included finding inexpensive apartments for homeless men, enrolling a meaningful proportion of them in night classes to earn a GED, and providing access to health and mental health services to overcome problems that prevented them from finding and maintaining employment. A process evaluation effort would examine whether these steps were taken. It would also ask whether the activities necessary to complete these steps were carried out, such as finding resources to assist with rent until the men found jobs, assigning responsibility for locating apartments, identifying or initiating night classes, and so on. In the logic model, it is assumed that outputs and outcomes cannot be achieved unless elements of the preceding process phase are completed, and determining this is the focus of process evaluation. However, even if results of a process evaluation indicate that the change effort has been appropriately implemented and process objectives have been achieved, it cannot be assumed that outcomes objectives will also be achieved.

Outcome evaluation focuses on both outputs and outcomes. As discussed earlier, outputs involve the administration of some service, such as providing mental health evaluations to a specific number of homeless men, or securing prescription medication for them. Outcomes arise from outputs, as when stabilization of

Evaluation

Behavior: Critically analyze, monitor, and evaluate intervention and program processes and outcomes.

Critical Thinking Question: Why do social workers have an ethical responsibility to critically monitor and evaluate change efforts?

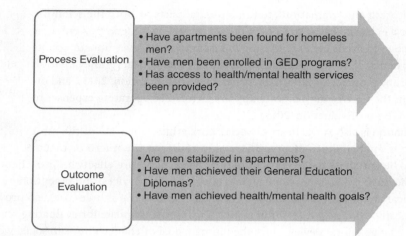

Figure 12.1
Process and Outcome Evaluation in the Centerville Example

Do an Internet search for "Promoting Social Responsibility in the Arab World." Search within the website for "Monitoring and Evaluation." Look at the first of the 12 manuals in English developed by Support for Training, Advocacy, and Networking for Development (STAND). Compare and contrast content in these manuals designed for introducing monitoring and evaluation to the civic sector in Kuwait and the region to what you are learning in this chapter. What are the differences and similarities?

mental health symptoms enables a specified number of men to find work within six months and to hold those jobs for a specified length of time. Again, however, the achievement of planned outputs does not guarantee that outcomes will be achieved. For example, receipt of mental health services may not be a sufficient condition for stable employment, because other problems such as substance abuse or lack of job skills are greater barriers. Figure 12.1 illustrates the differences between process and outcome evaluations in the Centerville example.

How Changes Can Go Wrong

In an article on the success and failure of change efforts, Burnes and Jackson (2011) note that as many as 70 percent of organizational change episodes fail. This figure includes commercial firms, where constantly shifting market forces may produce more frequent changes and more frequent failures than in human service organizations. Yet, just as in physics, where matter tends to resist change to its current state, few people and fewer macro systems leap to embrace every change that comes along.

Kegan and Lahey (2009) use a medical analogy to suggest that organizations have an "immune system" that tends to attack unfamiliar ideas. This is not always bad, as skepticism may arise from hard-earned lessons about what works and what doesn't. But excessive resistance to change means that an organization or community will eventually fail to adapt to new challenges or to adopt better ways of addressing them.

For these and other reasons, the first step in conducting a process evaluation is to begin monitoring even small aspects of the change episode immediately after it begins. The purpose of this is to determine if the desired changes are not being made or are being altered from what was originally planned. In doing this, it is helpful to be familiar with ways that change episodes fail. Box 12.1 offers a range of examples from the research literature. Many of these involve change failures in organizations, but some are from community settings as well.

Box 12.1 Examples of Why Change Episodes Fail

Leadership transitions	Parker, Alcaraz, and Payne (2011) conducted a case study of a community effort to reduce youth violence in a traditionally underserved neighborhood. Despite some initial successes, the change ground to a halt far short of its goals when members of the leadership team as well as local political supporters eventually left or turned their attention to other matters.
Lack of inspirational leadership	Nohe, Michaelis, Menges, Zhang, and Sonntag (2013) surveyed managers and workers at a large commercial firm undergoing major restructuring. Results indicated a positive feedback loop between a team leader's efforts to promote the change, team members' perception of that behavior as charismatic, and measures of success. The effect did not go directly from change-promotion to change-success, and only leaders who were seen as being able to promote the change in charismatic ways were successful.
Loss of attachment	A case study of hospital-based nurses by Grady and Grady (2013) revealed the existence of attachment bonds in working groups that mirror those among family members described by John Bowlby's (1969) attachment theory. Change episodes disrupted these bonds, and when they were not properly managed, led to lingering declines in service effectiveness.
Loss of middle-management role	Raelin and Cataldo (2011), in a case study of a large commercial firm, examined the role of midlevel managers during a major organizational change. They found that a top-down approach to the change caused executives and line-level workers to close ranks against each other. Middle managers, who could have served as mediators and facilitators, were left isolated and ineffective in moving the change forward.
Negative discourse about change	Using interviews and focus groups, Schwarz, Watson, and Callan (2011) studied an attempt to implement a new computer information system in a for-profit training firm. The attempt failed, and the authors' findings suggested that the nature of internal conversations among organizational members was a major reason for failure. Negative or pessimistic talk about the change can make its failure a reality, although this may be avoided by managers' skillful use of communication networks within the organization.
Cynicism about organizational change	Brown and Cregan (2008) found that pessimism about and resistance to change increase with poor sharing of information between managers and staff, along with lower involvement of staff in making decisions about change episodes. This supports earlier research (Wanous, Reichers, & Austin, 2000) showing that cynicism about change does not simply arise from employees who have negative or pessimistic personalities, but builds over time as a result of employees' experiences in the organization.

The purpose of the list in Box 12.1 is not to suggest that changes are doomed to fail. Instead, the point is that research continues to reveal a wide range of dynamics within communities and organizations that can interfere with successful change. These often appear after initiation of the change episode, so an important goal for monitoring activities is to assess their presence and make adjustments to counter their effects.

? Assess your understanding of the importance of monitoring and evaluation by taking this brief quiz.

A FRAMEWORK FOR EVALUATING THE CHANGE EFFORT

As noted in Chapter 11, activities consist of specific tasks undertaken to achieve objectives. In general, outcome evaluation is concerned with whether outcome objectives are reached; process evaluation focuses on whether activities were carried out to achieve process objectives that then led to achieving outcomes . Many macro systems, especially formal organizations, track such activities carefully as part of ongoing quality assurance procedures. Authors such as McFillen, O'Neil, Balzer, and Varney (2013) argue for a "diagnostic" approach, conceptualized for organizations along the same lines as preventive health-care checkups for individuals. These checkups show how the change process is going and what results are occurring.

Two tasks are highlighted in this framework. They are:

Task 1: Conduct a Process Evaluation
Task 2: Conduct an Outcome Evaluation

Task 1: Conduct a Process Evaluation

To the extent possible, process evaluation efforts for a change episode should mesh with existing tracking procedures to take advantage of information already being collected. However, since change efforts are, by definition, novel events, numerical data and other information needed for monitoring the progress of the change may be different from what is gathered on a normal basis.

Process evaluations allow decisions to be made as to whether the change effort is being carried out appropriately. This is based in part on information regarding whether process objectives are achieved. Of equal importance is information about whether the structures and activities created to achieve the process objective match those in the original plan.

Monitoring efforts focus on gathering information about four elements of the change episode: (1) technical activities, (2) interpersonal activities, (3) clients and beneficiaries, and (4) achievement of process objectives. In some cases, clients and other beneficiaries may be far removed from the change, such as when it is focused on internal operations of an organization. In other cases, they will be closely involved and crucial to determining whether the change succeeded.

Monitor Technical Activities

The key questions to be explored are:

- What is the appropriate sequencing for the activities that must be completed in order to achieve the process objective?
- Who will be assigned responsibility for completion of each activity?
- When must each activity be completed in order for the process objective to be achieved on time?

Technical activities are the steps described in the plan for the change episode that need to be completed in order to achieve a process objective. If these have been carefully itemized, preferably in Gantt chart form, monitoring is greatly simplified. Activities are often designed to happen in sequence, with the completion of one depending on completion of the previous one. As with dominoes in a line, if any individual domino is missing or fails to fall, progress stops. But when start and completion dates, together with a person responsible, have been established for each activity, monitoring simply requires confirming with the person responsible that the activity has been started or completed as of the date specified. This provides an early warning system in case any of the activities have not or cannot be completed on time.

When activities have not met deadlines, or when problems emerge, the lead person becomes involved in problem solving and decision making. Brody (2005) points out that **problem solving** involves formulating a problem statement and examining potential alternatives, whereas **decision making** requires choosing from among alternatives and implementing an approach to deal with the problem.

A critical issue in managing change efforts is staying on schedule. If the due date for scheduling appointments is missed, then each subsequent due date may slip, delaying implementation and possibly resulting in an inability to complete the project on time. The lead person is often the only individual who has a view of all of the activities that are going on simultaneously and therefore has responsibility for integrating component parts of the change effort.

In monitoring technical activities, it may be useful to add several columns to the activity chart, such as the following: Was the activity completed? Was it completed on time? What was the quality of the product? What adjustments are needed for this activity? What adjustments are needed for subsequent activities? By tracking each of these factors, the lead person will be in a position to be more proactive in anticipating problems and needs and in making the necessary adjustments.

The lead person should also be mindful of dynamics within the community or organization, such as those listed in Box 12.1, that can lead to noncompletion of one or more activities. An example is the work of Parker et al. (2011) showing how leadership turnover can undermine forward progress in a community change effort. In the Centerville case, it might be that a single city council member provided much of the driving force behind the contract with Community Senior Services and was also responsible for much of the oversight. If this person chose not to run for reelection or was defeated, momentum for completing the change and making it a lasting effort could be lost.

Monitor Interpersonal Activities

Key questions to be explored are:

- How enthusiastic and supportive are the designated implementers?
- Is there a formal or informal system for evaluating the performance of implementers?
- Is there a strategy for dealing with poor performance, apathy, or resistance?

Monitoring the implementation of a plan can be a highly rewarding experience when persons carrying out the plan are enthusiastic, hardworking, competent, compatible, cooperative, and committed to a common vision. Unfortunately, such a scenario is not always the case. Some participants may have been assigned without their consent. Personalities and styles of working may clash. Competition may emerge. Once again, Box 12.1 provides examples of these dynamics observed in various studies.

Interpersonal tensions can often be traced to uncertainty about roles and responsibilities or to feelings of being overly controlled. Good management practices should be promoted, encouraging participants to use their talents and abilities to the greatest extent while the lead person focuses on removing barriers to implementation activities. However, in spite of the manager's best efforts, competition and conflict are likely to surface at some point.

Strategies for dealing with performance problems, including interpersonal tensions, should be established and communicated to all participants. Within an organizational arena, performance should be evaluated regularly and consistently. In a larger, more permanent program, a formal appraisal will be conducted and placed in a personnel file. In a less formally structured effort (particularly with community change), regularly scheduled conferences, staff meetings, or peer review sessions can be encouraged in the interest of airing concerns before they affect morale and performance. Rewards and incentives should be commensurate with performance. Identifying all of these motivational factors for each participant at the point of selection and/or hiring (if applicable) can go a long way toward preempting interpersonal problems.

Community change efforts may involve coalitions of organizations or groups of people who do not work for one organization, and they may be almost totally dependent on volunteer commitment. Policy approaches to change may pull together disparate groups that are concerned about an issue but that are not formally related and may disperse once approval of the policy occurs. In some cases, employees of the organization responsible for implementing a change could not have been involved in the change process because they are not allowed to participate in advocacy efforts as part of their employment status, thus preventing the early involvement of implementers that is typically desired. When facing the complexities of a diffused implementation system, it is advisable for the lead person to spend a great deal of time communicating by phone, text, and email; in formally written reports; and in person to keep the project on track. Persistent and personalized attention to participants in the implementation process are critical if the full extent of the change effort is to be realized.

Monitor Clients and Beneficiaries

Key questions to be explored include:

- Are intended services being offered?
- Is there evidence that those services are reaching the intended targets?

Most change efforts are designed to make something useful happen for a target population, such as increasing the walkability of streets in a neighborhood or developing a new service for clients of an agency. Monitoring activities must examine whether activities are being completed that will lead toward these changes. They must also gather information to determine if activities are being directed toward the target population and not some other group.

In Chapter 7, we reviewed theory and research on *goal displacement*, through which organizational activities are pulled in unintended directions by influential individuals or groups seeking to serve alternative goals. The examples in Box 12.1 show additional ways in which change efforts can be undermined or misdirected. One way to avert this is to collect data from multiple sources about how the change is being implemented, also called **triangulation**. If different sources of information are used but results from those sources are consistent, the confidence with which conclusions can be drawn increases. Box 12.2 lists examples of data sources for monitoring and evaluation.

Box 12.2   Sources of Data for Monitoring and Evaluation

An after-school program is initiated in several middle schools in an urban area to reduce the frequency of vandalism occurring between the end of school and the time when most parents return home from work. The following are examples of data sources about participants in the program.

Source	Example
Key informant	A long-time local patrol officer is interviewed a few months into the program regarding evidence of reduced vandalism or other juvenile crime.
Focus group	A small sample of parents of children enrolled in the program is invited to offer comments after two months of operation. Focus groups often have a structured set of questions to which participants are asked to respond.
Community forum	Similar to the focus group example above, except all parents are invited. A less structured agenda is most common, so attendees can raise concerns or questions.
Case manager	The employee responsible for each case is contacted to obtain information on the participant's progress. The information collected can be gathered in an in-depth interview, a phone conversation, or a brief email or web-based survey.
Internal case record	The file maintained on each participant is reviewed to gather information on after-school attendance, behavioral problems, and other indicators.
Employee meeting	Staff members gather to discuss progress and report on individual cases.
External case records	Police records are accessed to record the number of vandalism reports or arrests of participants.
Accounting and billing records	Records of payments to after-school teachers show whether the sessions are remaining fully staffed.
Direct observation	After-school teachers and recreation leaders record which participants stay for the full duration of the sessions and which leave early.
Diaries and journals	Participants or parents write down or record accounts of their experiences with the program. Accounts from staff members can also be useful.
Case study	An intensive review of the progress of one or a small number of participants is completed using a combination of the above data sources.

Data collected from the sources described in Box 12.2 typically come in one of two forms—quantitative or qualitative. Quantitative data are numerical in form, ranging from a simple yes or no (0 or 1) regarding whether a particular activity occurred to complex ratings of managerial compliance. Qualitative data typically take the form of words and are able to tell a "story" that illuminates dynamics of the change effort or adds depth and context to numerical results. For example, using the sources listed in Box 12.2, data from billing records can show how many outside recreational staff were hired, but diaries and journals kept by supervisors can reveal whether a particular staff member was able to interact well with participants and keep conflicts to a minimum.

The domino analogy used earlier in this chapter is important to keep in mind with respect to monitoring efforts. Achievement of a particular objective may require that many preceding activities be completed. If eight such steps are necessary, but only the first seven are monitored, it is still possible that

Watch this video on monitoring and evaluation. What methods do London charities use to incorporate qualitative data into their monitoring and evaluation plans?

www.youtube.com
/watch?v=xDD2GZKPvys

the objective will not be reached. This argues for careful monitoring of every planned activity.

A countervailing force to constant monitoring comes from the demands that data collection places on employees. Despite the rapid transition over the past 20 years from paper forms to computer recordkeeping, the reporting burden for individuals has risen in many cases. This is due to the fact that, as organizations have become increasingly complex, demands for accountability have mushroomed, sometimes to the detriment of services. For example, Taylor (2013) found that workers submit to paperwork demands in part because doing so gives them a greater sense of accomplishment than does the reduced and often insufficient time available to spend with clients. Chang (2012) also notes the voracious appetite for documentation that modern organizations display, suggesting that the ability of computers and other devices to manage information has increased the demand for information more rapidly than technology can reduce it.

The dilemma faced by lead persons is that monitoring needed by the change effort may simply add to heavy demand for information that already confronts organizational members. Regardless of the data collection method or methods selected, the response to requests for still more data may be far less than enthusiastic, so monitoring efforts must balance the need for accurate information with limits to the organization's ability to collect it.

Assess Completion of Process Objectives

Key questions to be explored include:

- Does monitoring information show that the process objective was achieved?
- If not, at what point were the activities leading to it not completed or unsuccessful?
- What corrective actions are needed?

Using the activities, objectives, and timelines specified in a Gantt chart, the ultimate aim of monitoring efforts is to determine whether process objectives have been achieved. In the Centerville example, one process objective was:

> No later than six months after all participants have been selected, at least 90% of all participants will have completed their initial screening appointment with appropriate health clinics as documented by treatment plans provided by the providers at the clinic.

A well-crafted objective provides its own guidance concerning information to be gathered by monitoring efforts. In this example, the source of information will be providers of initial screenings and treatment plans. If the lead person or evaluator has made certain that necessary records are kept by providers to document screening appointments, then calling to retrieve that information should be straightforward and brief.

If it can be concluded that the process objective was achieved, the lead person or evaluator is free to proceed to other process objectives and then to outcome objectives. However, if information from monitoring efforts is inconclusive or indicates that the process objective was not completed, it will be necessary to ask a series of follow-up questions to determine what went wrong. Did too few participants show up for screenings? If so, did they lack transportation? Were they asked, contrary to arrangements with screening clinics, to pay for the service? Was the importance of the screenings insufficiently communicated?

These questions illustrate the value of collecting qualitative as well as quantitative data as part of monitoring efforts. In broad terms, quantitative information is useful for describing what happened, whereas qualitative data can answer questions like "What went wrong?" In this case, results from a focus group session with participants could reveal the presence of transportation problems that prevent them from keeping screening appointments. If regular sessions are held, the problem might be identified in time to make accommodations early in the change process. Similar information would be available if a small number of participants were asked to keep a diary or log. Crunkilton and Robinson (2008) and Teater (2011) provide examples of qualitatively focused program evaluations.

If the process objective was not achieved, answers to a variety of questions should be explored. Among these is whether the process objective and activities leading to it were appropriately conceptualized. If guidelines in Chapter 11 were incorrectly applied, it is possible that the process objective was not written in a way that makes it clear whether it was achieved. Consider these contrasting examples of how a process objective may be phrased:

- "By March 15, at least 30 homeless men in Centerville will have enrolled in a job skills program."
- "Job skills training will be made available to homeless men."

Monitoring information, if appropriately collected, should make it easy to conclude whether the first objective was met. The second example, however, lacks critical elements such as a deadline, and it is ambiguous about details such as what "made available" means and which homeless men are the focus of the effort (e.g., those in Centerville? Those in nearby towns?). The same need for clarity and precision applies to each entry in the list of activities; therefore, one result of monitoring efforts may be a conclusion that statements of activities and process objectives need to be revised and strengthened.

If monitoring results reveal that a process objective was not achieved, a systematic review should be initiated to find the cause. One possibility is that a single key activity was not completed, and as in the domino analogy, further progress stopped. Another possibility is that activities in the original list were insufficient to achieve the objective, and others are needed. Also possible is that activities believed to be appropriate were not, and a different approach will be required if the objective is to be achieved. Finally, it's possible that activities leading up to the process objective are sufficient to produce some change, but not as much as originally planned.

Failure to complete an activity or process objective does not mean the entire change effort is doomed to fail, and it is important to remember that few such efforts go exactly as planned. If the review process reveals that one activity was not listed or missed, completing it may be all that's necessary for progress to resume. The more time that passes between when progress stops and that fact is discovered, however, the more difficult it may be to restart the change effort. This means that monitoring cannot wait until the date the process objective is due to be achieved.

Another consideration is whether a partially achieved objective should be considered a failure or a less-than-hoped-for success. Much depends on whether the outcome objective toward which the process objective was targeted can still be achieved in full or in part. For example, if only 20 homeless men in Centerville—rather than the specified 30 men—receive job training, should the effort be abandoned? Suppose the outcome objective is for 25 of 30 men who receive job skills training to be employed within 60 days, and 18 of the 20 who are trained actually do find such work. Arguably, this is still a benefit to both the men and the community. In these cases, as we will discuss later in the chapter, efforts should be to determine if the benefit achieved by finding work for these men is worth the cost of the program. Resources are always scarce, and if a different program could have produced a more worthwhile outcome for the same amount of money, then the change effort's activities thus far cannot be considered a success.

Task 2: Conduct an Outcome Evaluation

In the logic model, inputs (clients and skilled employees) engage in various processes (assessment, counseling, and job training) to produce outputs (completion of GED and acquisition of technical skills). These outputs lead to outcomes (securing employment and housing), which produce impacts (economic self-sufficiency, and self-actualization). Outcome objectives may address not only outcomes but also impacts, and evaluation efforts must examine both.

The steps we discussed in Chapter 11 describe basic tasks to be completed in order to carry out both process and outcome evaluations. Essential elements include identification of a goal and outcome objectives, along with an intervention hypothesis that proposes what needs to happen in order to reach the goal. Major steps toward doing so are identified in the form of process objectives, and activities needed to achieve both process and outcome objectives are then specified. If monitoring activities and data collection are properly planned, implemented, and maintained, the task of completing an evaluation becomes one of interpreting results and making sure that conclusions are accurate.

With regard to the results of a process evaluation, three conclusions are possible. These are shown in Figure 12.2. If information gathered from monitoring efforts indicates that one or more process objectives were not achieved, attempts should be made to determine where progress stopped and to make corrections that will allow achievement of the objectives. If this cannot be accomplished, it is unlikely that outcome objectives will be achieved, and the change effort may need to be halted. However, if most or all of the process objectives were achieved, and if it remains plausible that this will result in achievement of one or more outcome objectives, the change effort should continue and evaluation efforts should enter the next phase.

Just as the achievement of process objectives is the focus of process evaluation, outcome evaluation seeks to determine if outcome objectives are achieved. Information to accomplish this is collected through monitoring efforts of the type used in the process evaluation phase. These efforts focus on whether activities leading toward outcome objectives are being carried out appropriately. At the same time, existing monitoring work may need to continue into this new phase to ensure that activities designed to be ongoing—such as new services, supervision, or billing and payment—proceed as planned.

In the Centerville example, one of the outcome objectives is "At least 80% of participants will have no more than one incident of disruptive behavior reported, as documented by a tracking system included in the monthly social services report."

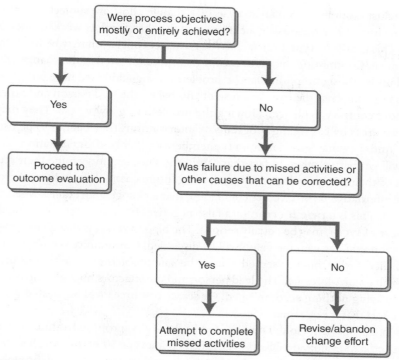

Figure 12.2
Decision Tree for Results of Process Evaluation

This addresses program impact, in that it assumes the social services provided to homeless men and women enabled them to change patterns of functioning that previously led to disruptive behavior. It also offers evidence to support the intervention hypothesis. When analyzing the results of an outcome evaluation, however, much of the work involves considering ways in which conclusions may be wrong.

Recognize Types of Error

Key questions to be explored include:

- Is there a risk of erroneously concluding the change episode succeeded?
- Is there a risk of erroneously concluding the change episode failed?
- Are evaluation efforts asking the right question(s)?

An intervention hypothesis uses information from theory and prior research to make an educated guess about what new actions, programs, or structures (e.g., community groups or organizational divisions) will lead to the achievement of a goal. The **null hypothesis** assumes the opposite—that any progress toward achieving goals and objectives happened not because of the change effort but simply because of chance. This means that evidence of achievement of outcomes must be sufficiently convincing to outweigh a contrary argument that the outcome was a random occurrence. This is the approach used by tests of statistical significance.

Evaluation

Behavior: Select and use appropriate methods for evaluation of outcomes.

Critical Thinking Question: What can you do if you discover that the methods you are using are not appropriate in fully evaluating a change effort?

Conclusions drawn from an analysis of a change effort are subject to two types of error. One involves erroneously concluding that the change effort worked when in fact it did not. This is called a **type I error**, and the incorrect conclusion may be thought of as a false positive. Committing this error means that those involved in the change effort may proceed under the assumption that the problems being addressed have been corrected, when in fact that's not the case. Because of this belief, the lead person and other actors may ignore contrary evidence, allowing the problem to grow worse. They may waste scarce resources by expanding programs or interventions they believe to be useful but are not. And they may give community members or clients of organizations hope that things will get better, when in fact that's unlikely. This can undermine their credibility and that of their group or organization, making future change efforts more difficult.

The alternative error involves concluding that a change effort failed when in fact it succeeded. This is a **type II error**, or a false negative. Its consequences, while different from those of type I, may be equally serious. The biggest threat is that a new program or intervention that has genuine value will be discarded. Community members or organizational clients who could be served will not be, and problems within the community or agency will go unaddressed. The lead person and other actors may give up on effecting change, leaving nothing accomplished. Or scarce resources will be wasted in a second change effort that is not actually needed.

Basch, Sliepcevich, Gold, Duncan, and Kolbe (1985) proposed a third type of error that is specific to evaluation efforts. They termed it a **type III error**, which they defined as evaluating a program that hasn't been properly implemented. This can produce results of unknown accuracy or inaccuracy, and thus of no value. Schwartz and Carpenter (1999) describe this as getting a correct answer to the wrong question.

Consider Sources of Error and Corrective Steps

Key questions to be explored are:

- Is there evidence that measures being used are reliable and valid?
- Is a sufficient number of measures of different types being employed?
- Are procedures in place for guarding against confounding variables?

Defending against the above errors requires keeping in mind that evaluation is a scientific endeavor and should employ the highest feasible level of methodological rigor. The same safeguards that one would expect to use in a research study are also desirable in evaluating a change effort. The following sections discuss common problems that can produce misleading results and erroneous conclusions, together with ways to combat them.

Measurement Unreliability   In the Centerville example, one outcome objective we have discussed involves limiting the number of disruptive behaviors among participants. This is an appropriate target for intervention, given its relationship to social skills and the ability to make placements in housing arrangements that will last over time, but the definition of *disruptive* may be ambiguous. Suppose that the source of information for measuring this objective is staff members at two single-room-occupancy hotels where many of the homeless men and women have been placed. Behaviors that one staff member finds disruptive may not be considered disruptive by another. The lead person or evaluator may discover after the fact that some participants were deemed to have failed due to comparatively minor behavioral problems, while others were considered successes despite several disruptive episodes.

Another problem is that over the period of observation, staff members may become more accustomed to participants' behaviors, meaning that a behavior that was considered disruptive soon after placement is not labeled as a disruption in later stages. These are examples of low interrater agreement and poor measurement stability, respectively, which are types of measurement unreliability (O'Hare, 2015). The only remedy to these problems is a two-stage effort to (1) initiate early training of staff members regarding what behaviors will be counted as disruptions, and (2) conduct tests throughout the change effort to ensure that staff members' ratings remain at acceptable levels of agreement with each other and with themselves over time.

The lead person or evaluator should be prepared to provide evidence to stakeholders of the reliability of measures being used in both the process and outcome evaluation stages. Box 12.3 provides examples of how reliability is assessed across different kinds of measures.

Measurement Invalidity   Other problems can arise from the use of measures that are not valid. The classic definition of **validity** is: Are you measuring what you think you're measuring? In the Centerville example, the reason for recording disruptive behaviors is to determine the ability of homeless men and women to make the transition from living on the street to living in some kind of group housing environment. The assumption is that their ability to avoid dysfunctional behaviors is a good indicator of their success in accommodating to a new living arrangement. However, it is possible that disruptive behaviors are caused not by difficulty transitioning to new housing but by other factors

Box 12.3	Indicators of Measurement Reliability
Interrater reliability	This involves the extent to which different observers agree on the presence or absence, intensity, frequency, or duration of behaviors being recorded. Although there are more sophisticated indicators, the most commonly used measure of interrater reliability is percent agreement.
Test–retest reliability	Some variables, such as mood, can rise and fall frequently over time. Others, such as personality traits or intelligence, change slowly and should show comparatively stable scores over time. If measures of presumably stable variables show dramatic variation, the measures may be unreliable. The most commonly used indicator of test–retest reliability is a correlation coefficient that shows the strength of the association between scores at two different points in time.
Alternate forms reliability	This typically applies to standardized scales such as achievement tests. If the measure is reliable, it should be possible to create more than one version of it, yet have the different versions yield similar scores. The most common indicator is a correlation coefficient measuring the strength of association between subjects' scores on different versions.
Internal consistency	This is also a measure of reliability in standardized scales. It is presumed that individual items in the scale will correlate reasonably strongly with other items and with the total score for all items. The most frequently used indicator is Cronbach's alpha, which is similar to a correlation coefficient but summarizes inter-item and item-total correlations across every item in the scale.

such as unresolved mental health or substance abuse problems. The new housing options may in fact be working well, but the lead person or evaluator might use information on the frequency of disruptions to erroneously conclude that the housing initiative failed (type II error).

A related issue involves the "fit" between measures and the individuals and environments in which they are being employed. Greeno, Colonna-Pydyn, and Shumway (2007) describe problems with evaluating community mental health efforts using measures that participants may find confusing, irrelevant, or offensive. Other problems include cognitive impairments that make self-report measures inappropriate, or participants may lack the necessary literacy skills to read and understand survey questionnaires. In addition, some participants may have difficulty with introspection or memory, and this may affect their ability to provide accurate information whether the method of data collection is self-report or some form of interview. Box 12.4 provides examples of issues that must often be addressed in choosing measures or evaluating results from measures already used in monitoring efforts.

Validity can be a difficult phenomenon to assess, as it cannot be measured directly and must be inferred from indirect evidence. The task of the lead person or evaluator is to examine such evidence with regard to measures being used in the change effort. One aspect of validity is **content validity**, which refers to whether characteristics considered to be part of a particular variable are actually present. In the Centerville example, reductions in disruptive behavior are believed to provide evidence of the effectiveness of social services. However, since other factors may influence disruptive behavior, it may be necessary to gather evidence of the content validity of this measure. One approach is to have a panel of experts review the measures being used and provide a rating for level of content validity (Bloom, Fischer, & Orme, 2009).

Box 12.4 Questions to Ask in Analyzing Measures

- **Is it practical?** Does administration of the measure require so much time or effort on the part of participants or staff that it is unlikely to be used or used appropriately? Also, are the measures being used affordable and as brief as possible?

- **Is it culturally appropriate?** Studies of standardized measures such as intelligence tests have found that they reflect the education, income, and racial/ethnic characteristics of their developers, meaning that they may provide misleading information when administered to those of other backgrounds. Also, many measures are available only in English, whereas social workers often undertake change efforts with immigrant populations and other nonnative English speakers.

- **Does it produce truthful responses?** Measurement "reactivity" occurs when participants or staff members seek to respond in ways that cast them in a more favorable light rather than being strictly accurate. Some measures are more likely than others to produce these reactions, especially when they address topics about which respondents may not want to be truthful.

- **Does it capture small but meaningful variation in key variables?** Different measures have different levels of sensitivity, as illustrated by the difference between 5- and 10-point scales. Do the measures used in this change episode allow participants or staff to record small variations while avoiding asking for information that is trivial or excessively detailed?

- **Is it a fit?** Do change-effort staff consider the data collected to be relevant, or do they feel it is simply imposed on them? Do they believe that results of data collection can be beneficial to them? Do the types of data collection mesh well with the atmosphere and mindset of the community or organization? Are interviews used when respondents cannot complete written forms on their own?

Another way of assessing the validity of a measure is to test it against some other measure or standard, which is termed **criterion validity**. In Chapter 11 we used the Rosenberg Self-Esteem Scale (SES) as an example of a standardized self-report measure. Criterion validity for the SES has been evaluated by comparing its performance against other measures of self-esteem that are presumed to be valid. Results indicate that, as hypothesized, SES scores correlate strongly with scores from those measures. All such measures should be reviewed for similar evidence prior to their selection, but as a normal course of an outcome evaluation, the lead person or evaluator should also confirm that this evidence exists and support the use of the measure. As discussed in Box 12.4, one example of such evidence is the extent to which different measures of a particular variable produce similar results.

Construct validity refers to whether a measure performs as predicted by theory or previous research. In standardized scales, this determines the type of items developed as part of the measures. In a scale measuring social isolation, for example, theory would identify properties of social isolation that a measure might address, such as discomfort in large groups, lack of attendance at parties or other gatherings, and so forth. One or more items would then be generated to address each property. A similar process is relevant to choosing and analyzing measures in evaluations of change efforts such as in Centerville. Ideally, the research literature will have been reviewed prior to choosing disruptive behaviors as a measure of success of social services provided to homeless men and women. Sometimes such reviews fail to occur, however, and the choice of measures is driven more by practical experience, ease of data collection, or other factors. If objectives relating to reduction of disruptive behaviors are not met, the evaluator may need to revisit the literature to determine whether a different measure might have performed better and if it is still possible to include it in monitoring efforts.

Inadequate Measurement Measures specified in process and outcome objectives should be part of a larger measurement scheme designed to provide sufficient information to judge whether a change effort is successful. In general, three principles apply:

- More measures are better than fewer measures;
- Different types of measures are better than measures that are all of the same type; and
- Too many measures will undermine evaluation efforts.

The rationale for using multiple measures is that the risk of error is greatly increased if conclusions about the success of a change effort are based on a single indicator, which might lack reliability or validity. Also, attempting to triangulate key variables by using more than one measure can increase both the accuracy of measurement and the depth of understanding of what occurred. Again, the measurement scheme for a change episode should be decided at its inception, but it may be possible after the fact to identify additional useful measures if too few were initially planned.

The goal of measurement triangulation is greatly aided by keeping in mind that many different approaches can be used to measure a particular variable. Box 12.5 shows major categories of quantitative and qualitative measures and describes how each might be used in a program to assist an organization's employees who have drinking problems. In planning the measurement scheme for a change episode, considerable attention

Box 12.5   Using Different Types of Measures

Case example: Outcome evaluation of a workplace initiative to assist employees who are seeking to control problem drinking.

Type of Measure	Subtype	Variable Measured	Example Measurement Approach
Behavioral measure	Self-report	Quantity consumed	Each participant submits weekly record showing number/type of drinks consumed.
	Observation by others	Quantity consumed	Each participant's spouse/partner records number of drinks participant consumes in a given period of time.
Self-anchored rating scale		Desire to drink	Each participant provides personalized anchors for a scale ranging from 1 to 10, where 1 represents no desire to drink and 10 represents the greatest craving participant can recall experiencing. Participants rate themselves on this scale three nights per week.
Standardized scale		Desire to drink	At intake and every two weeks thereafter, participants complete a standardized scale measuring desire to drink.
Unobtrusive measure	Archival or secondary data	Quantity consumed	Evaluator monitors outpatient clinic and/or ER records for pattern of visits.
	Behavioral artifacts	Quantity consumed	Each participant's spouse counts bottles in garbage and reviews checkbook to record amounts spent on alcohol purchases.
Electronic-mechanical-chemical measure		Alcohol use or nonuse	Participants undergo random urine screens.
Qualitative measure	Participant log	(Not specific)	Participants write down circumstances surrounding drinking or cravings.
	Knowledgeable judges	(Not specific)	Drinking companions record observations of participant's mood, apparent ability to handle cravings and/or ability to stay with treatment.
	Participant statements regarding change	(Not specific)	Participants record impressionistic observations about their progress and aspects of treatment that seem helpful.
	Staff observations and inferences	(Not specific)	Staff members record observations about participants' progress and aspects of treatment that seem helpful.

should be given to identifying ways to use measures from the various categories shown. For example, is it possible to measure disruptive behaviors through both reports by staff (behavioral observations) and accounts from participants about why they acted as they did (participant logs)? If this has not happened until evaluation efforts are well underway, the evaluator should still consider whether information from other measurement categories might be available.

If an evaluator discovers that one or more objectives of the change episode are not being met, one explanation may be that the measurement scheme is insufficient. A contrasting possibility is that the measurement scheme is excessively complex, cumbersome, burdensome, or some combination thereof. The axiom that "more measures are better than fewer" must be balanced against the ground-level realities of the change effort, where both participants and staff may have little remaining energy or enthusiasm for completing measurement tasks after other demands are met. The greatest risk is that animosity toward those tasks grows over time, corresponding to a gradual reduction in information available to evaluate the change effort. If the evaluator is careful in tracking results from monitoring efforts, this should become apparent, and difficult decisions may need to be made to discontinue collecting data on some measures.

Confounding Factors   The goal of an evaluation effort is to show that any outcomes achieved in the course of a change effort were in fact caused by that effort. Doing this requires that three conditions be met. First, it must be shown that the change effort and outcomes are associated with each other—that is, that commencement of the change effort and occurrence of the outcomes go together. Second, it must be shown that the outcomes did not appear until the change effort began, indicating that the presumed cause preceded the effect. Finally, it is necessary to show that the change effort alone produced the outcomes and not some other factor.

The most difficult to meet of the above conditions is the third, and the most important source of type I error is when events or circumstances make it appear a change effort was successful when in fact it was not. In their classic work on experimental research designs, Cook and Campbell (1979) describe these events or circumstances as *threats to internal validity*. In this case, *validity* refers not to whether you're measuring what you think you're measuring, but to the ability to assume that any effects arising from the change effort are due to it and not to extraneous factors. Box 12.6 lists seven examples of such factors and describes how each could produce erroneous conclusions in the Centerville example.

Other threats can also appear. One is the **placebo effect**, which occurs when outcomes are not due to the change effort but to participants' belief in its effectiveness. For example, homeless men and women in Centerville may change their behavior due to their belief that the social services being provided are useful, rather than to the services' actual effectiveness. Human nature is such that people often want so badly for things to go well that they convince themselves of this, especially in the absence of clear evidence. Evaluators must be aware of this and work to measure outcomes of change efforts above and beyond those associated with placebo effects.

In addition to the placebo effect, two other possible confounding factors are **evaluator bias** and **demand characteristics**. Evaluator bias does not refer to deliberate misrepresentation of evaluation results, but happens when participants detect subtle cues from staff members or others regarding the outcome they hope to achieve. Participants may then alter their behavior to make that happen. Staff members are unaware that they are exhibiting such cues, but they nonetheless influence results in ways that have nothing to do with the actual influence of the change effort. Demand characteristics are similar, but they refer to changes in participants' behavior that arise not from staff members' subtle cues but from factors such as participants' knowledge that they are being observed.

Detecting outcomes from an intervention or change effort requires making one of three types of comparisons: over time, against norms, or across groups. The most straightforward is the

Evaluation

Behavior: Apply evaluation findings to improve practice effectiveness at the micro, mezzo, and macro levels.

Critical Thinking Question: How would you go about acknowledging limitations in your evaluation of a change effort so that implications are not oversold?

Box 12.6   Threats to Internal Validity

Internal validity refers to the ability of an evaluation strategy to isolate the effect of the change effort and rule out confounding factors. Such factors can lead to an incorrect conclusion that the effort worked (type I error) or that it did not (type II error). Certain types of confounding factors appear regularly, and these are referred to as **threats to internal validity**. A few of the most common types are as follows:

History: An extraneous event that occurs at about the same time as the change effort. In Centerville, this might be something like the opening of a food bank close to an area frequented by many participants. If the lead person or evaluator is unaware of this, he or she could falsely conclude that improved nutrition among program participants was due to the change effort and not the food bank.

Maturation: The effect of natural processes that are confused with the effect of the change effort. Participants who are over a certain age at the start of the change effort may experience more rapid physical deterioration than others, leading evaluators to the conclusion that the program is ineffective, when in fact it may have worked reasonably well for all but the oldest participants.

Testing: When the act of being measured at Time 1 affects the results of later measurements. Staff members who are trained to record disruptive behaviors during an initial measurement phase may become hypervigilant about any

later disruptions, leading to the conclusion that participants' behavior has worsened when it has not.

Instrumentation: This occurs when measures change during the course of monitoring. The evaluator might decide that the wording of a survey used in initial measurements is ambiguous and thus makes changes prior to later measurements. This makes it possible that any differences observed are due to the changes in the survey rather than changes in the participant.

Statistical Regression: Refers to the fact that extreme scores tend to regress toward the mean over time. If the change effort focuses on selecting homeless men and women who are in greatest need, any change observed may simply reflect statistical moderation of scores rather than program success.

Mortality: Refers to problems that can arise when participants drop out. Suppose that Centerville participants who do not finish the program are those with more serious problems. If so, average scores at Time 2 will be higher than at Time 1, yet this may be due solely to the absence of those who left rather than to the effectiveness of services.

Selection: Applies to designs in which there is at least two groups. If the participants in one group are different in meaningful ways from those in another, the difference may be erroneously attributed to the effect of the intervention rather than to the fact the groups are actually not comparable.

---

first, and outcome objectives specified in the Centerville example reflect this. One calls for homeless men and women who were exhibiting disruptive behaviors at the start of the change effort to have greatly reduced these behaviors by the end of a certain period of time.

Do an Internet search for "FRIENDS National Center for Community-based Child Abuse Prevention." Click on the link for "Outcome Accountability," and read the definition and explanation about this subject. When an advocacy organization provides information about accountability and develops an evaluation toolkit, what potential evaluator biases and demands may be built into their resources?

Other objectives could have been written based on the second type of comparison, which employs norms. For example, if information were available in the research literature to indicate the average occurrence of disruptive behaviors in a typical homeless population, the outcome objective might have been to bring at least 80 percent of program participants to at least 25 percent below this number of disruptive behaviors by a certain date.

The difficulty with these two comparisons is that they are vulnerable to many of the threats described above and in Box 12.6. For example, suppose monitoring results indicate that the percentage of residents identified in the outcome objective did indeed show a reduction in disruptive behavior of the amount specified. The problem facing the evaluator would be to determine whether this change was the result of the change effort or a threat to internal validity. Some homeless men and women are not chronically homeless but episodically so, corresponding with deterioration in life circumstances. It might be argued that many of them were enrolled in the Centerville program when they were at a "valley" in life, but over the period followed by the change episode their functioning and circumstances improved above and beyond any effect of the program. This is an example of the statistical regression threat, and it offers a plausible alternative to the conclusion that the change effort worked. Other threats such as history, placebo effect, and demand characteristics could also be cited as possible explanations.

Controlling for these possibilities requires use of the third type of comparison—across groups. Suppose a nearby city that is similar to Centerville in many ways also has a homeless population in need of services, but no comparable change effort has yet been initiated there. The evaluator could seek to collect data on homeless men and women in the other city and compare their outcomes to those of Centerville's participants. If the reduction in disruptive behavior among Centerville residents is significantly greater than that among members of the comparison group, a much stronger case can be made that the improvement was genuine and not merely an artifact produced by one or more confounding factors.

The strongest type of comparison is between individuals who are sampled from the same population and then randomly divided between one group that is exposed to the intervention and another that is not. This is called a **randomized controlled trial (RCT)**, and if done properly it can counteract all of the above threats (Torgerson, Torgerson, & Taylor, 2010). As we noted earlier, lead persons and evaluators should seek to maximize the methodological soundness of their approaches, and RCTs are among the most powerful tools for doing so. Clearly, advance planning is required to incorporate these designs, and consideration must also be given to resources that will be needed for collecting and analyzing information on more than one group of subjects.

Change efforts are far removed from laboratory settings, however, and real-world limitations may undermine the use of RCTs. For example, too few participants may be available to divide them randomly across groups. It can also be challenging both ethically and practically to randomly divide members of a single group and then provide one subset with assistance while providing nothing to another. Moreover, RCTs may require that some staff members be trained to provide an intervention to their clients while other staffers receive no training and are supposed to do nothing different for theirs. People naturally share ideas and information, and it may prove impossible to keep elements of a new intervention from spilling over into what is supposed to be a pure control condition. For these reasons, quasi-experimental designs offer a viable alternative to RCTs. The example above, in which participants in Centerville were compared to those in a similar city, illustrates such an approach. The chief concern with quasi-experimental designs is the selection threat (Box 12.6), in which presumably comparable individuals actually are not. Quasi-experimental designs, while less able to rule out confounding variables than RCTs, are superior in most cases to approaches that include no comparison groups. The goal of evaluation efforts should be to employ the best approaches possible, despite limitations.

Other Problems   Lead persons and evaluators should be wary of positive results because, as discussed, there are many sources of type I error that can lead to a false conclusion of success. A careful review of these should be undertaken prior to making any decisions about the achievement of outcomes. With that caveat, it is often true that there are many more ways to fail than to succeed, so the conclusion of an evaluation effort may in many cases take the form of a postmortem analysis of what went wrong and how it can be corrected.

One area to consider if results are negative is the program or intervention. Among the questions to ask is whether **dosage** was sufficient, referring to whether participants received enough of the intervention to meet expectations and whether it was reasonable to believe that the program or service would bring about the outcome(s) sought. A related issue is **treatment fidelity**, which addresses issues such as whether the training of staff members produced the desired level of skill. Questions of these sorts may be answered in the course of the process evaluation, but they can be easy to overlook and difficult to assess.

Also of relevance in this context is the question of intervention strength and statistical power. If tools such as tests of statistical significance are used to determine if an outcome was achieved, the evaluator must keep in mind that detection of an effect requires either a powerful intervention or a large number of participants. A program or intervention that produces moderate but nonetheless positive results may not be recognized as useful if too few potential beneficiaries are served.

Another scenario that can occur is when results of the process evaluation indicate that the program was implemented as planned, but it still did not result in achievement of the outcome objective. This suggests that either the change was insufficient to bring about the desired outcomes—which could be due to problems of dosage or treatment fidelity—or that the intervention hypothesis was wrong and the change strategy was not the right one. In the latter case, it will be necessary to return to theoretical and empirical literature to see if assumptions leading to the intervention hypothesis are indeed correct.

Still another possibility is a variant of the type III error, which is to implement the wrong intervention. One reason for this may be that the diagnosis of the problem is wrong. When you visit a physician, it's possible that he or she will interpret your symptoms incorrectly, or you may fail to provide sufficient information and relevant details to enable an accurate diagnosis. The consequence is that a perfectly good medication might still have no effect because what it treats is not what you have. A more direct example might be a community change effort that focuses on demolishing drug houses in a troubled neighborhood when the greater need is to create job opportunities that provide an alternative to selling drugs. Or new administrative and supervisory structures are developed in an organization, when the greatest need is for better individual leaders whom employees will more readily follow. In a policy change, the focus of the policy may be misdirected and fail to address the identified needs of a particular target population.

Among the most critical concerns in this context is the quality of the stated objectives. As discussed in Chapter 11, objectives must be written in ways that make it easy to determine whether they've been met, but doing so can be more difficult than it seems. Consider this example: "By March 31, 80 percent of participants will have been served within 30 days of their first contact with the agency." At first glance this may seem sufficiently specific, but when the time comes to actually decide if the objective has been met, the task becomes more difficult. For example, what does "served" mean? Does it mean that services were completed or only started? And what is the definition of "participant"? Is it someone who has accepted services or who has only been referred? Finally, providing services is an output, not an outcome, and other objectives should follow this one to specify what the effect of receiving services is expected to be.

Evaluation efforts cannot begin until questions and concerns such as those listed above are resolved. Doing otherwise would be a waste of time and resources. For this reason, Wholey (2010) describes the process of completing an **evaluability assessment**, which seeks to determine whether it is possible to complete an evaluation on a particular initiative or change effort. As discussed, if the effort has not been planned properly, implemented properly, monitored properly, or guided properly by clear objectives, or has fallen prey to a variety of other potential pitfalls, the answer to that question will be "no."

Evaluate the Balance between Outcomes and Costs

Key questions to be explored are:

- Are outcomes appropriate in view of the cost?
- Is it feasible to conduct a cost–benefit analysis?
- Is it possible to conduct a cost-effectiveness analysis?

Because social work is almost always carried out in a context of scarce resources, every evaluation must ask difficult questions about whether the outcomes of a change effort are appropriate in view of its cost. For example, if a new counseling program allows the average participant to make 50 percent more progress toward therapeutic goals, it might be considered a success. But if the cost of the new program is almost three times that of the existing program, the question of whether the new program is worth the expense must also be considered. Similarly, in using a policy approach to change, the cost of implementing the policy must be weighed in light of the potential impact it will have on addressing the identified problem.

The evaluation literature discusses two approaches to assessing outcomes in the context of their cost. These are **cost–benefit analysis (CBA)** and **cost-effectiveness analysis (CEA)**. In general, CBA is used when the goal is to assess the overall value of a given program, whereas CEA is used to compare the costs of different approaches to achieving the same outcome (Boardman, Greenberg, Vining, & Weimer, 2010). The challenge for using CBA is that it requires the evaluator to "monetize" the impact of a particular program.

For example, in the Centerville effort, the goal of CBA would be to attach a dollar value to all benefits arising out of attempts to find housing for and provide social services to homeless men and women. Doing this requires a variety of calculations. For example, how much would be saved by the city if fewer police are required to patrol areas with high concentrations of homeless persons? How much would be saved by publicly funded hospitals that have to provide fewer emergency health or mental health services to homeless people who are now receiving preventive services in their new housing arrangements? How much more are local businesses earning in parts of town that customers previously avoided due to large numbers of homeless persons in the area, and how much are businesses earning in areas where homeless

Evaluation

Behavior: Apply knowledge of human behavior and the social person-in-environment, and other multidisciplinary theoretical frameworks in the evaluation of outcomes.

Critical Thinking Question: How would human behavior theory assist you in evaluating a change opportunity?

men and women have been assisted in finding housing? The goal in this approach is to arrive at a summary figure for all benefits of the program and then compare this to a figure for all monetary costs, which then allows a determination of whether benefits exceed costs.

The difficulty with CBA is that it requires attached value to benefits that may be difficult or impossible to monetize. For example, what is the dollar amount associated with the increase in self-esteem or life satisfaction on the part of a homeless person who now has a room and bed of their own? Or what is the value of their reentry into the workforce? In most cases, any attempt to calculate actual monetary figures for these benefits is likely to be highly speculative, meaning that the results may be subject to so much skepticism that the value of the effort is lost.

For this reason, the more common approach to analyzing the impact of change episodes in social work macro practice is CEA, which does not require monetizing all outcomes. Instead, CEA examines a particular outcome, such as the number of homeless persons housed, and calculates the cost associated with that accomplishment. This cost can then be compared to that of other approaches to see which method produces the same outcome for a lower price. The results are less informative than CBA, which might allow comparison of the value of creating a new program versus doing nothing at all. But CEA results are typically more straightforward and less subject to disagreement about whether accurate values have been assigned.

The most important point is that an evaluation effort does not stop with the determination of whether outcome objectives have been achieved. Consistent with the logic model, proper attention must be paid to program impact as well as program outcome, and one aspect of any change effort is whether the results can be justified in terms of cost. Figure 12.3 depicts the framework for evaluating the success of a change effort.

> **?** Assess your understanding of a framework for evaluating the success of a change effort by taking this brief quiz.

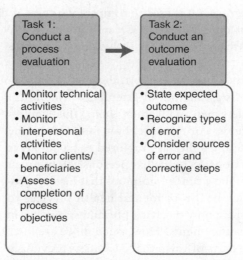

Figure 12.3
A Framework for Evaluating the Success of a Change Effort

SUMMARY

Principles of evidence-based practice dictate that social workers, whether they are assisting an individual client or initiating change in communities and organizations, must collect data to monitor the progress of their work. In this chapter, we describe the elements of two main tasks necessary to determine the success of a change effort in macro systems: process evaluation and outcome evaluation.

The goal of a process evaluation is to answer the question "Was the change effort implemented as planned?" Answering this requires developing and maintaining data collection efforts to determine if activities specified in the plan are taking place and if these are leading to accomplishment of process objectives. This requires being aware of ways in which change efforts go wrong and watching for signs that progress is slowing or activities are being directed toward goals and objectives other than those originally planned. Of particular concern in the monitoring process are technical activities necessary to initiate a change effort and keep it moving, such as finalizing program design, hiring personnel, recruiting participants, and commencing services. Also important are interpersonal considerations such as morale, commitment to the organization, and commitment to the plan for change. Finally, participants themselves should be monitored to determine if services are reaching them as planned and if those services are appropriate to participants' needs.

Outcome evaluation commences once evidence suggests that the change episode is being implemented as planned and process objectives are being achieved. If so, the focus shifts to whether outcome objectives are also being achieved. Determining this involves watching for pitfalls that can lead to mistaken conclusions, such as using measures that lack reliability and validity, or using too few or the wrong kind of measures to assess outcomes. Also of concern are ways in which extraneous factors can make it appear that the change effort succeeded when it did not, or vice versa. Toward the goal of combating those factors, the chapter reviews evaluation designs that add time and cost but provide effective means of ruling out alternative explanations. We conclude with an overview of ways to determine whether the cost for achieving certain results is reasonable and defensible.

 Recall what you learned in this chapter by completing the Chapter Review.

Appendix 1: A Framework for Monitoring and Evaluating the Intervention

Task 1: Conduct a Process Evaluation

Monitor Technical Activities

- What is the appropriate sequencing for the activities that must be completed in order to achieve the process objective?
- Who will be assigned responsibility for completion of each activity?
- When must each activity be completed in order for the process objective to be achieved on time?

Monitor Interpersonal Activities

- How enthusiastic and supportive are the designated implementers?
- Is there a formal or informal system for evaluating the performance of implementers?
- Is there a strategy for dealing with poor performance, apathy, or resistance?

Monitor Clients and Beneficiaries

- Are intended services being offered?

- Is there evidence that those services are reaching the intended targets?

Assess Completion of Process Objectives

- Does monitoring information show that the process objective was achieved?
- If not, at what point were the activities leading to it not completed or unsuccessful?
- What corrective actions are needed?

Task 2: Conduct an Outcome Evaluation

Recognize Types of Error

- Is there a risk of erroneously concluding the change episode succeeded?
- Is there a risk of erroneously concluding the change episode failed?

- Are evaluation efforts asking the right question(s)?

Consider Sources of Error and Corrective Steps

- Is there evidence that measures being used are reliable and valid?
- Is a sufficient number of measures of different types being employed?
- Are procedures in place for guarding against confounding variables?

Evaluate the Balance between Outcomes and Costs

- Are outcomes appropriate in view of the cost?
- Is it feasible to conduct a cost–benefit analysis?
- Is it possible to conduct a cost-effectiveness analysis?

Assess Your Competence

Use the scale below to rate your current level of achievement on the following concepts or skills associated with each learning outcome listed at the beginning of this chapter:

1	2	3
I can accurately describe the concept or skill(s) associated with this outcome.	I can consistently identify the concept or skill(s) associated with this outcome when observing and analyzing practice activities.	I can competently implement the concept or skill(s) associated with this outcome in my own practice.

_____ Describe the difference between process and outcome evaluation.

_____ Identify research methods employed to conduct evaluations.

References

Chapter 1

Abramovitz, M. (1991). Putting an end to doublespeak about race, gender, and poverty: An annotated glossary for social workers. *Social Work, 36*(5), 380–384.

Brody, R. (2000). *Effectively managing human service organizations* (2nd ed.). Thousand Oaks, CA: Sage.

Buila, S. (2010). The NASW Code of Ethics under attack: A manifestation of the culture war within the profession of social work *Journal of Social Work Values & Ethics, 7*(2). Retrieved June 17, 2014, from http://www.socialworker.com/jswve

Cimino, A. N., Rorke, J., & Adams, H. L. (2013). Supervisors behaving badly: Witnessing ethical dilemmas and what to do about it. *Journal of Social Work Values & Ethics, 10*(2), 48–57.

Council on Social Work Education (CSWE). (2012). *Educational policy and accreditation standards.* Retrieved from http://www.cswe.org/File.aspx?id=13780

Cummins, L. K., Byers, K. V., & Pedrick, L. (2011). *Policy practice for social workers: New strategies for a new era.* Boston, MA: Pearson Education.

Dominelli, L. (2014). Internationalizing professional practices: The place of social work in the international arena. *International Social Work, 47,* 258–267.

Garran, A. M., & Rozas, L. W. (2013). Cultural competence revisited. *Journal of Ethnic and Cultural Diversity in Social Work, 22*(2), 97–111.

Gates, A. B. (2014). Integrating social services and social change: Lessons from an immigrant work center. *Journal of Community Practice, 22* (1–2), 202–129.

Gelatt, J., Adams, G., & Monson, W. (2014). *Immigration and the changing landscape for local service delivery: Demographic shifts in cities and neighborhoods.* Washington, DC: Urban Institute.

Gilbert, N., & Terrell, P. (2013). *Dimensions of social welfare policy* (8th ed.). Boston, MA: Pearson Education.

Granado, C. (2006). "Hispanic" vs. "Latino": A new poll finds that the term "Hispanic" is preferred. *Hispanic Magazine.* Retrieved September 2006 from www.hispaniconline.com/hh/hisp_vs_lat.html

Gustafson, J. M. (1982). Professions as "callings." *Social Service Review, 56*(4), 501–515.

Gutiérrez, L. M., & Lewis, E. A. (1999). *Empowering women of color.* New York: Columbia University Press.

Hawkins, C. A., & Knox, K. (2014). Educating for international social work: Human rights leadership. *International Social Work, 57,* 248–257.

Healey, L. M., & Wairire, G. G. (2014). Educating for the global agenda: Internationally relevant conceptual frameworks and knowledge for social work education. *International Social Work, 57,* 235–247.

Jansson, B. S. (2014). *Becoming an effective policy advocate: From policy practice to social justice* (7th ed.). Belmont, CA: Brooks/Cole.

Johnson-Goodstar, K. (2013). Indigenous youth participatory action research: Re-visioning social justice for social work with indigenous youths. *Social Work, 58*(4), 314–320.

Karger, H. J., & Stoesz, D. (2013). *American social welfare policy: A pluralist approach* (7th ed.). Boston, MA: Pearson Education.

Kerson, T. S., & McCoyd, J. L. M. (2013). In response to need: An analysis of social work roles over time. *Social Work, 58*(4), 333–343.

Lee, P. (1937). *Social work as cause and function.* New York: Columbia University Press.

Native American Journalists Association. (2006). *Reading Red Report 2002: A report and content analysis on coverage of Native Americans by the largest newspapers in the United States.* Retrieved September 2006, from www.naja.com/resources/publications/

National Association of Social Workers (NASW). (2001). *Standards for cultural competence in social work practice.* Retrieved from http://www.naswdc.org/practice/standards.pdf

Netting, F. E., O'Connor, M. K., & Fauri, D. P. (2008). *Comparative approaches to program planning.* Hoboken, NJ: Wiley.

Pelts, M. D. (2014). A look back at the defense of marriage act: Why same-sex marriage is still relevant to social work. *Affilia, 29*(2), 237–247.

Powell, J. L. (2009). Editorial: IFSW code of practice in comparison to national codes. *Journal of Social Work Values, 6*(2). Retrieved June 17, 2014, from http://www.socialworker.com/jswve

Reamer, F. G. (2013). Social work in a digital age: Ethical and risk management challenges. *Social Work, 58*(2), 163–172.

Rothman, J., Erlich, J. L., & Tropman, J. E. (2008). *Strategies of community intervention* (7th ed.). Peosta, IA: Eddie Bowers.

Rothman, J., & Mizrahi, T. (2014). Balancing micro and macro practice: A challenge for social work. *Social Work, 59*(1), 1–3.

Sigelman, L., Tuch, S. A., & Martin, J. K. (2005). What's in a name? Preference for "Black" versus "African-American" among Americans of African descent. *Public Opinion Quarterly, 69*(3), 429–438.

Staniforth, B., Fouche, C., & O'Brien, M. (2011). Still doing what we do: Defining social work in the 21st century. *Journal of Social Work, 11*(2), 191–208.

Sullivan, W. M. (2005). *Work and integrity: The crisis and promise of professionalism in America.* San Francisco, CA: Jossey-Bass.

U.S. Bureau of Labor Statistics. (1995). *A Current Population Survey supplement for testing methods of collecting racial and ethnic information: May 1995.* Washington, DC: U.S. Department of Labor.

Warren, R. L. (1978). *The community in America* (3rd ed.). Chicago, IL: Rand McNally.

Zayas, L. H., & Bradlee, M. H. (2014). Exiling children, creating orphans: When immigration policies hurt citizens. *Social Work, 59*(2), 167–175.

Chapter 2

Becker, D. G. (1987). Isabella Graham and Joanna Bethune: Trailblazers of organized women's benevolence. *Social Service Review, 61,* 319–336.

Bender, D. E. (2008). Perils of degeneration: Reform, the savage immigrant, and the survival of the unfit. *Journal of Social History, 42,* 5–29.

Benish, A. (2010). Re-bureaucratizing welfare administration. *Social Service Review, 84,* 77–101.

Bernstein, J., Mishell, L., & Brocht, C. (2000). *Briefing paper: Any way you cut it—Income inequality on the rise regardless of how it's measured.* Washington, DC: Economic Policy Institute.

Boisson, S. (2006). When America sent her own packing. *American History, 41,* 20–27.

Brieland, D. (1987). Social work practice: History and evolution. In A. Minahan (Ed.), *Encyclopedia of social work* (19th ed., Vol. 3, pp. 2246–2258). Washington, DC: NASW Press.

Brieland, D. (1990). The Hull-House tradition and the contemporary social worker: Was Jane Addams really a social worker? *Social Work, 35*(2), 134–138.

Broughton, C. (2010). Bringing the organization back in: The role of bureaucratic churning in early TANF caseload declines in Illinois. *Journal of Sociology and Social Welfare, 37,* 155–182.

Brown v. Board of Education of Topeka, 347 U.S. 483 (1954).

Carlton-LeNey, I., & Hodges, V. (2004). African American reformers' mission: Caring for our girls and women. *Affilia, 19,* 257–272.

Centers for Disease Control. (2010). Early release of selected estimates based on data from the January–June 2010 National Health Interview Survey, *Percentage of adults aged 18 years and over who had five or more drinks in 1 day at least once in the past year: United States, 1997–June 2010.* Retrieved June 4, 2015, from http://www.cdc.gov/nchs/data/nhis/earlyrelease/201012_09.pdf

Chambers, C. A. (1985). The historical role of the voluntary sector. In G. A. Tobin (Ed.), *Social planning and human service delivery in the voluntary sector* (pp. 3–28). Westport, CT: Greenwood Press.

Chambers, C. A. (1986). Women in the creation of the profession of social work. *Social Service Review, 60*(1), 3–33.

ChildStats.gov. (2010). *America's children in brief: Key national indicators of well-being, 2010.* Retrieved January 2011 from http://www.childstats.gov/americaschildren/tables.asp

Chowa, G. A. N., Masa, R. D. V., Sherraden, M., & Weil, M. (2013). Confronting global poverty. In M. Weil, M. Reisch, & M. L. Ohmer (Eds.), *The handbook of community practice* (2nd ed., pp. 607–631). Thousand Oaks, CA: Sage.

Coleman, M. C. (1999). The responses of American Indian children and Irish children to the school, 1850s–1920s. *American Indian Quarterly, 23,* 83–112.

Collins, G. (2010). *When everything changed: The amazing journey of American women from 1960 to the present.* Boston, MA: Back Bay.

Corsini, R. J. (2002). *The dictionary of psychology.* New York: Brunner/Mazel.

Crompton, L. (2003). *Homosexuality and civilization.* Cambridge, MA: Harvard University Press.

Dominelli, L. (2014). Internationalizing professional practices: The place of social work in the international arena. *International Social Work, 57*(3), 258–267.

DuBois, E. C. (1999). *Feminism and suffrage: The emergence of an independent women's movement in America, 1848–1869.* Ithaca, NY: Cornell University Press.

Etzioni, A. (1969). *The semi-professions and their organization: Teachers, nurses, social workers.* New York: Free Press.

Facebook Pressroom Statistics. (2014). Retrieved August 2014 from http://www.facebook.com/press/info.php?statistics

Friedan, B. (1963). *The feminine mystique.* New York: Norton.

Fukuyama, F. (1999). *The great disruption.* New York: Free Press.

Garvin, C. D., & Cox, F. M. (2001). A history of community organizing since the Civil War with special reference to oppressed communities. In J. Rothman, J. L. Erlich, & J. E. Tropman (Eds.), *Strategies of community intervention* (6th ed., pp. 65–100). Itasca, IL: F. E. Peacock.

Gray, M., & Boddy, J. (2010). Making sense of the waves: Wipeout or still riding high? *Affilia, 25,* 368–389.

Griswold del Castillo, R. (2001). *The Treaty of Guadalupe Hidalgo: A legacy of conflict.* Norman, OK: University of Oklahoma Press.

Harrington, M. (1962). *The other America: Poverty in the United States.* New York: Macmillan.

Haynes, J. M. (2014). Safe third country agreement: Closing the doors on refugee women seeking protection. *Families in Society, 95*(2), 140–148.

Hildebrand, V., & Van Kerm, P. (2009). Income inequality and self-rated health status: Evidence from the European Community Household Panel. *Demography, 46,* 805–825.

Holt, S. (2006). *The Earned Income Tax Credit at age 30: What we know.* Washington, DC: Brookings Institution. Retrieved June 15, 2015 from http://www.brookings.edu/~/media/research/files/reports/2006/2/childrenfamilies-holt/20060209_holt.pdf

Huisman, M., & Oldehinkel, A. J. (2009). Income inequality, social capital and self-inflicted injury and violence-related mortality. *Journal of Epidemiology and Community Health, 63,* 31–37.

Jansson, B. S. (2015). *The reluctant welfare state* (8th ed.). Belmont, CA: Brooks/Cole.

Le, C. N. (2006). *Asian-Nation: The landscape of Asian America.* Retrieved June 4, 2015, from www.asian-nation.org/demographics.shtml

Lens, V. (2008). Welfare and work sanctions: Examining discretion on the front lines. *Social Service Review, 82,* 197–222.

Lindeman, E. (1921). *The community: An introduction to the study of community leadership and organization.* New York: Association Press.

Marwell, N. P., & Gullickson, A. (2013). Inequality in the spatial allocation of social services: Government contracts to nonprofit organizations in New York City. *Social Service Review, 87*(2), 319–353.

Marotta, T. (1981). *The politics of homosexuality.* Boston, MA: Houghton Mifflin.

Martin, L. L. (2005). Performance-based contracting for human services: Does it work? *Administration in Social Work, 29,* 63–77.

McCarthy, K. D. (Ed.). (1990). *Lady bountiful revisited: Women, philanthropy, and power.* New Brunswick, NJ: Rutgers University Press.

McCarthy, K. D. (2003). *American creed: Philanthropy and the rise of civil society 1700–1865.* Chicago, IL: University of Chicago Press.

McFadden, J. J. (2014). Discipling the "Frankenstein of Pauperism": The early days of charity organization case recording, 1877–1907. *Social Service Review, 88*(3), 469–492.

McKay, A. (2013). Crisis, cuts, citizenship and a basic income: A wicked solution to a wicked problem. *Basic Income Studies, 8*(1), 93–104.

McMurtry, S. L., Netting, F. E., & Kettner, P. M. (1991). How nonprofits adapt to a stringent environment. *Nonprofit Management & Leadership, 1*(3), 235–252.

Morris, P. M. (2008). Reinterpreting Abraham Flexner's speech, "Is Social Work a Profession?": Its meaning and influence on the field's early professional development. *Social Service Review, 82,* 29–60.

Moxley, D. P., Alvarez, A. R., Johnson, A. K., & Gutierrez, L. M. (2005). Appreciating the glocal in community practice. *Journal of Community Practice, 13*(3), 1–7.

National Center for Education Statistics. (2007). *Status and Trends in the Education of Racial and Ethnic Minorities.* Retrieved June 4, 2015, from http://nces.ed.gov/pubs2007/2007039.pdf

National Women's Law Center. (2009). *The Lilly Ledbetter Fair Pay Act.* Retrieved June 4, 2015, from http://www.nwlc.org/resource/fair-pay-frequently-asked-questions

O'Brien, G. V., & Leneave, J. (2008). The "art" of social work and the ADA's essential functions provision: Challenges and recommendations. *Administration in Social Work, 32*, 87–99.

Orgad, L., & Ruthizer, T. (2010). Race, religion and nationality in immigration selection: 120 years after the Chinese exclusion case. *Constitutional Commentary, 26*, 237–296.

Olson, M. E., Diekema, D., Elliott, B. A., & Renier, C. M. (2010). Impact of income and income inequality on infant health outcomes in the United States. *Pediatrics, 126*, 1165–1173.

Park, Y. (2008). Facilitating injustice: Tracing the role of social workers in the World War II internment of Japanese Americans. *Social Service Review, 82*(3), 447–483.

Parrott, S. (2006). *Testimony before the committee on ways and means, United States House of Representatives, July 19, 2006.* Washington, DC: Center on Budget and Policy Priorities. Retrieved June 15, 2015 from http://www.cbpp.org/archiveSite/7-19-06tanf-testimony.pdf

Patti, R. J. (2000). The landscape of social welfare management. In R. J. Patti (Ed.), *The handbook of social welfare management* (pp. 3–25). Thousand Oaks, CA: Sage.

Percy, S. L. (1989). *Disability, civil rights, and public policy.* Tuscaloosa, AL: University of Alabama Press.

Piketty, T., & Saez, E. (2014). Inequality in the long run. *Science, 344*(6186), 838–843.

Pimpare, S. (2012). Welfare reform at 15 and the state of policy analysis. *Social Work, 58*(1), 53–62).

Putnam, R. D. (2000). *Bowling alone: The collapse and revival of American community.* New York: Simon & Schuster.

Rapp, C. A., & Poertner, J. (1992). *Social administration: A client-centered approach.* New York: Longman.

Redelings, M., Lieb, L., & Sorvillo, F. (2010). Years off your life? The effects of homicide on life expectancy by neighborhood and race/ethnicity in Los Angeles County. *Journal of Urban Health, 87*, 670–676.

Rehabilitation Act of 1973, Pub. L. No. 93-112, 87 Stat. 335 (1973).

Reisch, M. (2013). Community practice challenges in the global economy. In M. Weil, M. Reisch, & M. L. Ohmer (Eds.). *The handbook of community practice* (2nd ed., pp. 47–71). Thousand Oaks, CA: Sage

Reisch, M., & Andrews, J. (2001). *The road not taken: A history of radical social work in the United States.* Philadelphia, PA: Brunner-Routledge.

Reisch, M., & Wenocur, S. (1986). The future of community organization in social work: Social activism and the politics of profession building. *Social Service Review, 60*(1), 70–93.

Richmond, M. (1917). *Social diagnosis.* New York: Russell Sage Foundation.

Shilts, R. (1987). *And the band played on: Politics, people, and the AIDS epidemic.* New York: St. Martin's Press.

Shipler, D. K. (2005). *The working poor: Invisible in America.* New York: Vintage Books.

Stern, M., & Axinn, J. (2012). *Social welfare: A history of the American response to need* (8th ed.). Boston, MA: Pearson Education.

Toffler, A. (1980). *The third wave.* New York: Morrow.

Trattner, W. I. (1999). *From poor law to welfare state: A history of social welfare in America* (6th ed.). New York: Free Press.

U.N. General Assembly (2011, October 17). United Nations Decade for the Eradication of Poverty (2008–2017). Retrieved June 15, 2015 from http://undesadspd/Poverty/UNDecadefor theEradictionofPoverty/Second

U.S. Bureau of the Census. (1970). *Population of congressional districts.* Retrieved June 4, 2015, from http://www2.census.gov/prod2/decennial/documents/42078080.pdf

U.S. Bureau of the Census. (2010a). *Intercensal estimates of the resident population by sex and age for the United States: April 1, 2000 to July 1, 2010.* Retrieved June 15, 2015 from http://www.census.gov/popest/cities/tables/SUB-EST2009-01.xls

U.S. Bureau of the Census. (2010b). *Current Population Survey (CPS): Annual Social and Economic (ASEC) Supplement.* Retrieved June 4, 2015, from http://www.census.gov/hhes/www/cpstables/032010/health/h01_004.htm

U.S. Bureau of the Census. (2011a). *Hispanics in the United States.* Retrieved June 15, 2015 from http://www.census.gov/population/www/socdemo/files/Internet_Hispanic_in_US_2006.pdf

U.S. Bureau of the Census. (2011b). *2011 Statistical Abstract: Black elected officials by office and state.* Retrieved June 15, 2015 from http://www.census.gov/prod/2011pubs/12statab/election.pdf

U.S. Bureau of Labor Statistics. (2010a). *Highlights of women's earnings in 2009.* Retrieved June 4, 2015, from http://www.bls.gov/cps/cpswom2009.pdf

U.S. Congress. (1964). *Act to Mobilize the Human and Financial Resources of the Nation to Combat Poverty in the United States,* Pub. L. No. 88-452, 88th Cong., § 2, 78 Stat. 508 (1964).

U.S. Congressional Budget Office. (2002). *The role of computer technology in the growth of productivity.* Washington, DC: Congress of the United States, Congressional Budget Office. Retrieved June 4, 2015, from www.cbo.gov/ftpdocs/34xx/doc3448/Computer.pdf

U.S. Internal Revenue Service. (2014). *Earned income tax credit statistics.* Retrieved June 15, 2015 from http://www.irs.gov/Individuals/Earned-Income-Tax-Credit-Statistics

Wagner, D. (1989). Radical movements in the social services: A theoretical framework. *Social Service Review, 63*(2), 264–284.

Waller, M. A., Okamoto, S. K., Miles, B. W., & Hurdle, D. E. (2003). Resiliency factors related to substance use/resistance: Perceptions of Native adolescents of the Southwest. *Journal of Sociology & Social Welfare, 30*, 79–94.

Warren, R. L. (1978). *The community in America* (3rd ed.). Chicago, IL: Rand McNally.

Weil, M., Reich, M., & Ohmer, M. L. (2013). Introduction: Contexts and challenges for 21st century communities. In M. Weil, M. Reisch, & M. L. Ohmer (Eds.), *The handbook of community practice* (2nd ed., pp. 3–25). Thousand Oaks, CA: Sage.

Westmoreland, T. M., & Watson, K. R. (2006). Redeeming hollow promises: The case for mandatory spending on health care for American Indians and Alaska Natives. *American Journal of Public Health, 96*, 600–605.

Wilkinson, S., & Kitzinger, C. (2005). Same-sex marriage and equality. *Psychologist, 18*, 290–293.

Witz, A. (1992). *The professions and patriarchy.* New York: Routledge.

Wolff, E. N. (2010). *Recent trends in household wealth in the United States: Rising debt and the middle-class squeeze—an update to 2007.*

Annandale-on-Hudson, NY: Levy Economics Institute of Bard College.

Wright, B. A. (1988). Attitudes and the fundamental negative bias: Conditions and corrections. In H. E. Yuker (Ed.), *Attitudes toward persons with disabilities*. New York: Springer.

Wu, C.-F., & Eamon, M. K. (2010). Need for and barriers to accessing public benefits among low-income families with children. *Children and Youth Services Review, 32*, 58–66.

Wynne, B. (2006). *Mississippi's Civil War: A narrative history*. Macon, GA: Mercer University Press.

Chapter 3

Appleby, G. A. (2007). Dynamics of oppression and discrimination. In G. A. Appleby, E. Colon, & J. Hamilton (Eds.), *Diversity, oppression, and social functioning* (pp. 51–67). Boston, MA: Allyn & Bacon.

Ashford, J., & LeCroy, C. (2013). *Human behavior in the social environment: A multidimensional perspective* (5th ed.). Pacific Grove, CA: Brooks/Cole.

Bell, L. A. (2007). Overview: Twenty-first century racism. In M. Adams, L. A. Bell, & P. Griffin (Eds.), *Teaching for diversity and social justice* (2nd ed., pp. 117–122). New York: Routledge.

Bourdieu, P. (1977). *Outline of a theory of practice*. Cambridge, MA: Cambridge University Press.

Bricker-Jenkins, M., & Hooyman, N. R. (Eds.). (1986). *Not for women only*. Silver Spring, MD: NASW Press.

Broido, E. M. (2000). The development of social justice allies during college: A phenomenological investigation. *Journal of College Student Development, 41*, 3–18.

Brooks, F. (2001). Innovative organizing practices: ACORN's campaign in Los Angeles organizing workfare workers. *Journal of Community Practice, 9*, 65–85.

Busch, N. B., & Wolfer, T. A. (2002). Battered women speak out: Welfare reform and their decisions to disclose. *Violence Against Women, 8*(5), 566–584.

Casey, E., & Smith, T. (2010). "How can I not?": Men's pathways to involvement in anti-violence against women work. *Violence Against Women, 16*(8), 953–973.

Cass, V. C. (1979). Homosexual identity formation: A theoretical model. *Journal of Homosexuality, 4*(3), 219–235.

Cass, V. C. (1984). Homosexual identity formation: Testing a theoretical model. *Journal of Sex Research, 20*(2), 143–167.

Cross, T. L., Bazron, B. J., Dennis, K. W., & Isaacs, M. R. (1989). *Towards a culturally competent system of care*. Washington, DC: Georgetown University Child Development Center, Technical Assistance Center.

Cross, W. E., Jr. (1971). The Negro-to-Black conversion experience. *Black World, 20*(9), 13–27.

Cross, W. E. (1991). *Shades of black: Diversity in African-American identity*. Philadelphia, PA: Temple University Press.

Doykos, B., Brinkley-Rubinstein, Craven, K., McCormack, M., & Geller, J. (2014). Leveraging identity, gaining access: Explorations of self in diverse field-based research settings. *Journal of Community Practice, 22*(1–2), 130–149.

DuBois, W. E. B. (1982). *The souls of black folk*. New York: New American Library.

Dudziak, S., & Profitt, N. J. (2012). Group work and social justice: Designing pedagogy for social change. *Social Work with Groups, 35*(3), 235–252.

Erickson, E. (1968). *Identity, youth and crisis*. New York: Norton.

Freeman, D. (2011). Teaching Obama: History, critical race theory and social work education. *Patterns of Prejudice, 45*(1–2), 177–197.

Giddens, A. (1979). *Central problems in social theory: Action, structure and contradiction in social analysis*. London, YK: MacMillan.

Gutierrez, L. M., Lewis, E. A., Dessel, A. B., & Spencer, M. (2013). Principles, skills, and practice strategies for promoting multicultural communication and collaboration. In M. Weil, M. Reisch, & M. L. Ohmer (Eds.), *The handbook of community practice* (2nd ed., pp. 445–460). Thousand Oaks, CA: Sage.

Haynes, J. M. (2014). Safe third country agreement: Closing the doors on refugee women seeking protection. *Families in Society, 95*(2), 140–148.

Hill Collins, P. (2000). *Black feminist thought: Knowledge, consciousness, and the politics of empowerment*. New York: Routledge.

Hook, J. N., Owen, J., Davis, D. E., Worthington, E. L., & Utsey, S. O. (2013). Cultural humility: Measuring openness to culturally diverse clients. *Journal of Counseling Psychology, 60*(3), 353–366.

Hooks, b. (1981). *Ain't I a woman? Black women and feminism*. Boston, MA: South End Press.

Hooks, b. (1989). *Talking back: Thinking feminist, thinking black*. Toronto, Canada: Between the Lines.

Hoyt, C. (2012). The pedagogy of the meaning of racism: Reconciling a discordant discourse. *Social Work, 57*(3), 225–234.

Hutchison, E. D. (2012). *Essentials of human behavior: Integration person, environment and life course*. Thousand Oaks, CA: Pine Forge Press.

Jeyasingham, D. (2012). White noise: A critical evaluation of social work education's engagement with whiteness studies. *British Journal of Social Work, 42*, 669–686.

Johnson, Y. M., & Munch, S. (2009). Fundamental contradictions in cultural competence. *Social Work, 54*(3), 220–231.

Kohlberg, L. (1984). *Essays on moral development: Vol. 2: The psychology of moral development*. San Francisco, CA: Harper & Row.

Kolivoski, K. M., Weaver, A., & Constance-Huggins, M. (2014). Critical race theory: Opportunities for application in social work practice and policy. *Families in Society, 95*(4), 269–276.

Leondar-Wright, B., & Yeskel, F. (2007). Classism curriculum design. In M. Adams, L. A. Bell, & P. Griffin (Eds.), *Teaching for diversity and social justice* (2nd ed., pp. 309–333). New York: Routledge.

Letendre, J., & Williams, L. R. (2014). "I hear you": Using focus groups to give voice to adolescent girls' experiences with violence. *Social Work with Groups, 37*(2), 114–128.

Link, B. J., & Phelan, J. (2001). Conceptualizing stigma. *Annual Review of Sociology, 27*, 363–385.

Maidment, J., & Brook, G. (2014). Teaching and learning group work using tutorial and community engagement. *Social Work with Groups, 37*(1), 73–84.

Marcia, J. E. (1993). The ego identity status approach to ego identity. In J. E. Marcia, A. S. Waterman, D. R. Matteson, S. L. Arcjer, & J. L. Orlofsky (Eds.), *Ego identify: A handbook for psychosocial research*. New York: Springer-Verlag.

Maslow, A. (1943). A theory of motivation. *Psychological Review, 50*, 370–396.

Mattsson, T. (2014). Intersectionality as a useful tool: Anti-oppressive social work and critical reflection. *Affilia, 29*(1), 8–17.

Mulroy, E. (2004). Theoretical perspectives on the social environment to guide management and community practice: An organization-in-environment approach. *Administration in Social Work, 28*(1), 77–96.

National Association of Social Workers. (2000). Cultural competence in the social work profession. In *Social work speaks: National Association of Social Workers policy statements* (5th ed., pp. 59–62). Washington, DC: NASW Press.

National Association of Social Workers. (2001). *NASW standards for cultural competence in social work practice*. Washington, DC: Author.

Narag, R., & Maxwell, S. R. (2014). Understanding cultural context when collecting field data: Lessons learned from field research in a slum area in the Philippines. *Qualitative Research, 14*(3), 311–326.

Norton, D. G. (1978). *The dual perspective: Inclusion of ethnic minority content in the social work curriculum.* New York: CSWE Press.

Nygreen, K., Kwon, S. A., & Sanchez, P. (2006). Urban youth building community. *Journal of Community Practice, 14*(1), 107–123.

Organista, K. C. (2009). New practice model for Latinos in need of social work services. *Social Work, 54*(4), 297–305.

Parham T. A. (1989). Cycles of psychological Nigrescence. *The Counseling Psychologist, 17*, 187–226.

Piaget, J. (1972). Intellectual evolution from adolescence to adulthood. *Human Development, 15*, 1–12.

Roby, J. L., Rotabi, K., & Bunkers, K. M. (2013). Social justice and intercountry adoptions: The role of the U.S. social work community. *Social Work, 58*(4), 295–303.

Rosenblum, K. E., & Travis, T. C. (2008). *The meaning of difference: American constructions of race, sex and gender, social class, sexual orientation, and disability* (5th ed.). Boston, MA: McGraw-Hill.

Ryan, W. (1971). *Blaming the victim.* New York: Pantheon.

Santrock, J. (2010). *Life-span development* (10th ed.). Boston, MA: McGraw-Hill Higher Education.

Savaya, R., & Waysman, M. (2005). The logic model: A tool for incorporating theory in development and evaluation of programs. *Administration in Social Work, 29*(2), 85–103.

Seck, M. M., & Helton, L. (2014). Faculty development of a joint MSW program utilizing Tuckman's model of stages of group development. *Social Work with Groups, 37*(2), 158–168.

Sewpaul, V. (2013). Inscribed in our blood: Challenging the ideology of sexism and racism. *Affilia, 28*(2), 116–125.

Skinner, B. F. (1971). *Beyond freedom and dignity.* New York: Knopf.

Sonn, C. C., & Quayle, A. F. (2013). Developing praxis: Mobilising critical race theory in community cultural development *Journal of Community & Applied Psychology, 23*, 435–448.

Staples, L. (2012). Community organizing for social justice: Grassroots groups for power. *Social Work with Groups, 35*(3), 287–296.

Strier, R. (2013). Responding to the global economic crisis: Inclusive social work practice. *Social Work, 58*(4), 344–353.

Tervalon, M., & Murray-Garcia, J. (1998). Cultural humility versus cultural competence: A critical distinction in defining physician training outcomes in multicultural education. *Journal of Health Care for the Poor and Underserved, 9*(2), 117–125.

Turner, J. C. (1982). Toward a cognitive redefinition of the social group. In H. Tajfel (Ed.), *Social identity and intergroup behavior* (pp. 15–40). Cambridge: Cambridge University Press.

Turner, R. H. (1990). Role change. *Annual Review of Sociology, 16*, 87–110.

Walker, L. A., & East, J. F. (2014). The benefits of including engaged residents and professionals in low-income neighbourhood redevelopment planning processes. *Journal of Community Practice, 22*(3), 342–364.

Way, N., Hernandez, M. G., Rogers, L. O., & Hughes, D. L. (2013). "I'm not going to become no rapper": Stereotypes as a context of ethnic and racial identity development. *Journal of Adolescent Research, 28*(4), 407–430.

Weil, M., Gamble, D. N., & Williams, E. S. (1998). Women, communities, and development. In J. Figueira-McDonough, F. E. Netting, & A. Nichols-Casebolt (Eds.), *The role of gender in practice knowledge* (pp. 241–286). New York: Garland.

Woodford, M. R., & Preston, S. (2011). Developing a strategy to meaningfully engage stakeholders in program/policy planning: A guide for human services managers and practitioners. *Journal of Community Practice, 19*(2), 159–174.

Chapter 4

Ashford, J., & LeCroy, C. (2013). *Human behavior in the social environment: A multidimensional perspective* (5th ed.). Pacific Grove, CA: Brooks/Cole.

Benford, R. D., & Snow, D. A. (2000). Framing processes and social movements: An overview and assessment. *Annual Review of Sociology, 26*, 611–639.

Blitz, L. V., Kida, L., Gresham, M., & Bronstein, L. R. (2013). Prevention through collaboration: Family engagement with rural schools and families living in poverty. *Families in Society, 94*(3), 157–165.

Borah, P. (2011). Conceptual issues in framing theory: A systematic examination of a decade's literature. *Journal of Communication, 61*, 246–263.

Chong, D., & Druckman, J. N. (2007). Framing theory. *Annual Review of Political Science, 10*, 103–126.

Dewulf, A., & Bouwen, R. (2012). Issue framing in conversations for change: Discursive interaction strategies for "doing differences." *Journal of Applied Behavioral Science, 48*(2), 168–193.

Diala, C. C., Muntaner, C., & Walrath, C. (2004). Gender, occupational, and socioeconomic correlates of alcohol and drug abuse among U.S. rural, metropolitan, and urban residents. *American Journal of Drug & Alcohol Abuse, 30*, 409–428.

Gitterman, A., & Knight, C. (2013). Evidence-guided practice: Integrating the science and art of social work. *Families in Society, 94*(2), 70–78.

Kettner, P. M., Moroney, R. M., & Martin, L. L. (2013). *Designing and managing programs: An effectiveness-based approach* (4th ed.). Thousand Oaks, CA: Sage.

National Association of Social Workers (NASW). (N.d.). *Evidence-based practice.* Retrieved June 8, 2015, from http://www.socialworkers.org/research/naswResearch/0108EvidenceBased/default.asp

Piven, F., & Cloward, R. (1971). *Regulating the poor: The functions of public welfare.* New York: Pantheon.

Roby, J. L., Rotabi, K., & Bunkers, K. M. (2013). Social justice and intercountry adoptions: The role of the U.S. social work community. *Social Work, 58*(4), 295–303.

Sabol, W., Coulton, C., & Polousky, E. (2004). Measuring child maltreatment risk in communities: A life table approach. *Child Abuse & Neglect, 28*, 967–983.

Sonn, C. C., & Quayle, A. F. (2013). Developing praxis: Mobilising critical race theory in community cultural development. *Journal of Community & Applied Psychology, 23*, 435–448.

Tashakkori, A., & Teddlie, C. (2009). Integrating qualitative and quantitative approaches to research. In L. Bickman & D. Rog (Eds.), *Applied social research methods.* Thousand Oaks, CA: Sage.

Trochim, W. (2006). Qualitative data. Retrieved June 8, 2015, from http://www.socialresearchmethods.net/kb/qualdata.php

Weil, M., Reisch, M., & Ohmer, M. L. (Eds.). (2013). *The handbook of community practice* (2nd ed.). Thousand Oaks, CA: Sage.

Chapter 5

Abramovitz, M., & Albrecht, J. (2013). The community loss index: A new social indicator. *Social Service Review, 87*(4), 677–724.

Adam, B. D. (1995). *The rise of a gay and lesbian movement.* New York: Twayne.

Aguilar, J. P., & Sen, S. (2009). Comparing conceptualizations of social capital. *Journal of Community Practice, 17*, 424–443.

Alinsky, A. (1971). *Rules for radicals*. New York: Vintage.

Alinsky, A. (1974). *Reveille for radicals*. New York: Vintage.

Almog-Bar, M., & Schmid, H. (2014). Advocacy activities of nonprofit human service organizations: A critical review. *Nonprofit and Voluntary Sector Quarterly, 43*(1), 11–35.

Benford, R. D., & Snow, D. A. (2000). Framing processes and social movements: An overview and assessment. *Annual Review of Sociology, 26*, 611–629.

Bessant, K. C. (2014). An interactional approach to emergent interorganizational fields. *Community Development, 45*(1), 60–75.

Breton, M. (2001). Neighborhood resiliency. *Journal of Community Practice, 9*(1), 21–36.

Broadbent, J., & Brockman, V. (Eds.). (2011). *East Asian social movements: Power, protest, and change in a dynamic region* (Nonprofit and Civil Society Studies). New York: Springer Science and Business Media.

Burrell, G., & Morgan, G. (1979). *Sociological paradigms and organisational analysis*. London: Heinemann.

Campbell, C. (2014). Community mobilisation in the 21st century: Updating our theory of social change? *Journal of Health Psychology, 19*(1), 46–59.

Case, C., & Hawthorne, T. L. (2013). Served or unserved? A site suitability analysis of social services in Atlanta, Georgia using geographic information systems. *Applied Geography, 38*, 96–106.

Chaskin, R. J. (2013). Theories of community. In M. Weil, M. Reisch, & M. L. Ohmer (Eds.), *The handbook of community practice* (2nd ed., pp. 105–121). Thousand Oaks, CA: Sage.

Chaskin, R., Brown, P., Venkatesh, S., & Vidal, A. (2001). *Building community capacity*. New York: Aldine de Gruyter.

Chaufan, C., Hollister, B., Nazareno, J., & Fox, P. (2012). Medical ideology as a double-edged sword: The politics of cure and care in the making of Alzheimer's disease. *Social Science & Medicine, 24*, 788–795.

Christens, B. D. (2012). Targeting empowerment in community development: A community psychology approach to enhancing local power and well-being. *Community Development Journal, 47*(4), 538–554.

Clark, D. C. (1973). The concept of community: A reexamination. *Sociological Review, 21*, 397–416.

Cohen, A. P. (1985). *The symbolic construction of community*. London: Routledge & Kegan Paul.

Collins, P. H. (2010). The new politics of community. *American Sociological Review, 75*(1), 7–30.

Conn, E. (2011). Community engagement in the social eco-system dance. In A. Tait & K. A. Richardson (Eds.), *Moving forward with complexity* (pp. 285–308). Litchfield Park, AZ: Emergent Publications.

Cramer, E. P., Brady, S. R., & McLeod, D. A. (2013). Building capacity to address the abuse of persons with disabilities. *Journal of Community Practice, 21*, 124–144.

Crozier, M., & Melchior, F. (2013). Perspectives in adult education—asset mapping: A course assignment and community assessment. *New Horizons in Adult Education & Human Resource Development, 25*(3), 125–129.

Delgado, M. (2000). *Community social work practice in an urban context*. New York: Oxford University Press.

Donaldson, L. P., & Daughtery, L. (2011). Introducing asset-based models of social justice into service learning: A social work approach. *Journal of Community Practice, 19*, 80–99.

Eikenberry, A. M. (2009). *Giving circles: Philanthropy, voluntary association, and democracy*. Bloomington, IN: Indiana University Press.

Emerson, R. E. (1962). Power-dependence relations. *American Sociological Review, 27*(1), 31–41.

Fellin, P. (2001). Understanding American communities. In J. Rothman, J. L. Erlich, & J. E. Tropman (Eds.), *Strategies of community intervention* (6th ed., pp. 118–132). Itasca, IL: F. E. Peacock.

Finn, J. L. (2005). La Victoria: Claiming memory, history, and justice in a Santiago Problacion. *Journal of Community Practice, 13*(3), 9–31.

Gallo, G. (2013). Conflict theory, complexity and systems approach. *Systems Research and Behavorial Science, 30*, 156-175.

Gamble, D. N., & Weil, M. (2010). *Community practice skills: Local to global perspectives*. New York: Columbia University Press.

Gerloff, R. (1992). Rediscovering the village. *Utne Reader*, 93–100.

Green, P., & Haines, A. (2002). *Asset building and community development*. Thousand Oaks, CA: Sage.

Greenspan, I. (2014). How can Bourdieu's theory of capital benefit the understanding of advocacy NGOs? Theoretical framework and empirical illustration. *Nonprofit and Voluntary Sector Quarterly, 43*(1), 99–120.

Gutierrez, L. M., & Lewis, E.A. (1999). *Empowering women of color*. New York: Columbia University Press.

Hannah, G. (2006). Maintaining product-process balance in community antipoverty initiatives. *Social Work, 51*(1), 9–17.

Hardina, D. (2002). *Analytical skills for community organization practice*. New York: Columbia University Press.

Hardina, D. (2003). Linking citizen participation to empowerment practice: A historical overview. *Journal of Community Practice, 11*(4), 11–38.

Hasenfeld, Y. (2010). *Human services as complex organizations*. Thousand Oaks, CA: Sage.

Hash, K. M., & Netting, F. E. (2007). Long-term planning and decision-making among mid-life and older gay men and lesbians. *Journal of Social Work in End-of-Life & Palliative Care, 3*(2), 59–77.

Hawley, A. (1950). *A human ecology: A theory of community structure*. New York: Roland Press.

Hawley, A. (1968). *Urban ecology*. Chicago, IL: University of Chicago Press.

Haynes, J. M. (2014). Safe third country agreement: Closing the doors on refugee women seeking protection. *Families in Society, 95*(2), 140–148.

Haynes, K. S., & Mickelson, J. S. (2006). *Affecting change: Social workers in the political arena* (6th ed.). Boston, MA: Allyn and Bacon.

Helms, J. (1984). Toward a theoretical explanation of the effects of race on counseling: A black and white model. *Counseling Psychologist, 12*(3–4), 153–165.

Hillery, G. (1955). Definitions of community: Areas of agreement. *Rural Sociology, 20*, 779–791.

Hillier, A. (2007). Why social work needs mapping. *Journal of Social Work Education, 43*(2), 205–221.

Hunter, A. (1993). National federations: The role of voluntary organizations in linking macro and micro orders in civil society. *Nonprofit & Voluntary Sector Quarterly, 22*(2), 121–136.

Hutchinson, R. N., Putt, M. A., Dean, L. T., Long, J. A., Montagnet, C. A., & Armstrong, K. (2009). Neighborhood racial composition, social capital and black all-cause mortality in Philadelphia. *Social Science & Medicine, 68*, 1859–1865.

Kayal, P. M. (1991). Gay AIDS voluntarism as political activity. *Nonprofit & Voluntary Sector Quarterly, 20*(3), 289–312.

Kelly, P. J., Rasu, R., Lesser, J., Oscos-Sanchez, M., Mancha, J., & Orriega, A. (2010). Mexican-American neighborhood's social capital and attitudes about violence. *Issues in Mental Health Nursing, 31*, 15–20.

Kettner, P. M., Moroney, R. M., & Martin, L. L. (2013). *Designing and managing programs: An effectiveness-based approach* (4th ed.). Thousand Oaks, CA: Sage.

Knickmeyer, L., Hopkins, K., & Meyer, M. (2003). Exploring collaboration among urban neighborhood associations. *Journal of Community Practice, 11*(2), 13–25.

Kretzmann, J. P., & McKnight, J. L. (1993). *Building communities from the inside out.* Evanston, IL: Northwestern University, Center for Urban Affairs and Policy Research.

Lazzari, M. M., Colarossi, L., & Collins, K. S. (2008). Feminists in social work: Where have all the leaders gone? *Affilia, 24*(4), 348–359.

Lohmann, R. A. (2014). *Voluntary action in new commons: Democracy in the life world beyond, market, state and household* (2nd ed.). Morgantown, WV: Roger A. Lohmann, Skywriters Press.

Lynd, R. S., & Lynd, H. M. (1929). *Middletown: A study in contemporary American culture.* New York: Harcourt & Brace.

Lynd, R. S., & Lynd, H. M. (1937). *Middletown in transition: A study in cultural conflicts.* New York: Harcourt & Brace.

Lyon, L. (1987). *The community in urban society.* Philadelphia, PA: Temple University Press.

MacNair, R. H., Fowler, L., & Harris, J. (2000). The diversity functions of organizations that confront oppression: The evolution of three social movements. *Journal of Community Practice, 7*(2), 71–88.

Martin, P. Y., & O'Connor, G. G. (1989). *The social environment: Open systems applications.* New York: Longman.

Marx, J. D. (2013). Ten emerging "communities" for social work education and practice. *Social Work, 59*(1), 84–86.

Maslow, A. (1962). *Toward a psychology of being.* New York: Van Nostrand.

McIntyre, E. L. G. (1986). Social networks: Potential for practice. *Social Work, 31*(6), 421–426.

McNutt, J. G., Queiro-Tajalli, I., Boland, K. M., & Campbell, C. (2001). Information poverty and the Latino community: Implications for social work practice and social work education. *Journal of Ethnic & Cultural Diversity in Social Work, 10*, 1–20.

Meyer, M. (2010). Social movement service organizations: The challenges and consequences of combining service provision and political advocacy. In Y. Hasenfeld (Ed.), *Human services as complex organizations* (pp. 533–550). Thousand Oaks, CA: Sage.

Mondros, J. B., & Wilson, S. M. (1994). *Organizing for power and empowerment.* New York: Columbia University Press.

Nkomo, S. M., & Cox, T., Jr. (1996). Diverse identities in organizations. In S. R. Clegg, C. Hardy, & W. R. Nord (Eds.), *Handbook of organization studies* (pp. 338–356). London: Sage.

Norlin, J., & Chess, W. (1997). *Human behavior and the social environment: Social systems theory.* Boston, MA: Allyn and Bacon.

Nye, N., & Glickman, N. J. (2000). Working together: Building capacity for community development. *Housing Policy Debate, 11*, 163–198.

O'Brien, G. V., & Leneave, J. (2008). The "art" of social work and the ADA's essential functions provision: Challenges and recommendations. *Administration in Social Work, 32*(4), 87–99.

Pantoja, A., & Perry, W. (1998). Community development and restoration: A perspective and case study. In F. G. Rivera & J. L. Erlich (Eds.), *Community organizing in a diverse society* (pp. 220–242). Boston, MA: Allyn and Bacon.

Park, R. E. (1983). Human ecology. In R. L. Warren & L. Lyon (Eds.), *New perspectives on the American community* (pp. 27–36). Homewood, IL: Dorsey Press.

Parsons, T. (1971). *The system of modern societies.* Englewood Cliffs, NJ: Prentice Hall.

Portes, A. (2000). The two meanings of social capital. *Sociological Forum, 15*(1), 1–12.

Putnam, R. D. (2000). *Bowling alone: The collapse and revival of American community.* New York: Simon & Schuster.

Quinn, P. (2004). Home of your own programs: Models of community collaboration. *Journal of Community Practice, 12*(1 / 2), 37–50.

Rine, C. M., Morales, J., Vanyukevych, A. B., Durand, E. G., & Schroeder, K. A. (2012). Using GIS mapping to assess foster care: A picture is worth a thousand words. *Journal of Family Social Work, 15*, 375–388.

Rogge, M. E., David, K., Maddox, D., & Jackson, M. (2005). Leveraging environmental, social and economic justice at Chattanooga Creek: A case study. *Journal of Community Practice, 13*(3), 33–53.

Rothman, J. (2008). Multi modes of community intervention. In J. Rothman, J. L. Erlich, & J. E. Tropman, & Cox, F. (Eds.), *Strategies for community intervention* (7th ed., pp. 141–170). Peosta, IA: Eddie Bowers.

Saegert, J., Thompson, P., Warren, M. R. (Eds.). (2001). *Social capital and poor communities.* New York: Russell Sage Foundation Press.

Saleeby, D. (1997). *The strengths perspective in social work practice* (2nd ed.). New York: Longman.

Salimath, M. S., & Jones, R., III. (2011). Population ecology theory: Implications for sustainability. *Management Decision, 49*(6), 874–910.

Seck, M. M., & Helton, L. (2014). Faculty development of a joint MSW program utilizing Tuckman's model of stages of group development. *Social Work with Groups, 37*(2), 158–168.

Smith, D. H. (1991). Four sectors or five? Retaining the member-benefit sector. *Nonprofit and Voluntary Sector Quarterly, 20*(2), 137–150.

Smith, D. H. (2000). *Grassroots associations.* Thousand Oaks, CA: Sage.

Solomon, B. (1976). *Black empowerment.* New York: Columbia University Press.

Stanfield, J. H. (1993). African American traditions of civic responsibility. *Nonprofit and Voluntary Sector Quarterly, 22*(2), 137–153.

Sun, X., Rehnberg, C., & Meng, Q. (2009). How are individual-level social capital and poverty associated with health equity? A study from two Chinese cities. *International Journal for Equity in Health, 8*, 1–13.

Tönnies, F. (1957). *Community and society* [Gemeinschaft und Gesellschaft] (C. P. Loomis, Trans., Ed.). East Lansing, MI: Michigan State University Press. (Original work published in 1887)

Van Til, J. (1988). *Mapping the third sector: Voluntarism in a changing social economy.* New York: Foundation Center.

Wahl, A., Bergland, A., & Løyland, B. (2010). Is social capital associated with coping, self-esteem, health and quality of life in long-term social assistance recipients? *Scandinavian Journal of Caring Sciences, 24*, 808–816.

Warren, R. L. (1978). *The community in America* (3rd ed.). Chicago, IL: Rand McNally.

Weil, M., Gambel, D. N., & Ohmer, M. L. (2013). Evolution, models, and the changing context of community practice. In M. Weil, M. Reisch, & M. L. Ohmer, (Eds.), *The handbook of community practice* (2nd ed., pp. 167–193). Thousand Oaks, CA: Sage.

Weil, M., Reisch, M., & Ohmer, M. L. (Eds.). (2013). *The handbook of community practice* (2nd ed.). Thousand Oaks, CA: Sage.

Weng, S. S., & Netting, F. E. (2014). Culturally responsive strategies used to deliver services to Asian Americans. *Families in Society, 94*(4), 253–260.

West, J. (1945). *Plainville, U.S.A.* New York: Columbia University Press.

Wineberg, R. J. (1992). Local human services provision by religious congregations. *Nonprofit and Voluntary Sector Quarterly, 21*(2), 107–118.

Wollebaek, D. (2009). Survival in voluntary associations, *Nonprofit Management & Leadership 19*(3), 267–284.

Yeneabat, M., & Butterfield, A. K. (2012). "We can't eat a road": Asset-based community development and the Gedam Sefer community partnership in Ethiopia. *Journal of Community Practice, 20*(1–2), 134–153.

Chapter 6

Alliance of Information and Referral Systems (AIRS). (2015). Retrieved June 22, 2015, from http://www.airs.org/i4a/pages/index.cfm?pageid=1

Almog-Bar, M., & Schmid, H. (2014). Advocacy activities of nonprofit human service organizations: A critical review. *Nonprofit and Voluntary Sector Quarterly, 43*(1), 11–35.

Bailey, D., & Koney, K. M. (2000). *Creating and maintaining strategic alliances: From affiliations to consolidations.* Thousand Oaks, CA: Sage.

Brady, S. R., & O'Connor, M. K. (2014). Understanding how community organizing leads to social change: The beginning development of formal practice theory. *Journal of Community Practice, 22*(1–2), 210–228.

Brudney, J. L. (2005). Emerging areas of volunteering. *ARNOVA Occasional Paper Series, 1*(2).

Chronicle of Philanthropy. (2013). Philanthropy 400 Data. Retrieved June 15, 2015, from http://philanthropy.com/article/An-Uneven-Recovery-for/142493/

Coulton, C., Chan, T., & Mikelbank, K. (2011). Finding place in community change initiatives: Using GIS to uncover resident perceptions of their neighborhoods. *Journal of Community Practice, 19*, 10–28.

Cross, T. L., Bazron, B. J., Dennis, K. W., & Isaacs, M. R. (1989). *Towards a culturally competent system of care.* Washington, DC: Georgetown University Child Development Center.

Dudziak, S., & Profitt, N. J. (2012). Group work and social justice: Designing pedagogy for social change. *Social Work with Groups, 35*(3), 235–252.

Estes, R. J. (2013). Global change and indicators of social development. In M. Weil, M. Reisch, & M. L. Ohmer (Eds.), *The handbook of community practice* (2nd ed., pp. 587–605). Thousand Oaks, CA: Sage.

Fortune.com. (2015). Fortune 500 2015. Retrieved June 22, 2015 from http://fortune.com/fortune500/

Green, G. P., & Haines, A. (2002). *Asset building and community development.* Thousand Oaks, CA: Sage.

International Social Work. (2014). Global agenda for social work and social development: First report——promoting social and economic equalities. *International Social Work, 57*(3), 3–16.

Jansson, B. S. (2011). *Becoming an effective policy advocate: From policy practice to social justice* (6th ed.). Belmont, CA: Thomson Brooks/Cole.

Jansson, B. S. (2015). *The reluctant welfare state* (8th ed.). Belmont, CA: Brooks/Cole.

Karger, H. J., & Stoesz, D. (2013). *American social welfare policy: A pluralist approach* (7th ed.). Boston, MA: Pearson Education.

Kettner, P. M., Daley, J. M., & Nichols, A. W. (1985). *Initiating change in organizations and communities.* Monterey, CA: Brooks/Cole.

King, S. W., & Mayers, R. S. (1984). A course syllabus on developing self-help groups among minority elderly. In J. S. McNeil & S. W. King (Eds.), *Guidelines for developing mental health and minority aging curriculum with a focus on self-help groups* (pp. 1–12; publication supported by National Institute of Mental Health Grant #MH 15944–04). Bethesda, MD: National Institute of Mental Health.

Kretzmann, J., & McKnight, J. (1993). *Building communities from the inside out: A path toward finding and mobilizing community assets.* Chicago, IL: ACTA.

Meenaghan, T. M., Gibbons, W. E., & McNutt, J. G. (2005). *Generalist practice in larger settings: Knowledge and skills concepts* (2nd ed.). Chicago, IL: Lyceum.

Nussbaum, M. C. (2006). *Frontiers of justice: Disability, nationality, and species membership.* Cambridge, MA: The Belknap Press of Harvard University Press.

O'Connor, M. K., & Netting, F. E. (2009). *Organization practice.* Hoboken, NJ: Wiley.

Rossi, P. H., Lipsey, M. W., & Freeman, H. E. (2004). *Evaluation: A systematic approach* (7th ed.). Thousand Oaks, CA: Sage.

Sen, A., & Williams, B. (1982). *Utilitarianism and beyond.* Cambridge, MA: Cambridge University Press.

Staples, L. (2012). Community organizing for social justice: Grassroots groups for power. *Social Work with Groups, 35*(3), 287–296.

Tannen, D. (1990). *You just don't understand.* New York: William Morrow.

Tobin, S. S., Ellor, J. W., & Anderson-Ray, S. (1986). *Enabling the elderly: Religious institutions within the community service system.* New York: State University of New York Press.

Warren, R. L. (1978). *The community in America* (3rd ed.). Chicago, IL: Rand McNally.

Weil, M., Reisch, M, & Ohmer, M. L. (Eds.). (2013). *The handbook of community practice* (2nd ed.). Thousand Oaks, CA: Sage.

Chapter 7

Acker, J. (1990). Hierarchies, jobs, bodies: A theory of gendered organizations. *Gender & Society, 4*(2), 139–158.

Acker, J. (2012). Gendered organizations and intersectionality: Problems and possibilities. *Equality, Diversity and Inclusion: An International Journal, 31*(3), 214–224.

American Society for Quality. (2006). *Total quality management.* Retrieved October 2006 from www.asq.org/learn-about-quality/total-quality-management/overview/overview.html

Argyris, C., & Schön. D. A. (1978). *Organizational learning.* Reading, MA: Addison-Wesley.

Argyris, C., & Schön. D. A. (1996). *Organizational learning II.* Reading, MA: Addison-Wesley.

Beddoe, L. (2009). Creating continuous conversation: Social workers and learning organizations. *Social Work Education, 28*, 722–736.

Bertalanffy, L. von. (1950). An outline of general system theory. *British Journal for the Philosophy of Science, 1*(2), 493–512.

Blau, P. M., & Scott, W. R. (1962). *Formal organizations.* San Francisco, CA: Chandler.

Bolan, R. (1980). The practitioner as theorist: The phenomenology of the professional episode. *Journal of the American Institute of Planners, 46*(3), 261–274.

Bolman, F. G., & Deal, T. E. (2013). *Reframing organizations* (5th ed.). San Francisco, CA: Jossey-Bass.

Bowen, G. L., Ware, W. B., Rose, R. A., & Powers, J. D. (2007). Assessing the functioning of schools as learning organizations. *Social Work in Education, 29*, 199–208.

Brazzell, M. (2003). Historical and theoretical roots of diversity management. In D. L. Plummer (Ed.), *Handbook of diversity management: Beyond awareness to competency based learning.* Lanham, MD: University Press of America.

Briggs, H. E., & McBeath, B. (2009). Evidence-based management: Origins, challenges, and implications for social service administration. *Administration in Social Work, 33*, 242–261.

Britton, D. M., & Logan, L. (2008). Gendered organizations: Progress and prospects. *Sociology Compass, 2*(1), 107–121.

Burns, T., & Stalker, G. M. (1961). *The management of innovation.* London: Tavistock.

Carr-Ruffino, N. (2002). *Managing diversity: People skills for a multicultural workplace* (5th ed.). Boston, MA: Pearson.

Castilla, E. J. (2008). Gender, race, and meritocracy in organizational careers. *American Journal of Sociology, 113*, 1479–1526.

Champion, D. J. (1975). *The sociology of organizations.* New York: McGraw-Hill.

Chang, C. C., Chiu, C. M., & Chen, C. A. (2010). The effect of TQM practices on employee satisfaction and loyalty in government. *Total Quality Management & Business Excellence, 21*, 1299–1314.

Chenhall, R. H. (2003). Management control systems design within its organizational context: Findings from contingency-based research and directions for the future. *Accounting, Organizations and Society, 28*, 127–168.

Cohen, P. N. (2007). Working for the woman? Female managers and the gender wage gap. *American Sociological Review, 72*, 681–704.

Collins-Camargo, C., & Royse, D. (2010). A study of the relationships among effective supervision, organizational culture promoting evidence-based practice, and worker self-efficacy in public child welfare. *Journal of Public Child Welfare, 4*, 1–24.

Cross, E. Y. (2000). *Managing diversity: The courage to lead.* Westport, CT: Quorum Books.

Cyert, R. M., & March, J. G. (1963). *A behavioral theory of the firm.* Englewood Cliffs, NJ: Prentice-Hall.

Deming, W. E. (1982). *Out of the crisis.* Cambridge, MA: Massachusetts Institute of Technology, Center for Advanced Engineering Study.

Dirsmith, M. W., Heian, J. B., & Covaleski, M. A. (1997). Structure and agency in an institutionalized setting: The application and social transformation of control in the big six. *Accounting, Organizations & Society, 22*, 1–27.

Drucker, P. F. (1954). *The practice of management.* New York: Harper.

Etzioni, A. (1964). *Modern organizations.* Englewood Cliffs, NJ: Prentice Hall.

Feigenbaum, A. V. (1951). *Quality control: Principles, practice, and administration.* New York: McGraw-Hill.

Fenby, B. L. (1991). Feminist theory, critical theory, and management's romance with the technical. *Affilia, 6*(1), 20–37.

Follett, M. P. (2005 [1926]). The giving of orders. In J. M. Shafritz & J. S. Ott (Eds.), *Classics of organizational theory* (6th ed.). Belmont, CA: Thomson Wadsworth.

Forester, J. (1980). Critical theory and planning practice. *Journal of the American Planning Association, 46*(3), 275–286.

Friedmann, P. D., Lan, J., & Alexander, J. A. (2010). Top manager effects on buprenorphine adoption in outpatient substance abuse treatment programs. *Journal of Behavioral Health Services & Research, 37*, 322–337.

Galbraith, J. R. (1973). *Designing complex organizations.* Reading, MA: Addison-Wesley.

George, C. S., Jr. (1968). *The history of management thought.* Englewood Cliffs, NJ: Prentice Hall.

Gibson, C. B., & Zellmer-Bruhn, M. E. (2001). Metaphors and meaning: An intercultural analysis of the concept of teamwork. *Administrative Science Quarterly, 46*, 274–303.

Giddens, A. (1979). *Central problems in social theory.* Berkeley, CA: University of California Press.

Glisson, C., Williams, N., Green, P., Hemmelgarn, A., & Hoagwood, K. (2014). The organizational social context of mental health Medicaid waiver programs with family support services: Implications for research and practice. *Administration & Policy in Mental Health & Mental Health Services Research, 41*, 32–42.

Gorman, E. H., & Kmec, J. A. (2009). Hierarchical rank and women's organizational mobility: Glass ceilings in corporate law firms. *American Journal of Sociology, 114*, 1428–1474.

Habermas, J. (1971). *Knowledge and human interests.* Boston, CA: Beacon.

Hakanen, J. J., Schaufeli, W. B., & Ahola, K. (2008). The job demands-resources model: A three-year cross-lagged study of burnout, depression, commitment, and work engagement. *Work & Stress, 22*, 224–241.

Hasenfeld, Y. (2010). *Human services as complex organizations.* Thousand Oaks, CA: Sage.

Herman, R. D., & Renz, D. (2004). Doing things right: Effectiveness in local nonprofit organizations, a panel study, *Public Administration Review, 64*, 694–704.

Herzberg, F. (1966). *Work and the nature of man.* Cleveland, OH: World.

Kang, H. R., Yang, H. D., & Rowley C. (2006). Factors in team effectiveness: Cognitive and demographic similarities of software development team members. *Human Relations, 59*, 1681–1710.

Katz, D., & Kahn, R. L. (1966). *The social psychology of organizations.* New York: Wiley.

Kelly, M. J., & Lauderdale, M. L. (2001). Public-private mentoring for leadership and service quality. *Professional Development: The International Journal of Continuing Social Work Education, 4*, 32–41.

Landsberger, H. A. (1958). *Hawthorne revisited.* Ithaca, NY: Cornell University Press.

Latting, J. K., Beck, M. H., Slack, K. J. Tetrick, L. E., Jones, A. P., Etchegaray, J. M., & da Silva, N. (2004). Promoting service quality and client adherence to the service plan. *Administration in Social Work, 28*, 29–48.

Lawrence, P. R., & Lorsch, J. W. (1967). *Organization and environment: Managing differentiation and integration.* Boston, MA: Graduate School of Business Administration, Harvard University.

Leana, C., Appelbaum, E., & Shevchuk, I. (2009). Work process and quality of care in early childhood education: The role of job crafting. *Academy of Management Journal, 52*, 1169–1192.

Lipsky, M. (1984). Bureaucratic disentitlement in social welfare programs. *Social Service Review, 58*(1), 3–27.

March, J. G., & Olsen, J. P. (1976). *Ambiguity and choice in organizations.* Bergen, Norway: Universitetsforlaget.

March, J. G., & Simon, H. A. (1958). *Organizations.* New York: Wiley.

Martin, L. L. (1993). *Total quality management in human service organizations.* Thousand Oaks, CA: Sage.

McGregor, D. (1960). *The human side of enterprise.* New York: McGraw-Hill.

Merton, R. K. (1952). Bureaucratic structure and personality. In R. K. Merton, A. P. Gray, B. Hockey, & H. C. Selvin (Eds.), *Reader in bureaucracy* (pp. 261–372). Glencoe, IL: Free Press.

Michels, R. (1949 [1915]). *Political parties* (E. Paul & C. Paul, Trans.). Glencoe, IL: Free Press.

Mikkelsen, E. N. (2012). An analysis of the social meaning of conflict in nonprofit organizations. *Nonprofit and Voluntary Sector Quarterly, 42*(5), 923–941.

Moore, S. T., & Kelly, M. J. (1996). Quality now: Moving human services organizations toward a consumer orientation to service quality. *Social Work, 41*(1), 33–40.

Morgan, G. (1986). *Image of organizations*. London: Sage.

Morse, J. J., & Lorsch, J. W. (1970). Beyond theory Y. *Harvard Business Review, 45*, 61–68.

Mouzelis, N. P. (1967). *Organization and bureaucracy*. London: Routledge & Kegan Paul.

Ouchi, W. (1981). *Theory Z: How American business can meet the Japanese challenge*. Reading, MA: Addison-Wesley.

Parsons, T. (1960). *Structure and process in modern societies*. Glencoe, IL: Free Press.

Peters, T. J., & Waterman, R. H. (1982). *In search of excellence: Lessons from America's best-run companies*. New York: Harper & Row.

Pfeffer, J. (1981). *Power in organizations*. Marshfield, MA: Pitman.

Pfeffer, J., & Sutton, R. I. (2006). *Hard facts, dangerous half-truths, and total nonsense*. Boston, MA: Harvard Business School Press.

Pfeifer, C. (2010). Impact of wages and job levels on worker absenteeism. *International Journal of Manpower, 31*, 59–72.

Rogers, R. E. (1975). *Organizational theory*. Boston, MA: Allyn & Bacon.

Rousseau, D. M. (2006). Is there such a thing as "evidence-based management"? *Academy of Management Review, 31*, 256–269.

Ruggiano, N., Taliaferro, J. D., & Shtompel, N. (2013). Interorganizational partnerships as a strategy for lobbying: Nonprofit administrators' perspectives on collaborating for systems-level change. *Journal of Community Practice, 21*, 263–281.

Saylor, J. H. (1996). *TQM simplified: A practical guide* (2nd ed.). New York: McGraw-Hill.

Schein, E. H. (2010). *Organizational culture and leadership* (4th ed.). San Francisco, CA: Jossey-Bass.

Scott, W. R. (1981). *Organizations: Rational, natural, and open systems*. Englewood Cliffs, NJ: Prentice Hall.

Selznick, P. (1949). *TVA and the grass roots*. Berkeley, CA: University of California Press.

Selznick, P. (1957). *Leadership in administration*. New York: Harper & Row.

Senge, P. M. (1990). *The fifth discipline: The art and practice of the learning organization*. New York: Doubleday.

Shafritz, J. M., Ott, S. J., & Jang, Y. S. (2011). *Classics of organizational theory* (7th ed.). Belmont, CA.: Wadsworth.

Sills, D. L. (1957). *The volunteers*. New York: Free Press.

Simon, H. A. (1957). *Administrative behavior* (2nd ed.). New York: Macmillan.

Simons, K. V., & Jankowski, T. B. (2008). Factors influencing nursing home social workers' intentions to quit employment. *Administration in Social Work, 32*, 5–21.

Sykes, A. J. M. (1965). Economic interests and the Hawthorne researchers: A comment. *Human Relations, 18*, 253–263.

Taylor, F. W. (1911). *The principles of scientific management*. New York: Harper.

Thomas, R. R., Jr. (1991). *Beyond race and gender: Unleashing the power of your total work force by managing diversity*. New York: AMACOM.

Thompson, J. D. (1967). *Organizations in action*. New York: McGraw-Hill.

Wamsley, G. L., & Zald, M. N. (1976). *The political economy of public organizations*. Bloomington, IN: Indiana University Press.

Weber, M. (1946). *From Max Weber: Essays in sociology* (H. H. Gerth & C. W. Mills, Trans.). New York: Oxford University Press.

Weber, M. (1947). *The theory of social and economic organization* (A. M. Henderson & T. Parsons, Trans.). New York: Macmillan. (Original work published in 1924)

Weick, K. E. (1995). *Sensemaking in organizations*. Thousand Oaks, CA: Sage.

Weick, K. E., Sutcliffe, K. M., & Obstfeld, D. (2005). Organizing and the process of sensemaking. *Organization Science, 16*, 409–421.

Williams, M. S. (2004). Policy component analysis: A method for identifying problems in policy implementation. *Journal of Social Service Research, 30*, 1–18.

Chapter 8

Abramovitz, M. (2005). The largely untold story of welfare reform and the human services. *Social Work, 50*, 175–186.

Almog-Bar, M., & Schmid, H. (2014). Advocacy activities of nonprofit human service organizations: A critical review. *Nonprofit and Voluntary Sector Quarterly, 43*(1), 11–35.

Acquavita, S. P., Pittman, J., Gibbons, M., & Castellanos-Brown, K. (2009). Personal and organizational diversity factors' impact on social workers' job satisfaction: Results from a national internet-based survey. *Administration in Social Work, 33*, 151–166.

Association of Fundraising Professionals. (2010). *Trends: In 2010, expect charitable donors to keep giving through long-term pledges*. Retrieved June 15, 2015, from http://www.afpnet.org/Audiences/ReportsResearchDetail.cfm?itemnumber=4289

Bach, S. (2009). Human resource management in the public sector. In A. Wilkinson, N. A. Bacon, T. Redmon, & S. Snell (Eds.), *The Sage handbook of human resource management* (pp. 561–567). Thousand Oaks, CA: Sage.

Bisgaier, J., Polsky, D., & Rhodes, K.V. (2012). Academic medical centers and equity in specialty care access for children. *Archives of Pediatric & Adolescent Medicine, 166*, 304–310.

Blackwood, A., Roeger, K. L., & Pettijohn, S. L. (2012). The nonprofit sector in brief: Public charities, giving and volunteering, 2012. Retrieved June 15, 2015, from http://www.urban.org/publications/412674.html

Bubar, R. (2010). Cultural competence, justice, and supervision: Sexual assault against Native women. *Women & Therapy, 33*, 55–72.

Burns, T., & Stalker, G. M. (1961). *The management of innovation*. London: Tavistock.

Casanueva, C., Fraser, J. G., Gilbert, A., Maze, C., Katz, L., Ullery, M. A., . . . Lederman, C. (2013). Evaluation of the miami child well-being court model: Safety, permanency, and well-being findings. *Child Welfare, 92*, 73–96.

Chaidez-Guttierrez, F., & Fischer, R. L. (2013). Reflecting on grantee evaluation accountability to funders: Exploring power dynamics with grassroots organizations in communities of color. *Journal of Community Practice, 21*, 304–326.

Chen, F. M., Fryer, G. E., Jr., Phillips, R. L., Jr., Wilson, E., & Pathman, D. E. (2005). Patients' beliefs about racism, preferences for physician race, and satisfaction with care. *Annals of Family Medicine, 3*, 138–143.

Chen, K. K. (2013). Storytelling: an informal mechanism of accountability for voluntary organizations. *Nonprofit and Voluntary Sector Quarterly, 42*(5), 902–922.

Chow, J. C., & Austin, M. J. (2008). The culturally responsive social service agency: An application of an evolving definition to a case study. *Administration in Social Work, 32*, 39–64.

Clark, R. H. (2007). A study of the relationship between job satisfaction, goal internalization, organization citizenship behavior, and mission statement familiarity. *Dissertation Abstracts International, A: The Humanities and Social Sciences, 67*(7), 2745.

Cordes, J., & Henig, J. R. (2001). Nonprofit human service providers in an era of privatization: Toward a theory of economic and political response. *Policy Studies Review, 18*, 91–110.

Cramm, J. M., Strating, M. H., & Nieboer, A. P. (2013). The influence of organizational characteristics on employee solidarity in the long-term care sector. *Journal of Advanced Nursing, 69*, 526–534.

Cross, T. L., & Friesen, B. J. (2005). Community practice in children's mental health: Developing cultural competence and family-centered services in systems of care models. In M. Weil (Ed.), *The handbook of community practice* (pp. 442–459). Thousand Oaks, CA: Sage.

Dennis, H., & Thomas, K. (2007). Ageism in the workplace. *Generations, 31*, 84–89.

Dill, W. R. (1958). Environment as an influence on managerial autonomy. *Administrative Science Quarterly, 2*(1), 409–443.

Eilbert, K. W., & Lafronza, V. (2005). Working together for community health: A model and case studies. *Evaluation and Program Planning, 28*, 185–199.

Fletcher, C. N., Garasky, S. B., Jensen, H. H., & Nielsen, R. B. (2010). Transportation access: A key employment barrier for rural low-income families. *Journal of Poverty, 14*, 123–144.

Forcadell, F. J. (2005). Democracy, cooperation and business success: The case of Mondragon Corporacion Cooperativa. *Journal of Business Ethics, 56*, 255–274.

Fung, K., Lo, H., Srivastava, R., & Andermann, L. (2012). Organizational cultural competence consultation to a mental health institution. *Transcultural Psychiatry, 49*, 165–184.

Gioia, D. A., & Thomas, J. B. (1996). Identity, image and issue interpretation. *Administrative Science Quarterly, 41*, 370–403.

Glisson, C., Landsverk, J., Schoenwald, S., Kelleher, K., Eaton Hoagwood, K., Mayberg, S., & Green, P. (2008). Assessing the organizational social context (OSC) of mental health services: Implications for research and practice. *Administration and Policy in Mental Health Services Research, 35*, 98–113.

Greenley, J. R., & Kirk, S. A. (1973). Organizational characteristics of agencies and the distribution of services to applicants. *Journal of Health and Social Behavior, 14*, 70–79.

Guo, C., & Saxton, G. D. (2014). Tweeting social change: How social media are changing nonprofit advocacy. *Nonprofit and Voluntary Sector Quarterly, 43*(1), 57–79.

Hasenfeld, Y. (2010). *Human services as complex organizations.* Thousand Oaks, CA: Sage.

Herbst, C. M. (2008). Who are the eligible non-recipients of child care subsidies? *Children and Youth Services Review, 30*, 1037–1054.

Hipp, L., & Warner, M. E. (2008). Market forces for the unemployed? Training vouchers in Germany and the USA. *Social Policy and Administration, 42*, 77–101.

Hodge, D. R. (2014). Assisting victims of human trafficking: Strategies to facilitate identification, exit from trafficking, and the restoration of wellness. *Social Work, 59*(2), 111–118.

Hodge, D. R., Jackson, K. F., & Vaughn, M. G. (2012). Culturally sensitive interventions and substance use: A meta-analytic review of outcomes among minority youths. *Social Work Research, 36*, 11–20.

Hopkins, K. M., Cohen-Callow, A., Kim, H. J., & Hwang, J. (2010). Beyond intent to leave: Using multiple outcome measures for assessing turnover in child welfare. *Children and Youth Services Review, 32*, 1380–1387.

Howard, D. (2013). *Human services in a market economy: Implications of program fee reliance among nonprofit human service organizations* UCLA Electronic Theses and Dissertations. Los Angeles, CA. Retrieved June 24, 2015 from http://www.escholarship.org/uc/item/9633t0ms

Independent Sector. (2014). *The value of volunteer time.* Retrieved June 25, 2015, from https://www.independentsector.org/volunteer_time

Jackson, K. F. (2009). Building cultural competence: A systematic evaluation of the effectiveness of culturally sensitive interventions with ethnic minority youth. *Children and Youth Services Review, 31*(11), 1192–1198.

Jaskyte, K., & Dressler, W. W. (2005). Organizational culture and innovation in nonprofit human service organizations. *Administration in Social Work, 29*, 23–41.

Jud, A., Perrig-Chiello, P., & Voll, P. (2011). Less effort in worsening child protection cases? The time-course of intensity of services. *Children and Youth Services Review, 33*, 2027–2033.

Kaldis, E., Koukoravas, K., & Tjortjis, C. (2007). Reengineering academic teams toward a network organizational structure. *Decision Sciences Journal of Innovative Education, 5*(2), 245–266.

Kettner, P. M., Moroney, R. M., & Martin, L. L. (2013). *Designing and managing programs: An effectiveness-based approach* (4th ed.). Thousand Oaks, CA: Sage.

Kirk, S. A., & Greenley, J. R. (1974). Denying or delivering services? *Social Work, 19*(4), 439–447.

Lebel, J. (2008). Survey says: Diversity-friendly workplaces are hard to come by. Retrieved June 15, 2015, from https://www.experience.com/alumnus/article?channel_id=diversity&source_page=additional_articles&article_id=article_1209399061931

Lee, R. D., & Johnson, R. W. (1973). *Public budgeting systems.* Baltimore, MD: University Park Press.

Levine, S., & White, P. E. (1961). Exchange as a conceptual framework for the study of interorganizational relationships. *Administrative Science Quarterly, 5*, 583–601.

Levitt, D. A., & Chiodini, S. R. (2014). Taking care of business: Use of a for-profit subsidiary by a nonprofit organization. Retrieved June 15, 2015, from http://www.americanbar.org/publications/blt/2014/06/03_levitt.html

Likert, R. (1961). *New patterns of management.* New York: McGraw-Hill.

Lipsky, M. (1984). Bureaucratic disentitlement in social welfare programs. *Social Service Review, 58*(1), 3–27.

Mallow, A. (2010). Diversity management in substance abuse organizations: Improving the relationship between the organization and its workforce. *Administration in Social Work, 34*, 275–285.

Marchevsky, A., & Theoharis, J. (2008). Dropped from the rolls: Mexican immigrants, race, and rights in the era of welfare reform. *Journal of Sociology and Social Welfare, 35*, 71–96.

Martin, L. L. (2000). Budgeting for outcomes in state human agencies. *Administration in Social Work, 24*, 71–88.

Martin, L. L., & Kettner, P. M. (2010). *Measuring the performance of human service programs* (2nd ed.). Newbury Park, CA: Sage.

McColl, M. A., Jarzynowska, A., & Shortt, S. E. D. (2010). Unmet health care needs of people with disabilities: Population level evidence. *Disability & Society, 25*, 205–218.

Merton, R. K. (1952). Bureaucratic structure and personality. In R. K. Merton, A. P. Gray, B. Hockey, & H. C. Selvin (Eds.), *Reader in bureaucracy* (pp. 261–372). Glencoe, IL: Free Press.

Miles, R. E. (1975). *Theories of management: Implications for organizational behavior and development.* New York: McGraw-Hill.

Miller, A. R., & Tucker, C. (2013). Active social media management: The case of health care. *Information Systems Research, 24*, 52-V.

Morse, J. J., & Lorsch, J. W. (1970). Beyond theory Y. *Harvard Business Review, 48*, 61–68.

Netting, F. E., McMurtry, S. L., Kettner, P. M., & Jones-McClintic, S. (1990). Privatization and its impact on nonprofit service providers. *Nonprofit and Voluntary Sector Quarterly, 19*, 33–46.

Netting, F. E., O'Connor, M. K., & Singletary, J. (2007). Finding homes for their dreams: Strategies founders and program initiators use to position faith-based programs. *Families in Society, 8*, 19–29.

Polivka-West, L., & Okano, K. (2008). Nursing home regulation and quality assurance in the states: Seeking greater effectiveness for better care. *Generations, 32*, 62–66.

Rank, O. N. (2008). Formal structures and informal networks: Structural analysis in organizations. *Scandanavian Journal of Management, 24*, 145–161.

Rao, D., Angell, B., Lam, C., & Corrigan, P. (2008). Stigma in the workplace: Employer attitudes about people with HIV in Beijing, Hong Kong, and Chicago. *Social Science & Medicine, 67*, 1541–1549.

Reeves, M. E. (2013) Brand partnerships as joint ventures: A comparison of two partnerships in the small non-profit arena. *Journal of Brand Management, 20*, 241–254.

Rodenborg, N. A., & Boisen, L. A. (2013). Aversive racism and intergroup contact theories: Cultural competence in a segregated world. *Journal of Social Work Education, 49*, 564–579.

Ruggiano, N., Taliaferro, J. D., & Shtompel, N. (2013). Interorganizational partnerships as a strategy for lobbying: Nonprofit administrators' perspectivs on collaborating for systems-level change. *Journal of Community Practice, 21*, 263–281.

Samples, M., Carnochan, S., & Austin, M. J. (2013). Using performance measures to manage child welfare outcomes: Local strategies and decision making. *Journal of Evidence-Based Social Work, 10*, 254–264.

Schmid, H. (2013). Nonprofit human services: Between identity blurring and adaptation to changing environments. *Administration in Social Work, 37*(3), 242–256.

Schmidt, M. J., Riggar, T. F., Crimando, W., & Bordieri, J. E. (1992). *Staffing for success.* Newbury Park, CA: Sage.

Shaefer, H. L. (2010). Identifying key barriers to unemployment insurance for disadvantaged workers in the United States. *Journal of Social Policy, 39*, 439–460.

Shier, M., Graham, J. R., & Jones, M. E. (2009). Barriers to employment as experienced by disabled people: A qualitative analysis in Calgary and Regina, Canada. *Disability & Society, 24*, 63–75.

Smith, G. H., III. (2013). The role of race concordance on prescription drug utilization among primary care case-managed Medicaid enrollees. *Research in Social & Administrative Pharmacy, 9*, 700–718.

Smith, L. A., McCaslin, R., Chang, J., Martinez, P., & McGrew, P. (2010). Assessing the needs of older gay, lesbian, bisexual, and transgender people: A service-learning and agency partnership approach. *Journal of Gerontological Social Work, 53*, 387–401.

Sussman, S., Skara, S., & Pumpuang, P. (2008). Project Towards No Drug Abuse (TND): Needs assessment of a social service referral telephone program for high risk youth. *Substance Use & Misuse, 43*, 2066–2073.

Taylor, F. W. (1947). *Scientific management.* New York: Harper & Row.

Thompson, J. D. (1967). *Organizations in action.* New York: McGraw-Hill.

Twombly, E. C. (2002). Religious versus secular human service organizations: Implications for public policy. *Social Science Quarterly, 83*, 947–961.

U.S. Bureau of Labor Statistics. (2014). *Volunteering in the United States, 2013.* Retrieved June 15, 2015, from http://www.bls.gov/news.release/volun.nr0.htm

U.S. Internal Revenue Service. (2014). *Individual noncash contributions, 2011.* Retrieved June 15, 2015, from http://www.irs.gov/pub/irs-soi/14insprbulnoncash.pdf

Van Slyke, D. M. (2003). The mythology of privatization in contracting for social services. *Public Administration Review, 63*, 296–315.

Wager, L. W. (1992). Organizational "linking pins": Hierarchical status and communicative roles in interlevel conferences. *Human Relations, 25*(4), 307–326.

Weber, L., & Dwoskin, E. (2014, September 30). Mood swings: As personality tests multiply, employers are split. *Wall Street Journal.* Eastern edition, New York, p. A.1. Retrieved October 2014 from https://ezproxy.lib.uwm.edu/login?url=http://search.proquest.com/docview/1566260695?accountid=15078

Weber, M. (1946). *From Max Weber: Essays in sociology* (H. H. Gerth & C. W. Mills, Trans.). Oxford: Oxford University Press.

Wiegand, B. (2014). Why celebrity iCloud hacking should matter to your nonprofit. Retrieved June 15, 2015, from http://forums.techsoup.org/cs/community/b/tsblog/archive/2014/09/09/why-celebrity-icloud-hacking-should-matter-to-your-nonprofit.aspx

Xu, H., & Morgan, K. (2012). Public-private partnerships for social and human services: A case study of nonprofit organizations in Alabama. *Public Administration Quarterly, 36*, 277–310.

Zhang, N., Li, Y., & Temkin-Greener, H. (2013). Prevalence of obesity in New York nursing homes: Associations with facility characteristics. *The Gerontologist, 53*, 567–581.

Chapter 9

Anderson-Carpenter, K. D., Watson-Thompson, J., Jones, M, & Chaney, L. (2014). Using communities of practice to support implementation of evidence-based prevention strategies. *Journal of Community Practice, 22*(1–2), 176–188.

Blitz, L. V., Kida, L., Gresham, M., & Bronstein, L. B. (2013). Prevention through collaboration: Family engagement with rural schools and families living in poverty. *Families in Society, 94*(3), 157–165.

Berg, M. T., Stewart, E. A., Schreck, C. J., & Simons, R. L. (2012). The victim-offender overlap in context: Examining the role of neighborhood street culture. *Criminology, 50*, 359–390.

Campbell, D. A. (2009). Giving up the single life: Leadership motivations for interorganizational restructuring in nonprofit organizations. *Administration in Social Work, 33*, 368–386.

Caplan, M. A. (2014). Communities respond to predatory lending. *Social Work, 59*(2), 149–156.

Cleaveland, C. (2010). 'We are not criminals': Social work advocacy and unauthorized migrants. *Social Work, 55*(1), 74–81.

Cohen, M. B., & Hyde, C. A. (2014). Empowering workers and clients for organizational change. Chicago, IL: Lyceum.

Conroy, S., & Williams, A. (2014). *Use of internet, social networking sites, and mobile technology for volunteerism.* Washington, D.C.: American Association of Retired Persons.

Decker, S. H., Melde, C., & Pyrooz, D. C. (2013). What do we know about gangs and gang members and where do we go from here? *Justice Quarterly, 30*, 369–402.

Everett, J. E., Homstead, K., & Drisko, J. (2007). Frontline worker perceptions of the empowerment process in community-based agencies. *Social Work, 52*(2), 161–170.

Freire, P. (1970). Pedagogy of the oppressed. New York: Continuum.

Hardina, D. (2014). The use of dialogue in community organization practice: Using theory, values, and skills to guide group decision-making. *Journal of Community Practice, 22*(3), 365–384.

Huebner, B. M., Martin, K., Moule, R. K., Pyrooz, D., & Decker, S. H. (2014). Dangerous places: Gang members and neighborhood levels of gun assault. *Justice Quarterly*, DOI: 10.1080/07418825.2014.984751

Ivery, J. (2014). The NORC supportive services model: The role of social capital in community aging initiatives. *Journal of Community Practice*, 22(4), 451–471.

Kissane, R. J., & Gingerich, J. (2004). Do you see what I see? Nonprofit and resident perceptions of urban neighborhood problems. *Nonprofit Voluntary Sector Quarterly*, 33(2), 311–333.

Kruzich, J. M. (2005). Ownership, chain affiliation, and administrator decision-making autonomy in long-term care facilities. *Administration in Social Work*, 29(1), 5–24.

Leung, T. T. F., & Lam, B. C. L. (2014). Challenges of partnership with mental health service users in service planning and management. *Human Service Organizations Management, Leadership & Governance*, 38(4), 320–335.

Lewin, K. (1947). Frontiers in group dynamics. *Human Relations*, 1, 5–41.

Linhorst, D. M., Eckert, A., & Hamilton, G. (2005). Promoting participation in organizational decision making by clients with severe mental illness. *Social Work*, 50(1), 21–30.

Luluquisen, M., & Pettis, L. (2014). Community engagement for policy and systems change. *Community Development*, 45(3), 252–262.

Majee, W., & Hoyt, A. (2009). Building community trust through cooperatives: A case study of a worker-owned homecare cooperative. *Journal of Community Practice*, 17(4), 444–463.

Medley, B. C., & Akan, O. H. (2008). Creating positive change in community organizations: A case for rediscovering Lewin. *Nonprofit Management & Leadership*, 18(4), 485–496.

Mullen, E. J. (2006). Choosing outcome measures in systematic reviews: Critical challenges. *Research on Social Work Practice*, 16(1), 84–90.

Papachristos, A. V., Hureau, D. M., & Braga, A. (2013). The corner and the crew: The influence of geography and social networks on gang violence. *American Sociological Review*, 78, 417–447.

Parrish, D. E., Harris, D., & Pritzker, S. (2013). Assessment of a service provider self-study method to promote interorganizational and community collaboration. *Social Work*, 59(4), 354–364.

Peerapun, W. (2012). Participatory planning in urban conservation and regeneration: A case study of Amphawa community. *Procedia – Social and Behavioral Sciences*, 36, 243–252.

Rycraft, J. R., & Dettlaff, A. J. (2009). Hurdling the artificial fence between child welfare and the community: Engaging community partners to address disproportionality. *Journal of Community Practice*, 17, 464–482.

Seck, M. M., & Helton, L. (2014). Faculty development of a joint MSW program utilizing Tuckman's model of stages of group development. *Social Work with Groups*, 37(2), 158–168.

Schneider, R. L., & Lester, L. (2001). *Social work advocacy*. Belmont, CA: Brooks/Cole.

Slocum, L. A., Rengifo, A., Choi, T., & Herrmann, C. (2013). The elusive relationship between community organizations and crime: An assessment across disadvantaged areas of the South Bronx. *Criminology*, 51, 167–216.

Staples, L. (2012). Community organizing for social justice: Grassroots groups for power. *Social Work with Groups*, 35(3), 287–296.

van der Smissen, S., Schalk, R., & Freese, C. (2013). Organizational change and the psychological contract: How change influences the perceived fulfillment of obligations. *Journal of Organizational Change*, 26(6), 1071–1090.

Walker, L. A., & East, J. F. (2014). The benefits of including engaged residents and professionals in low-income neighbourhood redevelopment planning processes. *Journal of Community Practice*, 22(3), 342–364.

Weiss, J. A., Dwonch-Schoen, K., Howard-Barr, E. M., & Panella, M. P. (2010). Learning from a community action plan to promote safe sexual practices. *Social Work*, 55(1), 19–26.

Woodford, M. R., & Preston, S. (2011). Developing a strategy to meaningfully engage stakeholders in program/policy planning: A guide for human services managers and practitioners. *Journal of Community Practice*, 19(2), 159–174.

Chapter 10

Banach, M., Hamilton, D., & Perri, P. M. (2004). Class action lawsuits and community empowerment. *Journal of Community Practice*, 11(4), 81–99.

Berlin, S. B. (1990). Dichotomous and complex thinking. *Social Service Review*, 64(1), 46–59.

Brager, G., & Holloway, S. (1978). *Changing human service organizations: Politics and practice*. New York: Free Press.

Brager, G., Specht, H., & Torczyner, J. L. (1987). *Community organizing*. New York: Columbia University Press.

Chen, B., & Graddy, E. A. (2010). The effectiveness of nonprofit lead-organization networks for social service delivery. *Nonprofit Management & Leadership*, 20(4), 405–422.

Cohen, M. B., & Hyde, C. A. (2014). *Empowering workers and clients for organizational change*. Chicago, IL: Lyceum Books, Inc.

Democracy Center. (2004). *Lobbying—The basics*. San Francisco, CA: Author.

Deschamps, R., & McNutt, K. (2014). Third sector and social media. *Canadian Journal of Nonprofit and Social Economy Research*, 5(2), 29–46.

Gutiérrez, L. M., Lewis, E. A., Dessel, A. B., & Spencer, M. (2013). Principles, skills, and practice strategies for promoting multicultural communication and collaboration. In M. Weil, M. Reisch, & M. L. Ohmer (Eds.). *The handbook of community practice* (2nd ed.), pp. 445–460. Thousand Oaks, CA: Sage.

Haynes, K. S., & Mickelson, J. S. (2010). *Effecting change: Social workers in the political arena* (7th ed.). Boston, MA: Allyn & Bacon.

Hoon, C., & Jacobs, C. D. (2014). Beyond belief: Strategic taboos and organizational identity in strategic agenda setting. *Strategic Organization*, 12(4), 244–273.

Knickmeyer, L., Hopkins, K., & Meyer, M. (2004). Exploring collaboration among urban neighborhood associations. *Journal of Community Practice*, 11(2), 13–25.

Lewin, K. (1947). Frontiers in group dynamics. *Human Relations*, 1, 5–41.

McPherson, E. (2015). Advocacy organizations' evaluation of social media information for NGO journalism: The evidence and engagement models. *American Behavioral Scientist*, 59(1), 124–148.

Menon, G. M. (2000). The 79-cent campaign: The use of on-line mailing lists for electronic advocacy. *Journal of Community Practice*, 8(3), 73–81.

Quinn, P. (2004). Home of your own programs: Models of creative collaboration. *Journal of Community Practice*, 12(1/2), 37–50.

Rothman, J., Erlich, J. L., & Tropman, J. E. (Eds.) (2008). *Strategies for community intervention* (6th ed.). Itasca, IL: F. E. Peacock.

Rubin, H. J., & Rubin, I. S. (2008). *Community organizing and development* (4th ed.). Boston, MA: Allyn & Bacon.

Schier, M. L., & Handy, F. (2015). Social change efforts of direct service nonprofits: The role of funding and collaborations in shaping social innovations. *Human Service Organizations: Management, Leadership & Governance*, 39, 6–24.

Schneider, R. L., & Lester, L. (2001). *Social work advocacy*. Belmont, CA: Brooks/Cole.

Takahashi, L. M., & Smutny, G. (2002). Collaborative windows and organizational governance: Exploring the formation and demise of social service partnerships. *Nonprofit and Voluntary Sector Quarterly*, 31(2), 165–185.

Tropman, J. E., Erlich, J. L., & Rothman, J. (2001). *Tactics and techniques of community intervention* (4th ed.). Itasca, IL: F. E. Peacock.

Waysman, M., & Savaya, R. (2004). Coalition-based social change initiatives: Conceptualization of a model and assessment of its generalizability. *Journal of Community Practice, 12*(1/2), 123–143.

Chapter 11

Anderson, L., Petticrew, M., Rehfuess, E., Armstong, R., Ueffing, E., Baker, P., Francis, D., & Tugwel, P. (2011). Using logic models to capture complexity in systematic reviews. *Research Synthesis Methods, 2*, 33–42.

Dessler, G. (2011). *Human resource management* (12th ed.). Upper Saddle River, NJ: Prentice Hall.

Dickson-Gómez, J. (2012). Substance abuse disorders treatment in El Salvador: Analysis of policy-making-related failure. *Substance Use & Misuse, 47*(13/14), 1546–1551.

Federal Register (2013). "Uniform administrative requirements, cost principles and audit requirements for federal awards: Final rule." www.federalregister.gov.

Fogel, S. J., & Moore, K. A. (2011). Collaborations among diverse organizations: Building evidence to support community partnerships. In M. Roberts-Degennaro & S. J. Fogel (Eds.). *Using evidence to inform practice for community and organizational change* (pp. 99–109). Chicago, IL: Lyceum.

Gantt, H. (1919). *Organizing for work*. New York: Harcourt, Brace & Howe.

Government Performance and Results Act of 1993. Public Law No. 103-62. www.whitehouse.gov

Hardina, D. (2002). *Analytical skills for community organization practice*. New York: Columbia University Press.

Kettner, P. M. (2013). *Excellence in human service organization management* (2nd ed.). Boston, MA: Pearson.

Kettner, P. M., Moroney, R. M., & Martin, L. L. (2013). *Designing and managing programs: An effectiveness-based approach* (4th ed.). Thousand Oaks, CA: Sage.

McCroskey, J., Picus, L. O., Yoo, J., Marsenich, L., & Robillard, E. (2004). Show me the money: Estimating public expenditures to improve outcomes for children, families, and communities. *Children and Schools, 26*(3), 165–173.

Montana, P. J., & Charnov, B. H. (2008). *Management* (4th ed.). Hauppauge, NY: Barron's Educational Series.

Mullen, T., & Resnick, B. (2013). Self-esteem among nursing assistants: Reliability and validity of the Rosenberg Self-Esteem Scale. *Journal of Nursing Measurement, 21*(2), 335–344.

Reis, E. P., & Moore, M. (2005). Elite perceptions of poverty and inequality. *Community Development Journal, 41*(2), 260–262.

Rosenberg, M. (1965). *Society and the adolescent self-image*. Princeton, NJ: Princeton University Press.

Savaya, R., & Waysman, M. (2005). The logic model: A tool for incorporating theory in development and evaluation of programs. *Administration in Social Work, 29*(2), 85–103.

Sherraden, M. S., Slosar, B., & Sherraden, M. (2002). Innovation in social policy: Collaborative policy advocacy. *Social Work, 47*(3), 209–221.

United Way of America. (1996). *Measuring program outcomes: A practical approach*. Alexandria, VA: Author

Weinbach, R. W., & Taylor, L. M. (2015). *The social worker as manager: A practical guide to success* (7th ed.). Boston, MA: Pearson.

Wholey, J. S., Hatry, H. P., & Newcomer, K. E. (Eds.). (2010). *Handbook of practical program evaluation*. San Francisco: Jossey-Bass.

Winter, C. L., & Ohmer, M. L. (2014). Using the best of research and practice to create an outcome measurement framework: A family service agency's experience. *Families in Society: The Journal of Contemporary Social Services, 95*(3), 155–162.

Chapter 12

Basch, C. E., Sliepcevich, E. M., Gold, R. S., Duncan, D., & Kolbe, L. (1985). Avoiding type III errors in health education program evaluations: A case study. *Health Education Quarterly, 12*, 315–331.

Better Evaluation. (2015). Determine and secure resources. Retrieved March 11, 2015, from http://betterevaluation.org/plan/manage _evaluation/determine_resources

Bloom, M., Fischer, J., & Orme, J. G. (2009). *Evaluating practice: Guidelines for the accountable professional* (6th ed.). Boston, MA: Pearson.

Boardman, A., Greenberg, D., Vining, A., & Weimer, D. (2010). *Cost-benefit analysis* (4th ed.). Englewood, NJ: Prentice Hall.

Bowlby, J. (1969). *Attachment and loss, vol. 1: Attachment*. New York: Basic Books.

Brody, R. (2005). *Effectively managing human service organizations* (3rd ed.). Newbury Park, CA: Sage.

Brown, M., & Cregan, C. (2008). Organizational change cynicism: The role of employee involvement. *Human Resource Management, 47*, 667–686.

Burnes, B., & Jackson, P. (2011). Success and failure in organizational change: An exploration of the role of values. *Journal of Change Management, 11*, 133–162.

Chang, C. (2012). Paperwork causes unintended distractions for physicians and nurses. Retrieved April 19, 2015, from http://www .kevinmd.com/blog/2012/01/paperwork-unintended-distractions -physicians-nurses.html

Cook, T. D., & Campbell, D. T. (1979). *Quasi-experimentation: Design and analysis issues for field settings*. Boston, MA: Houghton Mifflin.

Crunkilton, D. D., & Robinson, M. M. (2008). Cracking the "black box": Journey mapping's tracking system in a drug court program evaluation. *Journal of Social Work Practice in the Addictions, 8*, 511–529.

Grady, V. M., & Grady, J. I. (2013). The relationship of Bowlby's attachment theory to the persistent failure of organizational change initiatives. *Journal of Change Management, 13*, 206–222.

GrantsNorthwest. (2015). Matching evaluation to your project and organization. Retrieved April 2, 2015, from http://www .grantsnorthwest.com/matching-evaluation-to-your-project -and-organization/

Greeno, C. G., Colonna-Pydyn, C., & Shumway, M. (2007). The need to adapt standardized outcomes measures for community mental health. *Social Work in Public Health, 23*, 125–138.

Kegan, R., & Lahey, L. L. (2009). *Immunity to change*. Boston, MA: Harvard Business Review Press.

McFillen, J. M., O'Neil, D. A., Balzer, W. K., & Varney, G. H. (2013). Organizational diagnosis: An evidence-based approach. *Journal of Change Management, 13*, 223–246.

Nohe, C., Michaelis, B., Menges, J. I., Zhang, Z., & Sonntag, K. (2013). Charisma and organizational change: A multilevel study of perceived charisma, commitment to change, and team performance. *The Leadership Quarterly, 24*, 378–389.

O'Hare, T. (2015). *Evidence-based practices for social workers*. Chicago, IL: Lyceum Books.

Parker, R. N., Alcaraz, R., & Payne, P. R. (2011). Community readiness for change and youth violence prevention: A tale of two cities. *American Journal of Community Psychology, 48*, 97–105.

Raelin, J. D., & Cataldo, C. G. (2011). Whither middle management? Empowering interface and the failure of organizational change. *Journal of Change Management, 11*, 481–507.

Schwartz, S., & Carpenter, K. M. (1999). The right answer for the wrong question: Consequences of type III error for public health research. *American Journal of Public Health, 89*, 1175–1180.

Schwarz, G. M., Watson, B. M., & Callan, V. J. (2011). Talking up failure: How discourse can signal failure to change. *Management Communication Quarterly, 25*, 311–352.

Taylor, T. (2013). Paperwork first, not work first: How caseworkers use paperwork to feel effective. *Journal of Sociology and Social Welfare, 40*, 9–27.

Teater, B. A. (2011). A qualitative evaluation of the section 8 housing choice voucher program: The recipients' perspectives. *Qualitative Social Work, 10*, 503–519.

Torgerson, C. J., Torgerson, D. J., & Taylor, C. A. (2010). Randomized controlled trials and nonrandomized designs. In J. S. Wholey, H. P. Hatry, & K. E. Newcomer (Eds.), *Handbook of practical program evaluation* (3rd ed., pp. 144–162). San Francisco, CA: Jossey-Bass.

U.S. Department of Education, Office of Postsecondary Education. (2015). *Fund for the improvement of postsecondary education: FIPSE competitive grant evaluation requirements.* Retrieved April 16, 2015, from http://www2.ed.gov/about/offices/list/ope/fipse/evalrequirements.html

Wanous, J. P., Reichers, A. E., & Austin, J. T. (2000). Cynicism about organizational change. *Group and Organization Management, 25*, 132–153.

Wholey, J. S. (2010). Exploratory evaluation. In J. S. Wholey, H. P. Hatry, & K. E. Newcomer (Eds.), *Handbook of practical program evaluation* (3rd ed., pp. 81-99). San Francisco, CA: Jossey-Bass.

Glossary

Action system Composed of individuals from other systems who have an active role in planning the change and moving it toward implementation.

Activities Lists of tasks that must be undertaken and completed in order to achieve an objective.

Advocates Persons who argue for a cause or on another's behalf.

Ally A person of privilege who actively works to eliminate stigma and discrimination that occurs based on that stigma.

Amorphous structure Implies no persistent pattern of power relationships within the community.

Approaches Guidance based on experience and promising emergent processes; not always based on formal theories, and often altered as one learns in the process.

Arena An organization or community within which a change episode is undertaken.

Arenas Small groups, organizations, communities, and policy contexts in which macro practice occurs.

Artifacts Reflecting the climate of the organization, artifacts are the most visible structures, processes, and behaviors.

Asset mapping A process used to identify services, programs, resources, staff capabilities, values, and other factors that can be compared with risk factors in determining how to approach a community.

Assimilation Occurs when identity is tied to mainstream culture and the purpose of joining a movement is to become a part of the culture to which one has previously been denied access.

Assumptions In management by objectives, what is presumed about how meeting objectives will achieve expectations (e.g., that the use of better service techniques will improve outcomes).

Authority The term for power wielded with the consent of those being led (legitimized power).

Barrios Latino communities that have reasonably well-defined boundaries within a large metropolitan area.

Beneficence The desire to do good for others, as well as not doing harm.

Boundary clarity The variable that usually determines the level of formality within a community.

Boundary maintenance Monitoring and keeping established parameters in check.

Boundary setting The process of establishing criteria for the inclusion of individuals in a target population.

Bounded rationality The key to understanding organizational decisions is recognizing that there are constraints that limit decision making.

Bureaucratic disentitlement Describes situations in HSOs where clients fail to receive benefits or services to which they are entitled due to decisions based on rigid and sometimes illogical internal rules rather than client needs.

Bureaucratic disentitlement Situations in which workers within social welfare agencies neglect to take action or to inform clients about what they are qualified to receive.

Bureaucratic personality Persons who focus more on structural compliance than on responsiveness to human need.

Bureaucratization Growth in size and structural complexity of organizations, including human service organizations.

Campaign Strategy used when the target must be convinced of the importance of the change, but when communication is still possible between the two systems.

Capabilities perspective Recognizing that not all people have the opportunity to start at the same place and that consideration must be given to what it takes to get to the place where they can compete with others.

Capacity building An empowerment process at the individual, interpersonal, and community levels as participants gain knowledge and skills to effect action.

Catastrophic analogy Social systems defined by contentiousness and conflict taken to extremes with no stability.

Centralization The degree to which groups and organizations cluster in a location close to what is considered the community's center as opposed to decentralization in which they disperse beyond the area.

Charity Organization Societies Umbrella organizations that coordinated the activities of a wide variety of charities created to deal with the problems of immigrants and rural transplants who were flooding into industrialized cities in the United States in search of jobs.

Civil disobedience Engaging in activities that intentionally break the law.

Claimed domain The boundaries recognized by the organization.

Client-driven models An administrative or managerial approach in which the achievement of desirable outcomes for clients is the primary criterion for decision making.

Closed-system approaches Are more concerned with internal organizational structures and processes than with environmental factors.

Coalition A loosely developed association of constituent groups and organizations, each of whose primary identification is outside of the coalition.

Collaboration Strategy that implies a working relationship where the action and target systems agree that change must occur.

Communication The function that includes the use of a common language and symbols to express ideas.

Community Often characterized as space, people, shared values and institutions, interaction, distribution of power, and social system.

Community action field   Emerges when a number of social fields overlap.

Community development   Development that connects people to existing structures to engage in activities such as community building, economic development, neighborhood improvement, and developing affordable housing.

Community organizing   When multiple indigenous community residents use their strength in numbers to participate in empowering themselves to pursue social change.

Community values   Beliefs that are strongly held by persons who make up the community.

Competition   Groups competing for the acquisition or possession of land, jobs, votes, and other resources, moving from low to intense (even contentious) depending on the power dynamics.

Concept mapping   A process of brainstorming together, developing a problem statement, sorting through different perspectives on how to reframe the statement, and using whatever data and information are available.

Condition   A phenomenon that is present in a community or organization that may be troublesome to a number of people but that has not been formally identified, labeled, or publicly acknowledged as a problem.

Conglomerate merger   Occurs when units within the community form a confederation of multiple smaller units under a large umbrella agency.

Construct validity   Whether a measure performs as predicted by theory or previous research.

Content validity   Whether characteristics considered to be part of a particular variable are actually present.

Contest   Strategy used when, because of the strength of the opposition, neither collaboration nor campaign strategies are possible.

Cooptation   When one group persuades or manipulates another group to participant in or join a cause that the first group has typically opposed.

Cost–benefit analysis (CBA)   Used when the goal is to assess the overall value of a given program.

Cost-effectiveness analysis (CEA)   Used to compare the costs of different approaches to achieving the same outcome.

Creaming   Taking on less needy clients who can pay or clients who have a higher chance of success, over other more needy clients.

Criterion validity   Testing a measurement against some other presumably valid measure or standard.

Cultural competency   A process and a product that includes self-awareness and respect for diversity as well as effective practice behaviors at the micro, mezzo, and macro levels.

Cultural humility   An ongoing process that includes a continual commitment to learning and self-reflection, to altering the power imbalances in the interactions between helping professionals and service consumers, and to developing collaborative and equitable relationships with community members.

Culturally sensitive interventions (CSIs)   Interventions into which important elements that define a culture, such as values, practices, and standards of conduct, are incorporated.

Cyberactivism   The use of list serves, websites, message boards, petitions, blogs, text messaging, polling, mapping, and a host of other digital media such as Twitter, Facebook, and YouTube for the purpose of social change.

Cybernetic system   A self-correcting system, meaning that it is able to garner information from its surroundings, interpret this information, and adjust its functioning accordingly.

De factor domain   The actual boundaries set for the organization.

Decision making   Choosing from among alternatives and implementing an approach to deal with the problem.

Defended communities   Those communities that have to focus unusual amounts of effort toward looking after their members.

Defense   The way in which the community takes care of and protects its members.

Demand characteristics   Circumstances associated with the fact that evaluation efforts will always be intrusive to some degree, such as when improvements in participants' behavior arise not from the effect of the change but from participants' knowledge that they are being observed.

Demographic data   Variables such as socioeconomic status, age, race, and gender that characterize people.

Descriptive approaches   Theories that assist in analyzing what is happening within communities but do not provide the practitioner with methods to change a situation once it has been analyzed.

Descriptive theories   Sociological approaches intended to provide a means of analyzing organizations in terms of certain characteristics or procedures.

Dialogue   An ongoing process of action and reflection used to generate new ways of thinking in which organizational or community members engage with a professional planner as equals and co-learners.

Discrimination   Detrimental action or absence of action because of individual and group differences.

Domain   Organizational domain includes the boundaries within which services are delivered to clients.

Domain legitimation   Occurs when an organization wins acknowledgment of claims it makes as to its sphere of activities and expertise.

Dosage   Refers to whether participants received enough of the intervention to meet expectations and whether it was reasonable to expect that the nature of the change effort would bring about the outcome(s) sought.

Dual perspective   A framework that views an individual at the center of two surrounding systems, the nurturing system and the sustaining system.

Duration   The length of time a condition or problem has existed.

Effectiveness accountability   Focuses on the results, effects, and accomplishments of human service programs.

Efficiency   Carrying out tasks in the timeliest manner.

Efficiency accountability   The ratio of outputs to inputs or, more specifically, the ratio of volume of service provided to dollars expended.

Eligibility criteria   Those conditions established for clients to receive service.

Elitist structure   Assumes that a small number of people have disproportionate power in various community sectors and that this power remains constant regardless of the issue.

Empowerment   Comes from within the individual or community as a whole when there is an "aha" realization that there are inherent strengths on which to build and that using those strengths can result in desired change.

Episode of change   One phase in a longer term change process, in which immediate outcomes may be achieved; large changes may be composed of multiple episodes.

Espoused beliefs and values   What members of the organization say are important and are typically reflected in mission or vision statements.

Ethical dilemma   A situation in which a choice has to be made between equally important but seemingly conflicting values.

Ethics Guidelines for practice in carrying out values (the operationalization of values).

Etiology The underlying causes of a problem.

Evaluability assessment Determining whether it is possible to complete an evaluation on a particular initiative or change effort.

Evaluator bias Happens when participants detect subtle cues from staff members or others regarding the outcome they hope to achieve.

Evidence-based practice (EBP) The application of research and clinical evidence to decisions made about practice.

Evidence-guided practice (EGP) An alternative term to EBP, framing the concept of being guided as more action oriented than simply being "based on" or "informed by" research and clinical evidence.

Expectations In management by objectives, hoped-for outcomes.

Extracommunity affiliations Those relationships and networks that transcend geographical boundaries.

Extrinsic factors Motivators such as wages, hours, working conditions, and benefits that go beyond the immediate tasks of performing the job.

Factional analogy Social systems in which contentiousness is open and obvious and there is instability.

Field-interactional perspective An analysis of change dynamics in both place and nonplace communities.

Flash activists Free-agent advocates who emerge to mobilize large numbers of people to promote causes using social media such as Twitter, blogs, and Facebook.

Formal cooptation Involves a group agreement, through vote or some other formal means, to support an issue.

Formative evaluation Also referred to as a developmental evaluation, this occurs at early stages of a change effort to ensure that the necessary information is available to plan well.

For-profit agency An agency that is designated by its tax status to be a private business.

Frame of mind How one organizes data and information in a meaningful way.

Framing Presenting one's perspective in order to make sense of a situation, explain a condition, or label a problem.

Framing theory Based on the premise that any problem can be viewed from a variety of perspectives and can encompass multiple values.

Free-agent activists Advocates connected to causes rather than groups or organizations.

Frequency The number of times the condition or problem is likely to occur within a given time frame.

Full-pay clients Those who cover the cost of their services, either personally or through third-party reimbursement.

Garbage can analogy Used in decision-making theory to describe the rather chaotic process in which decisions emerge from a mixture of people, problems, ideas, and "choice opportunities" that are unique to every organization and situation.

Gemeinschaft Roughly translates as "community"; focuses on the mutual, intimate, and common bonds that pull people together in local units.

Geographic information systems (GIS) Electronic data used to develop maps and graphics as tools to analyze local communities.

Gesellschaft Refers generally to society or association.

Giving circles When community members form associations for the purpose of pooling their money and other resources for important causes

Glass ceiling Women and minorities can reach a level at which they have a view of functioning at the top but cannot get there because those who select persons for top positions often value sameness and fear diversity.

Global perspective When communities facing human challenges communicate across borders and learn from one another in addressing human needs.

Goal displacement Occurs when the formal goals of the organization—*stated goals*—are replaced by those of decision makers—*real goals*.

Goals A general statement that provides a beacon or focal point for the change effort and serves as a reminder of its purpose.

Government Performance and Results Act (GPRA) Law enacted in 1993 to alter how the federal government monitored and evaluated its grants and contracts by focusing less on how funds are spent and more on whether stated outcomes are achieved.

Hawthorne effect Refers to the fact that experimental subjects may perform in certain ways simply because they know they are being studied.

Homeostasis Maintaining balance or equilibrium within a social system.

Horizontal community Geographically bounded and represented by many linkages between and among organizations and neighborhoods that are located within the area and, in most cases, serve the community.

Horizontal merger Occurs, for example, when two organizations consolidate into a single organization

Human or population or social ecology Theories that examine structural patterns and relationships within place-based communities.

Human service organizations (HSOs) Have goals to improve the quality of life of persons outside the organization.

Ideal type A conceptual construct from which to assess organizational characteristics and to which no organization fits completely.

Incidence A phenomenon actually occurring over a period of time.

Informal cooptation Gaining support from an individual who was originally unsupportive of the proposed change.

Informal units Those structures that are not publicly incorporated as legal entities to deliver health and human services.

Information poverty Not having access to communication technology such as telephone, fax, email, computer, or text messaging on a regular basis.

In-kind contribution Nonmonetary materials or equipment such as food, clothing, physical facilities, real estate, vehicles, and office supplies contributed to an organization.

Inputs Resources, people, and processes that enter a system from the outside environment.

Institutional system Deals with interactions between the organization and the environment

Institutional theory Views organizations as incorporating externally driven rules, norms, values, and shared understandings that constrain action into their cultures.

Institutionalization Occurs when an organization takes on a life of its own that may have more to do with the interests of its own participants than with the instrumental goals it is supposedly serving.

Intensity The extent to which a condition or problem is considered threatening to individual, organizational, or community survival.

Intersectionality The complexity of multiple dimensions of difference that individuals occupy, and the isms related to those dimensions in understanding identity development.

Intrinsic factors   Motivators that lie within the work itself, such as satisfaction with successful task completion.

Introspective self-help   Used when separatism is too difficult to maintain; thus, community members focus on self-development and self-mastery.

Issue   Occurs when there is a disagreement.

Job redesign   A process that seeks to increase the intrinsic rewardingness of work.

Lead persons   Individuals who are responsible for oversight of the entire change process.

Learned incompetence   Occurs when employees in bureaucracies rely so heavily on a policy manual to make their decisions that they cease to think logically or creatively about their jobs.

Line-item budgeting   Identifying expenditure categories and estimating the dollars needed to cover expenses in each category for one year.

Logic model   A systematic approach to taking the data collected and compiled to this point, and organizing it in a way that makes clear what are the inputs, processes, and results that need to occur in order to plan an intervention

Macro practice   Professionally guided intervention(s) designed to bring about change in organizational, community, and/or policy arenas.

Macro-level change   Intervention in organizations or communities.

Mainstreaming   Providing assistance in such a way as to minimize the need for persons with disabilities to remain apart or operate separately from others in society.

Management by objectives (MBO)   An approach that involves both short-range and long-range planning, and it is through the planning process that organizational structures and procedures necessary to achieve an outcome are established.

Managerial system   Those structures and processes that manage the work of the technical core.

Manifest Destiny   The belief that God had willed the North American continent to the Anglo-Saxon race to build a Utopian world.

Meaningful participation   Authentic engagement of participants and the use of their input in decision making.

Mechanical analogy   Viewing a social system as a machine in which all the parts work closely together, are well coordinated, and integrate smoothly.

Militant direct action   Used to catch people off-guard through activism, with the intent of gaining a place within the community for persons involved in the movement.

Models   Prescriptions based on theories that provide direction for action.

Monitor   The collection of information on activities leading to achievement of objectives.

Monocultural system perspective   Treats conflict as though it were something deviant and undermines the concept of pluralism.

Morphogenic analogy   Social systems in which change is ongoing and the structure of the system is continually emerging.

Mutual support   The function that families, friends, partners, neighbors, volunteers, and professionals carry out in communities when they care for the sick, the unemployed, and the distressed.

Natural system   An entity that is aware of its own self-interest and acts to protect itself.

Need   Something that is necessary for living a quality life; it is different from a want, which is not necessary but is desired.

Needs assessment   A systematic way of gathering data and information to determine the needs of a particular group.

New commons   A term used to describe the third or voluntary sector in which collective identity gains momentum.

Non-full-pay clients   Service users whose payment must be derived from revenues generated from other sources (e.g., charitable donations or profits earned from full-pay clients).

Nongovernmental organization (NGO)   Nonprofit agencies that have emerged from the private sector, as opposed to being derived from government.

Nonprofit human service organization   A direct service providing agency with a voluntary (unpaid) board of directors, whose tax status requires any profits to be channeled back into the agency.

Normative antidiscrimination   A confrontational approach that stays within legal parameters and is used to gain access to community institutions that were previously inaccessible due to oppression.

Null hypothesis   This assumes that any progress toward achieving goals and objectives happened not because of the change effort but simply because of chance.

Nurturing system   The values of parents and extended family or substitute family via the community experiences, beliefs, customs, and traditions with which the individual was raised.

Objectives   These spell out the details of the planned intervention in measurable terms, including expected outcomes and the processes needed to achieve them.

One best way   The assumption that one can develop the best tools for completing a job by fitting workers' abilities and interests to particular assignments, and then finding the level of production the average worker can sustain, this becomes the "one best way."

Open system   One in which the environment is taken into consideration, as opposed to focusing solely on internal operations.

Oppression   Occurs when an individual, group, or society unjustly uses authority or power over others, including everything from institutional discrimination to personal bigotry.

Organismic analogy   Comparing social systems to biological organisms like the human body, with each organ having a different function.

Organizational culture   An interplay of artifacts, values, and underlying beliefs.

Organizational identity   What is unique, core, and enduring to the organization and to which organizational members cling when faced with major challenges.

Organizational image   How persons outside organizational boundaries see an organization.

Organizational structure   Refers to the way roles and relationships are constituted among persons within an organization.

Organizations   Collectives of individuals gathered together to serve a particular purpose.

Outcome   A measure of a quality-of-life change (improvement, stasis, or deterioration) for a client.

Outcome evaluation   Focuses on the achievement of outputs and outcomes.

Outcome objective   This specifies the *result* or *outcome* to be achieved on behalf of the target population.

Outcomes   Quality-of-life changes.

Outputs   Those resources, people, and products that exit a social system.

Performance-based contracting   A process in which agencies that receive contracts for services are required to meet specific targets for the quantity or quality of services provided.

Personnel   People who are constantly interacting with each other in communities and organizations.

Piece-rate wage   Paying workers for each unit they produce.

Pilot project   Short-term approach to test out the feasibility of a potential program idea.

Placebo effect   Occurs when outcomes are not due to the actual effectiveness of the change effort but to participants' belief in its effectiveness.

Pluralist structure   As issues change, various interest groups and shifting coalitions arise within the community, and the power dynamics change accordingly.

Pluralistic integration   Occurs when groups form communities that are confident in their own cultural identities and do not give up their distinctiveness.

Policy   A formally adopted statement about what is to be done and how it will happen—in other words, a course of action.

Politics   The reasons or motivation behind the different ways that individuals respond when asked to support a change effort.

Population at need   A group in which a problem already exists and for which change efforts may be more focused on intervention or treatment, than prevention

Population at risk   A group in danger of developing a particular problem and for which change efforts may be oriented toward prevention.

Power   The ability to influence actions and politics.

Practice   How an organization or individuals within it carry out basic functions in ways that are less formal than written policies.

Practice perspectives and models   Directions or guidance for persons wanting to change or intervene in a community arena.

Prejudice   Attitudes and opinions based on preconceived stereotypes, rather than on experience or reason.

Prescriptive approaches   How-to guides for taking action.

Prescriptive theories   Designed as how-to guides with the goal of helping to build better organizations.

Prevalence   The number of cases of a phenomenon that exist within a community at any one time.

Privatization   Reducing or ending direct provision of human services by public agencies and replacing it with purchase of service (POS) contracting, whereby governments pay private agencies (both nonprofit and for-profit) to provide those services.

Problem   A condition that has in some way been formally recognized and incorporated into the action agenda of a group, organization, or community.

Problem solving   Formulating a problem statement and examining potential alternatives.

Process evaluation   Also referred to as program monitoring, tackles the question of whether the intended changes were those that were actually implemented.

Process objectives   These describe the procedures to be followed to accomplish results or achieve outcomes.

Production, distribution, and consumption   The function that performs community activities designed to meet people's material needs, including the most basic requirements, such as food, clothing, and shelter.

Professional   Identifying with a set of values that places the interests of the client first; a professional relies on knowledge, judgment, and skill to act on those values.

Professional identity   A relational concept in which one identifies with a community of colleagues who share a common value base and whose joint efforts work toward a lifestyle having public value.

Professional judgment   The ability to skillfully apply and discern the quality of the best knowledge available in a workable manner.

Programs   Structured activities designed to achieve a set of goals and objectives.

Progressivism   An ideology that arose partly as a secular expression of Judeo-Christian values of egalitarianism and social responsibility, which were seen as ways to temper the excesses of laissez-faire capitalism. In this view, human rights supersede property rights, and society is seen as responsible for promoting the collective good.

Projects   Are much like programs but may be smaller in scale, have a time-limited existence, be more flexible, and can be adapted to the needs of a changing environment.

Public agency   A governmental organization.

Quality accountability   Focuses on the provision of services and differentiates between organizations that meet a quality standard and those that do not.

Quality circle   A technique in which employees set aside time to brainstorm ways to improve quality and productivity.

Randomized controlled trial (RCT)   The strongest type of evaluation design, wherein individuals who are sampled from the same population are then randomly divided between one group that is exposed to the intervention and one or more other groups that are not.

Requests for proposal (RFPs)   Official invitations to provider agencies from a potential funding source to submit an application for funding.

Resiliency   The capacity to maintain a sense of empowerment over time, to continue to work toward community betterment, and to resist the temptation to give up when there are conflicts, struggles, and setbacks; the ability to bounce back time and again.

Resource dependence   Refers to when organizations rely on elements in their environment from which they can obtain resources needed for survival.

Results   The result of an MBO process is measured by the extent to which actual outcomes match the original expectations.

Roles   Practitioner tasks that include clinical work as well as being a case manager, family counselor, group worker, supervisor, administrator, manager, coordinator, developer, organizer, activist, advocate, and analyst.

Satisficing   When the decision maker seeks to reduce uncertainty as much as possible in order to make a decision that has a reasonable likelihood of producing an acceptable outcome.

Scientific management   An approach in which managers analyze the workplace scientifically.

Segregation   Occurs as diverse groups either maintain or reduce their separation by characteristics such as race, religion, or age; the opposition of integration.

Semi-profession   A term originally used to describe fields in which training was shorter, status was less legitimated, the right to privileged communication was less established, a specialized body of knowledge was limited, and more supervision or social control was required than in older, male-dominated professions.

Separatism   An approach in which parallel communities are established and the identity of participants becomes tied to the alternative community.

Service accessibility Availability of what consumers need that is affected by such variables as population density, distribution of service need, the ability of area residents to pay for services, the existence of competition among service providers, and transportation options.

Settlement houses Community-based neighborhood centers targeting families new to the city and working to integrate immigrants into their new environments.

Small groups The smallest arena in which macro practice occurs and through which many organizational and community change occurs.

Social action groups Groups that are formed to pursue community change and political activism.

Social control The function by which community members ensure compliance with norms and values.

Social Darwinism The belief that income differences between rich and poor are natural and arise because the rich are more fit. A corollary is that services should not be offered to the poor since this would perpetuate the survival of those less fit.

Social field Occurs through an interactional process in which a sense of unity emerges as individual efforts turn toward collective action with common goals.

Social justice movement A broad term covering the philosophies of union organizers, anticapitalists, and social reformers who fought the excesses of the Industrial Revolution and advocated on behalf of laborers, immigrants, and persons living in poverty.

Social movements Small and large groups of people coming together for a common cause.

Social participation The function that includes interaction with others in community groups, associations, and organizations.

Socialization The function that reinforces the prevailing norms, traditions, and values of community members.

Standard An established specification widely recognized, used, and accepted by authorities; typically developed by accrediting bodies, governmental entities, and professional associations.

Stereotypes Generalizations about a group that suggest that all members of that group are the same and will exhibit the same behavior.

Strategic planning A process in which stakeholders establish broad goals, processes, and actions for the future.

Strategic taboo Strategic options initially disqualified and deemed inconsistent with the organizational identity beliefs of strategic actors.

Strategy The overall efforts designed to ensure that the proposed change is accepted.

Strengths perspective Focusing on identifying the possibilities within individuals and communities; recognizing their assets rather than focusing on their deficits.

Succession The rapidity with which one social group or set of organizations replaces another within the geographical area.

Sustaining system Surrounding the nurturing system, the sustaining system represents the dominant society and its cultural beliefs, values, customs, and traditions.

SWOT analysis Identification of strengths, weaknesses, opportunities, and threats in preparation for a strategic planning or revisioning process.

Systems theory This theory contends that any entity, whether it is a group, an organization, or a community, has multiple parts. Entities can be best understood as systems with interconnecting components.

There are resources that systems need in order to function, and they may come in the form of people, equipment, funding, knowledge, legitimacy, or a host of other forms. These resources interact within the system, producing something that becomes the system's product.

Tactics The specific techniques and behaviors employed in relation to the target system designed to maximize the probability that the strategy will be successful and the proposed change adopted.

Target population A group of persons who will benefit from a change opportunity.

Task environment External organizations on which an organization depends, either as providers of needed input (money, raw materials, and client referrals) or as consumers of its output.

Tax benefits Defined in part by official designation as charitable organizations under section 501(c)(3) of federal Internal Revenue Service, regulations that allow nonprofits to avoid paying taxes that for profit firms must pay.

Technical core The structures and processes within an organization's boundaries that allow it to carry out the principal functions for which it was created (e.g., the manufacture of an object or the delivery of a service).

Theories Sets of interrelated concepts and constructs that provide a framework for understanding how and why something does or does not work.

Theory X Assumes that people inherently dislike work and have to be pressured to put forth enough effort to do a job.

Theory Y Assumes that people are motivated and want to do well in their jobs.

Throughputs Involves the services provided by the agency—often referred to as its *technology*—and the way it is structured to apply this technology to inputs it receives

Time frame This is included in all objectives. and it is stated in terms of the month, day, and year by which the result will be achieved.

Total quality management (TQM) An approach toward maximizing customer satisfaction through quality service.

Trained incapacity Ways in which bureaucratic personalities lose focus on the needs of those they serve.

Transparency Keeping actions and decision-making processes in the open and available to scrutiny by the public and the media.

Treatment fidelity Degree of adherence to the intervention plan, such as whether new services are delivered in the way intended and by appropriately trained and skilled staff

Triangulation Collecting data from multiple sources.

Type I error Erroneously concluding that the change effort worked when in fact it did not.

Type II error Erroneously concluding that the change effort failed when in fact it succeeded.

Type III error Evaluating a change effort that hasn't been properly implemented.

Validity Whether what's actually measured is what one thinks is being measured.

Values Strongly held beliefs about what is necessary and worthy that many or most members of a social system perceive to be fundamental to quality social work practice.

Vertical community Calls attention to the fact that many important decisions may be made by parent organizations outside the boundaries of the local community, and these decisions may or may not be in the best interests of the community.

Vertical linkages   Connections between community units (people, groups, and/or organizations) with units outside the community.

Vertical merger   Occurs when a large organization absorbs a provider that feeds clients into the larger organization.

Voluntary action   Those activities in which collective action or group behavior occurs outside the confines of the market or government and away from the privacy of the domestic unit.

Voluntary association   A structured group whose members have united for the purpose of advancing an interest or achieving some social purpose.

Volunteers   Persons who donate their time and talent.

Wicked problem   One that is incredibly complex and cannot be easily tamed.

Index